CONSERVATION PLANTS

A USDA SUCCESS STORY

History of the Natural Resource Conservation Service

Plant Materials Program

W. Curtis Sharp

Table of Contents

Acknowledgments

A major source of information was from the National Archives at College Park, MD, which houses much of the Soil Conservation Service nursery records. They were most valuable for the period from 1935 through 1970. Additional historical information sources included individuals, published documents, and existing agency records, especially from the National PMC at Beltsville, MD, the office of the National Plant Materials Specialists in Washington, D.C., individual PMCs and the Plant Materials Program web site.

Special gratitude must be expressed for assistance provided by nearly every PMC staff person. They were extraordinarily generous of their time and effort to secure and provide answers to questions, or seek out small details. Their effort proved invaluable. John Englert, National PM Specialist spent many hours in interviews, sorting old records, tracking down additional documents and reviewing the manuscript. A special thanks also to my son, Mitchell Sharp, for his non-technical but objective review.

Several NRCS retirees warrant special recognition. Foremost among them were former plant materials specialists Robert MacLauchlan and Erling Jacobson. Each reviewed all or parts of the manuscript, and made additional contributions to several chapters. The published works, contribution of materials, and personal council of Douglas Helms, retired NRCS historian, was exceedingly helpful. The push to make this history a reality came from NRCS retiree Jack Carlson, who also contributed background information.

At the risk of overlooking someone, other contributing current and retired employees from the plant materials discipline were Bruce Ayers, Cluster Belcher, Herby Bloodworth, James Briggs, Jim Canterbury, Wayne Crowder, the family of Robert Craig, John Dickerson, Patricia Espinosa , Fred Gaffney, Bob Glennon, Donald Hamer, Wendell Hassell, Donald Henry, Jimmy Henry, Greg Hendricks, Richard Heizer, Larry Holzworth, David Lorenz, Gil Lovell, Mike Materne, Dan Merkel, Bruce Munda, Diane Naylor, Wendall Oaks, Mike Owsley, Scott Peterson, Robert Roush, Keith Salvo, Sam Sanders, John Scheetz, Bob Slayback, Joe Snyder, James Stevens, the family of Paul Tabor, Ash Thornburg, Dwight Tober, Kathy Valadez and Cliff Williams.

Picture credits are numerous. The cover is the flowering head of big bluestem from Jennifer Anderson via the USDA-NRCS PLANTS Database. The back cover is 'Imperial' Carolina Popular, releases by the Rose Lake, MI PMC and provided by John Englert. Those associated with a particular PMC came from that PMC's web page[1]. Figure 2.1 is credited to Wikipedia. Many pictures of individuals came from the National Archives, College Park, MD. The pictures associated with Dr. Abraham Stoesz were from the Beltsville, MD, National Agricultural Library Collection Number 350, and Paul Tabor's came from the Athens, GA, Hargrett Library, University of Georgia, Collection Number MS2163. The dedication picture of the James E. "Bud" Smith PMC was supplied from the archives of that Center, and the picture of Scott Peterson came from Facebook. The balance was from a personal collection belonging to the author.

INTRODUCTION

In 1492, Christopher Columbus reached the Western Hemisphere, initiating a massive change in the ecosystem of North America. The exchange of flora, fauna, and disease between the Old World and the New led historian Alfred Crosby to coin the term 'the Columbian Exchange'.[2] The long-term consequences are mixed. Food production and human populations increased enormously, but the ecological stability of vast areas was destroyed, erosion of the land increased, and many species were lost.[3] As a matter of fact, the impacts of human-kind on the earth are so great that many scientists believe we are no longer in the Holocene epoch period, which started 11,000 years ago at the end of the last ice age, but have entered the Anthropocene epoch, meaning man-new.[4] The effect of these changes has created the need for many tools, including conservation plants.

The Roosevelt Administration enacted the National Industrial Recovery Act of 1933, which authorized five million dollars for erosion control and employment programs.[5] This Act included funds that led to the creation of the Soil Erosion Service (SES) in the U.S. Department of the Interior. On April 27, 1935, Congress passed Public Law 74-46, in which it recognized that "the wastage of soil and moisture resources on farm, grazing, and forest lands is a menace to the national welfare", and it directed the Secretary of Agriculture to establish the Soil Conservation Service (SCS) as a permanent agency in the USDA.[6] The SCS absorbed the activities of the Soil Erosion Service and quickly developed numerous science-based tools and standards in agronomy, forestry, engineering, economics, wildlife biology and other disciplines. Field offices located in most counties have used these tools to help landowners plan and install conservation practices, including specialized conservation plants.

The search for such plants started in fourteen SES nurseries in 1933. The nurseries produced large numbers of trees and shrubs and were collecting seeds of native plants, These were used for soil and water conservation projects. Within each of these production nurseries was an observational nursery, each searching for superior conservation plants. This practice continued when the nurseries moved to SCS in 1935. By 1954 the production function of the nurseries was terminated and the observational nurseries became plant materials centers (PMC), collectively called the Plant Materials Program (PMP).

From its beginning, the Plant Materials Program has sought superior plants and methods for using them in the war against past and evolving natural resources degradation. It has changed over the years, always adjusting to meet evolving needs.[7]

This history discusses why such a program was needed, the efforts and accomplishments of conservation pioneers, how the Plant Materials Program came about, what it has accomplished, its star contributors, and where it may have strayed off course or could have done things better. The first seven chapters are generally in a chronological sequence with separate chapters providing details about different periods. The remaining chapters are about individual PMCs, special people, innovative accomplishments, and other issues affecting the Program. Principal sources of information include existing records at the National Archives, plant materials centers, SCS historians, others who have and are working in the Program, and the personal knowledge of the author.

Throughout this history many position titles, functions and even the name of the program and agency have changed. To the extent possible, all terminology reflects what these elements were called at that time in history. For example, the agency name, Soil Conservation Service, is used from 1935 until it changed in 1994. After 1994 the Natural Resources Conservation Service name is used. There will be some overlap in the terminology.

The Plant Materials Program has had a clear and unquestioned objective of finding and utilizing plants with superior characteristics for soil and water conservation applications. These plants are an important part of this history. Many are discussed individually and all appear in listings in Chapter 8 as an Output of the individual PMC. The Chapter 8 listings also include producer and ecological benefits resulting from the production and use for many of the new plants. A listing of the top producing ones, either in quantity or benefits, is near the end of Chapter 11.

Appendix 1 lists the definitions of acronyms used in the book. Scientific plant names are used according to the PLANTS database.[8] Generally, only common plant names are used in the text. Exceptions are made when plant names are a part of referenced publications. Appendix 9 is a listing of common and scientific plant names for all new conservation plants developed by the Plant Materials Program. They are ordered by common name to assist the reader in locating the scientific plant name of any new plants.

This history may exceed the norm in at least one aspect; that of including names of persons involved within the observational nursery or the Plant Materials Program. Initially an effort was made to present a complete roster of all former nursery and PMC fulltime professional and non-professional employees. This proved impossible, primarily because of the difficulties securing complete and accurate listings. As a result the names included are those of professional employees that can accurately be documented, plus the contributions of supporting staff in some discussions. Regrettably, some will have been missed. Names appearing in tables and in Appendix 2, 5 and 6 are not included in the index.

Source data is documented with End Notes. These are listed by heading and chapter following the index on page 472. The history does not contain a bibliography. However, Appendix 2, Partial List of Publications by SCS Nursery Division and Plant Materials Program Employees and Other Selected References Used in this History, includes most references that a bibliography would contain. Names of persons in the index are generally limited to those that appear in the text through Chapter 7, which encompass the chronological history. Names appearing in the other chapters, tables and appendices are not included in the index. Where tables overlap two or more pages,7 column headings are repeated on each page.

Chapter 1: WHY THE PLANT MATERIALS PROGRAM WAS NEEDED

The original people of North America lived in a wide range of environments. For several millennia they lived in small groups which were usually on the move hunting and gathering wild plant and animal foods. They did not establish permanent villages or clear land, leaving only a few scattered stone tools to indicate that they were here. This hunting way of life continued for thousands of years.

By around 4000 B.C., some Native Americans began to make clearings in the forest with stone axes, to encourage wild plant foods like berries and fruit trees. These clearings also attracted game that could be more easily hunted. By 1000 B.C., they started cultivating plants rather than relying completely on hunting and gathering. They cleared areas for gardens on floodplains along large creeks and rivers. The earliest plants grown were squash, gourds, and sunflowers. The Native Americans also established more permanent settlements and lived in larger groups. This altered the landscape more than their predecessors had.

The most intensive use of the land by the Native Americans was during the period from about 800 A.D. to the period of the 1600s or 1700s. By this time, they had developed large permanent villages and cultivated large fields of corn, beans, squash and pumpkins in stream and river bottoms. Populations were larger and impacts on the land were greater. In addition to agriculture, Native Americans intentionally burned portions of the woods in winter to keep the forest open for easier hunting and to stimulate plant growth that would attract deer. Burning also exposed mast for easier access to turkeys and deer. If and when they abandoned clearings, disturbances reverted to forests quickly.[9]

Following the introduction of Europeans in America, things rapidly changed. The impact on the land by the Native Americans was miniscule compared to the intensive agriculture that was to come.

CROPLAND EROSION

The early colonists settled primarily along streams, moving to upland areas only after lowlands were occupied. Land clearance and intensive cultivation led to severe soil erosion and land degradation in the late 1700s and early 1800s.[10] Fields were plowed down slope which made the work easier, but also increased the loss of soil. Plowing with the contour was hard work for both the animal and farmer. The usual depth of tillage was four inches with the use of a single-horse plow.

The invention of the cotton gin in 1796 stimulated large-scale production in the Piedmont and Southeast coastal plain.[11] Successful farmers acquired large land holdings. African-American slaves were brought to the region to work the fields. By the 1850s, cotton cultivation had left a large amount of the land in the area gullied and no longer useful for agriculture production. Population declined from 1850 to 1860 through migration to cotton lands further west in other southern states.

The magnitude of soil erosion during this period was enormous. Soil was stripped from the uplands, filled streams, raised water tables, and turned once fertile bottom lands into swamps. The lifespan of an average cotton field in Jasper County, GA for slave-holding plantations was about ten years. By then, the soil was eroded and depleted, and since new land was available they moved on.[12]

Early in the twentieth century, nearly ten million acres were used to cultivate row crops, and much of that land was losing soil with every rain. The Piedmont lost an average of about seven inches of topsoil; in many places all of it was lost. The resulting red hills were both the evidence and the heritage of generations of land mismanagement. In southwest Georgia, spectacular gullies, such as Providence Canyon, permanently ruined much of the land for farming.[13] As late as the 1980s PMC visitors to the area would be taken to these spectacular gullies.

Dr. Hugh Hammond Bennett reported in 1928 that certain Piedmont areas whose records were known, lost all their topsoil within a period of thirty years; ten inches or more of loam and clay loam were washed off down to the clay subsoil.[14] This clay subsoil, which replaced the departed topsoil, required from 400 to 600 pounds of fertilizer to produce as much cotton per acre as formerly was grown with 200 to 250 pounds of fertilizer, and was of no better quality.

When measuring soil loss on an open plot in the Piedmont region of North Carolina, 24.9 tons of soil per acre was lost each year, with an annual rainfall of 35.6 inches. On the same slope, soil erosion from grassland a year amounted to only 0.06 tons to the acre. In other words, the grass held back four hundred and fifteen times as much surface soil as was retained on untilled bare ground. The uncultivated plot retained 64.5 percent of the rainfall, a cotton plot 74.4 percent, and grassland 98.5 percent of the rainfall.[15]

A single county in the southern part of the Piedmont region was found by actual survey to contain 90,000 acres of land that had been largely cultivated at one time, and which had been permanently ruined by erosion.[16] The whole area was dissected by gullies, and bedrock was exposed in thousands of places. Here and there, islands and peninsulas of arable land had been left between hideous gullies, but most of these remnants were too small to cultivate. The land had been so devastated that it could not be reclaimed for cultivation until centuries of rock decay restored the soil.

Figure 1.1 A common site on abandoned cropland in the Southeast

The practice that caused one of our most precious resources to wash away was part of a larger culture that prevailed across the South and much of the nation well into the twentieth century. Pioneer agriculture, which took place in an era when land was cheap, and seemingly expendable, gave way to a combination of plantations, small farms, and eventually a sharecropper system that not only degraded the land but also kept farmers in debt and uneducated.[17]

Similar, but far less destructive, cropland soil erosion was commonplace through all the humid temperate regions of the eastern U.S.

There is no time or place in this country when cropland degradation was as rampant as during this period. Without a doubt, soil erosion on high quality cropland represented one of the greatest environmental threats facing the nation but, with rare exception, it stayed under the radar until it became a calamity.

MINING

To a great extent, the temperate regions of the Northeast escaped severe natural or human erosion-causing practices of the magnitude experienced in the Southeast. Timber resources were utilized extensively, but heavy litter and rapid re-growth minimized soil loss. Farming centered on either dairy or meat producing enterprises; small plowed fields intermingled with permanent pasture or woodlots. However, there was an exception, i.e., coal and other natural resource mining.

The U.S. has a long history of mining that even pre-dates the country's split from Britain. The coal industry, for instance, dates back to 1,000 A.D. when, the Hopi Indians, living in what is now Arizona, used coal to bake pottery.[18] To support the colonial iron industry in Pennsylvania in the mid-1700s, most mining activities disturbed small acreage, particularly underground mining. However, by the end of World War II, surface mining overtook underground mining as the primary way to extract the mineral.

Surface extraction has caused degradation of both arable and non-arable soil on a large scale. By the mid twentieth century, more than 740,000 acres of land in Appalachia had been directly affected by strip mining for bituminous coal, in addition to 59,000 acres in the anthracite region of Pennsylvania and 74,000 acres disturbed by mine-access roads. More than a third of this acreage was on steep slopes, and only one-fourth of the land was reclaimed. As a result, there were massive slides along 1,400 miles of strip-mine terrace benches. Even when operators attempted to reclaim sites, they often failed because mining reshuffled soil layers and exposed shale with much of the topsoil buried, and newly exposed soil was too acidic to sustain plant life.

The consequential failure of natural revegetation compounded erosion problems, which had an impact not only on actual mine sites, but also on adjacent land and riparian zones.

GREAT PLAINS LOSS OF PERMANENT VEGETATIVE COVER

During early European and American exploration the Great Plains was thought unsuitable for European-style agriculture;[19] indeed, the region was known as the Great American Desert. The lack of surface water and timber made the region less attractive than other areas for pioneer settlement and agriculture. However, following the American Civil War, settlement in the area increased, encouraged by the Homestead Act of 1862, and by the railroads. An unusually wet period in the Great Plains led settlers and government to believe that 'rain follows the plow', and that the climate of the region had permanently changed. The initial agricultural endeavors were primarily cattle ranching with some cultivation; however, a series of harsh winters, beginning in 1886, coupled with overgrazing, followed by a short drought in 1890, led to an expansion of land under cultivation.

Immigration began again at the beginning of the twentieth century. A return of unusually wet weather confirmed the previously held opinion that the "formerly" semi-arid area could support large-scale agriculture. Technological improvements led to increased automation, which allowed for cultivation on an ever greater scale. In the Llano Estacada, Texas farmland area, cultivation doubled between 1900 and 1920, and land under cultivation more than tripled between 1925 and 1930.[20] Farmers even used agricultural practices that encouraged erosion. For example, cotton farmers in the southern Great Plains left fields barren over winter months, when winds in the High Plains are highest. Others burned their wheat stubble, which deprived the soil of organic matter and increased exposure to erosion.[21]

The renewed immigration led to the plowing of the tall and short grass prairies, which unleashed the Dust Bowl. About 172 million acres of Great Plains cropland were eroded by wind and water at rates that exceeded twice the tolerance level for sustainable production.[22] On average, wind erosion was responsible for about forty percent of this loss,[23] and increased markedly during the drought years.[24] It impacted about seventy-four million acres leaving moderate to severe damage on approximately five million acres annually.

The increased exposure to erosion was revealed when an unusually severe drought struck the Great Plains in 1930.[25] The grass which covered the prairie lands for centuries held the soil in place and maintained moisture, but deep plowing and increased farming eliminated the grass holding the soil. The drought conditions caused the topsoil to become very dry and loose, and it was simply carried away by wind which, in turn, kicked up immense dust clouds that further prevented rainfall.[26]

On November 11, 1933, a very strong dust storm stripped topsoil from desiccated South Dakota farmlands in just one of a series of bad dust storms that year.[27] Then, beginning on May 9, 1934, a strong two-day dust storm removed massive amounts of Great Plains topsoil in one of the worst such storms of the Dust Bowl. The dust clouds blew all the way to Chicago where dirt fell like snow. Two days later, the same storm reached cities in the east, such as Buffalo, Boston, New York City, and Washington D.C. That winter, red snow fell on New England.

GREAT PLAINS AND BASIN GRAZING LAND

When the great herds of buffalo, elk, deer and other herbivores ranged across the Great Plains and Intermountain West it represented the perfect form of rotational grazing. When they passed over an area all the usable forage was consumed, so they moved on, maybe not returning for another year. The herd size represented what the resource could support.

Grasslands in the Great Plains were relatively tolerant of grazing because of their evolutionary associations with the continent's principal native grazer, the bison. In contrast, grasses of the intermountain West and Southwest have had less association with any intensive native grazing and were relatively intolerant of introduced domestic livestock activities. Native grasses and forbs in the Great Basin did not adapt to intensive grazing.[28] Perennial bunchgrasses in the Columbia Basin grew rapidly in the spring to set seed before summer. Heavy spring grazing prevented the plants from reproducing and eventually eliminated the native bunchgrasses. Grazing by large herds of introduced livestock after 1850 had a profound effect on the shrub-steppe plant population, greatly eliminating the grasses and palatable forbs. Richard Mack stated that cheatgrass (*Bromus tectorum*) was the most ubiquitous alien in the intermountain West during the 1889–1894 periods.[29] By 1928, the grass had reached its present distribution, as native grasses dwindled with overgrazing and cultivation. By the 1930s, federal range personnel estimated that eighty-four percent of the sagebrush-grass regions in the United States were severely depleted.[30]

The native animal herds disappeared as the west welcomed domestic livestock. Ranching became a staple of the Intermountain West culture and economy. As one of the first industries, cattlemen appeared in the western valleys in the 1860s to answer the demand of beef in a growing country. These early ranchers relied on the practice of open range grazing, where they grazed large areas of unsettled lands, continually moving their herds to fresher pastures. Its popularity waned with the introduction of the Homestead Act of 1862, and the expanded 1909 iteration. These two acts promised large parcels of land (160 and 320 acres, respectively) to applicants who could improve the land through agriculture practices. This led to an increase in fenced-in, privatized land. Managing livestock during bitter winters would lead to more intensive management of herds and signaled the curtain call of open range operations.[31]

This transition resulted in excessive amounts of livestock confined to a specific area, far exceeding what the resource could support. Even before the turn of the century, once-rich grasslands were seriously degraded after less than a human generation of use. By the early 1900s, overstocking of sheep on many middle-elevation grasslands had brought forest regeneration to a halt. The forest floor in some places was "as bare and compact as a roadbed."[32] Wildfires of the region drastically altered the once grass-rich ponderosa forest, causing severe erosion and long-term changes to the vegetative composition.

Large-scale cattle ranching began in the Little Colorado River Basin during the 1880s following the arrival of the Aztec Land and Cattle Company. Significant local range deterioration occurred shortly thereafter as it had elsewhere in the American West following the expansion of the livestock industry. Numerous local indications of overexploited grasslands persist throughout the region, even to this day. This is evidenced by bare soil, the low percentage of herbaceous vegetation that remain, the widespread invasion of juniper trees into the grassland community, and the overall reduction in range productivity. Significantly, the worst conditions prevailed on those lands which were owned and operated by the Aztec Land and Cattle Company.[33]

Although cattle and sheep were brought to the Southwest by the Spanish in the late 1500s, it only began to have a significant impact on the region's biota with the arrival of the railroads in the late 1800s. By 1890, hundreds of thousands of cattle and large numbers of sheep were grazing in the Basin: in pine forests, on grasslands, and along riparian corridors. Mouat and Hutchinson estimate that as much as seventy-six percent of dry land areas, such as the Great Basin, have been degraded to some extent.[34]

By the time federal forest reserves were proclaimed in the 1890s, ranchers had become accustomed to unregulated use of public lands as range for livestock.[35] As a result of these excessive stocking numbers, once-rich grasslands were seriously degraded even before the turn of the century.

By 1912, livestock pressures had penetrated the most remote, timbered and mountainous areas. Theodore Rixon, one of the first foresters in the Southwest, described the situation:

> At the beginning, the mountains and heavily timbered areas were used but little, but as the situation grew more acute in the more accessible regions the use of these areas became more general and in course of time conditions within them were more grave than elsewhere. The mountains were denuded of their vegetative cover, forest reproduction was damaged or destroyed, the slopes were seamed with deep erosion gullies, and the water-conserving power of the drainage basins became seriously impaired. Flocks passed each other on the trails, one rushing in to secure what the other had just abandoned as worthless, feed was deliberately wasted to prevent its utilization by others, and ranges were occupied before the snow had left them. Transient sheepmen roamed the country robbing the resident stockmen of forage that was justly theirs.[36]

The ultimate cause of regional grassland deterioration lay in the speculative nature of the nineteenth-century range cattle industry, and in the effect that livestock speculation had on local range management policies. Because range-stocking decisions were based on national market considerations rather than on local environmental conditions, the number and density of cattle that were maintained on local ranges was both excessive and unresponsive for local climatic conditions.[37]

Over one hundred years later, the effects of intense grazing in the latter part of the nineteenth century can still be readily seen in many parts of the Colorado Plateau.

Although riparian habitats represent less than one percent of the total acreage of public lands in the eleven western states, they are among the most biologically diverse and important fish and wildlife habitats. In Arizona and New Mexico, approximately eighty percent of all vertebrate wildlife use riparian habitats during part of their lives. The abundance of food, water, and shade which attracts wildlife to these areas also attracts livestock. Despite widespread recognition of the problem and attempts to remove or restrict livestock from riparian areas, degradation due to overgrazing was a serious problem on the Colorado Plateau. Destruction of streamside vegetation and hallowing of channels are some of the effects of poor grazing practices.

CALIFORNIA GRAZING LAND

California's twenty million acres of grasslands have also undergone dramatic changes during the last two centuries. Changes in grazing patterns from native herbivores to domestic livestock, followed by accidental and intentional plant introductions resulted in the conversion of perennial-dominated grasslands to introduced annual grasses.[38] The annual grasslands were also heavily invaded by deeply rooted late-maturing forbs, such as yellow star thistle. This series of invasions and conversions has changed the community structure, soil protection, soil water use and productive value of the grasslands. Native species are now only a minor component of the grassland flora, comprising less than 1% of the standing grassland crop.[39]

Overgrazing in the Mediterranean climate of California converted the native annual/perennial rangeland flora into almost entirely introduced annual grasses.[40]

COASTAL RESOURCES

Agricultural or other practices of the earlier settlers hovering along the east, gulf and western seaboard had minimal impact on soil erosion.[41] However, coastal resources were critical not only to the Native Americans, but even more so to the newly arriving Europeans. A combination of natural causes and abusive use along coastal regions created severe water erosion, threatening homes, farms and forests.[42] Much of the abusive use of coastal areas comes from the desirability of home sites, thus altering what would be the natural configurations of the shoreline. Two regions suffered the most, the Pacific Northwest and the central Atlantic states.

Coastal barrier dunes are formed by wave and wind action. Waves bring sand to shore from the adjacent inner continental shelf, or from upland sand brought to the coast by terrestrial streams, and it is transported landward. In a natural dune setting, vegetation reduces wind speed, causing sand to accumulate. As sand accumulates, plants adapted to the beach environment emerge, stabilizing the surface and promoting further dune formation. That process is frequently interrupted by natural activities, and in time mends itself. During storms, sand erodes from the beach-dune system and re-deposits as shallow sandbars offshore. In a stable beach- dune system, the sand moved offshore during storms is returned during calm weather. Thus, the dunes, beach, and near-shore sandbars act as a dynamic, integrated unit, often referred to as the beach-dune system.[43] As the population grew in coastal regions, human activity permanently interrupted these natural processes.

There was a big difference between how Native Americans and transplanted Europeans managed coastal resources. The Native Americans were passive managers while the transplanted Americans were manipulative; they altered the resource to fit their needs. The benefits of the dunes were no doubt well known by both groups, but the latter were sure they had more value for other uses, primarily for recreation and housing. Of course the coastal region was most valuable when the ocean was visible, so hundreds of miles of dunes were leveled to make this possible. However, the forces that created dunes kept on working, and the dunes kept trying to reform and re-vegetate.

Natural and human induced erosion along tidal streams and estuaries, particularly in the Mid-Atlantic States has become extensive. Approximately twenty-three percent of the shoreline was reported to have experienced some degree of erosion in Virginia in 1962. Approximately 21,000 acres of Virginia shoreline was lost between 1850 and 1950.[44] The study estimates the total volume of material lost by erosion into the Virginia portion of the Chesapeake Bay is 270 million cubic yards.

The erosion is the result of storm action, freezing and thawing, and waves eroding the toe of the vertical slope. The slope collapses, soil material is carried away and the process is repeated. The building of a sandy beach with groins, the use of a bulkhead to protect the slope, or a combination of both systems are the usual methods used to attempt to stop this erosion. These have worked with a varying degree of success, depending on site conditions, storm frequency and intensity. Both are expensive to install and have undesirable environmental impacts.[45]

Coastal estuaries exposed to tidal fluctuation and storm damage create a likelihood of shore bank erosion. Under natural conditions, the interface between the fluctuating water's edge and the upland is the zone where marshes develop. When the tide hits the marsh its energy is dissipated and the upland is protected from its erosive force. In the absence of marshes, the tide's energy is dispensed against a bare slope. Both natural and non-natural factors can accelerate the loss of marshes. It is estimated that fifty-seven percent of the total sediment load in the Chesapeake Bay is from tidal erosion. Maryland loses as much as twenty acres of land along the Chesapeake Bay shore in the wake of a tropical storm.

UPLAND STREAMS AND RIPARIAN AREAS

The impact of Native Americans directly on erosion from upland streams is assumed to be little or none. If streams erode due the acts of nature they continued to erode or heal themselves. To a reasonable extent, this was to be the case during the early centuries after the Europeans arrived. Over time, however, alterations in stream flow, roads, dredging, commercial fishing, boating, etc., along with nature's storms, have degraded the natural vegetation's ability to recover and provide adequate protection.

The occurrence of erosion on upland streams is relatively common. The severity depends to a great extent on the protection supplied by natural vegetation. Actions of developments adjacent to streams can accelerate erosion. Eroding streams contribute to in-stream and downstream sediment load, water turbidity, loss of land, and reduced recreational opportunities. Thirty three percent of Pennsylvania streams are considered impaired due to erosion.[46]

Associated with upland stream erosion is the presence or absence of a riparian area along the stream. Their presence is essential for many reasons. Over sixty-five percent of southwestern animals depend on riparian habitats during all or part of their life cycles. The riparian zone creates well-defined habitats within the drier surrounding landscape. According to Hoorman and McCutcheon, healthy riparian areas have many different characteristics depending upon location, geology, landscape, and climate. However, all healthy riparian areas have similarities that include the following:

- A thick growth of vegetation with diverse species of grasses, forbs, shrubs, and trees that cover the stream banks and provide shade.

- Land surrounding stream banks that generally remain wet throughout most of the year except where streams cut through rocky terrain.

- Stream banks that are more vertical and steep than flat and rounded.

- Stream flow levels which vary only moderately throughout the year.

- Stream water which is relatively clear but contains debris from stream banks (leaves, twigs, or logs) that create pools and other habitat for fish and aquatic insects.

- A diversity of wildlife including fish, aquatic life, mammals, and birds.[47]

Riparian area structure and composition changed due to irrigation diversions, reservoirs, farming, grazing, human settlement and natural storms. Replacing or improving riparian areas is critical to environmental, economic and recreational conditions.

LAND DISTURBANCE FOR ROADS, HOMES AND OTHER CONSTRUCTION

Native Americans traveled on foot using trails. Their footprints left few scars on the landscape. As early as fifty years after Columbus' arrival, the earth was moved to make a road accessible for buggies, then wagons, then motor vehicles. As the size and number of vehicles expanded the size of the trail expanded. Instead of moving a little earth, mountains disappeared, creating enormous erosion producers from sea to shining sea. All earth moving construction activity creates short to long-term erosion problems.[48]

WILDLIFE HABITAT

From the dawn of humans on the North American hemisphere, wildlife has been a source of food and visual enjoyment. As the Native American culture gave way to that which replaced it, the frequency and distribution of wildlife changed dramatically and permanently.[49] As this change took place, society came to a tipping point where it demanded some consideration to the continued elimination of the required habitat. Since terrestrial wildlife lives in and depends on vegetation, re-creating this environment is essential.

SUMMARY

Misuse of the land for the first three and a half centuries after settlement in what became the United States was a way of life. In the absence of some resistance to the land degradation juggernaut, this way of life would have in all likelihood, continued indefinitely.

Chapter 2: EARLY EROSION CONTROL EFFORTS

While limited in scope, attempts to control soil erosion in America date back to colonial times, particularly if it presented an immediate threat. For example, Provincetown, MA undertook an effort to stop the blowing sand that was threatening their town. The town is located on Cape Cod, which was formed entirely by drifted and wind-blown sand. Early Pilgrim writings describe Cape Cod as a forest of luxuriant woods containing juniper, birch, holly, vines, some ash, and walnut, mostly without undergrowth. After clearing these dense forests for fuel, fence posts and fish weirs, the population recognized that the lack of vegetation was causing the sand dunes to move, which in turn were threatening the town and harbor. Sand movement was so pronounced the harbor was in danger of being obliterated. In an effort to halt the dunes, in about 1714, the colonials began planting beach grass from existing stands, and placing pine branches to help the grass take root.[50]

CONSERVATION PRACTICES

Early observers of the need for conservation practices began proposing various solutions to the problem of cropland erosion. Jared Eliot, Samuel Deane, and John Taylor, among others relied on observations and personal experiences.[51] They advocated systems of pasture and legumes crop rotations, thus increasing fertility and lessening erosion by maintaining ground cover and improving the overall health of the soil. Eliot, a Connecticut farmer, observed

> When our fore-fathers settled here, they entered a land which probably never had been ploughed since the creation; the land being new they depended upon the natural fertility of the ground, which served their purpose very well and when they had worn out one piece they cleared another, without any concern to amend their Land, except a little helped by the fold and calf dung, whereas in England they would think a man a bad husband, if he should pretend to sow wheat on land without any dressing.

Samuel Deane promoted agriculture experimentation of crop rotations, methods of plowing to prevent erosion. Both Eliot and Deane knew the value of and encouraged the use of green manure crops. Deane seemed to stand alone with concern about wind erosion in the late eighteenth century in New England.

John Taylor of Carolina County, VA was a wealthy gentlemen farmer who, like Jefferson, wanted to preserve the old order of agriculture. He believed that the well-being of the nation was to be identified with the well-being of the farmers. What was good for the farmers was good for the country at large. His zeal for the cause of agriculture exceeded his time on earth.

> At the awful Day of Judgment, the discrimination of the good from the wicked is not made by the criterion of sects or of dogmas, but by one which constitutes the daily employment, and the greatest end of Agriculture. The judge upon this occasion has by anticipation pronounced, that to feed the hungry, clothe the naked, and give drink to the thirsty are the passports to future happiness; and the divine intelligence which selected an Agricultural state as a paradise for its first favorites, has here again prescribed the Agricultural virtues as the means for the admission of their posterity into heaven.[52]

MECHANICAL METHODS

Though he invented neither, Thomas Mann Randolph perceived the advantages of his hillside plow and horizontal plowing. More often called contour farming these days, this method of plowing involved running the furrows around the hillside on a horizontal plane, rather than up and down hills. A convert to the idea, Randolph's father-in-law, Thomas Jefferson, believed that, "In point of beauty nothing can exceed that of the waving lines and rows winding along the faces of the hills and valleys. The horses draw much easier on the dead level, and it is in fact a conversion of hilly ground into a plain."[53] According to Nicholas Sorsby, farmers could also build terraces or channels that ran around the hill to intercept and carry off water. He combined horizontal farming with the early precursor of the terrace, i.e., the hillside ditch, and greatly popularized "level culture" throughout the South.[54] Unfortunately, as observed in the last chapter, this idea may have been more popular than utilized.

After the Civil War, Priestly Mangum of Wake Forest, North Carolina, adopted broad-based Mangum terraces. By 1912, the system had been officially adopted and endorsed by the U.S. Department of Agriculture. Within another ten years it was utilized in nearly every state in the country.[55] Edmund Ruffin of Virginia developed the most elaborate system of what today might be called sustainable agriculture. He used a mixture of decaying sea-shells, clay and marl that made the acidic soils of the south more productive. He further demonstrated the value of crop rotations and legumes in maintaining fertility. Ruffin especially wanted to stem the tide of farmers leaving Virginia. The combination of these practices increased crop production, and, in his opinion, reduced soil erosion. Though he succeeded locally to some extent, he never revolutionized or reformed agriculture in the south. By the 1850s, his interests drifted to an independent south, which may have hindered widespread acceptance of his cropping systems.[56]

A few scientists and academics such as W. J. McGee and N. S. Shaler wrote about the soil erosion problem. McGee, in his 1911 *Soil Erosion,* discusses methodology for controlling erosion, like protecting the soil surface and enhancing infiltration. Although McGee was self-educated he achieved distinction in several scientific fields, including soil surveys as well as soil erosion. While on the staff of the Bureau of Soils, McGee organized the landmark Conference of Governors on Conservation of Natural Resources in 1908. In 1911, he published *Soil Erosion,* as complete a discussion of the subject as had been previously done.[57]

USING PLANTS

There are early examples of unintended use of plants for erosion control.[58] By the 1500s, Europeans from the Mediterranean region of Europe started arriving in California and accidentally brought with them non-native plants as ship ballast. Many of the plants were annual grasses. The number of native herbivores was nil compared to the rapidly expanding herds of domestic livestock. The existing native flora of mixed annual and perennial grasses and forbs soon gave way to overgrazing and the introduced annuals found their niche. The annuals became dominate but ironically, supplied erosion control. One can speculate what the erosion impact would have been had the introduced annuals not been present.[59]

Other examples abound where the destruction of a native flora opened the way for a plant to step forward and initiated an unintended conservation objective. Crested wheatgrass was introduced into the U.S. in 1887 from the windswept steppes of central Asia.[60] It fit well into the climate of the Northern Great Plains and much of the West's Great Basin. Having tolerated sheep grazing for thousands of years, it found a home following the intensive grazing of cattle. While it provided high quality spring grazing, palatability decreased as the season progressed. This was fortunate; otherwise it would have been eradicated like the native perennials.

The interest in the late 18th century of importing plants to America was high for crop production or ornamental use; their importation for conservation use came much later.[61] European beachgrass, *Ammophila arenaria*, was an early example, first planted in 1896 to stabilize sand in California.[62] It spread quickly along Washington's coast, both by natural means and cultivation. The native dunegrass, *Elymus mollis*, was the dominant grass along Washington's dunes before the arrival of European beachgrass. It produces a low, hummocky dune field, while American beachgrass, introduced from the east coast, produces a more defined and higher frontal dune. European beachgrass was extensively planted in the 1930s to halt dunes that were advancing inland. It appeared better suited for what was needed than either of the other two, because it was well adapted and produced much higher and steeper sided dunes. This allowed the stabilization of back dune areas with trees and shrubs.

Kudzu was first introduced into the United States in 1876 at the Philadelphia Centennial Exposition.[63] As a nitrogen producing legume, it was a desirable forage plant for livestock, which also helped it grow on the abandoned cotton land of the Southeast. Some say it escaped because it grew faster that a cow could walk. Then it was tried as an erosion control plant, and for that purpose it did reasonably well. It also does reasonably well for other things, like covering up junk cars. Its use by land owners, and later recommendations by the USDA, indicates how desperate the country needed conservation plants. [64]

VOICING CONCERN

A University of Chicago geologist, T. C. Chamberlain, spoke at the White House in 1908 about the dangers of erosion. Chamberlain convinced Hugh Hammond Bennett that he was right to be concerned about the relationship between soils and the survival of a people. Bennett often cited Chamberlain in his writings and credited him with giving legitimacy to erosion as a serious national issue. He ventured a guess that the mean soil formation in Illinois was no greater than one foot in 10,000 years. At such rates of formation, what he called 'surface waste' should not exceed one inch in a 1,000 years.[65]

It isn't as though the blight of soil erosion was being ignored by our founding fathers. It was Patrick Henry who said, "Since the achievement of our independence, wasn't he the greatest patriot who stops the most gullies."[66]

Historically speaking, improving crop production through plant breeding is a recent phenomenon. Not until 1908 did G. H. Shull of the Iowa State Agriculture Station first present the idea of inbred-hybrid lines. In some ways this and other technology advances may have worked against maintaining soil quality. They definitely increased production, which has a tendency to reduce soil stewardship unless given some special effort.[67]

A prolific USDA plants writer near the end of the nineteenth century was Frank Lamson-Scribner. Of his many papers, one relates to the use of plants for soil conservation: *Grasses as Soil and Soil Binders.* It describes the characteristics of plants which grow naturally in coastal dunes. Other plant related publications by Lamson-Scribner discuss plants that became prominent for conservation use, but the publications do not mention their value for that use.[68] Examples of Lamson-Scribner's writings include:

- Hungarian bromegrass; by F. Lamson-Scribner, 1894.

- Hairy vetch, sand vetch, or Russian vetch; by F. Lamson-Scribner, 1895.

- American grasses (v.) 1 (illustrated); by F. Lamson-Scribner, 1897. Rev. Ed. 1898.

- New species of North American grasses; by F. Lamson-Scribner, 1899.

- Flat pea: by F. Lamson-Scribner, 1899.

- North American grasses; by F. Lamson-Scribner, 1899.

- New and little-known Mexican grasses; by F. Lamson-Scribner, 1900.

- Cooperative range grass and forage-plant experiments at Highmore, S D; by F. Lamson-Scribner, 1900.

- Grass and forage plant investigations on the Pacific coast; by F. Lamson-Scribner, 1900.

- New or little-known grasses: by F. Lamson-Scribner, 1897.

- Records of seed distribution and cooperative experiments with grasses and forage plants; by F. Lamson-Scribner, 1902.

TAKING ACTION

In the early 1920s, William Boyce Thompson, who desired to establish vegetation to control erosion around his new Arizona home, contacted Dr. Franklin Crider of the University of Arizona for assistance. Thompson also wanted to experiment with re-vegetating the north slope of the mountain, which had been overgrazed by cattle. With Dr. Franklin Crider's help they sought to locate several species of groundcovers which could live long enough on the damaged hillsides and hold back enough soil to allow other species to become established. Their effort had long lasting consequences.[69]

Formal congressional recognition of soil erosion as a national emergency first came in 1929 in the Buchanan Amendment to the Agriculture Appropriation Bill of Fiscal Year 1930.[70] Much of this resulted from the 1928 USDA publication by Hugh Hammond Bennett, coauthored with William Ridgely Chapline titled, *Soil Erosion: A National Menace*[71]. The bulletin was not a manual on the methods of preventing soil erosion; rather it was a call to action, "...to the evils of this process of land wastage and to the need for increased practical information and research work relating to the problem." This led to finding an ally in the cause, A. B. Connor of the Texas Agricultural Experiment Station, who in turn enlisted the aid of Representative James Buchanan. The amendment Buchanan introduced provided $160,000 to be used by the Secretary of Agriculture for soil erosion investigations. In 1930, soil erosion experiment stations were set up under the direction of the Bureau of Chemistry and Soils.

Another wakeup call that came in the form of the 1930s Dust Bowl almost seems providential. To make sure we heard the message, the Dust Bowl was punctuated by the Great Depression. Indeed, for conservation purposes, it was a new beginning in more ways than one. The National Industrial Recovery Act of 1933 authorized five million dollars for erosion control and employment programs.[72] On September 13, 1933, the Soil Erosion Service was formed in the Department of the Interior, with Hugh Hammond Bennett as chief. A portion of these funds were

Figure 2.1 Texas dust storn, motivating Representative Buchanan to action

used to establish fourteen Soil Erosion Service nurseries. Their primary functions were

1. to produce or collect large quantities of proven conservation plants to be used in erosion control demonstration project, and

2. To conduct a systematic search and evaluation for superior conservation plants.

The fourteen nurseries are shown in Table 2.1, with their current status. Their transfer to the Soil Conservation Service two years later had planted the seed for the future observational phase of SCS nurseries. [73]

Table 2.1 Nurseries transferred from USDI, Bureau of Plant Industry to SCS April 1, 1935

No.	Location	Outcome	No.	Location	Outcome
1	Belle Mina, AL	Closed in 1938	8	San Antonio, TX	Closed in 1953
2	Statesville, NC	Closed in 1938	9	Shreveport, LA	Closed in 1938
3	Elsberry, MO	Functioning as PMC	10	Shiprock, AZ	Closed in 1939
4	Ames, IA	Closed in 1953	11	Placerville, CA	Closed in 1936
5	Cheyenne, WY	Never functioned as SCS nursery	12	Pullman, WA	Functioning as PMC
6	Mandan, ND	Functioning as PMC in Bismarck, ND	13	Stafford, AZ	Closed in 1939
7	Stillwater, OK	Closed in 1940	14	Tucson, AZ	Functioning as PMC

Chapter 3: CREATION OF THE SOIL CONSERVATION SERVICE AND EVOLUTION OF A PLANT EVALUATION CONCEPT

NEW AGENCY ESTABLISHED

Hugh Hammond Bennett, a soil scientist with the U.S. Department of Agriculture, became the director of the Soil Erosion Service (SES), U.S. Department of Interior on September 19, 1933. He had become the twentieth century crusader for soil conservation and later came to be regarded as its father.[74]

Several facets of Bennett's personality and background suited him to the role of crusader. First, he had the understanding of the problem due to experience; he grew up in one of the more erodible areas of North Carolina. He was a skilled writer and had a passion for the cause.[75] He published article after article. All of this contributed to his being an ideal promoter of the conservation cause. The crisis brought on by the Great Depression further provided Bennett with fodder for the fight.

Bennett had been a career employee in the Bureau of Chemistry and Soils, and had long recognized that a multi-disciplinary approach to the erosion problem was essential. Although the new agency was in the Department of the Interior, many of his staff had to be recruited from USDA with skills in soils, agronomy, biology, forestry and engineering. A few experienced people were scattered in federal and state agencies, and a fair nucleus was present on experiment farms set up earlier within the USDA.[76]

With the five million dollars in Soil Erosion Service emergency employment funds,[77] Bennett planned soil and water conservation demonstrations on farms in selected watersheds and established the fourteen soil erosion nurseries to supply the needed plant materials.[78][79] The original staff included experts in several technical fields. Others were recruited and trained. Because of the severe depression in 1933, many such individuals were available though they had little experience in erosion control work. Bennett's principal staff in 1933 is shown in Table 3.1.

Table 3.1 Original staff Soil Erosion Service

Vice Director	Walter C. Lowdermilk
Chief of Operations	William Stephenson
Technical Secretary	Robert A. Winston
Chief Agronomist	Lyman Carrier
Chief Agricultural Engineer	James G. Lindley
Specialist in Erosion	Glenn L. Fuller
Chief Forester	E. V. Jolter
Chief Fiscal Officer	Henry R. St. Cyr
Special Assistant	Charles W. Collie

PROVIDENCE PROVIDES AN OPPORTUNITY

It was not uncommon during the early spring for a Dust Bowl storm to be swept up into the atmosphere and to be carried across the country to the Atlantic seaboard.[80] Bennett, ever the showman, recounted the events years later about his testimony before the Senate Public Lands Committee in 1935.[81] He had followed the progress of the big duster from its point of origin in northeastern New Mexico, on into the Ohio Valley, and had every reason to believe it would eventually reach Washington. It did, in sun-darkening proportions, and at about the predicted time. This storm dramatized the need for soil conservation as it passed over Washington, just as he was testifying before the Senate Public Lands Committee, promoting a new agency committed to soil conservation. All this helped create the Soil Conservation Act of 27 April 1935, which transformed the soil conservation work into a permanent agency. On the same day, the Secretary issued Department Memorandum 673, establishing the Soil Conservation Service within the USDA, providing that the new agency include the activities conducted under the Soil Erosion Service, and designating H. H. Bennett Chief of the new agency.[82]

The Soil Erosion Service nurseries that transferred to SCS are listed in Table 2.1 in Chapter 2. The Soil Conservation Act of 27 April 1935 gave the Department and agency broad authority "To conduct surveys, investigations, and research relating to the character of soil erosion and the preventive measures…and conduct demonstrational projects." Authority to operate the nurseries was not included in the April 27 Act, but the authority came to the new agency with the transfer of the nurseries from the SES.[83]

Dr. Bennett had leveraged the Depression to gain his objective; a tool to address soil erosion. Creating the Agency became more palatable for the Administration because it could also serve as a conduit to improve job opportunities in rural America.[84]

Farmers first approached the Soil Conservation Act with skepticism, worrying that the federal government would over regulate them and essentially take direct control of the farms.[85] To overcome this concern, in 1935 Congress passed Public Law 46, establishing *soil conservation districts.* These conservation districts gave locally appointed directors, not federal officials, the authority to establish and manage local soil and water conservation work. The federal government, in turn, cooperated by granting the districts equipment and providing technical assistance to farmers. This arrangement left local areas with the authority to shape conservation projects, but encouraged them to undertake such projects with federal technical assistance and funding.[86]

Additional work-relief funds enlarged the conservation related programs so that by mid-1936 there were 147 demonstration projects and forty-eight nurseries, including carryovers from the SES, plus twenty-three experiment stations, 454 Civilian Conservation Corps camps, and over 23,000 Work Progress Administration workers on the different activities.[87]

The SES nurseries had evolved into two areas of responsibilities. The first and largest was to collect from native stands large quantities of woody seed, which was used to produce seedlings, and collect grass and forbs seed. Both were used for establishing demonstration projects and for direct conservation use on private lands. The second responsibility was finding new and better conservation plants through a comparative observational approach. The portion of the SES nurseries where that function was performed came to be known as the observational nurseries.[88] Although a functioning part of most production nurseries, these observational nurseries were not separate budgetary units, but depended on the nursery staff to carry out their program. Employees with special training were hired for this work at many nurseries, but nursery records do not separate observational personnel or activities from production activities.

While giving testimony to the U.S. House of Representatives Agricultural Subcommittee in 1953, the Chief of SCS at that time, Dr. Robert Salter, described observational nurseries in lay terms to the Congressmen. Although observational nurseries are discussed extensively in the following chapters, this simplified description warrants being presented here.

> At many of these (SCS) nurseries we have assembled strains of new grasses and legumes from plant breeders in state experiment stations and the Bureau of Plant Industry, and from a lot of natural collections. New grasses and legumes are studied in these nurseries in small plots. The seed of these which look like they have promise is

increased enough so that it can be put in a program of observational testing. The seed is distributed over various regions of the United States in small plantings in observational test plots. There are literally hundreds and hundreds of these tests. It is out of these tests that we determine the desirability of expanding any of these strains for commercial production. After observation tests show the value of a strain over a sufficient area, we blow it up and try to put it into commercial production.

BIRTH OF SCS OBSERVATIONAL NURSERIES

When SES was established in 1933, Charles R. Enlow moved from the USDA Bureau of Plant Industry to the USDI as an agronomist to head up the nursery development in the new agency, working under Dr. Bennett.[89] Born in Kingman County, Kansas, Enlow earned a B.S. in 1920 and an M.S. degree in 1927 at Kansas State University. After field work for the Great Western Sugar Company, he taught agriculture in Kansas high schools. In 1924, he became assistant professor of agronomy at Kansas State University; then in 1927 he joined USDA's Bureau of Plant Industry, in Gainesville, Florida. Two years later he was transferred to Washington, D.C., to direct the Bureau's grass and lawn research. From there he joined the SES in the USDI to head up the new Nursery Division.

Through the provisions of Plant Exploration and Introduction of the USDA Bureau of Plant Industries, the SES nurseries had obtained and tested seeds and plants of many introduced species.[90] According to Arnold S. Dahl, Associate Agronomist with the erosion control nurseries, they had been set up as conservation production nurseries, and also to conduct experiments with native and introduced grasses. Studies would be made of the time of planting, growth habits, root development, ability to withstand drought, hardiness, seeding habits, adaptability to cultivation, and erosion control possibilities. Physiological studies would be made of the processes in establishment and reproduction of the plants. These would involve studying the various factors affecting seed germination, the rest period of the seeds following harvest, how to break any dormancy, ability of the plants to reproduce vegetatively either by roots or rhizomes, the resistance of plants to extreme temperatures and drought, and other characteristics necessary for a plant to survive in a difficult environment.

When the SCS became a permanent agency two years later, Enlow came with the SES to the new agency and was initially given responsibility for directing the nurseries. An excellent scientist in his own right, Enlow had just returned from an extensive plant exploration trip with H. L. Westover to Russian Turkestan in the spring of 1935. Their exploration proved to be very timely and fruitful to the efforts of the budding observational nurseries.

On November 25, 1935, Enlow wrote Chief Bennett outlining sixteen tasks; he called them *types-of-work*, which covered the operation s that had taken place at the SES nurseries.[91] He recommended all sixteen should be included in the operations of the old and new nurseries that SCS currently manage,[92] and emphasized the need for each to have an observational component. This was based on the obvious need for conservation plants which the observational nursery could supply, and that conservation plants would not be developed by private industry. The concept of private companies producing conservation plants, let alone developing them, did not exist. By the late 1920s private seed companies were moving into the lucrative hybrid commodity crop arena.[93] Although environmentally critical, conservation plants would be used on only a fraction of the acres of an annually planted commodity crop, yet the cost of developing them would be similar. Private industry would have no incentive to get involved with developing plants uniquely suited for soil and water conservation uses.

The following is a detailed discussion about the sixteen tasks. The outcome of that discussion in late 1935 and early 1936 became the foundation for the observational nurseries and beyond, even into the twenty-first century.

Enlow told Bennett that the sixteen tasks were equal to what the SES nurseries had been doing when transferred to SCS. However, it seemed to him that the "general impression of the Soil Conservation Service was that the nurseries are merely growing large quantities of planting stock of a few species of trees and collecting enormous quintiles of a few grasses for use directly on the projects. This is not the original purpose for which the nurseries were established." He wanted to correct that impression. He continued

> I am particularly anxious that the Nursery Section be allowed to continue the collection of many hundreds of species of plants through our country as it has been done for the past two years, bringing the material into the nurseries in order to study methods of propagation and the possibilities of using these plants in an erosion control program. This, in my estimation, is the real work of the Nursery Section. It is very possible that the day might arrive that we would be obligated to suddenly discontinue the production of millions of trees and bulk collection of seed of grasses from the ranges. The developing work of promising species should be continued and I urge you to give your approval to a continuation of the program.

How prophetic. He concluded by re-emphasizing his position. "I urge you give your approval to a continuation of the program we have functioning very well at the present time."

It is obvious that Dr. Enlow was either a strong willed person, or had a great relationship with Dr. Bennett, or both. He strongly promoted observational nurseries and what had been happening there for a couple years. Enlow was the Nursery Section Director at that point, reporting to the head of the Conservation Operations Division, who reported to Bennett. He circumvented the chain of command to ensure his views were reviewed by Bennett.

Enlow's sixteen tasks are listed below, separated into three groups. One group embraced the observational nurseries concept, one focused on the mass collection and production of planting material, and the third group identified elements that potentially benefited both groups. The task numbers are those assigned by Enlow.

Observational nursery tasks included:

1. Securing, by systematic search, propagating and growing species and variations which are an improvement in erosion control value to materials now in use.

4. Determining, by appropriate nursery plantings, tests to identify the relative value of both native and introduced species for the purpose in mind.

6. Making small area and field transplanting tests of new and promising species and variations to determine the practicability of their use before being recommended and made available for project use.

7. Continuous investigation and practice to determine the simplest and most practical method of propagating and handling plants under the local conditions where they were used.

8. Continuous investigation and practice to determine the simplest and least expensive methods of harvesting, cleaning and handling seed, as well as securing other types of propagating material.

9. Making germination and purity tests of all seeds used, correlated with field practices, in an effort to regulate and simplify both planting and collecting operations.

10. Making continuous efforts towards improvement, by appropriate tests, method of treating and handling seed and other propagating material, so as to simplify planting operations and stand established.

Mass collection and production of planting material tasks included

11. Quantity production of proven nursery stock.

12. Quantity collection of proven native seeds and other propagating materials.

13. Increasing, through nursery production, valuable species of which limited propagating is available.

15. Technical supervision of all purchases of seed, fertilizer, limestone and inoculation materials for the projects including propagation of necessary specifications.

16. Keeping cost of production records on nursery stock and seed collection.

The following four tasks do not fit neatly into either of the first two groups but could have benefited either.

2. Making systematic search of species which have other economic uses combined with erosion control, such as forage, tannin, Indian food, fiber, rubber, game feed and cover, medicine, pulp, veneer, basketry and ornamentation.

3. Make surveys and mapping the distribution of native plants useful in the erosion control program and locating desirable areas of seed collection.

5. Establishing and maintaining arboreta of grass plantings of outstanding species for observation and a constant source of propagation material.

14. Preparing herbarium and root-system specimens of species and variations used or that offer promise, and sending duplicate samples to Washington.

Dividing them into groups facilitates tracking them through the process of becoming SCS policy, or falling by the wayside.

Concerns about parts of the Enlow memorandum to Bennett came on December 18, 1935 from C. B. Manifold, Chief, Conservation Operations. He was Enlow's boss. In a memo to Dr. Bennett, Manifold collaborated with Frank J. Hopkins, the Assistant Chief of Administration.[94][95] In the memo Manifold writes, "Mr. Hopkins has prepared the following comments on the particular points that are questioned." Apparently Manifold wanted the administrative viewpoint as well as his own presented to Bennett.

At the offset of the letter Manifold outlined what he saw as the four nursery functions in 1935. His number one is Enlow's number eleven, 'Quantity production of proven nursery stock'. Number two is Enlow's number twelve, 'Quantity collections of proven native seeds and other propagating material'. The next function Manifold listed was "actual establishment of the nurseries" and four was "the testing and propagation of this plant material in order to cover operations between research and field" which could include several of Enlow's recommendations. Manifold continued by pointing out that a number of the tasks listed by Enlow were "detailed explanations of the above group".

What was Manifold's understanding of his fourth function? Did he have in mind the9 same as what Enlow had written Bennett, "This, in my estimation, is the real work of the Nursery Section," or did he mean that the nurseries only had to do the 'testing and propagation of this material' that would allow the quantity production of his functions one and two? The use of the term *this material* certainly suggests it was the quantity production to which the 'testing and propagation' referred.

At that point in the Manifold to Bennett letter, Hopkins presented his objection to certain tasks listed by Enlow. The rebuttal blended Enlow's tasks one and two into the same argument, with two objections. First was whether SCS nurseries should be collecting plants with value other than erosion control at all. The second objection was the concept of systematically searching and collecting plants, for any reason. The objection was not whether it was a good idea, but rather whether it was an SCS responsibility. "Work of this nature should be arranged in conjunction with the Division of Woodland Management and conducted in cooperation with the Division of Plant Exploration and Introduction in the Bureau of Plant Industry which is charged with the responsibility of carrying on work of this type."

Hopkins next objection to the sixteen functions regarded task number three, 'making maps of the distribution of native plants'. He challenged whether this activity was even contemplated under the authority that established the SES nurseries. Next was an objection to task fourteen from Enlow's list, 'preparing herbarium and root -system specimens'. Hopkins could see the value of something like this for use by collecting crews for the purpose of identification, but thought it should not be stressed as a function.

The last objection was to task fifteen, 'technically supervising the purchase of seed, fertilizer, etc.' From Hopkins point of view, since the use of seed and plants coming from the nurseries was to be used on projects and district cooperator's land, this function should have been the responsibility of the Section of Agronomy, i.e., the section that would be using the nursery's agronomic products.

At that point in time, i.e., late in 1935, Dr. Charles Enlow faded from the observational nurseries picture. It must be said, however, whether he originated the 'observational nursery' concept of plant evaluations or not, he certainly served it well during this transition period from the Bureau of Plant Industries nurseries to Soil Conservation Service nurseries. He might be called 'the man of the hour'.

CRIDER ARRIVED IN WASHINGTON

Franklin J. Crider, formally employed by the Boyce Thompson Arboretum, Superior, Arizona,[96] became a Bureau of Plant Industry employee in 1934 at the erosion experiment station in Tucson.[97] With the creation of the SCS on April 27, 1935, the experiment station became an SCS nursery, and he changed employers but continued at that location until he transferred to Washington, D.C., arriving early in 1936, and was placed 'In Charge' of the Nursery Section. His exact arrival time is questionable, but it was well before late March, 1936, at which time he was authoring documents in Washington.[98]

Dr. Crider became a member of the University of Arizona Horticulture Department on June 1, 1918, and later became department head. During his years there, he was invited to visit Mr. Thompson. The two hit it off, so to speak, and Thompson picked Dr. Crider as the first Arboretum director. Crider resigned his position at the University on September 1, 1924.

Three years later, the Casa Grande Valley Dispatch contained an article announcing that Dr. Crider had been appointed regent of the University. On Friday, January 21, 1927, it contained an article titled, "New Regent U. of A. Specialist in Southwestern Horticulture," which provided a brief record of his work at the University before becoming arboretum director.[99]

> Director F. J. Crider of the Boyce Thompson Institute of Superior, Arizona, who had just been appointed regent of the University of Arizona, was regarded as one of the strongest horticulturists in the southwest. He was appointed professor of horticulture in the University of Arizona, College of Agriculture, and horticulturist in the agricultural experiment station June 1, 1918. He resigned that position on September, 1, 1924, after more than six years of hard work at the university, to accept the position of director of the Boyce Thompson Southwestern Arboretum, Superior, Arizona, at a greatly increased salary. Professor Crider was one of the strongest men on the staff of the College of Agriculture and during his work at the university prepared several valuable publications on horticulture, among which are the following:
>
> 1. The Olive in Arizona;
>
> 2. Planting a Citrus Grove in Arizona;

3. Propagation of the Date Palm, with Particular Reference to the Rooting of High Offshoots;

4. Establishing a Commercial Vineyard in Arizona.

When he left the university, he had several incomplete manuscripts ready for publication. Subsequently, one of these was published and another appeared as a bulletin entitled "Essentials to Successful Fruit Culture in Arizona".

Professor Crider's resignation in the college of agriculture was regarded as a great loss. Though offered the position of director of the Boyce Thompson Southwestern Arboretum in the spring, Professor Crider continued his work at the University until September to complete certain studies he had started. It was President Marvin's desire that he should continue as a member of the staff of the University of Arizona, College of Agriculture, and give lecture courses at times during the school year, in addition to his holding the position of director of the Boyce Thompson Southwestern Arboretum. However, this matter could not be arranged.

While at the university, Professor Crider made several important discoveries in southwestern horticulture, including:

1. The rooting of high date palm offshoots;

2. A new system of pruning known as the 'Intermediate' system;

3. A new variety of grape that is well suited for growing in the Salt River valley and in other southern Arizona valleys;

4. A study of the growth of roots; during the so-called dormant period of the tree;

5. The root growth of citrus trees;

6. The use of super-phosphates and blood meal as fertilizers to produce a superior quality of head lettuce.

Upon his appointment as director of the Boyce Thompson Institute, Director Crider began new lines of investigative work and also continued a few that he had already started at the university. His work at the Boyce Thompson Institute was a credit both to himself and to the state of Arizona and his appointment to the board of regents of the university greatly strengthened the agricultural and horticultural work at the university and in the state. The university and state of Arizona are to be congratulated upon having so strong a man in agriculture as a member of the board of regents.

Crider was recognized for his University of Arizona and Boyce Thompson work by receiving an honorary doctorate degree from the University of Arizona in late 1936.[100]

While in the position at Boyce Thompson Arboretum, Crider is credited to have held the belief that nature has evolved a plant for every purpose. Documentation of his having spoken or written these words is lacking, but his work at the Arboretum and with SCS suggests that he believed it was true. In an announcement of an upcoming speech by Crider, Prescott Evening Courier on June 30, 1930, said for several years he has devoted himself to the work at the arboretum. Here plants, imported from other countries, with climatic conditions similar to Arizona, have been grown to try their adaptability to this state."[101]

An article published by the Grassland Society of Southern Africa on January 30, 1986 discussed Crider's evaluation of Lehmann lovegrass (*Eragrostis lehmanniana*) at the Arboretum.[102] Crider's 1945 publication on Lehmann demonstrated the concept that nature had evolved a plant to stabilize overgrazed rangeland in Arizona, New Mexico and Texas.[103] Between 1937 and 1950, approximately 300 pounds of Lehmann seed were produced in Tucson and distributed to soil conservationists and scientists within the USDA for field plantings. By 1940, Lehmann lovegrass seed had been sown in

Arizona, New Mexico and Texas. Between 1940 and 1950 the grass began to appear on areas which had not been seeded.

Dr. Frank S. Crosswhite was Curator of Botany at Boyce Thompson Arboretum from 1971 until 2002.[104] He has written extensively about the Arboretum. Although he indicated that Aldo Leopold had met Dr. Crider at the arboretum this cannot be substantiated.[105] Another Crosswhite publication is a review of Dr. Crider's work on jojoba, *Simmondsia chinensis*.[106] Crosswhite states

> Director Crider became intensely interested in erosion control planting at a time when no such work had ever been done. After conducting extensive experiments in root growth, dry-land plantings, and reforestation at the Arboretum for five years, he agitated widely for conserving soil by planting covers on the land. He developed a cooperative program whereby a large nursery of erosion control plants was established by the Forest Service on Arboretum property for distribution largely to Indian Reservations. Labor was provided by the Civilian Conservation Corps.

To a great extent, Crider's research at the Arboretum was aimed at re-vegetating Arizona rangeland that had been degraded by domestic animal overgrazing. He enjoyed some success. Whether Crider talked the 'Nature has evolved a plant for every purpose,' he was walking it.

The best estimate of Dr. Crider's arrival in Washington is early January, 1936. The basis for this is that memoranda were circulating in December, 1935 within the Nursery Section in headquarters that he should have been sending or receiving, but Dr. Charles Enlow, his predecessor, was still identified as being in charge of the Nursery Section. The latest such memorandum was on December 18, 1935. Crider was in Washington on March 25, 1936 when Field Memorandum #SCN-4 was distributed by him. The magnitude of this document would certainly have required considerable time to converse with others and prepare, so the best estimate of his arrival time was around January, 1936. He replaced Dr. Enlow, who became the Chief SCS Agronomist until 1944 when he transferred to the Foreign Service.[107]

It is not known what conversations had taken place between Crider and Enlow relative to the types-of-work Enlow had listed for Bennett or the objections to them by Manifold and Hopkins. Most likely they were extensive, given Crider's work experience while at the Boyce Thompson Arboretum and his conviction that vegetation could play a dominate role in healing the soil erosion problems in America. Based on the Enlow-identified functions that the SEC nurseries had been doing, the concept could easily have been his. On the other hand, Crider's work at the Boyce Thompson Arboretum seems to embrace exactly what Enlow had set up at the SES nurseries. Had they met before 1935? Is it possible that Enlow steered the SES nurseries in the direction that nature had evolved a plant for every purpose because of contacts with Crider? Crider is on record of following that concept soon after he arrived at the Boyce Thompson Arboretum in the late 1920s. Or was it the case of two scientists with the same idea coming together at about the same time? The only evidence of contact found before Crider came to Washington took place in June 1935, when Enlow asked his secretary to send Crider in Arizona three copies of a publication.[108]

In 1935, Dr. Bennett was scrambling to find visionary employees. From where he sat Crider fit the bill; a logical choice for what they both had in mind, resulting in Crider becoming the first official leader of the observational nurseries as director of the SCS Nursery Section.

ESTABLISHING THE POLICY

Several policy-like documents relative to nursery operations were issued from the SCS Washington office during the next several months. The first and most critical one was on March 25, 1936, distributed about ten weeks after Crider's estimated arrival in Washington.[109] It clearly shows how well the tasks listed by Enlow made it into SCS nursery policy. Most are clearly identifiable but, in some

29

cases were watered down and less pointed than the way Enlow had presented them. The manner in which they appeared suggested that Crider may have run into some resistance and they were the best he could get. Of course, being new to the national scene may have created some hesitation about being as bold as Enlow had been. The record will show, however, that in the long view, he succeeded in making enough of the original sixteen tasks into formal policy to be effective.

It may be worthwhile to take a look at Dr. Crider's personality relative to his dealing with what was undoubtedly some fierce infighting between the large-scale production crowd and the observational nurseries supporters. More detail on Crider is presented in the Key Leaders chapter. Our best insight comes from Wilmer W. Steiner, who worked with him at the National Observational Project in Beltsville for six years. Steiner offered these thoughts at a memorial service held at Beltsville after Crider's death.[110]

> As you know, Dr. Crider was a quiet, modest, retiring individual who was completely absorbed in his work with plants. He was basically a researcher and disliked being bothered with administrative details or responsibilities.

Picture this man just off the Arizona range protecting his views on the future functions of nurseries. The inclination was to assume he would be consumed. In the short term, undoubtedly Enlow supported him. Crider must have had the confidence of Hugh Hammond Bennett, his exact personality opposite, and was also 'In Charge' of the nurseries when he replaced Enlow. Would this be enough?

In March 25, 1936, Crider authored FIELD MEMORANDUM #SCN -4, Functions and Activities of Nurseries, and sent it to Regional Conservators and Nurserymen. He signed it as F. J. Crider, In Charge, Soil Conservation Nurseries, and it was approved by C. B. Manifold, Chief of the Division of Conservation Operations.

It is necessary to digest the entire document to sort out the pieces pertaining to the observational nurseries. In the first three paragraphs he outlined why the memorandum was needed, the importance of the nurseries and their broad purpose, which was "...to provide planting materials, in the form of nursery stock, seed, cuttings, etc. of suitable species and varieties of plants for utilization in soil erosion and general revegetation." He proceeded to identify more specifically the details of the nursery responsibilities.

The following paraphrases the content of the March 25 Memo and its relationship back to Enlow's sixteen types-of-work (tasks). The major headings are labeled *A* through *H*, as they appear in the memo, and are underlined, with minor headings within each. Following most major and minor headings is a statement showing their relationship to Enlow's tasks, always in parenthesis.

A. Collection of Propagation Materials: The collection and propagation of materials, such as seeds, cuttings native seedlings, etc. an important activity, including:

(1) Collection for direct planting; largely -- grass seeds -- for general revegetation (Enlow's task twelve).

(2) Collection for nursery stock production -- to be grown in the nurseries for subsequent transplanting onto project areas (Enlow's task eleven).

(3) Collection of outstanding plants, to be propagated in quantity lots immediately for project use or handled as 'observational material' (single quotation marks are Crider's) until such time as the practical aspects of successful propagation and utilization are more fully understood (This is the first concrete reference to an 'observational phase' at nurseries and is Enlow's task one).

He followed under this heading with a fuller explanation. "The primary function of nurseries, contributing to the production of plants having the greatest usefulness in soil conservation work, is the finding and assembling of species and variations which are an improvement over plants commonly used. This may include forms which, because of special properties, such as soil binding, ground cover, self-reproduction, ease of propagation and transplanting, are singularly valuable for erosion control, or on account of certain inherent characteristics, such as drought resistance and general adaptation, are especially suited for revegetation purposes (Enlow's task one) also; plants which have other economic uses, combined with erosion control value, such as human food, forage, game feed and cover, medicine, fiber, tannin, oil, rubber, fence posts, fire wood, pulp, veneer, furniture, timber shade and ornamental" (Enlow's task two).

Our collectors will have abundant opportunity to locate material of this character and it is desired that they give special attention to this important phase of our work, keeping always on the outlook for, and the assembly of plants which in some outstanding particular way be worthy of special attention and utilization.

(4) Collections for inter-nursery, inter-regional and cooperating agencies.

This is to be based on requests from other nurseries as well as knowing what others need and being on the outlook for them. The potential for exchanging material with the Division of Plant Exploration and Introduction is emphasized because it -- offers opportunity-- for securing desirable exotic plants from foreign countries having similar climate to our own and that are anxious to cooperate with us in this particular project. The value of such exchange is seen in the large number of useful exotic plants being extensively used at present in our erosion control program and the promising outlook of many of the foreign species now under observation --" (This does not occur as an Enlow type-of-work, but certainly relates to the observation nursery work. Surely Enlow supported them).

(5) Locating and mapping collection areas, including description of plants and environmental conditions. In the case of herbarium material, typical specimens of all species utilized should be kept at the regional office and duplicates forwarded to Washington. It is particularly important that root-system specimens also be obtained when at all possible (Although Enlow's task fourteen did not require root specimens per se, root system work relative to grazing intensity done by Dr. Crider years later was one of his greatest contributions to soil and water conservation).[111]

(6) Seed harvesting and cleaning. (This is straight forward relative to acquiring methodology for managing the seed harvesting and cleaning of outstanding plants as well as building a body of knowledge. It is Enlow's task eight.)

B. Nursery Stock Production. (This heading covers all aspect of large scale production except the collections needed for it. It identifies the need for several of Enlow's types-of-work, including those exclusively geared for large scale production (tasks eleven and thirteen, as well as tasks seven, eight and nine related both to large scale production and observational nurseries).

C. Observational Plantings. (Here Crider covers all aspects of the subject)

"Determining the relative erosion control and other economic value of outstanding (native and introduced species) and as a constant source of propagating materials of proven species" (Enlow's tasks four and ten. He continues with what appears to be an unnecessary and even undesirable statement.) --- It is the purpose that observational plantings be maintained at one or more nurseries in each region where conditions warrant." (Why did he say this at all, or say instead 'observational plantings will be maintained at all nurseries'? As we will see, the decision making responsibilities of which nurseries would maintain observational nurseries left

31

an open door of questionable value. Who was to decide 'where conditions warrant'; was it to be Crider, the Regional Nurseryman, or someone else? It certainly does establish the significance, or maybe the potential insignificance, of observational plantings relative to other nursery activities. Was this wording freely offered by Crider, or forced into the memorandum by others? It may have paved the way for Chief Bennett to ask in 1949, in a memo to all regional directors, "Why not have all nurseries search for new legumes and other promising plants?"[112] Actually, by 1949 and well before that, most nurseries were enthusiastically conducting observational studies. After all, according to Enlow, they were the 'real work of the Nursery Section'.

D. <u>Seed and Stock Increase Plantings</u>. (This covers the large scale nursery production) "...multiplying production in the case of variations, as indicated by their behavior as observational material, that are worthy of being propagated in sufficient quantities for project use. (This relates somewhat to Enlow's task five, which included establishing an arboretum, but Crider omitted it).

E. <u>Field Observational Plantings.</u> (He calls this an) "...adjunct to nursery work proper" (They are to include evaluation plantings under natural conditions, presumably off of the nursery, to determine the relative value of the established plants and to) "...facilitate the development of successful establishment of plants under natural conditions (Enlow's task six).

F. <u>Selection of Plants for Nursery and Project Use</u>. (This deals entirely with the subject of selecting which species to produce in quantity on the nursery to meet project work requirements).

G. <u>Allocation of Nursery Stock and Seeds</u>. (This is a straight forward discussion of how the large scale collection and production of plant materials will be allocated to projects, etc.).

H. <u>Records and Reports</u>. (This section requires only one of Enlow's types-of-work, dealing with production costs, which was task sixteen).

When comparing the contents of FIELD MEMORANDUM #SCN -4 against the sixteen functions outlined by Enlow, it appears that task two 'Make systematic search for plants which have economic uses combined with erosion control value' is omitted. However, under the Observational Planting section Crider is specific, saying, "As a means of determining the relative erosion control value and other economic value..."it appears clear that the primary plant value must be erosion control, and ideally have other economic value as well." However under Section A <u>-Collection of Propagation Materials</u> he spells out most of the items Enlow listed as potential 'other' economic value, excluding only Native American food and basketry but adding human food, oil, fence posts, firewood, furniture, timber and shade, so it ends up awfully close to what Enlow recommended.

While systematic searches with the emphasis on economic value did not become a primary responsibility within the SCS Nursery program, it did lead to the requirement that the economic value of plants collected for erosion control be considered. Of greater significance was the establishment within SCS of the Hill Culture section within the Division of Research that continued until 1947.[113] Its mission was "The systematic search for and adaptation of superior strains of erosion resisting plants having an economic value". Whether the Hill Culture Program came into existence because it was rejected as a 'type-of-work' of observational nurseries is unclear. Although its focus was more economical, the evaluation concept on the two was similar.

Enlow's task three 'maps of the distribution of a native plant' is not in the memo. The objection by Hopkins may have kept the map making obligation out of the final observational nurseries responsibilities except that a map was to be made for collected plants.

Although task five, i.e., 'Maintain an arboreta of outstanding plants' is not mentioned, it is included under Section D - <u>Seed and Stock Increase Plantings,</u> but it isn't called an arboreta. Task fifteen, 'Technical supervision of all purchases' did not survive as a specific responsibility other than normal record keeping requirements of any Federal agency.

Even though Enlow did split some hairs to get his sixteen points, all except task three are included in some manner in the March 25, 1936 Functions and Activities of Nurseries Memorandum, even including the desirability of root samples. With all the associated detailed discussion, they may seem watered down relative to being so clearly articulated in the listing by Enlow. When reading both documents Enlow's sixteen types-of-work clearly convey that the observational phase was the purpose of the nurseries, while the Crider document coveys a blend, with the observation phase in the number two position.

On the same date as his directive, March 25, 1936, his boss C. B. Manifold sent a memorandum to regional conservators, under the subject of Nursery Work.[114] It is Memorandum #SCN-3, meaning it was probably prepared before #SCS-4, Functions and Activities of Nurseries. It contains two items that suggests Manifold, as Division Chief over several sections, including the Nursery Section, wishes to preempt the importance of the forthcoming #SCN-4. Prior to #SCN 3 the Chief of the Nursery Section, i.e., Crider, dwelt directly with the Regional Nurserymen, without going through the Regional Conservator. Memo #SCN-3 changes this. It conveys the decision that "nursery activities within each region be placed under the supervision of the Regional Conservator …", notwithstanding that the Nursery Section had up to forty-eight facilities scattered around the country, employing hundreds, and the other sections had none. The memo continues to suggest that this does not diminish the role of the Nursery Section but increases it because it will now have to coordinate its work with the other sections. Although discussed later, this arrangement lasted until 1939 when the nurseries became a division.[115]

Another interesting item in #SCS-3 states, "It should be kept in mind that the primary functions of the nurseries are the obtaining of seed and the production of nursery-grown stock required by the using sections (who were Sections of Agronomy, Woodland Management, Wildlife Management and Range Management)." Recall that Enlow expressed concerns in the fall of 1935 that the "…general impression of the Soil Conservation Service that the nurseries are merely growing large quantities of planting stock of a few species of trees and collecting enormous quintiles of a few grasses for use directly on the projects. This is not the original purpose for which the nurseries were established." Manifold did include in his memorandum what appears to be an afterthought, "Also, it is their function to secure untried planting materials which appear to have possibilities for erosion control…"

PROCEDURE ESTABLISHED

As a follow-up to #SCN 4, Functions and Activities of Nurseries, on July 27, 1937, Crider sent a Memorandum to Regional Conservators, to the attention of Regional Nurserymen, over the approval of Manifold, containing details on how to conduct the "Observational Phase of the Nursery Program".[116] It dealt with the "administrative and functional procedures, possibilities, and limitations." Crider offered, as his second paragraph, as simply as he could, what needed to happen at nurseries to realize his concept. He wrote:

> The observational phase of the Nursery Program is but a simple, direct approach to the major objectives of making available to the Service in quantity the best possible plant materials. The work entails constant search for species and variations within the species of plants with existent, outstanding erosion control values, which through appropriate (a) propagation, (b) cultural and (c) adaptation practices, can be effectively utilized in the further improvement of soil and moisture conservation operations.

The memorandum outlines much of the procedure used by observational nurseries and what became the Plant Materials Center Program, and continues to be its bedrock seventy-five years later.

What this document contains are the steps required for the "...development of the use of native and introduced erosion-resisting plants'" as well as adequate how-to details.

I. Assembly of Plant Materials (with erosion resisting characteristics)

    a. Native Plants

    b. Exotic Plants

    c. Exchange of Plant Materials

    d. Herbarium Materials (to be made only of plant cued in the observational phase)

II. Nursery Observation

III. Nursery Practices (developing cultural and management requirements)

IV. Supplemental Field Tests (referred to as Field Observational Plantings in 1936 memo, i.e., off nursery plantings on natural field conditions)

V. Field Trials on Demonstration Areas (plants ready for project utilization)

VI. Project Classification. (Required to facilitate budgeting and distinguishing from quantity production)

VII. Extra-Service Cooperation (emphasizes the need and desirability of close cooperation with multiple agencies, organizations, etc.)

VIII. Quantity Propagation (at SCS nurseries)

The comments following this last item deals with the "...proper use of nursery facilities to increase seed stock to a point where the planting requirements of the project can be met or until such time as other sources of supply are available." There appears to be an assumption here that the only conservation plantings to be made will be as a part of projects, and that the only source of planting stock will be from the nurseries, versus plantings being made by other public or private groups and with planting materials produced commercially. Maybe the 'other sources of supply' is assumed to be commercial. Nowhere, however, is the subject of commercial production mentioned. Step V, 'Quantity Propagation' addressed the need for large scale production once an outstanding plant had passed all the tests. This was to be accomplished by one or more nurseries producing large quantities of the new selection for project use. It may have been assumed that, as long as the nurseries existed, this step was not required. This is not how things worked out. As new and improved conservation plants emerged from the observational nurseries, farmers and ranchers involved in projects began to notice their superiority and inquired where they could get these new plants. This created a commercial demand, and created a requirement for nurseries to develop a process where new and improved plants could flow to growers.

In the early years, when the observational nurseries had selected a plant, it was given to the production side of the nursery, and they produced it for projects and soil conservation district cooperators. As time passed there was a need beyond this approach to get selected plants reproduced in quantity. Although the SCS observational nurseries represented a new entry into the realm of developing plants for specific uses, state universities had been doing it for commodity crops for years, as well as private firms. They had developed a process for the commercial production of seed producing grasses and forbs in the early twentieth century.[117] Their new plants were released to commercial growers, but the commercial firms were regulated through a state 'seed certification' program, specifically developed to assure the characteristics of the newly released plant would not be lost.

The evaluation concepts and procedures outlined by Crider in the March 25, 1936 and July 27, 1937 memorandums served observational nurseries well throughout the nursery years. Numerous directives and policy statements appeared during the 1939 - 1954 period that influenced policy in some way but none that altered the evaluation concept outlined by Crider in the aforementioned memorandums.[118] Crider did publish an article in Soil Conservation magazine in 1939, titled "Observational Planting" which reinforces and adds substances to the observational concept and process previously published.[119] It highlights that the "Plant must be chosen, in the first place, specifically on their known or potential conservational values." This view is reemphasized by his statement "our seed and plant collectors are constantly on the outlook for native plants which in some outstanding particular are worthy of being brought into the nurseries for further observations. Also, through special cooperative relations with the Division of Plant Exploration and Introduction of the BPI, and the efforts of our own Service, valuable introduced plants are being obtained for trial in the nurseries." Again, after asking, *what is an observational planting,* he states "...with a view to determining the plant's potential value and usefulness in connection with the various erosion control activities." The focus is on *what can this plant do for conservation,* as contrasted with an evolving concept of *here is an erosion problem, what plants might help solve it?*

From his days at Boyce Thompson Arboretum and the University of Arizona, Dr. Crider emphasized the desirability of developing close working relationships, and soliciting help from others, including Federal and state institutions doing agricultural research. He saw the observational nurseries approach relative to research as "occupying an essential intermediary place between research and practical field application."[120] If research was required, it should be done cooperatively with research agencies or institutions.

By 1937, SCS had two divisions that potentially could have overlapping plant related responsibilities. These were the Conservation Division which included the nursery section, and the Research Division which contained the Hill Culture section. To clarify any potential duplication, FIELD MEMORANDUM SCS #730 "Re: Coordination of activities to promote the use of superior plants and methods in erosion control" was issued on November 14, 1938 to all Regional Conservators and State offices over the signature of Chief Bennett.[121] It outlined the desirability of developing superior erosion resisting plants, and briefly what was required to accomplish this; it contained nothing new that was not already policy. The Memorandum outlined its intent with the following introduction:

> The nature and importance of this work are such that it should be participated in and helpfully implemented by all sections of these Divisions, and handled cooperatively with other interested Federal and State agencies.

Followed by:

> By reason of their functional duties and relationships, the Nursery and Hill Culture Sections are directly concerned with the study of erosion-resisting plants. Therefore, as active duties of the service in these cooperative activities, the related features of their work will be coordinated as close as practicable, and in turn with the work of the plant-using Sections, in order that a thoroughly intergraded program of plant improvement and utilization may be effected.

As a follow up to this Memorandum, Dr. Crider, with approval of C. B. Manifold, issued an unnumbered message to all Regional Conservators on March 2, 1939 on "Projecting Nursery Observational Work".[122] The purpose of this document was to provide additional details on how to develop and use cooperative agreements and work plans for conducting work with others. It emphasized that any cooperative activities requiring research would be spelled out in the work plan. Under the discussion of *Work Plans* Crider wrote, "Functionally the nursery observation work falls into four general classes, which constitutes the basis for the formation of work plans." They are A. Initial Observations, B. Supplemental Observations (adjuncts of major plant materials centers), C. Facilitating Studies, and D. Special Studies. The purpose of listing the four was to clearly identify what duties belong to SCS observation nurseries (A, B, and C) and which duties belong to the cooperator, which is item D. Expanding on item D, he summarized that when cooperative plant evaluations with state and Federal agencies is "of a distinctly specialized or research nature" the cooperating research agency will assume full leadership and responsibility for it.

An aside from the purpose of this document is Crider's use of 'plant materials center' and 'mother nursery', seemingly offering two optional substitutes for 'observational nurseries'. The term 'plant materials center' is used two additional times in the document under similar circumstances.

By 1939, the major foundation for conducting the 'observational phase' was over. The fundamentals established by these documents served to guide the operations of observational nurseries and plant materials centers with very little change into the twenty-first century.

One thing the developed procedures did not do, which would have been beneficial to at least the historian, was to create a clear administrative line between the large scale production and observational studies going on at the same facility. There is no evidence whether each worked from separate or joint pools of funds, personnel, equipment, etc. Personnel classification helped, such as an agronomist classification suggested an observation nursery employee, but some strictly production nurseries utilized agronomists also. Over time, publications, reports, attendance at meetings, etc. generally identify the observational workers from production workers. Like everything else, the really productive employees rose to the top, and many of them are recognized in the Key Leaders Chapter. However, there undoubtedly was considerable crossover between the two areas of nursery focus.

By 1939 it must have been most gratifying to Crider to observe the acceptance of the observational nurseries as a part of the ongoing program by most nurseries. It was a far cry from at least one nursery within a region conducting them, as he had suggested. In reality, by 1939 or 1940 reports were revealing that it was exactly the opposite; there were very few nurseries that had not established such studies. By the mid-1940s until 1953, all but three of the remaining twenty-four nurseries had a substantial observational program.

The final chapter in the evolution of the program development came when Dr. Crider moved to Beltsville, MD in 1939 to head up a new National Observational Nurseries Project.[123] Its purpose was to "increase the effectiveness of the soil and moisture conservation practices by bringing into use improved plant materials." Having permanently installed his concept into policy that "Nature has evolved a plant for every (conservation) purpose" he could now concentrate on putting his concept into practice by working with all observational nurseries scientists. While it is unclear exactly what motivated this move from his NHQ position, he returned to his true love of hands-on plant evaluations.[124] While Chief of the Nursery Division his responsibilities included overseeing the large scale production and the observational studies at nurseries. This move represented a significant shrinking of responsibilities. No clear reason was found explaining why he moved. He was replaced by Harry A. Gunning, the Senior Horticulturist on his Washington staff.

While there is no known connection to Dr. Crider, the Section of Nurseries became the Division of Nurseries at the end of 1939,[125] shortly following Crider's departure.

IMPACTS OF CRIDER AND ENLOW

How much impact, if any, did Dr. Charles Enlow have on the evolution of the observational concept? It is conceivable that his concept for the Soil Erosion Service came from his knowledge of the work Crider was doing in Arizona. A memo Crider wrote in 1949 to Dr. Maurice Heath, a new observational nurseries agronomist at the Big Flats, NY nursery, gives a clear view of his opinion. How this exchange between Heath and Crider came about is in itself an interesting story. Heath had written the regional nurseryman in Upper Darby, PA asking for suggestions on a paper he was preparing for publication on "Just how do the Soil Conservation Service Nurseries Contribute to the Soil and Moisture Conservation Program", a rather ambitious undertaking for a new employee.[126] The regional nurseryman forwarded it to the National Nurseryman, R. M. Ross, who gave it to Dr. Crider for answering. Crider drafted a reply and sent it to Chief Bennett for his review. Bennett's reply, one of the observational nurseries' all time highlights, is covered later. Using Bennett's suggestions and his own, Crider's reply to Heath takes on a father-to-son tone, explaining in detail how the observational nurseries work and how the concept originated. The majority of his reply is reproduced below. It is indeed an historical review of the observational nurseries program. As we will see later, by 1949 the track record of the observational nurseries was a shining star and the production nurseries were entering a downsizing mode. The subject was "Agronomy Society Paper". He wrote:

> Mr. Ross furnished me a copy of your letter to the Regional Nursery Division chiefs with the suggestion that I give you any available information considered helpful for the preparation of your paper for presentation to the American Society of Agronomy on "Just How Do the Soil Conservation Service Nurseries Contribute to the Soil and Moisture Conservation Program."

> As brought out in your letter, the most pronounced contribution of Soil Conservation Service nurseries to soil and moisture conservation is through our Nursery observational program. In thinking over your assignment, therefore, it seems to me you will want among other things to outline the history of development and fundamental procedures involved in this program.

> Having been intimately associated with the observational phase of our Nursery work since its inception, I can perhaps assist most by giving you a brief account of its early history and subsequent evolution. To do so, however, may be at the risk of seeming impropriety for, as you may or may not know, I was instrumental in initiating and shaping the development of this form of plant study as it applies to soil and moisture conservation in this country. The idea was some time in taking hold and the plan of procedure was not quickly understood and accepted even within our own Services. There were those who considered the methods as partaking too much of the nature of research to have a place in dynamic field operations. On the other hand, there were those who believed them too unscientific to find dependable results. The urgency of the erosion problems was such that it was not uncommon at first for the applicability of planting materials to be subordinated in favor of quantity production. Gradually, however, through the persistent effort of those who visualized its significance, the term "observational studies" has come to be understood as representing quality conservation performance. The simple, direct, cooperative, comparative evaluation of species, strains and methods such studies entail now is recognized as essential to the continuous improvement of soil and moisture consecration practices. Reflecting to our benefit in the exchange of seeds and helpful technical information, other Federal agencies, as well as a number of foreign countries, have adopted plant testing procedures patterned after our Nursery observational program.

> The use of vegetation long has been recognized as basis to successful erosion control. Realizing however, that no organized study has been made of vegetative materials for this purpose in this country, I conceived the idea of formulating a plan of plant assembly, testing and evaluation to meet the particular needs of the Soil Conservation Service. That was during the years 1934 and 1936 when, as head of the Nursery work of the Southwest Region, Soil Conservation Service, I had the task of providing suitable erosion control planting materials for one of the most difficult sections of the country. Here prolonged droughts, washing rains, hot drying winds, alkaline soils, varied topography and over grazing combined to create the ultimate in problems of erosion control and revegetation. Undoubtedly these adverse environmental conditions as

affect adaptation, establishment and survival stimulated my interest in devising the observational plan of plant testing, the purpose of which is to increase the effectiveness of soil and moisture consecration practices by bringing into use improved plant materials and methods.

Upon being transferred to the Washington office in January of 1936, one of my first acts as head of the Nursery Division was to present this plan informally to Dr. H. H. Bennett, Chief, Soil Conservation Service. He encouraged its further development and country-wide application and has continued as its staunchest supporter. Under the date of March 25, 1936, the plan was formalized in Field Memorandum SCN-4 as an integral function of the Nursery Division. It was explained in greater detail in a subsequent field memorandum dated July 27, 1936 and finally made a part of the Service manual.

I am enclosing copies of the above-named field memoranda which, with the Service Manual, make it unnecessary for me to go into further detail on this question.

Perhaps I can be of some further assistance by saying a word about our National Observational Project. As an integral part of our Nursery Observational Program, its main function is that of facilitating and coordinating our observational work generally. One of its major contributions is the maintenance of seed exchange and technical contacts with foreign countries. During the current year, for example, we obtained over 700 potential soil conservation accessions by direct seed exchange with twenty-five foreign countries. Among these accessions were species and strains entirely new to this country, including collections from unexplored (botanically) sections. Through this medium we already have secured a number of grasses and legumes that offer real promise for soil and moisture conservation. These, of course, will be reflected in the reports you get from the Regions. This type of work is greatly facilitated by our contacts with foreign countries that have initiated plant observational programs similar to ours.

Supplementing the statement in the Manual, I am enclosing a copy of a mimeographed sheet concerning our work at Beltsville and its relation to our observational work as a whole.

As you know, one of the strong features of our observational program is provision for close cooperation with State Agricultural Experiment Stations and related Federal research agencies, which you doubtless will emphasize.

You probably have a reprint of the Dr. A. L. Hafenrichter article on "Getting New Range Plants into Practice" which appeared in the October issue of the Journal of Range Management. It is an excellent presentation of the working of our observational program which you doubtless would find helpful. You are aware also of Hafenrichter and Stoesz' discussion of our observational program (not referred to as such) in the Yearbook of Agriculture, 1948, with the associated list of grasses and legumes brought into use through this means. As you know, there are other outstanding accessions in the advanced stages of evaluation.

I wish you success in the development and presentation of this timely and important subject. If I can be of further assistance, do not hesitate to call on me.

F. J. C.

cc: H. H. Bennett, R. M. Ross; Regional Nurserymen J. W. Keller, L. B. Scott, A. D. Slavin, C. B. Webster, A. D. Stoesz, C. G. Marshall, A. L. Hafenrichter

Considering the contents of the memorandum by Enlow to Bennett on November 25, 1935, it is difficult to square Crider's remark "I was instrumental in initiating and shaping the development of this form of plant study as applies to soil and moisture conservation in this country" without there being contacts between the two in the early 1930s. What did Enlow have in mind when he told Bennett, "I am particularly anxious that the Nursery Section be allowed to continue the collection of many hundreds of species of plants through our country as it has been done for the past two years, bringing the material into the nurseries in order to study methods of propagation and the possibilities of using these plants in an erosion control program. This, in my estimation, is the real work of the Nursery Section." Enlow then attached the 'types of work' that mostly ended up in Crider's foundation documents.

The reader will have to come to their own conclusion. Although the relationship between Crider and Enlow remains unclear, this letter does clear up Crider's opinion when he says, "the most pronounced contribution of Soil Conservation Service nurseries to soil and moisture conservation is through the Nursery observational project."

Chapter 4: PRODUCTION AND OBSERVATIONAL NURSERIES - THEIR PEOPLE, PRODUCTS, PROCESSES AND PERFORMANCE

The Great Depression, a horrendous misuse of land and abnormal weather created an unparalleled period of soil erosion in the 1930s. The Soil Conservation Service moved swiftly to develop a multidisciplinary program consisting of demonstrations, technical assistance to land owners and actual on-farm projects to reduce the rate of soil loss. Conservation planting was one of many tools. The number of mass producing nurseries expanded rapidly. By the spring of 1938, 112.6 million trees and shrubs had been shipped from fifty-four nurseries, and ninety-one million plants were carried over for the following year. Chapter 3 discusses a minor role of these nurseries, i.e., conducting observations to seek out superior conservation plants. This chapter is a brief history of their location, numbers, people and performance until the end of the observational nurseries in 1953. While the dollars spent on them was minor compared to the mass production side of the SCS, some of the originators of the concept viewed it as the main event.

OBSERVATIONAL NURSERY NUMBERS AND LOCATION

Table 4.1 shows the SCS nurseries that operated between 1933 and 1953, their locations and the time frame during which each nursery functioned, and whether the nursery participated in observational work, based on fragmented data. The opening and closing dates for many are estimates or are missing because verifiable records were not found. Nurseries listed as opening in 1936 may have opened in late 1935. Errors are also likely in regard to closing dates, since available records for the 1940 - 1946 periods are the most limited. To a great extent, the records showing the years of operation are used to estimate the opening and closing dates.

During the early years of nursery operations, regional numbers and boundaries changed frequently. As a result, the nurseries are not listed by administrative region, but rather grouped by section of the country. The last column shows the region they were in when they opened.

Figure 4.1 – Typical SCS tree and shrub production nursery. This is at Big Flats, NY

The observational nursery column in Table 4.1 indicates whether, based on the best available information, the nursery conducted observational studies during its existence. While SCS policy did not mandate they be conducted, evidence is lacking to show that this impacted the decision whether a nursery had an observational component or not. Evidence does show that many more than one per region, as Crider has suggested, carried out extensive studies.[127] On the other hand, records show that many nurseries were conducting these studies, but the absences of results over multiple years suggest they were minor contributors compared to several others. The outstanding producers will be easily spotted in the following narrative.

Six nurseries had been established in the Great Plains and Western States to serve as centers for the study of native vegetation and its use in erosion control, frequently designated on nursery production records as 'Grass' nurseries.[128] The studies included collection, identification, distribution, methods of propagation, and increases of all species having potential value as erosion-control plants. Their intent was to learn quickly how the production side of the SCS nurseries could produce large quantities of seed of selected natives, primarily grass. This was essentially a special task the nurseries needed to address as quickly as possible. These six 'grass' nurseries all had successful observational programs. Mandan, ND, Manhattan, KS, San Antonio, TX, Albuquerque, NM, Tucson, AZ and Pullman, WA were the six grass nursery locations. In the December 1935 issue of the *Soil Conservation* magazine Guy C. Fuller wrote the following about them.[129]

> One of the problems connected with the reestablishment of native sod in dust-blown regions concerns itself with the harvesting of seed. Grass nurseries have been set up by the Soil Conservation Services to collect native grass seed for the reseeding of large areas of abandoned land; to encourage reseeding and improvement of those areas that are approaching abandonment; to increase and encourage the use of valuable species never before introduced; to discover the best cultural methods and encourage proper management of vegetation. At the moment we are focusing attention on the lands west of the ninety eighth meridian-a significant line of demarcation because it is here that grasses divide into groups with the tall ones to the east and the short ones to the west.

Determining what nurseries were conducting observational studies, as shown in the observational nursery column, is difficult to confirm. A number of documents answer these questions partially, although some contain conflicting information or mistakes of omission or inclusion. Several nurseries were known to have had observational studies by 1936, in addition to the six 'grass' nurseries. In the south, this included Chapel Hill, NC, Americus, GA and Thorsby, AL. The Painted Post, NY nursery limited its observational studied to shrubs, and the Ithaca, NY nursery to grasses.

On a "Planned Use of Land in Soil Conservation Service Nurseries, May, 1951" listing, one column is 'Observational Use'.[130] All of the twenty-four nurseries functioning at that time have some acres devoted to this use. A February, 1960 report shows the location (nursery name) and indicates in a "Former Use by SCS" column whether they conducted observational studies.[131] It includes the Howard, PA nursery, although SCS had transferred Howard to the Pennsylvania Department of Forests and Water sometime earlier. A 1950 SCS Annual Administrative Report for Region 1 stated, "The Big Flats Nursery was the only SCS Nursery operated in Region 1 in 1950. Production of trees and shrubs and all nursery observational activities for grasses and legumes were conducted at this nursery."[132]

Another source of information regarding the number of nurseries conducting observational studies came from an inquiry in 1963 from Dr. A. L. Hafenrichter, Regional Plant Materials Specialist in the West to Dr. A. D. Stoesz, Chief National Plant Materials Specialist.[133] Dr. Hafenrichter asks if a list could be prepared that showed which nurseries were doing some 'grass work' at different times. Dr. Stoesz commented in his reply that the question "can hardly be answered to the complete satisfaction of everyone."[134] After Stoesz conducted a "considerable search of the files and consulted such minds as Max Hoover and Bob Thornton" he sent Hafenrichter a summary. Table 4.1 reflects its contents.

Other data included in the observational nursery column came from nursery and regional reports, names of known personnel that were associated with the observational nursery, output like new plants or publications, and certain assumptions such as the likelihood that a nursery did not have an observational component if they were only open a year or two.

Knowing how strongly Chief Bennett felt about observational nurseries, it is most likely any reply to "Are you conducting any observation studies?" would be yes, even if minimal. Nevertheless, the following table is marked Yes or No in the observational nursery column to indicate whether they did or did not, based on the best available evidence. For those that were open only a short period of time, it is relatively unimportant.

There are several nurseries listed at the bottom of Table 4.1 that have no regional association. These were identified by way of a letter from Chief Bennett to Richard P. White, Executive Secretary, American Nurserymen Association, in Washington D.C., dated March 29, 1939.[135] In the letter, Bennett explains that the nurseries on the list were transferred to SCS from the Division of Land Utilization, Bureau of Agricultural Economics by way of Secretary's Memorandum No. 785, dated October 6, 1938. The Bureau of Agricultural Economics transferred the Land Utilization Program to the SCS, effective November 1, 1938. Bennett tells Mr. White that all will be discontinued in the spring of 1940 with the possible exception of Hoffman, NC and Lexington, TN. Each nursery had an annual production capacity from one to four million plants. Only one of them appears on listings in later years, suggesting they were all closed by the early 1940s. The exception was Allegan, MI, which may have stayed open until 1946. It appears on SCS nursery lists well after 1939.

A note in the table in parenthesis refers to the line(s) above it.

Table 4.1 Location of SCS Nurseries that operated between 1934 and 1953*

Nursery Name	Year Opened	Year Closed	Observational Nursery	Region when opened
Beltsville, MD	1939	1953	Yes	Washington, D.C.
(This location opened in 1939 as the National Observation Project and Dr. Crider became the first manager. It never functioned as a production nursery.)				
Big Flats, NY	1940	1953	Yes	Upper Darby, PA
Clearfield, PA	1936	1938	No	Williamsport, PA
Glen Rock, PA	1936	1939	No	Williamsport/Upper Darby, PA
Howard, PA	after 1939	1950	No	Upper Darby, PA
(Operated on PA state land by SCS from 1936-1947; continued as a state run nursery.)				
Indiana, PA	1936	1938	No	Williamsport/Upper Darby, PA
Ithaca, NY	1935	1940	Yes	Williamsport/Upper Darby, PA
(Observational nursery only)				
Lancaster, PA	1936	1938	No	Williamsport/Upper Darby, PA
Milesburg, PA	1936	After 1941	Yes	Williamsport/Upper Darby, PA
(When Milesburg closed in not known, but was after 1941, when it reported an inventory)				
New Brunswick, NJ	1935	1938	No	Williamsport/Upper Darby, PA
Painted Post, NY	1936	Late 1940	Yes, shrubs	Williamsport/Upper Darby, PA
Saratoga Springs, NY	1936	1938	No	Williamsport/Upper Darby, PA
Spencer, PA	1935	1938	No	Williamsport/Upper Darby, PA
Tully, NY	1935	1940	Yes, shrubs	Williamsport/Upper Darby, PA
York, PA	1936	1938	No	Upper Darby, PA
In 1936 the NE Regional office was in Williamsport, PA, moving to Upper Darby, PA in 1936 or 1937.				
Appomattox, VA	1935	1936	No	Spartanburg, SC
Americus, GA	1935	1953	Yes	Spartanburg, SC
Athens, GA	1935	1938	No	Spartanburg, SC
Atmore, AL	1935	1938	No	Spartanburg, SC
Belle Mina, AL	1933	1938	Yes	Spartanburg, SC
Brooksville, FL	1940	1953	Yes	Spartanburg, SC
Chapel Hill, NC	1935	1952[136]	Yes	Spartanburg, SC
Chatham, VA	1937	1941	Yes	Spartanburg, SC

Nursery Name	Year Opened	Year Closed	Observational Nursery	Region when opened
Coffeeville, MS	1936	1939	Yes	Spartanburg, SC
(Nursery closed between 1939 and 1947. Reopened to close again in 1953.)				
Fairhope, AL	1935	1938	No	Spartanburg, SC
Friendship, NC	1934	1937	No	Spartanburg, SC
Georgetown, SC	1936	1938	No	Spartanburg, SC
High Point City Lake, NC	1934	1938	No	Spartanburg, SC
Jackson, TN	1936	1938	No	Spartanburg, SC
Monticello, GA	1936	1938	No	Spartanburg, SC
Polkton, NC	1934	1937	No	Spartanburg, SC
Rock Hill, SC	1935	1952	No	Spartanburg, SC
Sandy Level, VA	1940	1953	Yes	Spartanburg, SC
Spartanburg, SC	1937	1938	No	Spartanburg, SC
Statesville, NC	1933	1938	No	Spartanburg, SC
Thorsby, AL	1936	1953	Yes	Spartanburg, SC
Allegan, MI	1939	1946	Yes	Dayton, OH
Paducah, KY	1935	1952[137]	No	Dayton, OH
(Paducah reported having an observational nursery but there is no evidence of this by way or results.)				
Washington, IN	1937	1940	No	Dayton, OH
(Closed prior to 1947; exact date unsure)				
Zanesville, OH	1935	1953	No	Dayton, OH
Amarillo, TX	1935	1938	No	Amarillo, TX
Kentwood, LA	1935	1938	No	Fort Worth, TX
Dalhart, TX	1936	1953	Yes	Fort Worth, TX
(This location was a substation of San Antonio. It does not appear on inventory lists, yet reports of its observational nursery work continue until 1953.)				
Lubbock, TX	1937	1939	Yes	Amarillo, TX
Minden/Sibley, LA	1935	1950-52	Yes	Fort Worth, TX
Robson, LA	1935	1936	No	Fort Worth, TX
This location appears on a 1936 nursery list with two employees, but does not appear on subsequent lists.[138]				
Muskogee, OK	1939	1940	No	Fort Worth, TX
(Produced plants in 1939, cannot find evidence of production thereafter. Stigler and Stillwater was consolidated into Muskogee, or all three were closed in 1940 - 1941)				
Nacogdoches, TX	1935	1938	No	Fort Worth, TX
San Antonio, TX (Grass only Nursery)	1933	1953	Yes	Fort Worth, TX
Shreveport, LA	1933	1938	No	Fort Worth, TX
(Unsure of closing date. No evidence of production after 1940. It was a regional office briefly.)				
Stigler, OK	1937	1940	Yes	Fort Worth, TX
Stillwater, OK	1933	1940	Yes	Salina, KS/Fort Worth, TX
Woodward, OK	1939	1953	Yes	Fort Worth, TX
There is conflicting evidence as to the years where the regional office was located for nurseries in WI, IA, MO, and IL. Records suggest it was in Milwaukee, and then briefly moved to Des Moines, IA than back to Milwaukee.				
Ames/Ankeny, IA	1933	1953	Yes	Milwaukee, WI
Elsberry, MO	1933	1953	Yes	Milwaukee, WI
La Crosse, WI	1935	1938	No	Milwaukee, WI
Havana, IL	1936	1939	No	Milwaukee, WI
Winona, WI	1935	1953	Yes	Milwaukee, WI

Nursery Name	Year Opened	Year Closed	Observational Nursery	Region when opened
Lincoln, NE	1935	1946	Yes	Lincoln, NE
		(Closed between 1944 and 1949)		
Linder, WY	1937	1946	Yes	Mandan, ND
		(Closed between 1944 and 1949)		
Mandan, ND	1933	1953	Yes	Rapid City, SD/Mandan, ND
		(Mandan nursery moved to Bismarck, ND in 1952)		
Manhattan, KS	1935	1953	Yes	KS/TX/Lincoln, NE
		(This nursery shifted from regional offices, first in Salina, KS, then Amarillo, TX, then to Lincoln, NE.)		
North Platte, NE	1938	1943	Yes	Lincoln, NE
		(Grass only Nursery. Sub unit of Waterloo, NE.)		
Waterloo/Kearney, NE	1940	1953	Yes	Lincoln, NE
		(Waterloo nursery opened between 1940 and 1946, based on production figures. Moved to Kearney, NE in 1951.)[139]		
Vermillion, SD	1938	1946	Yes	Mandan, ND
		(Closed between 1944 and 1949)		
Albuquerque, NM	1935	1953	Yes	Albuquerque, NM
Colorado Springs, CO	1935	1938	No	Albuquerque, NM/Amarillo, TX
		(The Colorado Springs Nursery may have moved from the Albuquerque to the Amarillo region in 1937-39)		
Shiprock, NM	1933	1939	Yes	Albuquerque, NM
Stafford, AZ	1933	1939	Yes	Albuquerque, NM
		(Grass only nursery. It existed in the SES days as sub units of Tucson, 1933 - 1935)		
Tucson, AZ (Grass Nursery)	1933	1953	Yes	Albuquerque, NM
Littlerock, CA	1939	1943	Yes	Santa Paula, CA
Placerville, CA	1933	1935	While BPI	
		(The BPI Placerville Nursery did not function as an SCS nursery and does not show up in the any regional records)		
Pleasanton, CA	1939	1953	Yes	Santa Paula, CA
San Fernando, CA	1943	1953	Yes	Santa Paula, CA
		(Was initially at Littlerock and moved to San Fernando in 1943. In 1940 Santa Paula was treated as subunit of Littlerock.)		
Santa Paula, CA	1935	1940	Yes	Santa Paula, CA
		(There is no evidence of production at Santa Paula after 1940. Oswald K. Hoglund was manager there until 1939 when he moved to the Pleasanton, CA nursery. In the absence of another manager or any production, this nursery may have closed by 1940. It continued to serve as a regional office.)		
Watsonville, CA	1935	1940	Yes	Santa Paula, CA
		(Was either initially at Corralitos, or was the same nursery as Watsonville. There is no evidence of production at Watsonville after 1944. In 1940 Watsonville was treated as sub unit of Pleasanton.)		
Aberdeen, ID	1939	1953	Yes	Pullman, WA/Portland, OR
Astoria, OR	1936	1950	Yes	Pullman, WA/Portland, OR
Bellingham, WA	1937	1953	Yes	Pullman, WA/Portland, OR
Pullman, WA	1933	1953	Yes	Pullman, WA/Portland, OR
		(There may have been a regional office at Spokane, WA but the Regional Nurseryman was located in Pullman, WA from the beginning of the SESs in 1933, and remained there until 1943-44 when it moved to Portland, OR.)		
Tuskegee, AL	1936	1940	No	
Ozark, AL	1936	1940	No	
Milton, FL	1936	1940	No	
Hoffman, NC	1936		No	

Nursery Name	Year Opened	Year Closed	Observational Nursery	Region when opened
Princeton, KY	1936	1940	No	
Baudette, MN	1936	1940	No	
Muskogee, OK	1936	1940	No	(Appears above with note.)
Black Falls, WI	1936	1940	No	
Allegan, MI	1936	1940	No	(Appears above with note.)
Burns City, IN	1936	1940	No	
Hopkinsville, KY	1936	1940	No	
Lebanon, TN	1936	1940	No	
Lexington, TN	1936	1940	No	
(Transferred to SCS from the Division of Land Utilization, Bureau of Agric. Economics, March 29, 1939.)				

There were many nurseries opening and closing between 1935 and 1940. Although references can be found regarding the total numbers in operations during identified periods, no attempt has been made to track this number. A one paragraph note in the September issue of the *Soil Conservation* Magazine stated "Nineteen new nurseries will be established by the Soil Conservation Service to meet the pressing demand for trees, shrubs, and grass seed for use on erosion control demonstration projects, according to Charles R. Enlow, acting head of the Division of Nurseries. This brings the number of nurseries to 83".[140] The 1935 Annual Report to the Department from SCS does not list the number of operating nurseries other than the twenty from the Bureau of Plant Industries,[141] which is in conflict with earlier records, but the 1936 report says "Forty-eight major nurseries are now operated by the Service"[142]. By 1937, the same report states the number which operated that year was fifty-five but on June 30, 1937 there were forty-three operating, with an expected decline to thirty-five by the end of fiscal year 1938.[143] Needless to say the number was in flux.

The fourteen original SES nurseries had initiated observational studies by 1934.[144] By 1941, thirty-two were conducting studies, out of the existing thirty-eight[145][146] and twenty-one out of twenty-four conducted studies in 1952. There is confusion about the status of Rock Springs, SC, Paducah, KY and Zanesville, OH relative to whether they were conducting observational studies and are so identified in Table 4.1.

REGIONAL SUPPORT FOR OBSERVATIONAL STUDIES

A significant factor impacting the short and long term participation of nurseries in observational work was the support from the regional conservator (head of the regional office), regional nurseryman, and possibly the nursery manager. While we have seen that nearly all nurseries were participating, the degree of participation and their success is another story. Here the impact of the regional support may have been most telling. They selected the nursery personnel, to some degree controlled the allocation of funds, and, based on their interest became directly involved with the observational nursery program, or ignored it. For the most part, the early and continuing effort of observational nurseries involved the evaluation of herbaceous species; grasses and forbs, with emphasis on legumes. They were the erosion stoppers. In 1938, the four regional nurserymen serving that portion of the country with thirty inches of rainfall or more were three horticulturists and one forester. The other five regional directors were agronomists. Is there reason to believe a horticulturist or forester would be less supportive of grass and legume observational work than an agronomist? Initially at least, the observational program was predominantly agronomic in all regions.

As time passed and results from some observational nurseries began to emerge, it was obvious that the program was getting more support from some regional offices than others. Support for the observational nurseries also reflected the longevity of observational nursery personnel at a location. As we will see later, two excellent examples of this are the Pullman, WA and Albuquerque, NM nurseries.

Table 4.2 lists nurseries that the records show were conducting observational studies at different time periods. Of those listed in the '1952 Nurseries' column, eight (highlighted) were not credited with releasing a plant through 1953, but some contributed to releases from other nurseries.

Table 4.2 SCS nurseries in 1941, 1936 and 1952

1934 SES Nurseries	1941 Nurseries	Opened	1952 Nurseries	Opened
Albuquerque, NM	Aberdeen, ID	1939	Aberdeen, ID	1939
Amarillo, TX	Albuquerque, NM	1935	Albuquerque, NM	1935
Ames, IA	Allegan, MI	1939	Americus, GA	1935
Belle Mina, AL	Americus, GA	1935	**Ames, IA**	1933
Elsberry, MO	Ames/Ankeny, IA	1933	**Bellingham, OR**	1937
Ithaca, NY	Astoria, OR	1936	Beltsville, MD	1939
La Crosse, WI	Bellingham, WA	1937	**Big Flats, NY**	1940
Lincoln, NE	Beltsville, MD	1939	**Brooksville, FL**	1935
Mandan, ND	Big Flats, NY	1940	Chapel Hill, NC	1935
Manhattan, KS	Brooksville, FL	1940	Elsberry, MO	1933
Placerville, CA	Chapel Hill, NC	1935	Mandan, ND	1933
Pullman, WA	Chatham, VA	1937	Manhattan, KS	1935
San Antonio, TX	Dalhart, TX	1936	Pleasanton, CA	1939
Shiprock, NM	Elsberry, MO	1933	Pullman, WA	1933
Stillwater, OK	Lincoln, NE	1935	San Antonio, TX	1933
Tucson, AZ	Linder, WY	1937	**San Fernando, CA**	1943
Winona, MN	Littlerock, CA	1939	**Sandy Levels, VA**	1940
	Mandan, ND	1933	Thorsby, AM	1936
	Manhattan, KS	1935	Tucson, AX	1933
	Minden/Sibley, LA	1935	**Waterloo, NE**	1940
	North Platte, NE	1938	**Winona, MN**	1935
	Pleasanton, CA	1939		
	Pullman, WA	1933		
	San Antonio, TX	1933		
	Sandy Level, VA	1940		
	Thorsby, AL	1936		
	Tucson, AZ	1933		
	Vermillion, SD	1938		
	Waterloo/Kearney, NE	1940		
	Winona, WI	1935		
	Woodward, OK	1939		

Dr. A. L. Hafenrichter was appointed regional nurseryman in 1935, and for a short period was also nursery manager at Pullman, WA. Legendary producer of new plants, John Schwendiman, joined the staff in 1935 and remained until 1976. At Albuquerque, the first nursery to put a new plant onto the commercial market, Joseph Downs and Glenn Niner joined the nursery staff in 1936 and remained a part of it until 1962 and 1969 respectively. The regional nurseryman, Charles Marshall, and Niner were agronomists while Downs was a horticulturist.

Although the regional boundaries and headquarters changed, Dr. Abraham Stoesz was a regional nurseryman in the Northern Great Plains from 1936 until 1953. While he may have played a less dominate role in new plant development than Hafenrichter his longevity and steady hand had much to do with the observational nursery successes in his region. The great success of the nurseries in Pullman, WA, Aberdeen, ID and Pleasanton, CA under the direction of regional nurseryman Hafenrichter could not have been so successful without the help of regional conservator, J. H. Christ. He and Hafenrichter seemed to be on the same page, and Christ was particularly supportive during the transition period (see Chapter 5). Another regional nurseryman, L. B. Scott, who entered the SCS at

Shreveport, LA, soon moved to the regional nurseryman's position in Spartanburg, SC and remained in that position until the nursery closed. The South region, which had one of the largest erosion problems to tackle, and had more nurseries, was the only region to have a regional position committed exclusively to the observational nursery program. That position was held by agronomist, Paul Tabor. Three of their nurseries released eleven plants.

Longevity of employment was also commonplace in other regions. The South Region had several employees that entered nursery employment when they first started and became part of the Plant Materials Program in 1954. William Young, G. B. Blickensderfer, Paul Tabor and John Powell are examples. However, all worked at more than one nursery. Dr. Abraham Stoesz, Donald Atkins and Donald Cornelius are examples from the Midwest. Each had long periods of nursery service which carried over into the Plant Materials Program. None can be identified from the Northeast that had as much as five years of continuous observational nursery experience, except at the National Observational Project at Beltsville, MD.

Low observational nursery output and/or high observational nursery personnel turn-over suggested a lack of support at one or more levels. The best example of this came from Region I. Dr. S. M. Raleigh was employed as an agronomist soon after the nursery opened in 1940, but stayed less than a year. He later enjoyed a highly respected career at Pennsylvania State University. After the nursery had been open for six years a complaint arose from the National Office about the Big Flats, NY nursery. Chief of the Nursery Division, Dr. Gunning reminded the Chief of Operations, A. E Jones, on August 5, 1946 of "the difficulty we have had in convincing Region 1 that a nursery agronomy program (i.e., observational nursery) was necessary".[147] The Regional Agronomist, Dr. John Paul Jones contended that Region 1 did not need such a program and the Regional Conservator "had been inclined to concede...rather than make an issue out of the matter."[148] The letter to Jones included a survey of experiment stations in the Northeast that documented their support, as well as the need for such a program. While the outcome of this exchange is not specifically known, agronomic related observation studies showed limited results in the years that followed, although capable agronomist Dr. Maurice Heath came to Big Flats in 1948, initiated an aggressive program, and left in 1951.

In 1949, Robert Ross, then Chief, Nursery Division, asked all regional nurserymen for items that he could use in an upcoming 'Technical Operations Conference'.[149] John W. Keller, the new northeast regional nurseryman, wrote Ross on February 10, 1949 that he did not think Region 1 had much to offer, and then admitted they are uncommonly behind in meeting their tree and shrub quota. "As long as Region 1 is at the bottom of the list in regional nursery budgets, there is little hope for us to catch up." He is more optimistic about the observational work, however, pointing out that they are testing trees, shrubs, vines, legumes and grasses. Keller offers the point of view "we are really just getting started and do not have much to report". No doubt he was referring to the work Heath was starting. This certainly proved Gunning's observation.

Without a doubt, Heath had initiated an aggressive observational program, but, unfortunately did not stay long enough to realize any results. Because of his departure, Region 1 recommended that a GS-11 agronomist be employed immediately to replace Heath.[150] Agronomist Harry Porter, initially located in West Virginia, moved to Big Flats in early 1952. Sometime prior to that, Paul Lemmon, Forestry Specialist, Hillsboro, OR, who had years of experience with the observational nursery work in the Pacific Northwest, was asked to review the Big Flats program, which he did in February, 1952. His recommendations included an expansion of the agronomy work and some administrative realignment at the Nursery.[151] Reading between the lines, it appears Lemmon saw things as Gunning had earlier; regional support for a strong agronomic program at Big Flats was lacking. Instead, there was a strong biology program, led by regional biologist, Dr. Frank Edminster.

Soon after Lemmon's report and Porter's arrival, the shutdown of the nurseries was under way. In 1954, Porter became the Field Plant Materials Specialists, the nursery closed, and the PMC operated under a cooperative agreement with The Alfred Agricultural and Technical Institute until 1960.

One positive way to evaluate the impact of support at all levels is to look at the number of nurseries managed by personnel with observational nursery experience. For example, Table 4.6 lists the twenty-nine operating nurseries in 1949, plus the regional offices with known observational personnel. At least twenty-five of the twenty-nine had observational nurseries, and all were staffed with long term observational nursery employees except Big Flats. Individuals who had spent their entire career in observational-related studies were nursery managers at ten of the twenty-five.

FUNDING

Understanding the budget of an observational nursery is all but impossible. Firstly, all hiring, bill paying, salaries, etc. were managed at the regional office. Unfortunately, no figures have emerged that show a fiscal separation between nurseries within a region, let alone between functions within a nursery. Of course, the cost of observational studies was dwarfed by comparison to large scale production, particularly where the large scale plant production were trees and shrubs and observational studies was predominately grass and legumes. However, where large scale production and observational studies were predominantly grass and legumes it was difficult to tell where one started and the other stopped. While both feeding off each other, this did not help in identifying any separation of funds.

A 2005 Cost Benefit Analysis estimated the annual observational nursery costs.[152] Limited nursery budget information, plus a backward projection based on post-1953 allocations was used. Table 4.3 shows the 1950 estimated budget for those nurseries that became PMCs in 1953.

Table 4.3 Estimated 1950 observational nursery budget for nurseries which became PMCs

STATES	Estimated budget	STATES	Estimated budget
MISSOURI	$20,234	NEW YORK	$32,391
NORTH DAKOTA	$24,270	ARIZONA	$37,393
KANSAS	$26,199	WASHINGTON	$37,955
GEORGIA	$32,357	CALIFORNIA	$41,164

Based on a few known regional allocations and the number of nurseries per region, these estimates appear to be high, having a downward effect on benefit estimates.

Separating the production and observational costs would have been difficult, given that employees may have been carrying out work that benefited both, or personnel and equipment worked without a clear benefiting project. It might have been as difficult to estimate then as it is now. The $25,000 averages for 1950 may be as realistic as is possible without concrete information. The funding available between 1956 and 1958 supports this.[153] Over $1.3 million was allocated to seventeen receiving PMCs during that three year period, which is an average of slightly over $26,000 per year.

While the salaries paid to employees during the nursery years are of little value in determining the observational nursery budgets, they are a point of interest. Salary data in Table 4.4 is the highest salary at that professional grade and year for the information available.

Table 4.4 Nursery professional grade salaries

	Nursery Professional Grades			
Year	P-1	P-2	P-3	P-4
1936	$2,000	$2,600	$3,200	$3,800
1946		$3,650	$4,650	$5,900
1949		$3,850	$5,100	$6,235

NURSERY EMPLOYEES

The SCS employed about 150 professional persons from 1935 until 1953 to work in the Nursery Division. Archive listings of employee responsibilities are infrequently noted. Table 4.5 includes identified professional personnel working in the Nursery Division's national and regional offices and at nurseries, listed by 1953 regions. It is impossible to know whether, or to what extent, each employee was involved with observational nursery work. No doubt most were at some point in their employment with the Division. Some may have been included erroneously, but the intention was to err on the side of inclusion rather than exclusion. For example, there is scant evidence that two names under Region 1 (Hovey and Loughridge) worked in the observational nursery at Big Flats, except they were the only agronomists there, and logically would have been involved with the observational nursery work if there had been any.

The maximum number of regions from 1935 until 1942 was eleven, and then the number was reduced to seven. The first column in Table 4.5 identifies the region after the consolidation to seven. The second column contains the employee name and their location, and the third the year where the person first appears in a record at the identified location. This does not mean it was the only year the person was at that location; most likely it was not. If the number of years a person was at the same location is known it is shown as, for example, 1936-1953. Persons appearing several times are those that held positions at more than one location. This column shows the region number the nursery would have been in were they still operational in 1953.

The first persons listed in the Table 4.5 are the Chiefs of the Nursery Division, whose duties included the overall direction of the observational nurseries. Sources include archival records,[154] and personal communications, both written and oral.[155]

Table 4.5 Professional nursery employees - 1935 to 1953

	National Director of Nursery Section	First Year appears
	Charles R. Enlow, Acting, Washington, D.C.	1935-1936
	Franklin F. Crider, Washington, D.C.	1936-1939
	Harry A. Gunning, Washington, D.C.	1939-1948
	R. M. Ross, Washington, D.C.	1948-1952
	Grover F. Brown, Acting, Washington, D.C.	1952-1952
	Vacant	1953
	Beltsville National Observational Nursery Project	**First Year appears**
	Franklin F. Crider, Beltsville, MD	1939-1953
	Wilmer W. Steiner, Beltsville, MD	1948 -1953
Region*	**Regional Offices and Nursery Personnel**	**First Year appears**
1	J. Milton Batchelor, New Brunswick, NJ	1936
1	Dr. S. M. Raleigh, Big Flats, NY	1942, 1943
1	Kenneth L. Hovey, Big Flats, NY	1939
1	G. A. Loughridge, Big Flats, NY	1940, 1942-43, 1947
Region*	**Regional Offices and Nursery Personnel**	**First Year appears**
1	Charles M. Clements, Big Flats, NY	1943-1953
1	Maurice E. Heath, Big Flats, NY	1949 - 1952
1	Harry L. Porter, Big Flats, NY	1953
1	Robert Thornton, Ithaca, NY	1936
1	Charles F. Mann, Ithaca, NY	1936
1	Raymond E Culbertson, Ithaca, NY	1938
1	Kenneth L. Hovey, Painted Post, NY	1936, 1938
1	Edward H. Henry, Tully, NY	1936,1938
1	G. A. Loughridge, Glen Rock, PA	1938
1	Harry G. Eby, Howard, PA	1942

Region[*]	Regional Offices and Nursery Personnel	First Year appears
1	Vernal C. Miles, Howard, PA	1943
1	Harry G. Eby, Indiana, PA	1936,1938
1	Robert Thornton, Upper Darby, PA	1938-1953
1	Arthur C. McIntyre, Acting RN, Upper Darby, PA	1942
1	Frederick M. Trimble, RN, Upper Darby, PA	1936
1	John W. Kellar, RN, Upper Darby, PA	1949
1	Raymond E Culbertson, Upper Darby, PA	1942-1943
1	E. B. Coffman, Waynesboro, PA	1936
1	Harry L. Porter, Morgantown, WV	1950-1953
1	Charles M. Clements, Spencer, WV	1936
2	William G. Beatty, Atmore, AL	1936, 1938
2	John K. Boseck, Belle Mina, AL	1936
2	Douglas Cummingham, Fairhope, AL	1936
2	Hancell Rhodes, Fairhope, AL	1936
2	G. B. Blickensderfer, Thorsby, AL	1939
2	William C. Young, Thorsby, AL	1939, 1949-1953
2	R. L. Davis, Thorsby, AL	1949
2	Herbert Smith, Brooksville, FL	1949
2	William C. Young, Brooksville, FL	1936
2	G. B. Blickensderfer, Brooksville, FL	1936, 1948-1953
2	Lloyd Roof, Athens, GA;	1936, 1938
2	John Powell, Americus, GA	1939
2	Walter T. Mallery, Americus, GA	1939
2	Walter Guernsey, Paducah, KY	1936, 1938
2	William G. Beatty, Coffeeville, MS	1939, 1947-1953
2	Otto Veerhoff, Chapel Hill, NC	1936
2	Edgar L. Evinger, Chapel Hill, NC;	1936
2	Francis LaClair, Chapel Hill, NC	1939
2	Lloyd Roof, Chapel Hill, NC	1939, 1949
2	J. E. Ball, Chapel Hill, NC	1949
2	A. C. Matthews, Chapel Hill, NC	1938- 1953
2	John Powell, High Point, NC	1936, 1938
2	Francis LaClair, High Point, NC	1936, 1938
2	Carl A. Graetz, Statesville, NC	1936
2	Hancell Rhodes, Rock Hill, SC	1938, 1939, 1949
2	William H. Mann, Rock Hill, SC	1939
2	L B. Scott, RN Spartanburg, SC	1936-1952
2	J. L. Palham, Asst. RN, Spartanburg, SC	1938
2	Paul Tabor, Agronomist, Spartanburg, SC	1938-1953
2	J. L. Pelham, Chatham, VA	1936, 1938
2	Louis S. Houghton, Gretna, VA	1938
2	Carl A. Graetz, Sandy Level, VA,	1949
2	William H. Mann, Sandy Level, VA	1949
3	Albert F. Dodge, Ames, IA	1936
3	Ben B. Sprout, Ames, IA	1936, 1938
3	Virgil B. Hawk, Ames, IA	1949
3	Harold Reynolds, Washington, IN	1936, 1938
3	Kermit L. Olson, Winona, MN	1936, 1938
3	E. L. McPherron, Winona, MN	1949
3	Roger E. Sherman, Elsberry, MO	1936

Region*	Regional Offices and Nursery Personnel	First Year appears
3	Hugh A. Stevenson, Elsberry, MO	1935-1939
3	C. .J. Coukos, Elsberry, MO	1939
3	J. J. Pierre, Elsberry, MO	1949
3	John W. Sites, Dayton, OH,	1936
3	August E. Miller, RN, Dayton OH	1936
3	Tom O. Bradley, Zanesville, OH	1938
3	Charles W. Mann, Zanesville, OH	1939
3	John W. McQueen, Zanesville, OH	1939
3	Eldred M. Hunt, La Crosse, WI	1936
3	Arthur D. Slavin, RN, Milwaukee, WI	1936-1953
4	Emery A. Telford, Colorado Springs, CO	1936, 1938
4	Walter N. Schrader, Colorado Springs, CO	1938
4	Wm. Springfield, Kentwood, LA,	1936
4	Billie Rountree, Minden, LA	1952
4	Elbert O. Brown, Minden, LA	1948
4	J. L. Pelham, Robson, LA	1936
4	Charles R. Fernendez Robson, LA	1936
4	L. B. Scott, Shreveport, LA	1936
4	David H. Foster, Shelby, LA	1936, 1938, 1942
4	George T. Ratliffe, Shelby/Minden, LA	1943
4	Samuel T. Merrill, Shreveport, LA	1936
4	George T. Ratliffe, Muskogee, OK	1939
4	Lawrence G. McLean, Stillwater, OK	1936, 1938
4	Katie C. Kirkpatrick, Stigler, OK	1936
4	Herchel D. Price, Stigler, OK	1936
4	Wm. L. Giles, Stillwater, OK	1936, 1938
4	George T. Ratliffe, Stigler, OK	1938
4	Hershel D. Price, Stigler, OK	1939
4	Hershel D. Price, Stillwater, OK	1936
4	James E. Smith, Woodward, OK	1939-1950
4	Elmer G. Haynes, San Antonio, TX	1936
4	David H. Foster, San Antonia, TX	1943, 1948
4	James E. Smith, Amarillo, TX	1936, 1939
4	James E. Smith, Amarillo, TX	1939
4	Burton F. Kiltz, RN, Amarillo, TX	1939?
4	Simon E Wolfe, Fort Worth, TX	1949?
4	C. B. Webster, RN, Fort Worth, TX	1936-?
4	Simon E. Wolff, Fort Worth, TX	1939?
4	Gordon L. Powers, Lubbock, TX	1938
4	Emery A. Telford, Lubbock, TX	1939
4	David H. Foster, Nacogdoches, TX	1936
4	George T. Ratliffe, San Antonio, TX	1936
4	Dennis E. Griffiths, San Antonio, TX	1935-1943?
4	P. J. Choralet, San Antonia, TX	1936
4	R. C. Mauldin, San Antonia, TX	1939
4	Gerald O. Mott, San Antonia, TX	1936
4	James E. Smith, San Antonio, TX	1950-1953
4	Ashley Thornburg, San Antonia, TX	1953
5	Louis T. Moberly, Elkhart, KS	1941
5	Donald R. Cornelius, Manhattan, KS	1936, 1938, 1943, 1946
5	Dr. A. E. Aldous, Manhattan, KS	1936
5	George A. Rogler, Manhattan, KS	1936

Region*	Regional Offices and Nursery Personnel	First Year appears
5	Luther Jacobson, Manhattan, KS	1936
5	Fred P. Eshbaugh, Manhattan, KS	1944-1948
5	Donald M. Atkins, Manhattan, KS	1946, 1948
5	Wm. L. Giles, Manhattan, KS	1938-1943
5	Jesse L. McWilliams, Bismarck, ND	1948, 1949, 1950
5	Herbert Alexander, Mandan, ND	1936
5	Dr. Ernie George, Mandan, ND	1935
5	George L. Weber, Mandan, ND	1939, 1941
5	R. W. Carpenter, Asst. Agronomist, Mandan, ND	1941
5	Liard G. Wolfe, Mandan, ND	1936
5	Arthur E. Ferber, Mandan, ND	1936-1953
5	Jess L. Fultz, Lincoln, NE	1936, 1938
5	Dr. Lawrence C. Newell, Lincoln, NE	1936
5	Elverne C. Conrad, Agronomist, Lincoln, NE	1936, 1938, 1941
5	Dr. A. D. Stoesz, RN, Lincoln, NE	1936-1953
5	Wayne Austin, Assoc. Agron., Lincoln, NE	?
5	John W. McDermand, North Platte, NE	1946, 1948
5	G. J. Richmond, North Platte, NE	1941
5	J. E. Patterson, North Platte, NE	1941
5	Sulo O. Koski, Waterloo, NE	1946, 1948
5	John M. Stephens, Jr., Waterloo, NE	1946
5	Elverne C. Conrad, Waterloo, NE	1946
5	Liard G. Wolfe, Waterloo, NE	1948
5	John M. Stephens, Jr., Vermillion, SD	1938
6	Guy R. Sheets, Pima, AZ	1938
6	Louis B. Hamilton, Shiprock, AZ	1936, 1938, 1948, 1950
6	James H. Eager, Shiprock, AZ	1938
6	Theodore Spaller, Shiprock, AZ	1936
6	Guy R. Sheets, Stafford, AZ	1936
6	Charles C. Marshall, Tucson, AZ	1936, 1938
6	E. E. Hardies, Tucson, AZ	1936, 1938
6	Edward K. Vaughn, Tucson, AZ	1936
6	E. W. Hardies, Tucson, AZ	1936, 1938
6	Ellsworth G. Hendricks, Tucson, AZ	1948, 1950
6	Theodore Spaller, Tucson, AZ	1948
6	Louis B. Hamilton, Tucson, AZ	1938-1948, 1953
6	Andrew H. Purchase, Tucson, AZ	1939
6	Leslie N. Goodding, Tucson, AZ	1936
6	Louis Wankum, Tucson, AZ	1948
6	Joseph A. Downs, Albuquerque, NM	1935-1953
6	Glenn C. Niner, Albuquerque, NM	1936-1953
6	Theodore Spaller, Albuquerque, NM	1949, 1950
6	Darwin Anderson, Albuquerque, NM	1950 - 1953
6	Harry A. Gunning, RN, Albuquerque, NM	1936-1939
6	A. F. Kinnison RN, Albuquerque, NM	1939?
6	Charles C. Marshall RN, Albuquerque, NM	1936-1953
6	Harold R. Benham, Assoc. Botanist and Asst. RN, Albuq., NM	1946, 1948
7	Silvio Ronzone, Littlerock, CA	1941
7	Oswald K. Hoglund, Pleasanton, CA	1941-1953
7	Dirk J. Vanderwal, Pleasanton, CA	1941
7	Paul B. Dickey, Pleasanton, CA	1939 - 1946
7	Harold W. Miller, Pleasanton, CA	1946-1953

Region*	Regional Offices and Nursery Personnel	First Year appears
7	Donald F. Peterson, Pullman, WA	1944
7	Oswald K. Hoglund, Santa Paula, CA	1936, 1938,
7	Dirk J. Vanderwal, Santa Paula, CA	1936, 1938, 1941,1950
7	Lowell A. Mullens, San Fernando, CA	1946, 1949
7	Dirk J. Vanderwal, San Fernando, CA	1949
7	Paul Lemon, San Fernando, CA	1943
7	Silvio Ronzone, San Fernando, CA	1943
7	Dirk J. Vanderwal, San Fernando, CA	1943
7	Fred W. Herbert, RN, Santa Paula, CA	1936
7	Silvio Ronzone, Watsonville, CA	1936, 1939
7	Russell H. Stark, Aberdeen	1939-1943-1950
7	Roy A. Jansen, Aberdeen, ID	1846, 1949
7	Donald S. Douglas, Aberdeen	1950-1953
7	Lynn E. Guenther, Astoria, OR	1936-1943
7	B. L. Peters, Bellingham, OR	1938
7	R. L. Brown, Warrenton/Astoria, OR	1936-1942
7	W. E. Chapin, Bellingham, WA	1938-1943
7	Lynn E. Guenther, Bellingham, WA	1943, 1946, 1949
7	W. E. Chalpin, Pullman, WA	1936, 1938
7	Virgil B. Hawk, Pullman, WA	1936-1944
7	Robert S. MacLauchlan, Pleasanton, CA	1950-1952
7	Paul Lemon, Pullman, WA	1936, 1942
7	John L. Schwendiman, Pullman, WA	1936-1953
7	H. H. Rampton, Pullman, WA	1936
7	D. C. Tinsley, Pullman, WA	1936
7	Arthur J. Johnson, Pullman, WA	1939, 1943
7	Lowell A. Mullens, Pullman, WA	1939, 1942
7	Ronald F. Backman, Pullman, WA	1939
7	Harold W. Miller, Pullman, WA	1939, 1942, 1943, 1944
7	Donald S. Douglas, Pullman, WA	1946, 1949
7	Robert S. MacLauchlan, Bellingham, WA	1952-1953
7	Jack E. Woods, Pullman, WA	1946, 1949
7	Roland F. Sackman, Pullman, WA	1942
7	Dr. A. L. Hafenrichter, RN, Pullman, WA & Portland, OR	1935-1953
7	Paul Lemon, Asst. RN, Pullman, WA	1938?
7	Robert L. Brown, Asst. RN, Pullman, WA	1943

Many individuals in Table 4.5 transferred to new positions in the Plant Materials Program after the nurseries closed. They will appear in directories for either plant materials specialists, plant materials center managers, or a few as PMC employees in an agronomists or other position. An example is Glenn Niner, who was an agronomist at the Albuquerque, NM nursery from 1936 to 1953, and continued in that role at the Los Lunas PMC until his retirement.

Although some rosters are available, no attempt was made to record non-professional nurseries employees.

KNOWN OBSERVATIONAL NURSERY EMPLOYEES

In 1949, the Nursery Division developed a listing of Nursery Observational Personnel by location and classification.[156] Unfortunately, it omitted certain nurseries with a well-known observational nursery track record and omitted individual names from others. For example, James E. Smith, a leader in the search for conservation plants in the southern Great Plains, moved to San Antonio in 1949, which had a rich history of observational nursery work, but was not included in the 1949 list. Manhattan, KS is another obvious omission, based on the known presence of personnel assigned to observational work at that location. It also excluded known observation nursery personnel who had worked exclusively in that area before moving into management positions. As a result, Table 4.6 is a combination of several sources to produce a record of the operating nurseries in 1949, and the observational nursery personnel involved at that time. The last column shows that the nursery manager of ten of the twenty-five listed nurseries was an observational nursery person. The sources of the data are numerous, including personal communications,[157] archival records,[158] and annual reports.[159]

Table 4.6 All 1949 functioning nurseries and personnel participating in observational studies

Region	1949 Nursery Name	Persons Doing Observational Nursery Duties	Ex Observational Nursery Employees now Nursery Managers or Regional Nurseryman
NHQ	Beltsville, MD	Wilmer W. Steiner	Dr. Franklin Crider
1	Big Flats, NY	Maurice E. Heath	
2	Americus, GA	John Powell	John Powell
2	Brooksville, FL	G. B. Blickensderfer	G. B. Blickensderfer
2	Chapel Hill, NC	J. E. Ball, Lloyd Roof	
2	Coffeeville, MS	William G. Beatty	
2	Paducah, KY	(observational studies questionable)	
2	Rock Hill, SC	(observational studies questionable)	
2	Sandy Level, VA	Carl A. Graetz	
3	Spartanburg, SC (Regional Office)	Paul Tabor	
2	Thorsby, AL	R. L. Davis	William C. Young
3	Ames, IA	Dr. Virgil Hawk	
3	Elsberry, MO	J. J. Pierre, Roger E. Sherman	
3	Winona, MI	E. L. McPherron	
3	Zanesville, OH	(observational studies questionable)	
4	Fort Worth, TX (Regional Office)	Simon E. Wolff	
4	Minden, LA	Billie H. Rountree	
4	San Antonio, TX	Emery A. Telford	James E. Smith
4	Woodward, OK	Gordon L. Powers	
5	Lincoln, NB (Regional Office		Dr. Abraham Stoesz, RN
5	Bismarck/Mandan, ND	Jesse L. McWilliams,	
5	Manhattan, KS	Donald M. Atkins,	
5	North Platte, NE	John W. McDermand	
5	Waterloo, NE	Liard G. Wolfe	
6	Albuquerque, NM	Theodore Spaller Glenn C. Niner	Joseph A. Downs, Charles C. Marshall, RN

Region	1949 Nursery Name	Persons Doing Observational Nursery Duties	Ex Observational Nursery Employees now Nursery Managers or Regional Nurseryman
6	Tucson, AZ		Louis P. Hamilton
7	Aberdeen, ID	Roy A. Jansen, Russell H. Stark	
7	Astoria, OR	Lynn E. Guenther	
7	Bellingham, WA	Lynn E. Guenther	
7	Pleasanton, CA	Oswald K. Hoglund	Harold W. Miller
7	Portland OR (Regional Office)	Robert L. Brown	
7	Pullman, WA	Donald S. Douglas, Harold Miller, Jack Woods	John L. Schwendiman
7	San Fernando, CA	Lowell A. Mullens, Dirk J. Vanderwal	

Regardless of how the listing is interrupted, the most striking aspect of the results is that all but three functioning nurseries in 1949 had observational nursery studies underway of some significance. The three nurseries were in Rock Hill, SC, Zanesville, OH and Paducah, KY, and no doubt some observational work was going on at these three also.

PRODUCTS AND PROGRESS OF THE OBSERVATIONAL NURSERIES

The observational nurseries soon came to realize that their responsibility included more than just developing the plants. At the beginning, the concept was to develop a new plant, figure out how to propagate it and turn it over to the nursery to produce in quantity and use in SCS projects. To a great extent that is how it worked in the early years. Soon however, plants from the nurseries were ending up in the hands of individual farmers and ranchers, as well as other agencies doing conservation work. This required a complete package; one that was useful to multiple type users and one that delivered multiple products. As a result, this discussion covers the following deliverable observational nursery products, with emphasis on the first two:

- New Conservation Plants,

- Developed Technology,

- Large Scale Production of new plants and

- Delivering the Technology.

Product Number One: New Conservation Plants

As observational nurseries developed, starting at the SES nurseries in 1934, the clear and unquestioned objective was to find and utilize plants with superior characteristics for soil and water conservation applications. The 1936 policy restated this. Using Enlow's words, the product was: "Plants which are an improvement in erosion control value over currently used plants".[160] The arrow was pointed at getting new conservation plants with documented superior characteristics and broad adaptation into the hands of consumers.

What is meant by new plants? Using the concept, "Nature has evolved a plant for every purpose" new plants meant finding a superior accession to what was currently used, measured by all the desirable characteristics both Enlow and Crider established. In 1935, any list for which the new plants were needed, would have included these four overriding needs: (1) stabilize coal mining spoil in the Northeast, (2) convert eroding crop and pasture land in the southeast to productive use, (3) harness severe wind and water erosion on both crop and grazing lands of the Great Plains, and (4) rehabilitate millions of overgrazed and eroding acres of range land in the western U.S. The preponderance of 'new plants' that became available from observational nurseries were intended to be used to mitigate with these or closely related problems.

Observational nurseries made systematic searches for plants from any source that first and foremost appeared to have the potential of being good erosion control plants. Crider provided in his March 25, 1936 memorandum, some guidelines for identifying good erosion controlling plants. "As to what constitutes outstanding erosion resisting characteristics in a plant, which matter must be kept in mind whenever observations are being made, depends largely on how the plant is to be used, or the place it is to fill in the erosion control program; as, for example, (a) gulley slope stabilization, (b) prevention of sand blowing, (c) protection of terrace outlet, (d) control of sheet erosion, etc." Following that he lists twenty characteristics that give an indication of a plant's value for controlling erosion.

After the collection of many species, and multiple collections of most, each was evaluated for the twenty or so characteristics. The "Nature has evolved a plant for every purpose" concept put the emphasis on the plant rather than how the plant was to be used. Without a doubt, however, the scientist doing the evaluating kept in the back of his mind what problem it might help solve. The superior plants were selected, followed by more testing to be sure that they were better than plants currently used for solving the conservation problem. As a part of the process, it was determined if the selected plants could be reproduced in a manner that made it economically feasible to use.

Once all these criteria were met, the 'new plant' would be given a name or unique number. Then it was ready for release and large scale reproduction and use. Release meant the new plant was being released out of the total control of those responsible for selecting, evaluating and developing it, and was released to others for reproduction, which allowed it to become available for use by others. How well the release and large scale reproduction was managed often influenced how long the new plant would remain in demand and be used. Four principal management options were available to the observational nursery scientist for accomplishing this. They were:

1. Give the germplasm (seed, plants, etc.) to the SCS production nursery;

2. If the plant was a grass or forb, prepare documentation and provide the germplasm to commercial growers through the state seed certification process. This was the formal process, and the resulting release was called a cultivar (cultivated variety).[161]

3. Regardless of whether the plant was grass, forb or woody plant, just give it to producers. This was the informal process.

4. If the plant was a tree or shrub, document the superior characteristics of the plant, publish the results, including production requirements and obligations, and then provide material to reputable commercial producers. This constituted a 'formal' release of a tree or shrub. A certification process did not exist for trees or shrubs until early 1994.

The first option was used extensively during the early nursery days, without even putting a name on the new release. An example of this might be multiflora rose (*Rosa multiflora*). It never really went through any observational nursery selection process. As soon as it appeared to have characteristics that set it apart as a useful conservation plant, which was not erosion control but wildlife food and cover, it went immediately into large scale production by Big Flats and other nurseries. Tatarian honeysuckle (*Lonicera tatarica*) is another example from the same nursery, demonstrating the leadership influence of the regional biologist, Frank Edminster. At other locations the observational nurseryman might have walked across the hall to his production nursery counterpart and added it to the production schedule, without any concern for naming or releasing documentation. The nurseries produced several woody plants in the millions that demonstrated outstanding attributes, like the rose or honeysuckle, but were never officially released, while others were released years later. An excellent example of the latter is 'Streamco' purple osier willow which was produced in large numbers throughout the 1940s at the Big Flats, NY nursery and then released long after the nursery closed.

There were multiple drawbacks to this approach. First, the burden of avoiding contamination of the germplasm, thus losing any special qualities the selection had, would fall on the SCS nursery personnel, who had neither the tools nor the authority to do it. Second, the exclusive use of this approach limited the potential use of the new plant to what the nursery could produce, an approach that reduces+ its long term value. Third, and no doubt unrecognized at the time, was the economic benefit that could be accrued to commercial producers. The first option might have had the short term benefit of making the new plant available more quickly. Certainly the times and conditions encouraged expediency.

Nursery records show production of several grasses and legumes without release names, which later became cultivars. Additionally, some nurseries were producing seed of released cultivars while the same cultivar was being produced by commercial growers. For example, in 1950 SCS nurseries produced 45,000 pounds of 'Pensacola' bahiagrass and 9,660 pounds of 'Manchar' smooth brome. District cooperators produced an additional 1,187,000 and 111,700 pounds respectively.[162]

A blend of the first and the second option for releasing a plant seemed to be floating around in the mind of leaders very early in the observational nursery history. A 1938 archive document proposed procedures for the distribution of germplasm of selected grasses and legumes.[163] They would help (1) meet approved nursery production quota, (2) obtain, through limited field trials, new information about adaptation, planting, etc. of the selected plant, and (3) supply cooperating farmers with small amounts of pure germplasm stock from which to make further plantings on their farms. Number (3) was followed in some cases, which seems to suggest such plantings were really intended to expand production of the new accession. The 1938 document suggested the farmer may want to give some seed to his neighbor "occasionally to supply seed that may enter commercial channels." The authors, recognizing that this was likely to happen, proposed that, for all such germplasm stock, careful records be kept, which "will supply all the necessary information in the event that certification is desired". Unfortunately, this approach had let the cat (new release) out of the bag which could never be put back. It was a move in the direction of the certification process, option 2, but never appeared as the recommended national approach.

The release of 'Vaughn' sideoats grama (*Bouteloua curtipendula*) by the Albuquerque, NM nursery in 1940,[164] their first selected and named plant, was an excellent example of the second option.[165] The name comes from its collection location. Certainly the Albuquerque nursery anticipated years of potential use of 'Vaughn' sideoats grama. This required a plan to preserve the quality of the initial collection; a plan that would keep it from becoming contaminated with other strains of sideoats grama, potentially causing a loss of the desirable traits that led to its selection.

They opted to ensure that the quality of the subsequent generation would be preserved by releasing 'Vaughn' through the seed certification process. Crider recognized the desirability of this when he wrote the following in his 1937 foundation document, "Observational Phase of the Nursery Program."[166] "Also, it is a distinct function of the nursery section to maintain plantings of <u>pure seed stock</u>, as well as to maintain stock plantings in the nurseries of special material requiring vegetative propagation, as, for example, cuttings or tip layering". His last sentence, where he used the somewhat obscure tip layering as an example of vegetative propagation, certainly identified him as a horticulturalist as opposed to an agronomist. He had in mind the releasing of trees and shrubs with special conservation characteristics, but their certification was many years away.

One can only guess of the benefits that would have accrued to the observational nursery program had Crider in his Observational Phase of the Nursery Program established requirements that all grass and legume releases be through the state certification process. Doing this would require coordination with others. In the case of 'Vaughn', it was in cooperation with the New Mexico State University Seed

Certification Agency. The Certification Agency existed for that very purpose. Releasing it cooperatively through them assured that the reproduction would meet required standards for quality control. This opportunity existed in most, if not all states in 1940. Fortunately, this is the route the Albuquerque nursery chose.

The New Mexico State University Seed Certification office was the designated Official Seed Certifying Agency for the state in accordance with the New Mexico Seed Law. The agency was responsible for the promulgation of rules, regulations, and standards for all certification of seed and other propagating materials in the state.[167] This route required the nursery personnel to prepare documentation for the certifying agency showing why 'Vaughn' warranted release and certification. When the seed of 'Vaughn' was grown and sold commercially it carried a tag documenting this fact. For 'Vaughn', which is still sold today, the certification route guaranteed the buyer that they received the same quality sideoats grama as was selected and named in 1940. Before a plant was certified using this process, a standard for that plant had to have been developed. Many SCS releases had no standard at the time they were ready for release, but one could be developed through a joint SCS and certifying agency effort.

The desirability of certification warrants a discussion relative to the first plant released by an SCS observational nursery. The new plant was Arlington sericea lespedeza (*Lespedeza cuneata*) and the nursery was in Chapel Hill, NC. These folks, under the direction of Karl Graetz and Paul Tabor were quick and good. Sericea lespedeza became a very important conservation and forage plant in the Southeast. Although used in this country since 1898, its use increased rapidly through the SCS nursery efforts of the early 1940s.[168] They used the third release option for large scale production of Arlington. It was an informal release. Arlington was selected as a single plant from Arlington Farms, Arlington, VA by personnel at Chapel Hill.[169] The desire was to reproduce it in quantity as quickly as possible. Most likely, little or no consideration was given to a release plan, which should have included the certification process. Instead, they chose the quickest and easiest route. Seed was reproduced by the nursery and distributed to projects and local farmers. Once the local farmers saw how successful it was, they harvested some and replanted it on their property, or sold it to a neighbor, who did the same thing. Any control of quality was lost. A seed certification program had existed in North Carolina from 1929 and could have been used.[170]

Chapel Hill was an aggressive nursery with well qualified scientists, releasing four additional plants between 1939 and 1947. None were certified. All were introduced lespedeza species and most likely there was no standard developed for them, but this could have been done in cooperation with the certifying agency. Only one of the four is now commercially available. An even bigger fish was lost when the Chapel Hill nursery had the world's total supply of what then was called Suiter's tall fescue, and later released in Kentucky as 'KY-31' tall fescue. Had the nursery made contact with the North Carolina Seed Certification agency, it is highly likely a standard could have been developed for the species if it did not already have one, and 'KY-31' tall fescue could have been named 'Chapel Hill' and sold as such today. 'KY-31' can be purchased now in about any store selling seed.

Over time, releasing a new plant through the certifying agency became the desired choice and the norm. M. M. Hoover, writing to Nursery Chief H. A. Gunning in 1942, reported that he met with SCS Regional Nurseryman, nursery managers and "Dr. Keim and staff of the (Nebraska) College of Agriculture" concerning the "matter of certification of new and improved grass selections' and giving every encouragement to the…rapid development and commercial production of these improved plant materials."[171] Unfortunately, Hoover's enthusiasm did not take root quickly, particularly in the Southern Great Plains.

As we review the productivity of observational nurseries, it may not be obvious but important to know that there were no informal releases from western nurseries. The reason was simple, the regional nurseryman, Dr. Hafenrichter, forbid it. He had established a regional policy that required nursery personnel to complete several mandatory actions before a candidate received his approval. One, of course, was that the new plant would be released in cooperation with the state university agriculture experiment station and/or another appropriate agency. This automatically triggered the certification mechanism.

Participation in the certification program, as well as the preservation of the genetic quality of a cultivar, required that a limited number of generations separated it from the original 'new plant' germplasm. Understanding those requirements now will be useful in understanding the changes in procedure that have taken place over time. For most herbaceous, seed propagated plants three generations are the limit. The first generation is the most germplasm pure and is called *breeders seed*. As the name implies, this seed is controlled directly by the observational nursery personnel. The second generation is called *foundation seed*, produced from breeders, and is usually controlled and produced by the developer. Foundation seed is the material most often provided to the seed grower for the production of the third generation, *certified seed*, which becomes the commercial product. There is a registered class between foundation and certified, but it was used when the demand from commercial growers exceeded what could be provided from the foundation class. This rarely existed with conservation plants.

This entire certification discussion of new plants has been about grasses and legumes, with no discussion of the fourth release option, the certification of new woody plant releases. There are two reasons for this. No woody plant was released from observational nurseries, suggesting a limited need for a certification process. The second reason was the lack of any existing certification policy.

'Natob' bicolor lespedeza (*Lespedeza bicolor*), which is classified as a sub-shrub, was the only observational nursery, formally released plant that might be considered woody.[172] It was released by the National Observational Project at Beltsville, MD. Bill Steiner was the manager then and the release was done in the most desirable way possible at that time. Three additional sub-shrub lespedezas were released informally, two of them by the Americus, GA PMC in 1947. The third, VA-70 lespedeza, is listed as a 1952 release from Beltsville, but was actually from the Sandy Hill, VA nursery.

A few of the SCS nurseries were a continuation of SES nurseries, and logically had a jump start on the newly formed ones. Nevertheless, it is surprising how quickly new nurseries were able to initiate collections and establish observational plots. In 1935, there were eight nurseries in the Northeast. Only one was involved with observational studies; the nursery at Ithaca, NY.[173] This nursery had two sites. One was called Stewart Park, which evaluated shrubs and grasses. The other, called the Turf nursery, only evaluated grasses. It contained about 300 accessions under observation in 1937. Of the 300, 217 were being grown and evaluated in pots with an additional seventy-four legumes in pots. Additionally, 222 grasses and 131 legumes were being grown in forty-foot rows, and 118 grasses in one-hundredth acre plots. Nine had been selected for increase and additional study. At the Stewart site, 196 shrubs were under evaluation. This was a lot of activity from a 1935 beginning. The nursery closed in 1939. There is no record of what happened to these selected plants. Its manager, Robert Thornton, had moved to the regional office in 1938. What a shame the Ithaca nursery closed after such a promising start, not to mention the loss of Thornton, a number one scientist, and the selected germplasm that could have gone to the 1940 opening Big Flats nursery just 40 miles down the road.

A March 11, 1936 Work Project issued by the Section of a Conservation Nurseries in Washington, D.C., which is more of a report than work project, states that "Approximately 400 species of grasses were collected by crews of botanists working out of the nurseries. In addition to these native species, several hundred species of grasses collected by the Westover-Enlow Expedition to Turkestan and Turkey have been included."[174] Note that these numbers are by species. The number of collections per species is not given. The same 1936 work project states, "several thousand species and variations are under observation in the nurseries. "[175] The history of the Pullman Plant Materials Center by John Schwendiman records that, "An extensive observational grass nursery of more than 1,800 items was planted along with fifty-six one-eightieth acre triplicate plots of native and introduced plants."[176] Of course, Pullman had started in 1934, but their expansion remains impressive. See Figure 4.2, an outlying nursery in the Palouse Hills.

The observational nursery at Pullman was not the only thing that was extensive. By 1943, Pullman released their first cultivar, 'Manchar' smooth brome, collected in 1935 from the Kungchuling Experiment Station of the South Manchurian Railway, Manchuria, China.[177] It, as well as all of the

Center's future releases, was entered into the Washington State certification program. During the 1945-1946 period, four new native grass releases hit the market, each representing the first ever cultivars of these species. D. E. Stephens, superintendent of the Sherman Ranch Experiment Station, Moro, WA, collected the first, 'Sherman' big bluegrass from a native stand near Moro, Sherman County, OR, in 1932. It was re-collected by the SCS in 1935 and became a part of the extensive observational grass nursery.[178] The three other blockbuster cultivars in 1946 were 'Bromar' mountain brome, 'Primar'

Figure 4.2 1936, an outlying nursery site

slender wheatgrass and 'Whitmar' bluebunch wheatgrass. 'Bromar' was an improved strain of mountain bromegrass that was particularly suited for use in sweet clover-grass mixtures in pasture and green manure plantings. 'Bromar' was selected from a collection of mountain bromegrass on the campus of The State College of Washington at Pullman in 1933.

'Primar' slender wheatgrass occurs naturally from New Mexico to Alaska and from the Cascade Mountains east to Newfoundland. It was first cultivated in 1895 and used extensively in the Canadian Prairie Provinces and adjacent Dakotas. The native seed was collected near Beebe, MT, in 1933.[179] 'Whitmar' bluebunch wheatgrass is the awnless form of bluebunch wheatgrass. It was selected by the Pullman PMC from seed native to the Palouse grasslands near Colton, Washington. It performs best above twelve inches rainfall in high winter-low summer precipitation areas.[180]

During the remaining observational nursery years the Pullman nursery released four more grasses, all introduced. The foreign origin of 'Durar' hard fescue is unknown. It was reselected from an old planting on the Eastern Oregon Livestock Experiment Station at Union, WA in 1934. The collection resulting in 'Volga' mammoth wildrye was made by the Westover-Enlow expedition.[181] 'Alkar' tall wheatgrass was isolated after several generations of selections from PI-98526 introduced from the USSR in 1934.[182]

The Pleasanton, CA nursery, which opened in 1939, had in August, 1941 about 500 rows of plants being evaluated, consisting of about 200 species, and its sub-unit in Littlerock, CA "had more than a hundred species of grass and other plants under various stages of development."[183] The Pleasanton observational nursery added four new releases before it closed in 1953. 'Goar' tall fescue was their first, jointly released with the California Agriculture Experiment Station for use in irrigated pastures.[184] Its original germplasm came from Budapest, Hungary by way of the University of Manitoba, arriving in Davis, CA in 1925. Their second release, in 1949, was a native 'Cucamonga' California brome, a self-perpetuating winter annual, collected in 1939 near the Cucamonga, CA train station made famous by Jack Benny. It had its start at the Littlerock, CA nursery.

The third Pleasanton release was 'Akaroa' orchardgrass, originally from New Zealand. It was a late maturing cultivar with fine stems, leafy, and low growing. Its use is primarily for irrigated pastures in California and western Oregon and Washington. A fine article appeared in the Clatskanie Chief, Clatskanie, OR on April 3, 1953 extolling its value.[185] The author was SCS Work Unit Conservationist, Virgil Lance, who got his information from W. E. Chapin, the Bellingham, WA nursery manager. According to Chapin, it had been under evaluation there for fifteen years. Young Bob MacLauchlan, an agronomist at Bellingham reported that the test results with 'Akaroa' in twenty-eight plantings showed it to be definitely superior to common orchardgrass.

'Blando' brome, collected in 1940 by D. J. Vanderwal, is another self-seeding winter annual like 'Cucamonga', but is one of the numerous introduced annual bromes and is well adapted to the winter wet summer dry parts of California's rangeland. A most versatile conservation plant, it is used for annual range reseeding, vineyard and nut tree cover crop and replanting disturbed areas. While not released until 1954, it was a nursery product. It is highlighted in a www.youtube.com video as a cover crop in Napa Valley vineyards.[186]

The first release from the Aberdeen, ID observational nursery came in 1953, fourteen years after the nursery opened. It was 'P-27' Siberian wheatgrass, collected originally by the Westover-Enlow expedition. That same year the nursery released 'Topar' pubescent wheatgrass, from Turkestan, also collected by Westover and Enlow. It forms sod faster, is more adapted to poor fertility, higher elevations and saline conditions than most pubescent wheatgrasses. Its intended use was to combat soil erosion by stabilizing low fertility range sites. 'Topar' has been discontinued as a supported cultivar by SCS although it continues to be advertised for sale.[187] From 1977 through 2005, 4.7 million pounds of seed was produced commercially of these two cultivars.

Rounding out the Aberdeen observational releases was 'Sodar' streambank wheatgrass, collected by R. G. Johnson in a twelve-inch rainfall belt near Clayton City, OR. It remains a most popular option for rangeland revegetation, reclamation of eroding sites and, in recent years, a low maintenance and low rainfall lawn grass.

Another western observational nursery with an impressive release record was at Tucson, AZ where Dr. Crider started his SCS career. Crider's high regard for lovegrass was evident in their 1950 release of 'A-84' Boer lovegrass and 'A-68' Lehmann's lovegrass. Both were introduced from South Africa in the 1930s, and were released in hopes of restoring depleted rangelands in the Southwest.[188] They have a competitive advantage over native grasses because of early production of abundant seeds and a positive response to fire and grazing. Excessive overgrazing had created the need. Unfortunately, once the ground was stabilized, the lovegrasses over-filled their need by restricting the reinvasion of native grasses. They remain widespread in the Southwest.

The last Western nursery was Albuquerque, NM. 'Vaughn' sideoats grama, and 'Greenville' switchgrass, were both released in 1940. Both cultivars, named for their collection location, continue to be viable after seventy years. From 1977 (first year of records keeping) through 2005 there were 14,070,400 pounds of seed produced and sold for conservation purposes of 'Vaughn' and 'Greenville'.[189] In addition to 'Vaughn' and 'Greenville', another release, 'Amur' intermediate wheatgrass, released in 1952, originated from seed originally obtained from China, initially evaluated by the Pullman PMC. It was selected for leafiness, vigorous growth, strong seedling vigor, and good seed production. It was originally released for revegetation of disturbed lands and for pasture seedings at higher elevations.

Turning to the Great Plains nurseries, Mandan, ND and Manhattan, KS put several new plants into large-scale production. The nursery at Mandan cooperated in the releases of Mandan Canada wildrye, with the Agriculture Research Service and the North Dakota Agricultural Experiment Station.[190] It is often an early successional component of prairie mixtures, provides good forage quality during the early part of the grazing season, but is generally considered inferior forage after it matures.

Their second release was 'Nordan' crested wheatgrass with the same agencies as the Canada wildrye. It entered the observational system in 1937 from a selection made at an old nursery at Dickinson, North Dakota. Single plants were selected from two generations of the original plant collection. Seven plants within this open-pollinated progeny were bulked for seed increase and tested as Mandan 571.[191] It was released in 1953. Crested wheatgrass found a niche on the overgrazed western rangeland, making 'Nordan' one of the leading contenders for 'saving the west from erosion'.

Newhall, Rasmussen and Kitchen reported in 2009 on a study started in 1995 to reintroduce big sage into a sixty-three-year old stand of 'Nordan'.[192] That would suggest it had been in use at least ten years before it was released, unless the authors were mistaken on the cultivar name. Newhall, et al, pointed out that crested wheatgrass had been effectively used to stabilize arid and semi-arid range sites for decades and that it competes well with cheatgrass, halogeten, medusahead, Russian thistle and other introduced weeds. Replacing it with native plant materials would be desirable to improve wildlife habitat and ecological diversity. Due to its competitive nature, such attempts had met with limited success. Four years of data indicate that chemical control of crested wheatgrass prior to transplanting big sage resulted in some success.

The record at Manhattan is impressive, more because of the quality of their releases than the quantity. There were three. 'Blackwell' switchgrass and 'El Reno' sideoats grama have both been outstanding cultivars. Seed was harvested from a single plant near Blackwell, OK in 1934; ten years later, it was 'Blackwell', a cultivar. Figure 4.3 shows its area of known adaptation and use.[193] It was truly a broadly adapted cultivar. This switchgrass has been planted to well over a million acres, has a long history of endurance and has provided consistent benefits for restoration, pasture usage, wildlife cover, nesting, waterways, disturbed sites and levee seeding.[194] 'El Reno' sideoats, also originating in Oklahoma,

Figure 4.3 Adaptation areas of 'Blackwell' switchgrass

produces strong leafy plants that are excellent for forage. It grows rapidly and is noted for its disease resistance and winter hardiness.[195] Cheyenne Indiangrass, selected by James E. Smith and G. L. Powers at Woodward, OK, was informally released in 1945. These three cultivars are major contributions to the war on wind and water erosion on the central Great Plains.

The only nursery producing new conservation plants in the Southern Great Plains was San Antonio, TX. The first cultivar with which they were involved was King Ranch yellow bluestem. It was first reported in the Region 4 Annual Report for 1940, and appeared often for the next several years. In their combined third and fourth Annual Report for 1942 and 1943 a discussion of its merits appeared three times; first on page 5, stating "there is ample evidence here and elsewhere this strain is outstanding, and will prove valuable...stock food in many parts of this region."[196] It is so good, as noted on page 15, it spread into a field of native little bluestem.

Its history is as interesting as that of the ranch by the same name.[197] The origin of King Ranch blue stem in America as described by J. R. Harlan in Oklahoma Forage Leaflet No. 11, 1952, is as follows:

Nico Diaz noticed in 1937 a grass growing on King Ranch in a weakened Rhodes grass pasture. A collection was made and increased at the San Antonio nursery for distribution by SCS under T-3487. Recent inquiry into the history of Texas yellow beardgrass, which is apparently indistinguishable from King Ranch bluestem in all respects, leaves little doubt as to the original entry of this grass into the United States. History is briefly as follows:

- January 11, 1917 the California Agricultural Experiment Station, Berkeley, received a yellow bluestem accession from Amoy, China and gave it number TO 144 and later SPI number 44096.

- 1924, SPI 44096 was sent to Angleton Experiment Station, Texas, by V. E. Hafner, Bureau of Plant Industry, Washington, D. C, and given Texas number TS 8413.

- April 11, 1932--TO 144 (SPI 44096, TS 8413) was received by Division of Forage Crops and Diseases, BPI, Washington, D. C, from Agronomy Department, University of California, Davis, and given F. C. number 21785.

- April 11, 1935--F. C. 21785 (TO 144 SPI 44096, TS 8413) was sent to B. F. Kiltz, Oklahoma Agricultural Experiment Station, Stillwater, from Beltsville, Md.

- 1937, F. C. 21785 (TO 144 SPI 44096, TS 8413) obtained by United States Southern Great Plains Field Station, Woodward, Okla., from Stillwater.

- 1937, F. C. 21785 (TO 144 SPI 44096, TS 8413) was obtained by Texas AES, College Station, from Woodward.

- 1939, TS 8413 (F. C. 21785, TO 144 SPI 44096) was given the name 'yellow beardgrass' in Texas Agricultural Experiment Station Bulletin No. 570 and its performance at Angleton described.

- 1949, F. C. 21785 (TO 144 SPI 44096, TS 8413) was -- released for certification in Texas by Texas AES. All *Bothriochloa ischaemum var. songarica* furnished by Texas AES to individuals or substations since 1941 originated from this source. Since the original Chinese material had been grown at Angleton Experiment Station as early as 1924, there is little reason to suppose that King Ranch strain is any other than the Chinese accession that found its way from Angleton to King Ranch sometime during 1924-37.

The next important San Antonio nursery release is T-4464 buffelgrass, introduced from Kenya's Turkana Desert, and released informally in 1946. According to Smith, the San Antonio Nursery received an accession from the Beltsville Nursery in 1946 and planted it in rod rows.[198] Growth was outstanding and a small trial planting was made in Sutherland Springs, TX in 1948. The first market supply was available in 1950. Four years later it was estimated that there was in excess of 500,000 acres of buffelgrass in range, pasture and seed increase plantings in southern and SW Texas.

Buffelgrass solicits varying points of view. "T-4464 buffelgrass has changed desert scenery into Cattle Country for the last 7 decades."[199] "Buffelgrass is aggressively invading from southern Arizona."[200] "According to Valdez-Zamudiol and others (1995), the annual green forage production in pastures with this species increased forage production approximately three times in comparison to production in areas with native species."[201] "*Pennisetum ciliare* is regarded as one of six species that can potentially cause more ecological damage in the Sonoran Desert region than most of the non-natives present here."[202]NRCS has discontinued supporting T-4464 because it is "no longer produced."[203]

As mentioned earlier, the first observational nursery release in the Southeast was from Chapel Hill, NC, one of many nurseries that did not survive to become a PMC. Several talented plant materials personnel spent time there, with Karl Graetz having the longest career. Prior to their closing in 1953, the nineteen Southeast Region nurseries that functioned at one time or another had introduced twelve new plants into the culture of the region. Only five survived to be commercially available in 1977. By far the most successful from the region and one of the most successful nationally was 'Pensacola' bahiagrass. Its arrival as an outstanding cultivar is unique in a couple aspects. County agent E. H. Finlayson, of Pensacola, Florida, collected it around the old Perdido Wharf in 1941.[204] It is thought to have arrived in the U.S. by fruit boat from Central or South America. 'Pensacola' was the only cultivar from the Southeast region nurseries to be certified through the state seed certification program. However, that was not required for it to be successful; it found a niche stabilizing abandoned cotton land combined with its forage producing ability. It was a delight to Dr. Bennett.

The Northeast had as many as fifteen nurseries between 1935 and 1953, but only one was operating in 1953: Big Flats, NY. Neither it nor any of the others had released a new plant. While Dr. Maurice Heath was there in 1949, an accession of crownvetch, which had come from the Beltsville National Project, was in production on the nursery. It became the first release from that facility, but not until 1961. Ironically, Dr. Heath went from Big Flats to the Iowa State University, Ames in 1952 and met Dr. Virgil Hawk who had come from, what he called, "The stranglehold of Dr. Hafenrichter" at Pullman, WA in 1949.[205] At Ames, Hawk completed his PhD. and in 1961 he, the Elsberry PMC and Dr. Heath released 'Emerald' crownvetch. The Big Flats PMC page in Chapter 8 discusses this 'what might have been' story in greater detail.

The number of potential nurseries that could have been being conducting observational nursery studies was fluid during the 1935 - 1939 periods. Separate reports provided varying numbers in operation; from eighty-one in early 1936, which included Emergency Conservation Work and Civilian Conservation Corps camps, to fifty-five SCS "stock and grass seed production and observational nurseries" in fiscal year 1937.[206] As discussed earlier, it is unclear how many of these nurseries were actually collecting and evaluating plants for potential release. The best estimate is approximately twenty, which changed little by 1952. During 1948 – 1953, the number of nurseries stabilized at about twenty-four and all but three were conducting observational nursery work. However, by 1954 when all the nurseries closed, only fifteen observational nurseries had released or developed new plants ready for release.

An interesting observation on how Chief Bennett felt about nurseries conducting observational work is reflected in a ten-point questionnaire he sent to R. M. Ross, Chief, Nursery Division on October 26, 1949 titled "I would like to have."[207] He had just read a report titled "Main Work of the Soil Conservation Service for Fiscal Year 1949" dated October 24, 1949.[208] Ross had prepared the report based on what each regional nurseryman had sent him regarding their main items of work at their nurseries. Question seven on the "I would like to have" list was "Why not have all nurseries search for new legumes and other promising plants?" Number eleven told Ross, "See me on all ten of these things." Ross prepared a written reply in which he responded to question seven by stating his understanding of why all nurseries aren't searching for promising plants.[209] "Most of the nurseries still give attention to the finding of new and better soil conserving plants. Due, however, to differences in regional conditions and administrative evaluation of the importance of this type of work, greater emphasis is placed on this activity in some regions than in others." The balance of this two-page reply to question seven is a rehash of what was contained in his October 24 report. Other reports appear to indicate that three nurseries did not have an active observational nursery. This was known by Ross but he did not report it to Bennett.

Aside from Bennett's questions on the "Main Work of the Soil Conservation Service for Fiscal Year 1949" responses from several nurseries offered some interesting observations. Those nurseries, like Manhattan, KS, Albuquerque, NM or Pullman, WA, with strong observational programs, identified some equally strong accomplishments. Others, like Big Flats, offered one potential accomplishment that it fortunately never realized, i.e., to "find a hardy kudzu for the Northeast."

Observational nurseries took the lead in releasing fifty-one plants from the first in 1939 until the nurseries closed in 1954. They participated in twelve other releases cooperatively with other agencies or institutions, where SCS was not the lead releasing agency. Of the fifty-one releases, thirty were formally released and twenty-one informally, thirty-eight were introduced and thirteen native, five herbaceous legumes, two shrubs and forty-four grasses.[210] All are shown with the releasing nursery/PMC in Chapter 8.

The nursery most frequently using the informal approach was San Antonio, TX, with seven such releases. There was a general opinion in the Kansas, Oklahoma and Texas region that it was dangerous business to risk the production of SCS cultivars to other than SCS nurseries. It was the desire of the region to expand the size of nurseries and use the additional land to produce seed of new cultivates. Mr. Hoover, Chief Agronomist of the Nursery Division, recognized this resistance in a letter to A. E. Jones, Chief of the Conservation Operations.[211] He tells Jones that, in his opinion, "more beneficial and lasting results will accrue to the Service if...efforts and expense are directed towards the development of a seed production program by district cooperators" using the state seed certification agency.

Certainly there were many other outstanding selections residing at the nurseries that would be released after plant materials centers were established, but they are not included here. In reality any new cultivar released through about 1958 could be considered a child of the nurseries.[212] Foremost among these outstanding releases that would impact soil and moisture conservation for the next several decades included 'P-27' Siberian wheatgrass, 'Pensacola' bahiagrass, 'Blackwell' switchgrass and 'Blando' brome.

An observation of the releasing history of nurseries and PMCs offers at least one striking inconsistency. Hindsight certainly suggests the clear and unquestionable value of releasing grasses and forbs through the state seed certification program. As mentioned earlier Dr. Hafenrichter quickly developed a policy requiring observational nurseries in his regions to release all new plants through the certification program. On the surface, this appears as though it would include any woody plant releases, but this was not the case because such plants were not a part of the observation program in his regions. For more discussion on this topic, see Chapter 13. With the desirability of certification, and the policy existing in one region, why was it not national policy? Crider favored this approach. Why didn't they or other national leaders that followed him make it policy?

Although there were twenty-four nurseries in 1953, many of which had existed for ten years or more, all of the releases above came from only twelve nurseries, plus Astoria, OR which closed prior to 1953. The other twelve did not produce a single new plant to enter the commercial market.

Product Number Two: Detailed Technology on How to Grow, Establish and Reproduce

The second anticipated product from the observational nursery program was spelled out in several ways both by Enlow's 1935 and Crider's 1937 memoranda.[213]It can be summarized as the need for detailed technology on how to grow, establish and commercially reproduce the selected plant. Crider described it this way:

> Observational Phase of the Nursery Program - Nursery Practices. During the nursery observational period all data possible having to do with the handling of the plant, looking towards its practical establishment in the field or under natural conditions, as the case may be, should be obtained. This will serve not only as an indication of its practical value but furnish essential information for the subsequent use of both the nurseryman and the using agencies.

His use of the last phrase 'using agencies' suggested his view that the SCS would produce and SCS or some other agency would be planting it on the problem area. The role of the private land owner was not recognized at that time. Crider continued:

> Therefore, for those plants agreed upon as possessing the desired characteristics for field trials, studies must be made to determine successful methods of propagation, with the methods finally adopted being simple, easy applied, and lending themselves to quantity multiplication. Also, efforts should be made to find out, particularly in the case of plants like grasses and legumes, such facts as proper rate, depth, time, and method of planting, as well as any other facts essential to the successful establishment

of the plants where they can be most effectively used in a soil and moisture conservation program.

Many of the items listed by Crider were well known for commodity crops, but were lacking for the new plants that were being developed, including the difficulties of establishing new plants on harsh, eroding sites for which they were intended.

Developing this technology was as essential as finding new plants. Without it the superior plants would never have been successfully used. The new technology was also invaluable for replanting the large bulk collections the nursery crews were making all across the country, as well as for SCS, CCC, soil conservation districts and other crews planting the seed and plants grown or collected by the nurseries. The type of technology that needed to be developed varied across the country. Stabilizing eroding cotton land with 'Pensacola' bahiagrass required a totally separate set of tools than stabilizing the dunes in the Pacific Northwest. As a result, each participating nursery developed studies unique to their problems.

Recall Crider's March 25, 1936 policy memorandum where he allowed leeway relative to whether a nursery was obligated to have an observational nursery component.[214] Realistically, did they have an option? Nearly every nursery was producing or collecting native material to replant. How could the seed be cleaned and replanted? Every nursery had to struggle with the question, what to produce and how to do it? What better way to get answers to outstanding questions than via the observational nursery approach.

The need for this kind of technology is highlighted in a brief history written by James E. Smith in 1960.[215] Smith was in charge of making large-scale harvests of blue grama from native stands in New Mexico, Texas and Oklahoma. The first attempt was made in 1935 near Dalhart, TX. This area is often recognized as ground zero for the April 14, 1935 Black Sunday dust storm, striking Amarillo at 7:20 PM. Smith's best seed was collected about thirty-five miles southwest of Dalhart. The harvest was made with nine five-foot bluegrass strippers, towed in tandem sets of three machines each behind steel-wheeled tractors. Yields from the 2000 harvested acres ranged from around twenty to thirty-five pounds per acre, resulting in about 54,000 pounds.

During the cleaning and storage of the 1935 blue grama harvest, Smith became concerned about how much material could be metered out for planting, so he borrowed a cotton planter, a team of horses and soon found that it did a fine job of putting out the seed. While the cotton planter worked fine, the minimum seed it could put out was six pounds per acre in forty-inch rows. Considering all the effort involved in collecting and cleaning the seed, and the number of acres needing treatment, this seeding rate was too high. Discussion of this with the Woodward, OK field station led to the construction of the first grass drill made specifically to handle chaffy grass seed and meter it at the desirable rates. Built to field station specifications, the first custom-built grass drills were assembled in Amarillo and offered for sale. According to Smith, "Present (1960) models were essentially the same as the early ones built" in the late 1930s. The chief change, and a major improvement, was the addition of a small box to handle free-flowing and highly processed seed.

Smith now had the collected seed and the drill with which to plant it. The terrible dust storms continued making the preparation of a seedbed difficult. SCS and Bureau of Plant Industry scientists jointly devised a method of seedbed preparation to minimize weather hazards to establishing perennial grass plantings. The method featured growing a close-drilled sorghum crop into which the perennial grass was seeded the following spring, i.e., a nurse crop of sorts.

Local seed firms had entered the business of collecting seed from native stands and selling it to SCS or land owners. Smith convinced some of them to grow it as a crop. By 1938, following demonstrations by SCS that showed farmers how to produce more seed at lower costs; several took up the practice.

The first recorded combine seed harvest of native sand lovegrass took place along the North Canadian River near Woodward, OK in 1938, by SCS crews from the Bushland (Amarillo) nursery. This 300 pound harvest was used to increase the supply at Bushland and that was used to seed many thousands of acres in Kansas, Oklahoma, New Mexico and Texas.

As early as 1943, Don Cornelius, James Smith, and A. D. Stoesz were publishing methods of harvesting, storing, and processing native grass seeds.[216] Savage and Smith published *Regrassing Methods for the Southern Great Plains* and John Schwendiman contributed the *Effects of Processing on Germinative Capacity of Seed of Tall Oatgrass* in 1944.[217] R. H. Stark, J. L. Toevs and A. L. Hafenrichter published two papers in 1946 on cultural methods for establishing grasses in the Great Basin.[218] [219] Once a superior soil erosion and moisture conservation plant was spotted, its reproduction, establishment and management requirements were determined by observational nurseries. Appendix 2, which is a listing of pre-Internet publications, contains many articles from observational nursery scientists relating to the cultural requirements of plants.

In 1939, Dr. Charles F. Swingle, horticulturist on the Nursery Section staff in Washington, completed a major undertaking when he authored **"Seed Propagation of Trees, Shrubs and Forbs for Conservation Planting".[220]** This publication must have been on the desk of every nursery manager as soon as it was published, and it is likely it never left. Swingle was with the Bureau of Plant Industries and came over to the SCS probably in 1935. He outlines the need for this approximately 2000 species compilation in the introduction as follows: "At the beginning of the large-scale conservation work by the SCS the technicians of the Service were confronted with the necessity of producing large numbers of plants that had never before been grown. Of course the question arose immediately as to collection and handling of seed, including especially the amount of seed required to grow a given number of plants. During the past six years the technicians of SCS (which includes SES technicians) have accumulated a large amount of information …" It was a vital tool by many a PMC manager long after the nurseries closed. Of course this is the kind of essential information Dr. Crider had in mind. Other noteworthy publications by Swingle are included in Appendix 2.

In spite of the need for all observation nurseries to develop the technology for producing and establishing any conservation plant, policy developed in Region 5 came close to ruling it out. A 1940s policy statement (exact date unknown) presents, in detail, the existing national policy for conducting observational studies. Based on this, they summarize the meaning as they understood it in Region 5 (Lincoln). One summary item warrants repeating.[221]

> While not essential to any particular study, it will be generally assumed that such (observational) studies as are undertaken will lead to some phase of nursery production. While every consideration will be given to proposed studies, those which only involve cultural practices and utilization of existing plant materials will generally be considered the responsibility of the using division (i.e. agronomy, forestry, etc.) and the experiment station. This restrictive policy is necessary to prevent wholesale overlapping of division responsibility.

The policy continues to explain that if the study is to produce new plants the Nursery Division will actively participate. If it is only a how-to-do-it study it is not the responsibility of the observational nurseries.

Based on what was going on elsewhere, Region 5's interpretation of national policy relative to cultural practices was incorrect. Dr. Crider, in his July 27, 1937 Memorandum to Regional Conservators states "The work (of observational studies) entails constant search for species and variations within the species of plants with existent, outstanding erosion control values, which through appropriate (a) propagation, (b) cultural and (c) adaptation practices,…"[222] On page 5 of the same document, under Nursery Practices, he states "During the nursery observational period all data possible having to do with handling of the plant, looking towards its practical establishment in the field...should be obtained."

Chapter 8 contains information about each Plant Materials Center. Included with each is a featured non-release type accomplishment. Nearly all of them are a cultural accomplishment unrelated directly to the release of a new plant. Additionally, the annual reports by SCS to USDA, which are summarized in Appendix 3, also contain several stories of cultural advances.

Without a doubt, all observational nurseries were as concerned about cultural practices as about finding a new plant. They were essential for plants currently grown by the nursery or newly developed plants. In reality, cultural practice knowledge was being accumulated even if a quest for a new plant was unsuccessful. Appendix 2 identifies over 50 published works by nursery employees prior to the nurseries closing.

Product Number Three: Large Scale, Including Commercial, Production of New Plants

The need for large scale production of new plants was fully recognized by Dr. Crider in his July 27, 1937 memorandum. He states "these species and variations which pass the acid test of practicability...are propagated in sufficient amounts for general project use." He continues in the July 27, 1937 memorandum, "In this connection, it is very proper use of nursery facilities to increase seed stocks to a point where the planting requirements of the projects can be met or until such time as other sources of supply are available." His reference to 'project' suggests the observational nurseries' 'new plants' will have limited period of use. At the time of his writing that was a logical viewpoint. However, the potential value and use of these new plants beyond the projects and demonstration areas became evident and the demand exceeded the nursery's production capability. It was time for "other sources of supply" to become available. Quickly, commercial production supplemented the nursery supply. This was accomplished by either SCS informally giving planting stock to known or interested growers (informal release), or through the state certification process.

As discussed earlier, the West region was the first to require that the state seed certification process be used, although the Albuquerque Region under Charles Marshall was the first to use it.[223] Other regions were slower in accomplishing this process. Evidence is lacking to indicate whether there was any national concern about nurseries using the state seed certification process until the mid-1940s. It appeared that each nursery or region was making the decision on what approach to use as they went along. By the late 1940s, the regions encompassing the arid or semi-arid parts of the country were using the certification process, with the exception of the region including Oklahoma and Texas.

Recall the memorandum from M. M. Hoover, Nursery Division Agronomist, to A. E. Jones, Chief of Operations, which was dated January 2, 1946.[224] He had met with H. N. Smith, Regional Engineer and C. B. Webster, Regional Nurseryman, both from Fort Worth, to review a proposal to expand the production of seed to meet the regional requirements. The region supported the proposal on the basis that the nurseries had skilled and experienced technicians and their presence gave "greater assurance the seed will be available were and when and in the amount needed." Apparently, there were some reservations about whether the commercial market could manage new plants correctly and could provide the needed supply on a timely basis. While Hoover recognized the value of well trained technicians, irrigated land, etc., he felt the SCS would be better served in the long run by developing commercial sources. Hoover concluded his memorandum to Jones as follows: "With this thought in mind we will submit to you, in the near future, a review of the entire nursery program of the Service, particularly as it pertains to the observation and seed increase work with forage grasses. We believe a careful review of the entire program will result in procedures suitable to meet the present needs of Region 4 and, at the same time, conform to the national policy regarding the use of nursery production facilities for growing foundation seed of improved varieties of forage crops, and further increase through certification by state and certifying agencies."

Of course the certification program had grown out of the need for farmers, or anyone, to buy their seed with some knowledge of assured quality.[225] Hoover's reference to only 'forage grasses' and 'forage crops' may well reflect that certification standards did not exist for much else. It may also be, in part, because Hoover was an agronomist, seeing all plants as forages. While the use of 'forage grasses' may seem to be a narrow description of conservation plants in general, most new plants coming out of observational nurseries were grasses with forage value. As a matter of fact, at least thirty-six of the fifty-one releases credited to the observational nursery period were grasses with forage value. The first non-grasses were the two sericea lespedeza releases from Chapel Hill, which of course had forage value. If a new policy came from Hoover's recommendation, it was not found.

Looking back it appears that the planning for large scale reproduction of the new plant releases from nurseries had not been well thought out. At the beginning it is doubtful whether Bennett, Crider or anyone else, except maybe Hafenrichter, had any idea of the magnitude of success of the observational nursery new plants. All of a sudden, here were these new plants with a growing demand from projects and the public that the nurseries could not meet. In the end it worked out reasonably well, but during the process there were some lost motion and lost plants, such as those from Chapel Hill that did not survive.

Although slow, the commercial production of new releases was being realized. By 1953, thirty-one were in commercial production. The flow within SCS annual reports to the Department during the late 1940s and early 1950s, found in Appendix 3, documents how the production of new grass and legume releases became the darlings of the Nursery Division, replacing tree and shrub production. While unrelated, it is ironic to observe how successful the commercial production of new conservation plants became while the mass production of trees and shrubs continued at SCS nurseries. The net dollar value from the commercial production of most releases is shown in an Output table for each PMC in Chapter 8.

Product Number Four: Delivering the Developed Technology

In 1936 or 1937, the concept of delivering the technology from observational nurseries to potential users may not have seemed important to Crider. Why should it? The nurseries were producing the material and planting it. However, with the Soil Conservation Act in 1935, and the rapid establishment of local soil conservation districts across the country, SCS had a new partner whose members needed the technology.[226] Getting the observational nurseries' technology into the hands of SCS employees who were assisting district cooperators became imperative immediately.

The delivery of all types of technical assistance by SCS has utilized different approaches over time.[227] Demonstration Projects had their beginning in the Soil Erosion Service, where several disciplines combined their technology to establish and demonstrate multiple conservation practices. The demonstration area covered several farms where all types of conservation technology were used. The Coon Creek watershed in Wisconsin was selected as the first demonstration area, started in 1934 by the Soil Erosion Service.[228] Bennett wanted to show how farmers could plan farming operations to include soil conservation for long-term productivity. The Civilian Conservation Corps (CCC) worked as a partner on this and many of the other 173 demonstration areas. While such practices as contour farming and crop rotation were featured in Coon Valley, the role of proper vegetation was also demonstrated. James Smith records that, in 1935, the 54,000 pounds of blue grama seed was "distributed for planting in demonstration projects and CCC camp areas in Texas, New Mexico, Colorado, Kansas and Oklahoma."[229] Demonstration projects touched most areas of the country.

Once local conservation districts were formed, technical assistance would be delivered to land owners and managers through them.[230] SCS technicians would assist the conservation district and their cooperators. The first conservation district in the nation was chartered on August 4, 1937 in Anson County, North Carolina, birthplace of Hugh Hammond Bennett. Oklahoma, in the heart of the Dust

Bowl, became the first to enact the soil conservation district act.[231] As soon as SCS staffed the Districts, James Smith and others were available for assistance.

Regardless of the broad approach of delivering conservation assistance, the plant technology-related assistance reached the end user via three direct routes.

1. The one-on-one approach. If the SCS was the 'using agency' as Crider envisioned, the observational nursery developer of the technology may have directly transferred the required technology to the planting crew by participating in establishing the plantings in demonstration areas. As seed or plants of improved cultivars became available, either from SCS nursery production or commercial growers, SCS nursery employees provided direct, one-on-one assistance under some circumstances. One common example would be the assistance provided to a commercial seed or plant grower, or the same interaction with an SCS employee who would then work with the grower. One-on-one assistance was also commonplace in the exchange of information with a colleague from another agency.[232] While there was not a position established to conduct this or any other training within the observational nursery structure, nursery employees were in contact with end users of their product.

2. Formal Training, either one-on-one or by conference. Following the days when well-trained planting crews from SCS, CCC, or conservation districts made most of the plantings, organized training sessions became the norm. Nursery or non-nursery employees traveled around the state or region, providing training, or brought groups to a central location for training. The trainee may have been the land owner or another SCS employee who became the trainer of the individuals who would be making the plantings. An early example of this was the Regional Grass School held in the Pacific Northwest.[233] The first was held at Pullman, WA June 6-10, 1938, sponsored jointly by the SCS Agronomy-Range section and the Section of Conservation Nurseries. Sixteen presentations were made by national, regional or local technicians on conservation problems involving the establishment and use of conservation plants, primarily for reestablishing grass cover on rangeland. Proceedings of the Conference comprised 165 typed pages, which of course became a training tool. The second Regional Grass School was held at Condon and Seaside, OR in 1939.[234] Included were technical personnel of the SCS nurseries and agronomy field technicians. Results from grass evaluation nurseries, mixture studies from Pullman, and outlying nursery and field plantings were presented. Additionally, reports on palatability studies, and beachgrass plantings at Warrenton, Oregon, were included.

3. Published documentation and procedures. This has been, and remains, a main stay of delivering technology to all organizations, agencies groups, and individuals that are involved with conservation plant materials. The first results from observational nursery studies are found in annual and other more detailed reports. A summary of each annual report from 1936 to 1953 is available in Appendix 3. Nursery results became available via numerous reports, such as "The Observational Cottonwood Study, 1936-1939",[235] or "Technical Reports, Region 2, 1941- 1946".[236] The Regional technical reports exist for most regions and years, throughout the 1935 - 1953 periods. Many observational nursery scientists published articles in local, regional or national publications, conveying a piece of technology to fellow workers or the general public. Lists of many of these publications are in Appendix 2. Additionally, the Annual Report from the SCS Chief to the Secretary of Agriculture contained a brief review of observational nursery progress.[237] [238] While these do not represent direct transfer of conservation technical assistance, they alert broader agency offices and political representatives of what is available or on the horizon.

By 1946, SCS began a policy to reduce the distribution of nursery stock to SCDs but supplanting this with technical assistance. The need for high quality grass and legume seed increased with the curtailment of nursery stock production. More and more, the nursery facilities were being used for the growing of genetically pure foundation seed. "During 1947 the facilities of Service nurseries were used largely for maintaining foundation seed stock and the quantity production of newly evaluated conservation plants. The total seed production on the nurseries was 422,000 pounds."[239] This production was going to district cooperators for an expanding commercial seed production industry.

As a part of this transition more written accomplishments of nursery activities were documented. This varied from a one-page review to major publications. See Appendix 2 for major accomplishments developed by the observational nursery staff. Many which were prepared for short-term use will be missing, and a record of their existence lost, although their content may have been captured in other publications.

Historically the observational nurseries, and to a greater extent the plant materials centers, have been viewed by many as 'the best kept secret in SCS'. No doubt the nurseries did a poor job of drawing attention to their success, and were even more humble as time passed. Yet the rapid expansion of the use of new plants suggests the word was getting out. By 1954, the only part of the vast Nursery Division still functioning was the observational nursery program. It may be that the secret only existed within SCS.

TOASTS

Is it logical that a group of plant scientists would have reason to toast themselves and their work? Logical or not, they existed.

It is well documented that Dr. Hafenrichter was a taskmaster in more ways than one. However, it would be incorrect to suggest he did not enjoy the hearty fellowship of co-workers. The timing is unsure, but in the early years of the observational nurseries he provided, to whom he called the Hafenrichter boys, a toast they could collectively use during the evening happy hour or special occasion.[240] It was his habit to call on different members to give the toast. According to some old-timers, woe betides the person who didn't know it. Here it is.

Gesundheit, Gesellshaft und Langer Leben!

Weisen Fuchsen Schwantz

Mit unter der Erdeshen Auslavfer.

Translated:

Good health, fellowship and long life!

Creeping meadow foxtail with underground runners.

While the meaning may escape some, it was apparently clear to the Hafenrichter boys.

Years later, a toast was developed in the Eastern U.S. It reflected the desired result of our plant materials employment, and was certainly easier to learn. It went something like this.

Friends may come and friends may go.

And friends may peter out you know.

But we'll continue to evaluate and release,

Until all the erosion in the world shall cease.

Then we'll retire to that great PMC

Where there will be no weeds in our 'Lathco' flatpea.

As can be seen, the opportunities to develop a Plant Materials toast remain fertile.

SUMMARY

When Dr. Franklin Crider came to Washington in 1936 he met a blank sheet of paper upon which he was supposed to write a policy for operating well over fifty conservation nurseries. He was selected because he had a notion that plants could be found to solve most soil erosion and moisture conservation problems in the country. The nurseries for which he was writing policy were like two nurseries in one. One was to produce or collect enormous quantities of seed and plants. The other, through observation, was to find plants with superior qualities.

His policy survived nearly unscathed as late as 1953. The Eisenhower Administration USDA budget confirmed Enlow's prediction. The nurseries had been seeing a gradual attrition in their budget, numbers and production per unit. Their peak year for the numbers of operating and producing nurseries was 1937 with fifty-four[241], shipping 113 million woody plants.[242] The nurseries would be pared to thirty-six by the next year.

During the 1948 – 1952 periods, twenty-five producing nurseries averaged thirty-five million plants produced per year.[243] In 1952-1953, there were twenty-four nurseries. The existing nurseries in 1953 are shown in Table 4.7.

Table 4.7 Existing nurseries in 1953

Name and Location	Year Established	Name and Location	Year Established
Beltsville, MD	1939	Elsberry, MO	1934
Big Flats, NY	1940	Winona, WI	1936
Chapel Hill, NC	1936	Manhattan, KS	1936
Rock Hill, SC	1936	Waterloo/Kearney, NB	After 1940
Americus, GA	1936	Mandan, ND	1934
Thorsby, AL	1936	Tucson, AZ	1935
Sandy Level, VA	1940	Albuquerque, NM	1936
Brooksville, FL	1940	San Fernando, CA	1943
Paducah, KY	1935	Pleasanton, CA	1939
Zanesville, OH	1936	Pullman, WA	1934
San Antonio, TX	1934	Bellingham, WA	1937
Ames/Ankeny, IA	1934	Aberdeen, ID	1939

It is obvious from the draw-down of nurseries that SCS was either responding to pressure from the American Association of Nurserymen and others, or knew the ax was coming, or both. There is no reason to think SCS headquarters were surprised by the massive budget shortfall in the fiscal year 1954 budget. Contrast this with the observational nurseries output. In 1939, the first new plant was released. By 1944 there were nine, by 1948 there were twenty-eight and by 1954 there were fifty-one.

The birth of the Plant Materials Centers was on the threshold.

Chapter 5: TRANSITION PERIOD FROM OBSERVATIONAL NURSERIES TO PLANT MATERIALS CENTERS

BACKGROUND

The new 1953 administration of President Dwight D. Eisenhower promoted the idea that SCS should not be producing trees and shrubs to provide free to land owners, which in their view was not the responsibility of the Federal government, but of the private sector. While the large scale production nurseries were in direct competition with commercial growers, there is scant archival evidence of commercial grower complaints. Nor is any mention of this made during the budget hearings on the subject, and it was only casually mentioned as an alternative source to fill the void of trees and shrubs that was going to be temporally created by the closings.[244]

Actually, there is little evidence of much pushback by SCS on the closing of the production nurseries. The annual reports going to the USDA Secretary on nursery operations as early as 1952 left the impression that the nurseries were becoming obsolete. Additionally, in 1953 other agency changes were under way, maybe dwarfing the nursery closings.

On November 2, 1953, the regional offices were abolished and state offices established. At the same time, soil conservation research authority and stations were transferred to the Agricultural Research Service (ARS). At his own request, Robert M. Salter, Chief of SCS, was transferred to Chief of ARS. Donald A. Williams was appointed to succeed Dr. Salter. In 1952, Grover Brown had been the chief nurseryman, but the position that later became the National Plant Materials Specialist was vacant by late 1953.[245]

The nurseries were not closed by an act of congress, executive order or otherwise. The Bureau of the Budget guidance was that SCS would no longer operate nurseries. The guidance anticipated this responsibility would be taken over by state agencies. So, the nursery closings were the result of the guidance and a sharp reduction in the SCS nursery budget. The 1953 budget from the previous administration for nursery operations was $1.7 million. The House of Representatives Sub-Committee for Agriculture Appropriation first reduced the 1954 nursery proposed appropriation to $700,000, then to $425,000. While the elimination of the production part was clear, the pseudo research stepchild, the observational nurseries, was caught up in this elimination process.

THE DEBATE

During the hearings on April 1, 1953 of the House of Representatives Agricultural Sub Committee for the fiscal year 1954 budget, the debate centered around two things.[246] First was the SCS budget for 1954, and second was how the trees and shrubs formally produced by SCS nurseries were going to be available for conservation work. At no time was there any indication that private nurseries would pick up the slack. Rather, Chief Salter was pressed on whether SCS could transfer their nurseries to state agencies. Salter felt some would and some might not. The Congressmen did not oppose the nursery closings but were concerned what would happen if all twenty-four SCS nurseries immediately ended production without confirmed alternative producers. This concern included what would happen to all the plants ready to ship, but with no money to dig, pack and ship them. The conversation then seemed to bog down for a while with questions like the one from Mr. Horan, "What is the nature of this cooperative arrangement with the Federal state nurseries and schools of silver culture and so forth?" Salter assumed they existed, but wasn't sure of their contents. Congressman Laird wondered, "And what is the cost per tree of your stock?" Salter agreed to provide the requested information.

The position of SCS Chief Robert Salter (November 1951 - November 1953) relative to the observational nurseries was unclear prior to the 1953 congressional hearings. Of course, being a part of the Administration he needed to support its position on closing the production nurseries. However, Chief Salter, in the April 1, 1953 hearings, did present a persuasive argument for saving the observational nurseries.[247] When the House discussions seemed to be coming to a close, Chief Salter said "May I discuss one other aspect of this thing?" Chairman Carl Anderson agreed and Dr. Salter offered the following:

> The phase we have been discussing up to now is the production of seed and trees in quantity. There is another function of the nurseries which is vital to the soil conservation program. At many of these nurseries we have assembled strains of new grasses and legumes from plant breeders in state experiment stations, and the Bureau of Plant Industry, and from a lot of natural collections. New grasses and legumes are studied in these nurseries in small plots. The seed of these which look like they have promise is increased enough so that it can be put in a program of observational testing. The seed is distributed over various regions of the United States in small plantings in observational test plots. There are literally hundreds and hundreds of these tests.

> It is out of these tests that we determine the desirability of expanding any of these strains for commercial production. After observation tests show the value of a strain over sufficient area, we blow it up and try to put it into commercial production.

> Out of this program there are fifty-four new strains of grasses and legumes now in commercial seed production in the United States and certified by the responsible state agency, and sixteen more are in process of certification (*The figures and content of the statement was not exactly accurate, but his point was being made*).

> These are some of the most important plant materials we have for conservation. We are very anxious to maintain this phase of the nursery program, that is, the observational testing work and the planting and studying of new strains in the nurseries.

The presentation from Chief Salter is noteworthy from several points of view. First is the absence of any push back against closing the production side of the nurseries. Was this by prior agreement, or was Salter just toeing the Administration line? If that were the case, why bring up the observational program? Next, his presentation certainly solidified the opinion of Charles Enlow who told Bennett in December 1937 "this is the real work of the Nursery Section" and which Dr. Bennett came to acknowledge in 1949, when he said that the observational nurseries was "the *main work* of the Soil Conservation Service."[248] Salter had been well briefed, but by whom is not known.

Following the statement by Dr. Salter, there was an exchange of questions and answers about how many nurseries he was thinking about continuing the observational work, how much would it cost and who would operate them. Anderson thought three or four would be enough. Salter's reply was eight nurseries which would cost about $240,000, plus $165,000 "for the men who actually do the observation testing out in the field," referring to what later became the field or state plant materials specialists, $120,000 for one man each in the regional offices and one in the Washington office, for a total $525,000. Dr. Slater points out that the current allocation was set at $425,000. He went on to say that the SCS plan was to have the observational nurseries operated through cooperative agreements with state agricultural experiments or other non-Federal groups. Whether he really felt this was a good idea is unknown, but he did know the current administration was anxious to down-size the federal government, and that they would like the cooperative agreement arrangement.

It is interesting to speculate what were the eight nurseries mentioned by Salter. Hindsight makes it relatively easy. The eight turned out to be Beltsville, MD, then at least one per each existing region except Region 4, Western Gulf. They were Region 1 – Big Flats, NY (only one existed in that region),

Region 2 – Americus, GA, Region 3 – Elsberry, MO, Region 5 - Manhattan, KS, Region 6 – Tucson, AZ and Region 7 – Pullman, WA and Pleasanton, CA. Of course, the old SCS regional offices were being eliminated and replaced by five regional delineations without offices. This decision is examined in detail later. After a good bit of horse trading, the final number was ten. The other two were Aberdeen, ID and Bismarck, ND.

NRCS Historian, Douglas Helms, records that "SCS did not seem to protest the loss of the production function, but the nursery staff and cooperators in (Soil Conservation) Districts certainly wanted to continue the testing and selection functions." [249] As J. C. Dykes, the Assistant Chief, said after the fact, "It was necessary to determine what we could salvage."[250]The observational nurseries opened that door.

As hearings continued, members of the House of Representatives seemed insistent that the Government's investment in the observational nurseries and their valuable plant materials not be lost. The attitude was bipartisan, being supported alike by the Democrat Jamie Whitten of Mississippi, and Republicans H. Carl Andersen of Minnesota and Walt Horan of Washington. Horan recounted the plants selected at the Pullman nursery by their cultivar names.[251]

Apparently, after additional thought, the House Subcommittee advised the Secretary of Agriculture that the committee felt the liquidation of the remaining sixteen nurseries was too rapid and would result in unnecessary waste and "therefore allowed $1.2 million for the operation of all twenty-four of the nurseries by the SCS."[252] They pointed out that this was a reduction of $500,000 from the amount the nurseries had received the previous year, and encouraged the Secretary to work out arrangements with local sources to adequately maintain these nurseries.

Before a resolution was found there was, understandably, fear of the unknown. Dr. Abraham Stoesz inquired of his Washington boss on May 28, 1953 asking for a meeting so that you can "...explain to us more fully what we need to do to be set for adequate handling of the section beginning July 1."[253] He continued, suggesting that, "if you cannot meet with us could we be given a brief outline of the manner in which we are expected to operate." Mr. Brown replied, essentially, that there was no need for a meeting because, even though he had met frequently in an effort to develop the needed guidance, there were too many unanswered questions. At the top of the list of unanswered questions was the lack of a signed appropriation bill.

THE RESOLUTION

When a compromise was reached between both houses of congress the final fiscal year 1954 USDA appropriations for the nurseries was $800,000.[254] It was to be available for the orderly closing of the production nurseries and operating the observational nurseries. Chairman for the House Agriculture Subcommittee, Carl Anderson, wrote Secretary Ezra Benson on July 30, 1953 that SCS would continue the observational nursery work until an orderly transfer could be made to a non-Federal cooperating agency.[255] The Secretary replied that the Department intended to continue operating eight observational nurseries on a contractual basis. For fiscal year 1954 the regional allocation of the $800,000 for the orderly closing and observational nursery operations was as shown in Table 5.1. At that point there were twenty-four nurseries to be closed.[256] [257] Funds were allocated based on the old regions for orderly elimination of excess nurseries, but the allocation language identified ten observational nurseries to receive funding.

One fluctuation about the number of observational nurseries seems to have resulted from confusion in the Midwest over their location. The Manhattan, Kansas nursery was omitted from the funding list. The budget allocations were made on July 31, 1953, and included funds for Kearney, NE.

On September 3, 1953, F. G. Renner, Acting Assistant Chief of Operations, Washington D.C., wrote A. D. Stoesz, Regional Nurseryman in the Midwest, commenting, among other things, "We were rather surprised when we learned you were negotiating with Kansas State College for the operation of the Manhattan nursery as one of your cooperating units."[258] He goes on to explain that the Washington Office had been advised otherwise, and the funds had been allocated for Kearney, NE. Nebraska Senator Butler had expressed the interest of the city of Kearney for having the nursery located there, and that excellent land and facilities had been offered. Renner asked for an explanation why Stoesz had selected Manhattan for Region 5. While the explanation from Stoesz is not available, it is evident that Stoesz's explanation was adequate, and the Kearney site was disposed of and the Manhattan site was selected.

By early in fiscal year 1954 the $800,000 began to find its way down to the nursery/PMC level and things began to stabilize. See Table 5.1.

Table 5.1 Funding resolution for nursery closings

Region 1 - Big Flats, NY	$69,000
Region 2 - Americus, GA	$130,000
Region 3 - Elsberry, MO and Winona, MN	$120,000
Region 4 - No nurseries	$65,000
Region 5 - Mandan, ND and Kearney, NE	$135,000
Region 6 - Tucson, AZ	$75,000
Region 7 Pleasanton, CA and Pullman, WA	$165,000
Beltsville, MD	$20,000
National Headquarters	$21,000

FINDING COOPERATORS

Salvaging eight or so observational nurseries from the twenty-four production nurseries in 1953 was quite an accomplishment, but the Administration's requirement that all be operated by a non-Federal entity became more difficult than had been anticipated. By the beginning of fiscal year 1955, SCS was looking for suitors for a slightly changed list. Winona, MN and Kearney, NE had been dropped from the list, Manhattan, KS was added and a new site was in the works for Mandan, ND, located across the river in Bismarck, ND, which altered the number to nine.[259] They were: Big Flats, NY, Americus, GA, Elsberry, MO, Bismarck, ND, Manhattan, KS, Pleasanton, CA, Tucson, AZ, Beltsville, MD, and Pullman, WA.

When Don Williams testified in 1954 on the 1955 appropriations bill, he stated that agreements were complete on four of the nine nurseries. They were Americus, Georgia; Manhattan, Kansas; Mandan/Bismarck, North Dakota; and Tucson, Arizona. The agreement on the Big Flats, New York nursery was nearly complete. Agreements on another four observational nurseries seemed stalled for lack of cooperators.[260]

The lack of cooperators was not surprising, considering the amount of funds the cooperator would receive from SCS. The University of California at Davis advised the regional SCS director J. H. Christ that they "should not undertake the operation of the...nursery at Pleasanton, CA."[261] Washington State University at Pullman could see "little hope of carrying out an effective program, given the funds available."[262] Elsberry, Missouri found no interested takers. One prevailing point of view there is that Hugh Stevenson, a former nursery employee (1935 – 1939) who had developed a large commercial nursery in the Elsberry area, expressed strong objections to the right people, which blocked any potential of a cooperator being found. There is no evidence that the Beltsville nursery ever attempted to find a cooperator, although Administrator Williams told the Senate Subcommittee on one occasion that SCS was not in any final stage of completing agreements for the remaining "five production nurseries not yet transferred." He continued to list the five which included Beltsville.[263]

During the negotiations with the Department, SCS was authorized to operate the Aberdeen, Idaho nursery until legislation had been passed by the state to take it over.[264] The Aberdeen Chamber of Commerce advised Chief Williams, in an effort to gain more time to accomplish this, "Frankly, we die hard on a deal like this when we are thoroughly convinced that we have never seen money spent by the government to be more advantage on any project.", referring to the SCS observational nursery.[265] The Soil Conservation Districts were working hard to find a physical home and additional funding. By fiscal year 1955 they succeeded, finding a home consisting of land owned by the South Bingham Soil Conservation District and Idaho Department Game and Fish. The efforts of conservation districts in Idaho, Nevada and Utah contributed to accomplishing this feat. During this period, operations remained with the SCS. This arrangement continued and this rounded the number of surviving observational nurseries to ten.

"The USDA appropriations act for fiscal year 1954" was the first time a distinction was made between production nurseries and observational nurseries.[266] At the beginning of fiscal year 1955, five cooperative agreements would be funded and five facilities would be funded and operated by the SCS. They, and their cooperators, were

- Tucson, AZ operated by University of Arizona with $30,000 in SCS funding.

- Americus, GA operated by Georgia Agriculture Experiment Station with $30,000 in SCS funding.

- Manhattan, KS operated by Kansas State College, Agriculture Experiment Station with $15,000 in SCS funding.

- Big Flats, NY operated by the State University of NY, Alfred Agriculture & Technical Institute, Alfred, NY with $30,000 in SCS funding.

- Bismarck, ND operated by the North Dakota Assoc. of SCDs with $30,000 in SCS funding.

- Pleasanton, CA operated by SCS with $30,000 in SCS funding.

- Aberdeen, ID pending the completion of state legislative action.

- Beltsville, MD operated by SCS with $30,000 in SCS funding.

- Elsberry, MO operated by SCS with $30,000 in SCS funding.

- Pullman, WA operated by SCS with $30,000 in SCS funding.

No additional cooperative agreements were promulgated for the original nurseries. One reason five of the ten did not sign such agreements could be that the funding was inadequate. That and a combination of strong negotiating leadership by Dr. A. L Hafenrichter, with support from his boss J. H. Christ, may have been the deciding factor on the three of the five that were in his region. The House Subcommittee for the fiscal year 1955 appropriations contained the following statement:

> Of the nine nurseries which are being retained under Federal control to serve as permanent experimental stations in the various areas of the country; five will be operated by non-Federal cooperating agencies where satisfactory arrangements have been worked out. The remaining four will continue to be operated as research and observational nurseries by the Department.[267]

Helms wrote the following in a 2008 briefing paper:

> When Administrator Don Williams testified before the Senate appropriations subcommittee on agriculture, he pointed out this dilemma: that the House had directed SCS to operate the nurseries, but had not appropriated the funds needed to operate them. Senator Carl Hayden proposed adding money to operate the four

operational nurseries. Part of the issue was that the budget included up to $30,000 per nursery for obtaining planting materials from the State agency operating the nursery, but the cost of actually operating a nursery was higher. This fact may explain why some States did not agree to the proposed cooperative relationship with SCS. Williams did not offer any prospects of agreements on the other four observational nurseries. [268]

FATE OF CLOSING NURSERIES AND GERMPLASM

What was the fate of the other nurseries that had been conducting observational studies? In 1949, there were twenty-seven nurseries. By 1950, Astoria, OR had closed, and by 1951 two more had closed, Minden, LA and Woodward, OK, leaving twenty-four, with at least twenty-one of them conducting observational studies. Ten survived, leaving eleven that possibly held valuable plant materials that warranted additional evaluation. What was their fate?

- The Astoria, OR nursery reopened as the Corvallis, OR PMC in 1957.

- The nursery site at Albuquerque, NM closed, but two long term observational workers, Joseph Downs and Glenn Niner preserved the germplasm and led the effort for a PMC to be opened in 1957 through a cooperative agreement with the New Mexico State College of Agriculture, Middle Rio Grande Substation, at Los Lunas.

- The Brooksville, FL nursery closed in 1953 and the lease on the land on which it operated was terminated. After a four year lapse, an SCS-operated PMC opened in Acadia, FL in 1957, and moved back to Brooksville in 1963. No evidence of any surviving germplasm was found.

- The San Antonio, TX observation work survived through the efforts of James E. Smith, former nursery manager. SCS at the state level continued to provide funding to support the transition of observational studies from the San Antonio nursery closing to the Texas Agricultural Experiment Stations at San Antonio and Spur. The SCS nursery site was lost but valuable plant material was saved. This arrangement continued until 1965 when the James E. "Bud" Smith PMC opened in Knox City.

- The Chapel Hill, NC nursery closed in 1952. Long time observational studies leader in the Southeast, Karl Graetz, and W. W. Stevens, staff leader with SCS, wanted to take one last look to see if anything was worth saving.[269] On Thanksgiving Day 1953, the two visited the nursery and saw soybeans scattered over the ground. They cleaned the vines away, swept up leaves, beans and some dirt, and screened it through hardware cloth, salvaging about a gallon of the beans for future evaluation.

The balance of the nursery sites became the property of other public agencies. Stories persisted into the 1960s of SCS employees visiting old nursery sites to collect plants or to observe any outstanding plant performances.[270]

Another concern about the preservation of the valuable germplasm at SCS nurseries came from the former nursery owner, the Bureau of Plant Industry. The SCS Chief received a letter from A. H. Moseman, Chief; BPI dated June 10, 1951. Some BPI employees had visited the Beltsville nursery to determine if there would be any interest in them assuming any responsibility for the nursery activities in case SCS found it necessary to close it. They had not reached a decision on the point but were very concerned about maintenance of the "thousands of introductions in the course of their twenty years of operations."[271] Chief Moseman expressed intent for the BPI to assist in this preservation to the extent that it was desired and needed.

Any reply to this concern from SCS is unknown, but it undoubtedly would have given Chief Moseman assurances that SCS would take required action to be sure the germplasm would be maintained. Reports exist elsewhere in this history of the extraordinary efforts by some to do exactly this. Not included elsewhere, but mentioned here, are the hurry-up efforts that were made at various locations to be sure this potential loss was minimized, quite independent of the concern by Moseman. The Southeast Regional Director, L. B. Scott, instructed the observational nursery agronomist at Sandy Level, VA, Karl Graetz, to "within the next few days, give me a very complete outline of the observational work (at Sandy Level) which should be conducted at Americus."[272] Americus had been targeted as the contractual PMC in the Southeast. Regional Nurseryman Charles Marshall noted in a July 9, 1953 report that the SCS nurseries were to be liquidated by the end of fiscal year 1954 and that in Region 6 (Albuquerque, NM) it would be orderly to assure "that the new and promising plant materials are not lost but are placed where their testing and evaluation can be continued."[273] Anecdotal records suggest the valuable germplasm from the Albuquerque nursery spent a few years in the garage of Joseph Downs.

J. H. Christ, regional director in Portland, OR, wrote Chief Salter on October 26, 1953 of the status of work on nursery closings. He had five to deal with. His memo was not encouraging about finding cooperators, and went on the say, "The question of preserving some rare and promising introductions at San Fernando has not been resolved."[274] Although no solution was identified, the recognized need was explored with the Riverside Experiment Station to take some subtropical accessions.

However, with the mass nursery closings and the speed with which it was done, there is a high probability that some great accessions were lost. For example, when the North Carolina Wildlife Commission asked the SCS Regional Office if the equipment and plant materials at the Sandy Level, VA nursery could be moved to a nursery site in North Carolina operated by the Commission, he received a positive reaction but the final paragraph of the reply said "this office is to be closed within the next few months, it is imperative that we move as rapidly as possible…"[275]

A major factor involved in the orderly closing of the nurseries was the disposition of excess land. This included not only the operating nurseries in 1953 that were not transitioned to PMCs, but land holdings of previously closed nurseries. The land had been acquired in a variety of ways including the purchase of land to carry out the provisions of the 1935 act establishing the SCS, land transferred to the Secretary of Agriculture from other Federal agencies, and by conveyance to the Secretary from private individuals.[276] Other lands had been acquired with funds appropriated under Title III of the Bankhead-Jones Farm Tenant Act. To be able to dispose of these lands, Chief Salter wrote the Secretary, outlining the background and land holdings and proposed the Secretary seek an Executive Order from the President that would transfer all the lands in question to the Secretary through provisions of the Bankhead-Jones Act.[277] With that accomplished, the Secretary could then transfer "conveyed or leased land to state or local agencies on the condition that they continue to be used for nursery purposes or that arrangements be made for continued operations in an appropriate manner."

Executive Order 10516 was issued on January 29, 1954.[278] This greatly facilitated the transfer of land that was not needed. Some of those lands acquired by SCS under Title III went to the U.S. Forest Service January 4, 1954, and became the National Grasslands. Of the nine funded observational nurseries in 1954, Big Flats, NY; Elsberry, MO; Tucson, AZ; Americus, GA; Pullman, Washington, Pleasanton, CA and Beltsville, MD continued to operate on SCS-owned land. Only Aberdeen, ID and Bismarck, ND needed to make new arrangements.

An unofficially identified eleventh surviving PMC was in Texas. One could say it had existed under the radar. An observational nursery had been functioning at San Antonio but was closed. Records show that the SCS intended to continue it, and did, but records do not show that the Department was aware of it during this 1953-1954 time period. The San Antonio PMC is discussed in more depth later.

Summing up on the closed nurseries, reports dated September 1, 1954 and February 1, 1955 show the final disposition of the properties.[279]

1. Aberdeen was operating on land owned by the South Bingham Soil Conservation District.

2. The title for the Zanesville, OH land was transferred to the state.

3. Agreements with other public units to utilize Federal land was completed for Rock Hill, SC, Sandy Level, VA, Winona, MN, San Antonio, TX, Delhart, TX and Bellingham, WA. These agreements entitled the cooperator to use the land for a designated conservation purpose and receive the equipment by transfer.

4. Nurseries that had been on non-Federal land were liquidated, including Ankeny, IA, Albuquerque, NM, San Fernando, CA, Florence, OR, Paducah, KY and Honolulu, HI.

5. Pleasanton, CA, Elsberry, MO, Pullman, WA and Beltsville, MD continued to be operated by SCS on SCS land.

6. Tucson, AZ, Americus, GA, Manhattan, KS and Big Flats, NY PMCs continued to operate under a cooperative agreement on SCS-owned land. SCS headquarters had developed a standard cooperative agreement for these contractual arrangements. This was done because Headquarters was doubtful whether any contract could be developed with a cooperator which would permit accurate accounting of Service funds expended by a cooperating state agency in the carrying out of an observational program. For this reason, the SCS would make available a stated sum of money for a developmental and production program that would be mutually agreed upon by the involved parties. The contract was generally absent of specifics, such as pounds of seed, or accessions evaluated, but contained generic statements like 'Furnish adequate seed to fulfill the needs of Plant Materials Specialists for field plantings'. This provided latitude to the cooperator to either over achieve or under achieve. The cooperators were also entitled to use the land in excess of the need for SCS work for a designated conservation purpose and receive the equipment by transfer. The lack of specific items in these contracts opened the door for abuse. In all cases, except the New Mexico agreement, the contracting party had objectives in addition to those of SCS. This drained funds from carrying out desired SCS activities, setting the course for failure.

7. The original Mandan, ND nursery site consisted of 240 acres, and was subjected to flooding. [280] SCS acquired land on the old Fort Lincoln, ND military base in 1952, which replaced the Mandan site. Reestablishing the nursery there was in progress in 1953. The SCS nursery operation closed and was continued by the North Dakota Association of Soil Conservation District. In 1954, SCS transferred the Fort Lincoln land to them, which also became the PMC site; it continued to be operated by the Districts. In 1955, the original Mandan site was in the process of being purchased by the state of North Dakota.

8. The Brooksville, FL site was resolved by SCS discontinuing their lease with the owner, the U.S. Forest Service.

9. The 181.2 acres at Thorsby, AL were transferred by way of a cooperative agreement to the Alabama Polytechnic Institute, with SCS making no financial contribution.

10. The Waterloo, NE site was more involved. Two cooperative agreements disposed of 200 acres, one with the University of Nebraska and one with the Saunders Soil Conservation District. This left five acres with buildings. GSA sold the buildings and the five acres.

11. Cooperative agreements were developed for nurseries in Howard, PA with the PA Department of Fish and Game, and Kearney, NE with the municipal airport.

By the end of 1955, the land disposal was reasonably well resolved but just around the corner was the initiation of new PMCs, each requiring new arrangements for land.

CHANGING NAMES

It is unclear when the name 'observational nurseries' officially became 'plant materials centers'. As the SCS Nursery Division entered the 1952 - 1954 transition period, the name 'observational nursery' was commonly used, but the term 'plant materials nurseries' also began to be used. During this period, the first evidence of the use of 'plant materials' appears on October 26, 1952, when H. R. Wells of the University of California advised the SCS regional director, J. H. Christ, that they were not interested in operating the "plant materials nursery at Pleasanton, California."[281]

Generally, the observational nurseries continued to be referred to as nurseries as late as 1955.[282] On July 22, 1954, W. C. Young, Regional Plant Materials Technician for the south, wrote Dr. Stoesz, in Washington D.C., by transmitting the "Annual Report - Plant Materials, Southeast."[283] The report however, referred to the different locations as nurseries. Solidifying the name came when Chief D. A. Williams sent Assistant Secretary of Agriculture on July 16, 1956 a memorandum whose subject was "Soil Conservation Service Plant Materials Centers (Nurseries)."[284] The new name was officially adopted. However, the name 'nursery' did not die easily. The author recalls in 1957, after taking a job at a plant materials center, being asked by town folks, "Where do you work?" When he answered, "The plant materials center," the response was, "Where's that", then a pause, and, "Oh, you work at the nursery."

Oddly enough, the first identified use of plant materials centers, as discussed in Chapter 4, came in a March 2, 1939 memo from Dr. Crider, where he used 'plant materials center' and 'mother nursery' three times in the memo.[285]

CHANGING LEADERSHIP

This transition period represented a major upheaval in personnel. The nursery closings forced some employees to change agencies or switch to other types of positions within the SCS. However, many dedicated observational nursery employees remained with the new creation. The 1954 funding allowed for one National leader, one regional leader in each of the five regions and, in most cases one employee at each plant materials center who was not part of the PMC staff. Chief Salter called them "the men who actually do the observational testing out in the field."[286] This position became known as the *field plant materials specialist*. These employees, a PMC manager for SCS-operated centers and an advisor for cooperating PMCs rounded out the professional staff.

Selecting the first national leader was paramount. It was Dr. A. D. Stoesz, who moved from the regional nurseryman position in Lincoln, NE to Washington in mid-1954.[287] A memo sent by Dr. Stoesz from Washington on July 2, 1954 to W. C. Young was the earliest evidence of his presence there. Viewing other options for the first National Plant Materials Program leader might have included, in addition to Dr. Stoesz, C. B. Manifold, who had been Chief, Division of Conservation Operations, and Crider's boss in the late 1930s. In 1953, he became the National Forester and in 1955 he became the Northeast regional Plant Materials Specialist. Foremost however, among others was Dr. A. L. Hafenrichter. Not only was he an innovator but also an outstanding producer (see Key Leaders Chapter). Other regional nurserymen with excellent records were Charles G. Marshall from Albuquerque, New Mexico. He led the Arizona and New Mexico nurseries to many outstanding observational nursery accomplishments. The selecting officer had an excellent panel from which to select. There is no reason to believe that that any of the others could have done a better job than Dr. Stoesz. Nor has any specific explanation of this selection been found.

Wilmer Steiner became the manager at Beltsville, the only person in the SCS that knew Dr. Crider to any extent, other than Manifold. Steiner replaced Manifold, and his office was moved to the old regional office in Upper Darby, PA in 1955. Steiner was replaced at Beltsville by Robert Thornton, a long time Northeast Regional Assistant Nurseryman.

By the end of 1955, the transition from observational nurseries to plant materials centers was pretty well completed. Lingering turmoil created during the period would continue, especially at the five cooperating PMCs, but in time that would be resolved. National and regional leadership was in place, about fifteen field plant materials technicians were serving most of the states, and ten PMCs were in operation. Ten of the fifteen PM Technicians had observational nursery experience as did all five of the SCS-operated PMC center managers. Of the cooperative agreement centers, Tucson, AZ and Americus, GA retained the manager from the nursery, requiring each to change employers. The cooperators at Manhattan, KS and Bismarck, ND supplied new managers. Big Flats, NY had no designated plant materials employee until 1957.

The last vestiges of the SCS nursery days were fading. They could, however, be viewed with some pride for their observational output. By the end of 1954, they had placed fifty-one new plants on the market. The surviving PMCs had released thirty-one of the fifty-one. The closing Albuquerque, NM and San Antonio, TX units accounted for ten of the fifty-one releases, nine from closed Southeast nurseries Chapel Hill, NC and Thorsby, AL and one from Astoria, OR. Fortunately, the observation leaders from these closed nurseries continued employment in the new Plant Materials Program. Over the approximately eighteen years of their existence, the accumulation of knowledge and their outstanding products would pay great dividends to the conservation of natural resources in the coming years.

THE NEW STRUCTURE – LOST LEVERAGE

The production nurseries and the regional offices had disbanded in 1953-54. From 1935, all agency administration and line authority flowed from the National Office through the Regional Offices to the field activities, including the nurseries. Regional offices were the center for administrative direction, supervision, and technical excellence. During those years, existing state offices helped organize districts and the coordination with state and local agencies, but were under the direction of the regional office.[288]

A major part of the reorganization was the establishment of state offices, each headed by a State Conservationist. Prior to 1953, the supervision and technical expertise resided in the seven regional offices. Supervision and technical expertise was removed from the Regional offices to state offices. The initial reorganization plan called for SCS to buy technical services from the state extension services. After strong objections by the National Association of Conservation Districts and local conservation districts directors, the technical competence of the state offices was beefed up. The SCS administration held that this had been their plan from the beginning.[289]

Former Chief Bennett objected to the new arrangement. In a January, 1954 article titled, "They've cut the heart out of Soil Conservation," Bennett argued that the duplication of the technical and administrative staff in every state office as well as a compliment of Washington-Field personnel (regional linked to the national discipline leader) was not cost effective and it would be impossible to find qualified people to staff them. He said on the surface Secretary Benson's call for abolishing the seven regional SCS offices "probably seems like nothing more than a simple administrative shift. But actually it means tearing down a carefully built organization of skilled technical men and dispersing them to Washington, to state offices, or to the winds. The Secretary started putting this plan into effect almost immediately, despite strong protests from many of the nation's farm leaders."[290]

Some technical responsibilities for plant materials resided with a new Plant Technology Division at the national headquarters; the division's Director reported to the Assistant Administrator for Field Services. The division included a national leader for each plant science discipline. Additionally, attached to the division, were Washington-Field representatives for each plant science discipline. There were five Washington-Field Plant Materials Technicians (W-F PMT) in 1954; each served a group of states similar in geography to the old regions.[291] The different Washington-Field representatives for each discipline were not co-located initially but scattered within the states they served. For example, the W-F PMT for the northeast was initially located in Harrisburg, PA, the biologist was in Ithaca, NY and the agronomist was in Upper Darby, PA.

There was one exception to the elimination of regional offices. An Engineering and Watershed Planning Unit (E&WP Unit) was devised and located at the previous regional locations. The staff at the E&WP Units received their technical guidance from their counterparts in the Washington Office, and was administratively and technically responsible to the Director of the Engineering Division.[292] How fortunate it would have been if all positions in the plant materials discipline had operated the same way. Some newly appointed Washington-Field plant technologists who had been located in the old regional offices remained there with the E&WP Unit, including Dr. John Paul Jones, who was the regional agronomist and was appointed the Washington-Field agronomist for the Northeast. Other Washington Field plant technicians were scattered and were not necessarily assigned to the same areas as the E&WP Units.

Another new plant materials position was the Field Plant Materials Technician (FPMT), which served the states included in the PMC service area. Generally there was one FPMT for each PMC, but where one PMC served multiple states, a FPMT could be located in one or more of the other states. For example, the Northeast region, with a dozen or so states and one PMC had four FPMTs from 1955 through 1965. The FPMT coordinated the plant materials work between and within the states and with the PMC. Their supervisor was usually the state resource conservationist, a member of the state conservationist staff.

Under the new arrangement line authority was passed from the Chief to the state conservationist to the PMC manager. This was a critical change of the administrative configuration of how observational nurseries received technical, as well as supervisory input versus how PMCs would now receive it. See Figure 5.1 on the following page.

The disconnect between the regional plant technicians and the activities at the PMC is obvious. The new structure constituted a loss of line authority. All position heads in the Nursery Division structure were trained scientists with line authority, as contrasted with a new structure where the trained scientists were staff personnel, inputting their expertise through persuasion at the state office level.

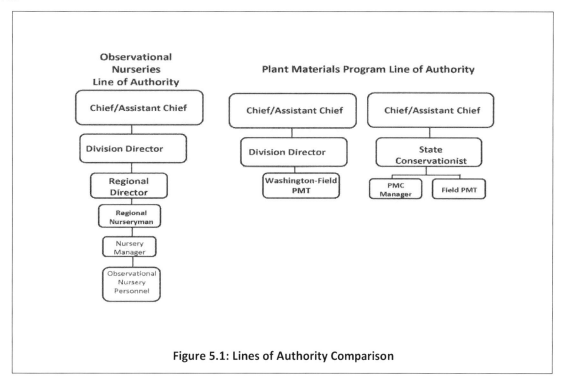

Figure 5.1: Lines of Authority Comparison

By April 30, 1955, the national, and five Washington-Field Plant Materials Technicians were

- National, Dr. A. D. Stoesz, Washington, D.C.

- Northeast Region, Courtland B. Manifold moved from National Forester to Harrisburg, PA

- Southeast Region, Crawford W. Young, moved from nursery manager, Thorsby, AL to Athens, GA

- Midwest Region, Harold W. Cooper, former range conservationist in Montana.

- Upper Midwest, Kenneth Welton, former state conservationist in Indiana

- West Region, Dr. A. L. Hafenrichter, remained in Portland, OR

Appendices 5 and 6 identify personnel by position and time of employment in their positions, to the extent that records could be located. Nursery and PMC Managers are shown in Appendix 5. Appendix 6 contains a roster of the plant materials specialist's positions, created in 1954, including national, regional and field positions.

RETENTION OF PERSONNEL

Two regional nurserymen remained in leadership roles with the new Plant Materials Program, Hafenrichter and Stoesz. Although Hafenrichter no longer had supervision over PMCs, his reputation and force of personality was such that he continued much as he had done before. Dr. B. R. Bertramson, Professor Emeritus, Washington State University, Pullman, WA, had commented about Dr. Hafenrichter, saying "One felt as though confronted by a prophet of biblical times..."[293] The PMC productivity within his area of responsibility until he retired in 1967 supports that argument. By the same token, the selection of Dr. Stoesz was equally wise. His background, training and pleasant disposition qualified him well for the National position (See Chapter 9, Key Leaders). Making the hard decisions and pressing them to conclusion was a desirable trait demonstrated by him on more than one occasion.

The prior experience of the other W-F PMTs was mixed. Steiner and Young had been nursery managers, and Cooper, Manifold and Welton had been in management/staff positions. They did not have the reputation or prestige of Hafenrichter when they entered the State Conservationist's office to give advice on how to run a PMC. Nor by temperament did they have a 'take charge' persona.

Closing the nurseries and regional offices put many employees in a holding pattern until things got sorted out. Dr. Stoesz on June 5, 1953 circulated a list of surplus professional employees in his region showing "Nursery Personnel Likely to Become Surplus."[294] The agency worked hard to help all displaced employees find new positions. One Regional Director told the SCS chief on July 24, 1953 that all nursery employees who might be separated had been notified.[295] Others in his region, such as four mechanics, resigned and entered commercial work and five agricultural aids found positions in SCS field offices. Two professional employees with over thirty years of Federal service remained at a PMC as biological technicians. Other personnel, particularly those in administrative positions, found jobs in the new and expanding state offices.[296]

Although some were lost, the majority of professional employees involved within the observational nurseries found positions with the Plant Materials Program. From these ranks the following positions were filled:

- National PMT,

- By 1960 all five W-F PMT positions,

- Twelve of the sixteen Field Plant Materials Technicians that were filled in the 1954-55 period,

- Managers at five of the eight PMCs functioning in 1954, which were Beltsville, MD, Americus, GA, Tucson, AZ, Pleasanton, CA and Pullman, WA. The other three, Big Flats, NY, Elsberry, MO, and Manhattan, KS were filled with inexperienced persons.

The manager/Field PMT breakdown is slightly misleading because John Schwendiman was a PMC Manager in 1954 and became a PMT in 1954, thus being counted twice. However, the core of the PMC Program was initially filled with experienced personnel.

- Wilmer W. Steiner, former National Observational Project Manager replaced Manifold in 1955 as the W-F PMT, and moved to Upper Darby.

- Crawford W. Young was the W-F PMT in the Southeast Region located at Fort Worth, TX

- Midwest Region – Donald Atkins replaced Cooper in 1955, at Denver, CO.

- Upper Midwest – Arthur D. Fladin replaced Kenneth Welton in 1960, and Donald S. Douglas replaced him the same year, all in Milwaukee, WI.

- West Region – Dr. A. L. Hafenrichter, located in Portland, OR.

The five individuals in the regional positions in 1955 remained leaders in the Plant Materials Program for the next fifteen years or so. What a wonderful time this would have been for Steiner, Young and Atkins to have had some training by former professor Hafenrichter. The three became close friends, as suggested by Figure 5.2. Had it been a quartet of friendship the Program would have benefitted.

The lack of clear organizational breaks between the production and observational personnel at the nurseries complicated identifying those employees that were considered in observational work. However, a 1949 listing plus additional reports and position rosters made it possible to compile Table 5.2. It shows who was retained to join the Plant Material Program after the nurseries closed, and in what positions.[297] This excellent group of carry-over employees represented the life blood of the program through most of the 1950s.

Figure 5.2 Crawford Young, Bill Steiner and Don Atkins in 1966.

One of the more interesting moves was that of Robert Thornton going from the regional office in Upper Darby to replace W. W. Steiner as National PMC Manager, who moved to Upper Darby as the W-F PMT. Thornton, trained as a botanist and employed at the Ithaca, NY nursery in 1936 before going to the regional office in 1938, had the reputation of an excellent mind and a caustic tongue. One of the responsibilities in his regional office position, as a member of a zone team, was to ensure, and enforce, technical quality of conservation work within the region. A certain PMC Manager can vouch for this, resulting from a call to the National PMC for some technical advice. Thornton advised the young fellow that the PMC program was going down the tube if the agency continued to employ such idiots that didn't know the answer to that simple question. Then of course he told the poor fellow far more than he needed to know to solve his problem. H. Wayne Everett, a trainee at the Beltsville PMC in 1963, tells of an experience Arnold Davis had soon after coming to Beltsville. Arnold had left a work unit conservationists position in Nebraska to come to Beltsville for training in anticipation of a career in plant materials. Wayne wrote of Arnold's son coming to the PMC to visit his father.[298] The son said in Thornton's presence "In Nebraska my dad was the boss". Thornton replied "Your dad isn't in Nebraska; and at Beltsville Bob Thornton is the boss". However, Thornton was a wonderful resource who assisted many a new employee entering the plant materials discipline.

Table 5.2 1953 Employees in Observational Studies

Region	Producing Nursery in 1950	Persons Doing OS Duties	Post 1953 Long-Term Plant Materials Position
1	Beltsville, MD	Dr. Franklin Crider	Retired
1	Beltsville, MD	Wilmer W. Steiner	NPMC Mgr. and NE Washington-Field PMT
1	Big Flats, NY	Harry Porter	Field PMT, NY
1	Ithaca, NY	Robert Thornton	Manager, National PMC, Beltsville, MD
2	Americus, GA	John Powell	Manager, Americus, GA
2	Brooksville, FL	G. B. Blickensderfer	Field PMT, FL
2	Chapel Hill, NC	J. E. Ball	
2	Chapel Hill, NC	A. C. Matthews	
2	Coffeeville, MS	William G. Beatty	Manager, Coffeeville, MS PMC
2	Sandy Level, VA	Carl A. Graetz	Field PMT, NC
2	Spartanburg, SC	Paul Tabor	Field PMT, GA
2	Thorsby, AL	William C. Young	South Washington-Field PMT
2	Thorsby, AL	R. L. Davis	
3	Ames, IA	Virgil Hawk	Field PMT, IA
3	Elsberry, MO	J. J. Pierre	
3	Winona, MN	E. L. McPherron	Field PMT, WI in 1954
4	Fort Worth, TX	Simon K. Wolfe	Transferred to US Corps Eng.
4	Minden, LA	Billie Rountree	Field PMT, MO
4	San Antonio, TX	Ashley Thornburg	TX WU, then Mgr., Bridger, MT PMC
4	San Antonio, TX	James E. Smith	Field PMT, TX
4	Woodward, OK	Gordon L. Powers	
5	Bismarck/Mandan, ND	Jesse L. McWilliams	Field PMT, WY
5	Lincoln, NE	A. D. Stoesz	National PMT, Washington, DC
5	Manhattan, KS	Donald M. Atkins	MW Washington-Field PMT
5	Waterloo, NE	Liard G. Wolfe	Was listed as surplus 7/1/1953
6	Albuquerque, NM	Joseph A. Downs	Field PMT, NM
6	Albuquerque, NM	Theodore Spaller	Returned to AZ PMC, later to Beltsville, MD
6	Albuquerque, NM	Darwin Anderson	Field PMT, AZ
6	Albuquerque, NM	Glenn C. Niner	Technical Advisor, Los Lunas, NM PMC
6	Tucson, AZ	Louis P. Hamilton	Manager, Tucson, AZ PMC
7	Aberdeen, ID	Roy A. Jansen	
7	Aberdeen, ID	Donald S. Douglas	Field PMT, ID
7	Bellingham, WA	Lynn E. Guenther	Field PMT, HI
7	Pleasanton, CA	Oswald K. Hoglund	Manager, Pleasanton, CA
7	Pleasanton, CA	Harold W. Miller	Field PMT, CA
7	Portland OR	Robert L. Brown	
7	Portland OR	A. L. Hafenrichter	West Washington-Field PMT
7	Pullman, WA	Jack Woods	SCS position in CA
7	Pullman, WA	John L. Schwendiman	PMC Mgr. to Field PMT, WA
7	San Fernando, CA	Lowell A. Mullens	
7	San Fernando, CA	Dirk J. Vanderwal	

NURSERY AND PMC ACTIVITIES DURING THE 1953 – 1954 TRANSITION PERIOD

Even though still in the middle of the transitional period, Director Christ was providing Chief Salter support and encouragement from Portland. On April 17, 1953, he sent Salter articles from Idaho, Oregon, Utah and Washington farm newspapers, and farm management magazines, which he summarized by saying, "They are evidence that the Service has recognized leadership in the field of grasses, legumes, browse, shrubs and trees. One attains that position only by much honest effort and high integrity".[299]

John Schwendiman was manager of the Pullman PMC during the 1953-1954 periods and gives a first-hand account in his First Fifty Years History of the Pullman PMC. He writes, "After seed harvest the technical staff was transferred. Agronomists R. A. Adlard and Edward Minick to the Washington State Extension Service and Forester R. J. Olson to the SCS at Elgin, Oregon; Mrs. Nellie Heath to the state office in Spokane and Ben Woolliscroft to the Plant Introduction Station in Pullman. At the end of 1954 only farm superintendent J. W. Baird and manager J. L. Schwendiman remained. Orders were to arrange transfers to Washington State College and close out operations by July 1, 1954."[300] Needless to say a similar situation was going on at most if not all other nurseries. However, by late summer fiscal year 1954, the $800,000 funds appropriated early in fiscal year 1954 became available, and Pullman, as well as other PMC sites, began to see a light at the end of the tunnel. The confusion did not keep Schwendiman from publishing Timothy Mite Becomes Problem for Seed Growers in the Northwest, followed by A Nursery Helps Put Conservation on the Ground in 1955.[301] The Pullman and Aberdeen nurseries joined forces to release in 1953 'P-27' Siberian wheatgrass, another Westover-Enlow winner. The actual selection of individual clones that formed the release was by Aberdeen Manager, R. H. Stark, in 1949.

The 'honest effort' discussed by Christ was continuing in spite of the tsunami-like disruptions caused by nursery closings. Production from the disappearing observational nurseries was being picked up by the new plant materials centers in spite of the unknown. At some nurseries, although things were not normal, there were plants to be evaluated, seed to be planted and releases to get out the door. James Smith in Texas was especially busy. His actions during this transition period give insight into his modus operandi. The San Antonio nursery was closing. One thing that needed to be done was to get two bluestems and a buffelgrass into the hands of commercial growers; i.e., Pretoria 90 and Kleberg bluestem, and Blue buffelgrass.[302] He reported that the buffelgrass was better adapted to heavy soils than T-4464 and was released to commercial growers in 1953, although the recorded release is listed as 1952.

Other potential releases, like the Indiangrass that was collected in the vicinity of Delhart, TX, had to be moved. A portion of the available seed was granted to the Cochran Soil Conservation District and used to establish a twelve-acre increase field near Morton, TX in 1953. Though not particularly interested, the land owner was persuaded by the local SCS work unit conservationist to harvest the seed in the fall of 1955. Yield was approximately 800 pounds of combine-run material and was bought at the field for seventy-five cents a pound by a Nebraska seedman. This gross return of fifty dollars per acre prompted many neighboring farmers to establish additional fields of Indiangrass in 1956 and later.

The San Antonio Nursery also informally released Medio Angleton bluestem. Their 1953 Regional report contains the history of this plant from beginning to end, which was not very long, and provides some interesting insight into how some plants ended up on the market. It is repeated here.[303]

> Medio bluestem, a form of Andropogon nodosus, (correctly identified as Dichanthium annulatum var. annulatum) was brought into the nursery by Simon Wolfe from an area on Medio creek near Seeville in February, 1951.[304] There is no way of learning just when this grass appeared nor its origin, but it now occupies the creek banks from above the US-59 highway bridge northeast to Seeville clear to Copano Bay. Medio bluestem resembles Angleton, but is shorter, has finer stems and leaves, and forms a very dense, heavy mat under dryland conditions in the nursery. In spite of the dry weather in 1951 and 1952 it produces good summer and fall seed crops here, which Angleton is not able to do at this location. Cattle relish the forage, as is evidenced by heavy grazing where available to them from Medio Creek. This grass should be ideal for terrace waterway control, and will likely prove valuable for range seeding. Because of the amount of growth shown in the nursery by Medio bluestem during the two dry seasons it has been on hand, it was decided to push increase immediately. Texas Grass

Growers and Pat Higgins were induced to get sod material from Seeville and put the grass in their production program. Higgins now has ten acres growing vigorously and should have seed by fall. Texas Grass Growers has a smaller field but expect to add to their acreage.[305]

Nursery closings or not, Smith was busy with several other things. He noted in this report that he made regular trips to Delhart, TX (1,300 plus miles round trip), appeared on the program of the Sixth International Grassland Congress held at State College, PA in August 1952, and assisted in the revision of Farmers Bulletin #1985.[306]

The Elsberry, MO PMC released an early maturing, southern type smooth brome cultivar 'Elsberry' in 1954.[307] An additional release in 1954 was an informal bicolor lespedeza from the Thorsby, AL nursery, which was closing. The departing manager, Crawford W. Young, no doubt had the same point of view as Smith, i.e., *let's get it out the door*. The 1952 soon-to-be-closed Astoria, OR nursery wanted to get 'Cascade' birdsfoot trefoil released but ran out of time. The Pullman nursery assumed the releasing responsibilities and finished it in 1954.[308] Other releases processed in 1954 were: 'Blando' brome, 'Sodar' streambank wheatgrass and 'Cascade' birdsfoot trefoil, in spite of the circumstances. 'Sodar', came from Aberdeen, ID, a landless PMC in 1954.

Based in a 1953 report about the Big Flats, NY nursery, great things were expected from the new PMC. They had reported that its 1953 operations "were at a high level...and the observational program was strengthened and expanded."[309] Their report prompted a congratulating note from Nursery Division Chief Ross.

The 1953 – 1954 periods turned out to be a most productive releasing two-year period. To give some meaning to the magnitude, 'Sodar' is number twenty-two among the most beneficial SCS releases and 'P-27' is number thirty. See Table 5.3.

Table 5.3 Total Benefit of Four, 1953 – 1954 Releases

Release Name	Scientific Name	Common Name	Release Year	Total Benefit*
P-27	*Agropyron fragile*	Siberian wheatgrass	1953	$17,303,800
Topar	*Thinopyrum intermedium*	pubescent wheatgrass	1953	$849,730
Blando	*Bromus hordeaceus ssp. Hordeaceus*	soft chess	1954	$6,148,200
Sodar	*Elymus lanceolatus ssp. Lanceolatus*	streambank wheatgrass	1954	$22,334,100
Total Net Producer and Ecological Benefit				**$145,010,900**

CONTRASTING LEADERS

A comparison between the arrivals of Dr. Crider in the spring of 1936 with the arrival of Dr. Stoesz in 1954 reveals parallels and differences. Crider arrived from a regional/manager's position of a nursery in Arizona and Stoesz from a regional nurseryman's position in the Midwest. Both faced program re-shaping challenges, Crider from the Bureau of Plant Industries nurseries and Stoesz from the SCS observational nurseries. Each had a jump start on formulating policy, Crider from the foundation of Charles Enlow's proclamations and his own background, and Stoesz from Crider's well thought and tested policy. Both were technically sound and benefited from a stellar reputation.

There were differences. Crider came to the position when the new agency was awash in pump priming money, while Stoesz was fearful about the budget. Crider's love was detailed plant evaluations, managing programs was Stoesz's. Crider was a private person, enjoying the rod rows far more than a budget meeting. Of course Stoesz loved and knew plants, but personality-wise he was more inclined to roll with the difficulties, mix, meld and compromise with friend and foe alike. This may have been their greatest difference. Remember, Crider fostered the establishment of the National Plant Materials Project at Beltsville and quietly became its director after four years in Washington. On the other hand, Stoesz stuck it out for ten years and retired from the position. However, as contrasted to Crider's arrival, getting policy in place was less urgent.

NEW PLANT MATERIALS POLICY

The first action towards developing new polices came on July 16, 1956 when Administrator Donald Williams sent the Assistant Secretary of Agriculture E. L. Peterson a memo advising him of the new SCS plant materials policy and the number and intended location for new PMCs.[310] Administrators Memorandum SCS PM-1, containing the policy of the new Plant Materials Program was issued soon after that.

It is assumed that Dr. Stoesz drafted this document and guided it through the review process which started with a March 15, 1956 draft.[311] Many of the fundamental procedural policies are similar or identical to the contents of the March 25, 1936 policy Field Memorandum #SCN-4, developed by Dr. Crider.[312] The role of the PMCs was essentially the same as those of the observational nurseries, but the new policy contained agency-wide procedures, such as the role of the new Washington-Field and Field Plant Materials Technician, and responsibilities of work unit (county) offices in carrying out the newly defined field plantings. A major objective of the observational nurseries was to feed the production nurseries with new products, and, of course, that objective had been terminated. New plant products would go exclusively to soil conservation district seed and plant growers and it would be produced commercially.

First, the new policy discussed the personnel structure. There was a national plant materials technician, located in the Washington office, and housed in a division with the other natural resource specialists in agronomy, forestry, etc. This was similar to the National Nursery Division staffing except the National Nurseryman was the chief of a division and had line authority down to the observational nurseries. The national PMT only provided leadership and coordination on plant materials matters between disciplines in the national office and between regions.

This SCS PM -1 identified five Plant Materials Program functions. Abbreviated, they are

1. Determining the need for new or better plant materials and cultural practices;

2. Developing plans for and evaluating promising plant materials on problem sites in soil conservation districts;

3. Encouraging the collection of promising native material;

4. Obtaining commercial production of proven materials; and

5. Bringing to the attention of research agencies the need for further plant improvement and development.

The section on Means for Carrying out the Functions follows, in abbreviated form.

1. The Service will maintain a small staff of competent plant materials technicians. The Washington-Field Plant Materials Technician will, under the guidance of line officers, assist the Plant Materials Technician (field PMT) serving one or more states in carrying out their functions. These functions were to

   a. Work with state program staffs and fields personnel of the Service to determine plant materials needs.

   b. Assist the manager of plant materials centers in his state or service area with the development and implementation of their program.

    c. Develop projects and plans and carry out, with Service personnel, a field planting program on district cooperator's lands as the final test of superior plants selected by the PMCs.

    d. Assist Service personnel and producers to establish and carry out a district seed and plant increase program of superior plants selected by the PMCs.

    e. Maintain close contact and working arrangements with other Federal and state agencies relative to plant materials work of the Service.

2. The Washington-Field Technologists and the other plant science disciplines will call to the attention of the Plant Materials Technologists plant materials needs in their discipline.

3. The Service will maintain or provide for essential PMCs in strategic locations serving resource areas where all kinds of plant materials may be assembled and evaluated for their conservation value, where initial growth of valuable plants can be increased for field planting in conservation districts, and where foundation seed or plants can be maintained and produced to be supplied to commercial growers. Whenever possible the PMC work will be done in cooperation with State Agricultural Experiments Stations.

4. Long range plans and annual plans of operations will be developed for the work of the PMC and cleared by line officers.

5. Field plantings will be used for the final evaluation of superior plants to determine its use and adaptation to multiple resource areas and use conditions. Assistance of cooperating agencies will be encouraged. The Field Plant Materials Technician will develop an annual plan for field plantings for each state served by the PMC and have it approved by the Washington-Field Technician.

6. Special plant materials problems for which plants cannot be adequately evaluated at the PMC may require off-site evaluation of several materials. Such plantings require the approval of the State Conservationist (These came to be called field evaluation plantings).

7. Proven plants for conservation usefulness will be moved into commercial production as quickly as practicable. The PMCs will not produce excess seed or plants other than is needed for evaluations and supplying commercial producers. Annual plans for District Increase are required, approved by line officers (This would have been a wonderful place to make it policy that all new releases to soil conservation districts producers be certified through the state certification agency where standards for the species existed. Nurseries in the Northern and Central Great Plains where Stoesz was a Regional Nurseryman used the certification process. All experiment stations in states where PMCs existed, or were to be established, had a certification process, so it seems so logical to have been done, but it was not).

8. There may be circumstances where large quantities of a conservation plants are in short supply, and with the administrators approval it might be produced at a PMC (This may have been in the policy as a way of authorizing production by the Coffeeville PMC, which opened in 1960, for the Yazoo-Little Tallahatchie Flood Prevention Project. The large seed and plant production continued at Coffeeville until 1982, at which time the plant materials function was strengthened. Since production quotas are easily measured, plant materials productivity of Coffeeville suggests the production quotas became the priority).

9. All plant materials technicians will participate in training, functional inspections of PMCs, field plant materials work and will report and publish their findings.

One final section on Relations emphasized the need for and requirement of close working relationships with multiple agencies, associations and institutions with related interest in the Service plant materials work. The document ended with, "Under the guidance of line officers, Service Plant

Materials Technicians" will maintain good working relationships with all representatives working in the field of plant materials.

Each PMC generally served regional resource areas, developing new plants and cultural techniques, basically the same as what the observational nurseries were doing. The field PMT also had the responsibility of being sure each states served by the PMC got their fair share of work. With the supervision of the PMC residing with the state conservationist in the state where it was located presented some challenges. Generally, it worked well, depending on the field PMT. The worst potential problem was that non-PMC states might lose interest in the program.

The technical management and coordination of the Plant Materials Program was weakened by the reorganization. Logically, the Washington-Field PMT should have been, and usually was, the strongest in both technical and leadership skills. The leverage this position now had to influence PMC direction was significantly reduced, and would be assumed by less technically qualified persons. The days of the technically strong regional leadership, exemplified by Dr. Hafenrichter, were diminished. As mentioned earlier, he maintained a significant degree of his influence until he retired, resulting from the prestige he had acquired from 1935 through 1953. No other Washington-Field PMT had that good fortune.

It is interesting to note that the policy contained three points about avoiding excesses of those things the Department wanted to curtail. It contained, in an abbreviated form, the following:

- provide field offices with only those plant materials needed for observation work,

- produce at PMCs only the amount plant materials needed for observation work, and

- use only the technique of observation, production and evaluation (not research).

SURVIVING PLANT MATERIALS CENTERS

In the Williams to Peterson memo of July 16, 1956, Williams identified five PMCs that SCS would operate.

- National PMC at Beltsville,

- Elsberry, MO, because a cooperator could not be found,

- Pullman, WA, Aberdeen, ID and Pleasanton, CA, the three former nurseries in old nursery Region 7. There was a delay in the re-opening of the Aberdeen PMC until 1955, during which time land arrangements were worked out with the South Bingham Soil Conservation District and the Idaho Department of Game and Fish.

  Dr. Hafenrichter had taken an active part in negotiating for a non-Federal cooperator to operate these three centers, as contrasted to all other regions where the newly appointed State Conservationist took the lead. Hafenrichter failed in finding a non-Federal home for all three. As discussed earlier Hafenrichter "usually got his way" and this was to be no different.[313] One could say that his poor negotiating skills got him exactly what he wanted.

The next listing in the Williams to Paterson memo stated "As long as satisfactory arrangements can be maintained...", which meant a cooperator would be found, "the following plant materials centers" could be established. They and their outcomes were as follows:

- Americus, GA was operated by Georgia Agricultural Experiment Station until 1977 when it returned to SCS operations. John Powell remained manager throughout the period.

- Big Flats, NY was operated by the State University of NY, Alfred Agriculture and Technical College, Alfred, NY from 1955 until 1960.

- Spur, TX entered the PMCs discussion with the Williams to Peterson Memo. It had not previously appeared. In a report to the Department on February 1, 1955, all the PMCs to be operated by SCS and those under cooperative agreements were listed.[314] Neither San Antonio nor Spur was included in either, but is listed under the liquidation heading. Limburg, on September 1, 1954 omitted Spur but included the same surviving PMCs as the February 1, 1955 report.[315] Yet an "Estimated Distribution of 1954 Funds for Nursery Work" in July 1953 includes $18,700 for Region 4 (Fort Worth, TX) designated for 'Field Observation Work'.[316] The same document normally identified by name the PMC to receive the funds, like Big Flats, Americus, etc.; except for Region 4 it was blank. In the 1956 Williams memo Spur was allocated $20,000 and an estimated $24,000 was allocated both in 1957 and 1958.[317] Starting with this memo, SCS clearly acknowledges the existence of Spur, TX as a PMC. This funding continued until 1965.

- Manhattan, KS was operated by Kansas State College until 1965 when it returned to SCS operations. Clarence Swallow, a Kansas State employee, was the first manager.

- Scottsbluff, NE was included on the July 16, 1956 memo from Administrator Williams to Assistant Secretary Peterson along with the other centers that would be established if suitable arrangements could be worked out with a cooperator.[318] During the search for PMC sites that would meet the plant materials needs of the central Great Plains, locations in Nebraska were considered. Recall the discussions in 1953 between the National and Regional office as to which location would be best for a PMC to serve the central region.[319] The Acting Assistant Chief of Operations on September 3, 1953 expressed surprise when he learned that Dr. Stoesz, then the Regional Nurseryman, was negotiating a cooperative agreement with Kansas State to operate the Manhattan PMC, rather than with Nebraska Experiment Station for a site at Kearney, NE, who had shown a strong interest. Of course, Manhattan, KS was selected.

By 1956, a decision had been made to establish another PMC to serve the northwestern Great Plains. Exactly who was promoting this or who made the decision is not clear. This new location was included in the July 16, 1956 memo from Williams to the Department that listed new centers to be established.[320] By 1958, the selection of the Scottsbluff site had moved along so far that $18,000 had been allocated to the University of Nebraska for its operations, and plantings had been made there. On March 31, 1959, Edward Graham, Director of the Plant Technology Division, advised J. C. Dykes, Deputy Administrator, that he and Dr. Stoesz had just met with Administrator Williams and resolved that the location of "the...Scottsbluff center...would not meet the plant materials needs of the Northern Great Plains as much as a move to a site further to the Northwest."[321] Continuing, Graham advised Mr. Dykes that Mr. Williams will be advising the Nebraska state conservationists by phone that the "Center would be moved out of Nebraska." It is obvious that SCS representatives in Nebraska and the University of Nebraska and had struck a deal for a PMC in Scottsbluff, based no doubt on the Williams to Peterson letter. Logically, Stoesz would have been aware of this, but for unknown reasons he became concerned two years later and he and Dr. Graham went to see Williams. Considering how things turned out, might Stoesz have had some encouragement from Hafenrichter to go see Graham?

Mr. Williams made the calls and discussed with the officials at the University that SCS would be making no more plantings there and that the "$16,475 now available to Nebraska for plant materials work (the balance left from the $18,000) will be re-allocated" by Dr. Stoesz to Montana.[322][323] During this same time period, discussions were held that lead to establishing a new PMC to serve that area at Bridger, MT. This, like the 1953 debate about a PMC to be at Manhattan or Kearney, suggests Dr. Stoesz to be strong-willed when necessary.

The Bridger center came about through the efforts of Stoesz, strong leadership of local Soil Conservation Districts in Montana and Wyoming; with support from Dr. A. L. Hafenrichter, the Washington-Field PMT for that area, and the SCS state offices in Montana and Wyoming. In 1959, Nebraska was in the SCS central region and Montana in the western. Thus Hafenrichter had a northern Great Plains PMC also. While no records were found, one can wonder what role, if any, Hafenrichter played in selecting the Bridger location and eliminating the Scottsbluff site. Fortunately, for several reasons, it was in Bridger and not Scottsbluff.

- In Bismarck, ND, a cooperative arrangement was made with the North Dakota Association of Soil Conservation District, to operate a PMC in conjunction with its tree and shrub nursery after the closing of the SCS nursery in Mandan. This continued until 1967.

- Tucson, AZ was operated by University of Arizona until 1962, managed by former SCS employee Louis P. Hamilton, Jr.

NEW PMCs BECOME A REALITY

The last category Administrator Williams listed in his memo to Peterson was for new PMCs to be opened and maintained in cooperation with suitable state agencies or operated by the Service if no suitable cooperator could be found, to serve the following areas.

- Southern Florida.

- Central Michigan.

- Northern New Mexico

- Western Oregon

- Hawaii

Their establishment process went as follows:

1. In Southern Florida, the Brooksville nursery closed with all the others in 1953. The land returned to the U.S. Forest Service, its former owner. Efforts started in August 1957 to find a new site for a PMC on the Florida peninsula which would also serve the plant materials needs in Puerto Rico. No state agency could be found that was interested in a cooperative agreement. No doubt some of Hafenrichter-like poor negotiating skills were used. A PMC was established on sixty acres of rented land near Acadia, FL in 1957.[324] Ten years later, SCS acquired 182 acres of land in Brooksville and the PMC relocated there, all under SCS operations.[325] Harry Haynesworth was the first manager at both places.

2. In Central Michigan, the Rose Lake PMC opened in 1958 under SCS control. Initially, cooperative agreements with Michigan State University at the Kellogg Farm at Battle Creek seem plausible. As discussions progressed difficulties were encountered in working out the cooperative features of the agreement so it was finally decided to drop the effort with the University.[326] Kenneth Welton, W-F PMT, learned that suitable arrangements might be worked out with the Michigan Conservation Department at their Experimental Farm near Rose Lake. Some of their activities parallel the typical work of a PMC. This knowledge led to establishing the Rose Lake PMC under SCS control. The first manager, Charles McDaniels, served for a little over a year and was replaced by Dorian Carroll.

3. In Northern New Mexico, after the Albuquerque nursery closing the search for a new site soon began. After an extensive search for suitable soil, water and available acres the New Mexico State College of Agriculture experiment station in Los Lunas was selected. The PMC was opened in 1957 with a cooperative agreement similar to that desired by the Department.[327] The cooperative agreement continues today, although changes have been

made that led to an SCS manager rather than cooperator manager. It has been one of the most productive PMCs nationally. It succeeded in part because of the cooperative agreement. The College wanted it to succeed, so they became enthusiastic and supportive cooperators. Of equal importance was their selected employee in 1957 to head up the work. James Anderson was an excellent choice. His objectives were the same as the SCS objectives, and his employer supported him.

4. In the Pacific Northwest, Astoria, OR, Warrenton, WA and Bellingham, WA had been nursery locations with observational studies in the coastal region of Washington and Oregon. All were closed in the 1952-54 period, but SCS continued to own the Bellingham property until the mid-1980s. Its disposition at that time brought grief to two National PM Technicians, which is discussed later. Able SCS negotiators consisting of R. L. Brown, a long time observational nursery employee, and Dr. Hafenrichter, soon found land and developed an agreement with Oregon State University. By 1957, SCS was able to lease fifty-seven acres of land and open the SCS-operated Corvallis PMC. Thomas A. Bown was the first manager.

5. In January, 1957, the SCS Administrator advised J. H. Christ, State Conservationist in Hawaii, that Morton Rosenburg, Director of the Hawaii Agricultural Experiment Station, was ready to enter into a memorandum of understanding with SCS to establish a PMC there. The Hawaii Station would provide suitable land on one of their substations, thus eliminating any responsibility to provide land not under their jurisdiction.[328] The PMC was established initially on Maui in 1957, then in 1972 moved to the fertile agricultural plains of Ho'olehua, on Molokai. It operates on eighty acres owned by the Hawaii Department of Land and Natural Resources. Lynn Guenther, who was the plant materials technician in Hawaii, also served as the first manager.

This brought the number of functioning PMCs to seventeen by the end of 1959. SCS leadership had followed Chief Donald Williams's 1956 commitment to Secretary Peterson almost verbatim. See Figure 5.3 and Table 5.4. The Williams to Peterson memo listed Spur, TX and Scottsbluff, NE as PMC sites. This was not accomplished for Scottsbluff, as previously discussed, or Spur, TX. No reason for the latter has been found. Maybe the Texas Experiment Station site at Spur was an unsatisfactory location for a PMC, or there was a desire on the part of SCS in Texas to avoid establishing a PMC through a cooperative agreement, so they

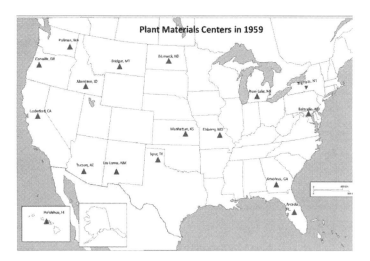

Figure 5.3: Map of PMC sites in 1959

delayed while seeking funds and an ideal site which resulted in the purchase at Knox City in 1965. Up until that point the plant materials program appeared to be functioning well with the combination of PMT James Smith and the work underway at Spur.

Table 5.4 Functioning PMCs in 1959

Name and Location	Year Established	Operation By	History before PMC	Center Manager
Americus, GA	1954	Cooperator	Americus SCS Nursery	John D. Powell
Beltsville, MD	1954	SCS	Beltsville SCS Nursery	Robert Thornton
Big Flats, NY	1954	Cooperator	Big Flats SCS Nursery	Edward Kenne
Bismarck, ND	1954	Cooperator	Mandan SCS Nursery	George Kary
Elsberry, MO	1954	SCS	Elsberry SCS Nursery	Roger E. Sherman
Manhattan, KS	1954	Cooperator	Manhattan SCS Nursery	Clarence Swallow
Pleasanton, CA	1954	SCS	Pleasanton SCS Nursery	Oswald Hoglund
Pullman, WA	1954	SCS	Pullman SCS Nursery	Robert J. Olson/Edwin O. Nurmi
Spur, TX	1954	SCS	San Antonio SCS Nursery	
Tucson, AZ	1954	Cooperator	Tucson SCS Nursery	Louis P. Hamilton, Jr.
Aberdeen, ID	1957	SCS	Aberdeen SCS Nursery	Harold L. Harris
Arcadia, FL	1957	SCS	Brooksville SCS Nursery	Harry Haynesworth
Corvallis, OR	1957	SCS	Astoria SCS Nursery	Thomas A. Bown
Ho'olehua, HI	1957	SCS	None	Lynn Guenther
Los Lunas, NM	1957	Cooperator	Albuquerque SCS Nursery	James E. Anderson
Rose Lake, MI	1958	SCS	None	Dorian Carroll
Bridger, MT	1959	SCS	None	Ashley A. Thornburg

PLANT MATERIALS CENTER BUDGETS

Formerly the Nursery Division received an allocation of appropriated funds which was divided among the regions to support production and observational nursery work. The budgets for each nursery were determined at the regional level. No evidence has been found to suggest funds were separated at the nursery level between production and observational nursery components. The last distribution from nursery funds was for the $800,000 congress had appropriated for winding down the nurseries.[329] The distribution of those funds was by region as shown earlier in this chapter. It reflected which potential nurseries might become PMCs.[330]

Because some nurseries were becoming PMCs the July 1954 allocations identified those nurseries as "Nurseries identified for operation by state agencies under contract to furnish observational planting materials."[331]

Starting with the 1954 allocation the plant materials centers received an allocation in the SCS budget as CO-46 funds (Conservation Operations-PMCs) for their operation. Each state office with a PMC received an annual allocation of these funds. Recommending the allocation amounts was the responsibility of the National Plant Materials Technician. One break the PMCs received was the gradual move for the national, W-F PMT and state PMT to be paid from other funds.

Table 5.5 shows allocations for 1956 through 1959.[332]

Table 5.5 Budget Allocations 1956 - 1959

PMC	1956	1957	1958	1959
Tucson, AZ	$25,000	$30,000	$30,000	$30,000
Pleasanton, CA	$28,310	$30,000	$31,500	$35,000
Arcadia, FL		$40,000	$40,000	$40,000
Americus, GA	$30,000	$40,000	$40,000	$40,000
Aberdeen, ID	$25,247	$25,427	$35,000	$36,700
Manhattan, KS	$15,000	$19,000	$19,000	$15,000
Beltsville, MD	$40,305	$40,000	$42,000	$42,000
East Lansing, MI		$10,000	$40,000	$25,000
Elsberry, MO	$28,506	$40,000	$42,000	$42,000
Bridger MT			$18,000	$34,000
Los Lunas, NM		$32,000	$40,000	$28,000
Big Flats, NY	$27,995	$30,000	$30,000	$30,000
Scottsbluff, NE*			($18,000)	
Bismarck, ND	$15,000	$15,000	$15,000	$20,000
Corvallis, OR		$20,000	$20,000	$20,000
Spur, TX	$20,000	$24,000	$24,000	$20,000
Pullman, WA	$40,305	$40,000	$42,000	$50,400
Hawaii		$20,000	$20,000	$20,000
* Scottsbluff, NE received $18,000 for 1959, which went from NE to the emerging Bridger PMC.				

UTILIZING NURSERY EMPLOYEES IN THE PLANT MATERIALS PROGRAM

Table 5.6 identifies the managers of the PMCs in operation prior to 1960. Nine of the sixteen were former nursery employees. Of the six PMCs operating under a cooperative agreement two managers had been nursery employees.

Table 5.6 PMCs Managers 1954 – 1959

PMC	Manager	ON Experience	PMC	Manager	ON Experience
Tucson, AZ	Louis P. Hamilton, Jr.	Yes	Manhattan, KS	Clarence Swallow	No
Pleasanton, CA	Oswald Hoglund	Yes	Rose Lake, MI	Charles McDaniels	No
Arcadia, FL	Harry Haynesworth	Yes	Bridger, MT	Ashley A. Thornburg	Yes
Americus, GA	John D. Powell	Yes	Bismarck, ND	Buck Worthington	No
Ho'olehua, HI	Lynn Guenther	Yes	Los Lunas, NM	James E. Anderson	No
Aberdeen, ID	Donald S. Douglas	Yes	Big Flats, NY	Edward Kenne	No
Beltsville, MD	William W. Steiner	Yes	Corvallis, OR	Thomas A. Bown	No
Elsberry, MO	Roger E. Sherman	Yes	Pullman, WA	Robert J. Olson	No
Spur, TX	James E. Smith	Yes			

The decade ended with eighteen PMCs, ten of them managed by individuals with observational nursery experience. There were a total of 28 Plant Materials Technicians, one National, four Washington-Field and 23 Field PMTs, all with observational nursery experience. This may have been an all-time high, both in numbers and experience.

From this list of twenty-eight plant materials technicians all but six of those serving prior to 1960 were employees of the nurseries. Additionally, Billie Rountree was briefly at the San Antonio, TX nursery and became a PMT in Missouri in 1960.

EMERGING PROBLEM

By the late 1950s, a weakness of the Plant Materials Program was emerging that haunted it beyond the end of the century. That problem was the shortage of qualified persons to fill vacancies. The fact that so many nurseries closed, leaving a pool of qualified persons to fill plant materials positions, delayed bringing new and younger employees into the program, thus postponing the problem for a while. Unfortunately, when it occurred, there was no immediate solution.

Of all the observational nurseries, none was more blessed with outstanding personnel than the Pullman, WA site. This was true from the regional nurseryman to the agronomist in the nursery. Yet, in 1959, even though Hafenrichter was still a Washington-Field PMT, the PMC manager position was hard to fill.

Realistically, this shortage was to be expected, and would get worse unless some action was taken to overcome it. It was due to several things that may not have been obvious in 1959. Although PMCs did not have the authority to conduct research (see Chapter 14), in reality the task of quantitatively documenting the superiority of one plant over another did require the same tools as used in research, and required qualified persons with the educational background and aptitude to do the job. During the nursery years, the right person needed for a specific position was employed directly from the general population. After the reorganization, PMCs became a small part of much larger organization and replacements for professional positions at the centers, e.g., the center manager, came from the existing pool of employees in field offices. The potential of finding a Schwendiman or Joseph Downs or James "Bud" Smith to fill these vacancies was limited. There may have been many qualified individuals in the field but, by the time a plant materials vacancy came open those individuals were established in a different career track and had lost interest. As a result, the bulk of the available agency personnel and the ideal PMC personnel were out of sync. Nevertheless it was done; much better in some regions than others. The principal weakness came from the loss of authority, influence and/or aggressiveness of the Washington-Field PMT. Selections were being made by state conservationists, who often lacked adequate knowledge of the necessary qualifications or which qualifying individuals were available. This is a responsibility most regional nurseryman would have filled but to a great extent was lost with the 1953-54 reorganization.

The state conservationist with a PMC in his state had the last word on who got the job. The state conservationists were generally hired because they were good administrative managers. Not that the PMC manager doesn't need good management skills, but they should take second place to plant-related technical and analytical skills. A typical PMC with a manager, one or two professional employees and a couple biological technicians isn't of the magnitude to require a full-time person to manage them. The truth is that the manager must be the chief on-site scientist. All too often management skills were given top billing and productivity suffered. All PMC managers should have prior experience in the scientific side of plant evaluation before becoming a manager.

One additional aspect of the selection process, although the rarest, was indeed the most troubling. It is easy to understand that in the course of employing a few or many people, a bad apple turns up once in a while. With federal personnel rules being what they were, the employee's supervisor had limited options. Training was one, but it did not always solve the problem. Demotions or firings were not something many supervisors were willing to tackle. A far easier option was to move the employee into a position where they would do the least harm, or to put it another way, move the individual out of sight. PMC's met those requirements better than most SCS units. Generally, employees at PMCs have less frequent contact with district cooperators, and thus met the out of sight requirement. With a four or five person staff, one unproductive person at a PMC could consume a quarter of the permanent staff resources for up to thirty years. Stopping or slowing this practice was difficult. An Assistant Chief who was being harassed by the National plant materials leader about such an action by a state conservationists under his supervision, finally, in exasperation explained, "What do you want me to do, eat him?" referring to the bad apple. In his opinion the state conservationist had no other option.

The uniqueness of the Plant Materials program made it difficult to have qualified employees standing in the wings ready when needed. Some efforts to overcome this have worked, and provided long term advantages. They will be discussed later.

In the case of filling a PMC manager's position at Pullman in 1958-59, Hafenrichter was kept informed by the state conservationist.[333] On December 31, 1958, he told Hafenrichter that no progress had been made, even though it had been offered to four SCS employees. The state conservationist offered several additional possibilities, none of which was successful. Later, in 1959, Edwin O. Nurmi was selected at age forty-seven, served nine years and retired.

PLANT MATERIALS PRODUCTIVITY AND OTHER HAPPENINGS - 1955 – 1959

There were ten PMCs that could potentially have released plants in the second half of the 1950 decade. Some were crippled by the transition from nursery to PMC. Big Flats, Americus, Manhattan and Tucson were under new management. Spur, TX had relocated from San Antonio. Yet the results were good; seven plants being released. Of the three Western PMCs that remained under the direction of Dr. Hafenrichter, Pullman released four and Pleasanton one. The other two were from Kansas with the Manhattan PMC making a contribution, but was not the lead releasing agency. All are shown with their releasing PMC in Chapter 8.

One of the outstanding cultivars in this group is 'Lana' wollypod vetch, a vigorous annual legume used for forage and hay or as cover crops throughout the winter wet – summer dry climate of California. 'Lana' vetch is a winter active plant, and is early maturing. When fall-planted in the California valleys it will produce most of its biomass in the winter and the early spring.[334] 'Lana' has been on the market for sixty years and widely used in California. MacLauchlan, Miller and Hoglund reported that over-seeding with Lana vetch, a self-perpetuating annual, appeared to be one of the most practical controls of medusahead, an invading annual grass that can reduce grazing capacity up to seventy-five percent.[335] Increased production and improved quality from infested annual range can be the results of seeding 'Lana' vetch. It is well adapted to all orchard and vineyard soils in California below 3000 feet in elevation where the operator does not expect to mow frequently.[336]

The most widely reproduced cultivar of the early 1950's group is 'Newport' Kentucky bluegrass. It came from selected seedlings collected along coastal bluffs at Newport, Lincoln County, OR. It has been the second highest commercially produced cultivar for the 1977 – 2005 production periods. Its value to producers and service value to ecosystems for that period of commercial production is $107 million. Another Pullman release in 1957 was 'Latar' orchardgrass. As the name implies this cultivar is late maturing, and with abundant light green leaves. The original seed came from the Institute of Plant Industry, Leningrad, Russia.

By 1955, the trauma of reorganization was over, The PMCs and plant materials technicians turned their attention to the future; finding vegetative solutions to soil and water conservation problems. Even though the period was disruptive, significant plant materials progress and accomplishments occurred. A few include

- Future discipline leader, Wilmer W. Steiner, finished and published the landmark work of Dr. Crider's *Root growth Stoppage Resulting from Defoliation of Grass,* which became the foundation for the range management concept of 'take half and leave half'.

- John Schwendiman and A. L. Hafenrichter published *A Nursery Helps Put Conservation on the Ground* in the Journal of S&W Conservation.

- James Smith reported that cultivated grass seed production in Texas in 1955 was about 28,000 pounds of five native species, (17,000 was the Indiangrass mentioned earlier) and seven introduced species had produced 885,000 pounds.[337] Buffelgrass, weeping lovegrass, KR bluestem and blue panic accounted for 878,000 pounds. By 1960, production was about 1,566,000 pounds of twenty-seven native and 408,700 pounds of ten introduced species. Six cultivars of sideoats, three of switchgrass, and one each of sand bluestem, green spangletop and plains bristlegrass produced 1.4 million pounds of seed. In 1960 there were 4,560 acres of seed production on the high plains.

- Future discipline leader, Don Douglas, one of Hafenrichter's boys, left the manager's position at Aberdeen in 1957 to become Field PMT in Idaho.

- Future discipline leader, Robert MacLauchlan, who had moved to the field office in Harrisburg, OR when the Bellingham nursery closed, returned to the plant materials fold in 1957 as PMT at the newly established Corvallis PMC.

- Future discipline leader, Curtis Sharp, took a position in the SCS East Aurora, NY field office for three months and then moved to Big Flats, NY, thanks to Harry Porter, PMT. There he became an employee of the cooperator who was operating the PMC.

- Donald Atkins, Midwest PMT, published *Plant the "go-back-land" to grass* in the Journal of S&W Conservation.

- John Schwendiman and others published *Pastures for Horse* and *Producing Grass seed in Washington* in a Washington Agriculture Experiment Station Circular, and *Improvement of Native Range through Introduction* in the Journal of Range Management.

- During 1957, Dr. Stoesz and Robert L. Brown published in the Year Book of Agriculture *Stabilizing Sand Dunes.*

- John Schwendiman continued in 1957 with *Well Managed Conservation Seedings Help Alfalfa* and *Good Land Management Supports Wildlife* in a Washington Experiment Station Circulars.

- During 1958 H. W. Cooper, James E. Smith, Jr., and Donald Atkins published *Producing and harvesting grass seed in the Great Plains* as USDA Farmers Bulletin No. 2112, and Atkins published *Cover on watershed dams* in the Journal of S&W Conservation.

- SCS published *Grasses and Legumes in Conservation Farming in Central Oregon and Adjacent Areas* by N. R. McClure, A. L. Hafenrichter and John Schwendiman in 1958.

- The Aberdeen PMC received a USDA Superior Service Award in 1958.

- In 1958, the California Department of Natural Resources augmented the funds available to the Pleasanton PMC.[338]

- Mr. Schwendiman published *Testing New range Forage Plants* in the American Association for the Advancement of Science – Grasslands in 1959.

- In 1959 the Beltsville PMC distributed seed packets of 732 genera and unknown species to PMCs.[339] The acquiring and distribution of foreign introductions was not only a major service to field PMCs, it was the principal source of new accessions for some. The National Center also signed a contract in 1959 with the U.S. Navy to find better erosion controlling plants for their earthen structures at their Propellant Plant at Indian Head, MD.[340]

- Dr. Hafenrichter received a Writers Award of $150 from SCS for his article in Advances in Agronomy in 1958.[341]

- In the 1950s, the PMC manager positions were at the GS-7 level; sixty years later they were GS-12 positions.

- Most W-F PMT, Field PMT, and national leaders met in 1957 in Pleasanton, CA. See Figure 5.4.

DEPARTING THE 1950s DECADE

The decade of the 1950s was a topsy-turvy period for the evaluations of conservation plants. Dr. Stoesz ended up in Washington as the Chief of the new Plant Materials Program with limited authority. However, by 1956 or 1957 the storm had quieted. With strong support from the agency at all levels, it looked like he would have ten or eleven PMCs. By decade's end he had seventeen.

An appropriate ending for the period may be contained in the minutes of a Plant Technology Division conference which was held on January 19-23, 1959 in Shreveport, LA.[342] Its purpose was to determine ways and means of making the Division and the work of its members more efficient. Each discipline, including plant materials, presented the status and needs of its discipline. Comments by Dr. Stoesz can be summarized as follows:

- The plant materials policy was okay, except some clarification was needed relative to the releasing of improved woody plants.

- Good progress was being made on the program's mission.

- Technical standards for the evaluation of plants at PMCs and in field plantings were needed.

- Plant materials training (for local employees) at training centers was inadequate and needed to be increased from two hours to eight hours.

- Funds for operating PMCs was inadequate.

- Three additional PMCs were needed. Their location: Central Tennessee, northern Mississippi and western North Carolina.

- The number of plant materials technicians was eroding and needed to be maintained.

No follow-up report on these needs have been found. An historical view for the next several years suggests:

- Policy had been expanded on all fronts, but policy for the release of improved woody plants had not.

- Progress on the program's mission was steady and good.

- Standards for the evaluation of plants at PMCs and in field plantings were improved, but the quality of the evaluation was no better or worse than the evaluator's ability.

- Funds for operating PMCs remained erratic, inadequate from the view point of the discipline.

- Two of the recommend areas for new PMCs was realized; the PMC in Kentucky to serve Tennessee and North Carolina, and the Coffeeville PMC in northern Mississippi.

- The number of plant materials technicians continued to erode.

- Most likely the plant materials training at training centers remained inadequate.[343] The author received a toy concrete mixer for pointing out that in the early 1980s the engineering discipline had more training time allotted to mixing and pouring concrete than all plant sciences disciplines together.

- Delivering technology to the end user continued to function at a high level from 1954 through the end of the decade. The principal publications of this period are included in Appendix 2.

Figure 5.4: Meeting in Pleasanton, CA 1957

Kneeling, Left to Right – Karl Graetz, Harold Miller, M. Donald Atkins, Murry Cox, James Smith, Robert Thornton, C. B. Blickensderfer, Robert S. MacLauchlan, Marshall Augustine, Bill Briggs, Robert Curtis, Harry Porter. Back Left to Right – Fred Haughton, J.C. Dykes, A.D. Stoesz, Harold Cooper, Crawford Young, Ken Welton, W.W. Steiner, A. L. Hafenrichter, Arthur Darsey, and Jack McCorkle. Location – Pleasanton, CA, 1957

The decade would not go quietly. Someone was always trying to consume someone else's pie. Such was the case in 1959 when W. C. Young called to the attention of Dr. Stoesz a proposal to join the state PMT and the state agronomist positions.[344] It may have been coincidental that this subject arose about six months after Dr. Stoesz warned of an erosion of plant materials technicians. This discussion harkened back to the 1953-1954 reorganization where line responsibility from Washington resided at the state level, rather than regionally. To some extent, each of the forty-nine state offices desired having a complete in-house technical staff. There were eighteen PMT's in the country at that time, most serving multiple states. This fostered a dislike for sharing a staff member with other states. If a state could not have their own PMT, many felt the duty should be given to an in-state staff person whom they completely controlled. From Young's point of view, this was a slippery slope that could consume most field plant materials technicians.

The proposal came up at a meeting of state conservationists, and was introduced by the representative from Arkansas. Dr. Stoesz opposed their proposal. It would place Morris Byrd, the current PMT serving Arkansas, Mississippi and Louisiana, in the new joint position of an Arkansas agronomist/PMT.[345] Stoesz pointed out that the Plant Materials Program sought solutions to all plant science disciplines, not just agronomy. Stoesz wondered how long it would be before other states proposed joint plant materials – agronomy combinations, or some other combination of the PMT with other plant science disciplines.

By November 11, 1959, Stoesz had drafted a letter from Administrator Williams to the state conservationist in Arkansas opposing the combination, and proposed instead reducing the states served by Byrd, and employing an additional PMT to serve the other states.[346] This memo was not sent, but the combining proposal was rejected. Byrd remained as the PMT until 1966, when he retired and the position was moved to Jackson, MS, which was logical once a PMC was established there. His replacement was Thomas A. Bown.

In spite of this bump in the road, by 1960 Dr. Stoesz had seventeen PMCs (see Table 5.7); Dr. Hafenrichter continued pretty much as usual and the other regional technicians were still sorting out people, cooperative agreements, and exactly how to operate in this new environment.

Table 5.7 PMCs by 1960

Plant Materials Centers	1st Year Operation as PMC	Comments
Aberdeen, ID	1954	Former Nursery
Beltsville, MD	1954	Former Nursery
Big Flats, NY	1954	Former Nursery
Bismarck, ND	1954	Former Nursery at Mandan, ND
Elsberry, MO	1954	Former Nursery
Jimmy Carter, Americus, GA	1954	Former Nursery
Manhattan, KS	1954	Former Nursery
Pleasanton, CA	1954	Former Nursery
Pullman, WA	1954	Former Nursery
Tucson, AZ	1954	Former Nursery
Corvallis, OR	1957	Former nursery at Astoria, OR
Ho'olehua, HI	1957	Newly authorized
Los Lunas, NM	1957	Former SCS nursery at Albuquerque, NM
Arcadia/Brooksville, FL	1958	Prior nursery at Brooksville, FL
Rose Lake, MI	1958	Newly authorized
Bridger, MT	1959	Newly authorized

Chapter 6: PLANT MATERIALS PROGRAM, 1960 - 1993

THE EARLY SIXTIES

The only remnants of nursery staff employees in the early 1960s were PMC managers John Powell at Americus, GA, Oswald Hoglund, CA and Robert Thornton, Beltsville, MD. However, several Field and Washington-Field PMTs were still contributing. See Table 6.1.

Table 6.1 Field and Washington-Field Carry-overs from the Observational Nurseries

Jesse McWilliams, WY	Charles M. Schumacher, NE
Donald H. Douglas, ID	Lynn Guenther, MI
C. B. Blickensderfer, FL	Ernest McPherron, NY
John Schwendiman, WA	Donald Atkins, NE
Paul Tabor, GA	Virgil B. Hawk, IA
Crawford Young, GA/TX	Ashley Thornburg, MT
Joseph A. Downs, NM	Billie Rountree, MO
Glen Niner, NM	Kenneth Welton, MI
Karl E. Graetz, NC	Harold Miller, CA
William W. Steiner, PA	A. D. Stoesz, DC
James E. Smith, TX	Robert MacLauchlan, OR
A. L. Hafenrichter, OR	

The individual PMCs received about the same funding in 1960 as they had in 1959. Elsberry, MO and Los Lunas, NM were cut and the new PMC in Bridger, which was given funds in 1959 from Nebraska, was increased. The annual operational allocations per PMC ranged from $15,000 for Manhattan, KS to $50,000 for Pullman, WA. The ranges appear extreme. Two PMCs received more than $40,000, seven between $30,000 and $40,000 and eight under $30,000.[347] The total congressional allocation for operating the eighteen PMCs was approximately $556,000 which averaged approximately $30,000 per center annually.[348]

Although the Coffeeville, MS PMC opened in 1960, they do not show up in the funds distribution for that year. Of course, they had the duel responsibilities to conduct the traditional plant evaluations and producing seed for the Yazoo-Little Tallahatchie Flood Prevention Project. Recall the exception in the Administrators Memorandum which allowed for this. Funds for the Coffeeville PMC may have come from Flood Prevention funds. How bad the SCS, i.e., Dr. Stoesz, and others really recognized a need for this PMC is unknown. Could it have been an avenue to get plant materials for the Yazoo project? Jumping forward a few decades and then looking back, the justification for a PMC remains problematic, based on the severity of conservation problems that could be solved with vegetation, which is reflected in the net benefits from plants released by the PMC.[349] By 2005, the net benefit from the Montana PMC, opening in 1959, was $150 million, Cape May, NJ, opening in 1965, had $17 million and Coffeeville releases was negative $3 million. Stoesz certainly could have made a strong argument in 1960 for Coffeeville funding from some source other than his budget. Of course, when the obligation to produce plants for the flood prevention project went away, its operating cost did come from the PMC budget.

With the 1961 change in Federal administrations it was necessary for SCS Administrator Williams to advise a new USDA Assistant Secretary what the different parts of the agency did. Williams wrote Frank J. Welch on March 7, 1961 about the Plant Materials Program, which contained standard policy comments except the last paragraph.[350] Here he pointed out that five PMCs were operated under agreements with state universities or, in the case of Bismarck, by the state association of soil conservation districts. He went on to say that some of these five would be better operated under SCS control and said that SCS expected to make some adjustments in 1961. The cooperative agreement with Big Flats, NY had already ended on April 1, 1960. Tucson, AZ terminated its agreement in 1962, Manhattan, KS did so in 1965, Bismarck did it in 1967, and Americus ended its contract in 1975. The agreement with Los Lunas continued, for reasons previously mentioned.

From late 1960, Dr. Stoesz allocated the lion's share of his efforts to participating in and following up on different national issues that impacted the National Plant Materials Program. The first project started sometime in 1960. Administrator Williams asked the State Conservationist Policy Committee "Are PM Centers serving a useful purpose?" The results were divided, so an Evaluation Committee was appointed, with Frank Joy Hopkins, long term Assistant Chief for Administration and Northeast Field Representative (assistant chief) as chairman.[351] The committee included three state conservationists, Stoesz and Hopkins. They reviewed the work of four centers. The first was Pullman, WA. The manager's position had just been filled with a new person to the Plant Materials Program. Of course, with the venerable Dr. Hafenrichter and John Schwendiman participating, the presence or absence of a manager would have been insignificant. Bismarck and Americus were numbers two and three, both being operated by cooperators. The Bismarck manager, according to the report, did not participate. The manager at Americus, John Powell, did participate, along with Paul Tabor, a PMT with a prestigious plant materials background. And the forth center was Beltsville, MD. Robert S. Thornton provided valuable input about what the National PMC is doing and should be expanding into doing.

Was the selection of Bismarck and Americus a follow-up to Administrator Williams' comments to the Assistant Secretary? Was the entire review a screen to correct a mistake made by the previous administration?

The committee report contained eight conclusions and seven recommendations. They are condensed below.

Conclusions:

1. There was a real and important need for the PMCs.

2. The current Plant Materials Memorandum #1, dated August 16, 1956, was adequate except it did not provide for an appropriate long range plan for each PMC.

3. The uncertainty of the place of the PMCs within SCS stemmed from (a) a lack of understanding of their current functions, (b) an adherence to previous organizational ideas, (c) limited participation in program planning by responsible administrators, and (d) inadequate long range planning.

4. The present contracting arrangements for the operation of PMCs wasn't working well.

5. PMC long range plans did not always reflect coordination with other SCS plans and operations.

6. One conclusion described the value of good cooperative relations the PMCs should have had with multiple named agencies and organizations. The assumed intent was to suggest PMCs should have developed them with the agencies and organizations.

7. More effective planning would result from full participation by responsible line officers in developing long range and annual plans.

8. The National PMC was desirable and its leadership should be extended and intensified.

Recommendations:

1. Issue an up-to-date statement on PMCs, further clarifying their function and relationship to lines of work and to provide for broader participation of line officers in planning.

2. Line officers should take an active and reasonable part in planning and carrying out plant materials work; state conservationists particularly should participle in planning the program and take a major role in relations with state agencies and groups, colleges, SCD associations, crop improvement associations and others.

3. Long range plans for PMCs should be reworked and tied in closely with the conservation needs of the area it served. Each state should have a planned Plant Materials Program that would feed the PMC long range plan, and work with the PMC to incorporate it into their plan.

4. Consider dissolving the contracts with cooperatively operated PMCs.

5. Special attention should be given to improving and extending relations with cooperating agencies, securing their understanding, advice and assistance.

6. PMCs should intensify their communications and information to be sure SCS offices, SCDs and others are familiar with their program, and let them know how the Plant Materials Program can help them (This was solidifying the 'best kept secret' opinion of officers).

7. Careful consideration should be given to the quality of personnel selected for plant materials work. (It goes on to identify the required characteristics of the selection, but one of them was not knowledge about plants.)

Some additional comments followed the recommendations. The committee felt there was real worth to the Plant Materials Program, and the need for it would continue. They also wanted to shorten the time period between discovery and when the plant could be used in applications. Developing cultural and management requirements were critical.

The report felt the lack of a "complete understanding on the part of some SCS personnel and others of the new role of the centers" was the problem. No specific examples were offered and it is difficult to know exactly what was meant by this. One real possibility was that some centers found difficulty forsaking the production part of the nurseries. Most likely this was because a few PMCs in the arid and semiarid parts of the country continued to harvest and process large quantities of released grasses, which had long ago been incorporated into the commercial seed trade.[352] Others in the higher rainfall areas had difficulty curtailing the production of run-of-mill woody plants which served no useful evaluation effort. Looking back, as a brand new PMC manager at Big Flats, NY in the 1957 - 1965 period, the author can easily identify with this concern.

The solution to this was full participation by line officers, particularly the state conservationists, in PMC activities. Had the Washington-Field PMT had any influence, this problem should and most likely would have been addressed by them, and the excessive production ceased.

After fifty years of hindsight, it is fair to say the committee conclusions and recommendations were right on, considering the current line-staff structure. More responsive attention to plant materials work by line officers, improving PMC long range plans, eliminating the agreements with cooperators, increasing the understanding of the purposes of PMCs and improving relations with others are all positive goals. As we will see, many of these points were addressed. The results may not have been all the committee had hoped to achieve, but significant progress was made on all stated goals.

The committee report concluded with some complementary comments about the Plant Materials Program as a whole.

The National and Washington Field PMTs met in Salt Lake City in January, 1961.[353] Needless to say, one item discussed was the committee report. Under Recent Advances in Plant Materials, Dr. Stoesz highlighted both old and new concerns.[354] He was worried about the availability of qualified employees to fill plant materials vacancies. Relative to the administrative role played by state conservationists, he shared some concerns with those of former Chief Bennett. Shifting administrative responsibilities to state offices rather than from four or five regional offices, at least in regards to operating the Plant Materials Program, was problematic.[355] Stoesz wondered in 1961, "It appears...that line officers (state conservationists) did not have close enough liaison and knowledge of center operations. Perhaps too much was taken for granted when the administrative responsibilities were shifted to the state office. In most instances the state conservationists inherited smooth operating units (nursery observational studies) that require little administrative direction."

The keeper of the minutes of this meeting follows that statement from Dr. Stoesz by concluding, "The Washington-Field PMT staff (Steiner, Douglas, Atkins, Young and Hafenrichter) had no suggestions for policy revision." Stoesz advises the Washington-Field PMTs that the Administrator (Williams) had ordered reviews of the remaining fourteen PMCs to determine if they were performing their required functions. He told his colleagues they should be prepared to direct the reviews to (1) men, (2) money, (3) facilities, and (4) support by people, no doubt meaning the state conservationists. As before, the qualifications and capabilities of the PMC staff seemed to be ignored.

As the meeting continued, each of the Washington Field PMTs reported on the work in their regions. Only Hafenrichter commented on any follow-up from the recent Evaluation Committee appointed by the administrator, who had visited the Pullman PMC in his region. Of course, the committee visited PMCs in the Midwest and south but neither Atkins nor Young mentioned any follow up. The report by Hafenrichter suggested that some states and PMCs in the West had addressed the committee recommendation to some degree. Considering the committee report date of January 9, 1961 and the February 7, 1961 date of the W-F PMT meeting, Hafenrichter had to be reporting on pre-Evaluation Committee results.

On April 17, 1961, Douglas gave a presentation to the state conservationists of his Cornbelt region that appears to be intended to address the conclusions from the Evaluation Committee relating to the need for line officers to take an active and reasonable part in planning and carrying out plant materials work.[356] It was an excellent presentation that covered the Plant Materials Program from beginning to end. The detail of his comments suggested that he assumed his audience had little or no knowledge of the program, yet they were its administrators. There is good reason to believe that what evolved into the State Conservationists Advisory Committee for each PMC was first articulated by Douglas in this presentation. An aside is that everything in it could be traced to the foundation memo developed by Dr. Crider in 1936 except the desired role of state conservationists.[357]

During the summer of 1961, most PMTs nationally held another conference at Beltsville, MD. See Figure 6.1.

On August 9-11, 1961 a review was made of the Rose Lake, MI PMC as a follow-up to the Evaluation Committee.[358] It was chaired by the Acting Director of the Plant Technology Division, Frank C. Edminster. He was a biologist by training and had been the regional biologist in Region 1 (Northeast) during part of the nursery years. Years later, it became evident that his interest and leadership shaped the positive side of the observational studies at Big Flats more than anyone else.

The review of Rose Lake addressed all of the Evaluation Committee's recommendations and reached conclusions to address each. One significant recommendation included the establishment of a state conservationist advisory committee, appointed by the administrator, which quickly became national policy. This committee would contain three state conservationist members from the PMC service area. They would meet annually, usually at the PMC, with the W-F PMT and others, and the meeting would be chaired by the state conservationist from the PMC state. Principal duties would be to develop or review the PMC long and annual plan, and evaluate the ongoing program relative to those plans. Other recommendations having broad applications to all PMCs included having a positive information program, and wider use of field evaluation plantings, an intermediate evaluation step between initial evaluations and field plantings.

Figure 6.1: National conference of PMTs in Beltsville, MD 1961

Left to Right: Frank Edminster, Joseph Downs, Donald Atkins, Joseph Ruffner, Ernest McPherron (front), Donald Douglas (back), Morris Byrd, Edward Ewaul (front), Edward Graham (middle back), Theodore Spaller (back), Kenneth Welton (middle), Paul Tabor, Bill Steiner (back), A. L. Hafenrichter (front), unknown, Virgil Hawk, Wilson Hill (back), Jesse McWilliams (front), Crawford Young (back), Abraham Stoesz, Bob Thornton (front), Ted Plier (back), Bert Fuss, J. C. Dykes, John Schwendiman. Location: Beltsville, MD PMC, 1961

The last national evaluation impacting the Plant Materials Program before Dr. Stoesz retired began in late 1963.[359] Recall that in 1954 the Washington Field PMTs were scattered, reporting to their Washington counterparts. This evaluation was a review of the organization and staffing of the Plant Science Technology Division. Administrator Williams charged the committee, headed by Dr. D. M. Whitt, Plant Technology Division Director, to find how the Division, from top to bottom, could deliver the required technology economically and with increased efficiently. Whitt started by asking all Plant Science Washington-Field Technologists six questions, well in advance of the actual meeting. Remember, these questions were submitted to all plant science disciplines. They were as follows verbatim:

1. List the Major Land Resource Areas that lie in two or more of the states you serve with continuing difficult problems in your discipline.

2. Identify the principal factors contributing to any program inadequacy in your specialty in these resource areas by the states making up each.

3. List states you serve in order according to your evaluation of the adequacy of the current activities in your specialty.

4. Identify factors contributing to your placement of the top two and the low two.

    a. As you view the present situation and trends, do you believe the same order of listing of states will prevail five years from now?

b. If not what order do you think will prevail; and from what will these changes in order result?

5. What actions in each state, and by whom, do you think would bring all the states you serve to the most adequate level (the top two states in Item 3 above) in your specialty?

Unfortunately, the only surviving reply from the W-F PMTs to the above questions is from Donald Douglas, who served the states of MN, WI, MI, OH, IL and IN. His answers were thoughtful but anticipated. He listed land resource areas, states within each area and the most continuing plant materials problems. Only Iowa and Illinois warranted special recognition because of a consistent, well-trained and long term PMT, an interested state conservationist, good teamwork within plant science staff, a good state plant materials committee, and excellent relations with State Experiment Stations. The reasons for program inadequacy in the other states were about the opposite of Iowa and Illinois, which he expected would stay that way for a while. He was confident that the anticipated revisions in the 1962 national memo would produce positive results.

It can be assumed all Washington Field Plant Technicians submitted replies to Whitt's six questions. However, when the meeting assembled, the six items did not seem to have much relevance. In the minds of some, they were a smoke screen for other pre-conceived objectives of the conference.[360]

During the run up to the January 1964 meeting, much debate was held on how the Plant Technology Division would meet the Administrator's charge. Douglas was pointed and forceful in expressing his views. There was a fundamental question relative to the efficiency of the Plant Science Technology Division which he asked and answered, i.e., "Why does a work unit conservationist (local SCS field office or county employee) spend so little of his time and effort on the vegetative phase? He assigns time priority to those things which pay off in recognition and reportable units."[361] Other points he made to Stoesz included the following:

1. Any evaluation of how the Plant Science Division can be more efficient should not be within the Division and between disciplines but between agency divisions. His argument was that making changes within Plant Science without considering the agency as a whole will make their implementation more difficult.

2. The autonomy of state offices isolated W-F PMTs and other specialists putting them in the "setting of interlopers or outlanders in most states." To him this was no surprise; it had been anticipated from the reorganization of the 1954-55 periods.

3. He supported some type of regional center. His concept was to place state offices administratively under a regional director, along with W-F technicians. In the same vain he opposed a regional center where the unit head would be a W-F staff. That "would simply further insulate us from the states." The old adage 'What goes around comes around' becomes a truism twenty-two years or so later when exactly what Douglas feared happened.

4. Another item to be discussed at the January meeting was the distribution of the Field PMT's duties to the other plant science disciplines. Douglas wanted to be on "record vigorously opposing" this.[362]

Once the conference got under way the original six questions asked by Whitt seemed to disappear. Discussions prior to the meeting may have focused their attention to the pitiful plight of the Washington-Field specialists, and a desire to find a way to get them in out of the cold. There may have been many results from this immense evaluation, but one really big item was accomplished; the establishment of the 1964 Regional Technical Service Centers. Maybe this was the preconceived intent. This strengthened the position of the Washington-Field positions greatly by putting them under an individual who was almost a line officer, and dramatically increased the opportunity for productive persuasion.

Some Leverage Returned – Regional Offices Opened

Administrator's General Memorandum-1, dated May 22, 1964 announced the establishment of four Regional Technical Service Centers. The locations were Upper Darby, PA (Northeast); Fort Worth, TX (South); Lincoln, NE (Mid-West); and Portland, OR (West). The memorandum stated that "each Regional Technical Service Center will be headed by a Field Representative who will report directly to the Administrator. The Field Representative is a major member of the Administrator's staff, but not a line officer. He will not provide regional administration to the states served by the Center but as a staff supervisor will coordinate the various technical services provided to the states."[363] In some ways the new Field Representative was like a Washington-Field Technician but was a member of the Administrator's staff. The Regional Technical Service Centers (TSC) were established to coordinate the technical expertise going to the states and to keep the technical specialists advised of program developments, policy changes, new procedures, and problems facing the service. This also consolidated the areas to four regions, eliminating the Cornbelt and moving Denver, CO personnel to Lincoln, NE. This impacted the plant materials discipline indirectly by eliminating the position Donald Douglas held, allowing him to replace Dr. Stoesz.

Figure 6.2 indicates the increased leverage the regional specialists had, if they chose to use it by lobbying their regional director. A much improved connection was established between the regional director, agency administrator and state conservationists.

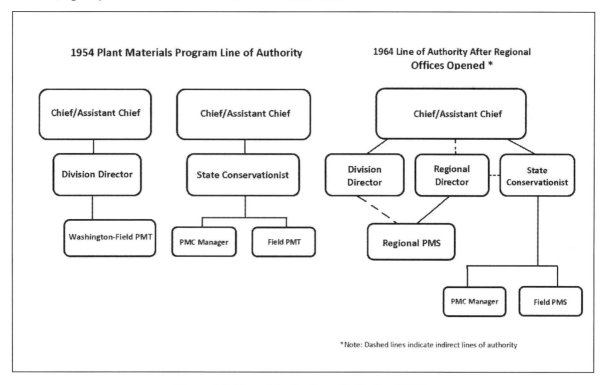

Figure 6.2: Line of Authority with Regional Offices

What had been discipline technicians were renamed to specialists, i.e. plant materials specialists, agronomy specialists, etc. The plant materials national and regional specialists and locations were

- National: Donald S. Douglas, Washington, D.C.

- Northeast, W. W. Steiner, Upper Darby, PA.

- South, Crawford Young, Fort Worth, TX.

- Midwest, Donald Atkins, Lincoln, NE.

- West, Dr. A. L. Hafenrichter, Portland, OR

What had been discipline technicians were renamed to specialists, i.e. plant materials specialists, agronomy specialists, etc. The plant materials national and regional specialists and locations were

- National: Donald S. Douglas, Washington, D.C.

- Northeast, W. W. Steiner, Upper Darby, PA.

- South, Crawford Young, Fort Worth, TX.

- Midwest, Donald Atkins, Lincoln, NE.

- West, Dr. A. L. Hafenrichter, Portland, OR

Personnel at the Technical Service Centers continued to receive guidance from their national counter-parts. The new Technical Centers did not increase the leverage of the National PM Specialist but did increase the influence of the former Washington-Field PMT positions. In 1954, the responsibilities of the new National PMT was to provide national coordination and leadership to what had become the National Plant Materials Program, but he had only his ability of persuasion to make anything happen. Of course, the Washington-Field PMT position was similar. Depending on personalities, etc., the Washington-Field PMT might not be invited to a state or asked for technical assistance or even have the opportunity to persuade the state conservationist.

Establishing the Technical Service Centers, with a director who had direct contact with the Administrator as his field representative, and who was the supervisor of the Regional PM Specialist, presented a new opportunity for influencing how things happened within the states they served. The director was not the state conservationist's supervisor, but the Administrator's representative carried weight with them. The establishment of Technical Service Centers was like bringing the Washington Field discipline representatives back into the fold. If the regional PM Specialist could now convince his boss of something, there was a good reason to think it would happen. It also strengthened the regional PM Specialist position with the PMCs and Field PM Specialists.

Accomplishments during the First Half of the 1960s Decade

While keeping a close eye on national issues and evaluations, Dr. Stoesz also gave thought and attention to more pleasant things. On August 30, 1963, not too far from retirement, he penned a short Developments and Accomplishments during the Past Decade.[364] He discussed the nursery closings, the plant materials centers' creation, and their expansion from the original ten to eighteen by 1963, and the poor experiences with non-SCS operation of PMCs. Although discussed elsewhere, it should be noted that he gave special attention to how the attitudes of plant materials scientists had changed from the fundamental concept of identifying a desirable conservation plant and then finding a problem for it to solve, to identifying the problem and finding a plant to solve it. It seems so obvious, yet the "Nature has evolved a plant for every purpose" concept had formed the basis of the Plant Materials Program.[365]

Dr. Stoesz also gave considerable discussion to the Plant Materials Memorandum SCS-1 of 1956 and the 1961-1962 evaluations that led to the development of Plant Materials Memorandum SCS-2 in 1962. From there he turned to the accomplishments of the decade.

'Emerald' crownvetch was released jointly by the SCS and the Iowa State University at Ames.[366] Dr. Hawk, long term PMT in Iowa was the guiding light behind 'Emerald', which entered the market place in 1961. It soon became the legume of choice for erosion control in the Corn Belt states and beyond.

Another 1961 release was 'Cardinal' autumn olive. As the name implies it was a desirable wildlife food plant, but much more. In the 1940s a plant was needed to grow on the acid mine spoil of Appalachia. It was described as needing to be easy to establish, tolerant to very acidic soils, competitive, and needing to produce soil nitrogen to enhance the growth of itself and other plants. Along came autumn olive, with these characteristics plus abundant seed production for wildlife food and its own multiplication. Its characteristics were so good, or so bad, that it did not limit itself to mine spoil. Its conservation value has been over shadowed by those characteristics that made it so valuable.

'Wimmera-62' ryegrass was a Pleasanton, CA release in 1962. From then until 2005 approximately 2.6 million pounds of seed was produced commercially for cover crops, erosion control and forage in the predominately winter wet – summer dry climate of California.

'Luna' pubescent wheatgrass became a blockbuster release for the Southwest and Great Basin states. It was released in 1963 by the Los Lunas, NM PMC, another product of the Westover-Enlow Expedition, and originally selected by the SCS nursery at Albuquerque, NM. Since its release, 11.1 million pounds of seed was produced through 2005, with a net producer and ecological benefit value of $21.6 million and a ranking of third of all SCS releases for net benefit.[367]

During the 1960-1964 time frame, seventeen releases were made, seven introduced and ten native species, with ten PMCs participating in them. Los Lunas released five. 'Garrison' creeping foxtail was a joint release by the Bismarck and Bridger PMCs. All but two were released formally. Big Flats contributed their first in 1961 and second in 1964. Relative to long term production 'Cardinal' autumn olive and 'Luna' pubescent wheatgrass far exceeded anything else.

Between 1960 and 1964 SCS Plant Materials Program authors published at least 25 times in various print media. These publication citations can be found in Appendix 2.

The sad cover of the 1964 Western States Plant Materials Center Annual Technical Report honored a lost conservationist.[368] The Yuma, AZ Daily Sun carried the following in its November 23, 1964 issue.[369]

> Arizona range and conservation societies are establishing a memorial fund in honor of the late Darwin Anderson, an expert on Southwest vegetation. Anderson was one of 29 persons killed when a Bonanza airliner crashed Nov 15 into a mountain near Las Vegas. The scholarship fund to be called the Darwin Anderson Memorial will provide scholarships to the annual Arizona Youth Conservation Camp. The memorial is under the sponsorship of the Soil Conservation Society of America and the Arizona Chapter American Society of Range Management. Anderson who was 53 was a native of Cochise. He had served southern Utah, Arizona and Nevada with the Soil Conservation Service since 1935.

Anderson had worked for the SCS Research Division, and, among other things, published his excellent work *Machinery for Seedbed Preparation and Seeding on Southwestern Ranges* in the Journal of Range Management in 1949.

Dr. Stoesz retired at the end of 1964, ending an SCS career of thirty-four years. More of his contributions and accomplishments can be found in the Key Leaders chapter.

THE DONALD S. DOUGLAS YEARS (1965 – 1970)

Dr. A. D. Stoesz was replaced by Washington-Field PMT, Donald S. Douglas, in early 1965. Donald started his SCS career in the observational studies work at the Pullman, WA nursery.[370] He was one of the individuals Dr. Hafenrichter had recruited and built into an excellent observational studies team, maybe the best then and throughout the Plant Materials Program history. All were disciplined, serious, reasonably private, hard-working, and loyal to the development of conservation plants.[371] Douglas represented somewhat of a departure from his leader, Hafenrichter, and most of the other Hafenrichter 'boys'; he was ambitious in a context of wanting to provide maximum contribution to the program, which he felt was possible through mobility and promotion. Douglas was a solid thinker, technically sound, and, based on his training at Pullman, had lots to offer other regions in the country.

Many factors influenced the selection of individuals for promotion, just like things influenced the productivity of the Plant Materials Program and individual PMCs. One factor that influenced the latter, and maybe the former as well, was the climate, with moisture availability being at the head of the list. This is examined in considerable detail in Chapter 13, Factors Effecting Observational Nursery and Plant Materials Center Productivity. Douglas' early training was in an area with millions of acres of eroding rangeland, created by overgrazing and limited rainfall. The need for conservation plants was overwhelming compared to the forty-inch annual rainfall of the east. Did the severe need for conservation plants create the greatness of one PMC or one regional specialist over another? The answer to that is not easy, but an opportunity created by environmental differences can reflect favorably on individuals at promotion time. Douglas was capable and took advantage of his opportunity.

Logic suggests Dr. Hafenrichter would have been the choice to replace Stoesz. Donald Douglas suggested after his retirement that the position was offered and Hafenrichter turned it down. Of the remaining regional PMSs one could assume Hafenrichter would have chosen Douglas, having been his boss for years. According to Robert MacLauchlan, Wilmer W. Steiner had been led to believe he was the first choice after Hafenrichter's refusal, even to the point of checking out homes in the Washington area. MacLauchlan recalls Steiner sharing the information that Chief Don Williams received a call from Hafenrichter which changed minds, and Douglas was selected. Although plausible, it remains speculation.

From about any point of view, Douglas arrived at an opportune time as head of the Plant Materials Program. Under Stoesz's leadership, production was accelerating, funding was reasonably good, new PMCs had been established on schedule and the Technical Service Centers were providing his regional PM Specialists with increased leverage. Another change was taking place within the Plant Materials Program which Douglas encouraged. He was an advocate of much broader input into the priorities at PMCs which led to their expanding into new work areas. This was a positive, but at times it was also a handicap to some.

During the nursery years, the needs of the local nursery determined the focus of the observational studies. These needs were identified from within the service area of at nursery. The stakeholder's included other plant science disciplines from all states served, and soil conservation districts. Determining the plant materials needs within a PMC service area was about the same. Beginning in the mid-1960s, new approaches to old problems and entirely new problems were being identified and consuming more and more PMC attention. For example, one is justified in wondering why Region I Nursery Division did not assign priority to observational studies on surface mine spoil. Big Flats began addressing this as soon as it became a PMC, and a new one was soon to be established with this problem as their number one priority. The focus of the new Cape May PMC was to explore vegetative solutions to coastal dune stabilization and eroding tidal shorelines. The other side of that coin was the potential for too much change, causing the loss of focus and leading to the accomplishment of very little. This may have haunted some PMCs, as is discussed in Chapter 8, which is an overview of each PMC.

Funding and New Centers

The funds identified in Table 6.2 were appropriations for PMC use while Douglas was Chief PM Specialist. Over the course of his tenure in NHQ the budget increased by sixty-four percent, partially resulting from newly appropriated money for new Centers. In addition to appropriated funding, the Los Lunas PMC received $25,000 annually from the State Highway Commission for the reimbursement of work and the state of Maryland received between $15,000 and $20,000 for similar work. This represented a beginning of reimbursable funding for several centers.

The percent of earmarks and offsets of the 'Total to Allocate' columns has been added to the table for the purpose of showing the drastic change that took place over time.

Table 6.2 PMC Funding 1964 - 1970

FY	Amount	% change prior year	Offset or EarMark	% of Total to Allocate
1964	$809,000			100.00%
1965	$914,000	13.00%		100.00%
1966	$1,128,000	39.40%		100.00%
1967	$1,280,000	13.50%		100.00%
1968	$1,007,962	-21.30%		100.00%
1969	$1,060,000	5.20%	$20,000	98.10%
1970	$1,330,000	25.50%	$20,000	98.50%

In 1965, the Cape May, NJ and the James E "Bud" Smith, Knox City, TX PMCs opened, the latter replacing the Spur, TX Center. This brought the number of PMCs to twenty. The Cape May PMC was the outgrowth of a March 1962 storm that struck the New Jersey shore but demonstrated the valuable role vegetation could play in mitigating real estate damage. Knox City was a planned replacement for the closed San Antonio and Delhart SCS nurseries. James Smith kept a semblance of a PMC going at Spur, TX in cooperation with the Texas Agricultural Experiment Station since the closing of those nurseries.

That semblance was impressive. The first Annual Progress Report from Knox City by Arnold Davis, their first manager, who was fresh out of training at Beltsville, listed the pounds of perennial grass seed that were shipped for field plantings in 1965[372] (Table 6.3). It showed, in a convincing way, what had been happening at the Spur Center. Several of these plants were later released, including klinegrass as 'Selection 75' in 1969. By 2005, 6.7 million pounds of seed had been produced commercially of this cultivar.

Table 6.3 Seed distributed for Field Plantings and Seed Increase from Knox City PMC in 1965

Species	Pounds	Species	Pounds
Cane bluestem	476	Rhodesgrass	88
Caucasian bluestem	268	Switchgrass	600
Sideoats grama	375	Little bluestem	172
Green sprangletop	62	Sand bluestem	610
Plains bristlegrass	92	Indiangrass	189
Arizona cottontop	140	Silky bluestem	80
Old world bluestem	101	Klinegrass	20

Arnold Davis (Figure 6.3) was a work horse of the first order. After holding the PMC manager's job for less than a year, he replaced the irreplaceable James "Bud" Smith as Plant Materials Specialist, and in 1973 became Regional PM Specialist for the South region. Did such rapid advancement result from the training he received at Beltsville, under Bob Thornton? Yes, that and his work ethic.

Figure 6.3 Arnold Davis

Dr. Virgil Hawk became the first manager in New Jersey. Virgil had a long career, starting as one of Hafenrichter's boys at Pullman, WA in 1935. He had a fellowship in the Department of Agronomy at Washington State University and was appointed a Bureau of Plant Industry agent in 1935. When the Bureau's nursery became an SCS nursery, Virgil went along. He became a Nursery Manager in 1943, and returned to his native Iowa to earn a PhD. at Iowa State. He remained in Ames, Iowa as an SCS Field PMT for many years, nursing the release of several plants. His career bookends stretched from the Palouse hills of Washington to the sand dunes in New Jersey.

The budget did increase as a result of the newly authorized Cape May Center. Knox City did not trigger additional funding on a continuing basis, because it was a replacement for Spur, TX which had been receiving an allocation.

Wilmer W. Steiner (Bill), the W-F PMT in the Northeast, knew the Big Flats PMC in upstate New York could not address two major problems in his region (See Wilmer W. Steiner in the Key Leaders, Chapter 9). Along with the New Jersey State Conservationist, Selden Tinsley, and NJ State Resource Conservationist, Edward Ewaul, he labored for support of a PMC in the mid-Atlantic area to deal with coastal problems. Two things came together to make it a reality; the 1962 storm that hit the coast and Senator Clifford P. Case of New Jersey. Ewaul found what he considered the perfect site which was purchased by the New Jersey Green Acres Program. [373]

With Cape May under his belt, Steiner then turned his attention to the second problem; a PMC to address the surface mining reclamation problems of Appalachia. He lacked the influential and aggressive support he had in New Jersey. Nevertheless, a new PMC was funded in 1967 to be located in Eastern Kentucky. The actual location was selected by a member of the House of Representatives Appropriations Committee from that area. The available acres for cultivation were limited to about fifteen, all subject to the potential of annual flooding. No doubt an exaggeration, but some visitors insisted that sunshine hit the site about 10:00 AM and departed by 4:00 PM.

Apparently, Steiner, or some other plant materials person, expressed reservations about the site that got back to J. C. Dykes, Assistant Administrator. These remarks appear to have prompted the following response by Dykes at a Washington Headquarters meeting, delivered by an unidentified person. A transcription of the remarks was stuck to an unrelated report in the archives. [374] It is reprinted below.

> SCS operates on a line and staff organization. Mr. Dykes has instructed us on the operation of this system on a number of occasions as only J. C. can. He described it this way: It is the job of the staff man to provide the line officer with information, counsel, and recommendations that bear upon the problem. It is the responsibility of the line officer to make decisions. Then it becomes incumbent upon the organization and all the people in it to support that decision by their words and actions.
>
> I think most of you know I'm referring to the Administrator's decision on the choice of site for the Appalachian PM Center. As staff people, we prepared what I believe was a very good and very objective report and recommendation. I'm sure the Administrator considered our recommendation as well as other factors, some of which may be beyond his control, before announcing his decision. It is a decision by which we can and will operate a Plant Materials Center.

My purpose in bringing this subject to your attention is this: The Administrator and his Deputies are receiving reports that people in SCS, and more particularly in Plant Materials, are critical of the Administrator's decision.

Communication to the Administrator through the usual channels or direct is open when you feel you have a valid protest. An expression of opinion or convictions in this manner is encouraged, but loose talk in the presence of Service and non-Service people who are not directly concerned cannot be tolerated.

Regardless of who was doing the loose talking, it was a mistake, and Douglas could not have been pleased. However, from a position of not very much hindsight, the administrator might well have taken the advice of his staff and said, "If this is the only site you can offer for a new PMC, no thank you". Steiner took his licks and moved on. In the 1990s the PMC was moved out of the Kentucky hollow to a larger one in West Virginia.

Increased State Conservationist Input

The desirability of increased participation of state conservationists emerged from the evaluations of the early 1960's, and culminated in the recommendations from the Rose Lake, MI review in 1961. This did not immediately become national policy, but Douglas vigorously supported and encouraged it. By 1962–63, most, if not all, PMCs had a state conservationist advisory committee. In a 1966 report by Douglas, this need and the progress being made was discussed twice. The report included "Strong interest and leadership displayed by State Conservationists through Center Advisory Committees is making PM work more effective."[375] It was mentioned again as, "The greatest contributing factor to the progress being made by PM work." In the same vein, the 1966 SCS Advisory MGT-2 required a PMC review at least every four years, led by the Administrator's field representative. These quickly became policy as Functional Inspections. The major stimulus supplied by the state conservationists advisory was not the result of their technical genius. Instead they created an environment which said, 'the boss cares about this program' and it gave assurances that decisions made would be implemented.

Added to the value of the state conservationists committee was the benefit of having the Administrator's Field Representative at the meetings. There are many examples. A state conservationist in one state convinced his counterpart in a PMC state to fill a position at the PMC with an employee deemed to be unsuitable for local field office work. The regional PM Specialist felt the same way about the employee's suitability for PMC work, and discussed it with the Field Representative, his supervisor. After observing the said employee at the advisory committee meeting, the Field Representative suggested the state conservationists needed to find a position where the employee in question would have greater opportunities. Of course, it was done.

Accomplishments during the Second Half of the 1960s Decade

Some other national activities which were occurring at the time, or were soon to occur during the Donald Douglas tenure, include the following:

1. The Manhattan, KS PMC returned to SCS operation on January 1, 1966.

2. The relocation of the Arcadia, FL PMC back to Brooksville was completed in 1967.

3. Douglas took special notice of the release and publicity associated with 'Cardinal' autumn olive, the first truly woody plant release, as being well-planned and executed. He pointed out that the decision to release it was made several years earlier, allowing ample time to establish seed orchards and pre-release publicity. This credit was due to Bill Steiner.

Between 1960 and 1970, many former nursery employees were lost from the Plant Materials Program, primarily by retirement. This was a group of individuals nearly impossible to replace, including Marshall Augustine, Joseph Downs, A. L. Hafenrichter, James E. Smith, Jr., Abraham Stoesz, Paul Tabor and Robert Thornton.

These losses and other things required fourteen of the twenty-two PMC managers to change positions during the tenure of Douglas as Head PM Specialist. Thirteen field PM Specialists and one Regional PMS also changed positions. Such turnover, naturally, affects output. The retiring of Dr. Hafenrichter in 1967 noted the end of a significantly fruitful contribution to the field of conservation plant science. His career and the careers of five members of this group are covered in more details in the Key Leaders Chapter. The good news however, is that seventeen former nursery employees continued employment into the 1960s, and a few well beyond that.

In spite of the best kept secret comment among administrators, year after year, publications reaching a wide audience continued to roll out. The 1965 --1970 period was no different. Many were refereed journal articles. They are shown in Appendix 2. One most noteworthy publication is:

Hafenrichter, A. L, J. L. Schwendiman, Harold R. Harris, Robert S. MacLauchlan, and Harold W. Miller. 1968. Grasses and Legumes for Soil Conservation in the Pacific Northwest and Great Basin States. AH 339, USDA, SCS, Washington, DC.

From the beginning of the observational studies in SCS nurseries, the broad intent was to find new plants that were better than what existed. When Conservation Beautification Memorandum-1 was issued in 1966, plant-related beautification took another leap. It called attention to desirable landscaping of SCS facilities, noting that wildflowers are not only pretty, they also control erosion. The Johnson administration triggered a major effort in the late 1960s to explore the use of wildflowers as a component in conservation plantings. Promoted by Lady Bird Johnson, PMCs responded with new cultivars of native wildflowers, the first one being 'Eureka' thickspike gayfeather from the Manhattan, KS PMC.

There were twenty-four releases during the years of 1965 through 1970. Production of the top five grasses exceeded 3.6 million pounds. 'Cape' became the immediate standard for beachgrass plantings on East Coast dunes; averaging 6.4 million plants produced annually for the twenty-eight years (1977-2005) records were kept.

'Cape' was one of those collections just waiting to be found. Late on a Friday afternoon, under long September shadows and eight hours from home a voice seemed to be saying to the collector 'give it up, give it up'. "Just one more dune" he thought. And there it was, spread out before him, a patch of beachgrass the likes of which were spectacular beyond belief. "Glory, glory", he thought, recalling the state conservationist charge, "Don't come carrying a lot of junk in here." Collection NJ-390 was only six years away from becoming the cultivar 'Cape'.

In addition to 'Cape' other noteworthy releases during this period included 'Regar' meadow brome by the Pullman PMC. Fifteen plants were selected from a 1958 irrigated nursery. The seed source for the nursery was from Zek, Kars province, Turkey, collected in 1949. By 2005 9.6 million pounds of seed had been produced. Four years after opening the Knox City PMC released 'Selection 75' klinegrass. By 2005 6.7 million pounds of seed had been produced commercially.

Douglas was acutely aware of the importance of having quality employees at all plant materials positions. He worked hard at influencing personnel placement. His success is hard to judge. One tool he used was to ask the regional PM Specialists of their opinion on persons ready for promotion or potential advancement. One archive shows his willingness to take a chance. An agronomist at a PMC had received very poor ratings by one PMC manager. The managers changed, and the next one rated the agronomist much higher. Based on this the regional PM Specialist advised Douglas that the agronomist might be ready for a promotion. The input by Douglas is unknown, but the agronomist was soon promoted to a PMC in another region.[376] Unfortunately, the new manager had used the rating system for the wrong reason, but realized his objective.

The tenure of Donald S. Douglas might be considered uneventful but successful; no major threats, no collapsing programs; nothing flashy, just steady progress. He may have been effective in introducing some of the desirable approaches of the West into other parts of the country. He viewed the state conservationist PMC committee as a major accomplishment, as well as boarding the input into PMC work, and his effort to get the Technical Service Centers established. All were positive accomplishments. Had Hafenrichter brought his prestige with him to the national position would he have been more effective?

Don stepped down at the end of 1970, and returned to the Northwest, where he completed his career, replacing another one of the Hafenrichter boys, Harold Miller, as regional PM Specialist. His returning to the West regional position was reflective of his first love. Always the straight arrow of the Schwendiman mold, he retired in 1973 and lived to be ninety-five, dying in 2006.[377]

Fortunately, thanks to Douglas Helms, SCS Historian, an interview with Don was recorded in about 1978[378], eight years after retiring. It allows some insight into his thoughts that may not have emerged during his years of employment. It consists of and is presented as multiple subject areas. Unfortunately, it has not been transcribed, thus limiting its value.

Interview with Donald Douglas by Douglas Helms

Operational differences between the West and the rest of the U.S.

> First Don discussed his work in the Midwest as a Washington-Field PMT. That was from 1960 through 1965. No doubt his answers also include his time as the National PMT. He emphasized that a pattern of testing, cooperation and release had been developed in the West that did not exist in the East. He thought some progress may have been made by himself in Iowa and Missouri, recalling that Dr. Virgil Hawk, PM Specialist in Iowa, had trained in the West. The West had concentrated on forage plants, but in the East the nursery history had been one of producing woody plants, and it was hard to get away from that. Helms then asked, "So you let the Midwest and the South concentrate on woody plants for their conservation work?" To which Douglas responded, "Yes, and they distributed them widely, paying little attention to the evaluation and testing process and virtually no relationship with the experiment stations…" Helms pointed out that some of the woody species were good for wildlife and Don agreed, "…and we were able to get some released."

> Helms suggested that after Don became the National PMT he had to learn a little more about the south, to which he replied, "I don't feel that I really enjoyed that (National PMT position) as much as I had working closer with people on the land. My job (in Washington) was working more with funds and…state conservationists, developing procedures, policy and memos and that sort of thing. I did enjoy working with the American Seed Trade Association and the American Nurserymen Association, and I think during my time the Service really developed better working relationships and understanding…(with them)." He continued to comment about the millions of woody plants SCS produced and how that led to the downfall of the nurseries, pointing out that most of the things SCS was producing, after the first few years, could have been produced commercially. Don was quick to recognize that the two Associations appreciated getting our releases. Helms then asked, "Weren't the nurseries closed by the time you came to Washington (1965)?" to which Don replied, "Yes, it (the production) had slowed down materially at any rate (suggesting he viewed the woody production of many PMCs as a continuation of the old nursery days) but there was still lingering antagonism" on the part of the Seed and Nurseryman's Associations.

Helms inquired if there was anything else he wanted to accomplish when he came to Washington? "Well yes, the national memo was rewritten to pretty much reflect those steps… that were used in the West. It was the desire of the Washington Chief that these procedures that had worked well in the west are extended nationally." "Oh, there had not been a national policy on that before?" Helms asked. "Yes and the western states had followed these procedures." Douglas then expounded to some degree on why it worked in the West. "Hafenrichter was primarily responsible. He was a good scientist and recognized by research people he had worked with and his working relationship with experiment stations was a lot smoother and easier than forsome of the people in the east who didn't have that background." "Did the Centers accept this change?" Helms asked. "Not easy," said Don. Helms asked why. The answer in the interview is garbled but, in short, it says it was because they hadn't done it before, lack of knowledge in how the system worked, and lack of confidence when working with experiment station researchers. Over time some progress was made and the West system was more adopted.

Helms asked about plant materials assistance to urban dwellers, such as plants which attract birds, etc. Douglas skirted his involvement, commenting on the use of windbreaks, saying he was aware of it but not much involved. The desirability of plant exploration, both domestic and foreign was discussed, which Douglas supported.

Helms asked if most of the new range plants in the west were an economic benefit to the region, to which he replied, "Released grasses to the Pacific Northwest would have more than paid for all the costs of the plant materials centers nationally" (He did not have the benefit of the analysis that was done in 2007.[379] It would more than document his statement as being correct).

Working with Hafenrichter

What was it like to work with him? Don replied that he was excellent at reasoning, and developing ideas. He was small and may have been a little self-conscious about it and compensated for it by being a little brassy. Those who knew him respected him highly, mentioning several of his boys; Miller, Hawk, Schwendiman, himself, etc. After the 1954 reorganization, when Hafenrichter became a Washington Field PMT, he was respected by state conservationists, and they usually accepted what he recommended.

Why didn't he become the National PM Specialist? When Dr. Stoesz took the job in 1954 it was offered to him, and again when Stoesz retired; he always declined. His reasoning was that working with the people was his 'pride and joy'.

Most Enjoyable Experiences

The association with people, both in the Service and with farmers, ranchers, and cooperating experiment stations were his top experiences. Pride associated with seeing the products of the program across the landscape also topped his list.

He mentioned the Washington office time associated with responding to letters written to the Secretary. All the old favorites were mentioned; multiflora rose, kudzu, etc. Two weaknesses in the program contributed to these and other introduced plants becoming pests; inadequate testing and mismanagement of the plant was his answer (Neither of these two plants were really the products of the observational nurseries or the PMCs. Northeast biologist Frank Edminster could be viewed as the principal promoter of multiflora rose, which is an excellent plant for wildlife).

THE Wilmer W. STEINER YEARS (1971 – 1973)

Bill Steiner came to the Beltsville SCS location in the early or mid-1940s.[380] He was a junior author of a 1944 publication on honey locust. He became manager of the National Observational Project in 1948, replacing Dr. Crider, who continued working there for a few years. In 1955, Bill became the Washington-Field PMT for the Northeast states, where he remained until transferring to Washington. The perfect description of his personality would be the opposite of pushy. Trained as a horticulturist, he saw beauty, if not conservation value, in all plants. Within the Northeast plant materials family, his annual participation in the Philadelphia Flower Show was a thing of joy and fear.[381] Working with the regional public affairs specialists, Bernard Roth, Bill directed the participation of SCS for several years in the show, each requiring some PMC input. In 1966, their display featured plant materials work on sand dunes, including twelve grasses and shrubs forced in the Big Flats and Cape May PMC greenhouses.

Retirements in the 1969 - 1970 time frames created a shuffle in regional positions. Steiner's move created a vacancy in the Northeast, as well as the retirement of Donald Atkins at Lincoln, NE and Harold Miller at Portland, OR. The positions were soon filled and Steiner had ample support and leadership capability in regional positions. They were:

- Northeast, Joseph D. Ruffner, replacing Steiner at Upper Darby, PA

- South, Crawford Young, Fort Worth, TX

- Midwest, Robert S. MacLauchlan, replacing Donald Atkins at Lincoln, NE

- West, Donald S. Douglas, Portland, OR replacing Dr. Hafenrichter.

Overall Donald Douglas had left the national position with the Plant Materials Program in good condition. The budget was better than holding its own against inflation, thanks to a twenty-five percent increase for fiscal year 1970 over the 1969 appropriation. See Table 6.4.

Former nursery staff employees still on the job in 1971 had diminished significantly from the early 1960s. The only PMC manager was John Powell at Americus, GA; additionally there were three regional and four field PM Specialists.

Table 6.4 Available Funds 1971 - 1973

FY	Appropriation	% change prior year	Offset or Ear-Mark	% of Total to Allocate
1971	$1,428,000	7.37	$0	100
1972	$1,472,116	3.09	$0	100
1973	$1,576,934	7.12	$0	100

Accomplishments

In the early 1970s it became apparent that the Pleasanton, CA PMC would have to be relocated. The Pleasanton site was in the path of urban expansion and encroachment by a race track. Efforts were initiated to locate a new site in the San Joaquin valley, which was completed and the center relocated by 1973 to Lockeford.

In 1971, there were twenty PMCs, all operated by SCS except Los Lunas, NM. The twenty-first center opened in 1972 in Palmer, AK. The first plant materials center assistance to Alaska was provided by the Pullman, WA PMC and the PM Specialist in Washington State. Because of distances and lack of funds this proved ineffective to address their needs. With support and assistance from SCS and encouragement from the University of Alaska, in 1972 the Alaska Legislature passed and Governor Bill Egan signed into law, a bill creating the Alaska Plant Materials Center at Palmer.[382] No additional funding was authorized by Congress. SCS provided and funded the first manager, James Stroh, for seven years. He was a seasoned SCS manager from the Bridger, MT PMC. Stoney Wright, an Alaska Department of Agriculture employee, replaced him. SCS funding has been erratic since then. More details are included in the Palmer PMC pages in Chapter 8.

From the very beginning, all SCS seed or plant collections from any source required that each be individually identified by number. Since there were many nurseries collecting many accessions the number for each nursery needed to be unique. For example the Americus, GA nursery may have started with AM-1, Manhattan, KS with KS-1, etc. When collections were traded between nurseries, and later PMCs, accessions began to acquire multiple numbers. Over time managing these numbers became a nightmare. The movement of seed of what became King's Ranch bluestem through the system, as discussed in Chapter 4, is an excellent example of what happened. A standardized numbering system was needed where only one number was assigned to an accession. Bill Steiner took on the job of creating such a national numbering system, similar to that used by the Agricultural Research Service, Plant Introduction office. Arrangements were made with ARS to assign a plant introduction number to each new accession. When the dust settled, there was a national policy for a uniform numbering process, which has been used successfully ever since.

While at the Beltsville, MD nursery in the mid-1940s, Bill became interested in some projects of the Hill Culture Research Section.[383] They were seeking new economic crops that could be grown in the 'hill country' of the eastern U.S., such as nut trees, wild grapes, etc. What attracted Bill was a collection of black locust clones made by Dr. Henry Hopp during the 1930s and assembled at Beltsville.[384] [385] Black locust, even in the 1930s, was recognized as a desirable plant for re-vegetating acid mine spoil and similar sites. Additionally, its decay resistance made it a favorite for split rail fencing, a product still in common use at that time. Unfortunately, a borer, *Megacyllene robiniae*, prevented the development of tall, straight trees. A borer-resistant black locust would represent a win-win situation.

To preserve any borer resistance in selected plants, they had to be propagated vegetatively. Through Bill's leadership, plantings of Hopp's clones were scattered around the eastern U.S., mostly in cooperation with other state and Federal agencies. It was a career-long endeavor, culminating years after his death with the release in 1987 of three cultivars called the Steiner Group, representing three of the original Hopp collections.[386] [387] The cultivar names were 'Alleghany', 'Algonquin' and 'Appalachian'.

Publications during the period were dominated by John Schwendiman and coauthors. He also joined former Hafenrichter boy, Dr. Virgil Hawk, to complete a chapter in the college text book *Forages*. These are listed in Appendix 2.

There were twenty-four releases for 1971 -1973 periods. Fourteen of the twenty-four were introduced plants. Three outstanding native grasses came on the market in about 1974, 'Critana' thickspike wheatgrass, and 'Rosana' and 'Arriba' western wheatgrass, just in time for the arrival of the Conservation Reserve Program in the next decade. From 1977 through 2005 17.5 million pounds of seed of these three was sold. Both 'Critana' and 'Rosana' were released by the twelve year-old Bridger PMC. Two introduced small trees, 'Pink Lady' winterberry euonymus and 'Midwest' Manchurian crabapple were readily accepted for windbreak and wildlife food and cover use in the Midwest and Corn Belt. Twelve of the twenty PMCs participated with at least one new plant.

Unfortunately, soon after his arrival in Washington in 1971, Bill learned he had an incurable throat cancer. He lost his voice to a great extent. There is no doubt that he was operating below par throughout the remainder of his time. His strengths had always been his gregarious and winning personality. The illness certainly would have hampered this and played to his reluctance to make difficult decisions. It can be assumed that many things slipped while Bill was fighting two battles at once. Nevertheless, he was able to implement the national accession numbering procedure and other required position responsibilities. He continued as best as his condition would allow, retired at the end of 1973, and died soon after.

The SCS proposed budget for fiscal year 1975 would have been developed in the fall of 1973. Bill logically would have had this responsibility for the PMC Program. Robert MacLauchlan, Regional PMS in Lincoln, NE was asked to assist Bill with this and other tasks. Working with the Plant Science Division Chief Victor Barry and the Budget and Finance Division, Bob developed a budget which gained support from assistant administrator Norman Berg. By the time it worked its way through the Department, the Office of Management and Budget and ended up in the president's budget that went to Congress there was a proposed 49.6 percent increase in the PMC allocation, which was passed into law. The development of this proposed budget happened on Bill's watch, with help from MacLauchlan and others.

Bill can be honored for his beloved personality, consistent demeanor and steady performance, which served the Plant Materials Program extremely well for twenty-seven years. See Chapter 9, Key leaders, for more details.

PROSPEROUS YEARS WITH ROBERT S. MACLAUCHLAN (1974 – 1984)

Robert MacLauchlan is highlighted as a Key Leader of the Plant Materials Program in Chapter 9.[388] Details are included there on his background and accomplishments.

In 1950 SCS offered Bob, living in Dennysville, Maine, a position in Pleasanton, CA. After two years at Pleasanton he moved to Bellingham, WA. With the 1953 reorganization and the closing of nurseries he landed in a field office for a short time, and then became Field PMT for Oregon and Washington, first headquartered in Hillsboro, OR and then Corvallis when the PMC opened in 1957. In 1966, he moved back to Pleasanton as the California Field PM Specialist and, four years later, moved to Lincoln, Nebraska as the Regional PM Specialist. From his initial employment in 1950 until he moved to Lincoln he worked under the technical direction of Dr. Hafenrichter, making him the second student of Hafenrichter's teachings to become the national leader.

As had been the case when Bill Steiner became National PM Specialist, MacLauchlan ended up with four new regional PM Specialists. Don Douglas, Joseph Ruffner and Crawford Young all retired at about the same time, and his move from Lincoln created the forth vacancy. The new ones were:

- Northeast, Curtis Sharp, Upper Darby, PA
- South, Arnold Davis, Fort Worth, TX
- Midwest, Ashley Thornburg, Lincoln, NE
- West, Sherrill H. Fuchs, Portland, Oregon.

Fuchs had been the Field PM Specialist in New Mexico before taking a multi-year overseas assignment in Algeria in 1966, returning home in 1970. When Donald Douglas retired from the regional position, Fuchs replaced him.

Former nursery staff employees still on the job in 1974 had diminished to five and only one was a PMC manager. Of course, that was the ageless John Powell at Americus, GA, who did not retire until 1982, after completing a forty-seven year career at the Americus observational nursery and PMC. The following Field and Regional Plant Materials Specialists remained in 1974.

- Karl E. Graetz, NC, retired in 1974
- Billie Rountree, MO retired in 1975
- John Schwendiman, WA retired in 1976
- Ashley Thornburg, Lincoln, NE retired in 1978

During the period while MacLauchlan was in Washington, manager positions at PMCs were quite stable. Ten PMCs had the same manager for the 1974 - 1984 timeframe; but two had four during the same period. The others changed two or three times.

Funding Bumps in the Road

While Bob was still at Lincoln, NE, he was asked to come to Washington a few times during 1973 to handle items Steiner was not able to get accomplished because of his illness. Although the 1974 appropriation was 4.32% higher than the 1973 budget, allocations made to the states were not adequate to keep all PMCs in the black. One minor cause for this was the $36,000 overhead charged by the National office which had not been done previously. Another and potentially larger cause was excess allocation to some PMCs for purchasing equipment or upgrading facilities. These funds were committed before the shortfall was recognized.

One solution proposed to solve the problem was not to MacLauchlan's liking. Plant Science Director Vic Barry, along with Budget and Finance Director, John Fish, were considering closing some PMCs. At the time, Americus, GA was still operating on a cooperative agreement. The logic was to close it because SCS had less control there than at other PMCs.

MacLauchlan's negotiating style was to first and foremost know more about the subject than the other negotiator, and second to see the big picture and the long-term implications that would be triggered by any action. He explained to Barry and Fish that closing one PMC would default the carefully designed national network of critically located Centers. His alternate approach was basically to hunker down, cut spending by eliminating all non-essential items, and seek additional funds. Bob laid out how this could be accomplished for the current fiscal year. While increased funds the following year was not in Bob's control, it was a possibility. If that failed, they would cross that bridge later. Table 6.5 shows the funds allocated to SCS for PMC operations, but does not include non-recurring funds Bob was able to secure from the Environment Protection Agency and the newly formed office of Surface Mining. Fortunately, things worked out well without closing any PMCs.

Table 6.5 Funding 1974 - 1984

FY	Appropriation	% change prior year	Offset or Ear-Mark	% of Total to Allocate
1974	$1,645,000	4.32	$36,000	98
1975	$2,461,000	49.6	$36,200	99
1976	$2,422,000	-1.58	$38,000	98
1977	$2,725,000	12.51	$21,600	99
1978	$3,047,236	11.83	$36,000	99
1979	$2,600,000	-14.68	$292,000	89
1980	$3,398,000	30.69	$130,000	96
1981	$2,933,000	-13.68	$297,000	90
1982	$3,486,000	18.85	$386,000	89
1983	$3,781,000	8.46	$182,000	95
1984	$3,895,000	3.02	$400,000	90

Funding is always a critical aspect of operating the Plant Materials Program. The program manager can control it to a limited extent by tweaking allocations up or down. Because the PMC budget is one of the smallest in SCS, tiny compared to some, positive relationships with all budget management people can pay big dividends. MacLauchlan instinctively knew this and quickly won their favor. Details of those kinds of benefits never come to the surface, but over time the sugar catches the fly. It served MacLauchlan well and any of his followers who understood its value.

<u>Readjusting Prior Accomplishments</u>

Recall the uniform numbering accession system spear-headed by Bill Steiner? When the new procedure was implemented in 1974 of ARS assigning a plant introduction number to each new accession, it quickly overwhelmed their office, leading to a major backlog of accessions at PMCs without a number. MacLauchlan guided this bottle neck to a successful conclusion by modifying policy to assign each accession a national temporary PI number, and only those accessions identified as having some superior conservation potential were assigned a permanent PI number.

The details are lost, but the memory is clear of a problem experienced by a PMC Manager in the late 1970s. He was dealing with a backlog of accessions at his PMC. From the employees point of view all he needed to know was that he had a problem and MacLauchlan was working on it. After months of waiting for a solution the employee grew wearisome, causing him to write MacLauchlan in which he laid out his burden. He opened by coming right to the point "You don't know the trouble you have caused me." As usual, MacLauchlan took the letter in stride.

<u>Expanding Need for Plants and Associated Technology</u>

The recognized need for new plant materials technology continued as a natural process of the Plant Materials Program. Some may have seemed futuristic in the mid-1960s and early 1970s, but new needs were being identified.[389]

- revegetation of land impacted by wildfires;

- controlling introduced weeds and restoring areas where weeds had invaded;

- reducing erosion from cropland by selecting cover crops and developing systems for their use to provide winter cover on low residue crops;

- increased plant diversity;

- improving and protecting the quality of surface and groundwater by developing filter strips, bio-terraces, and developing artificial wetlands for removing pollutants from waste water;

- creating, restoring, or managing wetlands;

- protecting upland riparian areas;

- saline soil reclamation;

- xerlscape plantings;

- developing plants and systems for their use that support low input, sustainable agriculture, and

- accelerating commercial production of previously released conservation plants in high demand.

The negative aspects of surface mining was gaining momentum, leading to the USDA Forest Service to initiate the Surface Environment and Mining (SEAM) program with the objectives of developing and applying technology to help maintain surface values and a quality environment while helping meet the Nation's mineral requirements.[390] A part of this program included revegetation. With the relatively new PMC in Eastern Kentucky and the Bridger PMC focusing on this critical need, MacLauchlan was able to secure about $100,000 annually from SEAM to support this work. This helped smooth out the erratic nature of appropriated funds in the 1970s and early 1980s.

Energy and the impact of mining increased to the point of arousing interest in establishing a new PMC in the central Great Basin region. The primary motivation came from a national interest in large deposits of oil-bearing shale in the area. This interest increased dramatically in the early 1970s with the decrease in oil available from foreign sources. The economic recovery of that oil and the need for re-vegetating the disturbed sites were the primary factors leading to the establishment of the Environmental Plant Center in Meeker, CO in 1975. Through the joint efforts of federal and state agencies, oil-related interest and conservation organizations, grants and other funds became available for two soil conservation districts to purchase land and construct facilities for the Center's operation. Unfortunately, the new center was not authorized by Congress, thus there was no new money for the PMC line item in the SCS budget. The need and local support for the center grew so fast the SCS leadership did not take the time to adequately pursue Meeker's funding through the appropriation process. The center has had continuing, though modest, financial support from SCS. SCS furnished a manager until 1995. Since then it has been managed by the White River and Douglas Creek Soil Conservation Districts, who depend on multiple funding sources.

In 1975, the Americus PMC returned to SCS operations. As had happened with other marriages cooked up in the 1954-55 period, the Americus one was also unsatisfactory. Bob MacLauchlan arranged for himself, the director of his division, Vic Barry, and the SCS state conservationist of Georgia to meet with the dean and others of the University of Georgia Agricultural Experiment Station to explore a separation. There was harmonious agreement. The Americus manager, John Powell, again changed employers by returning to SCS. This left only the Los Lunas, NM as a non-SCS operated center.

In 1978, James Anderson, the University of New Mexico Agriculture Experiment Station manager of the Los Lunas PMC retired. He had been a productive manager since 1955. While the cooperative agreement with the University was well run and both felt the agreement should continue, but a switch to an SCS manager was desirable. The first SCS manager was Wendall Oaks, recently transferred from the Big Flats Center. He accelerated the acquiring of reimbursable funds that enhance the productivity of the Center.

In the early 1980s, two new ad hoc PMCs were established in underserved parts of Texas. This is to say, they became established through a pooling of non-PMC funds with SCS Conservation Technical Assistance contributing the lion's share, with the balance coming from local sources. Neither PMC was congressionally authorized, thus no new funding was given to the PMC appropriation. The Kika de la Garza Center in Kingsville, TX was established in 1981 through the efforts of the Caesar Kleberg Wildlife Research Institute, the South Texas Association of Soil and Water Conservation Districts, and the Soil Conservation Service. James D. Ledbetter was the first manager. The East Texas Center opened at Nacogdoches in 1982, resulting from a cooperative agreement between Stephen Austin University, Deep East Texas and Northeast Texas Associations of Soil and Water Conservation Districts, SCS, the U.S. Forest Service, and a local Resource Conservation & Development Council. James Stevens was the first and third manager. Their funding was problematic for many years, but in recent years they share equally from the PMC appropriations.

Early in his tenure as National PM Specialist, MacLauchlan recognized another critical need and did something about it. Observational nurseries and PMCs had been releasing plants since 1939 but there was no record of how well they were being received and utilized. PMCs and field PM Specialists were aware of commercial production in their service area and MacLauchlan felt a need to capture this data. Its future use may not have been clear to him at that time, but knowing the magnitude of the utilization of new cultivars seemed important. This thought process led to a policy of a collecting and storing the annual amount of commercial production of each PMC release, stored in a database called the Plant Materials Annual Activities and Accomplishments. The first collection year was 1977. Data collection continued aggressively, with the exception of 1994, until the 2006 – 2007 periods when it was deemphasized. It has served the Program well.

"Phased and Orderly Transfer to Non-Federal Operations"

As outlined in Chapter 9, Key Leaders, Bob faced his biggest challenge in the 1978-1981 periods. It started during a routine congressional SCS budget hearing when a congressman asked SCS Chief Mel

Davis to list ways SCS could cut their budget. He said, "One thing we could do is transfer all plant material centers to non-federal entities. Just last week I was at the plant materials center in Colorado which is run by two soil conservation districts, with just one SCS employee." As a result, the USDA fiscal year 1980 budget directed SCS to develop a plan for the "… phased and orderly transfer" of PMCs to non-federal operations.

For the next three years, Bob ate, slept, agonized and acted on this crisis. By 1982 it was a dead issue. More details are provided in Chapter 9, Key Leaders.

Automation and the Bellingham Affair

The potential of computer automation made its appearance on the national scene in the early 1980s. National Plant Materials Program leader MacLauchlan was anxious to keep pace with any innovation that would benefit productivity. Fortunately for him and the discipline, young Wendall Oaks, the manager of the Los Lunas PMC, emerged as a Plant Materials leader in automation. He was anxious to see PMCs be the first discipline to have a uniform standard computer operating system.

As automation progressed, MacLauchlan could see a train coming; the need for funds with which to buy computers for each PMC. There were no surplus funds, but Oaks had to be dealt with. About that time, something wonderful happened. When the SCS nurseries closed, the properties of many were turned over to state agencies. In some cases, SCS continued to own the land. Such was the case with the nursery in Bellingham, WA. Since 1954, the Washington State Department of Agriculture had been using the land as a state nursery, and providing plants to local soil and water conservation districts. Because of its close proximity to the city there was great pressure to sell the land. Negotiations took place between the interested parties and a price was resolved. Since the only remaining vestige of the nurseries was the Plant Materials Program John Fish, Director of the Budget and Finance Division, led MacLauchlan to believe the funds would belong to them. The agreed to price was about $450,000. The cost of the required HP-250 computers was about $450,000.

Bob arranged for a meeting with the appropriate people to gain permission to purchase the computers with the Bellingham windfall. On his way to the meeting, he encountered Deputy Chief of Technology, Paul Howard, who was to attend the meeting. As they walked along Howard told Bob that since Wendall Oaks would be there and "if you have anything else you need to do, you need not attend." Of course Bob had lots of other things to do but he was the program manager and deadly interested in the fate of the Bellingham money. However, taking the hint from his boss's supervisor he stayed away. With Oaks present, he knew how it would turn out, and sure enough, the Bellingham funds were approved and the computers were purchased.

But that was not the end of the Bellingham story. The person who threw the red flag was Lynn Brown, State Conservationist in Washington. He was most displeased about the outcome. His logic was different than Bob's and the Budget and Finance Division. He argued that the money belonged to the State Department of Agriculture in Washington, the lessee of the land, who had been using the property for good conservation purposes, and had been maintaining it for more than twenty years. No doubt, Brown had led the soil conservation district association to expect some funds would be coming their way from the land sale and was working hard to save face. Unfortunately, with a situation like this, the PMC Program had zero political clout compared to the state soil and water conservation districts association. Attitudes changed. The money managers and Department attorneys concluded they had been hasty in awarding MacLauchlan the funds. However, each PMC had a computer with a plant materials software package. By the time this decision was finalized, MacLauchlan had decided to retire, leaving any resolution to his replacement.

From 1935 until 1954 SCS administration was from Regional Offices, which were closed in 1954, replaced by a loose configuration of Washington-Field Technicians serving regional areas. In 1965 Regional Technical Service Centers were established. Their director was a Field Representative of the

Chief, and technicians become specialists. On February 12, 1982 they were renamed National Technical Centers (NTC). The directors were reduced in stature and reported to the assistant chief for the region. The regional PM Specialist's leverage had been returned to that of the Washington-Field PM Specialists. To make matters worse, the specialists no longer reported to the director but to a section middleman. In reality, things didn't change much for the specialists in the positions who had good working relations with the states, but over time the 1954-65 events repeated themselves, and in 1995 the NTCs were abolished. The need for regional technical excellence was gone. One could argue that the leverage available to Regional Technical Service Centers specialists was so diminished by the National Technical Center structure, and their value had become invisible, why not close them.

Conservation Reserve Program makes SCS releases shine

The Food Security Act of 1985,[391] also known as the 1985 U.S. Farm Bill, was a five year omnibus farm bill, which made changes in a variety of USDA programs. Several enduring conservation programs were created, including the Conservation Reserve Program (CRP). It is a cost-share and rental payment program under the USDA. Technical assistance for CRP is provided by the U.S. Forest Service and the NRCS. The CRP encourages farmers to convert highly erodible cropland or other environmentally sensitive acreage to vegetative cover, such as cultivated or native grasses and grasslands, wildlife food and shelter plantings, windbreak and shade trees, and the like. CRP enrollment in 1985 was 1.9 million acres, increasing to thirty-six million by 1993.[392] By 2010 there were 31.3 million acres still enrolled.

CRP shined two bright lights on the Plant Materials Program. First was the good fortune that such a program of developing conservation plants existed. It almost seemed like the program was waiting until the PMCs had ample plants to re-vegetate any erodible land that might be enrolled. The second was the production explosion of PMC releases by commercial businesses. The following table provides a clue of how quickly producers and cultivars came together to meet the need. It shows the commercial production by three year periods for five widely used grasses in the central and southern Cornbelt and Great Plains regions. The data was provided from SCS records.

The commercial production of these five plants increased 5.2 times between the 1982-1984 periods and the 1985-1987 periods. See Table 6.6.

During the 1974 - 1984 periods nineteen PMCs participated in 102 releases. The vast majority were released in cooperation with others. Recall that Douglas worried about many PMCs failing to work cooperatively with other agencies. He would be pleased in the progress that had been made on this issue, not only by himself but by Steiner and MacLauchlan.

Table 6.6 CRP impact on the increased production of SCS Releases

A PMC Released Grass	Pounds of Seed			
	82-84	85-87	88-90	91-93
Cave-In-Rock switchgrass	168,300	725,000	495,105	457,750
El Reno sideoats grama	270,500	529,950	1,103,019	252,896
Blackwell switchgrass	181,700	578,180	1,170,225	454,300
Luna pubescent wheatgrass	1,104,905	7,819,102	3,211,820	883,340
Arriba sideoats grama	299,680	899,600	898,616	418,395
Totals	2,025,085	10,551,832	6,878,785	2,466,681

There were two informal, six germplasm and ninety-six cultivars; forty-one were introduced plants, one was a naturalized plant, and sixty were native plants. Types were as follows: one grass-like, fifty-one grasses; eight non-leguminous forbs, nine herbaceous legumes, twenty-six shrubs and seven trees.[393] The list included four native grasses whose commercial production from their release date through 2005 exceeded two million pounds each, with 'Secar' Snake River wheatgrass on top with 4.5 million. The new grass, forb and legume cultivars produced thirty-eight million pounds of seed from their release through 2005, or enough to reestablish vegetation on 3.8 million acres at the waste rate of ten pounds per acre. This time period also featured the release of several woody and herbaceous plants reproduced vegetatively for commercial use. Over twenty-eight million plants of 'Tropic Lalo', released by the Hawaii PMC, were produced, and Big Flats, NY finally released in 1975 the vegetative star of the 1949 Winooski River, Vermont project, 'Streamco' purple osier willow. All of this was going on while Bob MacLauchlan was fighting the Washington D.C. battles of the budget and the PMC's transfer to non-federal operations.

Being sure the technology developed by the Plant Materials Program reaches the end user is a constant challenge. In the 1970s and 1980s, publishing documents in journals, at conferences and as stand-alone publications was one important way. Appendix 2 lists about 45 publications by participating Plant Materials Programs authors for the time period from 1974 – 1984. Highlights among the group include the following. The publication by Joseph Ruffner was published five years after his retirement, while he continued as a volunteer.

Jacobson, E. T., D A. Tober, R. J. Haas, and D. C. Darris. 1986. The performance of selected cultivars of warm season grasses in the northern prairie and plains states. In Clambey, G. K and R. H. Pemble (ed.) The Prairie: past, present and future. Proceedings 9th North American Prairie Conference, July 29-Aug. 1, 1984, Moorhead, MN. Tri-College Univ. Cent. For Environ. Studies, ND State Univ. Fargo, ND. p. 215-221.

Ruffner, Joseph D. 1978. Plant Performance on Surface Coal Mine Spoil in the Eastern United States. USDA, SCS; SCS-TOP-155. Washington, D.C.

Sharp, W. C., C. R. Belcher, and J. A. Oyler. 1980. Vegetation for Tidal Stabilization in the Mid-Atlantic States. Broomall, PA, 19 pp. USDA-SCS, Broomall, PA, p. 17

Thornburg, Ashley A. 1976. Plant materials for use on surface-mined lands in arid and semiarid regions. U.S. Environmental Protection Agency, Washington D.C.

Regional Personnel

MacLauchlan provided strong national leadership, but he also depended on the regional plant materials specialists, as well as an assistant in his office from 1978 through 1983. Gilbert Lovell moved from manager of the National PMC to become MacLauchlan's assistant in 1978. Gil accepted a position with the Agriculture Research Service in 1980 and was replaced by Wayne Everett.

Wayne performed yeoman service as the assistant to MacLauchlan until mid-1982, when Assistant Chief Norman Berg decreed that Ecological Science specialists did not need an assistant, with the exception of agronomy, and Wayne was transferred to the National Office Program Evaluation Staff. His first assignment, strange as it might seem, was to evaluate the Plant Materials Program. His study showed, among other things, that some states with PMCs were off-setting much more of the PMC funds allocated to that state for administrative expenses than other states. It further showed the state offices had little or no guidance on this. Subsequent guidance was prepared to the effect that a state could off-set no more that than the percentage the PMC funds were to their total conservation operations budget. Little else came from the Plant Materials Program evaluation, and in 1984 Everett moved to the South Regional PMS position in Fort Worth, TX replacing the retiring Arnold Davis.

The regional positions were mostly stable during MacLauchlan's tenure in the Northeast and South but the West and Midwest were ever changing. In the West, there were five personnel changes from 1974 through 1984, four of the five served briefly in 1980, including Everett. The ever-mobile Kenneth Blan served as a Field PM Specialist in Mississippi and in the West and Midwest regional offices as PM Specialist within a four-year period. The Midwest position was vacant for nearly four years with regional specialists in the Northeast and South filling them. Details of these personnel movements can be seen in Appendix 6- Field, Regional and National Plant Materials Specialists.

Summary

The years Robert S. MacLauchlan served as program manager for the Plant Materials Program were marked by complete dedication and a desire to see the Program better off than when he started. In this he truly succeeded. From his very first days to his last, all persons that interacted with him became his supporter, as a result of his enthusiasm and commitment. The Key People chapter covers some accomplishments in greater detail.

THE FIRST NON-NURSERY PLANT MATERIALS PROGRAM LEADER

By April 1, 1985, a selection had been made for replacing Robert MacLauchlan.[394] Curtis Sharp was the choice, the Regional PM Specialist from the Northeast. Curtis had touched all the basics, starting in 1957 at the Big Flats PMC as an advisor to the Alfred Agricultural and Technical institute, which operated the Center until 1960, then served as manager until 1965. He then replaced the retiring Field PM Specialist Ernest McPherron, serving NY, PA and New England. That tour lasted about three months and he moved to the PM Specialist position for the Mid-Atlantic States, working out of the new Cape May, NJ PMC. After five years, he moved to Pleasanton, California as the PM Specialist in time for the PMC to re-locate to Lockeford three years later. A year after that, he replaced the retiring Joseph Ruffner as Regional PM Specialist in Upper Darby, PA. Sharp might be described as a plant materials activist. This is neither good nor bad, depending on what actions result from the activism. Before settling in, he pondered, 'What parts of the Program might best benefit from some fine tuning'.

As Dr. H. H. Bennett had said about the Division of Nurseries in 1954, when Sharp went to Washington in April 1985, he inherited a well-oiled Plant Materials Program. He had worked closely with MacLauchlan during his time as Regional PM Specialist in the Northeast. He knew MacLauchlan had left his successor a program with strong agency support and only a couple of small simmering fires. Additionally, Bob was always available for advice and council whenever Curtis needed it.

Following MacLauchlan as Program Leader had several national office advantages. Excellent working relationships with the Budget and Finance Office, Administrative Services, and International Divisions were examples. Another major asset to Sharp was the support he received from the Ecological Science Division Directors, Dr. Thomas Shiflet, who soon relocated after Sharp's arrival, and James B. Newman who was the director from 1985 until 1994. As a range conservationist, Newman understood the value of vegetation in conservation programs and supported the Plant Materials Program fully.

In 1985, there were twenty-four Centers, varying as always in capability and productivity. Two more were added within the next four years, both authorized by Congress, with funding. The first, in 1987, was the Booneville PMC in Western Arkansas. The driving force behind the congressional approval came from Arkansas Senator Dale Bumpers.[395] In addition to the PMC, Senator Bumpers was instrumental in co-locating units of the USDA, Agriculture Research Service and the Arkansas Cooperative Extension Service in Boonville, now called the Dale Bumpers Small Farm Research Center. The Golden Meadow, LA PMC opened in 1989, also authorized by Congress.[396] The conservation need motivating its establishment was the extensive erosion of tidal marshes in the western Gulf of Mexico. The success enjoyed by the Cape May, NJ PMC in this area provided encouragement. Because of the close relationship between State Conservationist, Horace Austin, and the U.S. Senators from Louisiana, plus support from Sharp, and no resistance from more senior people in SCS headquarters, the PMC became a reality.

Settling in to the Real World

While Bob MacLauchlan left a clean house with lots of positive happenings, there was one little speck of dirt under the Northwest corner of the rug. Recall the selling of the old Bellingham, WA nursery site and that Bob bought computers with the money? Washington State Conservationist Lynn

Brown remained adamant that the funds belonged to the Washington State Department of Agriculture. Attitudes changed and the money managers concluded he was the rightful owner of the money that had already been spent.

Soon after Sharp arrived in Washington, Brown raised the subject. Sharp realized future relations with the Pullman PMC were going to be non-existent until the standoff with Brown was resolved. The program at Pullman had languished since 1976, when the Plant Materials Program's most capable scientist at that time, John Schwendiman, retired. Sharp was anxious to see a turn around, but for that to happen, input from Lynn Brown was essential.

There was no slam-dunk solution to the $450,000 money problem. The PMC National Headquarters reserve was low. The tension broke when Sharp found $200,000 from other SCS sources, Brown agreed to a reduction of the full $450,000, and the PMC reserve paid the balance. While relations with Brown improved quickly, real changes at Pullman had to wait until the 1990s. In the end, the PMCs did get twenty computers at a good price.

Sharp soon got a bitter taste of being the new kid on the block. The National SCS office was always looking for positions that could be relocated elsewhere to reduce the appearance of being bloated. While Sharp was traveling, a messenger from the SCS Chief came around to the Plant Science Division. The Assistant Division Director thought the idea of assigning the supervision of the National PMC to the state conservationist in Maryland was okay and the deal was done.

Mistakenly assuming the whole affair was instigated by the brand new Maryland State Conservationist, Pearlie Reed, Sharp requested and was given an appointment with him. Pearlie said Sharp entered his office with fire in his eyes, but to no avail, the situation arose and was resolved closer to home, at the National Headquarters. In some ways the outcome could be viewed as positive. As long as Pearly was the State Conservationist in Maryland, it was possible to get things done at the National PMC that would have been more difficult in headquarters. Pearlie was positive about making the marriage work. Unfortunately this did not last very long.

One event that happened during the period when Reed was the state conservationist was seen by Sharp as a negative for the Plant Materials Program. Pearlie apparently had a high opinion of PMC manager James Briggs, relative to his SCS future and encouraged him to apply for a Resource Conservation & Development coordinator position in Maine. It was that or Reed had another person he wanted in the PMC manager's position. Either way Jim did apply and moved to Maine in 1989. He was less than enamored with his new position and soon applied for the PM Specialist position in Arizona. The selecting officer was State Resource Conservationist, Don Gohmert, an influential supporter of the Plant Materials Program for years to come. Jim was selected and served in that position from 1990 until 1996, then was promoted to Arizona State Resource Conservationist – Assistant State Conservationist, and later served as a regional PM Specialist in the West. His loss from Beltsville was acute, and the PMC remained awash until Scott Peterson became manager in 1991. Pearlie was soon promoted to be a state conservationist in California. His replacement in Maryland fell on hard times, was removed from the Service for a while, and replaced by Robert Klumpe.

Other activities that significantly impacted two PMCs were attempts to relocate them. The Tucson, AZ PMC only had forty-six acres, which was barely enough for it to function. The city of Tucson had grown around it, eliminating any potential for expanding at that location. The SCS leadership in Arizona decided to explore selling the downtown site and moving out into the country, much as the California PMC had done. Years passed. The PMC was at a standstill. At last, a new site and a buyer for the existing one was found. The appointed time for the closing of transactions was set; but the buyer did not show. Frustration won out, the relocation was abandoned and the existing site was renovated, which led to its being placed on the Register of Historical Places in 1996.

The other attempt to relocate a PMC was led by Sharp, but didn't start until 1991. Recall comments about the location of the Quicksand, KY PMC, and the scolding W. W. Steiner received for criticizing it. Maybe Steiner deserved the scolding but he was correct regarding the location. The potential opportunity to relocate Quicksand came when the Director of the ARS Appalachian Soil and Water Conservation Research Laboratory in Beckley, WV expressed an interest in closer working relationships with Quicksand. He supported a co-location, and so did Sharp. By late 1993, all parties concerned agreed. This milestone coincided with Sharp's retirement. The relocation took place, but the PMC found another site some thirty miles from the ARS Lab. Ironically, the new site was the one Steiner had identified as most desirable in 1967. It is on the grounds of the Federal Bureau of Prisons at Alderson, WV. While the new site is far superior to Quicksand, the synergy of co-location with ARS was lost.

Fortunately, there were virtually no policy issues external to SCS that required excessive attention during the late 1980s or early 1990s similar to those MacLauchlan had to deal with. The increasing awareness of environmental concerns about how the Federal government conducted their activities had limited program impacts because most parts of the Plant Materials Program were fully in compliance with new requirements. Actually, there were funds available to address issues needing to be corrected, like underground storage tanks. In stark contrast to SCS, the Environmental Protection Agency had deep pockets. One environmental nightmare that quickly blew away, after experiencing stiff resistance, was for PMCs to address pending fugitive dust regulations.

One major addition to the internal policy was the creation of a National Plant Materials Advisory Committee. This was a natural follow-up of the State Conservationist Advisory Committee for each PMC, created years earlier. It was created to provide guidance to the National PMC as well as to the national program. It consisted of five state conservationists, one from each of the four NTC service areas, the state conservationist from Maryland, who chaired the meetings, and representatives from the National Association of Conservation Districts and the Agricultural Research Service. The logic for the Maryland state conservationist being the chairperson stemmed from their supervision of the National PMC. This committee, which first met in 1991, was an excellent addition, and served the National PM Program well. Robert Klumpe served as the first chairperson. After a couple years he developed aspirations of assuming full responsibility for the entire national Plant Materials Program and lobbied the entire committee to that effect. There is no evidence of any committee support for this and the idea died an appropriate death.

In the absence of needing to put out fires, Sharp, with the help of the four Regional PM Specialists began to turn his attention what he felt were Program priorities. The individuals in the regional positions were well qualified, each with long experience as center managers and/or Field PM Specialists. In the Northeast, David Lorenz had work experiences in North Dakota and as manager of the Knox City, Texas PMC. Later, he was the Field PM Specialist in Pennsylvania. Wayne Everett, who served the South region, had experience at the Beltsville PMC on two occasions, served as the Kentucky PM Specialist, a brief stint as the West Regional PM Specialist, and as assistant National PM Specialist for three years. Erling Jacobson started as an agronomist at the Elsberry, MO PMC, was an outstanding manager at the Manhattan PMC, and spent nine years as the Field PM Specialist in North Dakota.

The forth regional specialist was Jack Carlson, who filled the revolving chair in the West. He started at the Lockeford PMC in California in 1973, became the PMC manager at the Big Flats, NY, Field PM Specialist in Spokane, WA and regional PM Specialist in just seven years. He had the intellect, personality and commitment to have become the regional plant materials leader as exemplified by Hafenrichter. But it wasn't to be; the 1953-54 reorganization had seen to that. Regardless of their technical knowledge they played second or third fiddle to line authority and politics.

An excellent example of this is an experience in which Carlson participated while in Portland. Southern Oregon farmers complained when they had to seed perennial grasses on their Conservation Reserve Plantings land in order to receive payment, while farmers in Siskiyou County, California, just across the state line, could seed or allow annual cereal rye to volunteer. The cost of seeding perennial grasses exceeded the cost of the cereal rye establishment by a substantial amount. Carlson was asked to provided Oregon and California documentation outlining the most desirable planting specifications for long term cover. This he did, but in the end Conservation Reserve Plantings in Oregon were planted with perennial grasses, and in Siskiyou County, California they were either planted with or allowed to volunteer to cereal rye. Technically he was correct, but under the circumstances, politically unwise. Such was the position of the regional plant specialist.

Figure 6.4 Jack Carlson

Jack left the discipline in 1992 to enter the expanding world of information technology, retiring in 2008 from the Senior Executive Service as the NRCS Chief Information Officer. In 1993 he was awarded the Distinguished Service Award, USDA's highest, for his Plant Materials work.

Plant Materials Awards

Everybody likes an award. Generally, the Plant Materials Program employees get their fair share, but there is something special about an award within your peer group. In 1986, an internal awards program was initiated. Regional Specialists submitted candidates annually in six categories along with their justification. Winners were selected, and to the extent possible, a joint ceremony was held to present the awards. The categories were

- Plant Materials Center of the Year

- Plant Materials Specialist of the Year

- Plant Materials Center Employee of the Year

- Meritorious Award Newcomer of the Year

- Special Plant Materials Service Award

The award categories were tweaked somewhat in later years, but continue today.

In addition to these awards, several plant materials employees have received USDA Distinguished Service and Superior Service awards. The winners of these and the winners of internal Plant Materials Program awards are included at the end of Chapter 9, following the Key Leaders—Productive Scientists, Productive Teams, and Other Major Contributors.

Expanded Plant Data Management

During his years at the SCS Regional office, Sharp had made extensive use of the USDA, SCS publication National List of Scientific Plant Names, which was the brain child of Dr. Thomas N. Shiflet, a range conservationist who rose to become Director of the Plant Science Division. This publication standardized the scientific name usage in SCS, and created a symbol that could be used as a shorthand for the scientific name. The publication also included some species attributes. In the mid-1980s, it existed only as a printed copy. Shiflet had a strong interest in seeing it automated, so he gave the task to the range conservation staff at the South National Technical Center in 1985. When Sharp moved to Washington it was still being developed there. He soon learned it had been renamed the Fort Worth Plant List, and little or no progress had been undertaken to automate it. With the automation of the entire Plant Materials Program well underway, the desirability of automating NLSPN became urgent. With the agreement and support of James Newman, the new director of the Ecological Science Division, responsibility for the management of NLSPN was moved to the Plant Materials Program and housed at the National PMC. Sharp asked Pearlie Reed for a position to be established there to lead the task of NLSPN automation. Pearlie agreed and Dr. Scott Peterson, brand new to SCS, was employed in 1987. Soon the Fort Worth Plant List was renamed by Scott and James Briggs, <u>Plant List of Attributes, Names, Taxonomy, and Symbols</u>, or PLANTS.

As PLANTS gained momentum and creditability within Federal agencies, academia and the general public, Sharp explored establishing a national plant data facility where all SCS disciplines, other agencies and the public using plant data could feed and retrieve what they needed. By 1993, secure funding and a facility location was in place and the agency established the National Plant Data Center (NPDC) under the Ecological Sciences Division at Southern University, Baton Rouge, LA. Scott Peterson was their first director. In 2009, the NPDC moved to the NRCS East National Technology Support Center in Greensboro, NC (new location of a regional office). For more detail on the evolution of PLANTS and the NPDC, which became one of the USDA's most widely used databases; see Chapter 11 – Great Innovations and Top Performing Cultivars.

Plant Materials Program Budget

The arc of funds appropriated by Congress for PMC operations has gradually been higher since 1955, with increases slightly above the rate of inflation. In 1956, the congressional allocation was $331,580 for twelve PMCs, or $27,632 per PMC. In 1990, there were twenty-six PMCs. Assuming all twenty-six were funded equally in 1989 with the $4.66 million available for allocation; each would have received $179,230. This included some funding going to the three PMCs for which no increase was made to the CO-46 allocation. One dollar in 1955 was worth $4.63 in 1989, or the 1955 allocation would be equal to $127,936 in 1989, using a Consumer Inflation Index Calculator[397], or $706 more than in 1955. In real dollars the PMC budget was increasing at a rate higher than inflation. Unfortunately the arc of deteriorating PMC facilities plus increasing demands on PMCs had greatly exceeded any budget adjustments. Meeting the need was consuming the budget, while personnel training, facilities, equipment and investment in new technology were being ignored. The most obvious, although not the most important, was the deteriorating condition of the physical plant and equipment. By the late 1980s, this problem was at the breaking point; the decision had to be made to do less work, close some PMCs or find more money.

Pushing a budget increase thru the vast USDA bureaucracy for a minuscule program like the PMCs was unlikely but Sharp thought it was worth an all-out try. He had two things on his side; the good will MacLauchlan had left and Assistant Chief Mack Gray, an economist and close personal friend and advisor to SCS Chief Wilson Scalings.[398] Gray made a name for himself as an economist who demanded that all projects be subject to a rigorous economic analysis.[399] Any proposed budget increase would have to go through Gray for sure. Sharp's approach was to do just what Gray liked; run an asset depreciation and maintenance schedule on every piece of equipment and every building at all PMCs. The task was daunting and the results were shameful. It showed that $1.89 million for ten years would be required for equipment and buildings to meet Federal standards.

Due to the lag in budget preparation and congressional enactment, the $1.89 million increase first appeared in the fiscal year 1990 allocation. Fortunately, the increase remained a part of the PMC budget past the estimated ten years.

The funds for the period covering 1985 through 1993 are shown in Table 6.7. The 'Offset or Earmarked' column shows funds withheld for the expenses incurred by the PMC program at the National Headquarters, which ran about five percent.

Table 6.7 PMC Budget from 1985 – 1993

FY	Appropriation	% change from prior year	Offset or Earmark	% of Total to Allocate
1985	$3,959,000	1.64	$409,000	90
1986	$4,089,000	3.28	$230,300	94
1987	$4,553,000	11.35	$184,000	96
1988	$4,856,000	6.65	$225,000	95
1989	$4,881,000	0.52	$218,000	96
1990	$6,884,000	41.03	$400,000	94
1991	$7,873,000	14.37	$0	100
1992	$8,055,990	2.32	$432,000	94
1993	$8,064,000	0.1	$505,500	94

Increasing Technical Capabilities

The success of most organizations, public or private, depends on the same two critical factors, adequate resources and qualified, enthusiastic people. The Plant Materials Program was no different. As discussed in Chapter 5, the difficulty of filling plant materials positions remained problematic. The variations in individual PMC productivity were obvious. This appeared to be due in part to lack of training and motivation of the PMC staff. How could these be improved?

The additional funding allowed for building and machinery upgrades, and freed up some funds to initiate a PMC trainee effort. In addition to increasing the technical capability at PMCs, another objective was to broaden the ethnic diversity in the Program. It was reasonable to think both could best be accomplished by going out of the agency for new PMC hires.

A plan was drafted and initiated in 1988. The persons were to be recruited and paid by the Program, and then placed at PMCs with both good leadership and a successful program. Since the hiring would be done by the state where the PMC was located, the state conservationist and the National PM Specialist would be the selection committee. The leverage that allowed the Plant Materials Program to guide the recruitment objective was simple: if the state conservationist was willing to receive the extra money and an employee, then they were willing to share in the selection process.

Funds were set aside to pay five trainees the first year and adjust the number thereafter as needed. A variety of ways were used to locate desirable candidates, but the best, by far, was by advertising in the American Society of Agronomy Journal. Many excellent candidates applied. The recruits were made to understand that their training would include relocating to positions for additional training or responsibility within a two-year period.

The first trainee was Dr. Richard L. Wynia, a 1987 graduate in Agronomy from South Dakota State University. His first assignment was at the Bismarck, ND PMC. After a couple of years he moved to an assistant manager's position at the Booneville, AR PMC. Then in 1991, he came to the Manhattan, KS PMC as manager. He remains there at the conclusion of this history. The productivity of that PMC attests to his capability. This was a most desirable course of events for a new PMC employee.

Other success stories exist. Two of the three regional PM Specialist positions in 2010 were former trainees; Joel Douglas in the South and Dr. Ramona Garner in the East. Both advanced through normal channels to arrive at the regional positions. Five PMCs were being managed by trainees. One trainee, who became a wetland ecologist, has retired. This was Chris Hoag, who became a trainee and then a wetland specialist at the Aberdeen, ID PMC. Chris became 'Mr. Wetland Restoration' in the upper Great Basin States. He is one of the three Productive Scientists honored in the Key Leaders Chapter. Dr. David Dreesen, agronomist with the Los Lunas, NM staff, is one reason the Albuquerque and Los Lunas, NM PMC Team was one of two most Productive Plant Materials Teams and is also included in the Key Leaders Chapter. His desire to be a scientist is paying off for the Plant Materials Program. The Bridger, MT PMC is the other most Productive Plant Materials Team, currently managed by a former trainee, Joseph Scianna. Other trainees are making contributions at PMCs. For example, Nancy Jensen of the Bismarck PMC has authored or co-authored seventeen web-published documents and constitutes a core scientist on the PMC staff. The work force diversity of PMC staffs changed from around two percent non-white males to fourteen percent in four years.

In 1988 when the trainee program started, the intent was to have four or five employees nationally on a continuing basis. Some trainees left the program, either to take another position in SCS or for employment elsewhere. To the extent funds would allow, this continued until 1993. In 2005, a trainee effort was restarted with three new trainees, and in 2009 three more were added to the program.

There were disappointments along the way; some trainees didn't like SCS and vice versa; also, the selection process got high jacked at least once, but the successful recruits are making contributions on a continuing basis.

Another attempt to increase technical capability was to establish four or five regional labs across the country to perform limited processes currently beyond the scope of PMCs. Of course, trained personnel were required, and that was built into the trainee selection process. The concept was that each lab would have a specialty and other centers would utilize it.

The initial plan was not realized on several fronts. No doubt the lack of funding or the perceived lack was the principal stumbling block, at least after Sharp left. These labs were never completed. Finding trained personnel was a second problem. The Corvallis PMC lab was designed and equipped for tissue culture and some secondary activities. Once built, it received operational funding for only about two years.[400] A horticulturist position was on the books for two years, and then eliminated when the individual transferred. That the concept existed until 1996 is indicated by a reference to them in a Quality Improvement Plan report published that year.[401] It asks the questions, "Laboratories - What is their role as a regional/national facility? What issues, opportunities and priorities should be considered?" The QIT is discussed in more details in Chapter 7.

Centers that completed labs used them for local activities, but the initial concept did not materialize. In hindsight, the lab establishment funds might better have been spent for computers, tractors or more trainees.

Conservation Center Concept

That the SCS owned 282 acres at the Beltsville Agricultural Research Center in Maryland, within a stone's throw from the nation's capital, was the catalyst that triggered the concept of an SCS National Conservation Center. It was not a Plant Materials Program idea, but the discipline was involved since it was the reason SCS owned the land. The concept was that the property could be converted into a demonstration farm of standard conservation practices; include a large SCS visitor center and meeting facilities that would attract movers and shakers across government and the private sector. A select group of forward thinkers were assembled in the late 1980s to develop a master plan. For a brief period in 1989, Paula Jones was brought to the Center by Pearlie Reed to serve as Coordinator. Of course, such a facility associated with the National PMC would be a major attribute towards reversing the best kept secret opinion. Over the months and years maps were made, concepts debated and master plans prepared. As the concepts became more grandiose, the least discussed ingredient was money, which was ignored, except near the end of each meeting when one of the heavyweights would ask Sharp, "The Plant Materials Program can contribute a couple hundred thousand dollars to get the show started, right?" Well, Sharp thought, which PMC will have to be closed? He hemmed and hawed and made no commitment: The handwriting was on the wall, *if this thing flies it will be with Plant Materials funds*.

At the time of Sharp's retirement the debate continued. The December, 1996 <u>Plant Science Quality Improvement Team</u> included the following Action Needed under CRITICAL ISSUE: STRUCTURE AND LINKAGES.[402]

> 5. Utilize Beltsville for something other than a National PMC and establish a Blue Ribbon Team to explore alternative options such as: a) location of a Plant Science Technology Institute, b) location to house visiting scientists (national and international), c) a training and/or demonstration center, and/or d) conventional regional plant materials focus, conferences, etc. New directions for the Beltsville center will require proper funding from sources not now available in the Plant Materials Program.

This action item has not been initiated other than to create a nice meeting room in the existing head house were the committee met. Although the potential for something in addition to the National PMC again became an issue in about 2004, it seems to be dormant at this writing.

International Activities

The relations Robert MacLauchlan had built in National Headquarters continued to pay dividends with the International Programs Division, and its director, Jerome Hammond. Jerry could easily see the win-win relationships of personnel exchanges between the Plant Materials Programs and foreign counterparts. Plant materials personnel carried a 'how to do it' story to and from each country visited, and explored the potential exchange of plants. Three notable success stories warrant a brief explanation.

The first is minor compared to the other two, but shows how receptive the 'how to do it' story can be. A two-person team went to Germany in the fall of 1984, focusing on continental shore erosion along the Baltic Sea. A German team returned to the U.S. the following year with pictures and stories of their initial evaluation plantings in the coastal area, typical in concept and design of PMC plantings.

The second is more far reaching. Jack Carlson, Regional Plant Materials Specialist in Portland, OR had developed a relationship with Grassland Research Institute, Hohhot (Huhehot), China. Climatic conditions are similar between Inner Mongolia and the Northern Great Plains. Jack was interested in the possibility of technical and plant exchange. On a visit to the Institute, the Chinese expressed an interest in one of their scientists spending a year at a Northern Great Plains PMC to study and work. In 1988 Gu Anlin came to the Bridger PMC and functioned as a member of their staff. The professional relationship with Anlin and the Grassland Institute continued long after she returned home. Carlson and the Montana plant materials team of Larry Holzworth, John Scheetz and Mark Majerus made frequent trips to China to make and evaluate plantings of grasses and legumes of mutual interest. Gu Anlin has continued her career, keeping in touch with her U.S. grassland friends, which has included revisiting the U.S. She added the following acknowledgement in her two volumes, <u>Atlas of Rangeland Plants in Northern China:</u> "Jack Carlson, Mark Majerus and Larry Holzworth, specialists with the NRCS of the USDA, assisted in the review of the species common names."[403] More recently she has provided Carlson with a similar volume; the <u>Tibetan Plant Book</u>.

In 1989, a team consisting of Wendell Hassell, the PM Specialist in Colorado, and Donald Hamer, the Cape May, NJ PMC Manager, visited Hungary, focusing on revegetation of mine land and reforestation activities. Hassell had the revegetation background, and, at that time, the Cape May PMC was the repository for the black locust clones that had been tested for superior borer tolerance. Black locust was introduced into Hungry between 1710 and 1720 and had become the most important exotic reforestation species in the country.[404] Through the continued interest and invitations of the Hungarians, Hassell returned in 1992 and 1994. He participated in organizing, as well as attending a Black Locust International Conference in 1996 in Budapest. Through his efforts NRCS also supported the conference financially. Wendell hosted Hungarian, Dr. Karoly Redei in November 1996 when he came to the U.S. to study poplar and black locust production.

National Park Service and U.S. Army Cooperative Activities

In 1987, the Yellowstone and Glacier National Parks Park developed an agreement with the Bridger, Montana PMC to produce seed of ecotypes collected on the parks. Starting in 1988, the Corvallis, Oregon, PMC successfully reproduced locally collected ecotypes for a road rehabilitation project in the Sol Duc Park. These experiences were so successful that an interagency MOU was signed in March 1989 that would allow other parks to make similar agreements with other PMCs. This is covered in greater detail in Chapter 11 -Great Innovations, and Top Performing Cultivars.

The U.S. Army Cooperative program came about through other than regular circumstances, building upon friendships with overlapping backgrounds and experiences. Through normal work activities, Billy Craft, State Resource Conservationist for SCS in Louisiana, became interested in the concept of building terraces with vegetation and shared his enthusiasm with Jackie Smith, Director of the Ecological Services at the U.S. Army base at Fort Polk, LA. Their joint work led to Smith's unit providing some funds to the Golden Meadow, LA PMC. Funding for such projects came from the U.S. Army Corps of Engineers, Construction Engineering Research Laboratory (CERL), with headquarters in Champaign, IL. Soon, Billy Craft assigned the leadership of this work with Fort Polk to Louisiana PM Specialist, Mike Materne.

Materne could see the parallel between what was happening in Louisiana with the U.S. Army and the cooperative agreement SCS had with the National Park Service. Maybe the Fort Polk – SCS arrangement in Louisiana could be used as a prototype for an U.S. Army – National Plant Materials Program agreement.

In July 1993, SCS and U.S. Army representatives initiated discussions of such a cooperative agreement, which became a reality in the spring of 1994. Former Northeast NTC regional PM Specialist, David Lorenz, filled the U.S. Army liaison position.

According to Lorenz, two additional Army liaison positions were established within SCS, one dealing with SCS Programs and another with the Soils Program. Lorenz described his principal duties as training army base biologists at individual bases and National Guard posts and recommending plant materials solutions for existing soil erosion issues. The cooperative agreement lasted six years and was terminated. The agreement did not live up to plant materials expectations.

Strategic Plan

The Plant Materials Program was required to develop a Strategic Plan in the early 1990s. The first was published in February, 1992.[405] It provided a window into what the current leadership was thinking and where the program was headed. It is provided below in abbreviated form.

The Vision Statement (1992):

A. The Plant Materials Program will:

  1. Employ highly trained, professionally qualified scientists;

  2. Create a work environment of excellence which attracts a diverse, enthusiastic and productive work force;

  3. Be customer oriented, anticipate and be responsive to emerging plant materials technology needs, and

4. Regard change as a dynamic and beneficial process.

B. Current and Future Plant Materials Technology Needs:

    1. Reduce cropland erosion and enhance production through

        a. Improved management of residue from crop and/or cover crops.

        b. Holding soil in place and trapping/tying-up nutrients and pesticides.

        c. Develop nitrogen fixing cover crops that hold chemicals and supply nitrogen.

    2. Expanded Water Quality Technology through

        a. Constructed wetlands to remove pollutants from waste water.

        b. Vegetative filter strip technology.

        c. Dryland waste utilization or grow-out plantings.

    3. Creation and Restoration of Wetlands and Riparian Areas.

    4. Reclaiming range and woodland sites infested with noxious weeds.

C. Emerging Regional and National Conservation Needs

    1. Sustainable Agriculture

        a. Crop conversion

        b. Terracing with vegetation

        c. Vegetative insectaria

        d. Improved germplasm to enhance biological nitrogen fixation.

    2. Preservation of Native Germplasm and Plant Diversity.

    3. Recovery of Threatened, Endangered, and Culturally Significant Plant Species.

    4. Bioengineering for Slope Stabilization.

    5. Conservation Plants for Urban Areas.

    6. Xeriscaping Plantings.

    7. Vegetative Management of Dredge Spoil.

Similarities to a much more broadly developed 2000 Quality Improvement Team efforts can be easily made, as well as the Reassessment of 2009.

New Releases and Publications

The PMCs addressing coastal erosion, Cape May, NJ, Brooksville, FL and Golden Meadow, LA, each contributed new and important releases. Other plants for stream erosion, high elevations sites, wetland restoration or windbreaks in Hawaii continued to broaden the base of the conservation problems that centers were addressing.

Many new releases warrant special attention. 'Niagara' big bluestem became the first SCS plant release to be sold under the Plant Protection Act provisions.[406] This Act allowed Certificates of Protection to be issued. These certificates provide legal intellectual property rights to breeders of new varieties of plants that are sexually reproduced by seed or tuber-propagation. The Act allows a restriction on the number of growers selected by the releasing agency. It is commonly used by state agricultural experiment stations and private developers of commodity crops. Growers of cultivars produced under the Act's protection will pay a royalty to the developers.

The SCS intent was to help keep new and highly valuable releases for critical but limited use available on the commercial market. Frequently, such releases may initially be produced by multiple growers, quickly exceeding market demand, resulting in no profit for any growers and the termination of the release. 'Niagara', a Northeast ecotype with a potentially limited market was a good example. The concept did not catch on for other cultivars for a variety of reasons. First, it required extra effort. Second, and the most telling, was the notion that taxpayers provided funds to PMCs to develop a critically needed conservation plant, and its availability to every interested grower should be maintained, even if the release were lost due to a lack of commercial production.

Ho'olehua, HI released 'Tropic Coral' tall erythrina for wind break use in 1985. Growers produced over seven million plants by 2005. For streambank and riparian area protection, the Corvallis, OR PMC released five and the Pullman, WA PMC four native willows, and the Big Flats, NY PMC released 'Ruby' red osier dogwood. By 2005, 4.7 million of these riparian plants were in use. The Americus, GA PMC released six new plants including two highly successful wetland plants. One is for coastal areas, 'Flageo' marshhay cordgrass, and the other for freshwater communities, 'Restorer' giant bullrush.

Americus and Big Flats added plants specifically for reducing cropland erosion, and the Golden Meadow PMC in Louisiana released its first cultivar to celebrate its opening, called 'Vermillion' smooth cordgrass. Three major native western grasses were released; 'Prior' slender wheatgrass and 'Trailhead' basin wildrye by the Bridger, MT PMC and 'Goldar' bluebunch wheatgrass by Aberdeen. 'Goldar', released in 1989, is a selection from a native plant collection made in Asotin County, Washington in 1934. The collection site was on a ponderosa pine-grassland plant community at an elevation of about 4,000 feet. Fifty-five years in the making, over two million pounds of 'Goldar' seed were produced commercially from 1990 through 2005.

Figure 6.5 'Vermillion' smooth cordgrass

Here and in other chapters, technical publications produced by the Program are highlighted, along with a good smattering of the popular ones, but they haven't been enough to quiet the critics. In an effort to attack the best kept secret shortcoming, the National PMC was allocated funds to employ a public information specialist to work exclusively with the Plant Materials Program. This, as contrasted to the PMC trainee program, did not have the opportunity of a two- or three-year training program. The desire and expectations were for instant success, but that didn't happen, and the next attempt with a public information specialist had to wait a few years.

A Shift in Policy

In the early 1990s, the SCS, the Agriculture Research Service and the U.S. Forest Service (USFS), i.e., the three USDA agencies most interested in plant releases, initiated an effort to address some needed changes in their plant release policy. Sharp, as the SCS representative, initiated the effort. The primary thrust was to broaden the releasing standards to address emerging interest in the use of local native ecotypes to solve conservation problems rather than widely adapted and tested cultivars. Another important objective was to provide a certification process for selected woody plants. Evaluating multiple generations of shrubs and trees to reach the cultivar level was unrealistic. Some type of certification program for superior woody plants was warranted. This effort was completed in late 1993, and included in the revised National Plant Materials Manual which was issued in January, 1994. Chapter 10 is devoted to the purpose, impact and management of this new policy.

Summary

A National Plant Materials program meeting was held in 1992 in Louisiana. The participants are shown in Figure 6.6.

Sharp retired at the end of 1993. Summing up his tenure of nine years is no easier than for any other national leader of the program. He may have been less traditionally-oriented than his predecessors who started their career working in a SCS nursery. He definitely saw loyalty to the Plant Materials discipline as an obligation and placed emphasis on doing new things and old things better. His focus concentrated on improving the technical quality and capability of the Plant Materials Program. While the Program improved in several areas, his pre-varietal release policy remained problematic. In the absence of science-based conservation plant releases, the need for the Plant Materials Program may come under question.

Figure 6.6 National Plant Materials Meeting in 1992 in Louisiana

Front Row: Wayne Everett standing, Bob Delzell, kneeling, Jack Carlson, Keith Salvo, Scott Peterson, Randy Mandel, Eric Scherer, Bill Fuller, Chris Hoag, Ray Cragar, unknown, Tommy Biles, Dwight Tober, Mark Majerus.

2nd Row: Mile Materne leaning over, James Wolfe, John Row, Wanda Robinson, Greg. Fenchel, Dan Lawson, Randy King, Joel Douglas, Jacy Gibbs, Harlan DeGarmo, Wil Fontenot, Laura Ray, Dave Lorenz, Gary Young, John Dickerson

3rd row: Bill Humphrey, unknown, Bruce Munda, Scott Lambert, Jimmy Henry, Gary Fine, Wendall Oaks, Curtis Sharp, James Stevens, Morris Houck, Dave Burgdorf, Mark E. Stannard , Malcolm Kirkland, Paul Salon,, Mike Owsley, Nancy Jensen, Erling Jacobson, Don Surrency, Rich Wynia. Martin van der Grinten

4th Row: Clarence Kelly, Sam Sanders, Wayne Crowder, John Scheetz, Bob Slayback, unknown, Tracy Raush-Anderson, Russ Haas, Cunningham, Larry Holzworth, Wendell Hassell, Don Hamer, Bob Glennon, Melvin Adams,, Dave Dyer, James Alderson, B. B. Billingsley, Dale Darris

140

Chapter 7: YEARS OF CHANGE 1994 – 2010

All National PM Specialists prior to the selection of Curtis Sharp had been selected by offering the position to the best qualified person, based on the judgment of the selecting officer, from a panel prepared by the national office. All had been from within the SCS and had observational nursery experience. That process changed in the late 1970s.[407] All positions became open to all interested individuals from other federal agencies. Sharp needed to apply for the position, as would his replacement.

A retiring National PM Specialist logically would have persuaded several qualified candidates to apply. There was no shortage. A technically and administratively qualifying panel might have included the following, all with broad, multiple location experience: Dave Lorenz, Wayne Everett, Jacy Gibbs and Erling Jacobson, Regional PM Specialists, James Briggs and Larry Holzworth, Field PM Specialists, and Wendell Hassell who did apply. The qualifying limitation included in the vacancy announcement may have eliminated some of these.

In early 1994, ECS Director, James B. Newman, asked Sharp to return to work temporarily to move along or wrap up three pending activities. They were the relocation of the Quicksand PMC, to solidify the agreement with Southern University, Baton Rouge, LA to house the new National Plant Data Center and to complete the cooperative agreement with the U.S. Army. During that period he learned of the pending retirement of Newman from the position of Director of the Ecological Science Division. He and the Plant Materials Program had every right to view this as a major negative event. Newman was a supporter of the Program long before he became director and continued to support Sharp while he was National PM Specialist. A change at this time created an uncertainty about who would be the selecting officer for the new National Plant Materials leader.

Newman was replaced by Peter F. Smith as acting Director of ECS in 1994. Smith had transferred from another agency to SCS, and for a period of time was Special Assistant for Strategic Natural Resource Issues in the Ecological Science Division. While both he and Sharp were Ecological Science Division members, they exchanged different points of view on the Plant Materials Program. Simply put, Smith thought the development of conservation plants should be the responsibility of private industry because most SCS plant releases proved profitable to producers and those benefiting should bear the costs. Besides, according to Smith, anybody could release a plant. Sharp disagreed, as did the USDA. Granted, private seed companies may realize huge profits from a new hybrid corn or other varieties of commodity crops that are planted on millions of acres annually. Conservation plants were not a commodity crop and there would be limited incentive for private industry to bear their development cost. Although environmentally critical, conservation plants are used on only a fraction of the acres of an annual commodity crop, and return only a fraction of the profit, yet the cost of developing the new varieties may be similar.

Sharp visited NHQ shortly after Smith became acting director. On this occasion, Smith had a panel for the new PM Specialist position, which he shared with Sharp. While disappointed that it did not contain the many highly qualified persons from the Plant Materials Program, it did contain one; Wendell Hassell. An earlier relationship between Smith and Hassell entered Sharp's mind as he viewed the list.[408]

Dr. Richard S. White, an ARS scientist from Colby, Kansas was selected and reported for duty in the late spring, 1994. He had arranged to maintain his office in Colby. He moved permanently to Washington sometime after December 1996.[409]

AGENCY NAME AND OTHER CHANGES

In 1994, the agency name was changed to Natural Resources Conservation Service (NRCS). The name change had no impact on the Plant Materials Program, but other circumstances created a difficult beginning for Dr. White. First of all, he was new to the agency with little or no knowledge of it or the Plant Materials Program. This was compounded by his not being at the National Headquarters. Managing the Plant Materials Program was a hands-on obligation. Located in an office void of any NRCS direct contact had to be a liability. Compounding this was the changing of two critical positions; his supervisor, the director of the Ecological Science Division, and the agency chief. Additionally, he must have begun to hear rumors of the closing of the four regional NTC offices soon after accepting the job. By early 1995, it appeared they would definitely be closed, thus eliminating a critical part of the national plant materials team. By the end of 1995, they were closed. All of these factors worked against the notion of Dr. White 'hitting the ground running', especially from Kansas.

Eight PMCs took the lead in releasing nine cultivars in 1994, plus cooperating with the Agricultural Research Service in releasing two more. And in 1994, the first year the pre-varietal release option was available, three were released, two by the Idaho PMC and one by the Golden Meadow, LA PMC. In 1994 the cultivar 'Rush' intermediate wheatgrass was released by the Aberdeen PMC and by 1995 it had produced 2.4 million pounds of commercial seed. Its release may have represented the beginning of the end of PMC association with the great introduced grass cultivars. Another wheatgrass, the native thickspike, was released from the Pullman, WA PMC, and named 'Schwendimar' for the late John Schwendiman. It produced a half-million pounds before it was discontinued because of contamination.

The increasing emphasis by NRCS and others on improving soil health, defined as how well soil does what we want it to do, found two friends in the new cover crops developed by the Americus, GA PMC, Auburn University and the Alabama Agricultural Experiment Stations. 'AU Early Cover' hairy vetch was selected for early development, vigor and disease resistance.

There were no informal releases in 1994. The pre-varietal releases eliminated the need for them. What could be more informal than Source Identified?

The quick utilization of the new pre-varietal release policy might suggest it was badly needed, and that the involved PMCs had plants in the evaluation process that fit well under the new policy provisions. It might also have raised a caution flag at the regional or national level of the potential abuse. Given its use over the next three years (five in 1995, fifteen in 1996 and forty-one in 1997) would have justified the caution. Unfortunately, a new National PM Specialist who had limited background in the Program and was located outside of the national headquarters, plus the closing of the regional offices at the end of 1995, had the effect of throwing caution to the wind.

By 1998 the Plant Materials Program began to have a web presence with a trickle of publications showing up on the PMC web pages, which grew rapidly over the next few years. Not surprising, by 1994 Chris Hoag, the wetland specialist from the Aberdeen PMC, had two ready and waiting.

PLANT SCIENCE QUALITY IMPROVEMENT TEAM (QIT)

In spite of these things, or maybe in part because of them, a thorough evaluation of the Plant Materials Program was launched in July, 1995, titled Plant Science Quality Improvement Team Study.[410]. It may be that a newcomer can see the shortcomings of a program much better than employees of the program. The findings of the QIT certainly suggest this. A close examination of the critical issues identified in the study does not reveal much that previous managers had not been struggling with for years. However, a new person carries no sins of past program actions or decisions. Under those circumstances, they enjoyed the freedom of correcting critical issues without self-incrimination.

While the use of Plant Science in the title and elsewhere is misleading, the sixty-five page QIT study clearly confines itself to the Plant Materials Program. No other NRCS plant science disciplines, including Range, Forestry, Biology and Agronomy are mentioned.

According to the authors, "The report provides the vision for how two critical elements of change can be best met to carry out NRCS's mission." The two elements were (1) how the program is organized and functions, and (2) how well it is integrated into agency strategic plans and operations at state, regional, and national levels. "The primary purpose of the QIT is to evaluate plant science (plant materials) activities in NRCS and make pertinent recommendations to improve program operation and quality."

The broad cross-section membership of the committee included two regional conservationists, two state conservationists, one assistant state conservationist, seven representatives from the plant materials discipline, and a resource conservationist. During the course of deliberation, sixteen critical issues were identified, each requiring multiple action items to correct, totaling ninety recommendations, each with its own time frame for completion. Additionally, eleven issues were identified that were to be "handled on an ad hoc basis." The ad hoc list appears to include fundamental elements of the Plant Materials Program, like foundation seed production, field plantings, long range plans, etc.[411] An issue with field plantings asked rather fundamental questions, like, "What is their role, when should they occur, how much effort is warranted?" Several members the QIT team would have known the answers to these questions, so they were undoubtedly being asked with the notion on making some fundamental alterations to the manner in which the program had been functioning.

The sixteen critical issues, somewhat abbreviated, were

1. Assessment of Customer Needs – There is a need to determine customers and characterize their needs on a continuing basis. *

2. Structure and Linkage - The current operational structure used to develop plant science (materials) information has several shortfalls: 1) it is currently not working well in all service areas; 2) there are insufficient linkages with new units in NRCS, 3) the Plant Materials Program is only one of several organizational units that deal with technology development and transfer. These shortfalls have high potential, therefore, for poor coordination, duplication, and not working on the "right" products.

3. Partner Participation – There is a lack of partner participation during the problem solving/project development process. This is hindered because the system does not allow for full partner involvement from the project beginning to the end.

4. Commitment by Management - The current commitment by Management varies from field to field. Improvement is needed.

5. Accountability – Accountability is currently a function of how line and program officers perceive the importance of the plant science (materials) activities. This perception results in variable accountability levels from poor to good.

6. Meeting New Challenges – New high priority needs from the Plant Materials Program are emerging. Some PMCs are responding and some are not.

7. Coordination and Management of resources – There is a need for better coordination and management of resources. This includes every one working on plant science (materials) issues.

8. Integration– Improved integration of plant materials work into "mainstream" NRCS is needed.

9. Service Area – Both PMC and PM Specialist service areas need to be defined so that all fields receive equitable assistance.

10. Technology Transfer – Role of the Plant Materials Specialist – Loss of PM Specialists and the lack of clearly assigning technology transfer to the PM Specialist, is causing poor technology transfer.

11. Products and Functions – PMCs need to improve quality and quantity of product delivery to field offices.

12. The Plant Materials Program needs to be marketed better.

13. Native Plant Species – Limit plant materials work to natives.

14. Holistic Approaches for Land Management – The Plant Materials Program can play a major role in helping NRCS develop a holistic approach to conservation planning.

15. Staffing – More money is needed as well as multi-field and regional coordination of plant materials work.

16.   Budget – The PMC budget is being hijacked by NRCS offsets and earmarks.

This is a comprehensive listing of critical issues. How to accomplish each is spelled out in the ninety action items. Collectively, any hope of accomplishing all ninety is staggering. Appendix 7 lists the Critical Issues from the plan and the required actions to address each. A summary of implemented actions fall into one of seven categories, shown in Table 7.1, each with a count.

It is difficult to determine what critical issues were resolved. Specific follow-up reports documenting implementation were not found. Fortunately, one or more of the action items were already policy and what was lacking was to follow what had been the practice for several years. Because of the nature of many critical issues, the frequent use of 'Ongoing' is understandable. Some are permanently ongoing, like budgeting, coordination and management, strategic planning, training, etc. Staying with the critical issues over time becomes difficult as they are replaced with other issues that, at the moment, seem more critical. It would have been unrealistic to expect implementation of all or most of the action items, or to totally complete any of them. As we will see, several action items were grappled with again in yet another internal evaluation called the 2000 Task Force Report. Regardless of the accomplishments the exercise did identify many things that would be desirable to accomplish.

Table 7.1 Summary of Actions Implementation Status

Action Item Status	No.
NI = Not implemented	2
I = Implemented	5
OG = On-going	33
TF = Passed off to the next study, the Task Force	18
Other/no status reported	25
Partial Implemented	4
I/OG = Implementation ongoing	3

PMC FUNDING STRIFE

PMC funding, as mentioned many times before, remains near the top of the concerns of the Plant Materials Program leader. Certainly Dr. White had his share of volatile budgets. This resulted from three things over which he had limited control. The first was a change in how the PMC and all other NRCS program appropriations were to be managed. The new decree mandated that all appropriated funds, except those extracted from each program for NHQ operations, were to be allocated to account holders out of the national office. The Plant Materials Center account holders were the states where a PMC was located. Prior to 1994, the program manager (National PM Specialist) could and did hold a reserve to be used for new initiatives or for unanticipated emergencies. For example, money was withheld in 1988 to initiate the PMC trainee initiative. This was no longer possible. However, over the years, ways around this handicap were resolved, such as allocating excessive funds to one state with the understanding that this fund was for the program manager's use. The second change impacting the budget started in 1996 when the amount of funds taken out of the PMC appropriation jumped from an average of five percent of the total appropriation from the 1954 to 1994, to sixteen percent or more. National PM Specialist MacLauchlan (1974 – 1984) had made a point to his replacement Curtis

Sharp (1985-1993) that he must work closely with the Budget and Finance Division in an effort to encourage and persuade them to give the small PMC program a break regarding this offset. His advice was good and NHQ overhead rarely exceeded the five percent from 1954 until 1994. Thereafter, it remained in the mid-teens to as much as twenty-four percent through 2010. Efforts by Dr. White to curb offsets are unknown. Being physically located in Kansas basically took him out of the game.

In 1999, a third financial drain emerged, the earmarks. This is a situation where Congress appropriates money to an agency, then specifies in the appropriation language that a prescribed amount must go to some unrelated project outside the agency. For example, in 2001 a congressional representative from Delaware earmarked $290,000 for a herbarium at Delaware State University, Dover, Delaware.[412] When the appropriation with this language arrived at SCS, the agency decided from which program they should take the funds for the herbarium. Because the herbarium was plant materials related the $290,000 came from PMC funds. During the years of 1999 through 2006, $13.4 million of PMC appropriated funds went to earmarks.

The impact of earmarks on the PMC allocation appeared to be excessive, relative to other NRCS program funding. For example in 2004, the NRCS Conservation Technical Assistance (CTA) appropriation was about $551 million and the PMC part of that was $11.5 million, or 2.09 percent of the CTA allocation.[413] However the PMC share of earmarks was 15.55% of their budget. The expression 'Someone is eating my lunch' might apply.

This changed, but not until 2010. The 2010 NRCS appropriation for CTA was $553,291,000 which contained $34.1 million in earmarks.[414] The PMC allocation within that CTA appropriation was $11,088,000 or two percent of the total, absorbing $240,000 or 2.16% of their budget. The difference from 15.55% to 2.16% represented a savings to the PMC budget of $1.6 million. This happened in part by some earmarks falling off and not being replaced. However, with the help of the Plant Materials Advisory Committee, earmark impact on the PMC budget was reduced. This was a stroke of good work by someone, no doubt the Plant Materials National PM Specialist, but why did it take so long? See these figures in Table 7.2. Note the change in the last figure in each line of data.

Table 7.2 Comparative Earmarks between PMC Appropriations and CTA

Year	NRCS CTA Appropriation	NTCS CTA Earmarks	PMC CTA Appropriations	% PMC Appropriations of NRCS Appropriations	PMC Earmarks	Percent
2004	$550,794,000	$102,200,000	$11,500,000	2.09%	$1,788,000	15.55%
2010	$553,291,000	$34,615,000	$11,088,000	2.00%	$240,000	2.16%

Independent of the earmarks, the NHQ offset also increased significantly during the 1994 – 2010 period. The average NHQ offset from 1980 through 1994 was 6.5%; from 1995 through 2010 it was 17.3%.

The one mitigating budget factor was that the appropriated funds for PMC use were going up substantially during the high offset and earmarking years. This is shown in Table 7.3 which provides the history of PMC appropriated funds from 1980 through 2010, including the NHQ offset and earmarked funds.[415]

Table 7.3 also shows what each PMC would have received in 2010 dollars had the available funds for allocation been divided equally among the number of existing PMCs. The last two columns in Table 7.3 are adjusted to 2010 dollars using the consumer price index.[416] Note that the five-year average of allocation per PMC from 1980 to 2010 varies only a small amount, less than the budgets of Douglas, Steiner or MacLauchlan. For example, the five-year average from 1980 through 1984 was $336,996 per PMC per year, while the average for the period between 2005 and 2009 is $352,595. The annual available funds per PMC between 1980 and 2010 fluctuated greatly. The average per PMC, in 2010 dollars, was $367,977. The average for the ten-year period between 1995 and 2004 was $358,978. Actually, in spite of the NHQ offset, the average PMC allocation for the eight-year period of 1990 – 1997 exceeded all others at $454,815 per PMC in 2010 dollars. At no time in the post-1996 period did the average PMC allocation drop as low as it was during the 1980–1989 period, which $336,503.

Table 7.3 PMC budgets, offset, earmarks and conversion to 2010 dollars from 1980 through 2010

Year	No. PMCs[4]	Appropriated Funds	NHQ Offset	Earmarks	Available to Allocate	CPI to 2010 $'s	2010 $ for allocation[2]	Funds per PMC[1]
1980	21	$3,398,000	$130,000	$0	$3,268,000	2.85	$9,313,800	$443,514
1981	23	$2,933,000	$297,000	$0	$2,636,000	2.4	$6,326,400	$275,061
1982	23	$3,486,000	$386,000	$0	$3,100,000	2.26	$7,006,000	$304,609
1983	23	$3,781,000	$182,000	$0	$3,599,000	2.19	$7,881,810	$342,687
1984	23	$3,895,000	$400,000	$0	$3,495,000	2.1	$7,339,500	$319,109
1985	23	$3,959,000	$409,000	$0	$3,550,000	2.03	$7,206,500	$313,326
1986	23	$4,089,000	$230,300	$0	$3,858,700	1.99	$7,678,813	$333,861
1987	24	$4,553,000	$184,000	$0	$4,369,000	1.92	$8,388,480	$349,520
1988	24	$4,856,000	$225,000	$0	$4,631,000	1.84	$8,521,040	$355,043
1989	25	$4,881,400	$218,000	$0	$4,663,400	1.76	$8,207,584	$328,303
1990	25	$6,884,000	$400,000	$0	$6,484,000	1.67	$10,828,280	$433,131
1991	25	$7,873,000	$400,000	$0	$7,473,000	1.6	$11,956,800	$478,272
1992	25	$8,055,990	$432,000	$0	$7,623,990	1.55	$11,817,185	$472,687
1993	25	$8,064,000	$505,500	$0	$7,558,500	1.51	$11,413,335	$456,533
1994	25	$9,506,192	$638,200	$0	$8,867,992	1.47	$13,035,948	$521,438
1995	25	$8,745,000	$592,200	$0	$8,152,800	1.43	$11,658,504	$466,340
1996	25	$8,875,000	$1,425,700	$0	$7,449,300	1.39	$10,354,527	$414,181
1997	25	$8,825,000	$1,546,685	$0	$7,278,315	1.36	$9,898,508	$395,940
1998	25	$8,825,000	$1,908,800	$0	$6,916,200	1.34	$9,267,708	$370,708
1999	25	$9,025,000	$1,736,900	$1,308,000	$5,980,100	1.31	$7,833,931	$313,357
2000	25	$9,125,000	$2,093,600	$750,000	$6,281,400	1.27	$7,977,378	$319,095
2001	25	$9,125,000	$1,832,043	$1,140,000	$6,152,957	1.23	$7,568,137	$302,725
2002	25	$9,849,000	$1,840,000	$2,235,000	$5,774,000	1.21	$6,986,540	$279,462
2003	25	$10,631,400	$1,841,400	$1,960,000	$6,830,000	1.19	$8,127,700	$325,108
2004	25	$11,500,000	$954,000	$1,788,000	$8,758,000	1.15	$10,071,700	$402,868
2005	26	$14,317,536	$1,957,363	$3,559,296	$8,800,877	1.12	$9,856,982	$379,115
2006	26	$10,441,530	$1,528,724	$700,000	$8,212,806	1.08	$8,869,830	$341,147
2007	26	$10,495,000	$2,114,786	$0	$8,380,214	1.05	$8,799,225	$338,432
2008	26	$10,782,000	$2,157,889	$377,340	$8,246,771	1.01	$8,329,239	$320,355
2009	26	$12,628,000	$2,437,591	$404,000	$9,786,409	1.02	$9,982,137	$383,928
2010	26	$11,088,000	$2,334,921	$240,000	$8,513,079	1	$8,513,079	$327,426

[1] Based on Consumer Price Index between 2010 and the year indicated.

TASK FORCE REPORT

The ink on the December, 1996 Quality Improvement Team report was barely dry when the Plant Materials Program organized a Task Force for "An Evaluation of Plant Materials Funding and Operational Relationships Consistent with Available Resources."[417] The stated goal "was to examine the current status of the program and provide a business strategy on plant materials operations consistent with available resources." Was this really the goal, 'to examine the current status' and 'develop a business strategy', or was it to 'stop the ridiculous offsets and earmarks and increase the base appropriation for PMCs'?

The Task Force membership was impressive; six state conservationists, four assistant state conservationists, two Plant Materials Program representatives, one District Conservationist, a strategic planner and a facilitator. The report outlined the rational for more base appropriation funding and a halt to what the committee felt were excessive and inequitable offsets and earmarks. The impacts on the Program are noted in the Task Force report. Section I identified three alternatives to reach the task force goal. They were as follows:

1. Secure additional funding or,

2. Supplement existing funds through 1) offset and earmark relief, 2) reimbursement of funds from other agency programs benefiting from plant materials products, and 3) other redirection of funds from within NRCS or,

3. Reduce the number of PMCs.

Not surprising, alternative one was identified as the most desirable, but the task force recognized that parts of all three might be implemented simultaneously to help relieve what appeared to be a funding crunch.

Recall that the QIT report included action items for critical issues that directly or indirectly related to the unstated Task Force mission of getting more money for the PMCs. Four QIT action items were included in the Task Force report in Section II, Strategy for Improving Program Operations. They were called Issues, which were expanded into several Sub-Issues with new Recommended Actions in the report. The Commitment by Management Critical Issue from the QIT was amended to include two Sub-Issues with ten new Recommended Actions. The other Critical Issues from the QIT included in the Task Force report were Accountability, Budget, and Structure and Linkage, each with Sub-Issues and Recommended Actions.

Recommended Action Four under Sub-Issue One (increase commitment by management) is "The National Plant Materials Advisory Committee will be reestablished as a part of national policy." The existence of this committee dates back to the 1980s and became national policy in the 1994 Plant Materials Manual revision (540.4 (b), p. 540-12).[418]

Should this report have reached persons that could have had an impact on the real goal of the Task Force, such as a member of the U.S. House of Representatives or Senate, or the USDA Secretary, the Section II Recommended Actions might have been enough for them to wonder if this program was worth saving, particularly in the absence of any positive comments. Without a doubt, many shortcomings identified in the QIT and Task Force reports needed to be identified and corrected. However, neither report contained any reference to the many accomplishments of the Program, such as the 354 commercially available cultivars, or the hundreds of printed and web page technical publications on every conservation plant from Tim Buck Tu to Tipperary, or that the measurable benefits of this Program produced a positive 3.65 ratio.[419] Why would a decision maker provide more funds for a program needing the combined 110 repairs?

Unfortunately, the Task Force report does not appear to have impacted the frequency or amount of offset or earmarked funds. They even increased, and funds available for PMC allocation remained about the same through 2010, thanks to continually increasing appropriations. In reality, the funding may not have been as bad as it appeared, but it sure gave cause for showing the underbelly of the Plant Materials Program through the QIT and Task Force evaluations.

DISCONTINUED RELEASES

The release of the first plant by the SCS observational nursery in 1939 to commercial growers has been duplicated about 720 times, if pre-varietal releases are counted, or about half that if they aren't. Logic, as well as seventy years of experience would suggest that some of the 720 varieties might be discontinued for one reason or another, like being replaced by newer, more effective plants or lack of commercial production. Because of these reasons, the 720 releases were justifiably reviewed in 2002 and 133 plants were removed from the releases PMC produced or maintained. They are shown in Appendix 8.

Another reason for discontinuing the 133 releases was that twenty-six were 'potentially invasive'. The first two reasons, replaced by newer and better plants and no commercial production, are simple and straight forward, easily supported by fact. This third reason is based on accurate observation and documentation, speculation and political opinion. The speculation and political opinion only applies to plants with a foreign origin. Had it not been many natives might have fallen for the same reason. All plants, regardless of their source, must have invasive characteristics to survive.

Fortunately, this designation was not absolute; some Bermuda grass releases were discontinued and some were not, some introduced fescues were discontinued and some were not. This appears to have depended on a measure of use. For example 'Pensacola' Bahiagrass is a tough grass capable of surviving in conditions that would destroy many grasses.[420] One important characteristic is its capability to withstand weather extremes, surviving periods of drought to heavy rains and back to drought again. Bahiagrass is very deep rooted, up to eight feet deep! This seems like it might have a potential for becoming invasive. Discontinuing it would have obviously been unwise, considering its abandoned cotton field stabilizing days of the 1930s when no native grass existed to do the job. Therefore, the decision to discontinue a plant based on its potential invasive characteristics had lots of wiggle room.

There will be a need to do some continual release weeding, particularly with the recent pre-varietal class of releases. The data presented later shows that fifty-nine have never been in commercial production and another forty-one had been but were no longer. They may be candidates for removal, thus reducing some fluff from the excessive release exuberances period.

Maintaining a current listing of only viable releases is a desirable accomplishment. It should have been done years before. No doubt it took outsiders not historically connected to all those old relics, or at least to the people who brought them to life. The more recent emotional and political advent of natives cannot be cast in the same light, however. Conservation plants are in some ways like people, if they are good they are good, regardless of where they came from.

Table 7.4 shows the discontinued releases as a part of the whole.

The word 'naturalized' is used to identify the source of some releases. The PLANTS database provides the following: "At PLANTS we use Introduced since it is widely known rather than

Table 7.4 Discontinued Releases

Release Type/Origin	% of all Releases Prior to Purging	% of Discontinued Releases
Cultivar	49	46
Informal	6	23
Pre Varietal and Germplasm	45	31
Native	77	49
Introduced	23	51

the similar term naturalized." Naturalized discontinued releases are those that evolved in a foreign land but now maintain themselves in the U.S. outside of cultivation.[421] So, introduced and naturalized appears to be about the same as used here.

Table 7.5 is the approximate status of viable releases. The horizontal totals show that the sixteen years of pre-varietal releases total 268 and the seventy years of cultivar releases and informal total 312.

Table 7.5 Status of Viable Releases

Source	Cultivar	Informal	Germplasm*	Tested	Selected	Source Identified	Totals
Native	197	5	4	15	149	101	471
Naturalized	15	1	0	1	2	0	19
Introduced	87	7	2	2*	1*	0	96
Totals	299	13	6	16	151	101	586
*= Previously carried as Cultivar							

THE PUBLIC AWARENESS PROJECT

Quick on the heels of the Task Force report, a public awareness effort was undertaken in concert with John L. McLain, Principal, Resource Concepts, Inc., Carson City, NV.[422] It came out of the Task Force effort to increase awareness and was presented to the National Plant Materials Program Advisory Committee meeting in March, 2001. The purpose was to build public awareness and support for the Plant Materials Program. The project was carried out through existing Memorandum of Understandings between NRCS, the Society of Range Management and Resource Concepts, Inc.

In early 2001, Resource Concepts developed 'Promo' sheets and an excellent Powerpoint presentation about the Plant Materials Program. Over the course of the year, working with NRCS employees, principally Dr. Richard White, Dr. Diane Gelburd, John Englert and John Scheetz, numerous meetings were held and presentations made. Foremost among these support and awareness building sessions were

- Western Governors' Association, who passed a resolution supporting additional funding for the PMP;

- National Cattleman's Beef Association;

- Ecological Society of America Office;

- Multi-Agency meeting, including representatives from USDA and USDI;

- Nevada state office of the Bureau of Land Management;

- Multiple state of Nevada natural resource related agencies.

Resource Concepts summarized the findings and recommendations from contacts that had been made during the year. The findings were about as expected. The Plant Materials Program was not well known to other conservation groups, there were inadequate cooperative agreements with other governmental groups to avoid duplication of efforts, those reached by this awareness effort felt the Plant Materials Program was worthwhile and should be supported, Plant Materials Program personnel were not good promoters of their own program, and allegedly internal budget constraints allow only one-half of the allocated funds to be utilized by the Plant Materials Program.

Recommendations were extensive, touching on many of the findings of the QIT. Follow up on these recommendations, or the results of the Public Awareness Project, are no clearer than those from the QIT or the Task Force. Of course, any effort that exposes the Plant Materials Program in a positive light is a good thing, something the QIT and Task Force certainly avoided. This effort may pay dividends that no one will ever know about.

By the late-1990s a major change was taking place that propelled the Plant Materials Program into the forefront of delivering plant materials technology: The Internet. Skilled individuals could craft a how-to-use article, with pictures, of every plant in the conservation tool bag and present it to the world in less time than it would typically have sat on an editor's desk in national headquarters. For example, by the end of 2011, the Aberdeen, ID PMC had about 230 plant-related publications on their web page, covering plants from creeping skunkbush to fernleaf biscuitroot.[423] The observational studies and PMC personnel did a creditable job publishing their work prior to the internet, as is evident in Appendix 2, which is a partial list of published technical documents produced during the first fifty-five to sixty years of plant materials work. It is dwarfed by online documents. Many previously published articles have been digitized and made easily available as well.

NATIONAL LEADERSHIP CHANGE

Following Dr. White's retirement at the end of 2003, the National PMC Manager, John Englert, filled the position as acting National PM Specialist until Robert Escheman was selected in June 2004. Bob served NRCS as a regional Landscape Architect before taking this new position. Whether qualified persons from within the plants materials discipline applied is not known. Advantages Bob had included knowledge of the agency and his ability and desirability to touch the right bases. What he may have lacked in technical knowledge he made up for with his positive attitude and a firm foundation in the concept of asking forgiveness rather than permission. While he was not able to completely turn around the financial quagmire of offsets and earmarks, they dropped significantly and his efforts to highlight the positive were commendable. His on-line *Agency Profile of the Plant Materials Program* presented the positive side; and willingness to fund and publish the *Plant Materials Program Costs and Benefits 1935 – 2005 Report* was commendable.[424]

During his four years, Bob steered a steady course, not endeavoring to reinvent the wheel, but avoiding any downward spiral. The desirable influx of new web-based publications continued, as did a definite slowing of the runaway pre-varietal releases. In addition, there were quality releases during the period, such as Opportunity Germplasm Nevada bluegrass or the joint release of 'Continental' basin wildrye.

One highly desirable agency change took place in the fall of 2004; the reestablishment of three regional offices, located in Portland, OR, Fort Worth Texas and Greensboro, NC. The regrettable aspect of the reestablishment was that the regional offices wielded limited influence. The regional director reported to the Washington Office Deputy Chief for Science and Technology. The leverage held by the plant specialists was about the same as during the 1954 – 1965 or the 1984 – 1995 periods, but reestablishment of regional offices was certainly a positive development. Those positions remain in place as this history ends.

In 2004 the new regional plant materials specialists were as follows:

- James Briggs, the often traveled, but always loyal plant materials team member, moving from an assistant state conservationist's position in Arizona.

- Joel Douglas, former PMC Manager field plant materials specialist from Coffeeville, MS

- Liva Marques, who served briefly and was replaced by Dr. Ramona Garner in October 2008, moving from the Tucson, Arizona PMC Manager position.

Joel was the first trainee at the James "Bud" Smith PMC in Knox City, TX, identified by then field PM Specialist, Richard Heizer, and what a find he was. He started in 1987. Ramona, also a trainee, joined the staff on the Los Lunus, NM PMC in 1989.

ECONOMIC VALUE OF NRCS CULTIVARS

In 1977, the Plant Materials Program started collecting yearly data on the commercial production of all released plants still on the market. This continued until about 2005 and gradually diminished after that. The data was used primarily as an indication of the potential use of each release. In 2006, Curtis Sharp, former Plant Materials Specialist, utilized a process developed by others to measure the economic benefit to the producer of conservation plants as well as the ecological services benefit from their use.[425] This data has been used in numerous parts of this history and is discussed in a 2008 publication *Plant Materials Program Costs and Benefits 1935 – 2005*.[426]

The measured benefits, from 1977 through 2005, are the net value to the growers who produced the improved plants, and the benefit to ecosystems in which they are used. Ecosystem benefit was determined using processes developed by Costanza and others.[427] Measurable benefits produce a positive ratio of 3.65. This is shown in Table 7.6.

Table 7.6 Measured Benefits from 1974 to 2005

Measured Benefit	Values	Ratio of Benefits to Cost
Cost of establishing and operating all Plant Materials Centers -1935-2005	$468 million	
Net benefits to producers of all released cultivars for 1977-2005 period	$518 million	1.11
Benefits to ecological systems of successfully established plantings from all released cultivars for the 1977-2005 period	$1.189 billion	2.54
Benefits to producers and ecological systems from the use of successfully established plantings from all released cultivars for the 1977-2005 period	$1.7 billion	3.65

These figures represent very conservative estimates for these reasons:

- The benefits derived from NRCS cultivars include production from 1977 through 2005, yet the PMCs costs are included from 1935.

- Although they may not be adapted, plants other than PMC-developed cultivars could be used for the conservation planting. This was addressed by reducing the benefit of each PMC cultivar by ninety-five percent, leaving a five percent PMC advantage factor over the anticipated performance of a plant of unknown origin, adaptation or performance. This was further reduced by subtracting the cost of establishing and maintaining each acre-year resulting from the PMC Advantage factor. This provided the net ecological benefit.

Greater detail of the methods used for these calculations are to be found in Appendix 4. Individual listings of all releases for which these calculations were made, as well as the benefit values, are found in Chapter 8 with each releasing PMC.

RELEASED CULTIVARS 1995 THROUGH 2011

The list of cultivar releases for the 1995 – 2011 periods is impressive for a number of reasons.

- Considering the number of pre-varietal releases (over 300) the 45 cultivars might have been unexpected.

- Of the 45 releases one was informal, 10 were from introduced sources and two were naturalized.

- Thirty were grasses, four legumes, seven shrubs and four trees.

- The Bismarck, ND PMC led the list with nine, Big Flats, NY with six and Manhattan, KS with five.

The Georgia PMC released two naturalized clovers for cover crops. 'Bannock' thickspike wheatgrass, released by the Aberdeen, ID PMC, is a long-lived, leafy, cool season native grass. It is moderately rhizomatous, with good sod-producing qualities. The original source of 'Windbreaker' big sacaton from the Los Lunus, NM center was selected from thirty-seven accessions collected by NRCS Field office staff in Arizona, New Mexico and Texas. From these thirty-seven accessions, ten accessions displaying the largest plants were selected. From their progeny, twenty of the most robust plants were selected during the fifth growing season, forming 'Windbreaker' big sacaton.

Foremost among the introduced grasses was 'Vavilov II' Siberian wheatgrass from Kazakhstan, also released from Aberdeen. It is a broad-based, fifty-clone synthetic, developed from clones of and genotypes from the original 'Vavilov' release. Siberian wheatgrass is very similar to fairway and standard crested wheatgrass, but has finer leaves and stems. Another introduced grass for the Northern Great Plains was 'Manifest' intermediate wheatgrass, released cooperatively by the Bismarck, ND PMC. It has exhibited consistent high forage yield over a wide geographic area and improved persistence under grazing, compared with current cultivars. It is a cool-season perennial sod forming grass introduced from Russia in the mid-1900s.

'Catskill' sand cherry, from the Big Flats, NY PMC is a native woody plant which attains a height of –twelve to eighteen inches, with a spread of approximately eight to ten feet. It is intended for use in shoreline and streambank stabilization, where low growing vegetation is preferred, and for riparian buffer plantings. 'Panbowl' river alder from the Appalachian PMC in Beckley, WV, is a nitrogen-fixing, thicket-forming shrub or small tree with dark, green foliage. It was observed to be outstanding in the Winooski, Vermont river project.[428] The species is native to the United States, found growing on streambank throughout much of the Appalachian region. The cultivar 'Panbowl' was collected on Panbowl Lake in Jackson, Breathitt County, Kentucky. It has flexible stems and fibrous root system, desirable traits for surviving the streambank environment.

The most frequently released species during this period was eastern gamagrass with five new cultivars from four PMCs. In field trials, 'Verl' equaled or surpassed standards set by a highly productive gamagrass called 'Pete'. Both were releasesd cooperatively by the Manhattan, KS PMC

ANOTHER EXPLOSION – PUBLICATIONS

Critical Issue ten of the 1996 QIT was Technology Transfer. Fifteen years later, the framers of that document could take pride in what happened with one segment of technology transfer – publications. By any mode of counting, the number of publications now available online from the PMCs and PM Specialists is little less than astounding. This has been an area of emphasis since at least the closing of the nurseries in 1953, but at no time has it been as prolific as in the last fifteen or so years. No doubt the QIT contributed, but other changes may have had an even greater impact.

First, responsibility for reviewing plant materials publications became a discipline and a state information specialist task. This eliminated excessive editorial review. A second event that made publishing easier and quicker was the Internet. Publishing roadblocks disappeared. Additionally, the combined pre-varietal releases and performance index (authors receiving performance points for publications) became a motivator, allowing a PMC five or more points for publications relating to each release. The bottom line, however, is that many individuals in the Plant Materials Program want to publish their good works and now with the roadblocks gone they can and are doing it.

Table 7.7 shows the approximate number of publications on the PMC web-site near the end of this history, listed by category. This output is shown for each center on their individual pages in Chapter 8.

Table 7.7 Online Publications

Publication Types	Number	Publication Types	Number
Books	3	PMC Annual Technical Report	57
Information Brochures and Flyers	161	Popular Journal or Magazine Articles	16
Major Publications	60	Propagation Protocols	11
Miscellaneous Popular Articles	79	Published Abstracts	62
Miscellaneous Technical Articles	115	Published Symposium Proceedings	53
Newsletters	142	Referred Journal Articles	31
Other Publication Types	64	Release Brochure	263
Plant Fact Sheets	311	Release Notices	197
Plant Guides	360	Technical Notes	378
Plant Materials Annual Report of Activities	65	Technical Poster	90
PMC Annual Technical Report	57		
		Totals	**2518**

CUSTOMER SATISFACTION STUDY

In contrast to the QIT of 1996, or because of it, the Plant Materials Centers received a higher consumer satisfaction study score than any of eight other NRCS programs, including two heavy-weights, Conservation Technical Assistance and the Soil Survey programs.[429] The study was conducted in 2006 by the CFI Group using the American Customer Satisfaction Index (ACSI) methodology, produced by the University of Michigan in partnership with the American Society for Quality.[430] ACSI is the only uniform, cross-industry/government measure of customer satisfaction. The study interviewed 1,160 respondents, made up of those in Table 7.8. Comparative results for PMCs with other programs are shown in Table 7.9. The PMCs provided the CFI Group customer of their program who became the respondents.

Among the Satisfaction Scores in Table 7.9, differences of three-points or greater are statistically significant at a ninety percent level. The PMC score was significantly greater than all others except the Resource Conservation and Development Program. The PMC score of 83 is well above the Federal Government's 2006 Customer Satisfaction Study results.

Whoever influenced the development of this study sure created a jewel. The 1,160 respondents certainly had not read the QIT or Task Force report.

Table 7.8 Groups responding to Customer Satisfaction Study

Group Name	% of Total
NRCS State Office	1
NRCS Field Office	1
Other NRCS	3
Non-Federal Office	15
Commercial/Business	17
Non-profit Agency	9
University/College	31
Other	23

Table 7.9 Customer Satisfaction Study Results

Program/Group	Satisfaction Score
Plant Materials Centers	**83**
Resource Conservation and Development Program	81
Soil Survey Program	79
Conservation Technical Assistance	79
Technical Service Providers	78
2005 NRCS Snow Survey Data	77
2005 NRCS Conservation Security Program	76
2005 Economic Research Service	75
2006 National ACSI	74
2006 Federal Government	72
Wetland Reserve Program	69
National Resources inventory	57

ANOTHER CHANGE IN LEADERSHIP

Not since the period when the nurseries were closing has there been the frequency of change that took place with the departure of Richard White and then Robert Escheman in 2008. His replacement was a return to the tradition of employing from within the discipline. John Englert, National PMC manager was selected and became the twelfth program leader in December, 2008. He came to the Beltsville Center in 1992 to manage the National Park Service projects in the Kentucky Cumberland Gap Historical Park. Because it was soft money, he did not become a permanent employee initially, but within a year, Scott Peterson, then manager, saw the worth of him. In 1994, when Scott became the director of the National Plant Data Center, John became National PMC Manager. Dr. Franklin Crider was the first manager at Beltsville and stayed from 1939 until 1948, or about ten years. Robert Thornton was there from 1955 until 1968, or about thirteen years. John Englert outlasted them all by at least a couple years.

After 2002, John Englert appeared to have become the right, and maybe the left hand of the national leader. At that time his collective knowledge of PMC activities may have exceeded anyone else in the discipline, given the absence of the regional PM Specialists. This, of course, increased until he was selected as National leader. Maybe, as in 1994, an outsider was needed, but the selecting officer, Ecological Science Director Michael Hubbs, a career NRCS employee, looked within first. Because John was the backup of departing national leader Escheman, he knew John well.

Dave White became NRCS Chief in early 2009. John was experienced with and knew the National State Conservationists Plant Materials Advisory Committee, all of whom were peers of former state conservationist White. Although White had just left Montana, a state with an excellent PMC and state program; John knew it would be desirable to give him a briefing. It was scheduled for April 14, 2009. State Conservationists Advisory committee members Niles Glasgow and Donald Gohmert, ECS Director Hubbs and agency historian, Douglas Helms, plus John all participated. Needless to say, budgets were a top subject.[431]

Among other things, the new chief was told that the Program either needed more funding for PMCs or they needed to seriously look at closing some of them. White's response, which came shortly after that meeting, was to redirect almost $1.8 million in agency funds to PMCs. That brought the 2009 Congressional funding level of $10.9 to $12.6 million less an approximate $2.7 million offset and earmarks.

Also in early 2009, Bill Puckett, Deputy Chief for Science and Technology, although supportive of the Plant Materials Program, was receiving feedback from others in leadership that PMCs were not financially sustainable and the discipline needed to take another look at the program. Even though the QIT and Task Force Study had identified some direction, a less ambitious assessment was warranted, dealing with fewer but broader and forward-looking issues. Early discussion became part of the talking points with White. When it was finished, it became the Reassessment of the NRCS Plant Materials Program, dated September 18, 2009.[432] The document had been prepared by the National Plant Materials Advisory Committee and the National and Regional PM Specialists under John's direction. An abbreviated preamble and the issues follow, along with four final actions needed by management to successfully address the issues:

Reassessment of the NRCS Plant Materials Program

The fiscal year 2009 Science & Technology Business Plan included tasks to reassess the structure and function of the Plant Materials Program and to position Plant Materials Centers (PMCs) as advocates of plant sciences in conservation activities. The recommendations below streamline current PMC activities and increase the focus of PMCs on NRCS needs. The future Plant Materials Program is anticipated to have a stronger national focus, will directly contribute to the scientific underpinnings of NRCS conservation practices, and will be geared to delivering products needed by the conservation field staff, while still retaining much of the grass-roots input and cooperative work that is a part of the program's seventy-plus year history.

Issue 1: New plants released to the public need to meet NRCS priorities and goals so that the expenditure of resources is justified.

Issue 2: PMCs initiate studies to respond to resource needs identified from many different sources. Studies at PMCs need to meet an NRCS priority and a significant portion of PMC activities should be focused on PM National Action Plans, such as for pollinators, energy, and climate change, transition to organics, air quality, and plant data collection.

Issue 3: Approximately twenty-five percent of PMC staff time and resources are expended on growing high-quality Foundation seed for distribution to commercial growers.

Issue 4: The PMC asset to NRCS has been underutilized in the past two decades.

Management Needs: In order to accomplish these actions and accelerate the Plant Materials Program's ability to address high priority NRCS concerns, the following are recommended for agency leadership consideration:

1. Direct states with PMCs to redirect activities to high priority activities of the agency.

2. Work with the National Program Leader on ways to reduce barriers which may inhibit or reduce the effectiveness of PMCs.

3. Incorporate a plant materials related element in the performance plan for all State Conservationists and State Resource Conservationists to encourage utilization, support and consistency in the management of Plant Materials Centers and state plant materials programs.

4. Continue to support Plant Materials Centers at a minimum of thirteen million dollars per year (appropriation amount) in fiscal year 2011.

Parts of the Issues and Management Needs are echoes from the past. Yet there are clear redirection threads running throughout the reassessment. It can serve as a guide for Englert. Sooner or later the assessments must become realities. This will remain his challenge.

THE FUTURE

A successful future for the National Plant Materials Program will hinge on the same things that have produced its successes for the past seventy-five years – a reasonable budget, strong national leadership and a work force of technically well-trained, strongly motivated and highly innovative personnel.

Chapter 8: OVERVIEW OF EACH PLANT MATERIALS CENTER — Their History and Output

While all Plant Materials Centers are a part of the same national program, each is unique. Many had their beginning as observational nurseries, while others were established long after the nurseries closed.

Information about each PMC includes the following parts:

HISTORY AND BACKGROUND

<u>Year and process leading to its establishment</u>

<u>History</u>

<u>Land tenure</u>

<u>Service Area</u>

OUTPUT

This section deals some of the accomplishments made by the plant materials team, consisting of the manager and staff, and the plant materials specialist.

<u>Conservation Plant Development:</u>

The first table in this section contains the PMC releases, and will denote the net production and ecological benefits through 2005 of plant releases for which calculations have been made.[433] The first column shows the name and type of release for which the PMC was the lead developer. The types are as follows: CV for a traditional cultivar and GP for pre-varietal releases. However, the use of GP, meaning germplasm, is a part of the release name, as with Franklin Bluffs Germplasm staghorn locoweed.

Any discontinued releases are also included in this table.[434] How these net production and ecological benefits were calculated is explained in Appendix 4. The Gross PMC operating budget covers all federal PMC funding from the year of establishment through 2005.

The second table in this section will denote other releases, including those by the PMC for which production or ecological benefit has not been determined because data was unavailable, they were released after 2005, or for which the PMC was not the primary releasing agency.[435] The latter means the PMC was one of the releasing contributors but was not the lead releasing agency. The definition of CV and GP are the same as described above.

Appendix 9 is a listing of common and scientific plant names for all released plants mentioned in this chapter. They are ordered by the common name to assist readers locate the scientific plant name of any new plants.

<u>Developed and Delivered Technology – Listed Publications:</u>

Each PMC web site contains a listing of publications which relate to vegetative solutions of conservation problems within its service area. The bulk of these were developed within the past twenty years by plant materials personnel, which reasonably well measures the life of the Internet. This output table does not include publications by the plant materials team that does not appear on the web page. Many of these can be found in Appendix 2 by author's name, and may also be referenced elsewhere in this history.

The publications on each PMC web site are divided into several types. This Output Table shows the number of publications developed through 2010 for each type. The types are shown with each PMC. While publication quality and significance varies, the quantity reflects the magnitude of work being accomplished, and even more important, that it is being summarized and made available. Each publication may contribute to the development of a Practice Standard and Specification for the NRCS Field office Technical Guide.

Developed and Delivered Technology – Featured Vegetative Accomplishments:

New conservation plants in commercial production may be the stars, but the how-to of seed and plant production, establishment, or management technology, are just as critical as the new conservation plants. This output is a selected vegetative accomplishment by the plant materials team. The selected accomplishment reflects a significant, high quality contribution, and is outlined in some detail.

Employees have been omitted from Chapter 8. Instead, all PMC managers appear in Appendix 5, which includes their tenure and comments about each PMC. The PMC supporting staff has not been included for a variety of reasons, primarily because of the difficulties securing complete and accurate listings, as well as reasons of privacy.

Field, Washington-Field and regional, and national plant materials specialists appear in Appendix 6.

Tables and Figures within Chapter 8 are numbered within each PMC discussion, rather than continuously throughout chapter.

Northern Latitude Plant Materials Center, Palmer, AK

HISTORY AND BACKGROUND:

Year and process leading to its establishment: The first plant materials center assistance to Alaska was provided by the Pullman, WA PMC. Because of the distance between Washington and Alaska and a lack of funds, this was not an effective way to address their needs. With support and assistance from SCS and encouragement from the University of Alaska, in 1972 the Alaska Legislature passed and Governor Bill Egan signed into law a bill creating the Alaska Plant Materials Center.436 This legislation directed the Plant Materials Center to fulfill several traditional agriculturally related PMC activities.

Their first manager was James Stroh, a seasoned SCS manager from the Bridger, MT PMC. He served as manager until 1980. Stoney Wright, an Alaska Department of Agriculture employee, replaced him and remains in that position.

Currently the PMC is a section of the Division of Agriculture within the Department of Natural Resources. Its major programs are as follows:

1. Revegetation and Native Seed Production,

2. Alaska Ethnobotany Research Project,

3. Foundation Seed Program,

4. Seed Growers Assistance Project,

5. Invasive Plants and Agricultural Pest Management,

6. Potato Seed Program, and

7. Other responsibilities for developing plant varieties and techniques for revegetation and erosion control and to provide technical reclamation assistance to industry.

In recent years, the majority of the Plant Materials Center's funding has come from non-state sources, primarily through congressional earmarks of the USDA NRCS Plant Materials Program budget. Between 1999 and 2009 the PMC received $6.2 million, nearly twice what each of the other PMCs received.[437] The web site advises, "The PMC has been very aggressive in securing grants and federal funds. This trend is not expected to decline. The PMC is unique in the fact that the enabling legislation encourages the facility to secure funds from cooperators." In the absence of any NRCS push back until about 2010 the earmarking for Palmer might have continued.

The majority of the remaining operating monies come from the State of Alaska. Additionally, the center brings in small amounts of revenue through cooperative projects with other agencies, the private sector, and through the sale of plant materials.

Land Tenure: Soon after the Plant Materials Center bill was enacted, a 285-acre tract near Palmer was selected for the center's site. An additional 120-acre parcel adjacent to the PMC was acquired through a land exchange with the Matanuska-Susitna Borough in 1982. This gave the PMC a total of 405 acres to accomplish its mandated duties, which then included revegetation work, horticultural development, foundation seed production, and disease-tested potato seed stock production.

Service Area: The PMC serves the entire state of Alaska, the largest in the U.S., roughly twice that of Texas and roughly one-fifth the size of the lower forty-eight states combined. Alaska has thirty-nine mountain ranges and seventeen of the twenty highest peaks in North America. Alaska has several major mountain chains and mountain ranges.

The climate of any given location in Alaska is largely determined by the climate region in which it lies. The influence of the Northern Pacific is largely responsible for the climate of the South Central and South Eastern regions of the state. The annual precipitation is very high in relation to the remainder of the state and the lack of extreme cold or hot temperatures speak of the maritime influence. The Bering Sea and high winds from strong storms are all features that influence the climate of the West Coast. Also, the climate is influenced from the extreme nature of air masses in the interior of the state, making the West Coast region a truly transitional zone. The climate of the interior region is the most extreme in terms of temperature range. Its continental location, isolated by the Alaska Range to the south and the Brooks Range to the north, allows temperatures in the summer to climb to 80°F and higher. Winter temperatures dip into the minus 40 to 50°F range. The mountain ranges also limit the amount of precipitation that falls in the interior by limiting the advection of moisture. Finally, the influence of the Arctic Ocean and the persistent sea-ice pack is felt in the Arctic region. Annual average temperatures in Barrow are on the order of 8-12° F and precipitation is very light, with only 4.5" on average falling at Barrow.[438]

Although limited, regional or field plant materials specialist assistance has been provided to the PMC and Alaska from the positions in Portland, OR and Washington State.

Conservation Plant Development

Due to the lack of production data no analysis was made of net production and ecological benefits from these releases. The Northern Latitude PMC has released the following plants:

Table 8-Palmer.1 Conservation Plant Releases

Release Name	Common Name	Release Year	Release Name	Common Name	Release Year
Egan, CV	American slougngrass	1986	Clam, GP	beach fleabane	2006
Gruening, CV	Alpine bluegrass	1986	Kotzebue, GP	Arctic Wild Chamomile	2006
Long, CV	mountain willow	1986	Shemya, GP	dusty Miller	2007
Wilson, CV	Bebb willow	1986	Attu, GP	longawn sedge	2007
Oliver, CV	grayleaf willow	1986	Kobuk, GP	dwarf fireweed	2007
Roland, CV	Pacific willow	1986	Tok, GP	Jakutsk snow parsley	2007
Caiggluk, CV	Tilesy Sage	1989	Slana, GP	tufted wheatgrass	2007
Benson, CV	beach wildrye	1991	Henderson Ridge, GP	red fescue	2007
Reeve, CV	beach wildrye	1991	Safety, GP	viviparous fescue	2007
Franklin Bluffs, GP	nodding locoweed	1995	Paxson, GP	alpine sweetvetch	2007
Mentasta, GP	staghorn cinquefoil	1995	Knik, GP	Jacob's ladder	2007
Twenty Mile, GP	boreal yarrow	2006	Cantwell, GP	tufted wheatgrass	2007
Solomon, GP	thickspike wheatgrass	2006	Nome, GP	glaucous bluestem	2007
Lowell Point, GP	meadow barley	2006	Ninilchik , GP	nootka alkaligrass	2007
Casco Cove, GP	beach lovage	2006	Nelchina, GP	spike trisetum	2007
Black Rapids, GP	field oxytrope	2006	Pioneer Peak, GP	nootka reedgrass	2008
Teller, GP	Alpine bluegrass	2006	King Salmon, GP	northern goldenrod	2009
Adak, GP	Arctic bluegrass	2006	Norton Sound, GP	alpine milkvetch	2009
Andrew Bay, GP	large glume bluegrass	2006	Sutton, GP	northern geranium	2009

Developed and Delivered Technology - Listed Publications. Publications on the Northern Latitude Plant Materials Center web site are numerous. No summary has been made. They can be accessed under publications at http://plants.alaska.gov/.

Developed and Delivered Technology - Featured Vegetative Accomplishments

The technical revegetation information of the Northern Latitude PMC is extensive. The 1987

Controlled Release Fertilizer Trials on Four Containerized Woody Plants is an example. This study was done by PMC staff member Donald R. Ross. A synopsis follows.

Producing vigorous, healthy woody plants for PMC experimentation is not unique to the Northern Latitude Center. The use of controlled release fertilizers offers an option to enhance their quality. Four treatments of controlled-release fertilizers were applied to four species of woody plants commonly used in PMC projects. A fifth treatment received no additional fertilizer and served as a control. Growth and mortality data were then collected and compared over two growing seasons.

159

The plants used in the trials were rooted, one year old cuttings of

- 'Roland' Pacific willow,

- 'Oliver' barren ground willow,

- Petrowsky poplar,

- red-osier dogwood.

Four slow release fertilizers were used. Three of the four are sold under the brand name Osmocote. The formulations used were 13-13-13, 18-6-12, and 0-40-0. All are designed to release nutrients over an eight to nine month period when the soil temperature averages 70°F. The fourth fertilizer was a controlled-release micronutrient mixture in granular form called Micromax. At the start of the trial in the spring all plants were transplanted into one gallon cans, using a uniform potting mix except for the fertilizer variables.

Four treatments plus a control were used.

- Treatment A was a combination of *Osmocote 13-13-13,* 0-40-0, and *Micromax,* each at the rate of one and one-half pounds per cubic yard of planting mix.

- Treatments B, C, and D used *Osmocote* 18-6-12 at increasing rates of 6, 8, and 10 pounds per cubic yard respectively.

- Treatment E was the control group with no additional fertilizer.

Table 8-Palmer.2 Results of Controlled Release Fertilizer Study

Measurements included height and girth of plants in July, 1984, again in February, 1985 during

Treatment	Avg. % Gain Ht.	Avg. Gain Girth (in.)	Range: % Gain Ht. (in.)	% Mortality
Salix brachycarpa spp. niphoclada				
A	61	0.02	5-217	25
B	230	0.083	85-379	3
C	208	0.073	43-394	5
D	268	0.093	57-500	13
E	24	0.01	0-57	3
Salix lasiandra				
A	29	0.016	0-125	10
B	122	0.073	35-271	38
C	110	0.068	18-377	53
D	109	0.072	0-337	18
E	13	0.01	0-60	13
Cornus stolonifera				
A	35	0.02	0-145	3
B	133	0.056	4-288	10
C	156	0.088	26-464	33
D	144	0.088	73-418	75
E	18	0.004	10 -73 O	
Populus x petrowskyana				
A	20	0.035	0-69	10
B	120	0.1	0-243	13
C	162	0.079	47-359	38

dormancy and last January, 1986 after the second growing season.

<u>Results</u>

Conclusions: Treatment B, *Osmocote* 18-6-12 at six pounds per cubic yard, was the most economically effective treatment. Using higher rates of controlled-release fertilizers on the unprotected containerized plants in these trials resulted in an increase in winter-induced mortality. Inducing the onset of dormancy by withholding nutrients is more difficult with controlled-release fertilizers. Extra winter protection may be necessary. No statistical analysis was made.

Controlled-release fertilizers are more convenient to use than liquid-feed fertilizers; however, the greenhouse operator has less control over the fertilization program. In comparing growth rates, further trials directly comparing a liquid-feed fertilizer program with controlled-release fertilizers should be conducted. These trials included only containerized plants. The effect of controlled-release fertilizers on field-transplanted plants should be explored in future trials.

Booneville, AR Plant Materials Center

<u>HISTORY AND BACKGROUND</u>

<u>Year and process leading to its establishment:</u> Funds were appropriated by congressional action in 1987 for a new PMC in Arkansas, based on the underserved area. The Center opened on April 12, 1987.

<u>History</u>: The driving force behind the congressional approval of the Boonville PMC came from Arkansas Senator Dale Bumpers. In addition to the PMC, Senator Bumpers was instrumental in co-locating units of the USDA, Agriculture Research Service and the Arkansas Cooperative Extension Service in Booneville, now called the Dale Bumpers Small Farm Research Center.[439]

The Center has focused on the enhancement of water quality, improved pastureland production, woodland protection, increased wildlife habitat, and critical area treatment. The Booneville PMC also works to reduce erosion from highways, reclaim mining sites, and assess the biomass production potential of grasses.

<u>Land Tenure</u>: The PMC operates on 282 acres. Approximately forty-four acres are owned by the State of Arkansas, and subleased from the USDA, ARS. The remaining 238 acres are owned by the State of Arkansas, and leased directly to NRCS.

<u>Service Area:</u> The area served by the Booneville PMC includes the Ozark Highland, Ozark border, Boston Mountains, Arkansas Valley and Ridges, Ouachita Mountains, and the Western Coastal Plain Major Land Resource Areas. Much of the Service area is characterized by rough terrain. The elevation ranges from 300 feet to 3,000 feet. The average annual rainfall varies from thirty-six inches in the west to fifty-three inches in the higher mountain areas of the east. Small family farms are characteristic of much of the area. Forage, poultry, and timber production are the major land uses. Soils are frequently shallow, stony and erosive. The economy of the area is supported largely by agriculture, coal mining, and tourism.

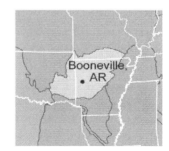

Conservation Plant Development

Plant releases from the Booneville PMC have not been in production long enough for economic data to be available. The plants they have released are listed in the table below.

Table 8-Boonville.1 Releases from the Booneville PMC

Release & Type	Scientific Name	Common Name	Release Year	Explanation
Hampton, GP	*Andropogon gerardii*	Big bluestem	2007	Post 2005, production unknown
Bumpers, CV	*Tripsacum dactyloides*	Eastern gamagrass	2005	Production data lacking

The Booneville PMC has been in operation twenty-two years. There are no easily identified impediments that identify why commercially available cultivars have not been developed.

Developed and Delivered Technology - Listed Publications

Table 8-Booneville.2 Number of PMC web site publications by type

Type of Publication	No.	Type of Publication	No.
Information Brochures and Flyers	1	Published Abstracts	2
Newsletters	8	Release Brochure	1
Plant Fact Sheets	1	Release Notices	2
Plant Materials Annual Report of Activities	3	Technical Notes	7
PMC Annual Technical Report	3		

The total number of publications is twenty-eight.

Developed and Delivered Technology - Featured Vegetative Accomplishments

Chicken farming is a large industry in Arkansas. What to do with the litter can be an asset to plant materials. The Booneville PMC set out to see how much. Here is their abbreviated three year report.

Dry-Matter Production of Eight Grass Species with Three Levels of Poultry Litter[440]

Other studies have been conducted using poultry litter on cool- and warm-season grass species.[441] However, there is limited information where variable rates of land-applied litter were used on both cool- and warm-season native grasses.

The purpose was to evaluate the effects of three poultry litter rates (0-, 4 and 8-tons per acre) on dry-matter production of perennial warm- and cool-season native and introduced grasses and a cool- and warm-season annual combination.

The four ton per acre of poultry litter was broadcast-applied as a single application in April and October for the warm- and cool-season grass species, respectively. The eight ton litter rate was applied as two four-ton/A split applications in April and June for the warm-season species and October and April for the cool-season species. Nutrient analysis of the poultry litter was approximately 80.1, 68.8, and 54.3 pounds per ton for nitrogen, phosphorus, and potassium, respectively.

Individual grass and fallow randomized subplot sizes were ten by twenty feet. Warm-season perennial grass species included 'Alamo' switchgrass (*Panicum virgatum*), 'T-587' Old World bluestem (*Bothriochloa caucasica*), 'Pete' eastern gamagrass (*Tripsacum dactyloides*), and 'Midland' bermudagrass (*Cynodon dactylon*). Cool-season perennial species consisted of

'Palaton' reed canarygrass (*Phalaris arundinacea*), 'Martin' tall fescue, and 'Boone' orchardgrass (*Dactylis glomerata*).

A cool- and warm-season annual subplot included a combination of 'Marshall' ryegrass (*Lolium multiflorum*) and 'Elbom' rye (*Secale cereale*) planted in the early fall and forage sorghum (*Sorghum bicolor*) planted in early summer. Establishment seeding rates for subplots were based on NRCS and University of Arkansas Extension Service recommendations. Cool-season perennials were seeded in March and warm-season perennials were seeded in June of the establishment year.

Litter was applied on the fallow subplots at the same rate and on similar dates as the grass subplots. The fallow plots were maintained free of plant material throughout the study.

Harvest regimes for seasonal distribution and total dry-matter production were based on best management practices for maximizing production for individual grass species. Clipping height for grass species were: six inches for switchgrass, four inches for Old World bluestem and sorghum, eight inches for eastern gamagrass, two inches for bermudagrass, and three inches for tall fescue, orchardgrass, reed canarygrass, and rye - ryegrass combination. Grab samples were obtained from subplots after each harvest for dry-matter determination. Results are reported on an oven dry-weight basis.

Production summaries of three year results are shown Table 8-Booneville.3.

Table 8-Booneville.3 Three year means for dry-matter yields of grass species as influenced by 0, 4 and 8-tons of applied poultry litter

Species	Litter application rate (tons/ac)		
	0	4	8
	DM yield in tons/acre		
Cool and warm-season annual	3.41	9.35	12.23
Bermudagrass	1.75	6.21	8.92
Tall Fescue	1.12	5.04	6.54
Reed Canarygrass	1.86	4.22	6.88
Old World Bluestem	0.82	3.57	5.76
Eastern Gamagrass	3.29	6.53	7.39
Orchardgrass	1.41	5.01	6.15
Switchgrass	1.75	6.27	8.11

Conclusions:

- Land application of poultry litter increased dry-matter production of native and introduced grass species.

- Generally, the warm-season perennial grasses produced more dry-matter than the cool-season perennial species.

- The majority of dry-matter, regardless of species, was produced during the first one-half of the growing season.

- Differences in dry-matter production were more pronounced and greater between zero and four ton/A than between four and eight ton/A poultry litter rates.

- The cool- and warm-season annual combination of rye, ryegrass, and forage sorghum produced 2.82 ton/A more dry-matter than eastern gamagrass and 3.31 ton/A more dry-matter than bermudagrass at the four and eight ton/A litter rates, respectively.

- Annual grass or grain crops may be used in the production of livestock forage. This is predicated on the selection of suitable soils.

Tucson, AZ Plant Materials Center

HISTORY AND BACKGROUND

Year Established: Established initially in 1934 by the Bureau of Plant Industry, it was moved to SCS in 1935, by congressional action.

History: The Tucson Nursery was established in 1934 by the Bureau of Plant Industry. In 1935 it moved to the Soil Erosion Service, and in April 1935 it was transferred to the Soil Conservation Service.[442] Dr. Franklin J. Crider, who is generally considered the father of what became the Plant Materials Program, entered Federal Service with the Bureau of Plant industry at Tucson, and then joined SCS as the Regional Nurseryman of the Southwest in 1935, located at Tucson.

The initial mission of the Tucson nursery was as a production nursery collecting large quantities of seeds for use on the Navajo, Gila, and Rio Grande regional revegetation projects.[443] The site originally consisted of seventy-eight acres of land. Eighteen acres was leased from the University of Arizona on the southern end of the University Experiment Farm located on Romero Road, and was later deeded to SCS. The remaining sixty acres was secured from the City of Tucson through the University of Arizona.[444] This was used rent-free until the late 1940s when the City expanded their water treatment plant and took the land back. At that time SCS purchased another thirty acres of adjoining land at about $350 an acre.[445]

The Tucson Nursery represented one of three nurseries serving the southwest. It was in a desirable location, close to the University of Arizona which had a strong agricultural research program. The other two were located in Safford, Arizona, and Shiprock, New Mexico.[446] The Tucson Nursery served as the headquarters of the three nurseries. Several buildings were constructed, blending with the local southwest architecture.[447] Joseph A. Downs was Superintendent of the Tucson Nursery following Crider, who moved to Washington in early 1936.

Between 1935 and 1953, the Soil Conservation Service operated the Tucson production and observational nursery. The Stafford, AZ and the Shiprock, NM nurseries were closed in 1939 and the production part of the Tucson nursery was terminated in 1953. The observational studies were transferred to the University of Arizona, with financial and technical help from SCS, and renamed the Tucson Plant Materials Center. In 1962, the operation was transferred back to SCS.

Fortunately, from a program perspective, the management during these years of change remained consistent. Louis P. Hamilton, Jr. had worked at the Shiprock and Tucson nurseries from 1938 and was the SCS nursery manager at Tucson in 1953. He then became a University of Arizona employee during their period of operation, returning to SCS in 1962.

After taking charge of the facility in 1962, the SCS initiated a three-year facilities rehabilitation program, which included re-roofing, repainting all of the buildings, installation of a new well and pump, and construction of some new buildings and a greenhouse. During the early 1990s management decided the PMC needed to be moved out of the Tucson metropolitan area where more land would be available. This progressed to the point of a scheduled closing on a new property but the seller did not show. At this point management changed, the move was abandoned and the office and other buildings were renovated and restored to their original southwest architectural style. In 1996 the buildings were placed on the National Register of Historic Places.

Several introduced lovegrasses were developed by the PMC. Although none are currently maintained or commercially produced, they are providing stabilizing cover and forage on thousands of acres in the PMC service area. Dr. Crider developed a major USDA Circular about them.[448]

Land Tenure: The PMC operates on 42 acres, owned by NRCS.

Service Area: The area served by the Tucson PMC encompasses the high, dry Sonoran, Chihuahuan, and Mojave deserts. These deserts represent a distinct and unique area. It includes parts of Arizona, California, Nevada, New Mexico, and Utah.

This area receives from two inches to thirteen inches of rainfall annually. Growing seasons range from 240 days to 360 days. Elevations range from 150 feet to 4,500 feet above sea level. Major land uses are irrigated farmland, rangeland, and mined land.

OUTPUT

Conservation Plant Development

In the mid-1930s the Southwest, as well as much of the country, was experiencing widespread soil erosion. There were many reasons for this, depending on location, but in the west one reason was universal overgrazing by domestic livestock. The lovegrass cultivars mentioned above provided, and are providing stabilizing cover and forage on thousands of acres. With much of the rangeland under protective cover, the PMC effort in recent years has turned to restoring native flora, riparian restoration and wildlife cover.

Table 8-Tucson.1 Net production and ecological benefits of releases

Release & Type	Common Name	Release Year	Total Production	Unit	Net Value to Producer	Net Ecological Value
A-130, CV	blue panicum	1950	192,600	LB	$340,631	$2,843,258
A-68, CV	Lehmann's lovegrass	1950	353,405	LB	$1,121,987	$10,096,781
A-84, CV	Boer lovegrass	1950	162,150	LB	$1,198,179	$6,229,803
A-67, CV	weeping lovegrass	1975	40,990	LB	$87,808	$1,450,021
Corto, CV	Australian saltbush	1977	1,552,600	LB	$9,836,389	$5,837,776
Cochise, CV	Atherstone lovegrass	1979	169,340	LB	$1,615,328	$9,195,162
Seco, CV	barley	1987	583,210	LB	$917,943	$9,069
Stevan, CV	plains bristlegrass	1994	533	LB	$(502)	$1,083
Totals					$15,117,763	$35,662,952
Production and Ecological Benefits from Releases:						$50,780,715
Gross PMC operating budget; 1935 - 2005						$20,402,321
Net Production and Ecological Benefits from Releases:						**$30,378,394**

The PMC has a cost benefit ratio of 2.49.

Table 8-Tucson.2 other releases

Release & Type	Common Name	Release Year	Explanation
Catalina, CV	Boer lovegrass	1969	NRCS not lead release agency
Palar, CV	Wilman lovegrass	1972	NRCS not lead release agency
Kuivato, CV	Lehmann's lovegrass	1976	NRCS not lead release agency
Puhuima, CV	Lehmann's lovegrass	1976	NRCS not lead release agency
Santa Rita, CV	fourwing saltbush	1987	Production data lacking
Rocker, CV	tanglehead grass	1992	Production data lacking
Loetta, CV	Arizona cottontop	2000	Production data lacking
Blythe, CV	desert saltbush	2002	Production data lacking
Saltillo Origin, GP	cane bluestem	2002	Production data lacking
Cochise, GP	spike dropseed	2005	Production data lacking
Pima, GP	whiplash pappusgrass	2006	Post 2005, production unknown
Vegas, GP	alkali sacaton	2006	Post 2005, production unknown
Moapa, GP	scratchgrass	2007	Post 2005, production unknown
Batamote, GP	desert zinnia	2008	Post 2005, production unknown
Bonita, GP	plains lovegrass	2010	Post 2005, production unknown

Developed and Delivered Technology - Listed Publications

Table 8-Tucson.3 Number of PMC web site publications by type

Type of Publication	No.	Type of Publication	No.
Information Brochures and Flyers	9	Popular Journal or Magazine Articles	1
Major Publications	1	Published Abstracts	1
Miscellaneous Popular Articles	3	Published Symposium Proceedings	2
Newsletters	7	Release Brochure	6
Plant Fact Sheets	6	Release Notices	6
Plant Guides	6	Technical Notes	11
Plant Materials Annual Report of Activities	3	Technical Poster	3
PMC Annual Technical Report	2		

The total of all web site publications is fifty six.

Developed and Delivered Technology - Featured Vegetative Accomplishment

Machinery for Seedbed Preparation and Seeding on Southwestern Ranges[449]

Darwin Anderson was an SCS employee located at the SCS Experiment Station in Tucson, AZ in the mid-1940s. A. R, Swanson, another SCS employee was located in a field office in Douglas, AZ. Both were working closely with the SCS Nursery, who were growing, collecting and developing new species, mainly grasses, for stabilizing range sites.

Conventional seedbed preparation did not work in this arid country. The germinating seed needed a break, like a little extra water. In semi-arid areas, like the Southwest, this preparation must provide for moisture conservation and soil compaction around the planted seeds. Anderson and Swanson accepted the challenge. Their objective was to create a seedbed which tilted the scant rainfall in favor of new seedings. Figure 8-Tucson.1 is their eccentric one-way disk which produced the kind of seedbed shown in Figure 8-Tucson.2.

It should be noted early on that what Anderson and Swanson accomplished seems common sense today, but because it had not been done before, so it was not so common in the 1940s.

Figure 8-Tucson.1 Eccentric one-way disk

Early trials showed that contour furrowing failed under range conditions because of the difficulty of keeping the furrows exactly on the contour. As a result, the water ran to the lower places resulting in spotted stands, and encouraged accelerated gully erosion. The problem was corrected by placing interruptions in the contour furrows which served as water storage basins, but creating them was difficult and costly. However, it was found that packing or firming the soil after the seed had been broadcast over the storage basins resulted in more uniform stands.

Benefits obtained by firming the soil led to development of the cultipacker-seeder, a commonly used seeder for many conditions today. It covered the seed and firmed the soil around it. It was observed that a superior stand of grass was usually obtained in the loose soil that had been thrown out on the undisturbed soil at the edges of the furrows. When loose soil is thrown over firm, undisturbed soil, water infiltration is increased, while simultaneously the firm soil holds the moisture in close proximity to the seed, thus making ideal conditions for seed germination and seedling establishment. Following this observation, a search was made for machinery which would make a series of short furrows or pits and at the same time leave a considerable portion of the seedbed area undisturbed.

Figure 8-Tucson.2 Pits produced by eccentric one-way disk

The eccentric one-way disk that was used for renovating blue grama grass sod in Wyoming appeared to almost fulfill the requirements of partial soil disturbance and water storage. With this in mind, a Wheatland one-way plow was equipped with eccentric disks and the cultipacker seeder was attached behind. The machine was set up so that every other disk was eccentric with a 3-turn lag. The eccentric disks were two inches larger in diameter than regular disks and were two inches off center, vertically.

This machinery was tested in a limited fashion on the San Simon Land Utilization Project in the summer of 1946 with fair results. In 1947, further trials were made and the machinery was modified to the extent that all regular disks were removed and replaced with spacing washers to prevent soil disturbance between the pits, thus producing the desirable condition of loose soil thrown over undisturbed soil. The Anderson and Swanson paper provides excellent details on how this was accomplished.

This arrangement was tested on soil that was rather impermeable and nearly bare of vegetation. The planting was done May 1, 1947, with the following species and rates per acre

- Wilman lovegrass (*Eragrostis superba*), two pounds.

- Boer lovegrass (*Eragrostis chloromelus*), one pound.

- Lehmann lovegrass (*Eragrostis lehmanniana*), three pounds.

The planting was done in strips nine feet wide and approximately eighteen feet apart.

No effective rainfall occurred at this site until August 7, when 1.73 inches fell during a three-day period. At this time germination occurred and the grasses were well up six days later when 0.22 inch of rain fell and again nearly filled the pits. The staggered pits were approximately twenty-four inches long, eight inches wide and four inches deep.

Rainfall during the remainder of the autumn was adequate and the seedlings went into the winter in good condition.

After two years of testing, the authors felt confident in making the following points about their results, each articulating the results of the experiment:

1. The machines are commercially available.

2. The machines are rugged enough to withstand operation under average range conditions.

3. Due to the staggered nature of the pits it is not necessary to stay on the contour.

4. The machine can be pulled by farm tractors.

5. The machine does seedbed preparation, planting and compaction with one operation.

6. The operation is fast and cheap.

7. The machine rather effectively controls competition from annuals and perennials.

8. Seed is well distributed to take advantage of varying moisture conditions.

9. With seed hoppers mounted on the eccentric disk, the combination of this and the cultipacker- seeder may be useful for seeding chaffy and clean seed mixtures simultaneously.

This technology, altered many times over, is the bedrock of all successful plantings in arid and semi-arid locations.

Anderson and Swanson used the following references:

Barnes, O. and A. L. Nelson. 1945. Mechanical treatments for increasing the grazing capacity of shortgrass range. Wyoming Agr. Exp. Sta. Bul. 273. 35 p.

Beutner, E. L., and Darwin Anderson. 1944, A method of seedbed preparation and reseeding deteriorated range lands. Jour. Amer. Sot. of Agron. 36: 171-172.

Flory, E. I. and Marshall. 1942. Regrassing for soil protection in the Southwest. USDA. Farmer's Bul. No. 1913. 60 p.

Pleasanton/Lockeford, CA Plant Materials Center

HISTORY AND BACKGROUND

Year Established: The Pleasanton PMC was established in 1939, by the congressional action authorizing SCS to establish nurseries.

History: The seed for what is now the Lockeford Plant Materials Center was planted in 1935 when the Soil Conservation Service opened a production nursery and initiated plant observational studies in Santa Paula, CA. The first observational studies scientist at the site was Oswald K. Hoglund, who became an illustrious leader in the quest for conservation plants in California. He was joined in 1936 by Dirk J. Vanderwal.

In 1939, a sixty-acre nursery site was purchased by SCS near downtown Pleasanton, California. The Santa Paula nursery continued under Vanderwal, with Hoglund moving to Pleasanton working under Paul Dickey. All the buildings were constructed with slump type adobe brick, cool in the summer and warm in the winter. At that time, Pleasanton was a sleepy little cow town, but by the end of the war it had been discovered as a desirable bedroom community for the Bay area. As the population grew, the real estate value of the land was too great for growing plants. The land was sold in 1972 and a 106 acre farm was purchased in the San Joaquin Valley near Lockeford. The relocation was completed in 1973.

When the nurseries closed in 1953, Pleasanton was one of the ten nurseries that continued as a PMC and one of five that remained under SCS control during and after the transition period.

While there were no plant releases from the Santa Paula nursery before its closing, there were two from Pleasanton before it became a PMC. It is worth noting that during the period following the transition from an SCS nursery to a PMC, the release of new plants at Pleasanton continued smoothly, with 'Blando' brome and 'Lana' vetch being released in 1954 and 1956 respectively. The reasons are obvious; the upheaval was minimized by remaining an SCS operation with experienced personnel.

Land Tenure: The PMC operates on the 106 acres owned by USDA, NRCS.

Service Area: The PMC serves the Mediterranean climate portions of California. This area is uniquely characterized by its dry summer and rainy winter seasons.

The service area has a complex topography composed of broad valleys, rolling foothills, upland plateaus and rugged mountains. Elevation extremes are from twenty feet below sea level to 14,400 feet above sea level. Agriculture in the service area is extremely diversified, including fruits and vegetables, extensive livestock production from native rangeland, and timber production.

OUTPUT

Conservation Plant Development

Over the course of the last two centuries, California grasslands have been converted to a community dominated by non-native, primarily Mediterranean-type annual grasses. Whether the conversion reflects a greater competitive ability for limited resources, or the non-native filling a void created by disturbances such as high-intensity grazing by introduced livestock, or a combination of the two remains unclear, and maybe is immaterial. Nevertheless, this explains why most plants developed by the Pleasanton PMC are introduced annual plants. Their performance convinced the nursery and PMC scientists that they were valuable conservation plants for the needs of that time.

Table 8-Pleasanton.1 Net production and ecological benefits of releases

Release & Type	Common Name	Release Year	Total Production	Unit	Net Value to Producer	Net Ecological Value
Cucamonga, CV	California brome	1949	480,000	LB	$1,799,249	$17,794
Akaroa, CV	orchardgrass	1953	401,000	LB	$6,706	$1,734,325
Blando, CV	soft chess	1954	2,910,000	LB	$4,343,942	$1,850,385
Lana, CV	wollypod vetch	1956	2,910,000	LB	$863,153	$797,522
Wimmera-62, CV	ryegrass	1962	2,655,000	LB	$435,853	$2,335,219
Perla, CV	koleagrass	1970	196,680	LB	-$55,653	$679,333
Zorro, CV	annual fescue	1977	1,252,500	LB	$5,320,292	$2,786,813
Casa, CV	quailbush	1979	99,620	LB	$14,646	$7,105
Dorado, CV	bladderpod	1979	81,320	PL	$19,282	$3,137
Marana, CV	fourwing saltbush	1979	109,198	PL	$19,377	$18,031
Berber, CV	orchardgrass	1981	503,030	LB	$483,040	$2,175,605
Duro, CV	California buckwheat	1983	47,004	PL	$24,021	$712
Panoche, CV	red brome	1985	263,500	LB	$1,030,601	$195,429
Sierra, CV	sulphur flower buckwheat	1987	69,300	PL	-$51,719	$5,299
Altura, , CV	greenleaf manzanita	1989	5,900	PL	-$2,806	$158
Maleza, CV	mountain whitethorn	1989	15,700	PL	-$6,125	$26,877
Cuesta, CV	ceanothus	1991	25,300	PL	$4,775	$359
Monte Frio, CV	rose clover	1991	65,500	LB	$171,432	$70,522
Rio, CV	beardless wildrye	1991	211,610	PL	$175,269	$114,475
LK115d GP	purple needlegrass	1998	5,720	LB	$72,357	$56,271
LK215e GP	purple needlegrass	1998	925	LB	$29,634	$7,280
LK315d GP	purple needlegrass	1998	770	LB	$21,679	$5,656
LK415f GP	foothill needlegrass	1998	1,020	LB	$26,649	$7,492
Mariposa, CV	blue wildrye	2002	13,100	LB	$66,708	$21,330
Total					$14,812,361	$12,917,128
Production and Ecological Benefits from Releases:						$27,729,489
Gross PMC operating budget; 1935-2005						$22,595,103
Net Production and Ecological Benefits from Releases:						**$5,134,386**

The PMC has a cost benefit ratio of 1.23.

Table 8-Pleasanton.2 Other releases

Release	Common Name	Release Year	Explanation
Mission, CV	perennial veldtgrass	1962	NRCS not lead release agency
Wilton, CV	rose clover	1967	NRCS not lead release agency
Lassen, CV	bitterbrush	1984	NRCS not lead release agency
LK621e, GP	western needlegrass	2006	Post 2005, production unknown
Central Coast 2600, GP	California brome	2008	Post 2005, production unknown
Central Sierra 3200 GP	California brome	2008	Post 2005, production unknown
Coastal 500, GP	California brome	2008	Post 2005, production unknown
Northern Cal 40, GP	California brome	2008	Post 2005, production unknown
Southern Cal 1000, GP	California brome	2008	Post 2005, production unknown

Developed and Delivered Technology - Listed Publications

Table 8-Pleasanton.3 Number of PMC web site publications by type

Type of Publication	No.	Type of Publication	No.
Information Brochures and Flyers	3	Plant Materials Annual Report of Activities	3
Miscellaneous Popular Articles	2	PMC Annual Technical Report	1
Newsletters	4	Release Brochure	10
Plant Fact Sheets	1	Release Notices	8
Plant Guides	14	Technical Notes	44

The total of web site publications is ninety.

Developed and Delivered Technology - Featured Vegetative Accomplishments

The Pleasanton/Lockeford PMC has a long and productive history. Two Featured Vegetative Accomplishments will be presented. The first one dates back to the nursery days.

1. Using Rice Hulls as Seed Diluents to Facilitate Seeding[450]

This is covered in detail in Chapter 11, Great Innovations.

2. Germination of High Elevation Manzanitas

In 1970, the Pleasanton PMC contracted with the California Division of Highways to test and develop plants for stabilizing California highway roadbanks in the Sierra Nevada. The project was under the direction of PMC staff member, George Edminson. Although the predominance of PMC work had been at the lower elevation of California, highways transected the High Sierras. Additionally, extensive land development was taking place there, particularly in the Tahoe Basin. These factors created a need for information on native shrubs for re-vegetating disturbed sites. Among the most important were two manzanitas; greenleaf (*Arctostaphylos patula*), and pinemat manzanita *(A. nevadensis)*. Although relatively easy to propagate from cuttings, propagation of the two species from seed would be much easier but was inconsistent and generally poor.

Agronomist Jack Carlson initiated a study to overcome this difficulty.[451] Despite scarcity of information, the literature indicated two basic requirements for germination: seed-coat scarification and breaking of internal dormancy with cold stratification. Therefore, Carlson studied the germination of both manzanitas, using sulfuric acid scarification plus cold stratification, and cold stratification combined with warm stratification.

The results demonstrate the importance of a high-quality seed source. Greenleaf manzanita seed was considerably superior to pinemat seed. One source of greenleaf seed came from

171

irrigated shrubs, which may have contributed to higher viability. Finding a good pinemat manzanita seed source was probably the greatest obstacle to successful germination. Based on the data, it is likely that greenleaf manzanita can be germinated easily in the greenhouse with forty to fifty percent success. Key factors in optimum germination are a good seed source, closely monitored scarification, removal of the carbon residue from the seedcoat after scarification, and adequate moisture during stratification.

Upper Colorado Environmental Plant Center, Meeker, CO

<u>HISTORY AND BACKGROUND</u>

<u>Year and process leading to its establishment</u>: The Environmental Plant Center was opened in 1975. The primary motivation for the Center came from a national interest in large deposits of oil-bearing shale in the area. The level of interest in oil shale increased dramatically in the early 1970s with the decrease in oil available from foreign sources. The economic recovery of that oil and the need for re-vegetating the disturbed sites were the primary factors leading to the establishment of the Center. The Center is located adjacent to the world's largest known deposit of this oil bearing shale.

<u>History:</u> Through the joint efforts of federal and state agencies, oil-related interest and conservation organizations, grants and other funds became available for two soil conservation districts to purchase land and construct facilities for the Center's operation. They were the White River and Douglas Creek Soil Conservation Districts. The Environmental Plant Center was not a federally authorized facility, thus no permanent federal funding became available at the time of its creation. However, NRCS has provided limited funding, and the balance comes from grants, and on-farm production of crops.

The Center is operated by the two the conservation districts.

<u>Land Tenure</u>: The 269 acres of land on which the Center operates is owned by the two conservation districts.

<u>Service Area</u>: The service area of the center is mountainous with high plateaus, open parks, foothills, mesas, and river valleys. The Plant Materials Center is characterized by sixteen inches of annual precipitation, a ninety-day frost free growing season, and an elevation of 6,500 feet.

Conditions change substantially from the high mountains to the dry desert areas. Soils are fragile and erosive. Plants are subject to drought, ice heaving, and wildlife usage.

Major land uses include dry cropland, irrigated cropland and hay land, rangeland, wildlife lands, and mined land.

<u>OUTPUT</u>

Conservation Plant Development

Considering its operational mode and the short time it has been open the positive net production and ecological benefit ratio of 1.21 is impressive. See Table 8-Meeker.1. The Center was hampered in its early years by administrative instability and drastic fluctuation and uncertainty of funds. A few years after becoming established, the priority of the oil shale reclamation diminished, requiring the Center to shift gears in program priorities and source of funding.

The two most prominent Center releases are 'San Luis' slender wheatgrass and Garnet mountain brome. The original seed collection was made by Glenn Niner, collector extraordinary, in 1975 in the San Luis Valley, Rio Grande County, Colorado. 'San Luis' establishes rapidly, and has good emergence success and spreading habit. Enough commercial seed was produced of 'San Luis' from 1984 through 2005 to plant 129,000 acres of rangeland or other denuded areas. Garnet has superior smut resistance to other mountain bromes and is longer lived. In its four years of commercial production (2001 - 2005), Garnet was planted on about 44,000 acres. It was initially collected in Powell County Montana near ghost town of Garnet. It is equal to or superior to other mountain bromes for ease of establishment, forage and seed production.

Table 8-Meeker.1 Partial net production and ecological benefits of the EPC releases

Release & Type	Common Name	Release Year	Total Production	Unit	Net Value to Producer	Net Ecological Value
Rincon, CV	fourwing saltbush	1983	4,000	LB	$11,484	$102,500
San Luis, CV	slender wheatgrass	1984	740,950	LB	$763,116	$1,825,634
Summit, CV	Louisiana sage	1986	255	LB	$ (36,996)	$6,158
Peru Creek, CV	tufted hairgrass	1994	329	LB	$ (46,566)	$161,742
Timp, CV	Utah sweetvetch	1994	11,180	LB	$92,382	$ 24,714
Garnet, GP	mountain brome	2000	444,000	LB	$ 45,736	$635,528
Total					$829,156	$2,756,276
Production and Ecological Benefits from Releases:						$3,585,432
Gross PMC operating budget; 1983 - 2005						$2,957,683
Net Production and Ecological Benefits from Releases:						$627,748

Table 8-Meeker.2 Other Releases

Release & Type	Common Name	Release Year	Explanation
Hycrest, CV	crested wheatgrass	1984	NRCS not lead release agency
Hatch, CV	winterfat	1985	NRCS not lead release agency
Hobble Creek, CV	big sagebrush	1987	NRCS not lead release agency
ARS 2678, GP	Kura clover	1988	NRCS not lead release agency
Maybell Source, GP	antelope bitterbrush	1997	Production data lacking
Pueblo, GP	bottlebrush squirreltail	2005	Production data lacking
Wapiti, GP	bottlebrush squirreltail	2005	Production data lacking
Long Ridge, GP	Utah serviceberry	2008	Post 2005, production unknown
Colorow, GP	black chokecherry	2009	Post 2005, production unknown

Developed and Delivered Technology - Listed Publications

Table 8-Meeker.3 Number of PMC web site publications by category

Type of Publication	No.	Type of Publication	No.
Information Brochures and Flyers	1	PMC Annual Technical Report	3
Miscellaneous Popular Articles	1	Refereed Journal Articles	1
Miscellaneous Technical Article	8	Release Brochure	7
Newsletters	5	Release Notices	2
Other Publication Types	1	Technical Notes	6
Plant Fact Sheets	12	Technical Poster	2
Plant Guides	11	Published Abstracts	1
Plant Materials Annual Report of Activities	3		

There are a total of sixty four web site publications.

Developed and Delivered Technology - Featured Vegetative Accomplishments

Maybell Propagation Projects:

For several years the UPCEPC has been studying, in cooperation with the Colorado Division of Wildlife, ways to successfully re-establish antelope bitterbrush in their service area.

Antelope bitterbrush is an important native browse shrub in the intermountain West. It occurs over most of the region, and is adapted to a wide range of soils and annual precipitation from eight to thirty-four inches per year and elevations of 4000 to 8500 feet. The shrub is slow growing with a moderate to very deep root system and wide ecotypic variations. It is normally two to six feet in height and up to eight feet in width with wedge shaped, three lobed leaves, some being persistent in winter. Flowering occurs in late spring to early summer with yellow to white blossoms.[452]

Antelope bitterbrush occurs most often as part of a mixed shrub community, but occasionally is found in nearly pure stands. It is associated with a variety of understory grasses and forbs. It can also be an understory plant in association with taller growing trees.

Natural establishment of antelope bitterbrush occurs in years with good seed production, often from seed stored in rodent's cache that was not eaten. Rodents normally cache seeds within fifty to seventy-five feet of an existing seed source. Continuous moisture is necessary the first few years of seedling growth for successful establishment. Unfortunately, suitable environmental conditions may allow natural revegetation in only one out of every twenty years.

The re-establishment efforts focused on an ecotype referred to as Maybell. Approximately 50,000 acres of a nearly pure stand of bitterbrush, near Maybell, Colorado, had burned in the previous two decades.[453]

Starting in 1998, the Center evaluated three major ways to re-establish bitterbrush in its area of adaptation.

I.   Reproducing the cache approach that occurs in nature.

This study involved artificially creating caches similar to what rats were doing, including several variables. These included:

- Two different seed lots with similar germination;

- Application of fungicides;

- Multiple dates for establishing the caches;

- Herbicide applications to planting area;

- Two planting locations, and

- Plot planting vs. row planting.

All caches were evaluated for appearance of continued dormancy, germination and seedling development.[454]

Considering the entire study, the caches resulted in 0.3% reestablishment. The cache in the herbicide plot averaged 0.7% establishment. This cache had plants fifteen centimeters tall after two years.

II.   Direct seeding of bitterbrush seed

The direct seeding study started in 1998. As with the cache approach, multiple direct seeding variables were used:

- Two different seed lots with similar germination;
- Application of fungicides;
- Multiple dates for making the drillings;
- Herbicide applications to planting area, and
- Two planting locations.

Seed germination and emergence was realized with most treatments. Unfortunately, ninety percent of the seedlings died from lack of moisture by the end of the first growing season. Any evaluation of these plots was terminated in 2002.

III. Establish plants which had been grown in tubes.

This first planting was made in 1999. Seed was germinated and seedlings were grown in ten cubic inch tubes for sixteen months prior to planting. The seedlings averaged about twelve inches. As with the other two studies, several variables were included.

- Herbicide applications to planting area;
- Two planting locations, and
- Plot planting vs. row planting.

Evaluations were completed in 2004.

Summary

The best survival after five years was planting in plots that had the herbicide treatment. It shows consistent survival averaging about twenty-five percent for this treatment.

Although two of the experiments were unsuccessful, the tube planting produced satisfactory results adequate for large scale field plantings of bitterbrush.

Brooksville, FL Plant Materials Center

HISTORY AND BACKGROUND

Year and process leading to its establishment: In 1947, the SCS opened a production nursery at Brooksville, with an observational nursery component. This served as the impetus for the PMC.

History: When the reorganization took place in 1953-54, the Brooksville nursery was closed. They were located on land leased from the U.S. Forest Service, and the lease was terminated. From this point until July 1, 1958, the Center ceased to exist. Then it reopened in Arcadia, FL on private leased land. In 1967, 182 acres of land in Brooksville, FL were purchased and the Center was moved back there.

Two individuals played a leading part in this period of transition. G. B. Blickensderfer was an early recruit into observational work, starting at the Thorsby, AL nursery in 1938 and then at Brooksville, FL from 1948 until 1953. Harry Haynesworth took a lead role in the establishment of the new PMC at Arcadia in 1957, moved with it to Brooksville, and later became a plant materials specialist in Georgia. With the establishment of the Arcadia PMC, Blickensderfer became the Florida PM Specialist, remaining in that position until 1963 when he retired.

Land Tenure: The Brooksville Center operates on 182 acres which are owned by NRCS.

Service Area: The Brooksville PMC serves Florida, the Caribbean Area, and coastal areas of Alabama, Georgia, and South Carolina. Rainfall varies from thirty inches per year in parts of the service area to more than 200 inches. Soil textures are predominately sandy and well drained, but large areas of clay and poorly drained soils are common. Elevations vary from sea level to a few hundred feet above it in Florida to more than 4,000 feet above sea level in Puerto Rico.

The climate ranges from warm and humid in northern Florida to tropical in the Caribbean. Major land uses include row crop production, rangelands, orchards, forest land, recreation and urban land.

OUTPUT

Conservation Plant Development

Table 8-Brooksville.1 Net production and ecological benefits of releases

Release & Type	Common Name	Release Year	Total Production	Unit	Net Value to Producer	Net Ecological Value
F-149, informal	American jointvetch	1969	7,406,100	LB	$6,673,922	$9,864,925
Bigalta, CV	Limpograss	1978	13,733,300	PL	$1,792,858	$36,072,801
Florigraze, CV	perennial forage peanut	1978	2,519,290	PL	$5,021,072	$1,202,624
Greenalta, CV	Limpograss	1978	1,647,700	PL	$79,715	$4,327,959
Redalta, CV	Limpograss	1978	4,984,500	BU	$388,449	$13,092,620
Flora Sun, CV	beach sunflower	1991	176,880	PL	$5,690	$97
Northpa, CV	bitter panicum	1992	2,918,550	PL	-$1,298,265	$5,137
Southpa, CV	bitter panicum	1992	263,035	PL	$207,401	$461
Sharp, CV	marshhay cordgrass	1994	401,600	PL	$95,943	$65,036
Chapingo, CV	Mexican teosinte	1995	55,700	LB	-$207,691	$34,821
Stuart, GP	switchgrass	1996	2,100	PL	-$231	$499
Wabasso, GP	switchgrass	1996	2,600	PL	-$242	$4
Citrus, GP	maidencane	1998	675,470	PL	$211,859	$458,475
Martin GP	eastern gamagrass	2000	7,225	PL	-$20,028	$13
St. Lucie GP	eastern gamagrass	2000	7,225	PL	-$2,185	$19
Brooksville 68 GP	perennial peanut	2002	25,280	PL	-$31,309	$11,367
Miami, GP	switchgrass	2004	3,200	PL	-$7,097	$5
Totals					$12,909,861	$65,136,862
Total Net Benefit Value to the production and Ecological Value						$78,046,723
Gross PMC operating budget; 1966 – 2005						$12,652,806
Net Production and Ecological benefits from cultivars:						**$65,393,917**

Over seventy-five percent of the net benefit was from two cultivars, 'Bigalta' and 'Redalta' limpograss, both making contributions to the forage production of Florida. The cost benefit ratio for the Brooksville PMC through 2005 was 6.17.

Table 8-Brooksville.2 Other releases

Release & Type	Common Name	Release Year	Explanation
Floral Passion, GP	blazing star	2003	Production data lacking
Ghost Rider, GP	chalky bluestem	2006	Post 2005, production unknown
Morning Mist , GP	hairawn muhly	2006	Post 2005, production unknown
Gator, GP	Muhlenberg maidencane	2007	Post 2005, production unknown
Fort Cooper, GP	splitbeard bluestem	2008	Post 2005, production unknown
Sea Islands, GP	gulfhairawn muhly	2009	Post 2005, production unknown
Osceola Blue, GP	lopsided indiangrass	2009	Post 2005, production unknown
Osceola Blue, GP	splitbeard bluestem	2009	Post 2005, production unknown

Developed and Delivered Technology - Listed Publications

Table 8-Brooksville.3 Number of PMC web site publications by category

Type of Publication	No.	Type of Publication	No.
Information Brochures and Flyers	7	Published Symposium Proceedings	6
Major Publications	3	Release Brochure	13
Miscellaneous Popular Articles	1	Release Notices	11
Newsletters	4	Technical Notes	5
Plant Guides	12	Miscellaneous Technical Article	2
Plant Materials Annual Report of Activities	3	Popular Journal or Magazine Articles	1
Published Abstracts	5	Refereed Journal Articles	1

Total number of web site publications is seventy-four.

Developed and Delivered Technology - Featured Vegetative Accomplishments

Florida Native Seed Production Manual[455]

The production of phosphate in Florida is a big deal. As with any mining operation, vast acres of land are disturbed, requiring reclamation. With the increasing emphasis on the use of native plants, land reclamation specialists are scrambling to meet this need.

Historically, plants that become commercially available have several desirable traits relative to their intended use. One of these is ease of commercial production. Many of the natives that would make logical reclamation plants are notoriously difficult to reproduce economically. While the production of several desirable natives may not be cost effective relative to other crops commonly available, their production is still possible. Additionally, the climate of the Brooksville service area is so unique the use of local ecotypes is highly desirable. All of these things culminate in the need for state-of-the-art information on the best way to produce these plants, not only for the phosphate industry but all land reclamation. Of course the first and foremost need was the how-to-do-it technology.

Between 1991 and 2002, the Brooksville PMC conducted research on native plants, under agreements with the Florida Institute of Phosphate Research (FIPR). From this and many other sources the Florida Native Seed Production Manual was developed. It contains comprehensive information about growing Florida native plants for large quantity seed production, including collection, planting and production technology. Planting and collection equipment currently available on the market is discussed, along with detailed information about seed conditioning equipment. Several native Florida species are showcased in this manual. All of them performed well on reclaimed mined lands, and are included in native upland seed mixtures.

Included in the manual are detailed instructions for

- Choosing a seed source;
- Selecting a seed producing field site;
- Seedbed preparation;
- Establishment of production fields;
- Production field management, and
- Seed harvest, cleaning and processing.

Detailed instructions, descriptions and adaptation of the following selected species are included in the manual.

- Bluestem, Chalky (*Andropogon capillipes* or *Andropogon glomeratus* var. *glaucopsis*).
- Bluestem, Creeping (*Schizachyrium stoloniferum* or *Schizachyrium scoparium* var. *stoloniferum*).
- Bluestem, Splitbeard (*Andropogon ternarius*).
- Eastern Gamagrass (*Tripsacum dactyloides*).
- Hairawn Muhly (*Muhlenbergia capillaris*).
- Lopsided Indiangrass (*Sorghastrum secundum*).
- Pinewoods Dropseed (*Sporobolus junceus*).
- Switchgrass (*Panicum virgatum*).
- Wiregrass (*Aristida beyrichiana*).
- Blazing Star, Handsome (*Liatris elegans*).
- Grassy-leaf Goldenaster (*Pityopsis graminifolia*).
- Partridge Pea (*Chamaecrista fasciculata*).

A sampling of the information provided for each species follows. The example species is wiregrass (*Aristida beyrichiana*).

SPECIES DESCRIPTION: Warm season perennial bunchgrass; leaf blades are narrow and rolled inward (wire-like), twelve to twenty inches long; seed stalks are one to three feet tall. Adapted to a wide variety of soils throughout Florida. Primary use is as a fine fuel for pine forest understory burn management programs; also an important source of nesting cover for upland game birds; livestock graze foliage after a burn when it is tender.

AVERAGE SEED/LB (KG): 907,000/lb. (2,000,000/kg) (bearded).

SEEDING RATE-DRILLED: (Pure live seed) 2 lb./ac for 12" rows, divide by 2, 3 or 4 for 24", 36" or 48" rows.

SEEDING DEPTH: 1/4" or less.

ROW SPACING: 24" to 48" (Planting double rows (6-12" spacing) within main rows is highly recommended to form a heavy canopy that will shade out weeds).

178

PLANTING DATE: Winter (November-January) plantings were successful in central Florida and the panhandle. Plantings during other seasons generally had lower stand densities.

WEED CONTROL: Prior to Establishment: Use herbicides and/or cultivation for 1 to 2 years to obtain a clean weed-free seedbed. Established Stand: Weeds can be a problem in this species because it is slow growing and shallow rooted. Spacing rows to allow for cultivation is recommended. Also hand weeding and labeled broadleaf herbicides can be used. In tests on reclaimed uplands applications at low to medium rates did not injure seedlings or mature plants.

INSECT/PATHOGEN CONTROL: Seeds commonly infected with smut-like fungus. Amount of damage to viable seed unknown; no known control measures available.

FERTILIZATION: During Establishment: Not recommended for direct-seeded stands. Fertilization may be beneficial to transplants if soil tests indicate nutrients are lacking. Established Stand: Fertilize according to soil test recommendations. In nitrogen deficient soils 30 to 50 lbs. nitrogen/ac may be applied in the early spring to maintain stands. Wire grass shows very little response to nitrogen fertilization, but it may be important for stand persistence.

IRRIGATION: During Establishment: Requires good soil moisture during establishment. Established Stand: Highly tolerant of droughty conditions once established. Irrigate during the growing season, if necessary, to keep plants vigorous. Good soil moisture is necessary for seed production. However, stands should not be irrigated when plants are pollinating or during the final stages of seed ripening.

HARVEST: Harvest Dates: Late November to early December. Collection Window: Approximately one to two weeks, barring high winds. Ripe seed is loosely held on seed head until it is dispersed by wind. Stripping: Preferable; harvest when conditions are warm and dry; damp seed won't strip off.

STAGE: When seed is easily hand stripped from the stalk - mature viable seed is very brittle and snaps when pressed with thumbnail.

- Brush Speed: 700 to 900 rpm.
- Forage Harvester: Adequate.
- Direct Combine: N/A
- Lodging: Low
- Shattering: Low

PRECLEANING TREATMENT/STORAGE: Stripped Seed: Usually not necessary if harvested during the dry period of the day.

Forage Harvest: Immediately air-dry for 3 to 7 days as necessary.

PROCESSING: Specialized Cleaning instructions: Debearding not recommended, as seed is brittle and easily cracked. Stripped seed can be scalped to remove large stems.

- Scalping: Clipper 2 screen fanning mill
- Top screen only: 32 round
- Preparation for Planting with a Hay Blower: (To break up large stems.)
- Hammer mill: 1/4 round

179

SEED YIELD: Irrigated: On research plots at the Brooksville PMC, production varied between 13 and 28 lb./ac pure seed with 17 to 29% germ. Yields may be increased with proper management and improved varieties.

STAND MANAGEMENT: Seed head production is influenced by the amount of light reaching the crown. Burn plants in the spring/early summer (May - July) or mow to 1 - 2 inch stubble height to remove old biomass. Burning or mowing in August will injure plants if they have already begun to flower. Plants do not need to be burned every year to produce seed, although viable seed production may be lower on unburned plants. Burning annually will reduce plant vigor, but proper fertilization may compensate for biomass removal.

EXPECTED PRODUCTIVE STAND LIFE: Stands persisted 6 years under irrigation at the Brooksville PMC. However annual biomass removal without fertilization severely reduced plant numbers after 4 years. Proper management will increase stand longevity.

Other included information includes:

- Seed and plant photos of each species. See Figure 8-Brooksville.1

- Additional Publications Addressing Native Species Production.

- Additional Sources of Useful Information.

- Equipment Dealers.

Figure 8-Brooksville.1 Seed and flowers of splitbeard bluestem, *Andropogon ternaries*

Jimmy Carter Plant Materials Center, Americus, GA

HISTORY AND BACKGROUND

Year and process leading to its establishment: What is now the Jimmy Carter PMC, located in Americus, GA, was one of the first SCS nurseries established by the congressional action in 1935.

History: The nursery became operational in 1935, with the primary emphasis on tree and shrub production but with an observational nursery component. Available records show that the nursery shipped 9,719,437 nursery stock plants in 1937.[456] The first personnel reference for the manager at Americus appears in 1938. It was John Powell. He started his SCS center career in 1936 as a junior horticulturist at the SCS nursery at High Point, NC. He moved to the Americus, GA nursery in 1937, and became the manager in 1938.[457] He served in this position until the nursery closed in 1953 except for a stint as a naval officer in the Pacific during World War II.

The nursery closed in 1954. When Don Williams, SCS Administrator, testified in 1954 on the 1955 appropriations bill, he stated that cooperative agreements were completed for the operation of four closed nurseries that had been selected to become PMCs.[458] Americus was one. A cooperative agreement had been worked out with the Georgia Agricultural Experiment Station, with SCS financial and technical help. John transferred from the SCS Nursery manager position to the PMC manager position as a University employee. This cooperative agreement with the University lasted until 1975 when the PMC returned to SCS operations, and with John as manager. He remained in this position until his retirement in 1982, serving as manager for forty-three years.

In 1995, the PMC name was changed to the Jimmy Carter PMC; President Carter was raised near Americus.

Hugh Hammond Bennett said, following a trip to the region in 1947, "Throughout this region (Southeast) there are great areas of land of variable soil and drainage conditions which are beginning to be brought into productive use by pasture man and rancher. The SCS has brought about this development....This has been done by fitting the various grasses which have proved to be good pasture grasses, into the right places:...Pensacola Bahiagrass on well-drained soils far down into Florida."[459]

Land Tenure: The Americus PMC contains 327 acres, which are owned by NRCS.

Service Area: The Plant Materials Center serves NRCS field offices, public agencies, commercial seed and plant producers, and the general public in Georgia, Alabama, North Carolina, and parts of Florida, and Tennessee. These states present a wide range of climatic and soil conditions and include a total of fourteen major land resource areas representing over 120 million acres across the southeastern U.S. Elevations in the service area range from sea level to 1000 feet. Temperatures range from a low of -20 degrees in the mountains to a high of 110 degrees. The frost-free growing season varies from 130 days in the mountains to more than 230 days along the coast. Annual rainfall over the area ranges from forty-five inches to eighty inches.

OUTPUT

Conservation Plant Development: While the Jimmy Carter PMC has had several outstanding releases, based on their total production and ecological benefits, 'Pensacola' Bahiagrass is the heavy hitter. It is among the top ten of all releases from all PMCs. Its benefits of $31 million exceed the total budget of the seventy year life span of the center. During the nursery years and for several thereafter their releases were mostly informal. Either the plants found their way onto to the market from nursery production or, after the nurseries closed, the informal releases just oozed into commercial production. Their cost benefit ratio is 3.09.

Table 8-Americus.1 Net production and ecological benefits of releases

Release & Type	Common Name	Release Year	Total Production	Unit	Net Value to Producer	Net Ecological Value
Arlington, informal	sericea lespedeza	1939	717,800	LB	$(177,647)	$1,537,887
Pensacola, CV	Bahiagrass	1944	36,813,261	LB	$4,815,422	$31,202,701
101, informal	bicolor lespedeza	1947	18,087,900	PL	$725,736	$738,102
Browntop, informal	millet	1950	535,900	LB	$26,015	$193,036
Ball	clover	1952	6,000	LB	$702	$780
Amclo, CV	arrowleaf clover	1963	854,300	LB	$278,342	$57,051
Thorsby, informal	cowpea	1964	1,567,600	LB	$27,381	$27,237
Ambro, informal,	virgata lespedeza	1971	6,533	LB	$3,836	$3,172
Wilmington, informal		1971	29,810	LB	$ (13,796)	$6,623
Athens, informal	sawtooth oak	1972	1,680,700	PL	$15,967,999	$999,727
Dove, CV	Proso millet	1972	1,971,000	LB	$21,535	$466,675
Ellagood, CV	autumn olive	1986	191,150	PL	$255,308	$17,970
Amquail, informal	Thunberg's lespedeza	1987	15,085,257	PL	$5,599,655	$69,337
Flageo, CV	marshhay cordgrass	1990	1,647,800	PL	$ (21,157)	$202,711
Big-O, CV	crabapple	1992	19,000	PL	$28,674	$1,607
Restorer, CV	giant bulrush	1993	3,114,750	PL	$296,694	$1,180,670
Sumter Orange, informal	daylily	1993	194,560	PL	$73,553	$1
Wetlander, informal	giant cutgrass	1993	2,163,750	PL	$276,360	$468,161
Total					$ 28,184,611	$ 37,173,446
Production and Ecological Benefits from Releases:						$65,358,057
Gross PMC operating budget; 1935 - 2005						$21,125,225
Net Production and Ecological Benefits from Releases:						**$44,232,832**

Table 8-Americus.2 Other releases

Release & Type	Common Name	Release Year	Explanation
Wild, informal	*Sudangrass*	*1950*	*Production data lacking*
Asheville, informal	tall fescue	1952	Production data lacking
101, informal	bicolor lespedeza	1954	Production data lacking
Thorsby, informal	bicolor lespedeza	1954	Production data lacking
Nakuru, informal	rescuegrass	1959	Production data lacking
Artex, informal	Texas millet	1960	Production data lacking
Davis, informal	hairy indigo	1962	Production data lacking
Dadeville, informal	smooth yellow vetch	1969	Production data lacking
Clanton, informal	tick clover	1985	Production data lacking
Georgia 5, CV	tall fescue	1992	NRCS not lead release agency
Americus, CV	hairy vetch	1993	Production data lacking
Doncorae, informal	Brunswickgrass	1993	Production data lacking

Release & Type	Common Name	Release Year	Explanation
AU Early Cover, CV	hairy vetch	1994	Production data lacking
AU Ground Cover, CV	caley pea	1994	Production data lacking
AU Sunrise', CV	crimson clover	1997	Production data lacking
Americus, CV	yellow indiangrass	2002	Production data lacking
Kinchafoonee, GP	Virginia wildrye	2004	Production data lacking
Newberry, GP	Indiangrass	2005	Production data lacking
Union, GP	purpletop	2005	Production data lacking
Muckalee, GP	woolgrass	2008	Post 2005, production unknown
Sumter, GP	soft rush	2008	Post 2005, production unknown
AU Sunup, CV	crimson clover	2009	Post 2005, production unknown
Penn Center, GP	switchgrass	2010	Post 2005, production unknown
Late, informal	hairy indigo	unknown	Production data lacking

These released, some with Auburn University, reflect not only the increasing cooperation between the two, but the shifting priorities to new plants for cropland protection and wetland restoration. Donald Surrency, a plant materialist specialist from 1984 through 2006, took a strong leadership role in the wetland restoration work.

Developed and Delivered Technology - Listed Publications

Table 8-Americus.3 Number of PMC web site publications by type

Type of Publication	No.	Type of Publication	No.
Information Brochures and Flyers	7	PMC Annual Technical Report	3
Major Publications	5	Popular Journal or Magazine Articles	1
Miscellaneous Popular Articles	6	Published Abstracts	1
Miscellaneous Technical Article	5	Release Brochure	13
Newsletters	9	Release Notices	5
Plant Fact Sheets	12	Technical Notes	5
Plant Guides	10	Technical Poster	4
Plant Materials Annual Report of Activities	3		

The total number of web site publications is eighty-nine.

Developed and Delivered Technology - Featured Vegetative Accomplishments

In recent years, the Jimmy Carter PMC has covered a broad spectrum of plant materials technology, a part of which has been outside the conventional privy of PMC work. Yet, all contribute to the body of knowledge about the use of plants for conservation work. Two are briefly reviewed.

1. Georgia Native Plant Material Guide for Longleaf Pine Understory[460]

Longleaf pine forests and savannas once covered approximately ninety-two million acres across the Southeast United States. Today, less than three percent of the original habitat remains. Throughout the historic range, the longleaf pine ecosystem is being impacted by forest conversion, fire suppression, habitat fragmentation, and invasive species.

Since 1936, longleaf pine acreage in Georgia has declined by over ninety

Figure 8-Americus.1 Longleaf pine plantation

percent. Most of the remaining longleaf pine habitat in Georgia is found on military bases and on large privately owned tracts and quail plantations in the Red Hills and Lower Dougherty Plain.

The Conservation Reserve Program (CRP) practice CP36 was created to restore the longleaf pine ecosystem on cropland that is within its historical range. The practice both restores the longleaf pine as well as the understory plant community, which includes the deerberry plant.

Provisions of the practice also deal with the control of invasive grasses and forbs that will out-compete native plant species that are naturally occurring or planted. This publication lends assistance to all land owners eager to improve their understory cover on land once occupied by longleaf pine.

2. Plant Materials Program Assisting Small Farmers in Alabama, Georgia and South Carolina[461]

The NRCS Small Farm Initiative specifically addresses small and limited resource farmer issues. The following are highlights of continuing efforts by the Plant Materials Program personnel to assist small farmers in Georgia.

Establishing on-farm demonstrations is one tool that works well for accomplishing this. For example, one small and limited resource farmer was assisted with establishing warm season grass plantings on his property and provided site specific information on establishment and management. This production of high quality forage helped sustain a low-input system. Another farmer was assisted in improving an on-farm wildlife habitat by constructing a duck pond and planting 'Dove' proso millet, sunflower, and 'Atlantic' coastal panicgrass, on eroding slopes adjacent to the pond. Even though one landowner

Figure 8-Americus.2 Alpaca pasture

grew up on a livestock farm in west Georgia, she needed professional plant materials help with forages for grazing her alpaca herd. The Plant Materials Program provided seed to establish a demonstration planting of native grasses for grazing, and provided other onsite assistance.

The Plant Materials Center increased the 'Trail of Tears' corn seed stock and helped reintroduce this very rare and special crop to the descendants of the Cherokee People that once covered the North Georgia Mountains. The corn was grown in a protected and irrigated area at the Plant Materials Center so that viable seed stock can be produced for future use. This special line of corn dates back to the 1830s, and accompanied the Eastern Cherokee

Figure 8-Americus.3 'Trail of Tears' corn seed stock

Tribes, known as White Eagle corn, on their 'Trail of Tears' west. This corn has been produced in small amounts for the past 163 years. The PMC produced 750 pounds of seed and returned it to the Georgia Tribes of the Eastern Band of Cherokee Indians.

Although some form of silvopasture management has been practiced for centuries, as an agroforestry practice it is specifically designed and managed for the production of trees, tree products, forage and livestock. Silvopasture results when forage crops are deliberately introduced or enhanced in a timber production system, or timber crops are deliberately introduced or enhanced in a forage production system. As a silvopasture, timber and pasture are managed as a single integrated system. Silvopasture combines trees with forage and livestock production. The trees are managed for high-value saw logs and at the same time provide shade and shelter for livestock and forage.

Figure 8-Americus.4 Field training conference

The silvopasture methodology offers diversity for small farmers by providing income opportunities from timber products, forages, and livestock. This field consists of pecan trees, forages, and livestock. The grazing area consists of Pensacola bahiagrass and crimson clover. From a conservation point of view, the practice not only impacts water quality by reducing soil erosion, but it addresses nutrient management and carbon sequestration, and other resource concerns.

Another successful tool used by the Jimmy Carter PMC includes conferences and field tours designed to meet the specific needs of small and limited resource farmers. The PMC, with support from Fort Valley State University, has held such conferences and tours with great success, not only with the numbers attending but quality and quantity of the subject matter covered.

Ho'olehua, HI Plant Materials Center

HISTORY AND BACKGROUND

Year and process leading to its establishment: The Ho'olehua, HI PMC was established by congressional action in 1957, initially on Maui, then in 1972 to the fertile agricultural plains of Ho'olehua, on Molokai. The Center has developed technology for cover crops, windbreaks, grazing systems, native plant production, and wildlife habitat. Controlling erosion, enhancing and protecting our natural resource base by using plant materials is the main mission. The Ho'olehua PMC has developed 'Tropic Coral' tall erythrina for use in windbreaks; 'Tropic Lalo' paspalum for use in ground cover in orchards, waterways, and roadsides; 'Tropic Sun' sun hemp for green manure, cover crops, and energy conservation; and 'Tropic Shore' seashore paspalum for stabilizing the shorelines and banks of aquaculture ponds, canals, and streams with brackish or salty water.

Land Tenure: The PMC encompasses eighty acres owned by the Hawaii Department of Land and Natural Resources.

Service Area: The area served by the Ho'olehua PMC include the Hawaiian Islands, Guam, Islands of the Commonwealth of the Northern Marianas, the Republic of Belau, Federated States of Micronesia, Marshall Islands and American Samoa, all of which owe their shape primarily to volcanic building. The islands all have been modified by erosion under strongly localized conditions. Elevations vary from sea level to more than 10,000 feet above sea level.

Hoolehua HI

Soils are derived from volcanic lava, eruptive deposits of ash, tuff and cinders, and limestone and alluvial deposits from coral reefs. Both the age and variety of parent material, plus extreme ranges in rainfall, have resulted in a complexity of soil types. Rainfall in the PMC service area ranges from less than ten inches to more than 390 inches annually. The driest areas are semi-desert.

Land use is diversified. Large acreages are devoted to ranching, sugarcane, macadamia nuts, coffee, and pineapple. Smaller acreages are used for truck crops, orchards and subsistence farming.

OUTPUT

Conservation Plant Development

Table 8-Ho'olehua.1 Net production and ecological benefits of releases

Release	Common Name	Release Year	Total Production	Unit	Net Value to Producer	Net Ecological Value
Kuiaha, CV	Desmodium	1969	80	LB	$245	$49
Tropic Sun, CV	sun hemp	1982	186,916	LB	$112,435	$67,788
Tropic Lalo, CV	Paspalum	1984	28,042,318	PL	$254,868	$179,597
Tropic Coral, CV	tall erythrina	1985	7,109,000	PL	$7,836,118	$1,485,795
Tropic Shore, CV	seashore paspalum	1988	312,321	PL	$30,427	$82,494
Kamiloloa, GP	Florida hopbush	2000	403	LB	$12,536	$ 4,282
Total					$8,246,629	$1,820,006
Production and Ecological Benefits from Releases:						$10,066,635
Gross PMC operating budget; 1957 - 2005						$14,384,323
Net Production and Ecological Benefits from Releases:						($4,317,688)

Their cost benefit ratio is (0.69).

Table 8-Ho'olehua.2 Other releases

Release & Type	Common Name	Release Year	Explanation
Tropic Verde, CV	perennial soybean	1992	Production data lacking
Kaho'olawe, GP	piligrass	2003	Production data lacking
Kaho'olawe, GP	kawelu	2005	Production data lacking
Makakupa'ia, GP	Aweoweo	2007	Post 2005, production unknown

Developed and Delivered Technology - Listed Publications

Table 8-Ho'olehua.3 Number of PMC web site publications by type

Type of Publication	No.	Type of Publication	No.
Information Brochures and Flyers	1	Published Abstracts	2
Miscellaneous Technical Article	8	Published Symposium Proceedings	2
Newsletters	7	Refereed Journal Articles	1
Other Publication Types	1	Release Brochure	3
Plant Fact Sheets	7	Release Notices	1

Type of Publication	No.	Type of Publication	No.
Plant Guides	2	Technical Notes	5
Plant Materials Annual Report of Activities	2	Technical Poster	3

The total number of web site publications is forty-eight.

Developed and Delivered Technology - Featured Vegetative Accomplishments

Use of Piligrass (*Heteropogon contortus*) Hay Bales for the Island of Kaho`olawe's Highly Erodible Sites[462]

Piligrass is an erect perennial native bunch grass found in the warm tropical regions of both hemispheres. It was once the main thatching material used by Polynesians for the construction of their homes. In Hawaii, it grows between one to three feet in height, mainly in arid and sometimes rocky areas from sea level to over a thousand feet. The long-awned seeds are sharp and pointed, forming tangled masses as they mature. When the seeds come in contact with soil moisture the long awns, which have sharp, barbed tips, arch and twist, which presses the seed into the soil.

The concept of using hay bales of piligrass for conservation comes from their physical value in stopping wind and flowing water erosion and the presence of seed in the bales that has the potential of germinating and producing a stabilizing grass stand.

Hay bales have been used for years for controlling erosion on Kaho'olawe, where overgrazing has created a desolate barren landscape. However, the principal reason for their use now is that the island was once littered with unexploded military ordinance. Though it has been partially swept or cleared of these ordinances, there are no assurances the island is completely void of them. If no ordinances were ever used on Kaho'olawe, implementing conventional conservation practices, with or without hay bales, would be relative easy. The use of machinery such as disks, tillers, and drills to prepare seedbeds is inadvisable because of the potential for the presence of ordinances, and much of the area that needs treatment is steep, gullied and rocky, and not accessible for mechanical treatment. Thus the use of bales, though tedious, time consuming and expensive, is much safer and environmentally desirable.

The top one third of the island is severely eroded and void of any significant vegetation. The area is extremely windy, dry, infertile and at times inaccessible by vehicle. The bales are available from the PMC as a by-product of the evaluation and seed increase process. Seed fields that are baled for use on Kaho'olawe Island are allowed to mature before baling. Each bale weighs approximately thirty pounds and is 27" x 18" x 15" in size. The bales are held together with polypropylene UV resistant baler twine.

Uses of baled piligrass: Once in place, the piligrass seed bales have multi-purpose uses. They include:

- Serve as a seed source of piligrass,

- provide physical barriers to trap sediment and divert water from roadways or other highly eroded areas,

- aid in protecting newly planted plants,

- serve as seedbeds for native plants,

- Physically control soil erosion, increase soil moisture retention, and provide a micro-environment for native plants to establish.

Methods used to test the value of the bales include:

- To create sediment traps, where the bales are placed in gullies and washouts. These structures utilized the entire piligrass bales and were placed end to end within shallow gullies, depressions or washouts. Depending on the size of the treatment area, anywhere between seven to twelve bales may be used.

- To construct berms. Due to the nature in which the bales are made, they can be peeled apart into various sized flakes or sections. This characteristic has allowed the fabrication of bundles, with piligrass flakes encased in commercially manufactured erosion control matting (geotextiles). Geo-textile matting is comprised either of straw, coconut fibers or polypropylene yarn, which are encased within polypropylene netting. Bundles are constructed by placing piligrass sheets or flakes within the geotextile matting and rolling it like a burrito. These bundles are placed across slopes on highly erodible sites and fastened in place with short wooden stakes.

- Piligrass seed bales have also been used to construct "planter boxes" to help establish native plants by creating a desirable microenvironment. Eight to ten bales are arranged to form a square (6' to 7.5' in length). Within the square, recycled potting mix from previous planting projects are utilized to provide a desirable planting medium. If available, water is sparingly applied. In some cases one end of the box was left open on the windward side of the square. This enabled the windblown soil to accumulate within the box.

- Other configurations, using the "planter boxes" concept have been used, such as creating a "C" or an "X". These configurations range in length of between ten to twelve feet. An "X" shape design is to trap windblown soil deposition and seed from the any direction. The center of the "X" with its square (18" by 18") hole acted as a planter box where seeds could be planted.

- Piligrass hay bales have also been used simply as mulch.[463] Flakes of the bales two to three inches thick were peeled away from the bales and laid directly on the surface. The flakes can be laid end to end across the slope. Due to the thickness and weight of the hay flakes, staking pegs were not necessary to prevent them from blowing away. Some results are shown below.

- Still another use for piligrass bales is the construction of water diversion structures. These structures are strategically placed along access roads and small waterways, to divert water off road shoulders to where it can exit to a safe outlet.

Results: Piligrass hay bales had a positive impact on the revegetation process of Kaho'olawe. It is clearly evident that the areas surrounding the outer rim of Lua Makika crater is beginning to look greener than a few years ago. See Table 8.Ho'olehua.4 and examples in Figures 8-Ho'olehua.1, 2 and 3. Though all of the greenery is not native plants, a good portion of it is, especially on the more severely eroded sections of northeast and southeast flanks of Lua Makika. Plants invading include Kamonamona (*Cenchrus agrimonioides*), wild leadwort *(Plumbago zeylanica)*; Maui chaff flower *(Achyranthes splendens)*, Aweoweo *(Chenopodium oauhense),* piligrass *(Heteropogon contortus),* and Florida hopbush *(Dodonaea viscose)*. The wild leadwort is showing remarkable growth within gullies, swales and the hardpan areas.

The implementation of various conservation methods utilizing native plants, have positively impacted the sensitive environment of Kaho'olawe. Success in the use of hay-bales has been realized, thereby allowing other native plants to establish as well.

Table 8.Ho'olehua.4 Average Vegetative Cover

Mulch Rate (lb./acre)	% cover after 63 days	% cover after 173 days
500	1.6	17.7
1000	1.6	17.9
1500	2.4	23.5
2000	6.5	49.2
4000	37.6	74.1
6000	9.8	49.3

Figure 8-Ho'olehua.1 X configuration   Three years later

Figure 8-Ho'olehua.2 Bales for water diversion -   Five years later

189

Figure 8-Ho'olehua.3 Diversion, one year's results   four year's results

---

Aberdeen, ID Plant Materials Center

HISTORY AND BACKGROUND

Year and process leading to its establishment: The Aberdeen Nursery was authorized in 1939, by the same congressional action which had established SCS production nurseries nationally.

History: Initially an outlying evaluation site for the Pullman SCS Nursery, Aberdeen became a full staffed nursery in 1939. SCS rented a thirty-five acre farm on the south side of Aberdeen for seed increase and seed production evaluations and constructed its first building.[464] Its first plantings were to evaluate grass and legume seed production under irrigation, and then they established an observational nursery in the 1940 crop year. The same year the nursery started, they began a range seeding evaluation with the University of Idaho on land at the local airport. Also in 1940 the nursery established what is called today a field evaluation planting at the Tetonia Branch Experiment Station to evaluate both species adaptation and various cultural and management techniques.

Aberdeen was one of ten facilities that continued operations as a PMC after 1953, when most soil conservation nurseries were discontinued and production was transferred to state/local governments and commercial entities. The Aberdeen nursery continued its operation on the rented land until it closed in 1953. Rental fees exceeded what was possible for the new plant materials center to pay. That meant seed fields were plowed under, evaluation plots were lost, and except for the valuable germplasm, most of the plant selection work of the nursery was also lost. The center was basically closed in 1953.

During 1953 and 1954 the South Bingham Soil Conservation District stepped forward and offered to borrow money and purchase land for the new facility. Just a year old itself, the district, without a source of income, found loan sources and by 1955 a property was leased to SCS and the first plantings were established. The District also built a Quonset type building for seed cleaning and equipment storage for $5,900, mostly from money borrowed from the North Side and Dry Creek Districts.

The center forged close working relationships with Agricultural Research Service geneticists at Logan, Utah and the U.S. Forest Service Shrub Sciences Laboratory experts at Provo, Utah to expand the portfolio of new conservation plants available to revegetation initiatives. Aberdeen pioneered riparian restoration and stabilization methods for semi-arid and desert zones. The Center has continued to support an active commercial seed production community in the region.

Land Tenure: The PMC operates on 112 acres; forty-five acres are owned by South Bingham Soil Conservation District. The remaining sixty-seven acres are owned by the Department of Idaho Fish and Game.

Service Area: The center is in the middle of the Snake River plain in southern Idaho and serves areas between the Rocky Mountains and the mountain ranges to the west. Elevation ranges from 1,700-12,000 feet through several vegetation zones. The continental climate changes rapidly with altitude, and is characterized as cold with wet winters, and dry summers with cool nights and warm days. Total precipitation varies from less than five inches to more than twenty-five inches annually. Vegetation zones range from desert shrub, grassland, shrub grassland, open woodland, and evergreen forest.

Land use includes livestock grazing, irrigated and dryland agriculture, recreation, wildlife refuge, timber production, hunting, mining, utility and transportation corridors, and urban areas.

OUTPUT

Conservation Plant Development

Table 8-Aberdeen.1 Net production and ecological benefits of releases

Release & Type	Common Name	Release Year	Total Production	Unit	Net Value to Producer	Net Ecological Value
P-27, CV	Siberian wheatgrass	1953	3,914,525	LB	$624,373	$16,679,421
Topar	intermediate wheatgrass	1953	271,500	LB	82,048	$762,666
Sodar, CV	streambank wheatgrass	1954	3,467,043	LB	$6,071,860	$16,262,143
Pomar, CV	orchardgrass	1966	14,700	LB	$3,146	$31,728
Regar, CV	meadow brome	1966	9,621,077	LB	$6,437,864	$14,161,254
Nezpar, CV	Indian ricegrass	1978	1,778,925	LB	$17,168	$1,450,318
Tegmar, CV	Dwarf intermediate wheatgrass	1968	558,500	LB	$20,421,836	2,189,908
Magnar, CV	basin wildrye	1979	3,189,719	LB	$16,771,128	12,826,209
Appar, CV	prairie flax	1980	1,330,261	LB	$8,358,865	$4,545,502
Delar, CV	small burnet	1981	1,540,465	LB	$2,161,726	1,185,965
Goldar, CV	bluebunch wheatgrass	1989	2,239,012	LB	$14,048,864	7,116,859
Clearwater, GP	alpine penstemon	1994	9,160	LB	$226,881	$54,273
Richfield, GP	penstemon	1994	26,600	LB	$645,833	$57,221
Rush, CV	intermediate wheatgrass	1994	2,414,500	LB	$5,177,139	$6,454,836
Bannock, CV	thickspike wheatgrass	1995	943,540	LB	$3,700,197	$3,338,339
No. Cold Desert, GP	winterfat	2001	300	LB	($9,511)	918
Snake River Plains, GP	fourwing altbush	2001	8,000	LB	($230,393)	$17,721
Totals					$84,509,024	$87,140,218
Gross Production and Ecological benefits from cultivars						$171,164,242

Release & Type	Common Name	Release Year	Total Production	Unit	Net Value to Producer	Net Ecological Value
Gross PMC operating budget; 1939 - 2005						$24,704,851
Net Production and Ecological Benefits from Releases						**$146,094,740**

The data shown above is based only on the production of the listed releases by commercial growers for the years of 1977 through 2005. The operating costs are for 1939 - 2005. The net benefit from the production of the Aberdeen releases exceeds the operating budget for that sixty-six year period by $2.21 million a year, or a benefit to cost benefit ratio of a super 6.9.

Table 8-Aberdeen.2 Other releases

Release & Type	Common Name	Release Year	Explanation
Ephraim, CV	crested wheatgrass	1983	NRCS not lead release agency
Paiute, CV	orchardgrass	1983	NRCS not lead release agency
Douglas, CV	crested wheatgrass	1994	NRCS not lead release agency
Vavilov CV	Siberian wheatgrass	1994	NRCS not lead release agency
Sand Hollow, GP	bottlebrush squirreltail	1996	Production data lacking
Aberdeen, GP	laurel willow	1997	Production data lacking
Bear Lake, GP	alkali bulrush	1997	Production data lacking
Bear River , GP	alkali bulrush	1997	Production data lacking
Camas, GP	hardstem bulrush	1997	Production data lacking
Centennial, GP	Nebraska sedge	1997	Production data lacking
CJ Strike, GP	creeping spikerush	1997	Production data lacking
Fort Boise , GP	alkali bulrush	1997	Production data lacking
Fort Boise, GP	common threesquare	1997	Production data lacking
Hagermans, GP	hardstem bulrush	1997	Production data lacking
Malheur GP	common threesquare	1997	Production data lacking
Market Lake, GP	common threesquare	1997	Production data lacking
Modoc, GP	Nebraska sedge	1997	Production data lacking
Mud Lake, GP	creeping spikerush	1997	Production data lacking
Ogden Bay, GP	hardstem bulrush	1997	Production data lacking
Roswell, GP	Baltic rush	1997	Production data lacking
Ruby Lake, GP	Nebraska sedge	1997	Production data lacking
Sterling, GP	Nebraska sedge	1997	Production data lacking
Sterling, GP	Baltic rush	1997	Production data lacking
Stillwater, GP	Baltic rush	1997	Production data lacking
Stillwater, GP	hardstem bulrush	1997	Production data lacking
Stillwater, GP	alkali bulrush	1997	Production data lacking
Railroad Valley, GP	Baltic rush	1998	Production data lacking
Wayne Kirch, GP	common threesquare	1998	Production data lacking
Fish Creek, GP	squirreltail	2003	NRCS not lead release agency
Toe Jam Creek, GP	squirreltail	2003	NRCS not lead release agency
Anatone, GP	bluebunch wheatgrass	2004	Production data lacking
Maple Grove, GP	prairie flax	2004	Production data lacking
Vavilov II, CV	Siberian wheatgrass	2008	NRCS not lead release agency
Recovery, CV	western wheatgrass	2009	Post 2005, production unknown

Of the twenty-nine non-cultivar releases made during this period, five are recorded as being produced commercially by 2010.

Developed and Delivered Technology - Listed Publications

Table 8-Aberdeen.3 Number of PMC web site publications by type

Type of Publication	No.	Type of Publication	No.
Information Brochures and Flyers	15	PMC Annual Technical Report	3
Major Publications	16	Propagation Protocols	4
Miscellaneous Popular Articles	27	Published Abstracts	2
Miscellaneous Technical Article	10	Published Symposium Proceedings	2
Newsletters	4	Refereed Journal Articles	3
Other Publication Types	6	Release Brochure	18
Plant Fact Sheets	21	Release Notices	22
Plant Guides	139	Technical Notes	55
Plant Materials Annual Report of Activities	2	Technical Poster	1

This total number of 350 web site publications is indeed impressive. Additionally, Aberdeen personnel have contributed with numerous other plant material teams in developing regional publications.

Developed and Delivered Technology - Featured Vegetative Accomplishments

The innovativeness of the Aberdeen PMC cannot be captured with one example, nor can space be allotted to mention all of them. Those that came out of the wetland work by Chris Hoag are so numerous that they are discussed in the Key Leaders chapter. As a result, two relatively recent innovations have been selected as examples.

1.   The Jet Harvester: A Shop Built Tool for Harvesting Forb and Shrub Seed[465]

The explosion of the use of native forbs for conservation use has increased the need for technology for all aspects of seed production, including harvesting. This is a significant obstacle to large-scale production of these plants. Many of our native forbs and shrubs bear light, easily-shattered seed which is not readily harvested by conventional processes, such as direct combining or by swathing followed by combining. Additionally, many native species have a pappus, awns or other appendages which further exacerbate the harvesting process. Many mature indeterminately, requiring multiple seed harvest dates which is not feasible when using common harvesting methods. These harvesting problems result in prices higher than can be justified for conservation work.

The authors at the Aberdeen PMC developed a machine, coined the jet harvester, which quickly and easily removes ripe seed from plants with minimal losses. The machine is non-destructive, resulting in reduced inert material in the harvested product. Features include:

- PTO driven
- Fully adjustable airspeed
- Easy cleanout
- Useable on numerous species
- Easy to manufacture
- Allows multiple harvests

From the prototype Jet Harvester developed by the PMC, specifications and measurements were developed, allowing others to manufacture equally effective harvesters.

Operation: The images below provide insight into the construction and operation.

Airflow is adjusted using the tractor PTO drive. Higher speeds are useful to pick up heavier or mature seed which is still clinging to the plant. Avoid excessively high speeds which will suck the seed through the fan without dropping it into the collection tank. PTO speeds of 1,000 to 1,600 rpm (fan speeds of 3,000 to 5,000 rpm) give good results for most species. Some minor experimentation is required with each species to determine the optimum operating speeds and techniques. Seed travels through the hose and is released into the collection tank without traveling through the potentially damaging fan impellers.

Seed is dumped into bins or garbage cans using the trap door located at the base of the collection tank. Cleaning the tank and hose between species or lots can be achieved by revving the PTO. Additional cleaning is done by scraping the inside of the tank or blowing air from a compressor, however this is rarely necessary. Occasionally, stems, sticks and other inert matter get lodged in the hose. This can usually be removed by increasing the rpm on the PTO.

Summary: The jet harvester significantly improves the harvest of many forbs and shrub species. It has been used at the PMC to harvest fourwing saltbush (*Atriplex canescens*), winterfat (*Kraschenninikovia lanata*), Gray's biscuitroot (*Lomatium grayi*), nine-leaf biscuitroot (*L. triternatum*), fernleaf biscuitroot (*L. dissectum*), Douglas' dustymaiden (*Chaenactis douglasii*) and sulphurflower buckwheat (*Eriogonum umbellatum*). It is much more efficient than hand harvesting and effectively reduces harvesting time well as post-harvest cleaning. The jet harvester is also very easy to clean between seed lots and species, and allows for multiple harvest of indeterminately maturing species.

Figure 8-Aberdeen.1 Examples of using the Jet Harvester - Clockwise from upper left: harvesting fourwing saltbush (*Antriplex conescens*), harvesting biscuitroot (*Lomatium sp.*), dumping seed from collection tank into a garbage can recepticle, and harvesting Douglas' dustymaide (*Chaenactis douglasii*).

2. Quick Methods to Estimate Seed Quality - The "Pop" Test[466]

For certified seed production, seed samples must be sent to an accredited seed laboratory for purity, germination, and/or viability testing. Getting these results back may take weeks to months depending on the lab, time of year, and species being tested. There is also a chance that the lab results will indicate viability less than the standard required for seed certification, in which case the seed must be re-cleaned and samples resubmitted for further testing. This can be very time consuming and expensive. In order to expedite this process, the Aberdeen PMC uses a novel technique that allow them to estimate seed quality during the cleaning process and thus reduce the chance of not meeting seed certification standards.

Healthy seed contains on average twelve to fifteen percent moisture content at the end of the cleaning process. When placed over sufficient heat this water is converted to a gas, which exerts tremendous pressure against the seed coat causing an explosion. In the case of popcorn, as the gasses escape, the inner starch fills portions of the endosperm and expands into a tasty treat. A more practical (but less delicious) use of this phenomenon is to estimate seed quality before sending seed off to a lab for testing.

The ability of seed to pop is dependent upon seed moisture content and the integrity of the seed coat. Even under good storage conditions, seeds lose this ability as the seed slowly loses moisture. In the case of popcorn, for example, optimum popping moisture content is about fourteen percent. As the moisture content declines to below approximately ten percent, popping performance goes down, and the number of unpopped kernels increases.[467]

Ogle and Cornforth compared the "popping" results of thirteen lots of eight native and introduced grass species with germination tests from the State Seed Laboratory and found a strong correlation between popped seed and overall viability.[468] The trial presented here expands the list of species tested by showing results from six native grasses, three native grass-like wetland species, three native forbs, and two native shrubs.

The hot plate used for the popping test has a sheet of steel welded with mounting brackets to sit over the heating element. Temperatures on the hot plate surface ranged from 126 to 327° C at the high setting with most of the plate lying between 200 and 260° C. Isolated hot spots of over 315 ° C (600° F) occurred at some of the weld points and along one edge of the hot plate.

Figure 8-Aberdeen.2 Hot plate mounted on a propane heater used for conducting "pop" tests.

Popping reactions were measured of eight replications of twenty-five seeds each of the lots tested. Seed was placed in the 200 to 260° C portion of the plate for up to fifteen seconds. Results were divided into three categories, 1) seeds that popped explosively and audibly, 2) seeds that rolled or moved but did not pop, and 3) no response. Means obtained from the pop test were used to create ninety and ninety-five percent confidence intervals (CI), and compared with results from the Idaho State Seed Lab. To provide additional comparisons, viability of some grass-like wetland species, *Penstemon* species and fourwing saltbush was determined using tetrazolium (TZ) tests. Viability comparisons between the pop tests were done using standard germination protocols.

References to the phrase 'combined response' means the sum of the seeds that popped and those that moved.

The combined response of sixteen out of twenty-one grass seed lots were within the ninety percent CI when compared to the standard germination protocols, while ten of twenty-one were within the ninety-five percent CI. The popping alone test tended to be significantly lower than lab results with only one seed lot being within the ninety percent CI.

All results from the grass-like wetland species were tightly correlated. Results from popping alone of hardstem bulrush were within the ninety-five percent CI, while the combined response slightly overestimated viability. Lab results of alkali bulrush and common three square fell within the combined response of ninety-five percent CI. Popping alone slightly underestimated lab results in common threesquare but was within the ninety-five percent CI for alkali bulrush.

Results of one of the two lots of the forb Lewis flax fell within the ninety-five percent CI of the combined response. Popping alone significantly underestimated viability in both cases. Both popping and combined response underestimated viability in the tested lots of firecracker and 'Venus' penstemon. The shrub winterfat seed did not react as visibly to heat as some of the other species tested, but careful observation did reveal swelling, rolling, and occasional popping. The combined pop and movement category correlated well with lab test results falling within the ninety-five percent CI. Popping alone did not correspond with lab viability test results. No response was detected from any seed of fourwing saltbush.

Summary: Our tests showed a reasonably close correlation (generally within ten percent) between seed quality and response to heat for newer lots of seed, but a significant overestimation of quality in older seed lots. Our tests also revealed several species for which the pop test was ineffective. The pop test is not one hundred percent reliable and will never replace actual germination or even TZ testing, but it can be used by seed producers and end users to provide a general indication of seed quality and reduce processing time.

Manhattan, KS Plant Materials Center

HISTORY AND BACKGROUND

Year and process leading to its establishment: The Manhattan Nursery was one of the first SCS nurseries established, and it survived during the closing of many nurseries in 1953 to become a PMC.

History: The present PMC had its origin as part of the first SCS national network of production and observational nurseries. The principal objectives of the Manhattan nursery were to produce woody plants and seed for re-vegetating the Great Plains. It was a national leader from the beginning in gross production and the identification of superior conservation plants.

The SCS nursery at Manhattan has had strong leadership from the start. Early leaders in the Administration were Warren Giles, who served as nursery manager for 1936-1939, and later became President of Mississippi State University. Charles Fletcher Swingle, a horticulturist, was another early leader who served the nursery from July 1939 to August 1943. He assisted in tree and grass seed production as well as grass germplasm collection and research. Donald Cornelius joined the nursery staff in 1936 and remained with it until 1948. He was the agronomist on the staff and provided leadership in the selection of superior grasses. The Lawrence Daily Journal - World of Lawrence, KS reported that on April 30, 1937, Cornelius made an experimental planting of a bluestem grass seed field.[469] By 1942 he published results of his Manhattan nursery work.[470] Fred P. Eshbaugh, another horticulturist, became manager of the nursery in 1944, and in 1954 became head of the National Arboretum in Washington D.C. M. Donald Atkins followed Cornelius, providing strong agronomic direction, which continued long after the nursery became a PMC.

At the peak of nursery operations, employee numbers ranged from 150 to 170. Later, the Council Grove CCC camp provided considerable nursery manpower and established a side camp on the nursery.

During World War II, nursery operations were reduced to the level that could be performed by twenty to twenty-five employees. In 1945, additional land was purchased and added to the nursery tract. Maximum woody production often exceeded five million seedlings annually. Piles of grass seed harvested from native stands were said to resemble small mountains. These mountains had to be cleaned and processed to plant on lands needing protection from soil erosion and to provide forage production for a more stable livestock industry.

Nursery scientists noted that great differences occurred in the way grasses responded when planted on different soils at different locations. They also noted that a seed's origin could affect the plants performance and limit its use or adaptability to certain conservation areas. It was observed that plants also varied morphologically with respect to height, spread, and seed production, environmental resistance and other factors even though they were the same species. Some species were also easier to propagate and reproduce than others. While all these things are common knowledge today, they were on the cutting edge in the 1930s and 1940s.

The Manhattan SCS nursery was closed in 1953. The facility became one of the first ten Plant Materials Centers, and was initially operated by Kansas State College for SCS under a reimbursable agreement. This continued until 1965 when SCS resumed their operation of the facility, with Erling Jacobson becoming the SCS manager. It is this rebirth that is considered by many to be the beginning of the modern era of plant materials work at the Manhattan PMC.

The facilities have had a dramatic upgrade since 1990, with the addition of a new office conference room facility, greenhouse, headhouse, lathhouse, seed storage building, an upgrade of the seed cleaning facilities, and remodeling of the former office into a laboratory. These improvements have allowed the Center to provide better services to their customers and to be more efficient and productive.

The observational nursery program at Manhattan was extremely productive in its early years. Three major cultivars were placed on the market by 1945. One was 'Blackwell' switchgrass. Over four million pounds of seed was produced of it from 1977 through 2005, and over 150,000 pounds were produced in 2005, sixty years after it was released.

Land and Tenure: The Center operates on 169 acres, owned by NRCS.

Service Area: The Manhattan PMC serves a diverse region of the heartland including Kansas, Nebraska, northern Oklahoma and eastern Colorado. This area of the country was originally native grasslands dissected by a number of major streams. Wooded riparian areas follow the streams and extend up the slopes. In the east there is precipitation sufficient to support a mixed hardwood community.

Annual amounts of precipitation can vary from forty-two inches in parts of Oklahoma and southeastern Kansas to fourteen inches in western Kansas and Nebraska. Temperatures fluctuate widely and are often accompanied by high winds and long periods without effective precipitation. Soil types also vary widely from the clays of northeastern Oklahoma to the coarse sandy soils found in the Nebraska sandhills. The extremes of climate and soil offer a challenging and varied environment in which conservation plants must survive and flourish to be effective. Today, this region's land use is largely devoted to agriculture. The production of food and fiber is the leading industry in the heartland.

OUTPUT

Conservation Plant Development

Table 8-Manhattan.1 Net production and ecological benefits of releases

Release & Type	Common Name	Release Year	Total Production	Unit	Net Value to Producer	Net Ecological Value
Blackwell, CV	switchgrass	1944	4,694,940	LB	$16,130,316	$28,539,242
El Reno, CV	sideoats grama	1944	3,963,651	LB	$13,321,828	$21,722,042
Cheyenne, CV	indiangrass	1945	681,900	LB	$3,918,137	$2,800,990
Garden, CV	sand bluestem	1960	289,600	LB	$2,370,995	$800,281
Barton, CV	western wheatgrass	1970	2,139,500	LB	$7,203,953	$8,005,138
Caucasian, informal	Caucasian bluestem	1972	138,650	LB	$1,259,173	$419,139
Pink Lady, CV	winterberry euonymus	1973	695,130	PL	-$52,388	$117,909
PMK-24, GP	eastern gamagrass	1974	75,750	LB	$209,699	$61,484
Eureka, CV	thickspike gayfeather	1975	10,780	LB	$491,847	$37,226
Kaneb, CV	purple prairieclover	1975	112,995	LB	$1,919,421	$624,501
Nekan, CV	pitcher sage	1977	21,908	LB	$538,751	$129,960
Prairie Gold, CV	Maximilian sunflower	1978	64,886	LB	$1,209,732	$1,200,365
Sunglow, CV	grayhead prairie coneflower	1978	30,279	LB	$470,767	$569,157
Cimarron, CV	little bluestem	1979	489,850	LB	$2,996,650	$3,618,021
Konza, CV	aromatic sumac	1980	557,416	PL	$13,936	$5,301
Midas, CV,	false sunflower	1984	10,850	LB	$440,207	$57,680
Pete, CV	eastern gamagrass	1988	812,200	LB	$4,943,696	$713,195
Lippert, CV	bur oak	1994	1,750	PL	$507	$1,273
Atkins GP	prairie cordgrass	1998	35,000	PL	$19,978	$62,643
Kanoka, CV	roundhead lespedeza	1998	382	LB	$21,188	$1,802
Southwind, CV	common reed	1998	57,000	PL	$42,993	$42
Reno GP	Illinois bundleflower	1999	800	LB	$5,466	$1,373
Riley GP	partridge pea	1999	6,766	LB	-$7,855	$1,893
Total					$57,468,996	$69,490,656
Production and Ecological Benefits from Releases:						$126,959,652
Gross PMC operating budget; 1935 – 2005						$19,666,490
Net Production and Ecological Benefits from Releases:						**$107,293,162**

198

It is most impressive that the first two releases, both made in 1944, represent forty percent of the centers net production and ecological benefits between 1977 and 2005. Of course, both were in high demand for reseeding, and both have proven over the years as outstanding selections. Their cost benefit ratio is 6.4, which is one of the highest.

Table 8-Manhattan.2 Other releases

Release & Type	Common Name	Release Year	Explanation
Kaw, CV	big bluestem	1950	NRCS not lead release agency
Kanlow, CV	switchgrass	1963	NRCS not lead release agency
Aldous, CV	little bluestem	1966	NRCS not lead release agency
Osage, CV	indiangrass	1966	NRCS not lead release agency
Bend, CV	sand lovegrass	1971	NRCS not lead release agency
Texoka, CV	buffalograss	1974	NRCS not lead release agency
GSF-I, GP	eastern gamagrass	1984	Production lacking
GSF-II, GP	eastern gamagrass	1984	Production lacking
Pronghorn, CV	prairie sandreed	1988	Post 2005, production unknown
Chet,* CV	sand bluestem	2004	NRCS not lead release agency
Verl,* CV	eastern gamagrass	2005	NRCS not lead release agency
Chisholm, GP	Chickasaw plum	2010	Post 2005, production unknown
El Kan, CV	yellow bluestem		Production lacking

* Jointly released by Manhattan and PMCs in Mississippi and Knox City, TX respectively.

Equally impressive is the management Manhattan PMC applied to the pre-varietal release policy, releasing only four, three of which had some commercial production, and the forth was released as a cultivar after such required data was collected.

Developed and Delivered Technology - Listed Publications

Table 8-Manhattan.3 Number of PMC web site publications by category

Type of Publication	No.	Type of Publication	No.
Information Brochures and Flyers	3	Published Abstracts	4
Major Publications	1	Refereed Journal Articles	1
Newsletters	12	Release Brochure	18
Plant Fact Sheets	24	Release Notices	2
Plant Guides	27	Technical Notes	9
Plant Materials Annual Report of Activities	3	Technical Poster	5
PMC Annual Technical Report	3		

The total number of web site publications is 112.

Developed and Delivered Technology - Featured Vegetative Accomplishments

Domesticating native grasses of the Great Plains

During the early periods of nursery operations, the SCS had limited knowledge or experience in harvesting, cleaning, or planting native grass species. The saying, "necessity is the mother of invention" was certainly true in this case. Many Rube Goldberg looking contraptions were assembled with torch, wire, bolts, scrap metal, and inspiration by the nursery crew. The resulting special equipment was used to harvest, clean, and plant the native grasses. Of course, with experience and additional ideas, more advanced equipment is available today. However, the contraptions worked then and in many instances their modifications are working today.

Throughout the period plant scientists observed the great differences that occurred in the way plants responded when planted on different soils and locations. Variations in plant morphology with respect to height, spread, seed production, resistance to environmental factors, propagation ease or difficulty and other factors suggested great potential for within species selections for conservation uses. These differences prompted studies that resulted in a disciplined methodology for the collection, evaluation, and reproduction of native plants.

The business of harnessing the value of native plants for both forage and conservation began to appear in print the mid-1930s. F. C. Gates published *Grasses in Kansas* in 1937,[471] which was more descriptive than a how-to-do-it paper, as was Warren Whitman's 1941, *Grasses of North Dakota*.[472] *Regrassing the Great Plains Areas* appeared in 1947 by M. M. Hoover and others which laid out the potential of grasses as the first line of defense against the raving dust storms.[473] In 1947, A. L. Hafenrichter and A. D. Stoesz published one of the first papers covering the domestication of grasses for conservation use, in which Stoesz covered the grasses of the Great Plains.[474] By the mid-1950s, adequate information had accumulated to publish an all-encompassing technical bulletin *Producing and Harvesting Grass Seed in the Great Plains*, authored by H. W. Cooper, James E. Smith, Jr. and M. D. Atkins in 1957.[475][476] Smith and Atkins followed up in 1967 with a more comprehensive treatment of the 1957 bulletin, allowing the Manhattan staff to develop adaptation maps for twenty-four different plants.

Throughout its existence, from 1935 until today, the Manhattan Nursery, and later the PMC, has been at the center of this evolving science. Of course, they had significant help, including SCS nurseries in Woodward, OK, San Antonio, TX and Mandan/Bismarck, ND, as well as from the State Agriculture Experiment Stations in the Great Plains. A thriving native grass seed industry stands as a testament to this effort, plus millions of re-grassed Great Plains acres.

The following paragraph was taken from an article by S. Ray Smith Jr. and R. D. B. Whalley, titled *A Model for Expanded Use of Native Grasses*, published in the Native Plants Journal in 2002.[477] They point out that interest in native grasses is increasing worldwide and proposed a step-by-step model to be used by plant breeders, ecologists, seed producers, and others interested in expanded uses for native grasses. According to Smith and Whalley the following steps have been used and are relevant for North America and Australia: 1) determine the need; 2) choose an appropriate species; 3) determine breeding system; 4) assess geographic and ecological range; 5) make a collection; 6) assess genetic diversity; 7) determine limitations of species; 8) develop appropriate breeding methods; 9) determine proper release strategy; 10) develop seed conditioning and establishment techniques; 11) develop management techniques; and 12) market development. It is not surprising that the M. D. Atkins and James E. Smith Jr., 1967 publication, *Grass Seed Production and Harvest in the Great Plains* was cited. Actually, although they did not list these items as such, it is a good outline of what they did.

Golden Meadow, LA Plant Materials Center

HISTORY AND BACKGROUND

Year and process leading to its establishment: Congress authorized the establishment of the Center in 1989. The conservation motivation behind it was the extensive erosion of tidal marshes in the western Gulf of Mexico. With NRCS support and the close relationship between State Conservationist, Horace Austin, and the U.S. Senators from Louisiana, the Golden Meadow PMC won the day.

History: Louisiana is losing approximately twenty-five square miles of coastal wetlands annually. It accounts for ninety percent of the nation's annual coastal wetland loss; land loss occurs as marginal erosion and interior marsh deterioration. Causes of this wetland loss have been attributed to a variety of things. Some of these may be slowed or reversed with appropriate vegetative technology. This potential was recognized in the mid and late 1980s, when the PMC Manager, Bob Glennon from Brooksville, FL, made some plantings near Golden Meadow. Congressional approval for the establishment of the Center came in 1989. Currently, efforts are in progress to develop plants and procedures to reverse this coastal wetlands loss.

Land Tenure: The Louisiana Land and Exploration Corporation owns ninety-three acres on which the Center operates.

Service Area: The Center develops plants and procedures to reverse the loss of coastal wetlands in the coastal regions of Louisiana, Mississippi, and Texas.

Galliano, LA

OUTPUT

Conservation Plant Development

Table 8-Golden Meadow.1 Net production and ecological benefits of releases

Release & Type	Common Name	Release Year	Total Production	Unit	Net Value to Producer	Net Ecological Value
Vermillion, CV	smooth cordgrass	1989	3,554,550	GP	$394,549	$1,078,165
Pelican, GP	black mangrove	1994	176,000	PL	$1,169,121	$225,042
Brazoria, GP	seashore paspalum	1999	80,000	PL	$58,953	$199,273
Fort Polk, informal	Vetiver grass	1995	215,000	GP	$177,903	$476
Fourchon, GP	bitter panicum	1998	177,900	PL	$124,662	$339
Total					$2,241,840	$1,503,282
Production and Ecological Benefits from Releases:						$3,745,122
Gross PMC operating budget; 1989-2005						$10,607,607
Net Production and Ecological Benefits from Releases:						($6,862,485)

The potential is great for this PMC to rapidly accelerate the net benefits resulting from its work. To date it appears lackluster. The need is so great that the availability of funding will not be a hindrance for applying real solutions. A 'where will vegetation work' investigation may be warranted. Their cost benefit ratio is 0.35.

Table 8-Golden Meadow.2 Other releases

Release & Type	Common Name	Release Year	Explanation
Gulf Coast, CV	marshhay cordgrass	2003	Production data lacking
Timbalier, GP	seacoast bluestem	2006	Post 2005, production unknown
Bayou Lafourche, GP	California bulrush	2007	Post 2005, production unknown
Caminada, GP	seaoats	2001	Post 2005, production unknown

Developed and Delivered Technology - Listed Publications

Table 8-Golden Meadow.3 Number of PMC web site publications by types

Type of Publication	No.	Type of Publication	No.
Information Brochures and Flyers	5	Published Abstracts	1
Newsletters	7	Published Symposium Proceedings	1
Other Publication Types	4	Release Brochure	8
Plant Fact Sheets	13	Release Notices	6
Plant Guides	8	Technical Notes	19
Plant Materials Annual Report of Activities	3	Technical Poster	2
PMC Annual Technical Report	3	Technical Poster	2

There are a total of eighty three web site publications.

Developed and Delivered Technology - Featured Vegetative Accomplishments

The major role of PMCs is to develop new plant materials technology and make it available for general use. In virtually all circumstances, a body of knowledge already exists on the subject. As the PMC develops new technology it adds to the whole.

A new PMC must first determine the priority needs within its service area, and then seek within the existing body of knowledge the role it can most effectively play. This process is most often very rewarding, both to the developer and, and if done well and preserved in a useful manner, to the general public. Maintaining and presenting the technology for public use is always challenging. However, it appears that the Golden Meadow PMC may be an exception.

The publication "Plants for Gulf of Mexico Coastal Restoration" reveals a body of knowledge that is well organized and presented in a useful manner.[478] Its level of completeness appears to qualify it as an outstanding accomplishment.

The introduction to this 'body of knowledge' represents an understatement for what awaits. It says "The information below will assist with coastal shoreline reclamation, revegetation, wildlife habitat enhancement, and phytoremediation." After some essential definitions, six links are offered:

- Coastal Wetland Definitions
- Grasses, Sedges, and Rushes
- Forbs and Wildflowers
- Trees and Shrubs
- Technical Documents
- Vendors and Growers

Within each is a bountiful amount of information. For example the "Grasses, Sedges, and Rushes" section lists nineteen useful species and technical papers on each relative to their use for "coastal shoreline reclamation, revegetation, wildlife habitat enhancement, and phytoremediation." Below is the listing for one species. The Scientific Name links to the database PLANTS and the Useful Documents heading list two sources of detailed information about the plant. A total of forty-eight species, including grasses, forbs, wildflowers, trees and shrubs are listed with similar information about each.

Below these tables the 'Technical Documents' heading list about a dozen sources, and the 'Vendors and Growers' links to commercial sources for most of the useful plants for marsh restoration projects.

Table 8-Golden Meadow.4 Plants for Gulf of Mexico Coastal Restoration example

Scientific Name	Common Name	Adaptation	National Wetland	Useful Documents
*Juncus roemerianus**	black needlerush	Saline and Brackish Marshes	OBL	Black Needlerush Plant Guide (PDF; 60 KB) Black Needlerush Plant Fact Sheet (PDF; 51 KB)

Current posting of publications on the Golden Meadow web page suggests some departure from what was the principal reason for the PMC establishment. Their listing of useful plants for marsh restoration projects should help them re-identify their original objective, and leave the warm and fuzzy native plant syndrome to others.

Norman A. Berg National Plant Materials Center, Beltsville, MD

HISTORY AND BACKGROUND

Year and process leading to its establishment: In 1939, a National Observational Nursery Project was created at Beltsville, MD. Dr. Franklin J. Crider was transferred from the In Charge, Nursery Division position in Washington D.C. to manager of the new project in late 1939 or early 1940. It was established uniquely to assist the observational studies at many production nurseries. In 1953 it was renamed to the Beltsville PMC.

History: The first SCS presence in Beltsville occurred in 1935 when the new agency established a Field Research station there on existing Federal land. The first researchers included Drs. Robert S. Salter and Clarence S. Britt[479]. Britt remained with SCS until their research capabilities were eliminated in 1953, and then transferred to the new Agriculture Research Service. Salter became Chief of SCS in 1951 following Dr. Bennett, and then became the administrator of the Agriculture Research Service.

Regional nursery reports from the mid-1930s omit listing Beltsville as a production nursery.[480] They do, however, indicate that the Beltsville location had the capacity of producing up to a thousand tree stock. This was a minor amount compared to the millions produced by other nurseries. This pattern continued over the years relative to capacity but on actual production records the statement "National Observational Nursery" appears.[481] No record has been found showing that an SCS nursery was located there until 1947 when a list of nurseries included Beltsville. Its budget of $37,323 in 1950 was a fraction of the budget of other listed nurseries.[482] In some years the Beltsville location was listed with nurseries but with a minuscule inventory.

It appears that the move of Dr. Crider to Beltsville in 1939 to head up the National Observational Nursery Project was intended as a major thrust for the observational studies program to become an integral part of the Nursery Division. By virtue of this act, the Beltsville location assumed a national leadership role, and maintained this role in 1953 when it became the National Plant Materials Center. Under Dr. Crider's direction, the National Observational Nursery Project conducted observational studies and rapidly became the central location for the collection and distribution of foreign introductions to regional nurseries.

Over the years, in addition to its national plant introduction work, the center also served other centers in several essential activities, such as cultivar name clearance, national automated data services or publication assistance. Working closely with the ARS Plant Introduction Office (later renamed to the National Plant Germplasm System) many introductions flowed through the process and became wildly used as outstanding cultivars.[483] As the rifle approach to PMC initial evaluations became the norm, the mass shipment of accessions, foreign or domestic, declined. In recent years it has assumed some regional plant materials development work, similar to the work of other Centers.

In 2009, it was renamed the Norman A. Berg PMC. Berg was an SCS Chief from 1979 until 1982, the last Chief selected from within the agency. If it needed renaming, logic might have suggested the Franklin J. Crider PMC, since he was the father of the agencies' plant materials program, served as chief of the Nursery Section, influenced its establishment and served as the center's first manager. Chalk up another one for lunacy.

Land Tenure: The PMC operates on 282 acres of NRCS owned land, which is located on the Beltsville Agricultural Research Center (BARC). The BARC facility is owned and operated by the USDA. BARC has approximately 7,500 acres that offers isolation from the metropolitan cities of Washington and Baltimore.

Service Area: Most of the duties of the NPMC are to serve the national network of PMCs. The regional service area is loosely defined as the Piedmont region and the edge of the Appalachian mountain range from southern Pennsylvania to North Carolina/Tennessee.

OUTPUT

Conservation Plant Development

While the purpose of the National PMC is different than other centers, which limits its potential for plant releases, it has released three plants for which some production data is available. Comparing this output to their gross operating budget would not be meaningful and is not shown.

Table 8-Beltsville.1 Net production and ecological benefits of the Beltsville PMC plant releases

Release & Type	Common Name	Release Year	Total Production	Unit	Net Value to Producer	Net Ecological Value
Natob, CV	bicolor lespedeza	1952	88,650	LB	($31,573)	$14,805
Tufcote, CV	bermudagrass	1962	43,320	PL	$524,004	$296,608
VA-70, CV	shrub lespedeza	1952	7,446,713	PL	$630,480	$383,059
Total					$1,122,910	$694,472

Not surprising, all three were introductions.

Table 8-Beltsville.2 Other releases

Release & Type	Common Name	Release Year	Explanation
Algonquin, CV	black locust	1987	No commercial data available
Allegheny, CV	black locust	1987	No commercial data available
Appalachia, CV	black locust	1987	No commercial data available
Mid Atlantic, GP	Florida paspalum	2009	Post 2005, production unknown

Three cultivars of black locust, listed above, are shown as Center releases on the NRCS web site. The PMC accumulated collections in the 1940s and the final date for their release was in 1987. The collections were made from many states and planted, evaluated and selected at the Big Flats, NY Center, who propagated them for field testing within the Appalachian region. This work started and remained under the direction of Wilmer W. Steiner until his death in 1974. The final selection was made from field work carried out by plant materials specialists in several eastern states where black locust is common. No production data is available. Additionally, one germplasm release of Florida paspalum was made in 2009.

Developed and Delivered Technology - Listed Publications

Table 8-Beltsville.3 Number of PMC web site publications by category

Type of Publication	No.	Type of Publication	No.
Information Brochures and Flyers	10	PMC Annual Technical Report	1
Major Publications	1	Published Abstracts	2
Miscellaneous Popular Articles	3	Release Brochure	3
Miscellaneous Technical Article	1	Release Notices	1
Plant Fact Sheets	26	Technical Notes	4
Plant Guides	3	Technical Poster	4
Plant Materials Annual Report of Activities	1		

The total number of web site publications is sixty.

Developed and Delivered Technology - Featured Vegetative Accomplishments

About four years after his retirement, the following publication was released by USDA.[484] Dr. Crider developed a part of the draft. It was completed and submitted for publication by Wilmer W. Steiner, who guided it through the review and printing process. All of the research was done by Dr. Crider. He had developed a root/shoot growth theory from observing jojoba roots and this interest lingered until he was in a position to make a thorough analysis. The magnitude and quality of this root growth study, and its far reaching impacts, represent a far better picture of who Dr. Crider was and what he loved than his program directing role from January 1936 until December 1939. It is highlighted as a non-release related work from the Beltsville PMC.

The publication citation is below.   Following that is a synopsis of the publication.

Crider, Franklin J. 1955. Root growth stoppage resulting from defoliation of grass. Technical Bulletin 1102. USDA, Washington, DC.

Purpose and rational: These studies attempted to determine to what extent removal of the foliage of grass causes root growth to stop, and the influence of this reaction upon root production. As early as 1927, Dr. Crider had observed in citrus seedlings, growing in glass-front boxes, that the main roots ceased to elongate and remained inactive for periods of four to six weeks during the yearly growth cycle of the plant, and the growth and rest periods of the roots alternated with growth and rest periods of the top.

Studies with glass-front boxes also disclosed that the root growth of peach, plum, privet, and pine seedlings stopped for a time after the tops of the plants were cut back severely. The roots of herbaceous plants likewise ceased to elongate when the foliage was shortened. Tobacco, tomato, and cabbage were among the soft-bodied plants tested, and removal of their tops also adversely affected root growth.

Grass was particularly sensitive to the removal of top growth, as indicated by the promptness with which root growth stopped. Because of the major role of grass in holding and building soils, as well as pasture or rangeland for livestock use, knowledge about the behavior of the roots in relation to top reduction was considered of fundamental importance by Dr. Crider.

Methods of observation: The details are included here to help understand the complexity of the experiment. It was essential to observe the roots in their growing state under as nearly natural conditions as possible to avoid undue interference with the normal functioning of the roots. Three methods of examination were employed:

Glass-Box Method. The grasses were grown in wooden containers two inches wide, twenty-four inches long, and twenty-four inches deep, inside dimensions. The boxes had heavy glass fronts which, between examinations of the roots, were protected from the light by sheets of tar paper. Small holes in the bottoms of the boxes and one-inch layers of pebbles provided drainage. The boxes were filled firmly to within one inch of the top with screened, uniformly mixed, fine sandy loam soil. They were kept in a forward-tilted position of approximately thirty degrees, which caused a higher percentage of the roots to remain visible on the face of the glass. The day-to-day recordings of root elongation were made directly on the glass by use of red grease pencils. All photographs are from the original 1955 publication.

Field-Excavation Method. This method represented a new way to observe root growth in a natural state, without disturbing the rest of the root system. The work was done in the field during midsummer. The soil was carefully washed away from one side of the plants, so as to reveal the freshly starting roots. Without undue exposure, small apical sections of the roots were blackened with moistened carbon and surrounded immediately with wet sphagnum. Moist burlap was then placed over the sphagnum and the hole recovered with soil to the ground level. Subsequent examinations to determine the growth status of the roots were made following clipping by lifting the burlap, gently removing the sphagnum and observing the white apical root growth.

Root-blacking Method. This exposed all the growing roots of the plant for observation. It consisted of growing the plants in small, movable, clay pots and blacking the roots so that the white apical root growth made between examinations could be seen. The blacking was done with moistened carbon, which is not injurious to the roots and dissipates slowly in watering. It was applied to the roots with a small, soft brush. The white, growing roots, which characteristically follow the inside perimeter of the pot, were easily seen and counted. To facilitate removing and handling the plants, shredded sphagnum was mixed with the potting soil. The pots also were lined with a thin layer of sphagnum. Alternate blacking and examination of the roots at definite intervals progressively revealed their growth status following clipping. See photos.

This work was done in a greenhouse, using the glass-box method. Eight grasses were studied. Three were cool-season species—smooth brome *(Bromus inermis)*, tall fescue *(Schedonorus arundinaceus)* and orchardgrass *(Dactylis glomerata)*. Five were warm-season species—Florida paspalum *(Paspalum fioridanum)*, King Ranch bluestem *(Andropogon ischaemum)*, switchgrass *(Panicum virgatum)*, blue grama *(Bouteloua gracilis)*, and bermudagrass *(Cynodon dactylon)*.

The observations covered a normal growing season, i.e., 247 days for the cool season and 146 for the warm-season grasses.

Results

Removals during the growing season of half or more of the foliage of grasses—cool- and warm-season species including bunch, rhizomatous, and stoloniferous types—caused root growth to stop for a time after each removal, with one exception. The exception was orchardgrass after the first clipping.

Aside from orchardgrass, a single clipping that removed most of the foliage caused root growth to stop for periods ranging from six to eighteen days. Stoppage occurred usually within twenty-four hours and continued until recovery of the top growth was well advanced. When these clippings were repeated periodically, as in a system of rotation grazing, root growth of all the grasses stopped for periods that ranged from twenty-five to forty-five days during the growing season.

The percentage of roots that stopped growth varied in proportion to the percentage of the foliage that was removed. A single clipping of a hundred percent of the foliage resulted in complete root-growth stoppage for seventeen days, and removal of eighty percent of the foliage caused complete stoppage for twelve days. Partial stoppage occurred after single clippings at the seventy, sixty, and fifty percent levels.

Effects of such clippings repeated frequently—similar to continuous grazing—were much more severe. All root growth stopped after the first clipping of ninety percent of the foliage, and the three-times-a-week clippings that followed prevented root growth during the whole test. Root-growth stoppage was somewhat less as lesser amounts of foliage were removed, but where seventy percent or more of the foliage had been taken repeatedly, no roots were growing at the end of the thirty-three-day test. Stoppage of root growth failed to take place in both the single and repeated percentage-clipping tests only when forty percent or less of the foliage was removed. The balance point in the relation of top reduction and root-growth stoppage was found to lie between the forty and fifty percent clipping levels.

Parts of bunchgrass plants were found to function independently so far as the effects of foliage removal on root growth were concerned. Clipping of the foliage of halves and individual culms of plants stopped root growth for only those parts. The habit of cattle grazing is to only graze that portion of the plant that seems desirable at that point in time.

Reduction of the foliage of the grasses affected root production adversely. In the single-clipping series, the number of growing roots at the end of the thirty-three-day test ranged from only thirty-two when ninety percent of the foliage was clipped to 132 when ten percent was clipped. In the repeated-clipping series, the range was strikingly greater—from zero at the ninety, eighty, and seventy percent clipping levels to 156 at the ten percent level. Among the seven types of grasses that were clipped periodically—two to four times during the growing season—the oven-dry roots of the unclipped plants weighed eight times as much as those of the clipped plants.

The drastic effects of the higher percentages of foliage removal in causing complete and prolonged root-growth stoppage, and correspondingly reduced root production, was reflected in poor development of the grass plants. See Figure 8-Beltsville.1, Figure 8-Beltsville.2 and Figure 8-Beltsville.3.

Figure 8-Beltsville.1 Rhodes grass removed from four inch pots thirty-three days after single clipping to different levels. Left to right, none, 10, 20, 30, 40, 50, 60, 70, 80 and 90 percent of the top of the plant had been clipped off. The white roots are new growth

Figure 8-Beltsville.2 Smooth bromegrass (above left) at the time of first clipping (2.5"). All visible roots of clipped plant stopped growing within two days and remained inactive for twelve days. Those of the unclipped plant continued to grow. The right image 23 days after the 1st clipping. The root response was identical to the 1st clipping.

Figure 8-Beltsville.3 The same smooth bromegrass as above (left) at the time of the third clipping (to 3"). This was done forty-six days after the second clipping. All visible roots of clipped plant stopped growing within the first day and remained inactive for eight days. Those of the unclipped plant continued to grow. The same smooth bromegrass (right) forty-six days after third clipping. The washed roots of the clipped plant on the left and unclipped on the right are shown forty-six days after the third clipping.

Summary

These data have particular application to soil conservation and pasture-management practices. They emphasize that the growing top cannot be reduced more than half without adversely affecting the functioning of the root system and the plant as a whole. They are striking evidence that close grazing or mowing during the growing season is at the expense of stand establishment and maintenance.

The complete stoppage of root growth is of particular significance in conservation farming. Because of the continuous suppression of aboveground growth and the inability of the plant to replenish food reserves, the effects of root inactivity are lasting. Thus weakened, the plant is less able to resist grazing, erosion, drought, cold, and disease.

The conclusion is that the successful use of grass for soil conservation and pasturage is contingent in large measure on the employment of practices that preserve the closest possible balance between top and root development.

In the photographs the white roots are the new growth. Note how the white roots disappear in Figure 8-Beltsville.1 as clipping intensity increased.

Rose Lake, MI Plant Materials Center

HISTORY AND BACKGROUND

Year and process leading to its establishment: The PMC was authorized by congressional action in 1958, with included funding.

History: Following the closing of SCS nurseries in 1953, the only PMC serving the climatic region in the northeast and the humid north central parts of the U.S. was at Big Flats, NY. A large service area void of PMC assistance was recognized by conservationists and political leaders alike. A combination of this led to the approval of a PMC in Rose Lake, MI to be included as part of the other federally funded Plant Materials Center Program.

Land Tenure: The PMC operates on forty acres which is owned by the Michigan Department of Natural Resources.

Service Area: The Rose Lake Plant Materials Center is located in the southern part of the Lower Peninsula of Michigan and provides plant solutions for the Great Lakes Region. The center serves Indiana, Michigan, Ohio, Wisconsin, and portions of Illinois. Agriculture is diverse throughout the Center's service area. It includes dairy, beef cattle, cash crops, truck-crop, and nursery operations. Timber production is important in the northern part of the service area. Large urban populations, making recreation an important enterprise, affect much of the area. The special problems throughout most of the service area are associated with glaciated soils, muck lands, sand dunes, and mine spoils.

Climatic conditions affecting plant growth include temperature extremes of minus thirty-five degrees to ninety-five plus degrees Fahrenheit, annual precipitation from twenty-five to forty-five inches, a growing season varying from fifty to two hundred days, and soil textures varying from light sand to very heavy soils. Major conservation concerns include stabilization of streambanks, shorelines, and roadbanks; improving pasture land; and increasing the availability and use of local native species.

Conservation Plant Development

Table 8-Rose Lake.1: Net production and ecological benefits of the Rose Lake PMC plant releases

Release & Type	Common Name	Release Year	Total Production	Unit	Net Value to Producer	Net Ecological Value
Mackinaw, CV	birdsfoot trefoil	1971	12,130	LB	$ 781	$ 26,322
Roselow, CV	Sargent crabapple	1978	1,591,652	PL	$ 378,324	$ 119,372
Imperial, CV	Carolina poplar	1979	7,852,372	PL	$ 4,231,194	$ 1,819,584
Indigo, CV	silky dogwood	1982	3,536,568	PL	$ 1,515,901	$ 2,592,164
Lancer, CV	perennial pea	1984	14,422	LB	$ 90,020	$ 32,623
Redwing, CV	autumn olive	1985	575,533	PL	$ 99,461	$ 56,557
Magenta, CV	hybrid crabapple	1990	72,042	PL	$ 37,491	$ 20,297
Affinity, CV	northern white cedar	1993	13,000	PL	$ 4,128	$ 128
Total					$ 6,357,301	$ 4,667,047
Production and Ecological Benefits from Releases:						$11,024,349
Gross PMC operating budget; 1958 - 2005						$11,463,640
Net Production and Ecological Benefits from Releases:						**($439,291)**

The cost benefit ratio is (0.96).

Table 8-Rose Lake.2 Other releases

Release & Type	Common Name	Release Year	Explanation
Leelanau, GP	highbush cranberry	1999	Production data lacking
Southlow Michigan, GP	big bluestem	2001	Production data lacking
Southlow Michigan, GP	switchgrass	2001	Production data lacking
Southlow Michigan, GP	little bluestem	2001	Production data lacking
Southlow Michigan, GP	indiangrass	2001	Production data lacking
Riverbend, GP	silky willow	2003	Production data lacking
Icy Blue, GP	Canada wildrye	2004	Production data lacking
Prairie View Indiana, GP	big bluestem	2005	Production data lacking
Prairie View Indiana, GP	little bluestem	2005	Production data lacking
Prairie View Indiana, GP	Indiangrass	2005	Production data lacking
Alcona,	Dellenius' ticktrefoil	2006	Post 2005, production unknown
Grant, GP	panicle leaf ticktrefoil	2006	Post 2005, production unknown
Koch, GP	prairie sandreed	2007	Post 2005, production unknown
Marion, GP	Dellenius' ticktrefoil	2009	Post 2005, production unknown
Vintage, GP	common elderberry	2010	Post 2005, production unknown

Developed and Delivered Technology - Listed Publications

Table 8-Rose Lake.3 Number of PMC web site publications by types

Type of Publication	No.	Type of Publication	No.
Information Brochures and Flyers	9	PMC Annual Technical Report	3
Miscellaneous Popular Articles	7	Published Abstracts	1
Miscellaneous Technical Article	1	Published Symposium Proceedings	1
Newsletters	9	Refereed Journal Articles	5
Other Publication Types	2	Release Brochure	7
Plant Fact Sheets	9	Release Notices	3
Plant Guides	2	Technical Notes	11
Plant Materials Annual Report of Activities	3	Technical Poster	3

Developed and Delivered Technology - Featured Vegetative Accomplishments

Community Garden Guide - Vegetable Garden Planning and Development[485]

In the late 1990s, the plant materials team in Michigan, along with others, initiated a cultural outreach project to assist the Red Cliff and Bad River Native American Tribes in Northern Wisconsin. These tribes were gardeners before they were relocated to reservations, growing a great deal of their vegetables, but their historic knowledge was lost. The result of the outreach program has been the development of a Community Garden Guide, hands on instructions, and numerous Plant Guides dealing with certain aspects of Native American family gardening.

The Guide flows from site selection to calculating the row length and width needed per vegetable to provide all family members with a yearly supply of garden vegetables. In between are all the steps needed to grow one's own garden, and how to do each step. An included process calculates the needed garden size, based on family numbers, followed by the required site preparation. The authors recognized that the procedure (shown graphically in Figure 8-Rose Lake.2) for turning the soil is extremely labor intensive, but they emphasized that "this manner will maximize rooting depths of plants and enhance percolation of water..."

Figure 8-Rose Lake.1 Native Americans gardening in Northern Wisconsin

Other site preparation options are provided, including a till-less option. It will require the following:

1. Begin by mowing all vegetation as close to the ground as possible.

Figure 8-Rose Lake.2 Soil Preparation Diagram

2. Place newspapers ten to fifteen pages thick directly over the mowed area. Be sure to overlap the newspapers three to four inches to prevent weeds from growing between the pages.

3. Spread compost, top soil or well-rotted manure to a depth of four to six inches over the entire newspaper area.

4. Plant garden seeds in the prepared garden bed.

Sections on Soil Testing, Fertilizing and Weed Control conclude the narrative. Always the home gardener's albatross, weed control, is handled nicely with three options for cleaning up the site a year or two ahead of time, and the use of:

- Smother crops, such as buckwheat or cereal rye;

- Solarization, using clear plastic, cover the area to be planted in the spring and until mid-season;

- Mulches, such as straw

The Community Garden Guide also includes some useful tables that tie things together, including

- Table 1. Family Garden Planning Guide - general guidelines for planning a family vegetable garden.

- Table 2. Row spacing (in feet) for selected vegetables

- Table 3. Garden Planner Worksheet

Elsberry, MO Plant Materials Center

<u>HISTORY AND BACKGROUND</u>

<u>Year and process leading to its establishment</u>: The origin of what became the Elsberry PMC happened in 1934 when the Bureau of Plant Industry established a nursery there. The Nursery then was transferred to SCS in 1935, and it survived the closing of most nurseries in 1953 to become a PMC. This may have been partly due to the lobbying efforts of Hugh Stevenson, the first nursery manager, who later developed a large nursery in Elsberry.

<u>History</u>: The present plant center had its origin as part of the first SCS national network of production and observational nurseries. The Elsberry site was producing seedlings as early as 1934. Its first director was Hugh Stevenson, who started with the Bureau in 1934, transferring first to the Soil Erosion Service and then to SCS.[486] His leadership continued until 1939 when he resigned and opened the Forest Keeling Nursery.

By 1937 the production of trees and shrubs reached 2,398,000 shipped and 2,278,000 carried over, at an annual cost of $10.23 per 1000 shipped.

In 1953 when the nurseries were closed, USDA was mandated to find a non-federal entity to operate them. This was not possible with Elsberry. Consequently, it remained under SCS control and became the first SCS-operated PMC. Roger E. Sherman, who entered employment at the nursery in 1936 as a Junior Horticulturist, became the first PMC manager, and continued in that position until 1958. Although the nursery had carried out an observational study program throughout the 1936 - 1953 periods, their first release was not until 1961. It was 'Emerald' crownvetch, released cooperatively with the Iowa Agriculture Experiment Station, through the leadership of Dr. Virgil Hawk, a long term PM Specialist located in Ames, Iowa. It had been under evaluation prior to the nursery closing, but the work was primarily conducted at Iowa State University. Hawk had returned to Iowa State to pursue his doctorate degree. He graduated in 1946 and returned full-time to SCS employment.

Land Tenure: NRCS currently owns 243 acres.

Service Area: The area served by the Elsberry PMC has a humid climate with precipitation ranging from twenty inches in the northwest regions to fifty inches in the southeast regions. Precipitation is unevenly distributed throughout the year with major portions received during the growing season. The average yearly high temperature for the region is between sixty and seventy degrees Fahrenheit. The average low temperature is between thirty-five and fifty degrees Fahrenheit. Topography of the area served by the Elsberry PMC includes glacial till prairies, Mississippi valley loess hills, Iowa and Mississippi deep loess heavy till plains, thin loess hills and plains, Mississippi valley slopes, and the Ozark highlands.

Major land uses include corn, soybeans, cattle, and hog farming. The primary conservation problems in the service area relate to soil erosion and water quality. They include cropland erosion, low forage production, streambank erosion, point sources of pollution from concentrated animal by-products, storm water and waste water run-off, wetland loss, and non-point pollution sources from agricultural lands.

OUTPUT

Conservation Plant Development

Table 8-Elsberry.1 Net production and ecological benefits of releases

Release and Type	Common Name	Release Year	Total Production	Unit	Net Value to Producer	Net Ecological Value
Emerald, CV	crownvetch	1961	8,744,697	LB	$16,916,653	$14,360,086
Cling-Red, CV	Amur honeysuckle	1971	495,500	PL	$67,939	$36,892
Cave-In-Rock, CV	switchgrass	1974	2,852,720	LB	$12,760,317	$17,308,071
Bobwhite, CV	soybean	1975	53,200	LB	$104,615	$67,531
Flame, CV	Amur maple	1978	2,982,558	PL	$1,685,511	$491,749
Elsberry, CV	autumn olive	1979	369,950	PL	$47,598	$37,077
Rountree, CV	big bluestem	1983	1,981,099	LB	$10,513,977	$6,698,793
Rumsey, CV	indiangrass	1983	780,000	LB	$5,472,922	$2,355,240
Elsmo, CV	lace bark elm	1990	218,665	PL	$855,869	$70,691
Redstone, CV	cornelian cherry dogwood	1991	103,265	PL	$140,291	$2,395
Central Iowa, GP	Canada wildrye	1995	30,240	LB	$80,206	$78,100
Central Iowa, GP	sideoats grama	1995	344	LB	$5,732	$1,173
Northern Iowa, GP	Canada wildrye	1995	61,083	LB	$90,326	$157,757
Northern Iowa, GP	sideoats grama	1995	1,180	LB	$906	$4,041
Southern Iowa, GP	Canada wildrye	1995	2,830	LB	($73)	$11,037
Southern Iowa, GP`	sideoats grama	1995	12,400	LB	$24,845	$42,463
Central Iowa, GP	roundhead lespedeza	1996	189	LB	$34,034	$43,596
Central Iowa, GP	oxeye false sunflower	1996	2,961	LB	$71,840	$7,205
Central Iowa, GP	tall dropseed	1996	27,267	LB	$119,999	$475,225
Central Iowa, GP	indiangrass	1997	40,637	LB	($62,586)	$247,886
Central Iowa, GP	little bluestem	1997	37	LB	$334	$192
Northern Iowa, GP	false sunflower	1997	5,432	LB	$158,122	$38,938

Release and Type	Common Name	Release Year	Total Production	Unit	Net Value to Producer	Net Ecological Value
Northern Iowa, GP	indiangrass	1997	9,420	LB	($1,333)	$44,545
OH 370, GP	big bluestem	1997	6,270	LB	$49,350	$49,049
Southern Iowa, GP	oxeye false sunflower	1997	215	LB	$7,626	$523
Southern Iowa, GP	roundhead lespedeza	1997	256	LB	$33,942	$1,208
Union, TS	tulip poplar	1997	48,644	PL/LB	$330,344	$132,402
Central Iowa, GP	big bluestem	1998	1,005	LB	$3,664	$8,728
Central Iowa, GP	purple prairieclover	1998	2	LB	$41	$7
Central Iowa, GP	rattlesnake master	1998	4,300	LB	$365,778	$21,548
Northern Iowa, GP	stiff goldenrod	1998	590	LB	$33,372	$579
Northern Iowa, GP	rattlesnake master	1998	1,771	LB	$254,424	$8,875
Southern Iowa, GP	indiangrass	1998	680	LB	$1,330	$4,362
Central Iowa, GP	thickspike gayfeather	1999	850	LB	$50,532	$4,370
Northern Iowa, GP	little bluestem	1999	6	LB	$48	$16,267
Northern Iowa, GP	thickspike gayfeather	1999	22	LB	$1,471	$113
Northern Missouri, GP	big bluestem	1999	2,090	LB	($6,688)	$18,152
Northern Missouri, GP	indiangrass	1999	5,831	LB	($4,206)	$35,569
Northern Missouri, GP	little bluestem	1999	8,680	LB	$48,846	$19,881
Northern Missouri, GP	Virginia wildrye	1999	1,800	LB	$6,215	$5,820
Southern Iowa, GP	big bluestem	1999	400	LB	$1,873	$1,560
Southern Iowa, GP	little bluestem	1999	300	LB	$947	$1,556
Southern Iowa, GP	rattlesnake master	1999	87	LB	$19,268	$615
Northern Iowa, GP	big bluestem	2000	600	LB	$2,190	$5,211
Northern Iowa, GP	roundhead lespedeza	2000	400	LB	$46,020	$1,302
Northern Iowa, GP	tall dropseed	2000	4,341	LB	$9,255	$75,657
Northern Missouri, GP	tall dropseed	2001	1,500	LB	$2,020	$26,143
Central Iowa, GP	stiff goldenrod	2002	553	LB	$20,321	$543
Cuivre River, GP	Virginia wildrye	2002	124,273	LB	$843,297	$401,816
Northern Iowa, GP	pale purple coneflower	2002	2,000	LB	$43,688	$5,927
Northern Iowa, GP	New England aster	2002	780	LB	$54,102	$17,487
Southern Iowa, GP	New England aster	2002	264	LB	$13,410	$10,736
Southern Iowa, GP	stiff goldenrod	2002	600	LB	$34,535	$589

Release and Type	Common Name	Release Year	Total Production	Unit	Net Value to Producer	Net Ecological Value
Southern Iowa, GP	New England aster	2002	525	LB	$51,901	$11,593
Southern Iowa, GP	tall dropseed	2002	265	LB	$833	$4,619
Northern Iowa, GP	purple prairieclover	2003	101	LB	$2,049	$2,253
OZ-70, GP	big bluestem	2003	12,125	LB	$19,570	$39,755
Missouri Covey, GP	false indigo bush	2005	5,450	PL	$19,389	$24,683
Total					$51,548,802	$43,540,181
Production and Ecological Benefits from Releases:						$95,088,983
Gross PMC operating budget; 1935 – 2005						$16,689,506
Net Production and Ecological Benefits from Releases						**$78,399,477**

The Elsberry PMC can be proud of the total financial benefit of their releases. Their cost benefit ratio is 5.69. The four blockbusters; 'Emerald' crownvetch, ' Cave-In-Rock' switchgrass, 'Rumsey' indiangrass and 'Rountree' big bluestem account for about fifty-four percent of it. 'Emerald', released cooperatively with Iowa State University, accounts for one-third of their net benefit. It has been discontinued because it was "replaced by others" and "potentially invasive" The forty-nine commercially produced pre-varietal releases accounts for 3.1% during their few years on the market.

All of the releases in Table 8-Elsberry.2 Other Releases except the first two, are pre- varietal releases made between 1994 and 2010. Of the eighty-one pre- varietal releases, forty-eight were produced commercially by 2005. The cultivar 'Elsberry' smooth brome has been discontinued because it is "no longer produced" or "replaced by others". Historically its production may have been limited to a few years soon after its release in 1954.

Table 8-Elsberry.2 Other releases

Release	Common Name	Release Year	Explanation
Elsberry, CV	smooth brome	1954	Production data lacking
Shawnee, CV	switchgrass	1995	Production data lacking
Alexander, GP	showy tick trefoil	1998	Production data lacking
Corinth , GP	roughleaf dogwood	1998	Production data lacking
Jefferson , GP	roughleaf dogwood	1998	Production data lacking
Nicholson , GP	roughleaf dogwood	1998	Production data lacking
Tazewell , GP	roughleaf dogwood	1998	Production data lacking
Western Missouri , GP	indiangrass	1999	Production data lacking
Northern Missouri , GP	thickspike gayfeather	2001	Production data lacking
Southern Iowa , GP	thickspike gayfeather	2001	Production data lacking
Western Missouri , GP	prairie coreopsis	2001	Production data lacking
Western Missouri , GP	thickspike gayfeather	2001	Production data lacking
Central Iowa , GP	New England aster	2002	Production data lacking
Southern Iowa , GP	pale purple coneflower	2002	Production data lacking
Central Iowa , GP	prairie Junegrass	2003	Production data lacking
Central Iowa , GP	rough blazing star	2003	Production data lacking
Central Iowa , GP	switchgrass	2003	Production data lacking
Central Iowa , GP	riged goldenrod	2003	Production data lacking

Release	Common Name	Release Year	Explanation
Northern Iowa , GP	prairie Junegrass	2003	Production data lacking
Northern Iowa , GP	rough blazing star	2003	Production data lacking
Southern Iowa , GP	rough blazing star	2003	Production data lacking
Southern Iowa , GP	wild bergamont	2003	Production data lacking
Northern Missouri , GP	grayhead coneflower	2004	Production data lacking
Southern Missouri , GP	little bluestem	2004	Production data lacking
Illinois Covey , GP	false indigo bush	2005	Production data lacking
Iowa Covey , GP	false indigo bush	2005	Production data lacking
Central Iowa , GP	pale purple coneflower	2006	Post 2005, production unknown
Midwest Premium , GP	American plum	2006	Post 2005, production unknown
Refuge , GP	big bluestem	2006	Post 2005, production unknown
Central Iowa , GP	wild bergamont	2007	Post 2005, production unknown
Northern Iowa , GP	wild bergamont	2007	Post 2005, production unknown
Sun Harvest , GP	Hazelnut	2007	Post 2005, production unknown
Northern Missouri , GP	sideoats grama	2008	Post 2005, production unknown
Northern Missouri , GP	pale purple coneflower	2009	Post 2005, production unknown
Western Missouri , GP	pale purple coneflower	2009	Post 2005, production unknown
Ozark , GP	little bluestem	2010	Post 2005, production unknown

Developed and Delivered Technology - Listed Publications

Table 8-Elsberry.3 Number of PMC web site publications by type

Type of Publication	No.	Type of Publication	No.
Information Brochures and Flyers	6	PMC Annual Technical Report	2
Major Publications	1	Popular Journal or Magazine Articles	1
Miscellaneous Technical Article	1	Published Abstracts	5
Newsletters	3	Release Brochure	25
Plant Fact Sheets	13	Release Notices	63
Plant Guides	22	Technical Notes	4
Plant Materials Annual Report of Activities	3	Technical Poster	5

The total number of web site publications is an impressive 154.

Developed and Delivered Technology - Featured Vegetative Accomplishments

Two Featured Vegetative Accomplishments of the Elsberry PMC are discussed below.

1. Source Identified Ecotypes for Commercial Production

The pre-varietal release policy became effective in 1994. No PMC has been more efficient in utilizing it than Elsberry. It has identified about seventy-six Source Identified releases from Missouri, Iowa and Illinois that are commercially produced or have the potential of being commercially produced.

Many of the source identified releases were done through a cooperative effort with the Iowa Integrated Roadside Vegetation Management (IRVM) and the Iowa Ecotype Project (IEP) of the University of Northern Iowa Tallgrass Prairie Center, as well as the Iowa Department of Transportation, and the Iowa Crop Improvement Association. The objective of the IRVM is as follows: "It is declared to be in the general public welfare of Iowa and a highway purpose for the vegetation of Iowa's roadsides to be preserved, planted, and maintained to be safe, visually interesting, ecologically integrated, and useful for many purposes."[487] Dove tailing with this objective is that of the Iowa Ecotype Project which is to

- Produce and increase regionally adapted Iowa Source Identified Foundation seed for commercial producers,

- Promote commercial availability and affordability of Source identified seed,

- Accession seed and plants derived from native remnant populations in Iowa for seed increase and research, and

- Increase seed of fifty species from 3,000 populations from three provenance zones in Iowa, and eighty-one 'ecotypes' of thirty-three species released for commercial production.[488]

2. Switchgrass for Biomass Production

The potential of burning biomass as an energy source has increased due to the rising costs of energy.[489] Switchgrass is a perennial and a large producer of biomass. The purpose of this study was to determine which of twelve switchgrass cultivars produce the most biomass at three locations over a five year harvest period.

Biomass yields at all locations were influenced by seasonal precipitation. Seed origin also influenced overall performance. 'Greenville', a New Mexico variety coming from an elevation of 4,938 feet, and 'Forestburg', the northernmost variety from South Dakota, ranked lowest in biomass yield at all three sites. Cultivars producing the most biomass varied across the plot locations, but generally, the more southern origin varieties produced the most biomass. 'Alamo', from Texas and 'Kanlow' from Kansas were the two highest yielding varieties for dry biomass, although 'Alamo' yields decline over time at the most northern location. 'Carthage' is a variety of eastern origin, which performed very well at all three locations, as did 'Cave-In-Rock' and 'Pathfinder'. Average yields from the three location and three years are shown in Table 8-Elsberry.4.

Table 8-Elsberry.4 Switchgrass for Biomass Production

Cultivar	3 Year, 3 Locations Pounds per Acre	Cultivar Source
Kanlow	11,800	Kansas
Alamo	10,700	Texas
Blackwell	9,300	Oklahoma
Carthage	9,200	North Carolina
Pathfinder	8,700	Nebraska
Cave-In-Rock	8,300	Southern IL
Shelter	8,200	West Virginia
Trailblazer	8,000	Nebraska and Kansas
Sunburst	7,100	South Dakota
Nebraska 28	6,800	Nebraska
Greenville	5,400	New Mexico
Forestburg	5,200	North Dakota

217

Jamie L. Whitten Plant Materials Center, Coffeeville, MS

HISTORY AND BACKGROUND

Year and process leading to its establishment: The beginning of what is now the Jamie L. Whitten Plant Materials Center is not clear. The first date in which the Soil Conservations Service grew plants at the facility started in January 1936.

History: The Coffeeville Nursery was one of many established in 1936 by the Soil Conservation Service with the mandate to produce seed and plants for re-vegetating eroding land in its service area. William G. Beatty was the first manager, making $2,700 per year. He continued in this position until 1942. During 1937 the nursery shipped over nine million plants and carried over 250,000. On October 31, 1939 the capacity at Coffeeville was estimated to be fifteen million, with a seed collection capacity of 5,000 pounds.[490] No records have been found that a nursery operated at Coffeeville after 1942.

The Coffeeville PMC was authorized by Congress and began operations on August 8, 1960, functioning both as a PMC and a seed production unit for the Yazoo-Little Tallahatchie Flood Prevention Project. The production unit seemed to carry the bigger stick. The seed and plant production unit was discontinued in 1982, and the plant materials function was reorganized and expanded. The name change from the Coffeeville PMC to the Jamie L. Whitten PMC occurred in 1990. Whitten was a long-term chairperson of the U.S. House of Representatives Agricultural Appropriations Committee.

In 1960 there were a limited number of selected plants that had survived from the 1936 to 1942 period that the PMC could consider releasing. Additionally, the seed production obligations from 1960 to 1982 had a negative impact on typical PMC functioning, all of this reflecting on their cultivar or other PMC output.

Land Tenure: The PMC operates on 360 acres owned by the U.S. Forest Service.

Service Area: The area served by the PMC is generally rolling except for a few nearly level floodplains and narrow cliffs along streams and rivers. It includes all of MS and parts of AL, AR, LA and TN. The climate is temperate and humid. Average rainfall is about fifty inches, and the temperature increases greatly from north to south. Frost-free days range from about 200 in the north to 340 in the extreme south.

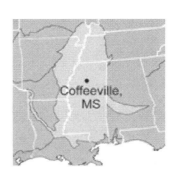

OUTPUT

Conservation Plant Development

Table 8-Coffeeville.1 Net production and ecological benefits of releases

Release & Type	Common Name	Release Year	Production	Unit	Value to Producer	Ecological Value
Chiwapa, CV	Japanese millet	1965	223,175	LB	$32,466	$61,353
Meechee, CV	arrowleaf clover	1966	338,454	LB	$ (217,097)	$22,082
Halifax, CV	maidencane	1974	2,817,601	PL	$2,006,025	$3,891
Indian Bayo, GP	powdery thalia	1996	2,500	PL	$28,298	$2,055
Quail Haven, CV	Reseeding soybean	1986	395,100	LB	$550,838	$260,525
Leflore, GP	creeping burhead	1996	600	PL	$5,325	$ 489
Lark, GP	partridge pea	1997	75,379	LB	$87,154	$19,034
Leaf River, GP	woolgrass	1996	6,650	PL	$28,755	$ 1,261

Release & Type	Common Name	Release Year	Production	Unit	Value to Producer	Ecological Value
Morton. GP	kori-yanagi willow	2001	27,100	PL	$43,333	$30,489
Total					$2,552,150	$490,070
Production and Ecological Benefits from Releases:						$2,953,369
Gross PMC operating budget; 1960 – 2005						$15,786,329
Net Production and Ecological Benefits from Releases:						**($12,832,960)**

It is reasonable to assume that the Jamie L. Whitten PMC had virtually no carry-over of potentially releasable plants from the work of the nursery. The emphasis on producing plants from 1960 until 1982 for the Yazoo-Little Tallahatchie Flood Prevention Project precluded much plant development work. This, combined with no clear and overwhelming demand for conservation plants, left the PMC with a negative net, relative to measurable ecological and production benefits.

Table 8-Coffeeville.2 Other releases

Release & Type	Common Name	Release Year	Explanation
Hopefield, GP	trailing wildbean	1997	Production data lacking
Highlander, CV	eastern gamagrass	2003	Production data lacking

Developed and Delivered Technology - Listed Publications

Table 8-Coffeeville.3 Number of PMC web site publications by type

Type of Publication	No.	Type of Publication	No.
Information Brochures and Flyers	1	Plant Materials Annual Report of Activities	3
Major Publications	3	PMC Annual Technical Report	3
Newsletters	9	Published Symposium Proceedings	2
Other Publication Types	1	Release Brochure	2
Plant Fact Sheets	4	Technical Notes	8
Plant Guides	2		

The total number of web site publications is thirty-eight.

Developed and Delivered Technology - Featured Vegetative Accomplishments

A major focus of all PMCs in recent years has been the methodology for reproducing commercially useful conservation plants. The Jamie L. Whitten PMC is no different. The Featured Vegetative Accomplishment will focus on Seed Propagation Techniques for Wetland Plants, a technical note developed in 1997 by Janet Grabowski, an Agronomist at the PMC.[491]

Introduction: Natural germination of most emergent wetland plants occurs during drawdown periods when water levels are severely reduced. In order to propagate these plants from seed, it is necessary to simulate the environmental conditions experienced during these drawdowns.

An excellent review of the literature showed several threads that would be useful in resolving the propagation of the selected species for this study.[492] They include the following:

Germination was improved in some species by:

- A period of cold, moist stratification.

- Maintaining the medium in a wet, but not inundated state.

- Exposing the seed to light.

- A night/day temperature cycle of 20/30°C.

- In a natural wetland, seed of *Sagittaria latifolia* (common arrowhead) germinates on the surface of shallow water and then the seedlings settle to the bottom and root in the substrate.

- Seeds with thick seed coats or hard surrounding fruit structures may be improved if the seed coat is broken or scarified before planting.

- Germination of common arrowhead can be improved by cutting the seed coat with scissors before planting.

- Changing the water weekly during a six month storage period gave slightly better germination than storing seed in water that was not changed regularly.

- Intact seeds of *Sagittaria variabilis* did not germinate, but high germination percentages resulted when the seed coat was ruptured.

- Only slight improvement in germination percentages for *Scirpus* species resulted from concentrated sulfuric acid used to reduce the thickness of the seed coat.

- Post-harvest seed storage conditions can also affect seed germination.

- Germination of *Scirpus* species that was stored dry and then stratified had similar or, in some cases, better germination then seed stored in water at 2-4°C.

- Germination of seed that was stored dry without stratification or in water at room temperature proved to be sporadic.

The PMC collected wetland plants from various locations in Mississippi that showed potential for use in wetland mitigation and restoration plantings or for constructed wetlands for waste water treatment.

The species collected are listed below. Seed of all these species ripen above, or in the case of creeping burhead, both above and on the surface of the water. As a result, all were   exposed to drying conditions before dispersal

A few of these species are not commonly marketed, so propagation methods have not been recorded. Limited propagation information is available on the others, but these southern ecotypes may respond differently than the northern ecotypes studied in the literature. For example, ecotypes of these species adapted to the climate of Mississippi would not be exposed to extended periods of cool, moist conditions appropriate for stratification.

Most of the species studied can be easily propagated by vegetative means, but production of seedlings may be more economical because they require less production space, and the use of seedlings in wetland plantings would increase the genetic diversity of the planting population. Therefore, a study was initiated to determine the best seed storage conditions; pre-planting seed treatments, and germination environments for them.

Common Name	Scientific Name
Woolgrass	*Scirpus cyperinus*
Soft-stem bulrush	*Scirpus tabernaemontani*
Longbeak	*Sagittaria australis*
Bulltongue	*Sagittaria lancifolia*

- Powdery thalia   *Thalia dealbata*
- Creeping burhead *Echinodorus cordifolius*

Seed of these accessions were harvested in late summer to fall. Collection dates varied between species and years of collection. Seed was collected when fully mature and before any significant seed shattering occurred. All necessary seed cleaning was performed before the seed was allowed to dry.

Storage treatments varied as follows:

- Dry storage in a cooler maintained at 55°F and 45% relative humidity, for a three to four month stratification period.
- Scarification treatments included using mechanical means or sulfuric acid, and combinations of stratification and scarification.
- Moist storage was in a cooler at 42°F with no humidity control.
- Water storage was in a cooler at 42°F with no humidity control.

Storage and pre-planting treatments were based on published references or on previous work with that species at the PMC. For example, only those species where moist or water storage appeared to be beneficial were stored in that manner.

All species were subjected to dry storage. Moist storage was tested on soft-stem bulrush, longbeak arrowhead, creeping burhead, powdery thalia, bulltongue, and for only the first year on woolgrass. Water storage was tested on soft-stem bulrush, longbeak arrowhead, bulltongue, and for the first year only, woolgrass. During the first year of testing the moist and water storage treatments did not prove to be beneficial, so they were dropped from the second year of the test.

All species except longbeak arrowhead and bulltongue were stratified. The late harvest date of these two made it impractical, time wise, to apply both stratification and dry storage treatments.

Seed from the dry storage and stratification treatments were counted and planted in the greenhouse at the same time.

An initial seedling count was made when it was deemed that a sufficient number of seedlings were present to justify counting.

The conclusions include:

Woolgrass: Woolgrass germination rates in this test were fairly high. Others also found that woolgrass seed placed in various storage conditions germinated readily. If equipment is not available to clean the seed from the surrounding fruit structures, a potential alternate planting method is to tear fruit clusters into smaller sections and plant them without further cleaning. The ecotype used in this study did not require stratification, although seed may germinate more rapidly if stratified. Although best germination rates were in the treatments with a saturated growing medium, later seedling growth may be improved if once the seedlings become established; the growing medium could be maintained in a moist, but not wet condition.

Soft-stem bulrush: Soft-stem bulrush germination rates were fairly low. Others had found that germination of larger-seeded *Scirpus* species, with thicker walled seed, was often less than satisfactory. Neither acid nor mechanical scarification substantially improved germination. Moist storage or dry storage followed by a three to four month stratification, preferably using peat moss as the stratification medium, are recommended for this ecotype of soft-stem bulrush.

Longbeak arrowhead: Longbeak arrowhead germination rates were also fairly low, so seeding rates should be adjusted accordingly. Seed germinated best when stored in water or in a moistened state, but there was also some response of dry stored seed to stratification. Seedlings germinated and grew best in a saturated growing medium.

Bulltongue: Bulltongue seed germinates more readily than longbeak arrowhead, but the germination rates were lower than would be expected by the reseeding potential exhibited in the PMC growing ponds. The seed germinated better in a wet growing environment, but germination rates possibly could be improved by elevating the water level above the surface of the growing medium. Seed germination rates were highest in the water storage treatment, but it appears that moist storage and probably even dry storage followed by a stratification treatment to re-hydrate the seed may provide acceptable germination rates. Mechanically scarifying the seed prior to stratification may also be beneficial.

Powdery thalia: Seed germinates slowly and sporadically over a long period of time. Dry storage is probably best for this seed but cold stratification for three to four months prior to planting is required for germination to occur. Germination may also be slightly improved if the seed is mechanically scarified before stratification. This species grew best when the growing medium was maintained in a moist, but not saturated condition.

Creeping burhead: Acceptable germination levels were not obtained with any combination of the seed treatments and growing environments tested. There was a slight trend towards improved germination with the saturated media conditions on the flood bench.

Literature used

Andersen, R. N. 1968. Germination and establishment of weeds for experimental purposes. Weed Science Society of America, Urbana, IL. 235 p.

Crocker, W. 1907. Germination of seed of water plants. Bot. Gaz. 44:375-380.

Garbisch, E. W. and McIninch, S. 1992. Seed information for wetland plant species of the northeast United States. Restor. and Manage. Notes. 10(1):85-86.

Harris, S. W. and Marshall, W. H. 1960. Germination and planting experiments on soft-stem and hard-stem bulrush. J. Wildl. Manage. 24(2):134-139.

Isley, D. 1944. A study of conditions that affect the germination of Scirpus seeds. Cornell Univ. Agric. Exp. Stn. Memo. 257, Ithaca, NY. 28 p.

Keddy, P. A. and Constabel, P. 1986. Germination of ten shoreline plants in relation to seed size, soil particle size and water level: An experimental study. Journal of Ecology. 74:133 141.

Muenscher, W. C. 1936. Storage and germination of seeds off aquatic plants. Cornell Univ. Agric. Exp. Stn. Bull. 652, Ithaca, NY. 17 p.

Sharp, W. M. 1939. Propagation of *Potamogeton* and *Sagittaria* from seeds. N. Am. Wildl. Conf., Trans. 4:351-358.

Shipley, B. and Parent, M. 1991. Germination responses of 64 wetland species in relation to seed size, minimum time to reproduction and seedling relative growth rate. Functional Ecology 5:111-118.

Bridger, MT Plant Materials Center

<u>HISTORY AND BACKGROUND</u>

<u>Year and process leading to its establishment</u>: The PMC was authorized by congressional action, which included funding in 1959.

<u>History</u>: When SCS closed all the nurseries in 1953, ten of the twenty-four locations became plant materials centers. Nationally, large un-served areas existed.

Through the strong leadership of local Soil Conservation Districts in Montana and Wyoming, regional support from Dr. A. L. Hafenrichter, a plant materials specialist, and the SCS state offices in Montana and Wyoming, a PMC was authorized at Bridger, MT in 1959. Initially, the PMC operated on eighty acres of privately owned land, and was later expanded to 140 acres. The land was leased by the Carbon County, MT Conservation District. In 1970, the 104 Conservation Districts in Montana and Wyoming purchased the 140-acre farm. The SCS now leases an additional 130 acres for PMC use.

<u>Land Tenure</u>: The Conservation District Associations in Montana and Wyoming continue to own the 140 acres leased by NRCS for PMC operations.

<u>Service Area</u>: The PMC serves the states of Montana and Wyoming. Environmental conditions in the area are diverse. The topography ranges from mountains in the western one-third of Montana and Wyoming, to rolling flat plains, desert basins, and plateaus in the remaining areas. Elevations range from less than 2,000 feet to more than 12,500 feet above sea level. Soils range from coarse sand to clay, with a majority in the loam, clay loam, silt loam, and silty clay loam textural classes.

The frost-free period ranges from less than forty days to 145 days. Average annual precipitation ranges from five inches in the desert basins of Wyoming to sixty inches or more at the higher elevations. More than fifty percent of the annual precipitation occurs in winter.

<u>OUTPUT</u>

Conservation Plant Development

The Bridger PMC has been one of the most productive centers in the Plant Materials Program. Its plant development output has been steady with one outstanding release after another, utilizing mostly native plant materials. 'Critana' thickspike wheatgrass ranks fourth of all PMC released plants in total benefits, although it was released later than all of those listed above it in value.

Table 8-Bridger.1 Net production and ecological benefits of releases

Release & Type	Common Name	Release Year	Total Production	Unit	Net Value to Producer	Net Ecological Value
Garrison, CV	creeping foxtail	1963	421,775	LB	$(263,259)	$1,488,747
Critana, CV	thickspike wheatgrass	1971	8,777,835	LB	$23,568,074	$45,220,480
Lutana, CV	Cicer milkvetch	1971	724,769	LB	$2,785,106	$1,293,585
Rosana, CV	western wheatgrass	1972	4,338,058	LB	$10,198,494	$19,822,752
Goshen, CV	prairie sandreed	1976	671,910	LB	$2,275,003	$3,918,552
Wytana, CV	fourwing saltbush	1976	17,330	LB	$112,092	$315,753

Release & Type	Common Name	Release Year	Total Production	Unit	Net Value to Producer	Net Ecological Value
Shoshone, CV	beardless wildrye	1980	217,818	LB	$432,185	$867,162
Pryor, CV	slender wheatgrass	1988	1,499,159	LB	$2,843,139	$6,978,113
Trailhead, CV	basin wildrye	1991	1,302,176	LB	$5,017,926	$5,208,149
Rimrock, CV	Indian ricegrass	1996	4,411,570	LB	$15,421,218	$16,245,498
Bridger-Select, GP	Rocky Mountain juniper	1998	115,196	PL	$(18,540)	$760,445
Antelope GP	white prairie clover	2000	20,380	LB	$244,948	$157,700
High Plains GP	Sandberg bluegrass	2000	5,400	LB	$(618)	$1,566
Hunter GP	ponderosa pine	2002	27,520	PL	$(6,247)	$227,853
Open Range GP	winterfat	2002	600	LB	$4,800	$1,809
Washoe GP	basin wildrye	2002	4,850	LB	$(5,731)	$27,179
Stillwater GP	prairie coneflower	2004	8,500	LB	$146,570	$743,112
Total					$62,755,158	$103,278,456
Production and Ecological Benefits from Releases:						$166,033,614
Gross PMC operating budget; 1967 - 2005						$15,668,045
Net Production and Ecological Benefits from Releases:						**$150,365,570**

With its consistently strong management, it has established a high bar for itself. Its cost benefit ratio is a whopping 10.6.

Table 8-Bridger.2 Other releases

Release & Type	Common Name	Release Year	Explanation
Bozoisky-Select, CV	Russian wildrye	1984	Production data lacking
Dupuyer, Streambank, GP	silverberry	2000	Production data lacking
Pondera Floodplain, GP	silverberry	2000	Production data lacking
Foothills, GP	Canada bluegrass	2001	Production data lacking
Old Works, GP	fuzzytongue penstemon	2002	Production data lacking
Prospectors , GP	common snowberry	2002	Production data lacking
Great Northern, GP	western yarrow	2004	Production data lacking
Spirit, GP	sweetgrass	2004	Production data lacking
Stillwater, GP	prairie coneflower	2004	Production data lacking
Trapper, GP	western snowberry	2004	Production data lacking
Copperhead, GP	slender wheatgrass	2006	Post 2005, production unknown
Opportunity, GP	Nevada bluegrass	2007	Post 2005, production unknown
'Continental', CV	basin wildrye	2008	Post 2005, production unknown
Ekalaka, GP	bur oak	2009	Post 2005, production unknown
Mill Creek, GP	silver buffaloberry	2010	Post 2005, production unknown
White River, GP	Indian ricegrass	2007	NRCS not lead release agency

Developed and Delivered Technology - Listed Publications

Table 8-Bridger.3 Number of PMC web site publications by type

Type of Publication	No.	Type of Publication	No.
Information Brochures and Flyers	6	Popular Journal or Magazine Articles	3
Major Publications	2	Published Abstracts	8
Miscellaneous Popular Articles	4	Published Symposium Proceedings	19
Newsletters	9	Refereed Journal Articles	5
Plant Fact Sheets	8	Release Brochure	21
Plant Guides	13	Release Notices	8
Plant Materials Annual Report of Activities	3	Technical Notes	67
PMC Annual Technical Report	3	Technical Poster	5

The total number of web site publications is 181.

Developed and Delivered Technology - Featured Vegetative Accomplishments

Two Featured Vegetative Accomplishments are included for Bridger. The first conveys the completeness with which the Plant Materials Program in Montana addresses reclaiming disturbed land. The second, though brief, also relates to reclaiming mine spoil, and demonstrates how one piece of the solution was accomplished. **.2**

1. Reclaiming Disturbed Land in the Western Coal Fields

In the eastern U.S., ten years before the establishment of the Bridger PMC, the Plant Materials Program was deeply involved in seeking better ways to reclaim surface mined land. In 1959 the Bridger PMC joined the effort; although, due to dramatically different climate, soils, and methods of mining, it was like starting over. This review demonstrates the magnitude of the contribution of the Bridger unit, not only in developing new plants, but developing a complete package of plants and procedures to totally reclaim mined land.

The first manager, Ashley Thornburg, soon emerged as the plant materials reclamation leader in the western coal fields as he worked his way from the center manager's position to the Montana and Wyoming PM Specialist, and then to the regional PM Specialist for the Midwest. Those who followed Ashley continued to build the knowledge base on coal spoil reclamation.

As a recognition leader Ashley was tapped to summarize the role of vegetation in the arid and semiarid regions of the country. This resulted in the following publication:

Thornburg, Ashley A. 1976. Plant Materials for Use on Surface-Mined Lands in Arid and Semiarid Regions. U.S. Environmental Protection Agency, Washington D.C.

This publication included plant materials technology for all the Great Plains states and from all sources, which consisted mostly of work performed by PMCs.

Reclamation related publications from the minds and hands of the Bridger crew, prior to Ashley's landmark publication, included

Stroh, James R. and Alvin G. Law. 1967. Effects of Defoliation on the Longevity of Stand, Dry Matter Yields and Forage Quality of Tall Wheatgrass, *Agropyron elongatum* (Host) Beauv. Agron J 59:432-435.

Stroh, James R. and Vernon P. Sunberg. 1970. Emergence of grass seedlings under crop residue culture. Journal of Range Management. p. 226-27.

Thornburg, Ashley A. and James R. Stroh. 1968. Cultural and Mechanical Seed Harvesting of Fourwing Saltbush Grown Under Irrigation. Am. Soc. of Rn. Mgt., Annual Meeting, Albuquerque, NM.

Thornburg, Ashley A. 1971. Grassland legume seed production in Montana. Agri. Expt. Sta. Bull. 333. Montana State University, Bozeman.

Reclamation remained a key focus between 1980 and 1990 with these new releases:

Pryor	*Elymus trachycaulus ssp. trachycaulus*	slender wheatgrass	1988	inclusion as a quick establishing species in seeding mixes, reclamation, highways, CRP.
Trailhead	*Leymus cinereus*	basin wildrye	1991	fall/winter livestock grazing, reclamation, wildlife food and cover
Rimrock	*Achnatherum hymenoides*	Indian ricegrass	1996	wildlife food and cover, livestock forage, and mixes on sandy soil for reclamation

The following publications are among those that continued the reclamation work:

Abstract--Revegetation Trials in the Pinedale Anticline Project Area. (PDF; 15 KB)

Winslow, S. R., K. J. Clause, J. S. Jacobs, and R. M. Hybner. 2009. 26th Annual Meeting American Society of Mining and Reclamation, Billings, MT. 11th Billings Land Reclamation Symposium.

Hybner, R.; E. Graham, M. Majerus and S. Majerus. 2009. Comparative Evaluation of Grasses, Forbs, and Seed Mixtures from "Local" versus "Non-Local" Origins at (Stucky Ridge) Anaconda, MT. Billings Land Reclamation Symposium, Billings, MT. 11th Annual 2009. 1 p.

Holzworth, L. K., J. Schaefer, G. Green, and T. Wiersum. 1993. The city of Anaconda erosion control and stabilization of C hill. In Proceedings: 10th National Meeting of the American Society of Surface Mining and Reclamation. Spokane, WA., May 1993. 8 p.

Scianna, J. D; E. Graham; R. Kilian, D. Zentner and R. Hybner. 2009. Effects of Sub-Irrigation Tubes and Cover Type on Woody Plant Establishment. (PDF; 17 KB) ASSMR-Billings Land Reclamation Symposium, Billings, MT. 11th Annual. 1 p.

Graham, E., S. Majerus, M. Majerus; J. Scianna and R. Hybner. 2009. Selection and Release of Indigenous Plant Materials for the Anaconda Superfund Site - 'Opportunity' Germplasm Nevada Bluegrass. ASMR - Billings Land Reclamation Symposium, Billings, MT. 11th Annual 2009. 1 p.

Holzworth, L. K., H. Hunter and S. R. Winslow. 2004. Disturbed Forestland Revegetation Effectiveness Monitoring - Results of 30 Years. 9th Billings Land Reclamation Symposium & 20th Annual Meeting of American Society of Mining and Reclamation, Billings, MT. June 3 - 6, 2003. 28 p.

Winslow, S. R. 2002. Native Plant Seed Collection and Seed Production for Reclamation. Inter-Tribal Native Plant Nursery Training, Pablo, MT. Jun. 2002. 1 p.

Majerus, M. 2000. Restoration with native indigenous plants in Yellowstone and Glacier National Parks. (PDF; 38 KB) Proc. 2000 Billings Land Reclamation Symposium, Pages 207-215. 9 p

Prodgers, R. A., T. Keck, and L. K. Holzworth. 2000. Revegetation Evaluations-How Long Must We Wait?. (PDF; 241 KB) Reclamation Research Unit and the Water Center, Montana State University, Bozeman, MT. Mar. 2000. 14 p.

Marty, L. 2000. The use of local ecotypes for the revegetation of acid/heavy metal contaminated lands in western Montana. Proc. 2000 Billings Land Reclamation Symposium, Pages 216- 228. 13 p.

When the time came for Thornburg to write his summary publication the task was made easier by his and the Bridger PMC's earlier accomplishments.

2. Revitalizing the Environment: Proven Solutions and Innovative Approaches

The following paper was presented at the 2009 National Meeting of the American Society of Mining and Reclamation, Billings, MT. The meeting title was Revitalizing the Environment: Proven Solutions and Innovative Approaches, held May 30 – June 5, 2009. The paper is a summary of an EPA sponsored Mine Waste Technology Program seeking Acid/Heavy Metal Tolerant Plants.[493] The Bridger paper citation follows:

Hybner, R. M., Elizabeth C. Graham, Mark E. Majerus, and Shannon G. Majerus. 2009. Comparative Evaluations of Grasses, Forbs and Seed Mixtures from Local versus Non-Local Origins at (Stucky Ridge) Anaconda, MT.

This Bridger PMC project included a study of a Nevada bluegrass collected near Anaconda, MT and tested at Stucky Ridge, which proved significantly superior to four other seed sources (two indigenous and two cultivars) for percentage stand and cover, vigor rating, and biomass production on a lime and fertilizer amended site. It was named and released as Opportunity Germplasm in 2007 for heavy-metal contaminated mine land reclamation, post-fire reclamation, native range restoration, wildlife habitat and logging road revegetation.

Figure 8-Bridger.-1 Opportunity Germplasm Nevada bluegrass

Opportunity germplasm bluegrass establishes easily and rapidly on sites characterized by low soil pH and moderate to high levels of heavy metals (relative to phytotoxicity levels) when these sites are properly amended. Evaluations of the accession have been conducted near Anaconda, Montana, where high levels of arsenic, cadmium, copper, lead, and zinc were present. It is best used as an inner-space species in native seed mixtures with other appropriate grasses, forbs, and shrubs. It exhibits superior performance on fertilized and lime-amended, acid/heavy-metal impacted sites under the ambient climatic conditions of the Upper Clark Fork Watershed (Deer Lodge County, Montana).

It's just another tool in the reclamation tool box.

Cape May, NJ Plant Materials Center

HISTORY AND BACKGROUND

Year and process leading to its establishment: The Cape May PMC was established in 1965, by congressional action.

History: In March 1962, a combination of high winds, high tide and driving rains washed tons of sand, soil and buildings into the ocean, causing billions of dollars' worth of damage along the Eastern seaboard. There were plant-bearing dunes with grasses, shrubs and trees holding the sand intact despite the violent elements. Consequently, Congress acted to protect the dunes from Cape Cod to the

Virginia and North Carolina Capes, and to increase the use of grasses, shrubs and trees to strengthen the dune structure.

In 1964 an eighty-eight acre farm was purchased by the New Jersey Green Acres program, on which the PMC was established.[494] Dr. Virgil Hawk, a long term plant materials specialist in the Northwest and Corn Belt, became the first manager.

The driving force behind the effort to secure authorization and financing for the center was New Jersey State Conservationist Seldom Tinsley, Regional PM Specialist Wilmer W. Steiner and Senator Clifford Chase of New Jersey. It was a team effort, with lots of supporting help. Construction started and Hawk worked in temporary quarters until August 1965.

The first plant collections were made between August and September, 1965 by Curtis Sharp, a newly appointed PM Specialist, who entered the position on August 16. He was instructed to report to the State Conservationist Tinsley, en route to the PMC. The instructions from Tinsley were simple. "As soon as you get down there to Cape May tomorrow, I want you on the road collecting every outstanding American beachgrass you can find, from Kitty Hawk to Cape Cod." One of the last collections he made, collection NJ-390, became the cultivar 'Cape'. By 1970, Seldom Tinsley had moved on but the first plants of 'Cape' American went into the hands of a commercial grower, and the official release soon followed.

Within twenty years of its establishment, the Cape May PMC had developed a host of tools to address the two high priorities that led to its creation. The plants and the technology for stabilizing sand dunes and eroding tidal shorelines had been accomplished.

Land Tenure: The four acres where the buildings are located are owned by NRCS. The additional and adjacent eighty-four acres of ideal coastal plain soil is owned by the State of New Jersey.

Service Area: The area served by the Cape May PMC consists of the coastal regions of the mid-Atlantic Coast from Cape Cod, Massachusetts through North Carolina, plus the upland area of the Piedmont regions of the eastern mountains. The soils, topography, climate, and land use combine to produce a distinct plant resource area. The climate is tempered by the Atlantic Ocean. There are wide fluctuations in annual precipitation, and to a lesser extent, in temperature. Drought years do occur, and hurricanes are common. Agriculture is predominantly cash row crops, orchards, truck crops, specialty crops and poultry. There are large areas of hardwood and pine forests. Extensive areas of tidal marsh are vital to the seafood and wildlife resources. Outdoor recreation is a major industry, which places extreme pressure on natural resources.

OUTPUT

Conservation Plant Development

Table 8-Cape May.1 Net production and ecological benefits of releases

Release & Type	Common Name	Release Year	Total Production	Unit	Net Value to Producer	Net Ecological Value
Cape, CV	American beachgrass	1970	179,250,874	PL	($50,006)	$748,397
Rem-Red, CV	Amur honeysuckle	1970	3,841,203	PL	$482,371	$556,139
Emerald Sea, CV	shore juniper	1971	6,796,163	GP	($34,066)	$22,792

Release & Type	Common Name	Release Year	Total Production	Unit	Net Value to Producer	Net Ecological Value
Atlantic, CV	coastal panicgrass	1981	20,354,355	PL/LB	$17,607,048	$139,695
Sea Isle, CV	Japanese sedge	1984	63,300	PL	$10,536,795	$72,676
Avalon, CV	saltmeadow cordgrass	1986	3,903,261	PL	$141,753	$1,384
Bayshore, CV	smooth cordgrass	1992	104,000	PL	$309,507	$361,101
Ocean View , CV	beach plum	1993	44,057	GP	$44,708	$8,931
Sandy, CV	rugosa rose	1993	303,035	PL	$5,862	$40
Wildwood, CV	Bayberry	1993	111,709	PL	$163,678	$3,279
Total					$29,207,650	$1,914,435
Production and Ecological Benefits from Releases:						$31,122,084
Gross PMC operating budget; 1966 - 2005					$13,665,506	$13,665,500
Net Production and Ecological Benefits from Releases:						$17,456,578

Most of the releases by the Cape May PMC are produced and replanted from vegetative parts. This is due to the nature of the conservation problems they are used to solve, i.e., coastal dunes and tidal stream erosion. The partial exception is 'Atlantic' coastal panic grass, which can be propagated by both vegetative parts and seed.

The impact of this phenomenon is that a lot of vegetative parts must be produced to establish a limited number of acres. This volume of production results in bumper net benefits to the producer but limited ecological benefits, which is based on the land use and acres planted. In the case of 'Cape' American beachgrass, the process used to calculate use benefits treated coastal sand dunes as 'stabilized land,' which yields $106 in ecological benefits per acre. The 179,251,000 commercially produced plants of 'Cape' only stabilize 309 acres, which seems small compared to, say, rangeland, but encompasses an enormous amount of the east coast sand dunes. Of course, the 309 stabilized acres may be protecting millions of dollars or real estate.

The cost benefit ratio of the Cape May PMC is 1.78.

Table 8-Cape May.2 Other releases

Release & Type	Common Name	Release Year	Explanation
Suther, GP	big bluestem	2002	Production data lacking
Suther, GP	Indiangrass	2002	Production data lacking
Suther, GP	little bluestem	2002	Production data lacking
Carthage, CV	switchgrass	2006	Post 2005, production unknown
High Tide, GP	switchgrass	2007	Post 2005, production unknown
Coastal, GP	Indiangrass	2007	Post 2005, production unknown
Dune, GP	coastal little bluestem	2007	Post 2005, production unknown
Timber, GP	Switchgrass	2009	Post 2005, production unknown
Monarch, GP	seaside goldenrod	2010	Post 2005, production unknown

Developed and Delivered Technology - Listed Publications

Table 8-Cape May.3 Number of PMC web site publications by type

Type of Publication	No.	Type of Publication	No.
Information Brochures and Flyers	1	Published Abstracts	2
Major Publications	1	Published Symposium Proceedings	3
Miscellaneous Popular Articles	4	Refereed Journal Articles	2
Newsletters	1	Release Brochure	11
Other Publication Types	2	Release Notices	2
Plant Fact Sheets	18	Technical Notes	3
Plant Guides	7	Technical Poster	6

There are a total of sixty-four web site publications.

Developed and Delivered Technology - Featured Vegetative Accomplishments

Keeping vegetation on tidal shores

In 1965 when the PMC became operational, there were two clearly defined conservation problems for the PMC to address. Without these two problems it is doubtful whether there would even have been a Cape May PMC. The massive March storm of 1962 had so devastated the Mid-Atlantic coast, it was evident man-made defenses were not the only answer. By far, the number one priority was to develop cultivars and the technology for their use to build and stabilize coastal sand dunes.

The second priority was the use of plants to halt or reduce erosion along tidal stream estuaries. See Figure 8-Cape May.1 This problem was great in terms of magnitude, even though it existed along less valuable real estate than the coastal dunes. Although previous work by SCS plant materials specialists gave a hint of a potential vegetative solution, the failures certainly left open whether any vegetative solution was realistic. In contrast to the establishment of vegetation on dunes, the nuances associated with the dynamic tidal beaches were much greater, each impacting the establishment and maintenance of vegetation. The work discussed in the following paragraphs was conducted between 1960 and 1970, as well as from previous work by others.[495]

The first question to answer was the best way to use vegetation; slope and stabilize the eroding bank, or establish a marsh on the beach which might trap sediments to protect the toe and allow the bank to stabilize naturally.

Figure 8-Cape May.1 Typical eroding bank

Sloping the bank and vegetating it was unsuccessful. When either normal or storm tides ran up the beach and hit the toe, it melted away making the entire bank vulnerable to erosion. Conversely, where there was a fringe of vegetation occurring naturally or from planting on the beach, from a few to many feet wide, the bank was always stable. On such sites the mean or storm tides did not reach the toe, because they ran into the vegetation. So the question of where to concentrate planting attention was resolved - on the beach. Where it existed, planted or natural, sand was trapped, building the fringe marsh higher and, in the process, pushing the mean high tide away from the toe, and reducing the energy that storm tides carried, thus keeping them away from the beach. A typical approach is shown in Figure 8-Cape May.2 and Figure 8-Cape May.3.[496]

By applying the logic of Crider, that a plant exists for every purpose, selecting the plant species was obvious. They naturally occurred in the zones shown in Figure 8-Cape May.2, American beachgrass above mean high tide, saltmeadow cordgrass in the intertidal area and smooth cordgrass from mean to low tide.

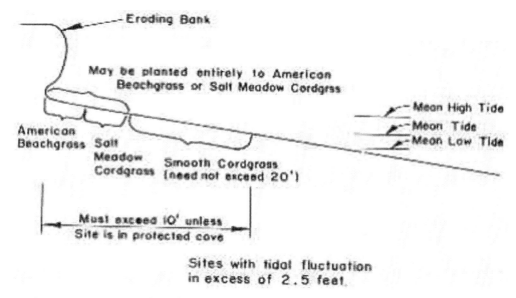

Figure 8-Cape May.2 Ideal planting arrangement on a tidal beach affronting an eroding

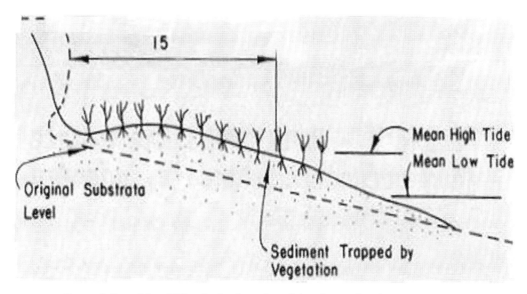

Figure 8-Cape May.3 The desired results of the above planting arrangement

While this was an important step, many questions remained. It was obvious that some potentially eroding banks had a fringe marsh on its beach and was not eroding, while others

231

looked the same and were eroding. What were the differences? There are energy levels, both in size and frequency, carried by waves that exceed what any adapted fringe marsh vegetation can endure. The key was to measure each eroding site in such a way that would indicate its potential for being stabilized with a fringe marsh.

Every eroding site was different in one or more of the shoreline characteristics that brought wave action to bear on the beach. Factors impacting the amount of delivered energy include the following. The underlined words are repeated in an assessment worksheet discussed later.

1. Fetch - the miles of open water perpendicular and at 45° either side of perpendicular to the shore of the eroding site.

2. General shape of shoreline for a distance of 200 feet on either side of the proposed planting site giving the desired results of the above planting arrangement.

3. Shoreline orientation.

4. Boat traffic within a half mile.

5. Width of beach above mean high tide.

6. Potential width of planting beach width.

7. On shore slope gradient of beach.

8. Presence of beach vegetation

9. Depth of sand at mean high tide.

The task got under way by measuring eroding and non-eroding shorelines for the above factors. Simultaneously, plantings were made to check what seemed to be a desirable site. The combination of these measurements from naturally stable sites, eroding shorelines, successful plantings and failed plantings provided reasonably clear guidelines how each factor and combination of factors delivered wave energy to the beach. From this an Assessment Guideline was developed to numerically measure the potential of a shoreline to be stabilized.

The Assessment Guideline is available from multiple sites:[497] including:

- http://www.mgs.md.gov/coastal/pub/tidalerosionChesBay.pdf

- http://www.dnr.state.md.us/ccws/sec/download/VegetationForShorelineStabilization2.pdf

- http://www.surfrider.org/artificialreef/artificial_reefs.htm

- https://habitat.noaa.gov/restorationtechniques/public/shoreline_tab4.cfm

- http://www.amazon.co.uk/Vegetation-shoreline-stabilization-mid-Atlantic-States/dp/B0006XED8Q

- http://www.dec.ny.gov/docs/water_pdf/sec3part4.pdf

Figure 8-Cape May.4 is the same site as Figure 8-Cape May.1 after establishing vegetation on the beach.

Figure 8-Cape May.4 Same site as Figure 8-Cape May.1 shown above five years later

Los Lunas, NM Plant Materials Center

<u>HISTORY AND BACKGROUND</u>

<u>Year and process leading to its establishment</u>: An SCS nursery was established at Albuquerque in 1936 by the same congressional action which established SCS. Early documentation following the closing of many nurseries conveyed the intent of establishing a plant materials center in northern New Mexico quickly.[498]

<u>History</u>: Actual production at the Albuquerque Nursery got under way in 1936, under the management of Joseph Downs. Downs previously worked with Dr. Franklin Crider in Tucson, AZ. Soon after he arrived in Albuquerque, Glenn Niner joined the staff. Their working relationship would continue for the next twenty-six years. In 1937 the nursery shipped 1,745,527 plants and carried over 2,190,902.[499] In 1937 all nurseries produced or collected only 222,040 pounds nationally of grass and legume seed. However, by 1950 the Albuquerque nursery alone produced or collected 165,090 pounds. In addition, the Albuquerque observational nursery got off to a fast start. In 1940 the nursery released 'Grenville' switchgrass and 'Vaughn' sideoats grama. 'Vaughn' has remained an outstanding cultivar, and was commercially available in 2010.

The 1953 nursery closings included the one at Albuquerque, requiring the lease for the land to be terminated. Fortunately, Joe Downs had the forethought to salvage propagating material of the most promising accessions, as well as the records, and save them in his garage for another day.

The ex-nursery employees, including Downs and Niner, were employed in other SCS activities.

In early 1957, through the efforts of Downs and Harbour Jones, superintendent of the NM State College of Agriculture, Middle Rio Grande Substation at Los Lunas, a basic agreement was drawn up between SCS and the College, whereby the College would operate a PMC at the substation. Funds and technical assistance would be provided by SCS and the cooperator would furnish the manager. James E. Anderson became the first manager in 1957. This arrangement continued until 1978.

Between 1978 and 1979 a new agreement between SCS and the University of New Mexico was developed. The most significant change was to switch management responsibility from the University to SCS. Of course, the sub-station continued to be managed by the University. The excellent cooperation between the two agencies continues.

Land Tenure: The PMC operates on 208 acres owned by the New Mexico State University.

Service Area: The Los Lunas PMC serves the semiarid and arid southwest region, including Northeast Arizona, Southeast Colorado, New Mexico, and Southeast Utah. Environmental conditions, including low precipitation, high intensity rainfall, wind, extreme topography, and varied land uses, combine to produce a variety of problems needing plant material solutions.

Elevations range from about 2,000 feet to more than 15,000 feet. Annual precipitation varies from six inches to more than thirty inches. Climatic conditions affecting plant growth vary from hot dry summers at low elevations, to those at high elevations where frost can occur at any date. Climate and soil conditions may vary within short distances.

The southern and western areas of the region are semi-desert with plateaus, plains, basins, and isolated mountain ranges. Land is primarily used for rangeland. Fruit and nut production is common in the southern area.

OUTPUT

Conservation Plant Development

Table 8-Los Lunas.1 Net production and ecological benefits of releases

Release & Type	Common Name	Release Year	Total Production	Unit	Net Value to Producer	Net Ecological Value
Grenville, informal	switchgrass	1940	11,000	LB	$9,301	$128,889
Vaughn, CV	sideoats grama	1940	2,475,714	LB	$12,145,453	$24,397,549
Amur, informal	intermediate wheatgrass	1952	357,940	LB	$418,182	$894,168
Largo, CV	tall wheatgrass	1961	6,400	LB	$(6,458)	$16,623
Elida, CV	sand bluestem	1963	28,056	LB	$262,529	$5,748
Lovington, CV	blue grama	1963	906,285	LB	$7,118,666	$13,052,479
Luna, CV	pubescent wheatgrass	1963	11,117,885	LB	$21,635,308	$24,301,844
Pastura, CV	little bluestem	1963	334,547	LB	$2,353,272	$3,381,314
Jose, CV	tall wheatgrass	1965	4,280,519	LB	$1,291,483	$11,117,675
Nogal, CV	black grama	1971	22,060	LB	$1,599	$651,322
Arriba, CV	western wheatgrass	1973	4,359,759	LB	$15,335,199	$21,164,437
Bandera, CV	Rocky Mountain penstemon	1973	214,839	LB	$1,250,023	$1,605,461
El Vado, CV	spike muhly	1973	93,007	LB	$397,078	$1,219,787

Release & Type	Common Name	Release Year	Total Production	Unit	Net Value to Producer	Net Ecological Value
Redondo, CV	Arizona fescue	1973	206,495	LB	$1,126,344	$2,234,368
Paloma, CV	Indian ricegrass	1974	563,339	LB	$1,199,376	$3,778,918
Barranco, CV	desert willow	1977	56,020	PL	$9,776	$105,146
Jemez, CV	New Mexico forestiera	1978	328,512	PL	$39,860	$3,930
King Red, CV	Russian olive	1978	526,100	LB	$376,123	$63,023
Montane, CV	mountain mahogany	1978	96,025	LB	$149,326	$185,940
Bighorn, CV	skunkbush sumac	1979	365,614	PL	$22,651	$21,973
Ganada, CV	yellow bluestem	1979	166,520	LB	$1,443,354	$2,392,706
Viva, CV	Galleta grass	1979	631,259	LB	$42,778	$4,810,595
Hachita, CV	blue grama	1980	1,599,364	LB	$14,351,625	$30,285,758
Salado, CV	alkali sacaton	1983	65,555	LB	$149,630	$1,123,799
Niner, CV	sideoats grama	1984	754,278	LB	$5,219,391	$7,424,260
Hatch, CV	winterfat	1985	16,184	LB	$(431,498)	$483,092
San Juan GP	narrow leaf penstemon	2000	700	LB	$17,500	$(7,385)
Grant GP	cane bluestem	2001	1,650	LB	$24,355	$34,983
Total					$85,952,225	$154,968,400
Production and Ecological Benefits from Releases:						$305,780,970
Gross PMC operating budget; 1935 - 2005						$21,923,110
Net Production and Ecological Benefits from Releases:						**$283,522,344**

In spite of its short shutdown from 1953 until 1957, the Los Lunas nursery/PMC has an admirable record, helped along with three releases before the PMC existed. There are three easily identified reasons for this. First is the clearly identifiable need. After that would have to be strong, and long term, technical and management leadership. The twenty-six year relationship of Downs and Niner, and the excellent partnering of SCS and NM State College of Agriculture head this list.

Their cost benefit ratio is a whopping 13.9.

Table 8-Los Lunas.2 Other releases

Release & Type	Common Name	Release Year	Explanation
Hope, CV	desert willow	1980	NRCS not lead release agency
Autumn Amber, CV	skunkbush sumac	1983	NRCS not lead release agency
Cedar, CV	Palmer's penstemon	1985	NRCS not lead release agency
Tierra, CV	bladder senna	1985	Production lacking
Regal, CV	desert willow	1989	Production lacking
Alma, CV	blue grama	1992	NRCS not lead release agency
San Juan, GP	narrow leaf penstemon	2000	Production lacking
Tusas, GP	bottlebrush squirreltail	2001	Production lacking
Star Lake, GP	Indian ricegrass	2004	Production lacking

Release & Type	Common Name	Release Year	Explanation
Westwater, GP	alkali muhly	2006	Post 5005, production unknown

Developed and Delivered Technology - Listed Publications

Table 8-Los Lunas.3 Number of PMC web site publications by type

Type of Publication	No.	Type of Publication	No.
Information Brochures and Flyers	6	Popular Journal or Magazine Articles	1
Major Publications	2	Published Abstracts	5
Miscellaneous Technical Article	4	Published Symposium Proceedings	9
Newsletters	1	Refereed Journal Articles	6
Plant Fact Sheets	2	Release Brochure	4
Plant Guides	1	Release Notices	5
Plant Materials Annual Report of Activities	2	Technical Notes	6
PMC Annual Technical Report	3	Technical Poster	2

The total number of web site publications is fifty-nine.

Developed and Delivered Technology - Featured Vegetative Accomplishments

The Los Lunas PMC, as well as others, has been a leader in developing new conservation plants. However, the Los Lunas PMC stands alone in the utilization of grant funding for the cooperative development with their University partner of an array of basic cultural practices that enhance the use of conservation plants throughout the Southwest. This approach has also permitted using PMC funds to concentrate on single subject vegetative problems. Several examples follow, presented as abstracts.

1. Basic Cultural Practices: Tumbling for Seed Cleaning and Conditioning [500]

Small rock tumblers can be used to clean and condition seeds both in an aqueous and a dry mode. During the process, grit and gravel remove fruit pulp and abrade seed coats.

Wet tumbling of seed aids imbibing of moisture, leaches water-soluble germination inhibitors, and may partially substitute for cold stratification for some shrub seed lots.

Small, hobby-size rock tumblers were used to accomplish a number of seed cleaning and seed conditioning treatments. The principal application of the tumbler has been maceration of dried or hydrated fruit pulp. We commonly use it to remove pulp from dried New Mexico olive (*Forestiera pubescens* var. *pubescens*)

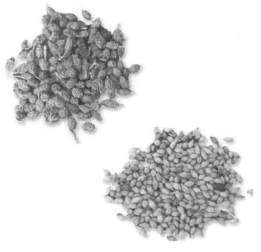

Figure 8-Los Lunas.1 Impact of tumbling

fruits. The fruits, collected in late summer or fall after the pulp has dehydrated, adheres tenaciously to seeds. A wet tumbling procedure employing pea gravel/crushed stone and water in a rubber lined tumbler vessel allows the rehydration of the pulp and slow abrasion of pulp from seeds. The amount of water is minimized so that the gravel and fruit makes slurry. This method is not quick, but the tumbler can be run overnight. After a course of tumbling, the contents are dumped into a sieve and the pulp is washed off, leaving clean seeds. The tumbling process is repeated until clean seeds are achieved. See Figure 8-Los Lunas.1.

2. Effect of Gibberellic Acid and Standard Seed Treatments on Mountain Snowberry Germination[501]

Acid scarification, warm stratification, cold stratification, and soaks in gibberellic acid (GA3) were effective in promoting germination in mountain snowberry (*Symphoricarpos oreophilus*) from New Mexico, but treatment levels and interactions were important. The combination of a thirty-minute acid soak, a twenty-one day warm stratification treatment, and an eighty-four day cold stratification treatment (the shortest duration evaluated) was highly effective in promoting germination. Increasing cold stratification from 84 to 168 days increased germination, as did incubation in all concentrations (250 to 1000 ppm) of GA3, but the benefit of longer cold stratification and GA3 incubation was reduced for acid-scarified seeds. Acid scarification breaks physiological dormancy of the embryo and may allow maturation of the embryo during cold stratification to begin sooner. Timing of GA3 application was also important. For seeds undergoing acid scarification followed by warm stratification followed by cold stratification, application of GA3 prior to warm stratification resulted in less germination compared to application following warm stratification. In snowberry, early GA3 application may result in GA3 catabolism during warm stratification, reducing the concentration available during cold stratification.

3. Refinement and Stratification of Thinleaf Alder and Water Birch Seeds from New Mexico[502]

For multiple seed collections of thinleaf alder (*Alnus tenuifolia*) and water birch (*Betula occidentalis*), response to IDS (incubation, drying, and separation), gravity separation, and stratification was highly variable among seed collections. In thinleaf alder, drying periods of eighteen or twenty-four hours following a twenty-four hour incubation period were comparable to dry seed separation in petroleum ether for increasing percentage of filled seeds. In water birch, IDS treatments resulted in lower percentages of filled seeds than separation in ninety-five percent ethanol. Overall, cold (5 °C (41 °F)) wet stratification for fifty-six days improved water birch germination from eleven percent to sixteen percent. In thinleaf alder, response to a fifty-six day stratification ranged from zero to sixteen percent germination improvement. Using separated seed in combination with appropriate stratification length achieved the largest improvements in germination. Treatment selection is discussed in relation to optimizing use of limited greenhouse space and seed supply.

4. Testing Native Grasses for Survival and Growth in Low pH Mine Overburden Pile Construction[503]

Overburden piles at the Molycorp Corp. molybdenum mine in North-Central New Mexico contain neutral rock types as well as mixed volcanic rocks, which are highly weathered materials with low pH and high salinity from pyrite oxidation. The mixing of rock types during overburden pile construction has resulted in heterogeneous substrates with a range of pH and soluble salt levels.

An experiment to determine grass species more likely to survive and grow in these low pH overburden materials used substrate treatments consisting of an unadulterated acid rock, an acid neutral overburden mixture ratio of 9:1, and an acid neutral overburden mixture ratio of 3:1. Containerized grass seedlings of fifty-four species/ecotypes, primarily cool-season natives of the western U. S, were transplanted into these substrates.

Species grown from seed collected at the Molycorp site having superior performance included *Muhlenbergia montana* (two ecotypes), *Blepharoneuron tricholepis*, *Festuca* species (three ecotypes), and a *Poa* species. A number of commercially available grass varieties had good survival and growth in these substrates: *Deschampsia caespitosa* 'Peru Creek', *Festuca arizonica* 'Redondo', *Festuca ovina* 'Covar', *Festuca ovina* 'MX-86', *Festuca* sp. 'Shorty', *Poa compressa* 'Reubens', *Pascopyrum smithii* 'Arriba, Barton, and Rosana', and *Elymus trachycaulus* 'San Luis'. Other native grass species that showed superior survival and growth results in these acid rock substrates included *Elymus canadensis*, *Danthonia intermedia*, *Sporobolus wrightii*, *Poa nemoralis*, and *Hesperostipa comata*.

5.   Longstem Transplants for Riparian Plantings in the Southwest[504]

This study is limited to the Southwestern Riparian Tree and Shrub Planting Methods, which the PMC has concentrated on for several years and developed adequate technology to address most circumstances.

Many Southwest riparian sites require revegetation following the removable of invasive woody species such as salt cedar. Many of these sites have shallow water tables and support established native riparian phreatophytic vegetation. However, because of flood control structures and flow regulations, the surface water hydrology has been altered disconnecting these sites from the flood plain and resulting in no overbank flooding. This supplemental water from flooding is critical in a desert climate for the recruitment of new seedling stands of common obligate riparian species such as cottonwoods (*Populus species*), willows (*Salix species*), New Mexico olive (*Forestiera pubescens*), indigo bush (*Amorpha fruticosa*), and false willow (*Baccharis salicina*). Generally these species require more than twice the water that hot desert climates can provide.

The Longstem Planting Method involves placing the lower portion of the root ball of a transplant in contact with the capillary fringe of the water table in the fall when the evapotranspiration demands of plants are reduced. Often this requires that the root crown of a transplant be buried as deep as four to six feet. By spring, new adventitious root growth has been initiated on the main stem of the plant, just below the soil surface where needed oxygen is available. More than 7,000 longstems of common riparian species have been planted during the past five years in riparian test areas of New Mexico and Colorado. Survival has ranged from seventy to ninety-three percent, generally without irrigation.

Big Flats, NY Plant Materials Center

HISTORY AND BACKGROUND

Year and process leading to its establishment: The Big Flats nursery was established in 1940, by the same congressional authorization that enabled the establishment of SCS production nurseries nationally.

History: "A Federal nursery was established at Big Flats in 1940, located on the Corning - Elmira road about one mile west of the community. Labor for development and production at this unit will be provided by a full CCC camp, now in process of development on the nursery track."[505] The nursery consisted of two farms, each 660 feet wide, for a total of one-quarter mile wide, and one and one-quarter mile long, running north and south, starting at the Chemung River in the south and ending at the base of the uplands in the north.

The nursery's primary function was to produce trees and shrubs for planting throughout the Northeast for conservation purposes. As with many other SCS nurseries, Big Flats had an observational nursery component. Unfortunately, the observational nursery program never functioned at the same high level as was true at other nurseries. It appears this was primarily due to the Regional Office Agronomist holding a negative attitude about observational studies because such work might either offend the strong experiment stations in the Northeast, or, in his opinion, the experiment stations were doing all the conservation plant work that was needed.[506]

As war clouds loomed the economy improved and the CCC program was closed. From then until late 1942, the production nursery personnel came primarily from the local community. In August 1942 the Civilian Public Service Camp was established at the nursery and a new supply of labor, although less cooperative, arrived and lasted until late 1946. These were individuals that refused to serve in the military but were obligated to serve in a civilian service.[507] The Civilian Public Service Camp was closed shortly after the war ended.

Charles Clements was the nursery manager from 1940 until it closed in 1953. Over the years different agronomists were on the staff, the last ones being Dr. Maurice E. Heath followed by Harry Porter. It is unclear exactly when Heath arrived or left. When he did leave he returned to Iowa State University to co-author the textbook *Forages* and to work with Virgil Hawk on developing 'Emerald' crownvetch. Because strong support for observational nursery work was lacking at the regional office, the Big Flats leader position may have stayed vacant for some time before and after Heath. Porter started in 1953 and served briefly as the lead observational nurseryman until the nursery was closed, then became a PM Specialist until 1960. The observational staff never exceeded two people, an agronomist and one aide, who was Carlton Dody.

Figure 8-Big Flats.1 Original farmhouse on left, which was the the nursery office. On the right is the 1946 flood. Note the office in the background, which later burned.

When the SCS nurseries closed in 1953, so did the one at Big Flats. However, it was one of the ten closed facilities that would become a PMC, and be operated by a state agency with funding from the Federal government. The State University of New York, through its two year Agricultural and Technical Institute at Alfred, NY, was selected to do the work. In addition to their carrying out the conservation plant work, the Institute developed a summer program for agriculture students, most of which came from cities. The plan was to do the conservation plant work with USDA funds, and the required funds for operating the student summer program would come from the production of vegetables, hay and tree seedlings produced by the students, and sold in the local market.

There is an interesting story that circulated in the Washington office at that time regarding what was happening at Big Flats.

One fellow said to another: "I understand they are growing strawberries on the old Big Flats nursery."

"Oh really" was his reply, "I sure hope they aren't selling them."

"For heaven's sake, no. What, from a federal facility? That would be awful embarrassing," the storyteller replied, but of course they were.

Unfortunately, the bulk of the USDA funding went for construction and related student costs. By 1957 the Institute was obligated to employ a full-time professional to provide technical leadership for conservation plant work. This was Curtis Sharp. While this helped move it along, it continued to lag and by 1960 SCS decided to terminate the agreement with the University, and SCS assumed full control of the operation on April 1, 1960.

The only employee that was a carryover from the nursery years that continued his employment with the cooperator was Robert Sherman. He started with SCS in 1948, became a Technical Institute employee in 1954, and returned to SCS in 1960. During his employment he survived twelve managers, serving as a thread of continuity from one to another. The last one he trained was Martin van der Grinten, who became manager in 1986. Sherman concluded 'he gets it' and retired in 1987. Apparently so, Martin is a continuing part of the Big Flats history.

Land tenure: The NRCS owns the 203 acres of the PMC.

Service Area: The area served by the Big Flats PMC contains both glaciated and non-glaciated soils. The Center provides service to Maine, Vermont, New Hampshire, Massachusetts, New York, and Pennsylvania. This cool, humid region consists of plateaus, plains and mountains. The elevations range from sea level to over 4,000 feet above sea level. Minimum temperatures range from 0 to -40 degrees Fahrenheit. The frost free season is 120 days to 160 days.

Dairies, fruit, and truck crops dominate the area's agriculture. Potatoes are a major crop in various parts of the region. Large areas are forested, which produce significant amounts of timber. Products include lumber, pulpwood, Christmas trees, firewood, and maple syrup. Non-agricultural activities which play a dramatic role in the use of conservation plants include surface mining, expanded land transportation systems, heavy urban development, and increasing recreational facilities.

OUTPUT

Conservation Plant Development

Table 8-Big Flats.1 Net production and ecological benefits of releases

Release	Common Name	Release Year	Total Production	Unit	Net Value to Producer	Net Ecological Value
Cardinal, CV	autumn olive	1961	36,706,654	PL	$3,204,987	$3,058,173
Chemung, CV	crownvetch	1964	257,150	LB	$1,151,905	$531,538
Arnot, CV	bristly locust	1969	3,697,760	LB	$237,126	$124,252
Lathco, CV	flatpea	1972	409,568	LB	$1,130,288	$1,607,759
Streamco, CV	purple osier willow	1975	9,646,792	PL	$261,656	$5,808,144
Tioga, CV	deertongue	1975	499,009	LB	$660,350	$861,133
Aroostook, CV	cereal rye	1981	1,221,203	LB	$420,779	$165,371
Golden Jubilee, CV	black-eyed Susan	1985	3,013	LB	$11,755	$8,994
Niagara, CV	big bluestem	1986	152,275	LB	$175,581	$609,481
Shelter, CV	switchgrass	1987	182,103	LB	$563,264	$1,431,770
Ruby, CV	red osier dogwood	1988	1,698,813	PL	$969,990	$2,736,128
SG4X-1, GP	eastern gamagrass	1995	100	PL	($6)	$0

Release	Common Name	Release Year	Total Production	Unit	Net Value to Producer	Net Ecological Value
Catskill, CV	dwarf sand cherry	1996	15,431	PL	($2,304)	$1,747
Keystone, CV	buttonbush	1996	83,306	PL	$130,688	$72,694
Spike, CV	hybrid poplar	1996	18,247	PL	$920	$240
Total					$8,916,981	$17,017,423
Production and Ecological Benefits from Releases:						$25,934,400
Gross PMC operating budget; 1940 - 2005						$21,566,950
Net Production and Ecological Benefits from Releases:						**$4,367,450**

The two heavy weights for the Big Flats PMC are 'Streamco' willow and 'Cardinal' autumn olive, equaling nearly half of their total production and ecological net value, and exceeding all others in total production. The centers net benefits are modest relative to some others, primarily related to the reasons mentioned above under Impacts. Their cost benefit ratio is 1.20. See Featured Vegetative Accomplishments.

Table 8-Big Flats.2 Other releases

Release & Type	Common Name	Release Year	Explanation
Glacial Lake Albany, GP	butterfly weed	2001	Production data lacking
Glacial Lake Albany, GP	wild lupine	2001	Production data lacking
Copper, CV	chinquapin	2005	Post 2005, production unknown
Meadowcrest, CV	eastern gamagrass	2006	Post 2005, production unknown
Greenbank, CV	sandbar willow	2008	Post 2005, production unknown

The two pre-varietal releases were in commercial production at one time.

Developed and Delivered Technology - Listed Publications

Table 8-Big Flats.3 Number of PMC web site publications by type

Type of Publication	No.	Type of Publication	No.
Information Brochures and Flyers	4	Popular Journal or Magazine Articles	1
Major Publications	3	Published Abstracts	7
Miscellaneous Popular Articles	7	Published Symposium Proceedings	3
Miscellaneous Technical Article	1	Release Notices	2
Other Publication Types	2	Technical Notes	6
Plant Fact Sheets	2	Technical Poster	11
Plant Materials Annual Report of Activities	2		

Their total number of web site publications is fifty-one.

Developed and Delivered Technology - Featured Vegetative Accomplishments

1. Ability of crownvetch to suppress woody plant invasion

Woody plants are undesirable on highway slopes and utility rights-of-way in the Northeast. Large trees and many smaller woody plants create safety and maintenance problems. Woody plants in utility rights-of-way areas hamper access of maintenance equipment and interfere with overhead electrical and communication lines, as well as under-ground pipelines and conductors.

In 1980, plant materials personnel associated with the Big Flats PMC, in cooperation with the Pennsylvania Department of Transportation, evaluated the ability of crownvetch to suppress woody plant invasion. The objective was to determine the competitive ability of crownvetch and other herbaceous groundcovers to restrict the invasion of woody plants on highway slopes.

In 1975, the Pennsylvania Department of Transportation identified fifty-one locations throughout the state where crownvetch had been seeded between 1955 and 1965. As you will see in the next section all the selected plantings had been seeded to 'Penngift'. The Maryland Highway Administration identified twelve locations in their state where plantings of predominately grass species were at least ten years old. They were well distributed from central to western Maryland, but all were within twenty-five miles of the Pennsylvania border.

Each of the sixty-three locations was surveyed. Several additional sites were surveyed at each location if a variety of exposures or cuts and fills were present. In all, 129 sites were surveyed on about 147 acres. Each individual surveyed site was 18.3 meters wide by the height of the slope.

The following was recorded at each: Location, exposure, percent slope, age of slope, existing woody species and land use adjacent to the site, soil texture, rooting zone, and soil pH.

Results: Where the percent of crownvetch was zero and some other erosion control mixture, primarily grass, had been used, there were sixty-seven woody plants per thousand square meters. The number of plants per thousand square meters gradually decreased as crownvetch percentage increased until it reached a low of seven plants per thousand square meters where the crownvetch cover exceeded eighty percent. In other words, one woody plant occurred within every fifteen square meters where there was no crownvetch and one plant occurred in every 143 square meters where the crownvetch cover exceeded eighty percent.

There was a gradual reduction in the number of woody plants as the percentage of crownvetch cover on the slope increased, irrespective of exposure. Exposures considered the least favorable for plant growth, the south, southwest, and west exposures, had by far the fewest woody plants. When the number of volunteer woody plants in crownvetch stands was considered, there were no dramatic differences between the cuts and fills.

While variations in the amount of crownvetch cover and the number of woody plants did vary somewhat by exposure, cut or fill slopes, soil texture and pH, age of slope and overhanging canopy, the reduction of woody plants relative to percent crownvetch cover was consistent.[508]

2. This is a 'what might have been' story

In 1953, after twelve years as a production and observational nursery, the Big Flats PMC inherited three plants that led to releases. They were single accessions of crownvetch, purple osier willow and autumn olive. No data existed of comparative evaluations of multiple strains of any of them. It would appear that happenstance resulted in three quite superior accessions just hanging around until the PMC came along. All were subsequently released. 'Streamco' purple osier willow had been extensively planted in comparison to other species and consistently performed well. 'Cardinal' autumn olive was released as a wildlife food and cover plant and for use on acid mine spoil for stabilization purposes. Its performance has exceeded all reasonable and unreasonable expectations. It is so good it is perceived, with some justification, of being bad. The third release was 'Chemung' crownvetch, which is another story.

By 1964 when 'Chemung' was released, another cultivar, 'Penngift', released in 1954, was well established in commercial markets. 'Penngift' had other things on its side; a savvy promoter who knew how to market anything and how to rapidly expand seed production to meet the growing demand he had justifiably created. 'Chemung' had none of those, and being late to the market it was doomed.

There is no doubt that crownvetch was, and remains one of the best critical area stabilizing plants for temperate regions to come out of any conservation plant effort. Crownvetch covers up the soil, eliminates erosion, and makes our highways and byways beautiful in May and June. It's just too bad that the cultivar wasn't 'Chemung'. Not because it was an SCS release but because, by comparison, it is significantly more vigorous and robust, from the moment it germinates.[509] McKee reported in 1969, "Cotyledons of the variety 'Chemung' were significantly larger than those of the variety 'Penngift', with those of 'Emerald' being intermediate in size." There is ample evidence recorded in the Big Flats Annual Technical Reports for 1961 and 1962 of the seed size, cotyledon and seedling vigor differences; all favoring 'Chemung' over 'Penngift'.[510]

Ironically, for 'Penngift' the less vigor was an advantage. Its lower profile and less vigorous growth proved valuable in seed production by not over growing itself and smothering the seed pods, a problem with the overly robust 'Chemung'. However, this handicap of 'Chemung' was easily overcome through careful site selection for seed production.

Smitten by the dominance of 'Penngift', production and sales of 'Chemung' languished. So what does this have to do with a Featured Vegetative Accomplishment?

One can speculate the more robust 'Chemung' has a much greater smothering effect on the invasion of woody plants as well as itself. And its tolerance to slightly lower pH levels would have extended its life on the slowly acidifying slopes. Had 'Chemung' been released first, associated with a strong promotional plan for use and seed production, 'Penngift' would have a hard time to break into the market. It is unknown when the accession that became 'Chemung' came to Big Flats, but it was in production prior to 1949. That year it was recognized as a valuable stabilizing plant by its performance on the PMC dike during one of their all-too-often floods. Why wasn't it released then, or earlier? Of course we will never know.

Great Basin Plant Materials Center, Fallon, NV

HISTORY AND BACKGROUND

Year and process leading to its establishment: A requested earmark by Senator Harry Reid for fiscal year 2006 provided funding for the establishment of the Center. It opened on June 26, 2006.

History: The Great Basin Plant Materials Center, located in Fallon, Nevada, is the newest PMC. Identified conservation needs in the Great Basin, including frequent and devastating wildfire, invasive weeds, and severe drought, have left the region on the verge of severe environmental degradation. Introduced plants have changed many ecosystems in the Great Basin. The Center's priorities include methods to reduce the harm done by introduced plants, reestablishment of desirable vegetation, and development of plant species to rehabilitate lands disturbed by fire and drought.

The soil, water, and air resources in the Great Basin face an environmental crisis. The Center strives to provide native plant materials that are adapted to the extremely harsh conditions found in the Great Basin. The PMC is developing native plants for the low precipitation and high salinity zones.

Land Tenure: The PMC operates on approximately 120 acres, owned by the University of Nevada.

Service Area: The Great Basin PMC Service Area covers approximately 139,000 square miles, i.e., almost eighty-nine million acres in four states: Nevada, Oregon, California, and Utah.

There has not been a field plant materials specialist serving Nevada since the PMC opened.

OUTPUT

Due to the newness of this PMC limited output is available to report. One exception is publications.

Table 8-Fallon.1 Number of PMC web site publications by category

Type of Publication	No.	Type of Publication	No.
Miscellaneous Popular Articles	1	Plant Materials Annual Report of Activities	3
Other Publication Types	1	Technical Notes	2
Plant Fact Sheets	2	Technical Poster	2

Their *Cover Crops for Green Manure in the Great Basin* publication is a thorough and well done evaluation of several introduced cover crops.

Bismarck, ND Plant Materials Center

HISTORY AND BACKGROUND

Year and process leading to its establishment: In 1934, USDI, Bureau of Plant Industry established a production nursery at Mandan, ND. This became the initial step towards establishing a PMC.

History: On March 27, 1935, a Bureau of Plant Industry nursery in Mandan was transferred to the USDA Soil Erosion Service. One month later, on April 27, 1935, the agency's name was changed to the Soil Conservation Service. The production nursery expanded rapidly. In 1937, over one million trees were produced. During fiscal year 1952-53, the SCS Nursery was moved to a new location in the bottoms between Bismarck and Mandan, called the Fort Lincoln Military Post.[511] A most interesting aspect of this move included re-locating one building from Mandan across the frozen Missouri River to Bismarck during February, 1953. The experience was published by the Tribune West newspaper staff writer Stan Stelter[512] on December 10, 1985, as recalled by former nursery manager Elmer Worthington. Five of eight buildings from the Mandan site were moved to Bismarck, four via truck and bridge and one by ice.

The Mandan Nursery initiated a vigorous observational nursery program from the offset, led by Dr. George Rogler, who directed this work until the nursery closed. Several plants entered the evaluation process during the nursery years that became commercially available cultivars. Two went onto the market before the nursery closed; 'Nordan' crested wheatgrass and 'Mandan' Canada wildrye. Others that came into the evaluation process during the nursery years, and were later released, include 'Garrison' creeping foxtail, 'Rodan' western wheatgrass, 'Lodorm' green needlegrass, 'Bison' big bluestem, 'Dakota' switchgrass and 'Oahe' hackberry.[513]

In November, 1953, the SCS closed the Fort Lincoln production nursery, as well as similar nurseries around the country. Since SCS owned the land, a semblance of a PMC continued to exist. In 1955 SCS transferred title of this land to the North Dakota Association of Soil Conservation District, who continued the production of trees and shrubs similar to when the nursery was operated by the SCS. With financial and technical assistance from SCS, the Association designated a small acreage to be used as the observational nursery. The valuable plant materials from the Mandan site were moved to this location, which became the Bismarck PMC. The Association continued to operate the PMC until 1967 when the agreement was terminated and the PMC's operation returned to SCS. However, a close cooperative arrangement continues between the PMC and the Association.

Over the past seventy-five years, the Bismarck PMC has provided a host of plant solutions for the diverse landscapes in North Dakota, South Dakota and northern Minnesota. The Center offers technical assistance for improving productivity of range and pasture lands, re-vegetating saline-alkaline soils, windbreaks, enhancing wildlife habitat and wetlands, and enhancing native prairie ecosystems.

Land Tenure: The PMC operates on sixty acres owned by the Lincoln Oakes Nursery, through a cooperative agreement with the North Dakota State Association of Conservation Districts.

Service Area: The Bismarck PMC serves the states of North Dakota, South Dakota and Minnesota. From the high plains and prairies of the Dakotas to the corn-belt and forests of Minnesota, the area is complex and productive. People depend on its cropland and rangeland for food and fiber, its coal and taconite mines for energy and steel, its lakes and woods for recreation and serenity, and its wetlands and open spaces for wildlife and beauty. However, satisfying the demands people make on natural resources often causes erosion and other environmental problems. Along with the right to use natural resources is the responsibility to protect and restore the land. Plants are one of the best tools for this job of conservation. Effective conservation plants must be adaptable to the extremes of heat, cold, wind and drought in the northern plains states.

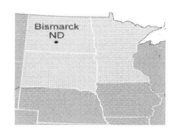

Average annual precipitation varies from fifteen inches in North Dakota to thirty inches in parts of Minnesota, with seventy-five percent of the total precipitation received between April and September. Extreme fluctuations in annual precipitation are common. Elevation ranges from 800 feet to 7,000 feet. Temperatures fluctuate widely from -60 degrees to more than 100 degrees Fahrenheit.

OUTPUT

Conservation Plant Development

Table 8-Bismarck.1 Net production and ecological benefits of releases

Release & Type		Release Year	Total Production	Unit	Net Value to Producer	Net Ecological Value
Nordan, CV		1953	32,400	LB	$1,281,396	$6,668,225
Pierre, CV		1961	450,801	LB	$1,959,606	$3,208,074
Garrison, CV		1963	496,691	LB	$284,271	$1,855,969
Killdeer, CV		1963	255,227	LB	$1,159,625	$1,805,731
Midwest, CV	Manchurian crabapple	1973	2,742,510	PL	$298,995	$220,054
Cardan, CV	green ash	1979	2,243,491	PL	$144,833	$375,785
Oahe, CV	hackberry	1982	655,435	PL	$104,046	$250,109

Release & Type		Release Year	Total Production	Unit	Net Value to Producer	Net Ecological Value
Sakakawea, CV	silver buffaloberry	1984	716,250	PL	$5,515	$93,071
Scarlet, CV	Mongolian cherry	1984	370,143	PL	$80,546	$30,820
Bonilla, CV	big bluestem	1987	607,408	LB	$3,423,285	$2,967,291
Centennial, CV	cotoneaster	1987	1,028,950	PL	$107,736	$155,171
Forestburg, CV	switchgrass	1987	1,406,540	LB	$3,400,158	$17,844,944
Tomahawk, CV	indiangrass	1988	730,475	LB	$5,758,694	$2,827,779
Regal, CV	Russian almond	1989	353,175	PL	$54,301	$27,200
McDermand, CV	Ussurian pear	1990	703,875	PL	$113,185	$102,200
Reliant, CV	intermediate wheatgrass	1991	12,500	PL	$80,814	$288
Homestead, CV	Arnold hawthorn	1993	1,649,685	PL	$490,267	$377,600
Bad River Ecotype, GP	little bluestem	1996	41,686	PL	$211,829	$688,600
Badlands Ecotype, GP	little bluestem	1996	14,264	PL	$93,951	$62,200
Bismarck Ecotype, GP	buffalograss	1996	8,000	PL	$5,408	$19
Bad River Ecotype, GP.	blue grama	1996	20,493	LB	$108,596	$283,828
Red River Natural, GP	prairie cordgrass	1998	43,800	LB	-$536,188	$12,620,289
Legacy, CV	late lilac	1999	2,242,450	PL	$364,493	$180,399
Bismarck GP	purple prairieclover	2000	7,540	LB	$68,821	$121,634
Medicine Creek, GP	Maximilian sunflower	2000	900	LB	-$124	$40,041
Itasca, GP	little bluestem	2001	90,000	LB	$610,870	$633,806
Prairie Red, CV	hybrid plum	2005	16,250	PL	$1,138	$1,324
Silver Stand, TS	Sandbar Willow	2005	2,775	PL	$250	$1,884
Total					$19,676,316	$53,444,411
Production and Ecological Benefits from Releases:						$73,120,728
Gross PMC operating budget; 1935 - 2005						$19,319,798
Net Production and Ecological Benefits from Releases:						**$53,800,930**

The early emphasis of the Bismarck PMC was to tame the ravages of wind erosion with vegetation, thus the early releases were of grasses and windbreak trees and shrubs. In recent years other environmental considerations have moved to the forefront, including wildlife habitat, wetlands, and native prairie ecosystems enhancement. A combination of these new plant cultivars and the excellent development of the needed technology for their use, place the Bismarck PMC near the top in any category. Their cost benefit ratio is 3.78.

Table 8-Bismarck.2 Other releases

Release & Type	Common Name	Release Year	Explanation
Mandan, CV	Canada wildrye	1946	NRCS not lead release agency
Lodorm, CV	green needlegrass	1970	NRCS not lead release agency
Rodan, CV	western wheatgrass	1983	NRCS not lead release agency
Bison, CV	big bluestem	1989	NRCS not lead release agency
Dacotah, CV	switchgrass	1989	NRCS not lead release agency
Mankota, CV	Russian wildrye	1991	NRCS not lead release agency
ND-WWG931,GP	western wheatgrass	1993	NRCS not lead release agency
ND-WWG932,GP	western wheatgrass	1993	NRCS not lead release agency
Canam, CV	hybrid popular	1995	NRCS not lead release agency
Sunnyview, CV	big bluestem	1998	NRCS not lead release agency
Bismarck, GP	narrow-leaved coneflower	2000	Production data lacking
Bismarck, GP	stiff sunflower	2000	Production data lacking
NU-ARS AC2, GP	crested wheatgrass	2002	Production data lacking
Haymaker, CV	intermediate wheatgrass	2003	Production data lacking
Survivor, GP	false indigo	2005	Production data lacking
Prairie Red, CV	hybrid plum	2006	Post 2005, production unknown
Manifest, CV	intermediate wheatgrass	2007	Post 2005, production unknown
McKenzie, CV	black chokeberry	2008	Post 2005, production unknown
Prairie Harvest, GP	common hackberry	2009	Post 2005, production unknown
Riverview, GP	American black currant	2010	Post 2005, production unknown
Mandan-759, informal	intermediate wheatgrass		Never officially released

Developed and Delivered Technology - Listed Publications

Table 8-Bismarck.3 Number of PMC web site publications by category

Type of Publication	No.	Type of Publication	No.
Books	3	PMC Annual Technical Report	4
Information Brochures and Flyers	16	Popular Journal or Magazine Articles	1
Major Publications	16	Published Abstracts	2
Miscellaneous Popular Articles	1	Published Symposium Proceedings	1
Miscellaneous Technical Article	1	Refereed Journal Articles	1
Newsletters	16	Release Brochure	28
Other Publication Types	3	Release Notices	11
Plant Fact Sheets	5	Technical Notes	11
Plant Guides	9	Technical Poster	9
Plant Materials Annual Report of Activities	2		

Their total of web site publications is 140.

Developed and Delivered Technology - Featured Vegetative Accomplishments

Staying In the Tree Buggy (referring to how long it takes to evaluate and release tree species)

When we think of the Northern Great Plains, or the prairies, we think of wind, grass, and a treeless plain. Why not? That's what it was like when the first settlers moved west. Slowly, and then not so slowly, the treeless grassland became a treeless cropland. More settlers arrived, and with them not only the desire, but the need for trees came with them.

Both scientists and settlers assumed the Great Plains environment could be altered to increase precipitation and improve their chances for agricultural success, because they believed that trees caused rainfall. Trees did so by drawing moisture from deep beneath the surface of the earth, which then evaporated from the leaves. As the moisture passed from the subsoil to the atmosphere through the intermediary of the trees, it condensed and fell to the earth as rain. Consequently, by planting trees on the Great Plains the environment could be altered. The environment of the Great Plains, however, proved more difficult to change in reality than in theory. Although settlers planted trees, rainfall did not increase and without irrigation from a nearby stream, the trees died by the score.[514]

In 1890, however, Bernhard E. Fernow, head of the Division of Forestry at the USDA, visited the Great Plains and told the Nebraska State Board of Agriculture: "I believe that forest planting is one of the necessary requisites to permanently reclaiming this vast domain; I believe that reforesting this large area, deforested by fire, buffalo, and consequent desiccation, is not impossible."[515] This changed federal policy, and from then until the mid-1930s the U.S. Forest Service with state agencies conducted many extremely large experiments up and down the Great Plains. Possibly the most successful was a reserve which became collectively known as the Nebraska National Forest in 1907. It was a national forest of 208,902 acres, protected from all agriculture activities, and mostly without trees.

Charles A. Scott, state project director for the U.S. Forest Service in Kansas, who had extensive experience with the mammoth experiment, grew skeptical.[516] In 1935 he stated, in no uncertain terms, that, "The shelterbelts (in Kansas) will not change the general climate of the entire region." However, the shelterbelts would "modify temperature, humidity, and wind velocity on portions of the adjoining farms."[517] Shelterbelts would not prevent drought, but they would lessen its effects. Moreover, shelterbelts would not increase the total amount of rainfall, but they would help conserve the moisture. Simply put, the shelterbelts would help control the local field environment. While experimentation continued, the focus narrowed to what would work in shelterbelts and windbreaks. By this time, SCS was thrown into the struggle. SCS considered tree planting as part of its other conservation work, rather than as a major independent activity. SCS officials also preferred to plant smaller windbreaks to protect farmsteads and livestock rather than the larger shelterbelts that primarily were designed to protect croplands, and it preferred that the initiative for tree planting be assumed by the newly organizing soil conservation districts at the local level.[518] The SCS role was to find the best plants.

Interest in woody plants for use in windbreaks and shelterbelts for the Northern Plains accelerated in 1934 when the Bureau of Plant Industry opened the soil erosion control facility in Mandan, ND. In the early years, planters had a limited selection. As one early publication on farm forestry stated, "It may take several years to show that trees are not adapted to a certain region or situation or soil. The ordinary planter cannot afford to experiment with trees."[519] Though there are many native trees and shrubs, people were looking for plants to increase the diversity in their species mix, or they needed cultivars with specific characteristics not currently available.

The SCS effort accelerated as soon as its nurseries closed and a PMC opened in Bismarck, ND. The state conservationists of the three states served by the PMC established the shelterbelt and windbreak as a priority. Their charge was simple. Find the best plants, from adaptation to shape to auxiliary value for use in windbreaks and shelterbelts. The PMC staff received assistance of many, including USDA Agricultural Research Service at Mandan, ND, USDI Fish and Wildlife Service, State Universities and Agricultural Experiment Stations, Soil Conservation District cooperators, seed growers and nurseries in the three states served by the PMC.

Creativity describes the major innovations implemented at the Bismarck PMC in recent years. Species identified by the state ecologist staffs as high priority for assembly and initial evaluation became part of the PMC's annual operations. A project plan was developed and the collection area to be sampled identified, as well as the number of plants or quantity of seed to be collected, and the time of collections. Potentially useful plants were collected from many locations. In 1954, PM Specialist John McDermand, made the first annual seed collecting trips to the Agriculture Canada Arboretum in Morden, Manitoba.

The large number of collections made were planted in greenhouse flats, and then transplanted to individual plant containers. These were grown out as 2-0 stock and transplanted to two or more sites on Major Land Resources in each of the three states. Figure 8-Bismarck.1 is an example. The planting plan includes four plant plots with five replications. Initial evaluations were made on each plant so that the data could be analyzed statistically.

Figure 8-Bismarck.1 Early plantings at Morris, MN

From these plantings the best were selected and went into advanced studies. Three or more locations in each of the states were selected. For example, starting in 1972, the McKenzie Slough Game Management Area (North Dakota Game and Fish Department) became the first location where these new selections were planted, followed in 1978 with a new location at the West Central Experiment Station (now known as the West Central Research and Outreach Center) at Morris, MN. See Figure 8-Bismarck.2. These plantings provide more control of weeds and animal and insects pests, and gave assurances that they would not be harmed and be available for observation for many years.

The final test was to establish the best of the best in actual used conditions in windbreaks and shelterbelts. From this final evaluation came the superior selections that became cultivars.

It takes a long time to evaluate a woody plant for the Northern

Figure 8-Bismarck.2 Morris, 2002

Great Plains, requiring long term commitment and the dedication to 'stay in the buggy'. The PMC effort has been successful for many reasons, but foremost has been the consistency, quality and longevity of their commitment. Erling Jacobson, PM Specialist who followed McDermand, Russell Haas, PMC Manager, and Dwight Tober, PMC manager, each contributed substantially to the release of many cultivars.

Over sixty years of annual evaluations, the PMC staff has found many adapted species and cultivars. Several are now on the commercial market for use by farms, ranches and homeowners that would not have happened without this long term consistency. The plants listed in Table 8 Bismarck.4 are among those that resulted from this dedication.

Table 8-Bismarck.4 Tree and shrub releases for windbreak and shelterbelt use

Cultivar	Common Name	Year Released
Midwest	Manchurian crabapple	1973
Cardan	green ash	1979
Oahe	hackberry	1984
Sakakawea	silver buffaloberry	1984
Scarlet	Mongolian cherry	1984
Centennial	cotoneaster	1987
McDermand	Ussurian pear	1990
Canam	Hybrid poplar	1995
Regal	Russian almond	1997
Legacy	late lilac	1999

Corvallis, OR Plant Materials Center

HISTORY AND BACKGROUND

Year and process leading to its establishment: The Corvallis PMC was established in 1957. It was authorized by congressional action, which included funding.

History: The current history of the Corvallis PMC started in 1957 when it opened on fifty-eight acres of land owned by the Oregon State University, but the entire history and productivity more accurately represents a continuation of plant materials work in western Oregon and Washington by SCS from the earliest days of the agency.

In 1935 the SCS, cooperating with the Civilian Conservation Corps, undertook the task of stabilizing approximately 3,000 acres of shifting sand dunes and barrens along the Oregon coast, with the objective of protecting several thousand acres of land and property valued at $10,000,000.[520] The Warrenton, OR CCC camp took the lead. This accomplishment is the Featured Vegetative Accomplishment for the Corvallis PMC. The CCC camp at Warrenton closed in 1942. However, SCS had opened a full scale nursery at Astoria, OR which continued support of the dune stabilization work until its closing in 1953.

Before the Astoria nursery closed, another person briefly joined the staff that was to play a significant and positive role in the future of the Corvallis and National PMC Program. That was Robert S. MacLauchlan, who was National Chief PM Specialist from 1973 until the end of 1984.

From the closing of all nurseries in 1953 until the Corvallis PMC was opened in 1957, the area was without plant materials assistance. It came into existence through congressional action, and appropriated funds became a part of the continuing PMC budget base for its operation.

Land Tenure: The PMC operates on fifty-eight acres are owned by the Oregon State University.

Service Area: The Corvallis PMC service area includes the northern Pacific Coast Range, Willamette Valley and Puget Sound, as well as the Olympic, Cascade, and Siskiyou Mountains of western Washington and Oregon. It provides plant solutions for northwestern California, western Oregon, and western Washington. Heavily forested coastal terraces, steep mountains, grass balds, foothills and valleys, woodland prairies, and Savanna vegetation typify the topography and natural vegetation.

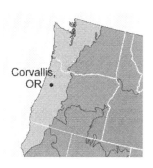

OUTPUT

Conservation Plant Development

Table 8-Corvallis.1 Net production and ecological benefits of releases

Release & Type	Common Name	Release Year	Total Production	Unit	Net Value to Producer	Net Ecological Value
Cascade, CV	birdsfoot trefoil	1954	19,300	LB	$20,245	$39,525
Marshfield, CV	big trefoil	1971	20,400	LB	$44,555	$23,117
Kalo, CV	birdsfoot trefoil	1976	51,700	LB	$54,749	$79,308
Hederma, CV	riverbank lupine	1981	76,700	LB	$ (74,590)	$ (35,435)
Clatsop, CV	Hooker willow	1988	1,084,555	PL	$ (165,879)	$251,836
Multnomah, CV	Columbia river willow	1988	24,562	PL	$ 4,429	$4,379
Nehalem, CV	Pacific willow	1988	161,040	PL	$37,687	$28,709
Placer, CV	erect willow	1988	395,500	PL	$14,873	$70,507
Plumas, CV	Sitka willow	1988	524,140	PL	$ (72,868)	$93,440
Bashaw, CV	Douglas spirea	1990	181,500	PL	$303,389	$448
Rogue, CV	arroyo willow	1990	421,100	PL	$ (92,402)	$75,071
Mason, CV	western dogwood	1992	292,500	PL	$488,713	$52,145
Arlington, CV	blue wildrye	1995	158,000	LB	$1,882,556	$337,966
Elkton, CV	blue wildrye	1997	93,000	LB	$1,029,839	$198,461
Baskett Slough GP	California oatgrass	2001	5,735	LB	$114,333	$28,331
Tillamook GP	tufted hairgrass	2002	2,000	LB	$10,613	$983,233
Willamette GP	tufted hairgrass	2002	4,000	LB	$18,151	$1,966,467
Total					$3,618,393	$4,197,506
Production and Ecological Benefits from Releases:						$7,815,899
Gross PMC operating budget; 1957 - 2005						13,857,809
Net Production and Ecological Benefits from Releases:						($6,041,911)

The net benefit from the many Oregon releases is disappointing. This is in part due to the nature of the landscape, climate and the lack or large areas of farm or rangeland. Heavy rainfall produces dense vegetation. As a result, conservation vegetation ends up being used primarily for small restoration projects.

Table 8-Corvallis.2 Other releases

Release & Type	Common Name	Release Year	Explanation
Skamania, GP	Sitka alder	2006	Post 2005, production unknown
Jackson-Frazier, GP	meadow barley	2008	Post 2005, production unknown

Developed and Delivered Technology - Listed Publications

Table 8-Corvallis.3 Number of PMC web site publications by category

Type of Publication	No.	Type of Publication	No.
Information Brochures and Flyers	4	Popular Journal or Magazine Articles	3
Miscellaneous Technical Article	20	Published Symposium Proceedings	1
Newsletters	2	Refereed Journal Articles	2
Other Publication Types	21	Release Brochure	9
Plant Fact Sheets	44	Release Notices	10
Plant Guides	7	Technical Notes	18
Plant Materials Annual Report of Activities	3	Technical Poster	3
PMC Annual Technical Report	2		

Their total number of web site publications is 149.

Developed and Delivered Technology - Featured Vegetative Accomplishments

The Warrenton, OR Project and its Aftermath:

The Cause – The Warrenton dune project intended to correct an unintended, yet man-made, situation. In the 1880s, navigation up and down the Columbia River was increasing. As it increased, the boats became larger and soon the millions of cubic yards of sediment which came down the Columbia River from upstream erosion created navigation hazards.[521] The many changes in the shoals and sand bars, and the shifting and changing depth of the deepest channel led Congress, by the River and Harbor Act of August 2, 1882, to authorize a board of engineers "to examine in detail the mouth of the Columbia River, Oregon, and report such plan, with estimates, for its permanent improvement." The board submitted its report on October 13, 1882. This led to several changes, all directed at the need for improved navigation.

Rapid construction of a jetty on the south side of the river commenced in 1889 and its effect was immediately noticeable. A new report recommended in 1893 construction of four groins on the north side of the jetty. All of these recommendations were carried out and the jetty was completed in 1895. The channel depth, which was twenty feet in 1889, increased to thirty-one feet in 1895, remained at thirty feet through 1896 and 1897, then began to decrease. An extension of the south jetty was started in 1903 and completed in 1913. As construction of this extension progressed, it became apparent that a north jetty would be necessary to stabilize the entrance and secure and maintain a channel forty feet deep. This addition progressed rapidly and was pushed to completion in 1917, by which time the controlling channel depth had increased to thirty-seven feet. Desirable navigation was accomplished.

A southern littoral drift across the face of the Columbia soon deposited its sediment load south of the jetty. This led to an initial accumulation raising the beach above the water line and advanced the shore line seaward. From about 1913 the collective impact was to blanket an area from the Columbia along the coast about sixteen miles, nearly to the rocky promontory known as Tillamook Head.

By 1935, sand was threatening to inundate the military preserves at Fort Stevens at the mouth of the Columbia River and Camp Clatsop, farther south. Lakes adjacent to the coast, lying on wildfowl migratory routes, and natural havens for these wildfowl, were rapidly disappearing beneath the blanket of shifting sand. Sitka spruce forests, fringing Clatsop Plains on the east, were succumbing as the sand moved slowly upon them. Here and there a few bricks and scattered boards marked the locations of former homes that had literally "gone with the wind." Hundreds of acres of rich pasture land were reduced to barrens of shifting sand and several thousand additional acres were endangered.[522]

Cooperating with the Civilian Conservation Corps, SCS undertook the task of stabilizing approximately 3,000 acres of these shifting sand dunes, with the objectives of stabilizing the dunes and protecting several thousand acres of land to the east. W. T. McLaughlin, a range examiner at that time proposed ways to stabilize the dunes while achieving some desirable topographic design.[523] With this knowledge, SCS scientists and CCC enrollees at the Warrenton, Oregon camp participated in a project that became internationally known to experts on stabilizing expansive areas of coastal sand dunes that had and were moving inland.

To begin to get a handle on what these early conservationists saw as a problem, CCC enrollees logged and split fire-killed timber, donated by the county, to build a picket fence along the beach. This slowed or stopped the sand movement where it could be stabilized. The question was…with what? An inventory of native sand stilling plants identified American dunegrass (*Leymus mollis*) as a logical choice, but was there something better? European beachgrass (*Ammophila arenaria*) had been planted and appeared superior in its vigor and rate of spread. After comparison plantings, which included American beachgrass (*Ammophila breviligulata),* this observation was confirmed, and it became the plant of choice. Planting European beachgrass on the dune that formed over the picket fence created the foothold in the restoration project. As time passed the stabilized areas quickly became a recreational site.[524]

When the project started, a forester named Robert L. Brown was the SCS onsite manager. Of course, he was under the general supervision of the regional nurseryman, Dr. A. L. Hafenrichter. In 1948 the two of them published the results, followed by another paper by Wilber T. MacLaughlin and Brown in 1942,[525] two more by Brown and Hafenrichter in 1948 and 1962,[526] [527] and the last in 1977 by John Schwendiman at an international conference dealing with sand dune reclamation.[528]

The objectives had been realized. SCS Historian Douglas Helms set the stage to understanding the background on this project in his 1985 publication.[529] Years after it was completed, two papers, Carlson, Rickendorf et al,[530] and Rickendorf et al utilized the results from this project and many other sources to put together a complete package on of how to stabilize sand dunes in the Pacific Northwest.[531]

In the early 1950s, Wilber E. Ternyik joined the staff of the Warrenton project. For more than a decade following World War II he worked on the project. An article appearing in the Eugene, OR 'The Register Guard', on May 1, 2006, had this to say about Ternyik, "He changed the actual face of the dunes during his time with the federal Soil Conservation Service in the 1950s, after discovering the power of European beachgrass to stabilize sand that was smothering houses and roads. Ternyik worked for the Soil Conservation Service upon his return to the states (i.e., following WW II). The agency was puzzling over how to stop shifting sands from invading unwanted territory on the coast. Before long, people were calling Ternyik the Johnny Appleseed of European beachgrass, which stays erect throughout the coast's harsh winters and created the foredune that now lines much of the shoreline."[532] Following this experience, Ternyik opened his own beachgrass growing and planting business. In 1991 he co-authored the USDA Agriculture Handbook 687 with others.[533] For his dune work and many other contributions, Ternyik's life-size bronze bust rests in the Gateway to Discovery building in Eugene.[534]

Beachgrass planting strategically placed to halt dune movement into lake and forest on other side.

Figure 8-Corvallis.1 Sand movement and control on the Warrenton, OR project

By the early twenty-first century American beachgrass was invading and replacing the European beachgrass, which had been the standby from the 1930s, but this was not the only change. Both American and European beachgrasses were considered invasive exotics and were being removed.[535] Both create a different dune environment than the native, American dunegrass which produces an irregular, hummocky dune line and landscape. European beachgrass builds a continuous and higher, steeper sided dune than either of the other two grasses. American beachgrass is somewhere in the middle, like European, it creates continuous dunes but like American dunegrass, they are lower and less steep.

Other serious questions about the impacts of the entire dune project are being raised, like the desirability of even stabilizing the site, and the impacts of doing so on the ecological purity of the native species. Additionally, a dune environment created by either American or European beachgrass may threaten the habitat of the Western snowy plover (*Charadrius alexandrinus nivosus*), an endangered species.[536]

So hindsight, depending on how important Western snowy plover is, may suggest the original mistake occurred when the jetty was built to keep the Columbia River open for navigation. This resulted in the scouring of the channel bottom and keeping the channel open, but dumping millions of cubic yards of sand on the beach to the south, carried from the vast Columbia watershed. Had the jetty not been built, maybe the area would not have required stabilizing. Were the objectives of stabilizing sand that was inundating military preserves, filling lakes lying on wildfowl migratory routes, and burying Sitka spruce forests just plain wrong?

Getting things back to their natural condition is complicated. There is certainly something to be said for allowing the waters to run free and the sand to accumulate in the mouth of the Columbia, as it was doing on March 23, 1806 when Lewis and Clark left Fort Clatsop and headed upstream for home. Perhaps it would have been better for the native community if they had just stayed home.

East Texas Plant Materials Center, Nacogdoches, TX

<u>HISTORY AND BACKGROUND</u>

<u>Year and process leading to its establishment</u>: The PMC opened in 1982. Its establishment resulted from a cooperative agreement between Stephen Austin University at Deep East Texas, the Northeast Texas Associations of Soil and Water Conservation Districts, the NRCS, the U.S. Forest Service, and a local Resource Conservation & Development Council.

<u>History</u>: The evaluation and selection of plants for conservation purposes was taking place at SCS nurseries in Texas from 1935 until they closed in 1953. The effort continued sporadically by SCS technicians at Texas Agricultural Experiment Stations, first at San Antonio and later at Spur, TX until 1965 when the Knox City PMC opened in north central Texas. The need for a PMC in the more humid eastern parts of the state was met in 1982 through the efforts of several groups.

While SCS was one of these, and has provided continuous funding, the PMC at Nacogdoches was not authorized by the U.S. Congress, meaning that there was no adjustment in the Federal PMC budget to support the Center.

<u>Land Tenure</u>: The PMC operates on seventy-five acres which is owned by the U.S. Forest Service.

<u>Service Area</u>: The East Texas Center has a service area of forty-two million acres that include eastern Texas and northwestern areas of Louisiana. Soils range from deep, coarse-textured sands to heavy clay inundated bottomlands. Elevation varies from fifty feet to approximately 700 feet above sea level, increasing from south to northwest.

The average annual precipitation of the area served by the PMC ranges from thirty-two inches to more than fifty-six inches, increasing from northwest to southeast. Seasonal rainfall patterns are established. Normally, rainfall, perennial streams, and ground water provide an abundance of available water; however, short droughts are common. Humidity and temperatures are usually high during the growing season. The average growing season ranges from 228 days to 260 days from north to south.

Principle conservation problems in this gently-rolling to hilly-forested land and prairies area include the need for plant materials and technology to provide soil protection, enhance production, and improve water quality on degraded pasture, rangeland, and cut-over timberland, and restoration of surface-mined areas, streambanks, and saline and high water table soils.

<u>OUTPUT</u>

Conservation Plant Development

No production data was available from the East Texas PMC released plants prior to 2005.

Table 8-Nacogdoches.1 Other releases

Release & Type	Common Name	Release Year	Explanation
Jackson, GP	eastern gamagrass	1999	Became a cultivar release
Harrison, GP	Florida paspalum herbaceous	2004	Production data lacking
Crockett, GP	mimosa	2006	Post 2005, production unknown
Pilgrim, GP	velvet rosettegrass	2007	Post 2005, production. Unknown

Developed and Delivered Technology - Listed Publications

Table 8-Nacogdoches.2 Number of PMC web site publications by type

Type of Publication	No.	Type of Publication	No.
Information Brochures and Flyers	3	Plant Materials Annual Report of Activities	3
Major Publications	1	PMC Annual Technical Report	3
Miscellaneous Popular Articles	1	Published Abstracts	3
Miscellaneous Technical Article	1	Release Brochure	7
Newsletters	5	Release Notices	2
Other Publication Types	4	Technical Notes	7
Plant Fact Sheets	18	Technical Poster	4
Plant Guides	6		

Their total number of web site publications is fifty-four.

Developed and Delivered Technology - Featured Vegetative Accomplishments

Constructed Wetlands for On-Site Septic Treatment - A Guide to Selecting Aquatic Plants for Low-Maintenance Micro-Wetlands

The following resulted from the PMC actually creating maintenance-free micro-wetlands in the front yard of the Center. Applicable state and county health regulations and required permits are an essential up front part of utilizing this approach.[537]

The use of constructed wetlands to treat domestic wastewater from single-family residences is a rapidly emerging and badly needed biotechnology. Such treatment systems, sometimes called micro-wetlands or rock/reed filters, have a media filter in which special plants grow to enhance septic treatment and create a pleasant landscape. Such wetlands allow both safe treatments of household wastewater and in low rainfall areas, the use of treated water to sustain a low-maintenance landscape.

How Micro-Wetlands Work: Micro-wetlands are an alternative or supplemental treatment for standard septic systems. Shallow, level earthen ponds are excavated, then lined with heavy plastic and filled with media such as river rock, purchased pebbles or even chipped rubber tires. Typical micro-wetlands are designed to contain two cells or zones. Septic water from the home flows into the first cell. A perforated pipe from the first cell allows water to enter the second cell or pond. It is essential the ponds be level to allow the water to spread uniformly across the entire media bed. As it passes through the media in both cells the plant roots, bacteria, enzymes, fungi and protozoa break down pollutants.

At the back, or outfall of the second cell is another perforated pipe that collects the treated water and sends it out for disposal. Figure 8-Nacogdoches.1 is the PMCs' micro wetland.

The quality of out-flow effluent is determined by how long the water takes to pass through the media, which in turn helps determine the size of each cell. This varies depending on many factors. The cell size at the East Texas PMC was determined from a known set of circumstances, including the

Figure 8-Nacogdoches.1 Front office lawn with two wetland cells

amount of septic water that must be treated and the physiographic conditions at the site, such as length of growing season, amount of rainfall, and the characteristics of the plants that can be used in the area. These factors vary from location to location.

Selecting Plants for the Low-Maintenance Micro-Wetland: The following plant selection guidelines used by the East Texas Center will be useful in many locations. In the typical two cell design, the first zone receives the strongest wastewater. Since this section is likely to be anaerobic, plants that pump oxygen to their roots, which accelerate decomposition of pollutants, and are nutrient-loving should be placed here. These plants are usually hard stemmed marsh plants that have tiny tubes for transporting oxygen to their roots. Most of these do not flower, but many stay green late into the fall or during the winter. In the second cell, or the back of the wetlands, the major nutrient reduction takes place. Here flowering, soft-stemmed, nutrient-tolerant plants work best. These plants transport water out of the system by evapotranspiration. However, a major benefit of these plants is that they beautify the garden and provide color. Using plants that flower in different seasons will keep the wetlands beautiful most or all year long.

As a rule, the right plant placed in the wrong zone will quickly display signs of stress, such as wilting, refusal to flower and other indications that it is not suited to the site. Such plants are easily removed and replaced with other species.

Many of the hard-stemmed plants, such as cattails and woolgrass, can be found growing wild in nearby drains and ponds. Other plants that tolerated the cell conditions may have to be purchased from a water garden source.

A wetland cell is no different than any other flower bed in that plants will needed to be replaced, thinned, harvested or re-transplanted. However, not only will the user have created a wetland, and have another attractive garden spot, but will be contributing to a healthier environment.

Kika de la Garza Plant Materials Center, Kingsville, TX

HISTORY AND BACKGROUND

Year and process leading to its establishment: This PMC was established in 1981 through a Memorandum of Understanding between the Caesar Kleberg Wildlife Research Institute, the South Texas Association of Soil and Water Conservation Districts, and the Soil Conservation Service.

History: The driving force for this Center was the need for commercially available conservation plant materials adapted to the unique climate and soils of the South Texas area. The James E. "Bud" Smith Center had attempted to meet these needs; however it was unable to adequately do so because of the physiological differences between the areas. While the SCS was a part of the Memorandum of Understanding, and has provided some continuous funding, the PMC at Kingsville was not authorized by the U.S. Congress, meaning that there was no adjustment in the Federal PMC budget to support the Center.

It is named the Kika de la Garza Plant Materials Center due to the extraordinary effort of the congressman who helped get It established, but unfortunately, not funded.

Land Tenure: The PMC is located on ninety-one acres; seventy-six acres are owned by Texas A&M University at Kingsville and fifteen are owned by the privately held King Ranch.

Service Area: The area served by the Kika de la Garza PMC comprises about twenty-seven million acres of the southern portion of Texas. Average annual precipitation ranges from seventeen inches in the western areas to more than forty inches along the coast. Average annual temperatures range from 68 degrees to 74 degrees Fahrenheit. The average growing season ranges from 260 days in northern areas to 330 days in the lower Rio Grande Valley. Topography is flat to rolling with extremely variable soils.

The major land uses in south Texas are rangeland, pasture, and hay land. These land uses support the production of beef cattle and high quality white-tail deer. Cropland is locally scattered through the south Texas region. Its heaviest concentration is in the lower Rio Grande Valley where irrigated citrus and vegetables are grown. Along the Gulf Coast Prairie where precipitation is enough to support annual crops, cotton and grain sorghum are grown. The Texas Gulf Coast is also an internationally significant migration and wintering habitat for North American water fowl. Strip mining areas, oil field exploration, and coastline urbanization are also land uses that require conservation plants.

OUTPUT

Conservation Plant Development

All plant releases from the Kika de la Garza PMC have been germplasm; there are no cultivars. They are listed below along with their intended uses.

Table 8-Kingsville.1 Germplasm releases by the PMC

Release & Type	Common Name	Release Year	Uses
Falfurrias, GP	big sacaton	1998	livestock forage, restoration of native vegetation, re-vegetating alkaline and saline sites, grass hedge terrace, wind strips for erosion control, and stabilization of watershed structures, stream banks and floodplain areas
Kinney, GP	False Rhodes grass	1998	early season forage and native range restoration
Falfurrias, GP	big sacaton	1998	livestock forage, restoration of native vegetation, re-vegetating alkaline and saline sites, grass hedge terrace, wind strips for erosion control, and stabilization of watershed structures, stream banks and floodplain areas
Lavaca, GP	Canada wildrye	2000	cool season forage on pastureland and rangeland
Mariah, GP	hooded windmill grass	2006	roadside plantings, range seeding, critical site revegetation
Welder, GP	shortspike windmill grass	2006	roadside plantings, critical area revegetation
Kika 677, GP	streambed bristlegrass	2006	rangeland planting, erosion control, wildlife habitat and water quality improvement
Kika 819, GP	streambed bristlegrass	2006	rangeland planting, erosion control, wildlife habitat, and water quality improvement

Release & Type	Common Name	Release Year	Uses
Kika 820, GP	streambed bristlegrass	2006	rangeland planting, erosion control, wildlife habitat, and water quality improvement
Kika 648, GP	plains bristlegrass	2006	range seeding, wildlife habitat
Chaparral, GP	hairy grama	2007	critical areas, roadsides and reclamation sites
Dilley, GP	slender grama	2007	critical area sites, roadsides, reclamation sites, buffers and filter strips
Atascos, GP a	Texas grama	2007	critical areas, roadsides, and reclamation sites
La Salle, GP	Arizona cottontop	2007	rangeland seeding
Goliad, GP	hairy wedelia	2008	range restoration, native landscaping and wildlife habitat
STN-561, GP	Hookers plantain	2009	cool season upland wildlife plantings and range seedling mixes
STN-496, GP	redseed plantain	2009	upland wildlife plantings and range seeding mixes
Zapata, GP	Rio Grande clammyweed	2009	upland wildlife plantings and range seeding mixes
Maverick, GP	pink pappusgrass	2010	rangeland seeding and highway right-of-way plantings
Webb, GP	whiplash pappusgrass	2010	rangeland seeding, highway right-of-ways, and for upland wildlife

Developed and Delivered Technology - Listed Publications

Table 8-Kingsville.2 Number of PMC web site publications by type

Type of Publication	No.	Type of Publication	No.
Information Brochures and Flyers	7	Published Abstracts	1
Plant Fact Sheets	28	Refereed Journal Articles	2
Plant Guides	9	Release Brochure	20
Plant Materials Annual Report of Activities	3	Release Notices	12
PMC Annual Technical Report	2	Technical Notes	17
Popular Journal or Magazine Articles	2	Technical Poster	2

Their total number of web site publications is 105.

Developed and Delivered Technology - Featured Vegetative Accomplishments

A Bioengineering System for Coastal Shoreline Stabilization[538]

For many years, the Shoreline Erosion Committee of the Texas State Association of Soil and Water Conservation Districts has implemented shoreline erosion control projects with smooth cordgrass, *Spartina alterniflora*. Due to the hazardous conditions along the coast, many of them were less successful than anticipated. This was particularly true where a bluff existed on the project. Either the planting would not become established or, in some cases, the bluff continued to erode. The development of geotextiles offered a potential to overcome the failures that were being experienced.

Geosynthetic turf reinforcement mats (TRM) provide a low-cost alternative of hard armor on eroding shore lines. The mats along with the root reinforcement of planted vegetation resist damage from wave energy. On high-energy wave sites, cellular concrete blocks are an alternative to concrete and rip-rap. Both helped establish adapted and native, stabilizing plants.

In partnership with the San Patricio Soil and Water Conservation District, the PMC implemented a shoreline project in October, 1997, under a grant from the Texas Coastal Management Program. They evaluated turf reinforcement matting and cellular blocks while testing several plants such as marshhay cordgrass (*Spartina patens*), gulf cordgrass (*Spartina spartinae)* and marsh elder (*Iva frutescens*), as well as smooth cordgrass, for adaptation and added environmental and engineering enhancement.

The location of the project was near Portland, Texas along the Nueces Bay. The shoreline had a bluff that ranged in vertical height from zero to eight feet. The soil of the site was Monteola clay. The slope of the tidal area was approximately five percent and had an open fetch of roughly three miles. The water salinity in July of 1997 had twenty-five parts per thousand.

On July 1, 1997, Tensar fence was installed at approximately the mean tide level, with three-inch diameter size posts every ten feet, as a wave barrier. It was secured to the post with 1" x 2" lathing and nailed at the top and bottom. 'Vermilion' smooth cordgrass that was 18-24" tall, 1-2 stems and with 6" bare roots was planted in four rows 2' apart at 2" below to 12" above mean tide, ten feet toward shore from the Tensar wave barrier.

From August 25-28, 1997, PROTEC 420 cellular blocks and North American GreenC-350 TRM were installed. The slope was shaped to a 2.5:1 grade. The toe was stabilized by installing three blocks at 4:1 grade and then backfilled. All blocks were underlain with a non-woven filter fabric. The blocks extended forty-eight feet in length and three feet in vertical height. The TRM was placed on the bank and extended for 152 feet in length and ranged from zero feet to eight feet in vertical height. The toe and the top of the bank were trenched to a one and one-half foot depth and the TRM was secured with either eight-inch staples or six-inch (60d) nails with tin caps, and buried. The TRM was secured every eighteen inches with a six inch overlap of the mats.

On October 27, 1997, an alternating sequence of a grass and a shrub were planted. The grasses were gulf cordgrass and marshhay cordgrass. The shrubs were marsh elder armed saltbush (*Atriplex acanthocarpa)* and wax myrtle (*Myrica pusilla*). The grass and shrub sequence was chosen to provide a root network of fibrous and tap roots to secure the bank slope. The plants were also chosen for abundant top growth to cushion the bank against wave energy.

The TRM was easy to install and has stayed stable since planting. The estimated wave energy for stability at this site, based on their experience, was when the beach was protected at two feet above mean tide with a secure offshore wave barrier or a mature cordgrass stand. Without wave barrier protection, they would only recommend using the TRM at three feet or more above mean tide. The cost of the material was relatively inexpensive, making this option very attractive.

The cellular blocks have also remained stable. However, the corner where the blocks made a transition to TRM did not, and repairs were made with a "Terracell" cellular confinement system. The cost of cellular blocks is expensive, making it desirable only where other material is inadequate.

The four-inch "Terracell" cellular confinement system is a flexible material, making it easy to install. It has provided better stability then the TRM at low tide elevations and is less expensive than cellular blocks. Furthermore, on high shrink-swell clay soils, the cellular confinement system may give added protection against riling and gullying of the bluff slope. It appears to be adapted to one foot above mean tide and higher.

In February 1998, the transplants were surveyed for survival and found forty dead plants out of 1400. Most of the dead plants were at the shoreline of the cellular blocks, smothered by shoal grass (*Halodule wrightii*). By April of 1998, the shoalgrass was one to two feet thick along the shoreline, smothering the shoreline plants, especially at the deep corner of the blocks.

On July 9, 1998, and again in February 5, 1999, survival and growth was excellent. The grasses performed exceedingly well with all having survival rates over ninety percent. Both gulf cordgrass and marshhay cordgrass have grown well at this site and appear to be adapted to one and one-half to two feet above mean tide and higher. Marshhay cordgrass not only survived well but had rhizomes on many plants.

The shrubs did not perform as well as the grasses. Wax myrtle had an eleven percent survival rate. Overall, Marsh elder had a seventy-two percent survival rate. However, at sites that were two feet above mean tide, it had a ninety-three percent survival rate. The majority of its mortality occurred at the shoreline. Shoalgrass smothered many of these plants.

Conclusions: It is recommended that smooth cordgrass be planted on sites where little shoalgrass is encountered and tidal slopes are less than five percent. See Figure 8-Kingsville.1. Once the cordgrass is well established, bluffs less than eight feet in elevation can be shaped and planted to adapted plant material. With the added toe protection, the bluff treatment has improved chances of success.

Where a smooth cordgrass stand is established, a combination of TRM and cellular confinement system should provide good shoreline stabilization. If smooth cordgrass cannot be established, then a bluff treatment that includes cellular concrete blocks for toe protection will be needed.

On high value commercial or residential property where adjacent landowners are protecting their shoreline, this system appears to have promise. Also, this system may have particular value for soil stabilization and wildlife habitat enhancement on man-made spoil islands along the Texas Gulf Coast.

Figure 8-Kingsville.1 Vermillion Smooth cordgrass

James E. "Bud" Smith Plant Materials Center, Knox City, TX

HISTORY AND BACKGROUND

Year and process leading to its establishment: Because of the recognized need, the PMC was authorized by congressional action and established in 1965.

History: In 1935, the Bureau of Plant Industry opened a nursery in San Antonio, TX. The same year it was transferred to SCS. Its principal function was to produce or collect grass seed for range revegetation, and to conduct an observational studies program. The nursery closed in 1953, and the land was transferred to the Texas Agricultural Experiment Station. Many of the desirable plants from the observational nursery continued to remain for a short time at the San Antonio nursery, under the watchful eye of SCS employee James E. Smith, who had been the manager of the San Antonio Nursery and became the plant materials specialist serving Texas in 1954. After a period of years, Smith relocated the plants to the Texas Agricultural Experiment Station in Spur, TX, where they continued to be reproduced and evaluated state-wide in field plantings.

Dr. A. B. Corner was the State Director of the Texas Agricultural Experiment Station at College Station, Texas, and as such he was in constant contact with the Spur sub-station. He and the late R. E. Dickson, superintendent of the Spur sub-station, wrote the original draft of the national law which founded the Soil Conservation Service, so that Spur could boast of being the birthplace of the SCS.[539]

When the Knox City PMC was authorized and established in 1965 these valuable accessions were the first items planted there. Four cultivars from this group, which had their beginning years earlier at the San Antonio nursery, were released by the PMC. Another release was collected and tested at Spur before the PMC came into existence.

The new Center was renamed the James E. "Bud" Smith Center in 1967, in honor of the individual who had contributed so much to the program, not only as a plant materials specialist from 1954 - 1965 where he constantly lobbied for a PMC, but as an SCS nursery employee in Oklahoma and Texas, before moving to Texas. See more on Smith in the Key Leaders chapter.

Land Tenure: The PMC operates on 137.5 acres of privately owned land.

Service Area: The PMC provides plant solutions for central Texas, southern Oklahoma, and parts of Kansas, Colorado, and New Mexico. The wide range in topography, climatic factors, and vegetation has resulted in a diverse and unique area served by the Center.

Rainfall varies from forty inches in the northeast to less than eight inches in the far west. Seasonal patterns are established, but frequent droughts and major storms of high intensity are common. Seventy-five percent of the precipitation is received from March to October. The growing season is 280 days in the south part of the area and 179 days in the most northern part of the area.

OUTPUT

Conservation Plant Development

Table 8-Knox City.1 Net production and ecological benefits of releases

Release & Type	Common Name	Release Year	Total Production	Unit	Net Value to Producer	Net Ecological Value
King Ranch, informal	yellow bluestem	1941	445,037	LB	$303,272	$1,397,416
T-4464, informal	Buffelgrass	1949	2,927,283	LB	$3,229,244	$30,160,773
Kleberg, Informal	bluestem	1954	78,485	LB	$108,147	$246,443
Medio, Informal	bluestem	1954	53,440	LB	$70,739	$280,346
Gordo, Informal	bluestem	1957	56,028	LB	$76,483	$102,802
Llano, CV	Indiangrass	1963	8,240	LB	$5,537	$47,083
Selection 75, CV	kleingrass	1969	6,747,544	LB	$27,260,359	$139,044,390
Mason, CV	Sandhill lovegrass	1971	5,900	LB	$25,460	$112,375

Release & Type	Common Name	Release Year	Total Production	Unit	Net Value to Producer	Net Ecological Value
Marfa, Informal	green sprangletop	1974	599,500	LB	$247,930	$913,438
Alamo, CV	switchgrass	1978	897,308	LB	$2,132,576	$19,190,524
Aztec, CV	Maximilian sunflower	1978	36,280	LB	$207,296	$330,148
Shoreline, CV	common reed	1978	2,734,720	PL	$89,235	$8,517
Lometa, CV	Indiangrass	1981	276,529	LB	$64,326	$1,437,795
Rainbow, GP	wild plum	1981	98,411	GP	$56,164	$25,460
Saltalk, CV	alkali sacaton	1981	1,000	LB	$2,668	$51,067
T-587, GP	Old World bluestem	1981	459,632	LB	$187,355	$11,911,524
Yellowpuff, GP	littleleaf lead tree	1981	315	LB	$2,421	$57
Haskell, CV	sideoats grama	1983	2,397,714	LB	$7,216,063	$20,648,117
Sabine, CV	Illinois bundleflower	1983	376,375	LB	$2,012,759	$287,659
Comanche, CV	partridge pea	1985	269,798	LB	$1,514,040	$221,346
Eldorado, CV	Engelmann daisy	1985	21,300	LB	$272,598	$31,709
Plateau, CV	awnless bush sunflower	1987	23,136	LB	$114,698	$70,654
Van Horn, CV	green sprangletop	1988	394,708	LB	$1,857,807	$6,517,994
Earl, CV	big bluestem	1996	26,680	LB	$93,744	$106,231
Borden County, GP	sand dropseed	2000	9,500	LB	$34,516	$249,769
Cottle County, GP	sand bluestem	2002	4,000	LB	$14,280	$18,970
OK Select, GP	little bluestem	2002	7,000	LB	$19,403	$93,252
San Marcos, GP	eastern gamagrass	2005	100	LB	$271	$96
Total					$47,219,390	$233,505,954
Production and Ecological Benefits from Releases:						$280,725,344
Gross PMC operating budget; 1935 - 2005						$19,354,667
Net Production and Ecological Benefits from Releases:						**$261,370,677**

The first five releases listed above were developed during the nursery days. Note all are informally released, meaning, in this case, that these plants had been selected as superior by the observational nursery staff, reproduced on the production side of the nursery and/or provided to land owners and managers, who in turn began producing and selling the seed; all this without any formal releasing process.

The net benefits from the James E. "Bud" Smith Center exceed the cost of operations thirteen times. 'Selection 75' klinegrass alone had earned seven times more than the costs to release it. As a matter of fact, the benefits from four cultivars each exceed their costs. The nursery/PMC output has been consistent for seventy-five years. King Ranch yellow bluestem went on the market only five years after the nursery opened. The cost benefit ratio of the PMC is 14.7.

Table 8-Knox City.2 Other releases

Release & Type	Common Name	Release Year	Explanation
Angleton, informal	bluestem	1942	NRCS not lead release agency
Blue, informal	buffelgrass	1952	Production data lacking
Pretoria 90, informal	bluestem	1954	Production data lacking
Gordo, informal	bluestem	1957	Production data lacking
Premier, CV	sideoats grama	1960	NRCS not lead release agency
Llano, CV	buffelgrass	1977	NRCS not lead release agency
Nueces, CV	buffelgrass	1977	NRCS not lead release agency
Verde, CV	kleingrass	1981	NRCS not lead release agency
Brazos, informal	bermudagrass	1982	NRCS not lead release agency
Marfa, informal	green sprangletop	1990	Production data lacking
Overton R18, CV	rose clover	1991	NRCS not lead release agency
Boomer, CV	bur oak	1994	Production data lacking
Duck Creek, GP	Texas dropseed	2000	Production data lacking
Kerr, GP	Texas swampmallow	2000	Production data lacking
Potter County, GP	spike dropseed	2000	Production data lacking
Cuero, GP	purple prairieclover	2003	Production data lacking
Hondo, GP	velvet bundleflower	2003	Production data lacking
Plains GP	prairie acacia	2008	Post 2005, production unknown

Developed and Delivered Technology - Listed Publications

Table 8-Knox City.3 Number of PMC web site publications by type

Type of Publication	No.	Type of Publication	No.
Information Brochures and Flyers	15	Plant Materials Annual Report of Activities	3
Major Publications	1	PMC Annual Technical Report	3
Miscellaneous Popular Articles	1	Published Abstracts	6
Miscellaneous Technical Article	7	Published Symposium Proceedings	1
Newsletters	11	Release Brochure	20
Other Publication Types	8	Release Notices	2
Plant Fact Sheets	16	Technical Notes	10
Plant Guides	12	Technical Poster	3

Their total of web site publications is 119.

Developed and Delivered Technology - Featured Vegetative Accomplishments

The productivity of blockbuster cultivars of the James E. "Bud" Smith PMC should be enough output. But their output did not stop there. Remember that two of the earliest products identified for the Plant Materials Program were

- Product Two – Detailed Technology on How to Grow, Establish and Reproduce

- Product Four – Delivering the Developed Technology

James Smith and Arnold Davis were legendary for roaming their field offices with how-to-do-it technology.[540] [541] Smith wrote an undated dissertation,[542] which apparently was prepared for soon-to-be-visiting SCS Administrator Williams. It reviewed briefly the history of the observational nursery work in Texas and his work as a PM Specialist from 1954 until 1960. Reading the document tells one a lot about Smith, including his keen desire to simplify and then advocate better ways to use vegetation for soil conservation. Here is an example from his 1960 document.

"During the cleaning and final storage of the 1935 blue grama harvest at Dalhart, Smith became concerned about how such material could be metered out in planting. He took some seed to the Dalhart Field Station Supt. B. F. Barnes to see whether the station cotton planter would distribute it. They harnessed a team, hooked up to the planter, and soon found that it did a fine job of putting out the seed. This machine was one of the picker wheel type and, with the high quality of seed on hand, could only be cut down to six pounds per acre in 40-inch rows. That rate was too high, but the idea was okay." Discussion of this fact with the BPI men at Woodward Oklahoma Field Station resulted in the construction of the first grass drill made specifically to handle chaffy grass seed material. Smith was a great plants person but even better at figuring how to get seed into the ground and growing.

The James E. "Bud" Smith PMC web site lists 105 publications of Developed Technology. How is the best way to package sound technology for NRCS Field Offices use? How about wrapping it inside the basic plant materials related Standard and Specifications. This is exactly what James Alderson did which he calls a Plant Materials Fact Sheet. Each outlines in detail a definition, purpose, planting considerations, management and then identifies the desirable plant species for use. The eight which he developed are as follows:

- Contour Buffer Strips - Conservation Practice 332

- Cross Wind Trap Strips - Conservation Practice 589C

- Field Borders - Conservation Practice 386

- Filter Strips - Conservation Practice 393

- Herbaceous Wind Barriers - Conservation Practice 422A

- Riparian Forest Buffers - Conservation Practice 391

- Streambank and Shoreline Protection - Conservation Practice 580

- Windbreaks and Shelterbelts - Conservation Practices 380 and 650

One page of the Filter Strip Fact sheet is shown below.[543]

Table 8-Knox City.4 Filter Strips Conservation Practice Plant Identification Chart

MANAGEMENT

Before establishment apply fertilizer and other soil amendments according to a soil test. Plant into a firm, weed-free seedbed. Inspect FS periodically to insure unwanted weed do not become a problem. Mowing or grazing should be scheduled to encourage dense growth and to accommodate wildlife. Inspect after storm events to ensure the effectiveness of the practice. Restoration may be required after the strip has accumulated so much sediment that it is no longer effective.

The Plant Materials program has looked at several plant species and their use in vegetative filter strips.

The chart below identifies various plant materials and their use in FS.

PLANT SPECIES *1	WILDLIFE USE FOOD(F),COVER(C)	GROWING SEASON	RECOMMEND USES (SEE CODES BELOW)
Switchgrass	F/C	Warm	1,2,3,4,5,6
EasternGamagrass	F/C	W	1,2,4,5
Big Bluestem	C	W	1,2,4,5
Indiangrass	C	W	1,4
*Bermudagrass	C	W	1,2,3,4,5,6
*Old World Bluestem	C	W	1,4
*Tall Fescue	F/C	Cool	1,3,6
*Tall Wheatgrass	F/C	C	1,2,3,4,6
Maximillian sunflower	F/C	W	1,2,5
Commom Reed	C	W	1,2,4,5,6
Canada Wildrye	F/C	C	1,2,5
Virginia Wildrye	F/C	C	1,2,5
*Bahiagrass	F/C	W	1,5,9
Plains Bristlegrass	F/C	W	3,6,10
*Dallisgrass	F/C	C	1,2,4,5,8
Illinois Bundleflower	F	W	1,5,6,10
Partridgepea	F	W	1,2,4,10

* Denotes an introduced species.
*1 - Different ecotypes of the same species may have different use codes check local guides for final use.

Recommended Use Codes
1 = Nitrogen Uptake
2 = Phosphorus Uptake
3 = Saline/Alkaline Soils

4 = Sediment Retention
5 = Adapted for Use Along Streams
6 = Adapted to High Water Tables
7 = Flood Tolerant
8 = Shade Tolerant
9 = Resistant to Traffic
10 = Drought Tolerant

Contact your local conservation district office for additional information related to the installation and management of each plant type and others that may be locally adapted.

Pullman, WA Plant Materials Center

HISTORY AND BACKGROUND

Year and process leading to its establishment: The nursery at Pullman, WA was created in 1935 by the same congressional action which had established the SCS.

History: Under President Franklin D. Roosevelt in the spring of 1933, the Civilian Conservation Corps (CCC) program was established to do emergency conservation work. H. H. Bennett obtained authorization to establish erosion control demonstration projects. Through the influence of the Dean of the College of Agriculture, E. C. Johnson, the Palouse demonstration project was headquartered at

Pullman under the leadership of William Rockie with E. C. Johnson as Chief Engineer.[544] The location of the Pullman Nursery became the PMC.

During the winter of 1933, a need for plant materials was contemplated. Harry Schoth, with the Bureau of Plant Industry, Soils, and Agricultural Engineering from Oregon State College at Corvallis was called upon for assistance.[545] He organized a native seed collection program under Dr. Lowell Mullen, a Washington State College graduate, and also made available seed from two foreign plant expeditions to Mongolia and Russia, the Westover-Enlow and Roerich Expeditions. During 1934, four teams of two men each spent the late summer collecting native plant seeds throughout the Pacific Northwest.

During 1934 and early 1935, negotiations with the Agronomy Department of Washington State College were completed for the use of some college land on which to plant the new introductions. A group of local citizens, led by banker George Gannon, backed the purchase of additional acres. Through a cooperative agreement, land plus office space in Wilson Hall was made available for grass and tree testing and production.

At the time of purchase, the land was planted with winter wheat. Two acres were plowed out and re-planted with foreign plant introductions and a block of slender and crested wheatgrasses. Wheat was grown for the next several years on land not used for nursery work. Virgil Hawk, a graduate student at WSC did the field work, and was later employed as manager of the outlying nurseries.

A 200-man CCC camp had been established at the present Pullman Airport and a labor force of twenty-five men with a foreman was assigned to the Pullman nursery. The Pullman camp was closed in October 1938 and labor was then supplied by the Moscow, Idaho camp. CCC labor was supplemented by hiring as many as twenty high school or college students for summer work. A 2.2 acre building site was purchased by the U.S. government on scabland south of the college land. Government ownership was a prerequisite for the expenditure of building funds. Construction of the residence, seed house and shop was completed in 1937 at a cost of $75,000.

Dr. A. L. Hafenrichter, WSC Agronomy Department Professor, was hired as the Palouse Demonstration projection agronomist in 1933 and in 1935 he was appointed regional nurseryman with Dr. Paul Lemmon, a forester, as assistant. In June 1935, Clair Swendby was hired from the WSC Forestry Department to grow trees and H. W. Miller, a WSC Forestry senior, became his assistant. Hank Rampton, assistant to Harry Schoth from Corvallis, was hired to make initial plantings and get the nursery started. Dr. Del Tingey, an Agronomy professor on leave from Utah State University at Logan was in charge of local planning and operations during 1936. Arthur J. Johnson was the first farm manager. Junior agronomist John L. Schwendiman was employed Sept. 3, 1935. Harold W. Miller became the Junior Forester after graduation from WSC in June 1936.

By December 1935, the USDI, Soil Erosion Service, under which the demonstration project had been started, was transferred to the Soil Conservation Service. This reorganization put Project Supervisor Mr. Rockie in charge of all Demonstration projects in the Northwest. He chose Pullman as headquarters for the Soil Conservation Service.

It is unclear exactly who was nursery manager during the 1935 - 1939 time frame. Virgil Hawk is listed as Outlying Nursery manager, and Arthur J. Johnson as Farm Manager. Hafenrichter served as Regional Nurseryman, and was located at Pullman, so he may well have assumed this role during the nursery's organizational years.

For the next seventeen years the Pullman nursery, with regional direction by Hafenrichter and onsite leaders Schwendiman, Hawk, Miller and others, set a high bar for fulfilling the concept of Dr. Franklin Crider for finding plants to solve conservation problems. When 1953 rolled around, and all nurseries were closed, again Hafenrichter used his influence to be sure Pullman observational program would become, and remain an SCS-run PMC. The high bar of productivity remained until the mid 1970s, when output slowed for the next twenty or so years.

Land Tenure: NRCS owns 157 acres and the remaining 163 acres are owned by Washington State University.

Service Area: The Pullman PMC lies in the heart of the Palouse Hills region which is internationally recognized for outstanding wheat yields and, sadly, some of the highest soil erosion rates in North America. The Center provides plant solutions for parts of Idaho, Washington, and Oregon. Eastern Washington, Oregon, and northern Idaho is a mosaic of cropland, orchards & vineyards, rugged scablands, native range, and mountains.

The service area of the Center faces many resource challenges. Winter winds strip unprotected topsoil and create dust clouds that degrade air quality for people living downwind. Melting snow erodes unprotected soil that pollutes receiving waters. Many of the region's streams are important for salmon and steelhead trout spawning and rearing. Riparian areas in the Center's service area frequently lack desirable vegetation that provides shade and woody debris for fish habitat. Invasive plants hinder streambank revegetation. Annual weeds have replaced native vegetation in many areas, and noxious weeds such as spotted knapweed are invading forested areas. These undesirable plants impede natural revegetation and threaten healthy wildlife environments.

The annual rainfall ranges from six inches in the Columbia Basin to more than sixty-five inches in the mountainous regions of Kittitas County, Washington. Summers are warm and dry. Wind is common in the plains regions of Oregon and Washington resulting in wind erosion of soils in these low rainfall areas. There are many acres of rangeland and irrigated cropland in the eight to fourteen inch annual rainfall zones, and many acres of dry-land cropland in the fifteen to twenty inch rainfall areas. While wind erosion is prevalent in the eight to twelve inch precipitation areas, water erosion predominates in the higher precipitation zones, particularly from water running over frozen ground. The frost-free growing season ranges from 70 days at Pierce, Idaho, to 213 days in Benton County, Washington. Elevations range from 350 feet in the plains regions to 9,675 feet in the Eagle Cap Wilderness area of Union County, Oregon. Most of the agricultural land is below the 2,800 foot elevation.

OUTPUT

Conservation Plant Development

Table 8-Pullman.1 Net production and ecological benefits of releases

Release & Type	Common Name	Release Year	Total Production	Unit	Net Value to Producer	Net Ecological Value
Manchar, CV	smooth brome	1943	9,775,273	LB	$1,911,172	$16,575,772
Sherman, CV	big bluegrass	1945	4,455,236	LB	$15,466,105	$82,449,674
Bromar, CV	mountain brome	1946	2,748,980	LB	$ (229,637)	$3,281,259
Primar, CV	slender wheatgrass	1946	56,000	LB	$124,786	$222,973
Whitmar, CV	bluebunch wheatgrass	1946	1,304,430	LB	$3,756,205	$125,312
Durar, CV	hard fescue	1949	1,628,221	LB	$1,081,827	$5,930,286
Volga, CV	mammoth wildrye	1949	259,555	LB	$ 271,393	$534,680

Release & Type	Common Name	Release Year	Total Production	Unit	Net Value to Producer	Net Ecological Value
Alkar, CV	tall wheatgrass	1951	1,222,240	LB	$1,898,844	$8,342,661
Draylar, CV	upland bluegrass	1951	32,400	LB	$(11,632)	$273,294
Greenar, CV	intermediate wheatgrass	1956	1,636,350	LB	$3,253,869	$3,257,700
Latar, CV	orchardgrass	1957	3,651,805	LB	$2,161,718	$7,460,824
Newport, CV	Kentucky bluegrass	1958	22,508,470	LB	$3,158,084	$106,840,204
Covar, CV	sheep fescue	1977	1,582,757	LB	$ (240,966)	$1,106,397
Canbar, CV	Canby bluegrass	1979	342,075	LB	$221,592	$1,559,807
Secar, CV	Snake River wheatgrass	1980	4,494,801	LB	$9,645,988	$13,870,908
Umatilla, CV	snow buckwheat	1991	75,500	PL	$33,305	$655,769
Curlew, CV	Drummond willow	1993	224,035	PL	$56,427	$352,882
Palouse, CV	Lemmon's willow	1993	181,450	PL	$ 82,467	$147,627
Rivar, CV	Mackenzie willow	1993	289,084	PL	$101,127	$235,197
Silvar, CV	coyote willow	1993	195,630	PL	$19,679	$128,278
Schwendimar, CV	thickspike wheatgrass	1994	455,400	LB	$54,600	$1,923,885
Blanchard, Origin, GP	blue elderberry	1996	16,610	PL	$20,343	$ 878
Cheney Selection, GP	western dogwood	1998	3,050	PL	$ 5,279	$8
Total					$42,842,572	$255,276,278
Production and Ecological Benefits from Releases:						$298,118,849
Gross PMC operating budget; 1935 - 2005						$22,258,626
Net Production and Ecological Benefits from Releases:						$275,861,103

Pullman leads all other PMCs relative to total Net Production and Ecological Benefits from Releases. They do so as a result of the nursery effort. Nine of their releases were made before the nursery closed in 1953, and 'Greenar' intermediate wheatgrass, 'Latar' orchardgrass and 'Newport' Kentucky bluegrass, released in 1956, 1957 and 1958 respectively, were children of the nursery effort. The net benefit of these cultivars represents seventy-nine percent of the total benefit from all their releases. On the other hand, there have been no releases since 1998 that were included in the 2005 economic study. The team that assembled at Pullman between 1935 and 1940 saw an opportunity and took advantage of it. Their cost benefit ratio is 13.4.

Table 8-Pullman.2 Other releases

Release Name & Type	Common Name	Release Year	Explanation
P-4874, CV	bulbous bluegrass	1956	Production data lacking
Cougar, CV	Kentucky bluegrass	1965	Production data lacking
Pomar, CV	orchardgrass	1966	Production data lacking
Trailar, CV	western clematis	1992	Production data lacking
Okanogan, GP	common snowberry	1997	Production data lacking

Release Name & Type	Common Name	Release Year	Explanation
Wallowa, GP	red osier dogwood	1998	Production data lacking
Harrington Origin, GP	red osier dogwood	1999	Production data lacking
Kendrick, GP	Saskatoon serviceberry	2000	Production data lacking
Newport, GP	Saskatoon serviceberry	2000	Production data lacking
Okanogan, GP	Saskatoon serviceberry	2000	Production data lacking
Colfax, GP	Lewis' mock orange	2002	Production data lacking
St. Maries, GP	Lewis' mock orange	2002	Production data lacking
Union Flat, GP	blue wildrye	2008	Post 2005, production unknown
White Pass, GP	blue wildrye	2010	Post 2005, production unknown

Developed and Delivered Technology - Listed Publications

Table 8-Pullman.3 Number of PMC web site publications by category

Type of Publication	No.	Type of Publication	No.
Information Brochures and Flyers	20	Plant Materials Annual Report of Activities	1
Major Publications	3	PMC Annual Technical Report	2
Miscellaneous Popular Articles	3	Published Abstracts	1
Miscellaneous Technical Article	29	Refereed Journal Articles	1
Newsletters	9	Release Brochure	7
Other Publication Types	5	Release Notices	8
Plant Fact Sheets	19	Technical Notes	38
Plant Guides	29	Technical Poster	6

Their total number of web site publications is 181.

Developed and Delivered Technology - Featured Vegetative Accomplishments

Two Featured Vegetative Accomplishments are discussed for Pullman. The first is as follows:

1   The Concept of Outlying Nurseries

The following summary is from the 1990 book, History of the Pullman PMC - Its First 50 Years by John L. Schwendiman.[546]

The first Featured Vegetative Accomplishment started even before SCS became an agency. In 1934 Virgil B. Hawk became a graduate student at Washington State University in Pullman, and was employed there by the Bureau of Plant Industry. He had two acres of wheat plowed out and in the spring of 1935 planted some native collections, foreign plant introductions and a block of slender and crested wheatgrass. In December 1935 Virgil became an employee of the new SCS Pullman Nursery and Dr. A. L. Hafenrichter became regional nurseryman. By 1936 a full nursery staff was assembled and Virgil was put in charge of Outlying Nurseries.

Outlying Nurseries consisted of a standard list of commercial grasses and legumes along with limited native and introduced grasses at various locations. They were conceived as a "means of measuring the adaptation of various grasses and legumes for soil conservation use in the widely different ecological areas of the Northwest" by the Pullman Nursery staff. They soon became an official part of nursery observational work and later PMP policy. Over the years they have been called several things but their objective has not changed.

Off Center Evaluations - Off-center evaluations are plantings and evaluations used by the PMC or sometimes PM Specialist as part of a study to evaluate plant releases or technology away from the center. Typically they consist of cultural or management studies established at locations that represent a land resource area or a site having soil, climate, and other conditions not represented at the PMC. Although initial testing is sometimes conducted off the PMC, these sites generally are used for advanced testing.[547]

Initially, at Pullman, the Outlying Nurseries were used more for initial screening. In later years when Dr. Hawk was Manager of the Cape May PMC, he graciously shared some of his early experiences in Pullman.[548] It sounded like a wonderful life for a young man, employed in a brand new program with a dynamic leader like Hafenrichter. His reminiscence included how the concept of Outlying Nurseries was hatched. It evolved out of an unscheduled team meeting, including him, Schwendiman, Dr. Paul Lemmon, and of course Hafenrichter, making a long car trip in the heat of the summer. Not to waste time, the day-long conversation dwelt on how to round out the evaluation process. Dr. Hawk recalled that just a few years later the concept of Field Plantings, which become a final step in the evaluation process of cultivars, took life in a similar way, although the team had lost Lemmon but gained Donald Douglass.

2.   Development of Alternate Row Seedings

Alternate row seedings seem so commonplace today one might ask why discuss something that has been a standard practice for decades. The reason is simply; the concept was not common before it was first used in 1937 in conservation plantings, and by none other than Virgil Hawk. He made the first plantings on the Pullman nursery in 1935. In 1936 he made grass and legumes plantings at Lind, Goldendale and Dayton, WA, and at Moro, Pendleton, Conoon and Union, OR. In 1937 he established more plantings at Pullman and at outlying locations, using alternate row grass-legume seedings for the first time as an evaluation tool. On page 103 of John Schwendiman's <u>History of the Pullman PMC - Its First 50 Years</u> is a March 21, 1983 letter written to John by Dr. Hawk. It contained the following, "Part of the drill tubes plugged up at Dayton and the alternate row method of seeding alfalfa-grass mixtures was born."[549] Figure 8.Pullman.1 is an excellent example of an alternate row grass-legume seeding.

Regular annual technical reports were begun in 1938 and were required of each project, including RN-l; <u>Observational Testing of Native and Introduced Grasses, Legumes and Forbs - Uniform Rod Row Strain Trials</u>. This was the first report on the evaluations from Outlying Nurseries. From then on the use of alternate row plantings as an evaluation tool became a common practice for outlying nurseries.

Some examples:

A.   A study of 136 grasses planted alone and in alternate rows with sweet clover, was established in 1942. Root samples were taken from the sweet clover rows. Sweet clover alone produced 2400 pounds of dry matter per acre in the surface six inches of soil and sweet clover-grass alternate row produced 3200 pounds.

B.   The first recorded field-sized test using alternate row seedings involving alfalfa-perennial grass mixtures, and was made in 1945 (During that year John L. Schwendiman became nursery manager when Virgil B. Hawk left for advanced study at Iowa State University). This was done by plugging alternate seed outlets in the grass part of the drill and in the legume seeder, alternating In such a way so that alternating rows of grass and legume were seeded. The seeding rate was reduced so close so that in-row competition between grass and legume seedlings could be avoided.

C.   Also in 1945, new outlying nursery plantings were established, including twenty-seven grasses seeded in alternate rows with 'Ladak' alfalfa at four locations: Pullman, Pendleton,

Union and Sandpoint, WA. New mixtures were included in the 1948 outlying nurseries. Fifteen grasses each in alternate rows with 'Ladak' alfalfa replicated and randomized in plots eight feet wide. Seedings were made both on a gentle south slope and a steep north slope. After hay harvest a sled-type sod cutter six inches wide by eight inches deep was used at right angles to the alfalfa grass mixture plots. Three samples per plot were washed and dried. Intermediate and crested wheatgrass with the alfalfa were best with six tons of air dry roots per acre; about sixty percent of the roots from these mixtures were from grass.

D. By 1949 nearly 10,000 plant accessions had been tested in outlying observational nurseries, include those planted in 1941, 43, 45 and 1949. In dry years, the twelve-inch spaced alternate grass-legume row plantings produced more than closer row spacing. Alternate row spacing allowed a greater contribution from the grass fraction of a mixture than conventional seedings. The orchardgrass - sweet clover mixtures, which contained the earliest maturing grass, were most satisfactory for use in green manure mixtures.

E. In 1951 sweet clover grass mixture studies were continued using fifteen different grasses. Drilling five pounds per acre of sweet clover in alternate, six-inch rows with five to eight pounds of grass was proven to be the best method of establishment. This allowed grass to make its greatest contribution to the mixture, approximately a thousand pounds per acre of additional dry matter, over conventional seeding methods. As a result of these studies, farmers of the northwest started planting annually acreages of sweet clover grass mixtures for green manure, an excellent method of returning organic matter to the soil.

Figure 8-Pullman.1 Alternate row grass and sweet clover

F. At Pendleton, OR sweet clover-grass mixture studies patterned after those at Pullman confirmed that Spanish sweet clover and 'Bromar' mountain brome in alternate rows was the best green manure combination for use in the local winter wheat green pea crop rotation. These plantings were utilized by plowing and sweep tillage, followed by cropping to wheat.

G. In 1957 the first harvest was made on twenty-six different grasses planted in alternate rows with alfalfa. Mixtures averaged two and one-half tons per acre. 'Greenar' and 'Amur', wheatgrass and 'Bromar' were the most dominant grasses. Alternate rows seedings allow grass to make its greatest contribution to a mixture. Best production was achieved when sweet clover - grass was planted without a companion crop.

H. MacLauchlan and Hafenrichter reported in 1961 that the alternate row seeding technique was widely used in the Pacific Northwest in the 1940s and 1950s for establishing mixed stands of grasses and legumes for hay, forage, and green manure.[550] It resulted in better stands of both species by reducing inter specific competition compared to plantings where both species were sown in the same drill row.

I.   In 1962, grass legume mixtures for use as hay, pasture and longtime conservation rotations under irrigation were established for the second time at Pullman and Rockford, WA. Included were twelve legumes seeded in alternate rows with 'S-143' orchardgrass. Hairy vetch at 5.29 tons/acre, followed by sweet clover, alfalfa and red clover were most productive.

J.   A five year summary was made in 1971 of ten orchardgrass varieties, four meadow foxtail and four creeping foxtail varieties, planted alone and in alternate rows with birdsfoot trefoil and 'Vernal' alfalfa. Irrigation was adequate. The orchardgrass/legume averaged from 3.93 to 5.11 tons per acre, and the foxtails from 4.23 to 4.99 tons per acre.

Appalachian Plant Materials Center, Alderson, WV

HISTORY AND BACKGROUND

Year and process leading to its establishment: The PMC was established by congressional action in 1967, based on the recognized need for new conservation plants to stabilize Southern Appalachian surface coal mining spoil and increase production from Appalachian forage land. The authorization received a push from building pressure to pass the Federal Surface Mining Act.

History: The southern Appalachian region had been underserved for years by the existing plant materials center network. The increasing dependence on coal from Appalachian sources and low production from forage land highlighted the need for new plant materials.

The thrust for the establishment of a new center came from Wilmer W. Steiner, the regional plant materials specialist in the Northeast. Steiner had searched the problem area for a suitable site and, in his judgment had identified one. However, a member of the U.S. House of Representatives on the Appropriations Committee wanted it in his congressional district which included Breathitt County, KY. A site was selected in the community of Quicksand on property owned by the University of Kentucky. Tillable land was limited to less than twenty acres, which was subjected to annual flooding.

The limitations of the initial site in Quicksand were soon recognized. In 1980 the USDA, Agricultural Research Service established a laboratory in Beckley, WV, and in the early 1990s extended an invitation to co-locate the PMC at Beckley. At the same time Curtis Sharp, National PM Specialist, was lobbying SCS to relocate the PMC to Beckley. Fortunately it was relocated but it did not co-locate with the ARS Lab. This appears regrettable because of the loss of facilities that would have been available to the PMC as well as access to staff specialists in many disciplines otherwise not available. Instead the PMC is located on property formally owned by U.S. Department of Labor, Federal Women's Prison in Alderson, WV. Ironically, this was the original site identified by Steiner, years before the ARS Lab opened in Beckley. The agreement to move from Quicksand was made in 1993 but not completed until 1998.

Land Tenure: NRCS owns 185 acres. The valley setting is similar to Quicksand but much larger.

Service Area: The Center serves parts of eleven states in the southern Appalachian region. The topography of the region is rugged, with steep slopes terminating in narrow, flat valley bottoms along perennial streams.

Elevations range from 400 feet to 6,500 feet. Average annual rainfall ranges from thirty-two inches to fifty-five inches. The minimum temperature reaches -24 degrees Fahrenheit. The growing season is from 130 days to 203 days, increasing in the southern states.

The area is humid and mostly forested, with soils derived from sandstone, limestone, or shale. Urban development and agriculture tends to be concentrated in or along the floodplains and valley bottoms.

OUTPUT
Conservation Plant Development

Table 8-Alderson.1 Net production and ecological benefits of releases

Release & Type	Common Name	Release Year	Total Production	Unit	Net Value to Producer	Net Ecological Value
Appalow, CV	sericea lespedeza	1978	1,184,350	LB	-$377,713	$953,402
Bankers, CV	dwarf willow	1983	2,382,528	PL	$672,772	$1,127,353
Gobbler, CV	sawtooth oak	1986	1,499,704	PL	$674,701	$1,030,745
Golden, CV	chinquapin	1987	1,500	LB	$4,319	$2,163
Golden, CV	golden chinquapin	1989	135,500	PL	$250,856	$6,918
Rhizo, CV	Kura clover	1989	1,500	LB	$4,319	$2,163
Quickstand, CV	bermudagrass	1992	137,000	PL	$255,175	$9,081
Total					$1,484,429	$3,131,825
Production and Ecological Benefits from Releases:						$4,616,254
Gross PMC operating budget; 1966 – 2005						$17,479,745
Net Production and Ecological Benefits from Releases:						**($12,863,491)**

A host of reasons help explain the negative net production and ecological benefits. They include the short life of the PMC, frequent turn over in PMC managers, its undesirable initial location, limited acreage of conservation problems and the productive time lost in moving from one location to another.

Table 8-Alderson2 Other releases

Release & Type	Common Name	Release Year	Explanation
Panbowl, CV	hazel alder	2007	Post 2005, production unknown
Augusta, CV	orchardgrass	2008	Post 2005, production unknown
Ruffner, CV	tall oatgrass	2009	Post 2005, production unknown

Considering the nature of these three releases, and their intended use, they have great potential for outstanding results if adequate promotion can be obtained. The authors of the Vermont Winooski River project report, discussed in Chapter 10, felt speckled or hazel alder should be evaluated further for streambank stabilization purposes.[551] Recognizing this was a long time in coming, but 'Panbowl' has unlimited use potential throughout the PMC service area and beyond.

Developed and Delivered Technology - Listed Publications

Table 8-Alderson.3 Number of PMC web site publications by category

Type of Publication	No.	Type of Publication	No.
Information Brochures and Flyers	1	PMC Annual Technical Report	2
Miscellaneous Popular Articles	7	Popular Journal or Magazine Articles	1
Miscellaneous Technical Article	16	Propagation Protocols	7

Type of Publication	No.	Type of Publication	No.
Other Publication Types	3	Release Brochure	2
Plant Guides	11	Release Notices	1
Plant Materials Annual Report of Activities	2	Technical Poster	3

The total number of web site publications is fifty-six.

Developed and Delivered Technology - Featured Vegetative Accomplishments

The following is a summary of three PMC outreach activities that promote good conservation through the use of native plants.[552]

1   Native Plants for Kentucky Food Security Act Programs: The Kentucky Food Security Act contracts are placing emphasis on wildlife benefits, obtained through the use of native plants. Unfortunately, the commercial availability of locally adapted native plants is poor. The Kentucky Plant Materials Committee approached the PMC for assistance with this dilemma in 2004. As a result, the PMC increased five native species. They are: *Liatris spicata*, spiked blazing star, *Rudbeckia hirta*, black-eyed Susan; *Desmanthus illinoensis*; Illinois bundleflower; *Lespedeza capitata*, roundhead lespedeza; and *Lespedeza virginicus*, Virginia lespedeza. Seed produced by the PMC was provided to Kentucky seed producers who will establish production fields and market seed of these species in Kentucky. The first commercial fields were established in 2010. All of these species are potential Kentucky ecotype releases.

2   U.S. Army Corps of Engineers – Marmet Native Plant Mitigation: The Appalachian PMC has assisted the U.S. Army Corps of Engineers - Huntington District with restoring a native plant community at the Marmet Locks and Dam Project, located on the Kanawha River in West Virginia upstream of Charleston. All vegetation within the approximately 150 acre site was destroyed during the course of construction.

Six native woody species were harvested from the site prior to the start of construction. Those species are: *Acer saccharinum,* silver maple; *Lindera benzoin,* spicebush: *Sambucus canadensis,* elderberry; *Asimina triloba,* pawpaw; *Sassafras albidum,* sassafras; and *Aesculus octandra,* yellow buckeye. Plants of each species were grown and maintained as containers at the PMC until completion of construction. In the autumn of 2005, 128 pawpaws, 104 elderberries, ten sassafras, 100 spice bushes and thirty-eight silver maples were returned and reintroduced to the Marmet site. Additional plants grown at the PMC were reintroduced to the site upon completion of all construction in 2009.

3   Camp Dawson Native Grasses Project: In 2004, the PMC agreed to produce local ecotypes of warm season grasses for the Natural Resources Staff at Camp Dawson, the Army National Guard Training Camp near Kingwood, WV for re-vegetating areas disturbed by annual training activities. Much of the training conducted at the camp involves earthmoving equipment, which inevitably leaves a lot of bare ground to be re-vegetated. Previous revegetation efforts have focused almost exclusively on use of introduced grasses and/or legumes which have often proven to be less than satisfactory aesthetically or have wildlife value and adequate erosion control. This has accelerates the Camp's Natural Resource Staff to created to increase use of locally adapted warm season grasses.

Several warm season grasses are indigenous to the Camp. Four are *Sorghastrum nutans,* Indiangrass; *Andropogon gerardii,* big bluestem; *Schizachyrium scoparium,* little bluestem; and *Panicum virgatum,* switchgrass. Seed from each of these was collected at Camp Dawson in 2004 and 2005 and planted to establish seed production blocks at the PMC in 2006. Seed harvested from the PMC production fields will be returned to Camp Dawson to be used in re-vegetating areas disturbed by troop training exercises. All four species will also be evaluated at the PMC as potential Central Appalachian ecotype releases for use as forage and wildlife values. Seed increase activities continued in 2009, and limited amounts of switchgrass and little bluestem were available to the Army National Guard in 2010.

Chapter 9: KEY LEADERS, PRODUCTIVE SCIENTISTS, PRODUCTIVE TEAMS, OTHER MAJOR CONTRIBUTORS AND AWARDS

The history of any associated group of people, regardless of the cause, must take note of key individuals who have contributed in ways that significantly exceed the norm. The seventy-five year history of the National Plant Materials Program is no different. Identifying these individuals is difficult, not because their numbers were few, but for the exact opposite – there are so many, and the number will continue to grow as the history of the Program lengthens. With those points in mind this chapter discusses those persons who warrant special recognition. Their contribution to the formation, evolution and productivity of the National Plant Materials Program stand apart. Needless to say, the lion share come from the earlier years of the program. To be sure, there are many employed today that over time will stand apart along with those discussed on the following pages.

Key individuals impacting the Plant Materials Program cannot be complete without mentioning the contributions of three early SCS Administrators.

- It goes without saying that the contributions made by Dr. Hugh Hammond Bennett to the Plant Materials Program exceed all others; without his there would have been no such program. Near his retirement he continued to see the main work of SCS nurseries as the products from the observational studies.

- The "May I discuss one other aspect of this thing" statement by Administrator Dr. Robert M. Salter must be highlighted as a singular event that salvaged the observational nurseries. It seemed to have been an afterthought in his testimony to the House of Representatives Agricultural Sub Committee for the fiscal year 1954 budget, but it obviously was not. See the section titled 'THE DEBATE' in Chapter 5 for his statement.

- Of parallel importance to the Salter testimony was the July 16, 1956 memorandum from SCS Administrator Donald Williams to the Assistant Secretary of Agriculture E. L. Peterson advising him of intended SCS policy regarding the new Plant Materials Program, and the number and recommended location for new plant materials centers. Administrator Williams was supportive of the Program until his retirement in 1969.

One characteristic of many productive Plant Materials Program workers was the publication of their work, which are generally omitted from Chapter 9, but are included in Appendix 2, Partial List of Publication by Soil Conservation Service Nursery Division and Plant Materials Program Employees. Exceptions are primarily where the author published before or after their employment in the Program, or a publication of exceptional importance.

This chapter is organized into the following categories:

Key Leaders: Persons whose leadership was crucial to developing and maintaining the National Plant Materials Program

Productive Scientists: Exceptionally productive individuals.

Productive Teams: Exceptionally productive teams of individuals.

Major Contributor: The combination of scientific accomplishment and leadership.

Other Noteworthy Contributors: Those persons whose contributions may be singular or seemingly small but over time highly beneficial. They are discussed in the order of their chronological occurrence in the agency.

Awards: Many of the persons recognized in this chapter and many others have been the recipient of awards from USDA and from within the Plant Materials Program.

These persons and units are recognized in Tables 9.11 and 9.12 at the end of this chapter.

Key Leaders: Persons whose leadership was crucial to developing and maintaining the National Plant Materials Program

Dr. Franklin J. Crider- Key Leader

William Boyce Thompson Arboretum Director,
Director of Erosion Plant Studies, University of AZ,
Regional Director Soil Erosion Service,
In-Charge SCS Nursery Division,
Manager National Observational Project

<u>Introduction</u>

Where does history start? There are endless extenuating circumstances that mark a beginning. For example, what is the starting point of the Plant Materials Program in the Soil Conservation Service? Many scenarios can be offered, like the birth of SCS, or the election of the New Deal, or even the creation of USDA. Any of these beginnings could be used, but the history of the SCS Plant Materials Program would eventually lead to one name, Franklin J. Crider.

Figure 9.1 Dr. Franklin Crider

Dr. Crider was born December 1, 1883 in St. Matthews, South Carolina.[553] He graduated with a Bachelor of Science degree from Clemson University, and taught horticulture at Clemson and North Carolina State University for a few years. Later, he received a Master's degree from the University Minnesota, and in 1936 he was awarded an honorary Doctor of Science degree from his former employer, the University of Arizona for his outstanding work at that institution.[554]

His interest in the practical use of plant materials started early, when in 1915 he published his first paper:

Crider, Franklin J. 1915. Home canning of fruits and vegetables. Circular / South Carolina Agricultural Experiment Station of Clemson Agricultural College.

<u>Early Contributions in Arizona</u>

Dr. Crider moved west in 1918 and became a member of the University of Arizona Horticulture Department, of which he later became Department Head. His contributions during this period can be partially measured by the following:

Crider, Franklin J. 1922. The olive in Arizona. AZ Agric. Exp. Stn. Bul. No. 94

Crider, Franklin J. 1924. Planting a citrus grove in Arizona: Timely hints for farmers. AZ Agric. Exp. Stn.

Crider, Franklin J. 1925. The adobe sweet potato storage house in Arizona. AZ Agric. Exp. Stn.

Crider, Franklin J. 1926. Essentials to successful fruit culture in AZ Agric. Exp. Stn.

Crider, Franklin J. 1926. Propagation of the date palm: With particular reference to the rooting of high offshoots. AZ Agric. Exp. Stn. Bull No. 95.

Crider, Franklin J. 1926. Pruning deciduous fruit trees in the Southwest. AZ Agric. Exp. Stn.

Crider, Franklin J. 1927. Effect of phosphorus in the form of acid phosphate upon maturity and yield of lettuce. AZ Agric. Exp. Stn. Bul. No. 121.

In the early 1920s, William Boyce Thompson, after years of mining in Montana and making his fortune on Wall Street, found his greatest interest in a new home he was building in the Arizona hills, near the town of Superior in what came to be known as his Picket Post house. His desire to plant a few trees in this new climate led him to contact the University of Arizona. Dr. Crider was the head of the Horticultural Department at that time. He came up to assist Colonel Thompson and what started as an idea for a few trees became an idea for an arboretum of all the plants and trees of the Southwest.[555]

Colonel Thompson established the Boyce Thompson Southwest Arboretum in 1924 and picked Dr. Crider as its director, who started his employment there on September, 1, 1924. The initial mission of the Arboretum was to study the plants of desert countries and to make the results available to the public. The articles of incorporation of the Arboretum allowed for all forms of "experiment, research, study and investigation of plant and animal life" and called for "broadening the public interest therein and knowledge thereof." Management now is through a cooperative effort by Arizona State Parks, the University of Arizona, and the Arboretum's private nonprofit corporation, which owns the physical facility.[556] These three managing partners maintain a balance between public events, academic endeavors and conservation. The arboretum gardens represent the living museum of plants capable of living in the Sonoran Desert of southern Arizona. Many were native species; others were introduced. The arboretum now contends it is "the oldest and most spectacularly situated arboretum and botanical garden in the American Southwest."

Jojoba Interest

Frank S. Crosswhite, who had a long association with the Arboretum, provides a review of Crider's work on Jojoba while there.[557] "On April 5, 1925, the first jojoba seedlings came up in the Arboretum nursery. The next day Colonel Thompson and Crider personally staked out an experimental jojoba planting east of Picket Post House, along the road near the Indian Village." This area was seeded on April 16 followed by a slow soaking rain on April 22 that measured 1.6 inches. Emergence of the seedlings started May 12. Although jojoba started germinating in ten days, stragglers continued to come up until the end of a month. It was later found that seed held at low temperatures before planting germinates more regularly. The plants on the dry lands were watched and compared with those started under cultivation and irrigation. By September 30, the cultivated plants had tripled their size over those in the wild and by 1931, F. J. Crider wrote that he had gotten jojoba to come into bearing in five years from seed, and that they produced satisfactory oil-bearing nuts. These Arboretum plants produced about a half pound of seed the first year after coming into bearing. These had been grown following Crider's opinion that for the plants to do best under irrigation, they should be given water comparable to about thirty inches of rainfall. Crosswhite continued:

> At an early date it was discovered that jojoba plants will not live if dug up and transplanted, regardless of how small the plants might be. This is because the taproot grows rapidly and important feeder roots may be eighteen inches deep before significant shoot development occurs. These feeder roots are invariably lost in digging out the plant. It was found that if rains are likely or irrigation possible, the plant should be directly seeded in the field. When planting arid hillsides, where irrigation might be difficult, plants started in gallon cans may be set out as year old transplants. Director Crider found that very tall pot substitutes allowed best growth of the long taproot. Roots of jojoba were studied by Crider in specially-designed concrete lysimeters, having glass windows for observation. Significant winter growth of roots was observed. Crider developed a theory that growth of the root alternated with growth of the shoot.

On January 21, 1927 Dr. Crider was appointed to the board of regents of the University of Arizona.[558] The Casa Grande Valley Dispatch offers the following endorsement to that appointment:

> Upon his appointment as director of the Boyce Thompson Institute, Director Crider began new lines of investigation work and also continued some of those that he had already started at the university. His work at the Boyce Thompson Institute is a credit both to himself and to the State of Arizona and his appointment to the board of regents of the university will greatly strengthen the agricultural and horticultural work there and in the state. The university and State of Arizona are to be congratulated upon having so strong a man in agriculture as a member of the board of regents.

Aldo Leopold spent time in the Arizona Territory working for the U.S. Forest Service in the Apache National Forest beginning in 1909 before going to New Mexico in 1911.[559] It is reported, but unconfirmed, that he met Franklin Crider years later and helped create the plant nursery at the Arboretum to grow native plants in the Southwest for conservation purposes, and for growing arid-adapted, non-native introductions for landscaping.

Frank Crosswhite wrote

> Boyce Thompson wanted to experiment with re-vegetating the north slope of the mountain, which had been overgrazed by cattle. Assisting Thompson in this effort was Arboretum Director Franklin J. Crider. Together they believed that they might reverse the vicious cycle of de-vegetation on Picket Post. They reasoned that they should locate species of groundcovers which could live long enough on the damaged hillsides to hold back enough soil to allow other species to become established. At the Arboretum, Crider masterminded a conservation project of enormous proportions. He developed a cooperative program at the Arboretum whereby a large nursery of erosion control plants was established for planting on government land where erosion had become a problem. This soil conservation nursery became so successful at the Arboretum that the federal government saw need of replicating it many times over the United States. Success for Crider meant consolidation of the program under a new agency, which became the U.S. Soil Conservation Service. In 1934 Crider left the Arboretum to become one of the founding fathers of this new government agency. He worked for many years at SCS in charge of the Plant Materials section headquartered at Beltsville, Maryland. When the achievements of Thompson, Crider, and the Arboretum are added up, it must be reckoned that they contributed a major impetus to formation and success of the U.S. Soil Conservation Service.[560]

The Arboretum web site explains, "The original Arboretum Director, Franklin J. Crider, left to become the first head of the Plant Materials Section of the SCS. As such, he was one of the important founding fathers (of the Soil Conservation Service)."[561] It was at the Arboretum that Dr. Crider formulated that, "Nature has evolved a plant for every purpose." Whether he articulated it at that time is not known.

Crider Joins the Soil Conservation Service

Franklin J. Crider became a Bureau of Plant Industry employee in 1934 at the erosion experiment station in Tucson.[562] Crosswhite writes, "In 1934 Crider organized a series of screening tests at the Plant Materials Nursery."[563] Some results were found in the Annual Report of Southwestern Nurseries for FY 1934-1935. The screening test was with Lehmann lovegrass accessions. Following the creation of the SCS on April 1, 1935, Crider became an SCS employee in Tucson as a regional director of nursery work. Being the responsible scientist that he was, his short Bureau of Plant Industry and SCS work at Tucson was well summarized before he departed.

Crider's arrival date in Washington appears to be after late December, 1935. The basis for this is that memoranda were circulating within the Nursery Section in headquarters that he should have been sending or receiving, but Dr. Charles Enlow's name was appearing on them. Dr. Enlow was Dr. Crider's predecessor as 'In Charge', Nursery Section Leader, serving in that capacity only a few months. The latest such memorandum was dated December 18, 1935. Crider was in Washington on March 25, 1936 when Field Memorandum #SCN-4 was distributed by him. The magnitude of this document would certainly have required considerable time to prepare. So the best estimate of his arrival time is early January, 1936.

Incorporating the Idea of 'Nature has evolved a plant for every purpose'

It is apparent from dates on memos that C. R. Enlow, Acting In Charge of Nurseries in 1935, was passing Crider's concepts, or his own, to Chief Bennett before Crider's arrival in Washington.[564] On November 25, 1935 Enlow wrote Chief Bennett outlining sixteen "types of work" that should be included in the operations of the Nursery Section. He stated:

> I am particularly anxious that the Nursery Section be allowed to continue the collection of many hundreds of species of plants through our country as it has been done for the past two years, (inherited from the Bureau of Plant Industries) bringing the material into the nurseries in order to study methods of propagation and the possibilities of using these plants in an erosion control program. This, in my estimation, is the real work of the Nursery Section. It is very possible that the day might arrive that we would be obligated to suddenly discontinue the production of millions of trees and bulk collection of seed of grasses from the ranges. The developing work of promising species should be confirmed and I urge you give your approval to a continuation of the program.

Many of the individual items of work related directly to what became the observational studies at production nurseries. For example the first item reads "Securing, by systematic search, propagating and growing variations which are an improvement in erosion control value of materials now in use."

Dr. Crider's concept undoubtedly encountered resistance from NHQ leaders. For example F. J. Hopkins, Assistant Chief for Administration in 1935 when reviewing the sixteen "types of work" that Enlow had sent Chief Bennett, objected to the first one, "Securing, by systemic search, etc." Hopkins argued "It hardly seems the responsibility of the Soil Conservation Service to conduct any systematic search for plants."[565] Of course, this 'Type of Work' was the bedrock of the observational phase of the Nursery Program and Bennett was not persuaded to stop or slow it down.

Although there were objections, on March 25, 1936 FIELD MEMORANDUM #SCN-4 was released regarding "Functions and activities of Nurseries" containing, in one manner or other, all sixteen types-of-work Enlow had outlined. Six related specifically to observational studies. The Memorandum was signed by F. J. Crider, In Charge, Soil Conservation Nurseries, and approved by C. B. Manifold, Chief, Division of Conservation Operations.[566]

On July 27, 1937 Crider sent a Memorandum to Regional Conservators, to the attention of Regional Nurserymen, over the approval of Manifold, containing the details on how to conduct the "Observational Phase of the Nursery Program." The concept had been sold and was from that point forward enshrined in policy.

Implementing the Process

Having permanently installed his concept into the policy of the SCS, Dr. Crider transferred to Beltsville in late 1939 or early 1940 and headed up the National Observational Nursery Project. It is unclear exactly what motivated this move from his NHQ position of "In Charge, Soil Conservation Nurseries." It was about at this time that the Section of Nurseries became the Division of Nurseries.

As we will see, Dr. Crider was a quiet, retiring person, a scientist, not well suited for a large bureaucracy. His earlier transfer from a department head at Arizona State University to the Boyce Thompson Arboretum out in the desert suggests a personality that wanted to be alone, to do things with his own hands. Another clue to this personality may be that he never had a co-author on any of his publications. Additionally, getting flack or disagreement from an administrative person, such as Hopkins, most likely was not his cup of tea.

His move to Beltsville allowed him to concentrate on putting his concept into practice, instilling the methodology throughout the SCS nursery system, and returning to his true love of hands-on plant research including his root – top defoliation study, published long after his retirement.

In December 1947, Harry A. Gunning, Chief, Nursery Division, Washington D.C. wrote Chief of Operations A. E. Jones recommending a promotion for Dr. Crider. Gunning pointed out that Crider had not had a promotion since he was appointed to BPI in 1934. He goes on to say "If there is any value or worthwhile accomplishments received from our Observational Program, the credit is due Dr. Crider."

In a 1967 Soil Conservation Magazine, a prefatory note by Dr. H. H. Bennett, Chief of SCS reads:

> Prefatory Note.-The observational method of plant study as applied to the development of soil conserving plants and techniques represent the first organized, systematic effort in this country to bring together, to study, and to evaluate plants for the specific purpose of soil and water conservation. The method was born of necessity. Dr. Franklin J. Crider took the lead in its formation.

> During this early period, Dr. Crider, as regional leader of nursery activities had the important task of providing suitable planting materials for conservation use in the Southwest. Undoubtedly, the adverse environmental conditions of this section as affecting plant adaptation, and ease of establishment, stimulated his efforts in the direction of the nursery observation method evaluation. On being transferred to the Washington office in 1936 as head of the nursery section, Dr. Crider was ready with a plan which won instant approval and enthusiastic support as an integral part of Service activities.

The Later Years

In 1951, shortly before his retirement, Dr. Crider received the USDA Superior Service Award.[567] In part the citation read:

> Dr. Crider is regarded by Service personnel and others as the father of the observational nursery studies as carried on through the SCS. Since the inception of the studies, he has provided outstanding leadership and inspiration to the nursery personnel throughout the Service.

It is apparent from the following letter how Dr. Crider was viewed at the highest levels of SCS, and how well the observational studies were viewed. Somewhat condensed, this letter was written April 15, 1949 by the SCS Chief, H. H. Bennett. Dr. Crider had asked the Chief how he felt about the advice Crider had given a colleague.[568]

> I have just read your memorandum of April 13 to Maurice E. Heath, offering suggestions in connection with his perspective paper on "Just How Do the SCS Nurseries Contribute to the Soil and Moisture Conservation Program?" It is a good statement and should help Mr. Heath in preparing his article, but I am inclined to feel that Heath would need something specific with respect to how the nurseries have gone out and picked up thousands of varieties, strains, and species of grasses and other plants for use in some part of the country in connection with our national soil and water conservation and good land use program. I think in such a paper as Heath

has in mind it would be too bad not to bring out that the observational work of this kind has undoubtedly advanced our range and pasture work in the United States more than anything that has ever been done in this direction. For example, I have just returned from a trip mostly through the Flatwoods section of the South Atlantic and SE Gulf Coast area. Throughout this region, there are great areas of land of variable soil and drainage conditions which are beginning to be brought into productive use by pasture men and ranchers on both small and large scale. The SCS has brought about this development which, I am sure, is going to put this part of the country, all the way from Fort Myers FL to VA, into the livestock business. This Flatwoods region has long been considered more or less unfit for agriculture and livestock because of poor soil and poor drainage.

Well, I think the SCS is rapidly solving the problem – or has already solved it on thousands of acres in the Carolinas, Georgia and Florida. This has been done by fitting the various grasses which have proven to be good pasture grasses into the right places. Suiter's (tall fescue) grass is one of the principal winter grazing on good, well-drained soils; 'Pensacola' Bahiagrass on well-drained soils well down into Florida.

I think the article might very well point out that some 19 or 20 grasses which the SCS has brought from the wild into domestication are quoted in this year's catalogues. You can get from my 1948 annual report some further discussion on what has been done with respect to some of the other grasses that have been brought to the U.S. by various agencies from other countries. The SCS has taken the better of these grasses by the nap of the neck and scattered them far and wide over the nation to the great advantage of our American grass industry.

H. H Bennett

PS.

This is my birthday and I can tell you I'm feeling pretty good because of what I have just seen in the Flatwoods country to the south of Washington. Pretty good birthday gift, no?

Dr. Crider retired from the Soil Conservation Service in January 1952 shortly after his sixty-seventh birthday.[569] The final years of his life are related in the following letter. It was written by Wilmer W. Steiner, who worked with Dr. Crider for years at Beltsville, and succeeded him as manager of the Beltsville National Observational Project. The letter was written in a response to a request for information that became a part of the Franklin J. Crider Memorial Garden dedication on July 7, 1967.[570] It too has been condensed.

As you know, Dr. Crider was a quiet, modest, retiring individual who was completely absorbed in his work with plants. He was basically a researcher and disliked being bothered with administrative details or responsibilities. I can still see him spending endless hours (usually his own) walking about the observational rows of grasses and legumes, poking at various plants with his old stick he almost always carried. He had a constant habit of chewing on leaves or stems or fruits of all the various plants in the nursery. He was a keen observer of plant performance and characteristics and was quick to sense where various species and strains fit in the conservation program.

Over the years, Dr. Crider had built up an unbelievably large group of foreign and domestic contacts and correspondence with whom he exchanged plant materials and information. Through the 1940s 'Doc' was a one-man plant introduction division which appeared to rival the Bureau of Plant Industry in the manner and importance of new accessions brought in.

In addition to his plant exchange and evaluation activities at Beltsville, 'Doc' managed to squeeze in some of the real research which so obviously intrigued him. A result of this was his publication "Root-Growth Stoppage Resulting from Defoliation of Grass": USDA Technical Bulletin No. 1102, published in 1955. This was at least partially written after his retirement.

In 1950, 'Doc' fell victim to a particularly virulent form of viral pneumonia. He was very sick for a long period. The disease seemed to affect his nervous system to such a degree he could not settle down to work again. He tried working part time, then gave up and retired from the Service. Typical of his quiet ways, he just walked off one day and didn't show up again. I found out he had retired several days later when I called his home to see how he was.

After retirement, Dr. and Mrs. Crider moved from Silver Spring, Maryland, to Daytona Beach, FL. They bought a small home and 'Doc' gardened and worked with papaya in an effort to improve the fruit through breeding and selection. I was told his health improved considerably under the Florida sun and that he actually took time out from plant work to do a little fishing.

Mrs. Crider had suffered from a heart ailment and passed away at Daytona Beach sometime during 1960. Then, after October 1960, 'Doc' moved to Sherman Oaks, CA, to live with his daughter, Dorothy. Franklin J. Crider passed away at Sherman Oaks on January 23, 1961.

Wilmer W. Steiner

The Crider Memorial Garden was established at the National PMC in 1967 by then Manager Robert Thornton. [571] Bob, who started his SCS employment at the Ithaca, NY nursery in 1936, moving to the Northeast Regional Horticulturist position in 1938, had worked closely with Dr. Crider and had great admiration for him. To the extent possible, a specimen of all the plants released by the nurseries and PMCs were to be displayed in the Garden. The year of its establishment, a bermudagrass tolerating winter temperatures of minus 17°F, which had been selected by Crider, was released from the Beltsville Center, and called 'Tufcote'. It became a part of the Garden, all of which was a grand showplace until the early 1990s, when it was discontinued. A plaque to Dr. Crider remains on the site.

The Memorial Garden still exists, and has been relocated closer to the building complex, highlighting some newer releases. Additionally, there are millions of acres of gardens, as Dr. Bennett put it, "scattered...far and wide over the nation" from the coastal dunes of the Atlantic seaboard to the slopes of the Cascades, each in its own way is solving a conservation problem. They are the legacy of Dr. Franklin J. Crider.

Dr. A. L. Hafenrichter- Key Leader

Assistant Professor, Washington State University,
Projection Agronomist, Soil Erosion Service,
Regional Nurseryman,
Regional Plant Materials Specialist

<u>The Man</u>

Persons entering the SCS Plant Materials Program any time prior to the mid-1970s, and anywhere in the country, soon heard about Dr. A. L. Hafenrichter. The first impression depended on who was sharing their point of view about him. To be sure, it was never neutral; he was always described with strong adjectives, like brilliant, opinionated, bold, overpowering, workaholic, dictatorial. An opinion was quickly formed.[572] Fortunately, we now have the benefit of a life's work on which a balanced judgment can be made.

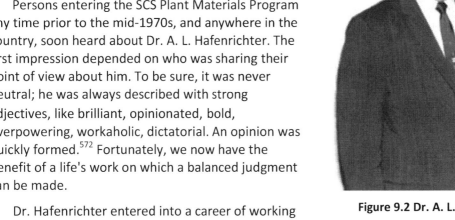

Figure 9.2 Dr. A. L. Hafenrichter

Dr. Hafenrichter entered into a career of working with plants in 1930 when he became an assistant professor of Farm Crops at Washington State University.[573] In 1933 he was hired as the Palouse Demonstration projection agronomist with the newly created Soil Erosion Service in the Department of the Interior. By 1935 the Soil Erosion Service became the Soil Conservation Service in the USDA. The Conservation Nurseries from the SES were transferred to SCS. One was located at Pullman, WA. Dr. Hafenrichter was appointed Regional Nurseryman, located first in Spokane, WA and later in Portland, OR. From this position he would provide technical and administrative direction to the Pullman Nursery.

The initial thrust and responsibilities of all nurseries was to produce large amounts of seed and plants for use in large conservation projects. In the western part of the country, this production leaned more towards grasses, as contrasted to trees and shrubs in the higher rainfall areas. As regional nurseryman, Hafenrichter had the responsibility of this large scale production as well as the observational studies. However, the identification of the best conservation grasses, and how best to mass produce them was widely unknown. This was not true of the production of trees and shrubs. As a result, from the very offset, the western nurseries took up the evaluating side of conservation plants before they could get to the large scale production.

The *History of Agronomy and Soils, WSU* by former Chairman B. R. Bertramson, and Professor Emeritus, Pullman, WA, provides an early window through which we can see why Dr. Hafenrichter stood apart from his colleagues.[574] The following is a quote from Dr. Bertramson:

> The SCS Nursery at Pullman was first headed by Dr. A. L. Hafenrichter-formerly a faculty member of the WSU Agronomy Department. He was an intense, dramatic, colorful, and able scientist. Those who worked under him, lovingly and respectfully described him in such terms as 'that dictatorial little Dutchman'. But they bore the title of Hafie's Boys proudly, and they profited in later years by his teachings and supervision. In later years when I was Chairman of the Department of Agronomy and Hafenrichter was in a supervisory capacity officially in Portland, he often came to see me, to reinforce some earlier commitment from the Department. One felt as though confronted by a prophet of biblical times when he would intone, 'Bert, we covenanted

(binding agreement, compact) with you.' He always made his point well and usually got his way!

During those early years of the evolving plant materials program another outstanding attribute of Dr. Hafenrichter emerged; his ability and insistence on employing only outstanding personnel who would contribute for years to the well-being of the effort. Here is the roster of employees at Pullman in the mid-1930s and 1940s that started with Hafenrichter.[575]

- John L. Schwendiman

- Harold W. Miller

- Virgil B. Hawk

- Paul Lemmon

- Donald S. Douglas

He kept the following motto on his desk: "There is much good that can be done if you don't worry about whom gets the credit." It appears he was entitled to and got his fair share of credit. Rarely a publication emerged from any office in the region without him being one of the authors.

Initially, Pullman was the only nursery in Hafenrichter's Region. Just before all the nurseries were closed in 1953, his region included the nurseries in Washington (Pullman and Bellingham), Oregon (Astoria), Idaho (Aberdeen) and California (Pleasanton). By then observational studies were being conducted at all these locations.

Performance

Between 1935 and 1953, the plants in Table 9.1 entered the commercial market as new releases from these locations, or had been substantially developed during this time period and were later released.[576] This list is a testimony to this 'intense, dramatic, colorful, and able scientist'.

Table 9.1 Plant Releases Developed by West Regional Nurseries 1935 - 1953

Cultivar	Common Name	Year Released	Cultivar	Common Name	Year Released
Manchar	smooth brome	1943	Volga	mammoth wildrye	1949
Sherman	big bluegrass	1945	Wimmera	annual ryegrass	1949
Greenar	intermediate wheatgrass	1945	Lana	wollypod vetch	1956
Bromar	mountain brome	1946	Alkar	tall wheatgrass	1951
Primar	slender wheatgrass	1946	Akaroa	orchardgrass	1953
Whitmar	bluebunch wheatgrass	1946	Topar	pubescent wheatgrass	1953
Blando	soft chess	1949	P-27	Siberian wheatgrass	1953
Cucamonga	California brome	1949	Sodar	streambank wheatgrass	1954
Durar	hard fescue	1949	Latar	orchardgrass	1956

He authored or co-authored many publications before and during his Regional Nurseryman days, all for the purpose of demonstrating the width and depth of knowledge resulting from the observational studies. Foremost of these was:

Hafenrichter, A. L., Mullen, L. A. and R. L. Brown. 1949. Grasses and Legumes for conservation in the Pacific Northwest. USDA Misc. Publ. 678. U.S. Gov. Print. Office, Washington, DC.

Many additional ones are included in Appendix 2.

From Nurseries to Plant Materials Centers

In 1953 the production part of the nurseries was closed and regional offices were consolidated. The Regional Nurseryman position was eliminated, but replaced by a Regional Plant Materials Technician position. Dr. Hafenrichter filled the position at Portland.

The observational studies conducted at these selected nurseries survived, becoming plant materials centers. There were ten closing nurseries authorized to become PMCs. According to the U.S. Department of Agriculture the ten were to be operated by a non-Federal agency or institution, with SCS financial and technical assistance. This applied to all except what was to become a National Center at Beltsville, MD. Three of the four nurseries in Dr. Hafenrichter's nursery region would become PMCs, Pullman, WA, Pleasanton, CA and Aberdeen, ID.

Figure 9.3 Dr. Hafenrichter and John Schwendiman in background

However, the 'intense, dramatic, colorful, and able scientist', Dr. Hafenrichter, thought this approach was illogical and technically unsound. Because PMCs served geographic areas, which included multiple states, he felt they should be operated as a Federal facility. Additionally, since the products of PMCs would find their way to conservation plantings through SCS field offices providing technical assistance to land owners, it was logical for both to be in the same agency.[577] Consequently, he coordinated efforts that assisted in altering the Department mandate.[578][579] He made sure the senators, congressmen, and potential institutions for operating the PMCs in Washington, California and Idaho knew how he felt and his reasons. In congressional debate, a senator from Washington referred to Pullman releases by name. To what extent Hafenrichter really impacted the outcome we do not know, but of the four that remained in the fold of SCS-operated centers, three were in his region. The other one was Elsberry, MO, and that was because a cooperating state agency or institution could not be found.

When the dust settled in 1954, five PMCs were to be operated by a non-federal cooperator.[580] Before Dr. Hafenrichter retired, four of the five of the cooperator-operated centers had returned to SCS. By 1963, as region boundaries changed and new Centers opened, there were eight centers receiving his able leadership. The newly opened ones included Los Lunas, NM, Bridger, MT, Corvallis, OR and Ho'olehua, HI. Tucson, AZ was one of the original ten and was moved into the West Region.

The Quiet Years

With the transition from observational nurseries completed it was time to return to the responsibilities at hand. First was to get all PMCs in his region trained and focused on the priorities. Hafenrichter had developed his way and system of developing new plants back in the old nursery days. It worked well then, and was implemented as new Centers came under his leadership. The system is discussed in considerable detail in Chapter 13, Factors Affecting Productivity. Understandably, his system was built around one conservation problem, which was re-vegetating degraded range land. Its simplicity as well as effectiveness presents the question of why was its use confined to the west, also debated in Chapter 13.

Shown in Table 9.2 are the new plant releases that came from the PMCs in his region from 1954 until a few years after his retirement. They were undoubtedly influenced by his leadership and technical savvy.[581]

Table 9.2 Plant Releases Developed by PMCs after Nurseries Closed

Cultivar	Common Name	Year Released	Cultivar	Common Name	Year Released
Cascade	Birdsfoot trefoil	1954	Perla	koleagrass	1970
Newport	Kentucky bluegrass	1958	Critana	thickspike wheatgrass	1971
Largo	tall wheatgrass	1961	Lutana	Cicer milkvetch	1971
Elida	sand bluestem	1963	Marshfield	big trefoil	1971
Lovington	blue grama	1963	Nogal	black grama	1971
Luna	pubescent wheatgrass	1963	Rosana	western wheatgrass	1972
Pastura	little bluestem	1963	Arriba	western wheatgrass	1973
Jose	tall wheatgrass	1965	Bandera	Rocky Mountain penstemon	1973
Pomar	orchardgrass	1966	El Vado	spike muhly	1973
Regar	meadow brome	1966	Redondo	Arizona fescue	1973
Kuiaha	desmodium	1969			

In 1947 Dr. Hafenrichter received the Superior Service Award from USDA, was honored as a Fellow in the American Society of Agronomy in 1954, and in the Society of Range Management posthumous in 1977. In 1963 he received the Distinguished Service award from USDA, their highest honor.

During the post nursery years his writing and publications continued. One collaborative effort that has stood the test of time for excellence was:

Hafenrichter, A. L., Schwendiman, J. L. Harris, H. L., MacLauchlan, R. S. and H. W. Miller. 1968. Grasses and legumes for soil conservation in the Pacific Northwest and Great Basin. USDA Agr. Handb. 339.

Summary

In conclusion, as in the beginning, what do others think? In 1994, Steven E. Phillips and Douglas Helms of the Economics and Social Sciences Division, SCS, interviewed former Chiefs of the Soil Conservation Service.[582] Following are the thoughts of Donald Williams.

> In the Pacific Northwest, the entire Pacific Coast area actually, we had one of the most outstanding plant materials specialists that the Service ever had, a man by the name of Dr. A. L. Hafenrichter, an agronomist with tremendous experience in reseeding plants for conservation objectives, and special grasses and legumes to fit different climatic and soil situations. I think that the greatest contribution to conservation and perhaps to agricultural production came about through the plant materials. Call it research if you want to. But it was applied research--developing these plants on Service areas and then getting the seed out to farmers to try. It gradually brought into the picture changes in the types of legumes and grasses that were being used throughout the western states. We did not get into such things as breeding wheat varieties or crop varieties. That was the job of the research service (Agricultural Research Service) or the state experiment stations. But we did get into the job of developing conservation plant materials. This was one of the strongest things that were done.

For all who have labored, or will labor in the Plant Materials Program, you can be proud of his legacy, and hope the leadership he provided is not only still contributing but being mimicked by the leaders of today.

Robert L. MacLauchlan – Key Leader

PMC Agronomist,
State Plant Materials Specialist,
Regional Plant Materials Specialist,
National Plant Materials Specialist

The Beginning

When the sun first touched the continental United States in January 25, 1950, as it had been doing since the beginning of time, it also touched Dennysville, ME.[583] However, that day was different. A young resident of Dennysville, Robert S. MacLauchlan, was going to receive a telegram from R. C Fury, personnel office in Portland, OR to report for a job on one of the last places the sun touches the continental U.S. – California. The telegram told Bob he had been selected from a Civil Service Register and he was to report to the Pleasanton, CA, Soil Conservation Service Nursery, right away. His father was less than enthusiastic. "Son that must be a hell of a poor job if they have to come all the way to Maine to get someone to accept it." Bob went to Pleasanton and the Plant Materials Program was the benefactor.

Figure 9.4 Robert MacLauchlan

Pleasanton was a sleepy little town in the Livermore Valley, about thirty miles from San Francisco. Although he had limited knowledge about the nursery business and less about the vegetation of California, he looked forwarded to his new job with the same enthusiasm that characterized his entire working career. He certainly made a good first impression on an assembled group at the nursery. They included Dr. A. L. Hafenrichter, his assistant Dr. Paul Lemmon, manager of the San Fernando nursery Dirk J. Vanderwal, and Oswald Hoglund, Pleasanton nursery manager, who would be his boss. He showed up five days early.

SCS Nurseries in California had been conducting observational studies and seeking outstanding conservation plants for years, under the regional guidance of Dr. Hafenrichter. Bob's association with Hafenrichter and others, combined with his intellect and work habits, landed him a new nursery job in 1952 with more responsibilities. He was instructed to report to the Bellingham, Washington nursery. Bob's role was to assist with management duties and become familiar with the observational studies underway at Bellingham. Unfortunately, it was short lived.

When the nurseries closed in 1953, Bob was transferred to the SCS field office in Harrisburg, Oregon. This lasted about as long as his stay in Bellingham. From there he returned to the plant evaluation work as plant materials technician for Western Oregon and Washington. He was first located in Hillsboro, OR, then in Corvallis, OR following the establishment of a new PMC at that location in 1957.

Increasing Responsibilities

After four locations in five years Bob was ready to settle down and accomplish something. Actually, his plant materials technician position, the Corvallis PMC, and for that matter the entire PMC program was new. Bob had entered the PMC Program on the ground floor. Carrying out the PM Specialist responsibilities and providing technical direction to the PMC, all under the leadership of Dr. Hafenrichter, became part of the building a future Program Leader.

By 1966, Bob was ready for a relatively short stint as plant materials specialist in California, sort of back where he had started, but with increased knowledge and the same or increased level of enthusiasm. During his stay an aggressive orchard cover crop study was initiated and two plants were released or readied for release.

Bob's leadership and management skill were being recognized beyond the west, and, in 1970, he accepted the position as Midwest National Technical Center Plant Materials Specialist in Lincoln, NE. Bob was following another plant materials westerner to move into the Midwest. In 1960, Donald Douglas had filled a similar position in Milwaukee, WI, and he shortly became the Chief PM Specialist in Washington D.C.

Crisis Management

Soon after his arrival in Lincoln, Bob was being asked to go to Washington to carry out some of the duties of the Chief PM Specialist, Bill Steiner, who had become gravely ill. Bob made several trips to deal with emergencies or near emergencies which limited his ability to get on top of his regional responsibilities. After only a little over three years in Lincoln, Bob replaced Bill in 1973. Little did he know his Washington time would be filled with one crisis after another, and neither did he know how well equipped he was for the challenge.

Bob was the National Plant Materials leader from August 1973 through 1984. His performance in that position is also discussed in Chapter 6 relative to program actions and accomplishments. His key contributions of crisis management are the principal focus here.

Crisis Number One

Upon Bob's arrival in Washington he had to deal with a budget crisis that had been simmering for several months. There was a shortfall and something needed to be done or PMCs would be closing. His supervisor was of that mind, suggesting Bob develop a 'hit list' of PMCs to close until the short fall was eliminated. Bob didn't like that idea. By 1974 there were twenty PMCs nationally, and the thought of closing one or more ran opposite to his passion for the Program. Besides, it would look like he was retreating; not a good example to set on the first weeks of a new job. He looked for a different solution.

An effective communicator, Bob tested the waters for other sources of funding, shuffled funds from center to center, eliminated all possible expenditures, and when the dust settled the crisis was over. All PMCs remained open. From then on, by effectively working with all levels in SCS, especially the finance office, budgets slowly improved. For the next few years the turbulent waters had quieted. Three new PMCs opened during this period, Meeker in Colorado, East Texas in Nacogdoches and South Texas in Kingsville.

Crisis Number Two

Although the 1974 budget crisis appeared to be a torrent of trouble, by 1980 it looked like only a trickle. Here's what happened. SCS 'shoot from the hip' Chief Mel Davis was testifying before a congressional budget subcommittee. A congressman asked Mr. Davis to list ways SCS could cut their budget. He responded by saying "Transfer all plant material centers to non-federal entities. Just last week I was at the plant materials center in Colorado which is run by two soil conservation districts, with just one SCS employee." He omitted telling the committee that the Colorado PMC was one-of-a-kind, born out of the energy crisis of the early 1970s, and thus was receiving most of their funding from other Federal and state agencies, oil shale related energy companies, and the local soil conservation districts farming operation. Needless to say, the congressman thought that was great, as did the rest of the committee, and so the USDA FY 1980 budget directed SCS to develop a plan for the "... phased and orderly transfer" of PMCs to non-federal operations. It was to be led by USDA Assistant Secretary Dr. M. Rupert Cutler, formally a Michigan extension specialist in natural resources policy.

Can you imagine? The last failed marriage with non-federal operation of PMCs had just been put to rest. Is it possible for a former state conservationist to be that out of touch?

Chief Davis told Bob he didn't want to be getting a lot of letters from disgruntled supporters. "Just get the job done," he said. He might have added, which was what he was thinking 'and don't let me look bad'. By this time he might have talked with cooler heads and realized his blunder.

Typical of his workmanlike manner, a plan began to evolve. Of course, to develop a plan that transferred all PMCs to non-federal entities required finding willing entities. Why not send a survey to all likely candidates that also measured the preference for other approaches for operating PMCs? If transferring them was such a good idea a survey would identify willing co-operators. Soliciting help from any and all sources, the questionnaire was ready to go. On January 19, 1980, a notice describing the details of the study appeared in the Federal Register. The notice also established the response period through April 4, 1980, and a final report to the Department by May 1, 1980. It offered four options for PMC operations.[584]

> Option 1: The continuation of the present program with adequate SCS funding, supplemented with funds and "in-kind" assistance from other Federal, state, and local agencies and organizations.
>
> Option 2: The continuation of present program funding, with definite arrangements for obtaining the additional needed financial, technical, and/or "in-kind" assistance from other Federal, State and local agencies.
>
> Option 3: Reduce the number of PMCs or reduce the level of ongoing programs at some or all PMCs.
>
> Option 4: Where suitable arrangements can be specifically identified, transfer the operations of some PMCs to non-federal control.

Distribution of the questionnaire was extensive. Each SCS state and regional office was supplied copies for distribution to any potentially interested party, a large mailing was sent to Federal agencies, national and regional agriculture associations, agriculture companies, colleges and universities, and similar groups. Additional requests for the questionnaires resulted from the Federal Register notice.

Responses came from farmers, ranchers, Federal agencies like the Agriculture Research Service, state agriculture experiment stations, the American Seed Trade Association, the American Nurserymen Association, the National Association of Conservation Districts, and PMC Advisory Committees; all knowledgeable about the PMC Program. Public participation resulted in 2,212 responses to the questionnaire. Other non-public responses arrived. Ninety letters were sent from congressional offices to USDA, letters were sent directly to Secretary Berglund, and letters were sent directly to Congress, all of them supported Option 1.[585]

See the summary in Table 9.3. Support for the first option was overwhelming; it received 84.8 percent of those responding. A summary of the results of the questionnaire, which appeared in MacLauchlan's questionnaire report, are shown below:

Table 9.3 Questionnaire Summary

Response Category	Total Responses	Alternatives Favored				Other or No Preference
		1	2	3	4	
Private Citizens	568	510	39	14	12	11
Private Companies	147	125	121	6	3	1
Other Federal Agencies	180	146	15	5	6	8
State & Local Governments	1,162	980	88	40	23	31
Organizations & Associations	137	115	12	6	3	1
Grand Total	2212	1876	166	71	47	52
Percent of Total	**100%**	**84.80%**	**7.70%**	**3.30%**	**2.10%**	**2.40%**

With this documentation it was time to report to Dr. Cutler. Bob laid out the relevant background, including the disastrous experience of those cooperative agreements with PMCs in Big Flats, NY, Americus, GA, etc. Relative to Option 4, the report stated "The study…identified no viable alternatives for transferring PMCs without full Federal funding on a continuing basis." It went on to say that even the non-Federal entities that might operate a PMC for SCS "were strongly supportive of the need for the continuation of this program as an SCS activity."

Over the following months Bob prepared status reports and met with Dr. Cutler and others in the Department, always displaying the support for the existing program and the complete lack of interest on the part of others willing to operate a plant materials center. Naturally, Cutler was not pleased. At every opportunity Bob continued to remind Dr. Cutler of the results when five PMCs were turned over to non-federal groups following the closing of the nurseries in 1953. This had no effect. "Keep trying" was always the response, which Bob did. Meeting after meeting, report after report, all wasting useful time, or so it seemed.

Sometimes wasting time is as asset. Elections come and elections go. By mid-1982 a new assistant secretary of USDA was on the job. Bob continued to send requested reports, but as time passed the requests dwindled, and then there were none. It was all over. The PMC Program came out of the experience more confident and stronger than it went in. MacLauchlan had used the exercise as a way of promoting the good works and informing others about the PMC Program. He was becoming an expert in crisis management.

Crisis Number Three

All PMCs do not function equally. In an effort to deal with one laggard PMC, a Regional PM Specialist suggested to the State Conservationist PMC Advisory Committee of that PMC that they hold the next meeting at an adjacent PMC to see how a more productive center functioned. This turned out to be a mistake. The committee from the laggard center concluded they could never do such a good job and proposed to MacLauchlan's old pal Chief Mel Davis that their center be closed.

Another one of those "Over my dead body" situations now faced MacLauchlan. Mel was still stinging from his last 'PMC experience'. Nevertheless, logic, generated support and a bulldog conviction of his cause won the day and the laggard PMC survived.

The Non-Crisis Robert S. MacLauchlan

To measure the career of Robert MacLauchlan only in terms of his ability to manage crisis would be a major injustice to him. The various qualities that made it possible for him to steer the Program through difficult times are the same qualities that encouraged, uplifted or counseled all employees of the program, and opened doors to potential adversaries and supporters alike. The entire Plant Materials Program prospered during his tenure as its Chief. His experience was broad and his wisdom sound. 'What would MacLauchlan think?' was a standard judgment consideration throughout the Program. The question was not asked in fear but because everyone knew his response would be reasoned and balanced.

Bob's exemplary service was recognized by the SCS when he was awarded the USDA Superior Service Award in 1979.

Summary

The sun still strikes Dennysville first, and the sun still sets on the twenty PMCs that existed when Bob went to Washington, plus a few more. He chose to retire at the end of 1984; after thirty-five years of totally committed service to the Plant Materials Program. All who hold the PMC Program in high esteem can thank their lucky stars that R. C. Fury, personnel office in Portland, OR, got that telegram to Dennysville, ME that chilly January morning in 1950.

Productive Scientists: Exceptionally Productive Individuals.

John L. Schwendiman– Productive Scientist

Center Manager
Plant Materials Specialist

An Introduction

"Hafenrichter was followed as Nursery Manager by John L. Schwendiman, whose personality and presence came to be embodied in the Soil Conservation Nursery--later called the Plant Material Center. He literally lived with the forages in the Nursery. Any damage to them, or the Program there, was a direct pain to John".[586] A close cohort of John on the faculty, Prof. Alvin G. Law, who was well known for his incisive and often witty pronouncements, spoke these words one day, in a fit of frustration because some people in Range Management were challenging John's philosophy. Al declared, "John Schwendiman has forgotten more about range management than they will ever know!"

Figure 9.5 John Schwendiman

Background

John L. Schwendiman was born September 18, 1909 in Sugar City, Idaho. He entered the University of Idaho in 1927. After serving as a missionary in Switzerland and Germany (1929-1932), he farmed for a year and returned to the University of Idaho where he graduated in 1935. He then taught agriculture at Rexburg, Idaho, and worked at the Idaho Experiment Station.[587]

Late in 1935, he entered the Soil Erosion Service as a technical foreman; and then in SCS became a junior agronomist at Pullman, Washington. He continued to serve as the agronomist at the Pullman nursery until 1939 when he became temporary nursery manager until 1940, when Dr. Paul E. Lemmon took over. In 1945 when Virgil Hawk left for graduate school John became permanent manager. He continued in this position until 1954. From 1954 until 1977 he was the plant materials technician/specialists for western Washington, northern Idaho, and eastern Oregon, and after 1970, for Alaska. He retired from SCS on December 31, 1976, and died June 6, 1982.[588] He was 82.[589]

Legacy

The Conservation legacy John created in forty years of USDA service falls into two areas:

- The new conservation plants he assisted in developing that are today used throughout the west.

- The use and management of conservation plants, which remains with us through trained individuals and his publications.

New Conservation Plants

When John Schwendiman arrived at Pullman, WA in 1935, two other plant materials giants were already with SCS. First, Dr. Franklin Crider had arrived in the SCS Washington D.C. office and was selling the concept that "Nature has evolved a plant for every purpose." The second giant, Dr. A. L. Hafenrichter, was busy at work in Pullman, WA, and later at Spokane and Portland, OR, putting together a process whereby the observational studies at the Pullman Nursery could implement Crider's concept.

The observational studies staff at Pullman had many advantages. The most important, although it may not have been recognized at the time, was that conservation problems that could be solved with vegetation abounded in their service area. Additionally, there was assembled a staff of scientists, as time would demonstrate, that may have exceeded the quality of any staff thereafter at any nursery or plant materials center. It included Schwendiman, Virgil B. Hawk, then a student at Washington State University, Dr. Paul Lemmon, a forester, Harold W. Miller, a forestry student, Donald Douglas, a recent agronomy graduate from WSU, and Dr. Lowell A. Mullen, a trained botanist. A close working relationship had evolved with the Agronomy Department at WSU, even increasing the nursery's capabilities.[590]

Figure 9.6 John with his beloved grasses

John participated in the introduction of no less than sixteen new conservation plants into the Northwest. A combination of these led to the commercial production of fifty seven million pounds of seed, and a net conservation value of $2.8 million.[591] These sixteen new releases can be seen in Chapter 8 on the pages about the Pullman, WA PMC.

Use and Management of Conservation Plants

In 1934 John was junior author on his first publication, a referred article in the Agronomy Journal. Over the years he became one of the most prolific authors in the Soil Conservation Service, writing or co-authoring over sixty journal articles, experiment station bulletins and circulars, USDA publications, and technical guides. He co-authored his last publication three years after his retirement.[592] In addition to delivering twenty-five technical papers at professional meetings, he sought to inform the public about new plant materials in over forty magazine and newspaper articles.

For the first seventy-five years of the Plant Materials Program, John Schwendiman can be considered the most prolific publisher of printed technical documents. Most are shown in Appendix 2. They convey the depth of his knowledge and his commitment to dispense it, both for the scientist and the farmer-rancher.

Recognitions

John was active in several professional organizations. He was a registered professional agronomist, a member of the American Society of Agronomy, a life member and fellow of the Society of Range Management, a charter member of the Soil and Water Conservation Society of America, and director of the Northwest Scientific Association.

Individual honors include:

- USDA Superior Service Award in 1967

- Honorary in Alpha Zeta and Sigma Xi

- President Northwest Section of the Society of Range Management

- Received Sears Foundation-Washington State Junior Chamber of Commerce Award

- Recognized in American Men of Science and Who's Who in the West

- Trustee of the Northwest Scientific Association

- Outstanding Achievement Award from the Society of Range Management in 1976

- Fellow in the Society of Range Management in 1979

- Received the Orville A. Vogel, Washington State Crop Improvement Award. The award is given annually to an individual in Washington State University's College of Agricultural, Human, and Natural Resource Sciences, WSU Extension, or USDA who has made significant contributions to the pure seed program or crop production in Washington state

- Sunday school teacher, Stake president and Stake Missionary

Conclusion

John worked for forty years, retiring at age sixty-seven on December 31, 1976. It was not his choice to retire. Conflicts between he and a new PMC manager led to an administrative decision to locate John away from the PMC. He chose retirement. The problem was solved. SCS lost a plant scientist giant and the Pullman PMC languished for twenty plus years. Talent, technical knowledge and productivity often become secondary to whimpering.

If there was a Plant Materials Program scientist in the first seventy-five years of its history that epitomized what a scientist should be, it was John Schwendiman.

James E. "Bud" Smith, Jr. – Productive Scientist

**Nursery Agronomist,
Nursery Manager,
Regional Nurseryman,
Plant Materials Specialist**

The Beginning

James E. "Bud" Smith, Jr. was the founder of conservation plant development in Texas and Oklahoma. His career started with the Soil Conservation Service in 1935 as an Assistant Agronomist at the Woodward, OK Field Station. From 1936 to 1939 he was regional nurseryman at Amarillo, TX, and then from 1939 until 1950 he was the nursery manager at Woodward. In 1950 he moved to San Antonio, TX to manage both the San Antonio and Delhart production and observational nurseries.[593] He

Figure 9.7 'Bud' Smith (right) with a pose of satisfaction, as a father with a favorite child (new release) soon to marry well.

continued in this position until the nurseries closed during the 1953-54 period. Then he assumed statewide responsibility for the plant materials work as the Texas plant materials technician/specialist.

The Evaluating Years

During his years as manager of the Woodward and San Antonio nurseries, Smith was accumulating both knowledge and plant accessions that would be useful in converting eroding rangeland to protected and productive cover in the southern Great Plains. When the San Antonio nursery closed, the land and the assembled accessions were transferred to the Texas Agricultural Experiment Station. Smith knew the value of the accessions, and through his efforts, and desirable working relationship with the Experiment Station, they were preserved and some level of evaluations and production continued.

From 1953 or 1954 Smith became the plant materials technician, and until 1965 he was the plant materials program in Texas, soliciting support from the state experiment stations, SCS county and area employees, other agencies, and, most importantly, the SCS State Conservationist H. N. Smith. Some SCS accessions still existed at the San Antonio Sub Station He was the person watching over them, as well as work done at another Experiment Station in Spur, Texas. Extensive observational studies took place there, undoubtedly with the assistance of Experiment Station personnel.[594] Smith also carried out a large scale field testing of several promising plants from 1954 until his retirement in 1965. Several of these later were released, some as cultivars.

Figure 9.8 The plant materials person is not hard to spot in this picture – second from the left. This was taken at the PMC dedication in 1967. His wife is next to him, and then the Administrator of SCS, Donald Williams. H. N. "Red" Smith, STC of TX is on the left.

In a previous reference James Smith stated "Plant materials center operations were organized in Texas in 1955, with first production in the fall of 1956."[595] He proceeded to point out what the state conservationist said to put major emphasis on getting soil conservation district cooperators involved in grass seed production, and that he had instructed the area conservationists on how to do it. Within the Plant Materials Program, the PMC at Knox City is viewed as the first one in Texas, yet one could argue that from 1954 until 1965 there was a PMC wherever Smith was standing, which was mostly in Spur.

Reports were prepared by him between 1961 and 1963 about plant materials activities at the Spur, TX Experiment Station and the sub-station in San Antonio.[596] Activities at both locations were related predominately to the production of multiple accessions carried over from the nursery days. The only non-production activities which he carried out involved a 300 accession initial observation block established in 1960 at Spur, and production enhancing studies. Remnants of the initial observation block remained in 1963. Of course, this story ends with a new PMC being established in 1965 at Knox City, named the James E. "Bud" Smith Center. Throughout the period, Smith labored continuously for its establishment. In 1965 those valuable accessions that Smith had herded for fifteen years were the first items planted there.

Actually, about 260 of the first accessions planted at Knox City were ones carried over from the San Antonio Nursery and the Spur Agriculture Experiment Station.[597]

At the dedication ceremony of the new PMC on September 7, 1967, the contributions of Smith were recognized by SCS Administrator Donald A. Williams by announcing that the PMC would be officially named the James E. "Bud" Smith, Jr. Center, citing Smith as "the driving force behind the development here."[598]

Two superior plants, King Ranch yellow bluestem and 'T-4464' buffelgrass found their way into commercial use before the nurseries closed in 1953. Four more had been selected as superior plants prior to the nursery closing and were field tested and released by Smith between 1953 and 1965; before the new PMC opened. Production at the Spur and San Antonio stations allowed Smith to make final evaluations of these four, assemble the data and get them released. They were Kleberg, Medio and Gordo bluestem and 'Llano' Indiangrass. Regrettably, only 'Llano' was formally released.

Other plants he had selected and nurtured for years were the first production fields established at the new PMC. Several of these reached release status and entered commercial production. One, 'Selection 75' klinegrass, has proven to be one of the most successful releases of the "Bud" Smith, Jr. PMC can be seen in Chapter 8.

To get a sense of the impact of Smith's work, it is well to look both forward and backward from the 1965 establishment date of the PMC. The ecological and production value of these cultivars exceed the operating costs of the combined observational studies and Knox City PMC costs from 1935 – 2005 fourteen times over. Actually, the value of 'Selection 75' alone was seven times these costs.

Acknowledgements

Smith was recognized widely in the Southern Great Plains for his knowledge of how to solve conservation problems with vegetation. Although he published sparingly he is acknowledged frequently by other authors for his contributions to their publications. One major publication, completed after his retirement, is

Atkins, M. D. and James E. Smith Jr. 1967. Grass Seed Production and Harvest in the Great Plains, Farmers Bulletin 2226. Washington, DC: U.S. Department of Agriculture. 30 p.

Previously, all PMCs that have been named for a person were named for non-plant materials people. The cynic might say such actions were motivated by selfish, non-plant materials related reasons. To be sure, such is not the case with the James E. "Bud" Smith PMC. For as long as that PMC survives, the employees will wear that name with honor.

In a document prepared by the PMC staff for the dedication of the James E. "Bud" Smith, Jr. PMC, the following is noted in the closing paragraph.[599]

"Since retiring, Bud has continued to work in the plant materials field. He travels the Southwest in the continuing search for, and evaluation of promising plants. Everywhere he goes; he sees the harvesting, planting and growing (of the plants) and techniques he helped develop in the 1930s still in use – a silent tribute to this plant materials pioneer."

No history of plant materials work in Texas can be written without mentioning Smith. Both Chapters 5 and 6 include much of his contributions.

J. Chris Hoag – Productive Scientist

Range Conservationist
Riparian Plant Ecologist

Looking back over the history of the Aberdeen PMC one can see many accomplishments, like 'P-27' Siberian wheatgrass or 'Sodar' streambank wheatgrass. They are the stars. Collectively, the ecological and production value of these two cultivars exceeded the total budget of the PMC by $8.2 million. What is not seen is the development of how to do things, like how to produce seed, how to plant, etc. As new needs for conservation plants were identified, and PMCs undertook the challenge to find solutions, the how-to always loomed as the first hurtle. Such was the case with the thrust of the Aberdeen PMC into developing methods for reestablishing or restoring riparian and wetland vegetation.

During the past twenty years the PMC has made giant progress in developing a complete package for addressing this need. The effort was led by Chris Hoag, a range conservationist, who transferred to the PMC as a trainee in 1991. His actions were never like a trainee; he hit the ground running. Jacy Gibbs, Regional PM Specialist, had nominated him. Experience had taught those associated with Jacy that his thinking was sound, so Chris was hired.

Working through the Interagency Riparian/Wetland Plant Development Project, which he organized, he took the leadership of the center's riparian and wetland vegetation project. While the emphasis of the project was on the Great Basin and Intermountain West regions, much of the developed information is applicable throughout the U.S. The following highlights some of the accomplishments and new techniques developed by Hoag and his team.

Each of the footnotes in this section represents a publication. They are all listed in Appendix 2.

Willow Clump Plantings

Willow clump plantings are a soil bioengineering technique that can be used when a large stand of willows are available to the project area.[600] The entire dormant plant is lifted with a backhoe including

Lift the clump   After placement, anchored with rock
Figure 9.9 The clump willow planting

soil, stems and roots, plus any clinging grass or other plants. A hole of similar size has been prepared. The lifted plant is placed in the hole, and the backhoe is used to pull soil around the plant and firmly pressing it into the hole. The backhoe can also be used to water the plant if needed. As soon as the plants are in place several of the branches should be trimmed. The clump being lifted is shown in Figure 9.9. The bank which received several is on the right. Note some large stone have been placed to help keep the willows in place.

The Stinger: a tool to plant unrooted hardwood cuttings

This tool was used for multiple applications.[601] First, it is a tool for pole planting of unrooted cuttings. Additionally it can facilitate the same practice through riprap or other bank protecting material. Below right the tool is shown opening a hole in riprap to make room for the pole, the middle picture shows the pole being planted and on the right the same process is used through a bale of

Opening a hole in riprap   **Planting a pole**   **Planting a pole through a bale of straw**

Figure 9.10 How the Stinger works, with Chris Hoag in the center picture

straw. See Figure 9.10.

An additional twist to the use of the Stinger is the waterjet stinger. It is a hydrodrill that uses high pressure water to drill a hole in the streambank. This tool is composed of a high pressure water pump with 2 probes that have stainless steel nozzles that increase the water pressure so it comes out the holes in the nozzle at 80 psi. When the nozzle is placed on the streambank, the water liquefies the soil and cuts a hole as it goes down.

Harvesting, Propagating, and Planting Wetland Plants

This outstanding Technical Note supplies extensive information on the harvesting, propagating, and planting wetland plants, with emphasis on sedges, *(Carix spp.)*, bulrushes *(Scirpus spp.)*, and spikerushes *(Juncus spp.)*. [602] All are used extensively in riparian and wetland revegetation because of their dense and aggressive root system. The following subjects are covered in detail.

- Direct seeding of wetland plants

- Collection and propagation of wetland plants

- Greenhouse propagation

- Wild transplant collections

- Wetland transplant plantings

It has an excellent literature citation section.

301

Newsletters and guidelines published by Chris and the Aberdeen Wetland group were equally packed with old and new information. By 1998 guidelines were published for establishing and maintaining constructed wetlands. Project Information Series No. 12 discusses 21 factors that help assure a successful outcome. These factors may seem fairly simple, but experience has shown that all must be addressed during the planning stages of the project. By addressing them in the planning stages of the project, the chances that they will be done well by the planting crews are greatly increased.

A 2007 copy, among other things, discusses a three day bioengineering workshop that focused on the use of old and new tools for riparian restoration. Figure 9.11 is a class installing vertical bundles which are long unrooted cuttings bound together and placed vertically in a shallow trench up the streambank with the base in the water and the tops sticking above the top of the bank.[603] The bundles are staked into the bank so they won't float or wash away during high flows. The bundles are then covered with soil and the soil is washed in around the cuttings to ensure good soil for stem contact. The stems in contact with the soil will grow roots and the parts that are exposed to the air and sunlight will sprout leaves and stems. Vertical bundles differ from a fascine in that fascines are staked and established horizontally at the streambank toe rather than vertically up the streambank.

The lower right picture in Figure 9.11 is the result of dormant brush mattress parallel along an eroding stream. As the picture shows the proof is in the pudding as the initially buried twigs, stems and trunks sprout sprout roots and produce new vegetation.

Figure 9.11 Top left; class installing a brush mattress with dormant material; right parallel installation. Bottom left severely eroding bank, right, re-vegetated results.

Pre-soaking hardwood willow cuttings for fall versus spring dormant planting

The proposal here was to compare the benefits of pre-soaking or not pre-soaking cuttings of two willow species that were fall and spring harvested and fall and spring planted.[604]

There was 100% survival from from all the peachleaf willow variables. Root and shoot production, however, did show differences between treatments. In terms of roots and shoots, the pre-soaked cuttings harvested and planted in the fall had better root and shoot production than all other treatments. The poorest producer of roots and shoots was the spring harvested cuttings that did not receive a pre-soaking treatment. Unsoaked cuttings harvested and planted in the fall had root and shoot production similar to spring harvested and planted cuttings that had been soaked. Also, for fall and spring collected materials, soaked cuttings performed better than non-soaked cuttings harvested and planted within the same season, e.g., fall soaked cuttings out performed fall unsoaked cuttings, .spring soaked cuttings out performed spring unsoaked cuttings.

Two cuttings of coyote willow died in the fall soaked treatment of the coyote willow trial reducing survival to 92%. The reason for the cutting mortality isn't known. All other cuttings from the three remaining treatments survived. Despite the somewhat lower survival, fall harvested and presoaked cuttings had significantly greater root production than the other treatments (fig 5). Similar to the peachleaf willow trial, the pre-soaked cuttings had better root production than their non-soaked counterparts. Shoot production for coyote willow was essentially the same for all treatments.

Wetland Sodmats[605]

Wetland plants such as sedges and rushes have very large and dense root systems. This kind of root density translates into excellent stream bank protection.

Wetland sodmats are large pieces of intact wetland soil and vegetation removed from a donor wetland site. Wetland sodmats are an excellent way to establish both small and large areas of wetland plants. The sodmats are harvested out of a wetland that is scheduled to be destroyed. Since relatively large areas of the donor wetlands are impacted, this method should be used only as a salvage technique.

The sodmats are harvested with shovels, backhoe, or a front-end loader modified with a sharp-edged steel plate that undercuts the sod, producing nice uniform sod squares. A backhoe with a large bucket can harvest sodmats quickly, but they typically will not be a uniform, in-tack square. Best results are achieved when the soils are moist but well drained at the time of cutting. Wetland sodmats can be up to 8 foot square depending upon the equipment that is used for harvest. Generally, the sodmats should be 6-8 inches thick. The harvested sodmats are then loaded onto a dump truck, flatbed truck, or trailer for transport to the planting area.

The harvested sod should be placed in a matching hydrological zone similar to the donor site. They should fit tightly together, similar to laying sod for a yard. Firm the sodmats into their new site.

Sodmats can be transplanted successfully about any time provided sufficient moisture is available in the recipient wetland. Dormant planting is not necessary as long as water is available immediately after replanting. Do not transport the sodmats uncovered for long distances because they will dry out. Sodmats can be stored for long periods if they are kept wet. Store them on an impenetrable surface. Do not stockpile during periods of high temperature.

Summary

The Plant Materials career of Chris was like a broad jumper who doesn't use a running start. Entering the discipline as a trainee, he leaped in a few years of employment to creating new technology that is applicable throughout most of the western region and beyond. This brief summary touches only a small part he and the Aberdeen accomplished in a short time. Following his retirement from NRCS, he formed the Hoag Riparian & Wetland Restoration, LLC Company.[606]

Productive Plant Materials Teams

No two PMCs are created equal. Consequently, the potential of their productivity will vary greatly, for many reasons. These include the presence or absence of major conservation problems within PMC service areas, longevity and capability of the PMC staff, size of budget, and non PMC leadership. Each factor can play a role.

Ways have been devised to approximate the economic value of some PMC products, like their releases. Centers are evaluated annually for their activities and accomplishments, using multiple factors like number of plant assemblies, number of publications or number of new plant releases, etc. Educational outreach, ecological impacts on the landscape, and economic impacts on commercial producers are additional factors indicating productivity.

While any historical evaluation using these or other factors of productivity is risky, in the mind of the author, the performance of two PMCs, throughout their years of operations, warrants special recognition. Two other Centers, Pullman, WA and Aberdeen, ID, both opening and remaining under the leadership of Hafenrichter for many years, have excellent output records. Unfortunately, both experienced an extended downturn before regaining their footing.

Albuquerque and Los Lunas New Mexico – Productive Team

Joseph A. Downs,   **Wendall Oaks,**
Glenn Niner,   **Gregory Fenchel**
James Anderson,

Founding

This team began to assemble even before Dr. Franklin Crider introduced the observational nursery concept to production nurseries. Crider joined the Erosion Control Service in 1934 at Tucson, AZ.[607] A year later; Joseph Downs joined the staff. The following year, in 1936, Downs joined the newly opened Albuquerque, NM Nursery staff as an agronomist, and Crider moved to Washington D.C. Downs was joined the same year by Glenn Niner as assistant agronomist.[608]

Downs and Niner continued their employment at Albuquerque until the nursery closed in 1953, and beyond. By 1938 Downs was the nursery superintendent.

Early Outputs

Between 1936 and 1953 the Albuquerque nursery collected seed from native grass stand, which was reproduced on some of the nursery lands. In 1939 they collected 25,000 pounds of seed and produced another 2,000 pounds for conservation plantings on ranches in the region.[609]

The team of Downs and Niner were also identifying superior ecotypes they found in the landscape as they made their collections. Their first three were released during the production/nursery days, which ended in 1953.[610] [611]

Vaughn' sideoats grama was "… collected from native stands near Vaughn, NM in 1935 and released in 1940."[612] 'Grenville' switchgrass was collected at Grenville, NM at 5900 feet elevation and sixteen inches of precipitation, and was released in 1940. 'Amur' intermediate wheatgrass was a plant introduction from Manchuria, China, and was released in 1952. The value of these three releases, when measured in net value to the producer and net ecological value exceeds $25.4 million. [613]

Post Nursery Outputs

In 1953 all nurseries were closed, including the one at Albuquerque. The nursery had been operating on leased land, which was terminated and all aspects of the nursery operation were closed. Fortunately Joe Downs had the forethought to salvage propagating material of the most promising accessions, as well as the records, and save them in his garage for another day.[614] In the meantime the ex-nursery employees, including Downs and Niner, were employed in other SCS activities.

In early 1957, through the efforts of Downs and Harbour Jones, superintendent of the NM State College of Agriculture Middle Rio Grande Substation, at Los Lunas, a basic agreement was drawn up between SCS and the College, whereby the College would operate a PMC at the substation. Funds and technical assistance would be provided by SCS and the cooperator would furnish the manager.

By the end of 1957, several increase plantings of superior strains from the observational nursery selections that Downs had stored were established on the new PMC. Additionally, even before the PMC was established, Joe Downs was making new collections.

James E. Anderson, NM State College of Agriculture became the first manager of the PMC in 1957. Glenn Niner provided the SCS technical assistance until his retirement in 1968 and Joe Downs became the first plant materials technician in New Mexico in 1954 and served in that position until 1962 when he retired. Anderson continued as manager until 1979.

Four new cultivars were released from the carry-over selections from the observational nursery over the next few years, and three from the post-nursery collections by Downs. These are shown in the Los Lunus PMC Pages in Chapter 8.

Although retired, the impacts of Downs and Niner continued to be reflected in the Los Lunas PMC output. James Anderson continued to complete the evaluation and release process of nine more cultivars of collections and/or selections made by the three. After Anderson's retirement in 1979, at least six more were released that had been selected by him, with the able assistance of Leaford Windle, who provided SCS Technical assistance from 1968 until 1977. Fifteen new

Figure 9.12 Top Joseph Downs, middle Glenn Niner, bottom Glen Anderson

cultivars, including 'Niner' sideoats grama, collected by Niner and Anderson in 1957, plus the balance of the releases by the PMC through 2005 are shown on the Los Lunus pages in Chapter 8.

The Albuquerque nursery closed in 1953. Los Lunas, which opened in 1957, became was one of the five to be operated through a cooperative agreement with another institution or agency. Of the five, only the Los Lunas PMC excelled, actually exceeding most if not all other centers, whether operated by SCS or someone else. The cooperative agreement remains intact. This success rests on the leadership of those early leaders, Downs and Anderson.

Table 9.4 summarizes the net values from the Los Lunas releases through 2005. It shows the Net to Producer and Ecological Benefits from releases that produce a benefit to cost ratio of thirteen to one. The net value of cultivars 'Hachita' blue grama, 'Arriba' black grama, 'Luna' pubescent wheatgrass and 'Vaughn' sideoats grama each exceeded the $21.9 million in observational nursery and PMC operating costs.

Table 9.4 Net value from Los Lunas releases

Production and Ecological Benefits from Releases:	$305,780,970
Gross PMC operating budget; 1935 – 2005	$21,923,110
Net Production and Ecological Benefits from Releases:	$283,522,344

New Operating Procedure, New Direction

During 1978-79, a new agreement between SCS and the University of New Mexico was developed. The most significant change was to switch management responsibility from the University to SCS. Wendall Oaks (Figure 9.13) came to the PMC in 1978 as the first SCS manager.

The focus of the Los Lunas PMC began to change in the early 1980s in three ways. The first change was a gradual shift from an overwhelming emphasis on restoration of grazing lands to other conservation needs. Foremost among these were

- Riparian restoration

- Stabilization of mining and other manmade disturbed sites

- Enhanced vegetative food and cover for wildlife

Figure 9.13 Wendall Oaks

The second change was increased collaboration with public and private groups which led to a significant increase in the PMC budget and an enlarged staff and program.

The third way was the leadership role of the Los Lunas PMC in automating all centers.

Impact of Refocusing - New Plants

New cultivars were developed for these new conservation needs, plus processes and procedures for their use, resulting in complete restoration packages. Eighteen or more new cultivars released in the past twenty years could be considered non-traditional. The magnitude of these accomplishments resulted in part from the new funding through cooperative agreements with others. Additions to the staff of talented personnel like Dr. David Dreesen helped make this possible. In the early 1990s Gregory Fenchel replaced Oaks but the momentum continued. Many publications appearing in Appendix 2 by the Los Lunas staff indicate this new emphasis, as well as accomplishments.

Impact of Automation of the PMCs Effort

This innovation started in the early 1980s, led by manager Wendall Oaks. It resulted in the automation of all centers nationally. Over the years the hardware and software technology changed, but this early effort, coming out of Los Lunas, impacted not only the PMC Program, but the entire agency. Wendall Oaks received the USDA Superior Service Award for this and other efforts.

Conclusion

When Joseph Downs joined the Soil Erosion Service in 1934 the first stone was laid for the success story of the Los Lunas PMC. The addition of Glenn Niner in 1936 was a second block which propelled the Albuquerque Nursery through the 1940s and until the early 1950s. Some time and effort was lost with the nursery closing in 1954, but Downs, Niner and the addition of James Anderson in 1957 made it seem like they never missed a beat. Then Wendall Oaks picked up the reins, built an enlarged staff with new money, and moved the program in other directions. Gregory Fenchel continues the tradition. Throughout its history, innovation and output has been their hallmarks.

Bridger, Montana – Productive Team

Ashley Thornburg,
James Stroh,
Robert G. Lohmiller
Larry Holzworth,
John Scheetz,
Mark Majerus,
Gu Anlin

Founding

When SCS closed all the nurseries in 1952-53, great un-served areas existed, and, over time many were filled. Through the strong leadership of local Soil Conservation Districts in Montana and Wyoming, support from regional plant materials specialist Dr. A. L. Hafenrichter, and the SCS state offices in Montana and Wyoming, a PMC was authorized at Bridger, MT in 1959.[615]

Figure 9.14 Ashley Thornburg

Leadership

The first manager was Ashley A. Thornburg, who started his SCS career as a lab technician at the San Antonio nursery, working under James E. Smith, Jr. From 1953 until 1959 he was a Soil Conservationist in Victoria, TX. Then he moved to Bridger, and continued in the position of manager until 1965, when he became the plant materials specialist serving Montana and Wyoming. In this position he continued to provide technical direction to the Center.

Ashley was replaced as manager by James R. Stroh in 1965; a bright fellow who carried on the excellent work started by Thornburg. In 1973 Stroh became the manager of a new PMC in Alaska.

Stroh was replaced by John Scheetz, who provided twenty-five years of strong and technically sound leadership. In 1988 Gu Anlin, from the Grassland Research Institute, Hohhot (Huhehot), China joined the staff for a year to continue mutually beneficial studies on grasses equally well adapted to the Northern Great Plains and Inner Mongolia. John continued as manager until 1998 when he became the National PMC Information Technology Specialist, located at the Bridger center.

Figure 9.15 John Scheetz

John was also greatly assisted and supported by two excellent Plant Materials Specialists. First was Robert G. Lohmiller from 1974 until 1979, who became the Montana State Resource Conservationist. Larry K. Holzworth moved from the PMC manager's position in Arizona to replace Lohmiller and continued in the position until his retirement in 2007.

Mark E. Majerus, a longtime understudy, replaced John as PMC manager in 1998. Mark continued the unbroken years of outstanding leadership from the founding of the PMC in 1959.

Measurements – Educational Outreach

Educational outreach to SCS employees in other agency personnel, farmers, producers and ranchers was accomplished in Montana and Wyoming through personal lectures, demonstrations, one-on-one contact, evaluation and demonstrational plantings and printed documents. From the beginning this has been a hallmark of the Bridger PMC, with plant materials specialists Thornburg, Lohmiller and Holzworth taking the lead. Their tireless pursuits in this area are legendary. Additionally, Thornburg and Holzworth, as well as PMC staff members, have published an astonishing number and array of publications about their products, which include new plants and the technology for using them. They can be identified in Appendix 2 by author name. One however requires special recognition.

Thornburg, Ashley A. 1976. Plant materials for use on surface-mined lands in arid and semiarid regions. U.S. Environmental Protection Agency, Washington D.C.

Production and Ecological Benefits from Releases

No PMC has been more consistent in the development and release of widely accepted and reproduced new plants than Bridger. When the benefits calculated from the Bridger PMC releases are compared to all PMCs, it ranks fourth. The three higher ranking PMCs had the benefit of observational studies starting in the mid-1930s at SCS nurseries, which contributed to their pool of releases. Bridger started from scratch in 1959. The first released plant with which Bridger was associated was 'Garrison' creeping foxtail, a joint release with another PMC. The first cultivar developed at Bridger was 'Critana' thickspike wheatgrass. It ranks fourth in terms of net benefits among all releases from all PMCs. Three of the top thirty 'net benefit' cultivars from the entire program, were released by Bridger: 'Critana', 'Rimrock' Indian ricegrass, and 'Rosana' western wheatgrass. Table 9.5 shows the production and value of their top seven releases. These accomplishments speak volumes about quality and quantity of accomplishments. Greater details are available in Chapter 8 in the section on Bridger.

Figure 9.16 Larry Holzworth

Conclusion

Table 9.5 Major grass and legume cultivars released by Bridger PMC

Release	Common Name	Release Year	Total Production	Unit	Net Value to Producer	Net Ecological Value
Critana	thickspike wheatgrass	1971	8,777,835	LB	$23,568,100	$45,220,500
Lutana	Cicer milkvetch	1971	724,769	LB	$2,785,100	$1,293,600
Rosana	western wheatgrass	1972	4,338,058	LB	$10,198,500	$19,822,800
Goshen	prairie sandreed	1976	671,910	LB	$2,275,000	$3,918,500
Pryor	slender wheatgrass	1988	1,499,159	LB	$2,843,130	$6,978,100
Trailhead	basin wildrye	1991	1,302,176	LB	$5,017,900	$5,208,100
Rimrock	Indian ricegrass	1996	4,411,570	LB	$5,421,200	$16,245,500

From 1959 through 2005 the Bridger Montana PMC team of Ashley Thornburg, James Stroh, Robert Lohmiller, Larry Holzworth, John Scheetz, Mark Majerus, and Gu Anlin has established a standard not likely to be challenged. The current manager, Joseph Scianna, a former trainee, is carrying the torch. They have published an astonishing number and array of documents, including information about new plants and the technology for using new and old plants for a wide variety of conservation measures. The quantity and quality of their plant releases stand second to none for the time of their operation.

Major Contributor: Accomplishment and Leadership

Selecting Major Contributors from the dozens of employees within the seventy-five year history of the Plant Materials Program was extremely easy. The difficult part was not selecting so many more. The simple criteria of combined scientific accomplishment and leadership fit so many. Those selected could fairly ask, "Why me when so many others were omitted?" The eleven selected represent the best among many.

Abraham D. Stoesz – Major Contributor

Nursery Agronomist,
Regional Nurseryman,
National Plant Materials Technician

Background

Dr. Abraham D. Stoesz was born in Minnesota, in 1894.[616] After a short term in the U.S. Army he studied at Tabor College, Hillsboro, KS, Bluffton College, OH and the University of Minnesota, where he earned his Master of Arts and Doctor of Philosophy degrees. He spent several distinguished years as a botanist in a number of universities, and then entered the Soil Conservation Service in 1936 with the Nursery Division in North Dakota.[617] He soon rose to the position of Regional Nurseryman, first at Rapid City, ND, then Mandan, ND, and later moved to Lincoln, NE in the same position.[618]

Dr. Stoesz was emblematic of his northern Midwest conservative upbringing. Those who traveled with him soon learned now emphatic he was about not paying more than a dollar per hour for sleeping arrangements.

Early Years

It was not surprising, with the observational studies authorization from Headquarters, that the Great Plains region would take a lead role, not only in native grass seed collection and nursery production, but also in new cultivar development. From the initiation of observational studies in 1936, new cultivars were significantly developed under Stoesz's supervision in the Midwest. Table 9.6 shows four such native grass releases.

His commitment to publishing the results of his work started prior to his SCS employment.

Table 9.6 Releases from Observational Nurseries in Midwest

Cultivar	Scientific Name	Common Name	Release Year
El Reno	Bouteloua curtipendula	sideoats grama	1944
Blackwell	Panicum virgatum	switchgrass	1944
Cheyenne	Sorghastrum nutans	indiangrass	1945
Mandan	Elymus Canadensis	Canada wildrye	1946
Kaw	Andropogon gerardii	big bluestem	1950
Nordan	Agropyron desertorum	crested wheatgrass	1953

Cooper, William S. and Abraham D. Stoesz 1931. The subterranean organs of *Helianthus scaberrimus*. *Bulletin of the Torrey Botanical Club*, Vol. 58, No. 2 (Feb., 1931), pp. 67-72

Challenge

There is every reason to believe that Dr. Stoesz did an outstanding job as Regional Nursery Manager, but that was peanuts compared to the challenge he would face between 1953 and 1955.

The position of SCS Chief Robert Salter (November 1952 - November 1953) relative to the observational nurseries was unclear prior to the 1953 congressional hearings.[619] Chief Salter, in hearings with the House or representatives Agricultural Subcommittee did present a persuasive argument for saving the observational nurseries. Helms records that "SCS did not seem to protest the loss of the production function, but the nursery staff and cooperators in (Soil Conservation) Districts certainly wanted to continue the testing and selection functions."[620] As J. C. Dykes, Assistant Chief said after the fact, "It was necessary to determine what we could salvage."[621]

Figure 9.17 Dr. Stoesz shown in his final years as National PM Specialist.

Following the statement by Dr. Salter there was an exchange of questions and answers including how many observational nurseries would be required and how much it would cost. Salter's reply was eight nurseries which would cost about $525,000 plus some other costs including $120,000 for one man each in the regional offices and one in the Washington office.[622] Thus the position of National Plant Materials Specialist became a reality.

In the final analysis it was Congress that salvaged the observation studies.[623] H. Carl Andersen, chairman of the House Subcommittee on Agricultural Appropriations, wrote to Agriculture Secretary Benson on July 30, 1953, stating the committee's position that essential observational work be continued.

So, in 1954 Dr. Abraham D. Stoesz was named the first Chief of what was becoming the Plant Materials Program in the SCS. He had ten PMCs, a little different than the congressional testimony indicated. Five were to be operated by SCS and five by a mishmash of cooperators.

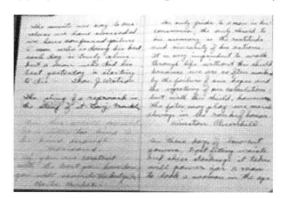

Figure 9.18 Dr. Stoesz was a copious note taker. A typical note book page is provided above, taken from an Abraham D. Stoesz collection at the National Agricultural Library.

The Results

We cannot be sure of the entire role Dr. Stoesz played during the transitional period between 1953 and 1955. Nevertheless, he was given the leadership of what had been salvaged.

The success or failure of that may be the best measure of his accomplishments. Let us start by looking at what the facilities for evaluating conservation plants were immediately before and immediately after the nursery closings, what the program was when Dr. Stoesz retired in 1964, and what it is today.

There were twenty-four nurseries conducting observational studies in 1952. Ten survived the upheaval. By the time Dr. Stoesz retired in 1964, two of the five PMCs operated by cooperators had returned to SCS operation, Big Flats and Tucson. All centers enjoyed some modest upward adjustment in all their budgets. Of greater significance, seven new or reopened centers were authorized with federal funding. Many contributed to this effort, but the support and guidance from Dr. Stoesz, and the success of the existing ten gave evidence of his leadership. The new ones were as follows:

- Reopened Arcadia, FL in 1957, which later moved to Brooksville.

- Reopened Astoria, OR in 1957 at Corvallis.

- Opened new at Maui, HI, 1957, later moved to Ho'olehua

- Reopened Albuquerque, NM in 1957 at Los Lunas.

- Opened new at East Lansing, MI, 1958.

- Opened new at Bridger, MT, 1959.

- Reopened on Coffeeville, MS, 1960.

By 2010 there were twenty-seven PMCs, twenty-five of which were operated by NRCS, and they could boast a seventy year (1935 – 2005) cost-benefit ratio of 3.65.[624]

Based on that evaluation, Dr. Stoesz would go to the head of the class. Maybe he was motivated by the story of the Boyce Thompson Arboretum in the Arizona desert, created by Dr. Franklin Crider, that "it became so successful...that the federal government saw a need of replicating it many times over the United States."[625]

Summary

The success or failure of maneuvering through the pitfalls of closing twenty-four large nurseries and opening eighteen PMCs in eleven years depends on multiple ideas, and decisions and actions made by multiple people. However, success will hinge on the quality of the guidance provided by the leader. That was Dr. Stoesz. He was the man for the times.

Donald S. Douglas – Major Contributor

PMC Manager,
Field Plant Materials Specialist,
Regional Plant Materials Specialist,
National Plant Materials Specialist

Donald S. Douglas first entered Federal service in 1935 as an SCS employee with the Civilian Conservation Corps at Goldendale, WA as an agronomist, and later at the CCC camp at Yakima, WA. He joined the staff of the Pullman PMC in 1947 as the agronomist. He served in this position for about three years, and then became manager of the Aberdeen PMC in 1950. Don left the manager's position in 1957 to become a plant materials specialist in Idaho. He held this position until 1960.

During Don's years at the Aberdeen PMC he and his staff received national recognition for their outstanding work. In 1958 the PMC received a USDA Superior Service Award, a year after Don moved from PMC manager to plant materials specialist. There can be no doubt, however, that his leadership had a great deal to do with the PMC receiving the Award. The following is taken from the History of the Aberdeen PMC.[626]

The Award for Superior Service

On June 20, 1958, members of the Aberdeen Plant Materials Center Staff were presented with a Superior Service Award from USDA and Secretary of Agriculture Ezra Taft Benson. Harold E. Tower, SCS western field representative, Washington, D.C., made the presentation during ceremonies at the Center.

The citation read: "For developing a run-down farm into an efficient unit producing new and improved plant materials, providing leadership in seed increase, and intensive use of these materials in Idaho, Utah and Nevada.

In the tradition of Hafenrichter and Schwendiman, Douglas knew the importance of publishing his works. While at Pullman and Aberdeen he did just that, which is included in Appendix 2.

Two new cultivars were released from Aberdeen while Don was manager and two others shortly after his departure. They are shown in Table 9.7.

Douglas was the plant materials specialist in Idaho for only three years, moving on to Milwaukee, WI in 1960 to become a Washington-Field Plant Materials Technician. He remained in this position for five years before replacing Dr. Abraham Stoesz as the second Chief PMT in Washington D.C. Don arrived in Washington in 1965, finding a stable budget and seventeen operating PMCs. He provided strong leadership while in this position, solidifying the gains made by Dr. Stoesz, and improving the overall budget. The Quicksand PMC was authorized during his tenure in this position, and the Bismarck PMC returned to SCS operations.

Table 9.7 Great releases with a close association to Douglas

Release	Common Name	Release Year
P-27	Siberian wheatgrass	1953
Sodar	streambank wheatgrass	1954
Pomar	orchardgrass	1966
Regar	meadow brome	1966

In 1970 Don returned to the West as the regional PM Specialist in Portland, from which he retired in 1974. He belonged to the American Society of Agronomy and was a lifetime member of the Society for Range Management.

The tenure of Donald S. Douglas might be considered uneventful but successful. He was anxious, with mixed success, in introducing some of the desirable approaches of the West into other parts of the country. Given the existing lack of leverage of the regional specialist, creating the the state conservationist PMC advisory committees was a major accomplishment, as well as his contributions to get the Technical Service Centers established. All were positive accomplishments.

Don stepped down at the end of 1970, and returned to the Northwest, where he completed his career, replacing another one of the Hafenrichter boys, Harold Miller, as regional PM Specialist.

Figure 9.19 Donald Douglas

313

His returning to the West regional position was reflective of his first love. Always the straight arrow of the Schwendiman mold, he retired in 1973 and lived to be ninety-five, dying in 2006.[627]

Don Douglas was cut from the same cloth as were the other Hafenrichter boys. They were ever steady, totally dedicated, and dependable to a fault. After twelve years with the Civilian Conservation Corps and twenty-seven years and six positions with the SCS, Don warrants recognition for his leadership, dedication and productivity within the Plant Materials Program.

Wilmer W. Steiner – Major Contributor

PMC Manager,
Regional Plant Materials Specialist
National Plant Materials Specialist

Early Years

Wilmer W. Steiner, known as 'Bill', joined the Soil Conservation Service prior to 1944 and in 1948 became manager of the Beltsville, Maryland Nursery.[628] Working at that location at that time would have been a great privilege because of the association with Dr. Franklin Crider. Additionally, Bill was a horticulturist, as was Dr. Crider. To the extent that it is possible to know, Bill Steiner and Dr. Crider were identical in their love of plants, conservation or otherwise.

Bill continued his management responsibilities at Beltsville throughout the nursery closing period. In 1955 he replaced C. B. Manifold as Washington Field Plant Materials Technician in Upper Darby, PA.[629] Manifold had been in the position for only a few months. Bill was replaced at the National PMC by Robert Thornton, also a horticulturist.

The Middle Years

In 1955 the Northeast was served by only one PMC. It was at Big Flats, NY, and was being operated through a cooperative agreement by the Alfred Agriculture and Technical College, sixty miles west of Big Flats. The College was using the property as a summer training farm for their agricultural students. Harry Porter, the PM Specialist for New York, was the SCS technical advisor. Curtis Sharp, an employee of the Technical College, was hired to do the on-center plant materials work.

Figure 9.20 Wilmer W. (Bill) Steiner

When Steiner first visited the Center he was disappointed to find very few selected plants or large assemblies that had been carried over from the Nursery's observational studies. They had released no plants from their beginning in 1940. There were several reasons for this. First, the Big Flats Nursery had not been blessed with the kind of long term scientists that were typical in other regions: No Paul

Tabor, Joseph Downs or John Schwendiman's existed in Big Flats. Additionally, during the nursery days there was strong resistance from the SCS regional office for Big Flats to engage in any evaluation of plants that might infringe on the role of the experiment stations. And lastly, the Northeast lacked the single focus, overriding conservation problem that could be solved with plants, such as rangeland in the west or eroding cotton land in the south. Problems abounded, such as plants for surface mine spoil reclamation, eroding streambanks, or the coastal erosion along in the Atlantic seaboard but all seemed outside the nursery vision.

When Bill arrived in the Northeast, he had four outstanding field plant materials specialists: Harry Porter, Wilson Hill, Marshall Augustine and Joseph Ruffner. With these four, plus Sharp at Big Flats, Bill soon began to turn the Northeast program around. By 1961 they released 'Cardinal' autumn olive and in 1964 'Chemung' crownvetch.

It may be worth noting that personality wise, Bill and A. L. Hafenrichter, his counterpart in the west, had absolutely nothing in common. Sometimes it was hard to get Bill to make his point, always fearful of offending someone. Instead, he worked in quiet ways, rarely raising his voice, but winning the day through logic, gentle persuasion and a pleasing personality.

A long term plan seemed to have evolved in Bill's mind as a way to accelerate the program in the Northeast. First was to get a person hired at Big Flats who was dedicated to conservation plant evaluations. This was accomplished with the employment of Sharp in 1957. Next was to get the operation of Big Flats back under the wing of SCS. This was accomplished by April 1, 1960.

Bill recognized that neither the coastal erosion problem nor the surface mine spoil erosion problem could be well served from Big Flats. So, on both fronts he initiated the effort to establish two new PMCs. Bill's quiet ways, consistency, and knowing where and when to apply the pressure, resulted in one being authorized in southern New Jersey in 1965 and another in eastern Kentucky in 1967.

In 1970, five years after opening, the first release was made from the Cape May Center, 'Cape' American beachgrass, and it was a blockbuster. However Bill was less than happy with the Quicksand PMC, being particularly unhappy with its location. That situation was corrected long after Bill retired. When it did happen, it was moved to Bill's initial selection site in West Virginia.

Final Years

Following the departure of Donald Douglas from the National PM Specialist position in 1970, Bill replaced him. Unfortunately, soon after his arrival in Washington he learned he had an incurable cancer. Nevertheless, he was able to implement a national uniform accession numbering procedure, to be used by all PMCs and other parts of USDA. While he continued as best as his condition would allow, he retired at the end of 1973, and died soon after.

Bill can be honored for his beloved personality, consistent demeanor and steady performance, which served the Plant Materials Program extremely well for twenty seven years.

Paul Tabor and John Powell – Major Contributors

Assistant Nursery Agronomist,	Junior Horticulturist
Regional Nursery Horticulturalist,	Nursery Manager
Nursery Director	Nursery Director
Plant Materials Specialist	Plant Materials Center Manager

Introduction

In the 1930s there were millions of acres of eroding, abandoned cotton land and other farm land in the Piedmont and Coastal Plain states of the South. While the Dust Bowl of the 1930s provided a major thrust for the creation of the Soil Conservation Service, Dr. Hugh Hammond Bennett, the "Father of Conservation" observed the need to be just as great in his native North Carolina. The great opportunity to become 'conservation heroes' within a new agency beckoned Paul Tabor and John Powell.

Paul Tabor was born in Danielsville, Georgia in 1893 and received a Master's Degree from the University of Georgia in 1915. After several years work as extension agent, pilot in WW II, and Professor of Agronomy at the Georgia State College of Agriculture, he became a project agronomist for the Sandy Creek Demonstration Project with the Soil Erosion Service. In 1935 he joined the SCS, and in 1938 moved to the regional office in Spartanburg, South Carolina as Assistant Regional Nurseryman in charge of the observational studies in Region 2 nurseries.[630] He continued in this position until the nurseries closed in 1953; then he became a plant materials specialist, located in Athens, GA. The overall thrust of his career was to determine what agronomic practices and plants could best be used to reduce soil erosion in the South, and how to get them into use.

John Powell was born in North Carolina in 1911 and graduated in the early 1930s from Furman University, SC with a botany degree. He started his nursery/plant materials career in 1936 as a junior horticulturist at the SCS nursery at High Point, NC. In 1937 he moved to the Americus, GA nursery, and soon became the manager. He served in this position until the nursery closed in 1953 except for a stint as a naval officer in the Pacific during World War II.[631]

When the Americus Nursery closed in 1953, it soon reopened as the Americus PMC, operated by the University of Georgia with SCS financial and technical help. John just changed employers. This

316

cooperative agreement with the University lasted until 1975 when the PMC returned to SCS operations, and John returned as manager. He remained in this position until his retirement in 1982, serving as manager of Americus for about forty-five years. John died in 1992.

To dramatize how bad the erosion had been during pre-SCS days, John loved to take nursery and PMC visitors out into the rolling Piedmont to show them what he called the "Canyons of Georgia". They were monstrous gullies that had formed over the past seventy-five to one hundred years on abandoned cotton land, several times deeper than his visitors were tall.

Contributions

The horrendous erosion problem that conservationists found in the south resulted from an abundance of land and 150 years of abusive farming practices. The farmers removed the protective forest cover and grew cotton until the first two or three soil horizons were gone, and then they moved on to another piece of land. When Paul Tabor, John Powell and others first viewed the task of healing the canyons they unfortunately found that the ecosystems of the Southeast had not evolved plants that could deal with such a situation. When the farms were abandoned, natural revegetation did not happen and the soil remained bare for decades.

Back at the nurseries, John and other managers were evaluating every native tree, shrub, and the few native forbs and grasses that were available, but no magic or near-magic bullet was found. So what to do? Paul and John had been casting around for introduced plants, as well as the natives. They had many candidates.

Foremost among these candidates was bahiagrass, *Paspalum notatum*. The early beginning of this exotic grass is thus recorded as a quote from county agent E. H. Finlayson, of Pensacola, Florida, in 1941:

> Because it was distributed around the old Perdido Wharf (destroyed in 1926) and had not been observed in other places, he suggested that it had been introduced in ballast dumped in the low land adjacent to the wharf before it was destroyed. Named Pensacola Bahia and believing the grass had pasture potential, Finlayson and Paul Tabor, of the Soil Conservation Service, began to promote it as an improved pasture grass for the Deep South. The excellent seeding habits, aggressiveness, persistence, and adaptation of 'Pensacola' Bahia helped the Soil Conservation Service to spread it widely in Florida and the Coastal Plain of adjacent states. Today, it occupies well over a million acres, where it has been planted and hundreds of acres where it has been unintentionally spread by man and beast. It is generally recognized as a good pasture grass, an excellent road-shoulder grass, and a serious pest in lawns and fine turf. There is good reason to believe that 'Pensacola' bahiagrass is now so well distributed and so well adapted that it will soon be found wherever grass grows in the deep south, whether man planted it or not.[632]

Based on additional research by Burton, 'Pensacola' Bahia may have reached Pensacola, Florida, in a sea-borne cargo ship from Argentina prior to 1926.

A second plant, adapted further north, is currently known as 'Ky-31' tall fescue, *Schedonorus phoenix*. Although this plant is adapted and used widely in the U.S., its path to wide spread use also went through Paul Tabor. The following is quoted from page 59 of the *History of Soil and Water Conservation in North Carolina.*[633]

> In the early years (nursery) work was centered on the production of pine seedlings, kudzu, bicolor lespedeza, and a variety of shrubs and trees. Later as the SCS began to extend its work...to farm pasture and cropland, better grasses and legumes were needed. The period was marked by the discovery, successful testing, and large scale

317

increase of 'Ky-31' tall fescue and…Bahiagrass. Paul Tabor, the eminent SCS regional agronomist, was instrumental in spreading the use of both plants. In 1943 he purchased sixty pounds of tall fescue seed from Mr. Suiter, a Kentucky farmer who had found this unusual grass growing near his farm pond and had started increasing the seed supply. Mr. Tabor's purchase represented the entire supply available in 1943. Half of the seed was sent to a SCS nursery in South Carolina and the remaining thirty pounds went to the Chapel Hill nursery. That fall it was used to establish the first planting of tall fescue in the state.

It is interesting to note that during these years Kentucky grew certified seed from seed produced in Chapel Hill. For four or five years, North Carolina officials would not certify the original 'Ky-31' fescue at Chapel Hill mainly because of the North Carolina State University's negative attitude toward this grass.

So, how important were the two exotic grasses introduced and widely tested by SCS throughout the south? Let the words Hugh Hammond Bennett, the fighter of the good fight, sum up his opinion of the two, Suiter's grass and 'Pensacola'. He wrote this in 1949 in response to an inquiry from an SCS employee asking what he might write for a paper on "Just how do the SCS Nurseries contribute to the Soil and Moisture Conservation Program."[634]

In a paper such as Heath has in mind it would be too bad not to bring out that the observational (Nursery) work…has undoubtedly advanced our range and pasture work in the U.S. more than anything that has ever been done in this direction.

H. H Bennett

At a special ceremony of the Soil Conservation Society of America in 1980, Paul Tabor was honored for his life's work in conservation.[635] A part of the citation reads as follows:

Tabor personally collected over 1,000 plant accessions for SCS, about one-half as many as all other southeastern SCS nursery personnel combined. He is credited for the development of two major new soil conserving crops for the Southeast - tall fescue and Pensacola bahiagrass. Today (1980) over five million acres in the South are planted to Pensacola for pasture and conservation.

By 2005 'Pensacola' bahiagrass, which was certified for commercial production in Georgia through the efforts of the Americus PMC, had contributed $31,202,000 through it ecological and commercial value to the economy of the south.[636] It is currently used extensively on the type of soils cotton farmers were abandoning in the nineteenth and early twentieth century. The potential value of Suiter's grass, or 'Ky-31' tall fescue, had been recognized before Tabor came on the scene, but he initiated its explosive use for converting highly eroding land back into pasture production.

Over the years the Americus PMC, under the direction of John Powell, and with the University of Georgia agronomists, has continued the evaluation of 'Pensacola' for cattle forage. Other important work by the PMC has resulted in the release of 'Dove' proso millet for wildlife use and 'Amclo' arrowleaf clover for cattle forage. Today 'Dove' is a widely used dove food, and of course 'Pensacola' bahiagrass is one of the dominant forage grasses in much of the coastal plain of the Southeastern U. S, particularly on less productive soils.[637] Paul Tabor also contributes to the environmental resurrection of abandoned farm land in the south through his educational and publication efforts, shown in Appendix 2. He also salvaged conservation related papers in the Southeast in:

Collection Number MS2163 of papers, notebooks, pictures, etc. of the Soil Conservation Service, Region 2 Regional Nursery Division, housed in the Hargrett Library, University of Georgia, Athens, GA.

Summary

Paul Tabor was one of that rare breed of people that could see the big picture, and combined scientific inquiry with the ability to get the job done. During his early career he saw what careless farming practices had wrought. While his contributions to soil and water conservation were varied and many, in the span of a couple decades he steered the use of two obscure grasses, in the words of H. H. Bennett, into "rapidly solving the problem...by fitting the various grasses...into the right places." Today some of their luster may have vanished, as a result of the 'native only' mania. Fortunately, Paul did not wait for the evolution of a Bahiagrass or tall fescue type plants in the southeast. Society today is the benefactor of their foresight.

The contributions of John Powell and the Americus PMC were critically important to the required research that made 'Pensacola' and other plants valuable conservation tools. John's forty-plus years had, and continue to have a huge payoff. His legacy will be long lived.

Erling T Jacobson – Major Contributor

PMC Agronomist,
PMC Manager,
Plant Materials Specialist,
Regional Plant Materials Specialist

Introduction

Erling T. Jacobson was born and raised on a farm in Deuel County, South Dakota.[638] He served in the US Army Air Section, 1953-55. Upon returning home, he utilized the benefits of the GI Bill to earn a Bachelor of Science Degree in 1958 from the University of Minnesota and went on to graduate studies in Plant Science. His professional career began with a training position for the Soil Conservation Service at Redfield, South Dakota in 1961. A strong interest in plants led him to a position at the PMC in Elsberry, Missouri as a Soil Conservationist.

Figure 9.21 Erling Jacobson

Manager, Manhattan, KS Plant Materials Center

Erling transferred to the PMC at Manhattan, Kansas, as Manager in 1965. For the previous twelve years the Center had been operated through a cooperative agreement with the Kansas State Agricultural Experiment Station. Erling gradually transformed the appearance and productiveness of the Center into a place that reflected pride, professionalism, and production. This was accomplished by the hard work of the PMC staff, and Erling's leadership. Plant Materials Specialist Robert T. Lippert provided technical support for the states served by the center.

With enthusiasm Erling continued the evaluation of all ongoing projects. Soon, however, he and Lippert initiated a program change to broaden the magnitude through increasing the number of species and the methodology used to evaluate them. Heretofore the emphasis had been primarily on

319

range grasses. Many of the new species were forbs, some of which were nitrogen producing legumes, and most had beautiful flowers. All were native to the rangeland flora and could be used for this purpose. Interest in their use was growing, with national emphasis being provided by Ladybird Johnson's promotion of wildflowers. This had a profound and positive effect on the Manhattan program for several years.

While manager, Erling developed a standard format for evaluating non-grass components of the native prairie, which has been used extensively by other PMCs and other agencies.[639] Of greater importance were the eleven new plants placed on the market for which Erling had either completed or initiated and completed the evaluation, or had left to be completed by his successor. He, like most new managers, benefited from the good work of his predecessors. Six cultivars went into commercial production during his stay and five additional ones followed shortly after his departure. The eleven are shown in Table 9.8.

Table 9.8 Releases Associated with Jacobson as Manager

Cultivar	Common Name	Year Released
Barton	western wheatgrass	1970
Caucasian	Caucasian bluestem	1972
Pink Lady	winterberry euonymus	1973
PMK-24	eastern gamagrass	1974
Eureka	thickspike gayfeather	1975
Kaneb	purple prairieclover	1975
Nekan	pitcher sage	1977
Prairie Gold	Maximilian sunflower	1978
Sunglow	grayhead prairie coneflower	1978
Cimarron	little bluestem	1979
Konza	aromatic sumac	1980

The process mentioned above is included in

Jacobson, E. T. 1974. The evaluation, selection, and increase of prairie wildflowers for conservation beautification. In Wali, M. K., Prairie: A multiple view. American Prairie Conf. No. 4, Grand Forks, ND, University of North Dakota Press. P. .349-404.

Plant Materials Specialist, Bismarck, North Dakota

In 1975 Erling transferred to the Plant Materials Specialist position at Bismarck, North Dakota. He replaced John McDermand. Here, he provided technical direction to the Bismarck PMC in their program of developing native grass and other cultivars for the Northern Great Plains. Shortly after his arrival in Bismarck, he developed a project plan for the Bismarck PMC in cooperation with the ARS Mandan Research Center to collect large assemblies of western wheatgrass and blue grama throughout western North and South Dakota. His experience in Manhattan provided the Center with the leadership and interagency coordination required to make this ambitious undertaking a success. The success of this project was later followed by the Bismarck PMC using similar techniques to make large assemblies of big and little bluestem and other species.

Following the assembly and selection of superior plants, large scale, replicated field evaluation plantings were conducted at a total of six locations in Minnesota, North Dakota, and South Dakota where extensive evaluations were conducted for six to ten years. Procedures evolving from this proved useful for future use by other PMCs and other agencies.

Because of the multidisciplinary application of this work, it has been published and widely used. A summary was first presented at the 1984 Prairie Conference at the Tallgrass Prairie Center in Cedar Falls, IA. Other publications relating to this work are in Appendix 2.

A 66-page booklet published in 2010 by USDA, NRCS, Bismarck, ND, titled *Grasses for the Northern Plains: Growth Patterns, Forage Characteristics, and Wildlife Values (Vol. I and II)* by Kevin K. Sedivec, Dwight A. Tober, Wayne L. Duckwitz, David D. Dewald, and Jeffrey L. Printz also used the performance data from these six sites. The latter publication, because of its blue cover and popularity, has come to be called the "blue book" and is the standard guide in seeding grasslands in the northern plains.

New performance information obtained from these studies created a baseline for species and variety adaptation recommendations for the region, and supporting documentation for the final release of five new warm-season grass cultivars. They are listed in Table 9.9.

Table 9.9 Major new grass cultivars for the Northern Great Plains

Cultivar	Common Name	Year Released
Dacotah	Switchgrass	1989
Bison	big bluestem	1989
Bonilla	big bluestem	1987
Forestburg	Switchgrass	1987
Tomahawk	Indiangrass	1988

Improved trees and shrubs for shelterbelt programs in the Northern Great Plains was also a high priority of the plant materials program. Erling and the PMC staff, working with Agricultural Research Service windbreak geneticist Dr. Richard Cunningham, made many large provenance seed collections of trees and carried out extensive plantation type evaluations. Resulting from this effort, and associated woody plant evaluations for joint shelterbelt and wildlife use, several important tree and shrub cultivars were cooperatively released. They are shown in Table 9.10.

Table 9.10 Major new woody plant cultivars for the Northern Great Plains

Cultivar	Common Name	Year Released
Cardan	green ash	1979
Oahe	Hackberry	1982
Sakakawea	silver buffaloberry	1984
Scarlet	Mongolian cherry	1984
Centennial	Cotoneaster	1987
Regal	Russian almond	1989
McDermand	Ussurian pear	1990
Homestead	Arnold hawthorn	1993

Regional Plant Materials Specialist

Erling accepted the Regional Plant Materials Specialist position at Lincoln, Nebraska in 1984. He provided technical leadership for the next ten years to four PMCs in the region. While in Bismarck he had developed a strong working relationship with Ducks Unlimited Canada and this carried over into his new regional position. Ducks Unlimited Canada had initiated a major native reseeding effort, primarily in the Canadian Prairie Provinces, and was developing a native plant collection and release program. Erling's assistance was invaluable. A publication he co-authored is having a major impact on native plant revegetation activities. It is

Jacobson, E. T., D. B. Wark, R. G. Arnott and D. A. Tober. 1994. Sculptured seeding: An ecological approach to revegetation. Restoration and Management Notes. 12:46-50.

Erling participated in the publishing of additional articles by virtue of his participation in work with other authors. They are also listed in Appendix 2.

Summary

The Society for Range Management in 1992 presented Erling with the Outstanding Achievement Award for technical support to Great Plains PMCs and for sharing technical expertise with scientist in China, the Soviet Union, and Canada. He was presented the Lifetime Achievement Award, sponsored by Ducks Unlimited of Canada, for "Advancing technology in establishment and management of native grasses, and fostering technical exchange across the border."

Erling retired in 1994. During his thirty-five years of service characterized by creativity and cooperation, he found ways for controlling Great Plains erosion, beautifying the landscape and providing wildlife habitat with plants that will stand as an inspiration to others.

Joseph D. Ruffner – Major Contributor

Work Unit Conservationist
Field Plant Materials Specialist
Regional Plant Materials Specialist

Background

Joseph Ruffner was a Work Unit Conservationist in WV for many years before he joined the plant materials ranks.[640] Joe replaced Frank Glover as the plant materials technician in WV in 1955. Frank had been making plantings since 1946, and was truly a pioneer in surface mine revegetation.[641] Joe's service area included WV, western PA, southwest VA, and the eastern parts of OH and KY. He knew what new plant technology was needed in his service area; stabilizing surface mine spoil was the first, second and third priority.

Figure 9.22 Joseph Ruffner

Challenge

In the 1950s, and for years before, coal was king in Appalachia, and restrictions on how to mine or what to do with the spoil once mined were all but non-existent. Nor were there any requirements for revegetation. Joe told of the frequent times he would seek help from SCS field office personnel and others; they told him he was wasting his time. "Those sites will never be replanted" was a common response. He recalled on one occasion he was carrying a fifty pound bag of fertilizer up a slope too steep to traverse by vehicle, when a local resident asked what he was doing. Joe told him and the neighbor responded, "What damn fool would be doing a thing like that?"

Products

It was a challenge but Joe thought he was up to it. Identifying the most appropriate plants to test was the first step. Native Americans had not created such conditions as the mine spoil, and no plants for growing on that sort of land had evolved. In nearly all of the densely forested regions of the East, the kinds of herbaceous, ground covering plants that are desirable to stop erosion and cover mine spoil, and allow the re-invasion of natives, did not exist. That combined with the acidic, low moisture holding spoil made the task more than challenging.

Joe assembled every possible plant he felt might have a chance at stabilizing the spoil, including non-native and native plants. Of course, all the native trees, most of the shrubs and the few native grasses were included. The total number of different species tested was 290, plus several collections of most species. Once the plants to test was resolved, subsets of the collections were planted in eight different Major Land Resource Areas, and on three levels of spoil quality; very acid, acid and slightly acid. Collectively, there were twenty-four site types, and potentially multiple collections of 290 species per site. To be able to make knowledgeable recommendations, such a magnitude of testing over several years was essential.

By the early 1960s the Big Flats PMC had released two plants Joe could use, 'Cardinal' autumn olive and 'Chemung' crownvetch. 'Arnot' bristly locust soon followed. Joe's tests identified other desirable species as well, like the native black locust, European black alder, and sericea lespedeza for use in more southern locations. More promising plants were on the way from Joe's tests and PMC evaluations: deer tongue, the only native grass with promise, and flat pea. Both were released in the early 1970s. Tall fescue was a consistent, short-lived grass useful as a nurse plant in a mixture.[642] Other plants showed promise but had problems, like tall oatgrass. Needless to say, cultural establishment studies proceeded along with the species testing.

It is interesting to note of the plants mentioned above, only deer tongue and tall fescue do not produce nitrogen, and the only natives are black locust and deer tongue. Actually, the autumn olive is such a prolific producer of both seed and nitrogen, even on acid spoil, it has become a pest.

Success breeds success. As Joe's work continued, and the body of knowledge grew, by the mid-1960s it became more acceptable to commit resources to re-vegetating mine spoil. Mine soil stabilization became believable. Others joined the hunt. State Experiment Stations and Federal Agencies with land holdings in Appalachia joined the effort as a national consciousness about destroying the landscape gained strength. Their efforts built on the foundation Joe had and was building. By the late 1960s he didn't feel so much like the lone wolf.

Figure 9.23 Joe among his plots at an outlying nursery

One most notable publication

Ruffner, Joseph D. 1978. Plant Performance on Surface Coal Mine Spoil in the Eastern United States. USDA, SCS; SCS-TP-155. Washington, D.C.

New responsibilities

In 1970 Joe was promoted to the Northeast Regional PM Specialist position, from which he could continue some direction of the mine spoil effort. In 1974 he retired. Once the position that he had vacated was filled, Joe offered to become a volunteer, which he continued for fifteen years. One of the first tasks as a volunteer was to summarize and publish his and Frank Glover's twenty years of knowledge about stabilizing surface mine land.[643] His publication coincided with the passage of the 1977 Surface Mining Act, requiring that all such lands, including abandoned mine land, be returned to as near as possible their original vegetative condition.[644] Thanks to Joe and others the plant technology for accomplishing this was in place.

Summary

The magnitude of Ruffner's contribution to surface mine reclamation is impossible to measure. He, like many SCS plant materials persons, toiled alone until a foothold was gained, bringing encouragement for others to join. We can be sure that there is no plant being used today that did not show up numerous times in the thousands of plots Joe scattered across Appalachia. It had been tried and retried, planted and replanted, tested and retested, until Joe knew if it could play a stabilization role. The tall oatgrass mentioned above was one grass he planted and replanted and knew it would work if its limitations could be resolved. It is pleasing to note the naming and release in 2009 by the Alderson, WV PMC of a tall oatgrass cultivar, named 'Ruffner'.[645]

As we survey the sweep of re-vegetative history of surface mine spoil, Joe might think, and with some justifiable satisfaction, "Maybe I wasn't such a damn fool after all."

Robert D. Lippert – Major Contributor

**Work Unit Conservationist,
Plant Materials Specialist**

Background

Soon after the Soil Conservation Service came into existence in 1935 a production nursery was located at Manhattan, Kansas. It concentrated on the collection and production of native grasses and forbs that might help harness the raging dust storms. In association with production, the nursery carried out a vigorous observational studies program. Typical of other nurseries, Manhattan had its core of outstanding agronomists, including Lawrence C. Newell, Donald R. Cornelius, and M. Donald Atkins; the latter two serving in the quest for outstanding conservation plants their entire career.

With the closing of the nursery program in 1953-54 old employees were scattered and new ones appeared. With the closing, the observational studies became the Manhattan Plant Materials Center. Initially it was operated by the Kansas State University, Agriculture Experiment Station, with funding and technical assistance from SCS. The first manager was Clarence Swallow, an employee of the Experiment Station. From 1953 to 1957, M. Donald Atkins and other SCS employees provided technical assistance to the PMC operations.

Figure 9.24 Robert (Bob) Lippert

Robert D. Lippert was a SCS Work Unit Conservationist in 1950 in Meade County, Kansas.[646] He transferred to the SCS Area Office in Hays, Kansas as a Plant Materials Technician in 1953, serving northwestern Kansas, and in 1957 he became PMT for all of Kansas, Oklahoma and Nebraska. This location also allowed him to provide technical assistance to the PMC, while carrying out a field testing program in his three-state service area. Although lacking in the technical training of his peers, Bob quickly developed a network of cooperation with Agricultural Experiment Stations and others interested in conservation plants, which paid dividends for years to come.

324

Lippert and Jacobson Become a Team

To a great extent Lippert was the Plant Materials Program in Kansas, Nebraska and Oklahoma until 1965, when the cooperative agreement with Kansas State was terminated and SCS resumed operations of the Manhattan PMC. Erling T. Jacobson was selected as the first manager. When Erling arrived additional staff was employed, new buildings were constructed, and equipment was purchased to make the center fully functional. Bob filled a key role in accelerating the PMC program following the transition to SCS operations. The program was revitalized by Bob and Erling.

A major contribution was Bob's leadership in identifying plant materials needs and priorities and incorporating them into a long range plan for the PMC. The plan he developed envisioned making large assemblies of plants in the late 1960s and early 1970s, followed by PMC evaluation and final testing of the selected accessions. This effort was launched across the multi-state region, which Bob directed, and indeed made many collections himself.

It is evident from the following list that Bob and Erling were creating an ambitious undertaking. All of the 'Wildflowers' listed below do indeed have attractive flowers. They are also native forbs which make up a portion of the rangeland flora. Consequently, their collection represents a potential use beyond the beautification component. Through Bob's leadership and his excellent working relationships with the SCS field staff in the three states where he worked, the following fourteen major native plant assemblies were made:

- Grass collections of;
  - blue grama
  - buffalo grass

- Wildflower collections, somewhat in response to Lady Bird Johnson's highway beautification program;
  - thickspike gayfeather,
  - purple prairieclover,
  - pitcher sage,
  - Maximilian sunflower,
  - grayhead prairie coneflower,
  - false sunflower,
  - Illinois bundleflower,
  - partridge pea,

- Woody plant collections of;
  - bur oak,
  - aromatic sumac,
  - American plum
  - hackberry

These assemblies proved very successful, providing fresh new plants for the initial evaluation phase and selected material for Bob to use in his final testing program. Through the close and hard working relationship between Bob and Erling, several new cultivars were soon made ready for release.

One key to the success of getting the new releases on the market was Bob's close working relationship with several commercial seed growers. Over the years they had come to have a high level of respect for his technical ability, and when the time came for the PMC to put a new plant on the market they accepted it anxiously, knowing it would be high quality and a money maker. Sharp Brothers Seed Company, Healy, KS; Miller Seed Company, Lincoln, NE; Wilson Seed Company, Polk, and Stock Seed Company, Murdock, NE were among those he worked with.

Another area which contributed to the success of the Manhattan PMC program was the excellent relations Bob had developed with the agricultural university communities throughout Kansas, Nebraska and Oklahoma. Among Bob's strong supporters were Dr. Kling Anderson and Dr. Frank Barnet of Kansas State University; Dr. Robert Ahring and Dr. Charles Taliaferro of Oklahoma State University; Dr. L. C. Newell and Dr. Satero Salac of the University of Nebraska; Walter Bagley, a windbreak forester at the University of Nebraska and Dr. Jerry Tomanek from Fort Hays State University in Hays, Kansas. All the tools were in place for an exceptional period of new conservation plant development.

The End Product

The Manhattan PMC has an admirable list of new cultivars that have reached the commercial market. The guidance supplied by Bob Lippert paved the way for many of them. The assemblies he initiated along with Erling Jacobson led directly to the release of several. It is for sure that the release and success of all of the following, Table 9.11, were influenced positively by Bob.

Table 9.11 Releases Influenced by Bob Lippert's Guidance

Cultivar Name	Common Name	Release Year
Osage	Indiangrass	1966
Barton	western wheatgrass	1970
Bend	sand lovegrass	1971
Pink Lady	winterberry euonymus	1973
Texoka	buffalo grass	1974
Eureka	thickspike gayfeather	1975
Kaneb	purple prairieclover	1975
Nekan	pitcher sage	1977
Prairie Gold	Maximilian sunflower	1978
Sunglow	grayhead prairie coneflower	1978
Cimarron	little bluestem	1979
Konza	aromatic sumac	1980
Midas	false sunflower	1984
Pete	eastern gamagrass	1988
Pronghorn	prairie sandreed	1988
Lippert	bur oak	1994
Kanoka	roundhead lespedeza	1998

To accomplish what he did required long weeks. Leaving early Monday morning, traveling across one or more states, evaluating plantings, collecting seed or plants, or conducting a workshop; he would return to the PMC late Friday, drop off collected materials and to prepare for the following week. He was always enthusiastic about what he had seen the week past, and what he would be seeing the next week. These work habits help explain the magnitude of his accomplishments.

Summary

Bob retired in 1977. Travel anywhere across Kansas, Nebraska or Oklahoma and you will most likely see a plant in the landscape that Bob Lippert helped develop. Bob was an example to all other plant materials employees for his excellence in leadership, building relations, and dedication to the program.

Marshall Augustine – Major Contributor

Plant Materials Specialist

Introduction

Marshall Augustine, or Augie as he was known, was one of those rare persons who carried with him an air of self-confidence and invincibility.[647] Whatever Augie did or wherever Augie went he created an environment of opportunity. Augie always had his eyes open for erosion problems that could be solved with vegetation, and he figured out how to get it done, both technically and administratively.

Figure 9.25 Marshall Augustine

Augie joined the Soil Conservation Service in the late 1930s, and worked for more than twenty years at various field offices and the SCS State Office in Maryland. In 1954, because of his well-known love for plants and how to use them in conservation work, he was selected as the plant materials specialist serving New Jersey, Delaware, Maryland and the eastern part of Virginia.

Building a Reputation

Some years prior to 1953, Augie was working in the counties of Southern Maryland; the area that lies east of the Potomac River and west of the Chesapeake Bay. As an SCS employee providing assistance to Soil Conservation District Cooperators, he frequently encountered the massive erosion problem common in that area, as well as throughout the mid-Atlantic region. It was commonly referred to as tidal shoreline erosion. Augie could see where vegetation was stabilizing some of the shoreline, but other areas with similar characteristics were still eroding. He saw this erosion as bad but something plants might help solve. He knew that SCS had broad responsibilities for soil erosion, but he also knew that addressing tidal shoreline erosion was a no-no because it was "turf" belonging to the U.S. Army Corps of Engineers. Nevertheless, he said, "Let us make a few plantings just to see what would happen," and based on the outcome advised landowners on what they might do.

Chief Hugh Bennett liked to come to Maryland to view conservation progress and to enjoy fellowship with district supervisors. Marshall told an amusing episode that happened during one of these visits. A farmer in Southern Maryland told Hugh how much he appreciated Augie helping to solve his shoreline erosion problem. Augie could see the redness beginning to spread round the Chief's big neck and face. He merely replied that Augie was typical of all his high quality employees. Later, when they were alone, Augie said, "The Chief put his big hands around my neck and bellowed, 'Augustine, if I ever hear of you working on shore erosion again I'll fire you on the spot!" A few days later, Augie received a phone call from Ed Davis, Maryland's State Conservationist. Mr. Davis told Augie that the Chief had called him about a Congressman having a shoreline erosion problem on land he owned in Southern Maryland and wondered if Augie might stop around and take a look at it. Then Mr. Davis added, "But Augie, if you get into trouble, I'll deny I ever called you about this."[648]

When Augie became the plant materials specialist he had moved out of providing advice about tidal shoreline erosion control and into the evaluation of a solution. From this position he launched a crusade.

His Passion and Legacy

Augie was a seven days a week PM Specialist. Located in College Park, MD he had limited assistance from the Big Flats, NY PMC which served his area. He did the best he could without PMC assistance; running his test plots close to home so he could get to them on weekends.

One of his most endearing passions was sand dune stabilization along the mid-Atlantic coast. Wherever he went he promoted the idea that well vegetated sand dunes were the best protection against storms. Specific contributions in this area included proving that dunes could be vegetated more quickly and better by using first, fertilizer, and second, fertilizer containing magnesium. Another innovation included the initiation of the commercial production of American beachgrass, as contrasted to robbing one sand dune to plant another. Without a doubt, his promoting sand dune stabilization value through his work contributed to the establishment of the Cape May PMC.

His passion for sand dune work is conveyed by two experiences.

1.   Bill Steiner was the regional PM Specialist in the 1950s and 1960s in the area where Augie worked. Typically, he visited field sites of the PM Specialists in the region. On one such occasion they were reviewing some plantings of American beachgrass on New Jersey dunes. At the time Augie had a broken leg in a cast, and was on crutches. On the way to the site Augie assured Bill he had had all the help he needed to get the planting done, and that his broken leg was not a handicap. As the review unfolded Bill noticed something strange. Many of the culms of beachgrass were in the sand upside down. Bill pressed the point. Turns out, Augie's help had left about 4:00 PM and he finished it alone, some after dark.

2.   For several years Augie organized and ran a Sand Dune Revegetation tour, covering parts or all of the NJ, DE, MD and VA shoreline. Their purpose was to build support for the practice and to provide education on how to do it. These tours were so popular multiple busses were employed to move the crowd from site to site. Although popular, they were expensive, not only in dollars but the involvement of various SCS personnel's time. Augie's boss, the state conservationist in Maryland, Edward Keil, was not always sure of the priority of sand dunes, compared with other conservation priorities.

Each year the tour had a starting point. On the way to the starting point one year, Mr. Keil told Augie to announce at the start of the upcoming tour that this was to be the last sand dune tour, and be sure to make it clear. When the crowd had assembled, Augie called the group to order, said a few things, then introduced Mr. Keil by telling everyone all the wonderful things the he had done, was doing, and was going to do, and how great a boss he was. Then Augie said "And to prove it he has invited us back next year." Given the circumstances, Augie figured the state conservationist would not repudiate the beloved Augie in front of all his friends, and he was right. The tours went on.

Augustine's work also initiated an accelerated effort to stabilize eroding tidal shorelines with vegetation, instead of exclusively using structures. Augie made many plantings on tidal shorelines, primarily in Virginia. He found eroding sites that, in his judgment, looked like similar sites that were not eroding. The slopes were graded and planted from the waterline to the top of the slope; varying the plant selection from cordgrasses at the waterline to non-aquatic plants above. Many failed but some performed magnificently, dramatically indicating that vegetation would work in some locations.

A third area where his efforts made a major contribution was the use of decomposing fabric to protect waterways while the vegetation became established. This was a typical example of his approach, planned or coincidental, of latching onto a problem and living, eating, talking and sleeping with it twenty-four hours a day until it was solved. Close friends would avoid him just because they didn't want to hear another jute fabric story. In typical fashion he sold the notion, which became an accepted and standard practice.

Fortunately, a part of his contributions to the use of vegetation to control erosion was captured in these publications. He was the instigator of the potential of plants to help solve both subject areas covered in these publications. Yet, when it came time to publish he was off attacking another problem.

Augustine, Marshall and W. C. Sharp. 1969. Effect of Several Fertilizer Treatments on the Production of American Beachgrass Culms. *Agron J* 61:43-45.

Sharp, W. C., M. Augustine and Joseph D. Vaden. 1970. Ten-year Report on Sloping Techniques Used to Stabilize Eroding Tidal River Banks. *Shore and Beach*; 38:31-5.

Sharp, W. C., C. R. Belcher and J. A. Oyler. 1980. Vegetation for Tidal Stabilization in the Mid-Atlantic States. USDA-SCS, Broomall, PA. 19 pp.

Summary

Three big areas on which Augustine left his most indelible mark was tidal shoreline erosion and sand dune stabilization in the Mid-Atlantic area, and the use of jute for protecting waterways anywhere. Today the vegetative standards and specifications, and erosion control manuals in the states where he worked, reflect the efforts of this short fellow who talked a mile a minute, knew everyone, was loved by all, and worked like a horse.

Below is a portion of a statement pulled from the *Conservation in Maryland* history by A. C. Hawkins.[649]

> Marshall Augustine was one of the early pioneers in plant materials for use in erosion control. He spent long hours with many people working with plants for controlling erosion on beach areas, waterways, streambank, strip mines and developing areas...Mr. Augustine was widely recognized in his field and after retiring, worked as a special advisor to the Department of Natural Resources in Maryland to help them get started in sediment erosion control work.

Augie retired in 1970. Those who knew and appreciated him were blessed. While not a giant in the scientific or publication arena, he accomplished marvelous things through force of personality, absolute dedication, and hard work. He was an institution unto himself. Augie viewed his zeal for the use of conservation plants as an opportunity, and he made the most of it.

John McDermand – Major Contributor

Nursery Agronomist,
Plant Materials Specialist

Background

On, April 27, 1935 a Bureau of Plant Industry seed/plant production and observational nursery in Mandan, ND was transferred to the USDA Soil Conservation Service. The production nursery expanded rapidly. In 1937, over one million trees were produced. Later SCS purchased land in the bottoms between Bismarck and Mandan for a new nursery. During 1952 and 1953 the Nursery was moved to this new location, called the Fort Lincoln Military Post.

In November, 1953, the SCS closed the Fort Lincoln production nursery. The North Dakota Association of Soil Conservation District continued the production of trees and shrubs similar to when the nursery was operated by the SCS. With financial and technical assistance from SCS, the Association designated a small acreage to be used as the observational nursery. Although limited, valuable plant materials from the nursery became the foundation of the Bismarck PMC in 1954. By 1967 the agreement with the Association was terminated and the PMC's operation returned to SCS. However, a close cooperative arrangement continues between the PMC and the Association.

Figure 9.26 John McDermand

Productive Years

John McDermand was first employed by the Soil Conservation Service in 1946 as an agronomist in North Platte and Waterloo, Nebraska.[650] From there he went to the nursery in Kearney, Nebraska, and in June 1954 when the nurseries closed he was transferred to the SCS State Office, Bismarck, ND as plant materials technician.

John, being the only full-time plant materials employee in North Dakota, had the dual role of providing the technical assistance to the nursery, as well as the role of plant materials technician. According to Erling Jacobson, who replaced him as PMS upon his retirement in 1974, John held the semblance of a plant materials effort together until SCS assumed operations of the PMC in 1967. His responsibility included the collection, initial evaluation, and increase of plants used in the field testing program, as well as responsibility for the field testing.

Several valuable plants that had been selected by the nursery staff as warranting additional study became a part of his initial and continuing work load. From that group the following were ultimately released:

- 'Garrison' creeping foxtail with the newly established Bridger, MT PMC in 1963

- 'Rodan' western wheatgrass

- 'Lodorm' green needlegrass

- 'Bison' big bluestem

- 'Dakota' switchgrass

- 'Oahe' hackberry

John spent his first summer (1954) inspecting grass plantings established by Nursery employees. He also made an assembly of sideoats grama from South Dakota, from which became a widely produced cultivar called 'Pierre'.

In September 1954 he made the first of many trips to the arboretum at Morton, Manitoba. There he made collections of improved trees and shrubs to be evaluated for use in farmstead and field windbreaks in the Northern Great Plains.[651] As with the sideoats grama, John had a keen eye for identifying superior plants. One of the very first from Morton which he collected was the Ussurian pear, later released in 1990 as the cultivar, 'McDermand'.

Between 1954 and 1967 John established hundreds of conservation field plantings in the three states of North Dakota, South Dakota, and Minnesota, many of them contributing to the release of the new plants.

The operations of the Bismarck PMC became more independent in 1967 when Sheridan Dronen became the first SCS manager, and funds became available to expand the program. This allowed John to work full-time as a field plant materials specialist.

The real legacy of John McDermand was the quality and number and outstanding accessions he left for those who followed. John retired in 1974. He had collected and initiated the evaluation of all of these. This is an amazing accomplishment.

- 'Cardan' green ash, released in 1979
- 'Oahe' hackberry, released in 1982
- 'Sakakawea' silver buffaloberry, released in 1984
- 'Scarlet' Mongolian cherry, released in 1984
- 'Centennial' cotoneaster, released in 1987
- 'Forestburg' switchgrass, released in 1987
- 'Tomahawk' Indiangrass 1988
- 'Bonilla' big bluestem, released in 1989
- 'McDermand' Ussurian pear, released in 1990
- 'Regal' Russian almond, released in 1997
- 'Legacy' late lilac, released in 1999

Summary

In addition to the plant materials that John passed on was a work ethic that few can match. After long hours on the road to make and evaluate field plantings, he would return late Friday afternoon, and on the weekend make evaluations at the PMC, weed the seed and plant increases plantings, and prepare for the next week on the road. On top of that, the quantity and quality of documentation he recorded on adaptation and performance was a model for those who followed him.

John left an enduring mark on the conservation of the Northern Great Plains and on the Bismarck Plant Materials Center program. Even after retirement he continued his contact with the Plant Materials Program as a volunteer at the PMC until health problems forced him to quit.

M. Donald Atkins – Major Contributor

Nursery Agronomist,
Regional Plant Materials Specialist

M. Donald Atkins joined the Manhattan Regional Nursery staff as an agronomist in 1946.[652] He remained in this position until the Nursery closed and the Manhattan PMC assumed the continuation of the observational studies. He remained at the PMC until 1955, providing technical assistance to the Kansas State University personnel who were operating the Center under a cooperative agreement with SCS.

In 1955 he replaced Harold Cooper as Regional (Washington-Field) Plant Material Technician located in Denver, Colorado, and later in Lincoln, Nebraska. In this position he provided technical direction to plant materials work in the Midwest Region and PMCs in Manhattan, Kansas; Bismarck, North Dakota; Elsberry, Missouri; and East Lansing, Michigan until his retirement in 1970.

Figure 9.27 Donald Atkins

During the early operations of the Manhattan Regional Nursery, there was limited knowledge about the technology of collecting, harvesting, cleaning, and planting native grass seed. As experience broadened, it was noted and documented in numerous publications authored or co-authored by Atkins. These publications also discussed the extensive morphological variation that occurred within species, how different grasses responded when planted on different soils and locations, and the impact that seed origin had on plant performance and conservation use. All of these encouraged and led to the collection and selection of superior strains within several species throughout the Great Plains. Atkins was in the forefront of this evolving technology.

These and other important scientific and technological advances are well documented in a variety or publications shown in Appendix 2. Two stand-alone Farmers Bulletins are listed here.

Cooper, H. W., J. E. Smith, Jr., and M. D. Atkins. 1957. *Producing and harvesting grass seed in the Great Plains.* Farmers Bul. No. 2112. U.S. Govt. Printing Office, Washington, DC.

Atkins, M. Donald and James E. Smith, Jr. 1967. *Grass seed production and harvest in the Great Plains.* Farmers' Bulletin 2226: USDA, Washington, DC. 30 p.

M. Donald Atkins was a dedicated professional, respected as an outstanding teacher and role model for younger employees. He provided steady guidance to the budding PMC Program in the mid-1950s, and specifically to the two that were initially in his region, Manhattan and Bismarck. Their exemplary record speaks well for the foundation they received from M. Donald Atkins.

Other Noteworthy Contributors

The following three persons appeared early in the evolution of the Plant Materials Program. Each contributed significantly to its long term success.

Dr. Charles R. Enlow – Other Noteworthy Contributors

Agronomist, Bureau of Plant Industry
Agronomist, Soil Erosion Service
Acting, In Charge, Nursery Division, Soil Conservation Service
Agronomist, Soil Conservation Service
U.S. Foreign Service

The contribution of Dr. Enlow is one of those singular happenings when the right person is in the right place at the right time. His contributions are discussed in detail in Chapter 3, and the purpose here is to highlight this contribution.

Recall that he joined the Soil Erosion Service in 1933 and helped get the fourteen nurseries established. When SES moved to SCS in April 1935 his position was Acting, In Charge, Nursery Section, which he held until the end of 1935. During this nine-month period he vigorously defended the purpose of and need for the nurseries.[653] In addition to outlining the "Types of work" the nurseries should be doing, he advised Dr. Bennett, "(the) general impression of the Soil Conservation Service is that the nurseries are merely growing large quantities of planting stock of a few species of trees and collecting enormous quintiles of a few grasses for use directly on the projects. This is not the original purpose for which the nurseries were established." He continues "I am particularly anxious that the Nursery Section be allowed to continue the collection of many hundreds of species of plants through our country as it has been done for the past two years, bringing the material into the nurseries in order to study methods of propagation and the possibilities of using these plants in an erosion control program. This, in my estimation, is the real work of the Nursery Section. It is very possible that the day might arrive that we would be obligated to suddenly discontinue the production of millions of trees and bulk collection of seed of grasses from the ranges. The developing work of promising species should be continued and I urge you give your approval to a continuation of the program."

While it took until 1953 for his predictions to be fulfilled, he was dead right on both.

Dr. Enlow was born in Kingman, KS June 28, 1893.[654] He attended Kansas State University, majoring in Agronomy, and received a B.S. in Agriculture in 1920. In 1927 he received an M.S. degree from the same institution. He moved to Washington D.C. in 1929 and took a position with the Bureau of Plant Industries in the Interior Department. He joined the Soil Erosion Service, and Dr. H. H. Bennett, in 1933. The same year he joined Dr. Harvey L. Westover for the plant expedition to Russian Turkestan, bringing back 2,124 lots of seeds.

After temporally filling the position of Head, Nursery Section from April 1935 until Dr. Crider arrived in January, 1936; Enlow became the Chief Agronomist for SCS until 1944. He spent the balance of his career with the U.S. Department of State, Foreign Service, retiring in 1965. Over the course of his career he published over forty agronomic related mimeographs and publications, including twenty articles in the Soil Conservation Magazine.

Dr. Crider guided the nurseries through the early years of getting organized and establishing policy. That policy which he established relating to observational nursery work looked a lot like the contents of the November 1935 memo Enlow wrote to Bennett.

M. M. Hoover – Other Noteworthy Contributors

West Virginia University Agronomy Professor
Bureau of Plant Industries
Chief Agronomist, Section and Division of Nurseries
ARS PI Station Coordinator and Professor of Agronomy, Ames, Iowa

In 1935 Max M. Hoover, an agronomist, was working in Spencer, West Virginia on a Bureau of Plant Industries Project. On February 12, 1935 Walter C. Lowdermilk, then vice director, Soil Erosion Service, asked Hoover to survey Midwestern SES nurseries and other facilities, including erosion control stations and experiment stations.[655] Lowdermilk was anxious to get a complete report dealing with all aspect s of the soon-to-be SCS units.[656] He told Hoover "I am especially interested in information which you are accumulating on methods of harvesting the seed of native grasses." Lowdermilk also advised him of his $5.00 per diem.

This proceeded on schedule with Hoover returning several trip reports to Lowdermilk. According to John Schwendiman in the First Fifty Years, The Plant Materials Center, Pullman, WA, Dr. Hoover came all the way there in the summer of 1936, no doubt on his inspection trip, and interviewed Dr. Hafenrichter for the job as Regional Nurseryman.[657] Schwendiman also observes that "Hafenrichter organized the nursery division in the Northwest under Max Hoover of Washington D.C." In a letter included in the Pullman History, dated March 21, 1983, Virgil Hawk wrote "On April 15, 1935 I was transferred to the new USDA, SCS organization with Charlie Enlow in charge with Dr. Max Hoover as his assistant."

Upon his return to the new office location in Washington D.C. Hoover became the Chief Agronomist on the staff of first the Section of Nurseries and then in 1939 of the Division of Nurseries. Did Hoover think he was going to replace Enlow?

Prior to his joining the Bureau of Plant Industries, Hoover was employed by the Agronomy Department of West Virginia University. There he had an extensive publication record dealing primarily with agronomic crops. A few of them follow:

Garber, R. J., N. J. Giddings and M. M. Hoover. 1928. Breeding for disease resistance with particular reference to the smut of oats. Scientific Agriculture, Vol. 1X (2):l03-1l5

The Relation of Smut Infection to Yield in Maize, Garber, R. J. and M. M. Hoover Agronomy Journal 1928 20: 7: 735-746.

Hoover, M. M Wheat-Rye Hybrids, Jour. Heredity Vol. 20: p. 171, No. 4. April 1929.

Garber, R. J., and M. M. Hoover. 1929. Natural Crossing between Oat Plants of Hybrid Origin. West Virginia Agri. Exp. Stn., Morgantown, WV

The Effect upon Yield of Cutting Sweet Clover (Melilotus alba) at Different Times and at Different Heights, R. J. Garber, M. M. Hoover and L. S. Bennett, Agro. J. 1934, 26: 11: 974-977

Hoover was apparently a prolific writer of technical papers. In 1935 he moved from WVU to the SES, made an extensive western trip for SES/SCS, met Franklin Crider in 1936 and by February 1937 he authored the following 44-page bulletin:

M. M. Hoover. 1939. Native and Adapted Grasses for Conservation of Soil and Moisture in the Great Plains and Western States. Farmers Bulletin No. 1812, USDA, Washington, DC.

Hoover was the sole author, listed as senior agronomist, Section of Conservation Nurseries, Division of Conservation Operations, Soil Conservation Service. Later that year he published with Crider:

Collection of native grass seed in the Great Plains, USA, F. J. Crider, M. M. Hoover, Imperial Bureau of Plant Genetics: Herbage Plants September, 1937. Aberystwyth. Bulletin No. 23.

From an economic crop agronomist to a conservation plant agronomist in two or three years is indeed impressive.

During the tenure of Dr. Crider as Chief of the Nursery Section, and continuing after Crider left and was replaced by Dr. Harry A. Gunning. Hoover served the nurseries well as their chief agronomist. Writing to Nursery Chief H. A. Gunning, in 1942, he reported that he met with the SCS Regional Nurseryman and nursery managers and, "Dr. Keim and staff of the (Nebraska) College of Agriculture" concerning the "matter of certification of new and improved grass selections" and giving every encouragement to the "rapid development and commercial production of these improved plant materials."[658]

In 1946, after an extensive trip through the southern Great Plains, spending time with James E. Smith, Jr., A. E. Faber, and Donald R. Cornelius, Hoover wrote to A. E. Jones, Chief of Operations, dated January 2, 1946.[659] Hoover was sending Jones a trip report about his attending the International Crop Improvement Association, and a meeting with H. N. Smith, Regional Engineer and C. B. Webster, Regional Nurseryman, both in Fort Worth. The purpose was to review a proposal from the region to expand the production of seed on the nurseries to meet the regional seed requirements. Hoover was a proponent of nurseries producing certified seed of new cultivars, which the Fort Worth region resisted. This is discussed in greater details in Chapter 4 - Production and Observational Nurseries: Their People, Products, Processes and Performance. Hoover knew the importance of certified seed and took every opportunity to promote it. An unrelated but interesting point about the memo from Hoover is why he sent it to Jones rather than his boss, Dr. Gunning. No clear explanation was found.

Hoover includes in his memo to Jones that he, Smith, Faber and Cornelius had met in Woodward, OK and "assembled material for a farmers' bulletin." In 1947 the following 37-page publication appeared that addressed collecting and processing seed of grasses being used extensively for conservation:

Hoover, M. M., James E. Smith, Jr., A. E. Faber, and D. R. Cornelius: Seed for Regrassing Great Plains Areas, USDA Farmers' Bulletin 1985, 1947.

Why was Hoover the principal author? Smith, Faber and Cornelius and others had done the work. It may have been because of the age-old story of the scientist being too busy to publish the results of his work. It is not difficult to imagine that Hoover went to Kansas and Oklahoma, knowing the likes of Smith, Faber and Cornelius were loaded with information of the type Lowdermilk wanted, so they agreed to publish as a team with Hoover doing the writing.

The following year Hoover, using old and new information, included an article in the 1948 Yearbook of Agriculture

Hoover, Max M., M., A. Hein, and C. O. Erlanson. 1948. The Main Grasses for Farm and Home. 1948 USDA Yearbook of Agriculture, Washington, DC. p. 639-700.

It is unclear exactly when Dr. Hoover left the SCS. In 1954 he was Regional Coordinator for the PI Station, USDA in Ames Iowa.[660] He may have left prior to the 1953 nursery closing. Regardless, he continued his agronomic publishing activities, with a variety of co-authors. The first article below was published in May 1953, meaning it was prepared slightly in advance of the actual nursery closings. At that time Hoover was a graduate Assistant in Farm Crops at the Iowa Agriculture Experiment Station in Ames, IA. The last listed publication suggests he had moved into the upper tier of eastern university forage agronomists as shown by these co-authors.

Scholl, J. M., W. H. Hale and M. M. Hoover. 1957. Feeding Value of Smooth Bromegrass, *Bromus Inermis* and Meadow Bromegrass, *Bromus Erectus*. Agron. J. 49: 5: 276-277.

Sprague, M. A., M. M. Hoover. W. A. Wright, H. A. MacDonald, B. A. Brown, A. M. Decker, J. B. Washko, V. G. Sprague, and K. E. Varney. 1963. Seedling management of grass-legume associations in the northeast. Northeast Regional Publication No. 42, New Jersey Agr. Exp. Sta., Rutgers, New Brunswick, NJ.

Harry A. Gunning – Other Noteworthy Contributors

Horticulturalist, Bureau of Plant Industry
Chief, Nursery Division, Soil Conservation Service
Assistant Director, National Arboretum, Washington D.C.

Harry A. Gunning was born in Kansas on February, 28, 1893 and passed away on October 14, 1960. Trained as a Horticulturist, from 1919 to 1935 Dr. Gunning was in the Division of Plant Exploration and Introduction of the Bureau of Plant Industry, Soils, and Agricultural Engineering. It is unclear exactly when Mr. Gunning joined the SCS. He appears on the Permanent Personnel record of Soil Conservation Nurseries, dated January 30, 1936 as being on the Albuquerque, NM staff.[661] Records are available to document his collection of specimens for the University of Arizona herbarium as late as June, 1936.[662] These could have been collected on a visit either as an employee of the Bureau of Plant Industry or as an SCS employee. Considering the events taking place in 1936, and the urgency of activities in SCS, one could speculate that he joined SCS after that. The collections included species of the *Poa*, *Astragalus* and *Chamerion* genera.

The February 1938 USDA Miscellaneous Publication 304 personnel listing of people in the Section of Nurseries include Dr. Crider, M. M. Hoover, PhD, Senior Agronomist, Harry A. Gunning, Senior Horticulturist, and Charles F. Swingle, PhD, Horticulturist.[663] This publication had to have been drafted weeks or months earlier. In December, 1939 Dr. Crider transferred to the position of Manager, National Observational Project at Beltsville, MD. Harry A. Gunning replaced him as Chief of the Nursery Division. Even though it does not appear that Gunning was a dynamitic person during those formable years of nursery development, he obviously impressed someone in the upper echelon of SCS. Mr. Gunning continued as the Chief, Nursery Division until 1948 when he returned to the USDI as Assistant Director of the National Arboretum.[664]

His tenure as the Nursery Division Chief is marked with steady and productive attention to progress in the observational studies as well as the production side of nursery responsibility. Any national leadership tenure of nine years warrants recognition. There was a constant effort on his part to improve nursery production efficiency.[665] Some examples of Mr. Gunning's positive impacts are discussed in Chapter 4. An example is the survey he conducted in the Northeast of experiment stations to document the support for SCS developing conservation plants, contrary to the view of the SCS regional office. Another was his strong support for observational studies in developing certification

336

standards for released grasses or legumes, and their commercial production under these standards through the state certifying agency. Unfortunately, he did not make it a policy.

Near the end of his time as Nursery Division Chief he teamed with Floyd M. Cossitt and C. A. Rindt to write *Production of Planting Stock*.[666]

Plant Materials Program Awards

This section identifies recipients of Department awards plus awards given by the Plant Materials Program. It does not include awards given locally, such as those within units or states.

<u>USDA Awards</u>

Recognizing worthy employees has been a part of the USDA from its beginning. Its purpose is to "to recognize organizational, individual, and group performance that exceeds performance and/or public service expectations, especially that which contributes to the core values, mission, and goals of the Department."[667] The Distinguished Service award is the highest award available in Federal civilian service and the Superior Service award is second to it. For an employee to receive either a Distinguished or Superior Service award requires considerable work on the part of someone willing to prepare the documentation. It usually is and should be the employee's supervisor.

Dr. Hafenrichter's outstanding performance is recognized throughout this history. It is not surprising that he would be the first of only two Plant Materials Program employees to receive this award. Jack Carlson was the other. Both were holding the same position when they received the award.

The first superior service award received by an employee of an observational nursery or PMC, which again was Dr. Hafenrichter in 1947. On three occasions there were two in the same year. One might speculate that there are two reasons for this. First, the Plant Materials Program was awash with outstanding employees, and second, adequate initiative was present to develop the required documentation. Although there has been neither a Distinguished nor Superior Service Award since 1993 it cannot be for the lack of outstanding employees. The current National PMS and one of the most Productive Scientists preformed their good works during that period.

See Table 9.12 for observational nursery and Plant Materials winners of the two Departmental awards.

Table 9.12 Department Awards: Distinguished and Superior

USDA Distinguished Service Award			
Name	**Year**	**Position**	**Location**
A. L. Hafenrichter	1963	Regional PM Specialist	Portland, OR
Jack R. Carlson	1993	Former Regional PM Specialist	Portland, or
USDA Superior Service Award			
Name	**Year**	**Position**	**Location**
A. L. Hafenrichter	1947	Regional Nurseryman	Portland, OR
Maurice E. Heath	1947	Nursery Agronomist	Big Flats, NY
Aberdeen Nursery	1950	Observational Nursery	Aberdeen, ID
David H. Foster	1950	Nursery Manager	San Antonio, TX
Franklin J. Crider	1951	Nursery Manager	Beltsville, MD
Pleasanton Nursery	1952	Observational Nursery	Pleasanton, CA
Marshall T. Augustine	1958	Field PM Technician	College Park, MD
Sherrill H. Fuchs	1966	Field PM Technician	Albuquerque, NM
John L. Schwendiman	1968	Field PM Technician	Portland, OR

USDA Superior Service Award			
Name	**Year**	**Position**	**Location**
Karl E. Graetz	1972	Field PM Technician	Raleigh, NC
Robert S. MacLauchlan	1979	National PM Specialist	Washington, DC
Arnold G Davis	1981	Regional PM Specialist	Fort Worth, TX
W. Curtis Sharp	1984	Regional PM Specialist	Broomall, PA
Wendall R. Oaks	1988	PMC Manager	Los Lunas, NM
Richard C. Russell	1988	Biological Technician	Beltsville, MD
Wendell G. Hassell	1989	Field PM Specialist	Denver, CO
James S. Alderson	1992	Field PM Specialist	Temple, TX
W. Curtis Sharp	1992	National PM Specialist	Washington, DC

Plant Materials Awards

In 1986 the Plant Materials Program initiated an internal awards program. They were:

- Plant Materials Center of the Year – In recognition of best overall performance by a plant materials center.

- Plant Materials Specialist of the Year – The best overall performance of a plant materials specialist.

- Plant Materials Center Employee of the Year – The employee who has demonstrated leadership and skills contributing to the production of the PMC in excess of their responsibility.

- Meritorious Award – The plant materials employee who has made the greatest contribution to the discipline and agency outside of their area of responsibilities.

- Newcomer of the Year – The best performance and contribution during the initial three years within the discipline.

- Special Plant Materials Service Award – A non-plant materials person whose efforts are substantially advancing the Plant Materials Program.

There was a lapse in this program from 1994 until 2001, when it was restarted. Six internal awards were available. Awards over the two time periods were blended together to produce the following:

Table 9.13 Plant Materials Program Awards

Outstanding Plant Materials Center Award			
Name	**Year**	**Position**[1]	**Location**
Bismarck PMC	1986	PMC Unit Award	Bismarck, ND
Bridger PMC	1987	PMC Unit Award	Bridger, MT
Cape May PMC	1988	PMC Unit Award	Cape May, NJ
Manhattan PMC	1989	PMC Unit Award	Manhattan, KS
Jimmy Carter PMC	1990	PMC Unit Award	Americus, GA
Los Lunas PMC	1991	PMC Unit Award	Los Lunas, NM

Outstanding Plant Materials Center Award			
Name	Year	Position[1]	Location
Elsberry PMC	1992	PMC Unit Award	Elsberry, MO
National PMC	2002	PMC Unit Award	Beltsville, MD
Elsberry PMC	2003	PMC Unit Award	Elsberry, MO
South Texas Natives	2005	PMC Unit Award	Kingsville, TX
Bismarck PMC	2006	PMC Unit Award	Bismarck, ND
Kika de la Garza PMC	2007	PMC Unit Award	Kingsville, TX
Aberdeen PMC	2008	PMC Unit Award	Aberdeen, ID
Florida PM Specialist and PMC	2009	PMC Unit Award	FL State office & Brooksville, FL
James E. "Bud" Smith PMC	2011	PMC Unit Award	Knox City, TX
Outstanding Plant Materials Employee Award			
Name	Year	Position[1]	Location
Richard Heizer	1986	Field PM Specialist	Temple, TX
Wendall Oaks	1986	PMC Manager	Los Lunas, NM
Cluster Belcher	1987	Field PM Specialist	Somerset, NJ
Wendell G. Hassell	1987	Field PM Specialist	Denver, CO
Larry Holzworth	1988	Field PM Specialist	Bozeman, MT
Jack R. Carlson	1988	Regional PM Specialist	Portland, OR
Edward D. Surrency	1989	Field PM Specialist	Athens, GA
Mark E. Majerus	1989	Agronomist	Bridger, MT
Rachel H. Bergsagel	1989	Biological Technician	Bismarck, ND
Sue Roach	1989	Biological Technician	Americus, GA
John Dickerson	1990	Field PM Specialist	Syracuse, NY
Russell Haas	1990	Field PM Specialist	Bismarck, ND
Chris "CL" Hacker, Jr.	1990	Biological Technician	Knox City, TX
Jerrald M. Massey	1990	Farm Foreman	Meeker, CO
Jacy L. Gibbs	1991	Field PM Specialist	Boise, ID
Brent Cornforth	1991	Biological Technician	Aberdeen, ID
James A. Wolfe	1992	Field PM Specialist	Jackson/Coffeeville, MS
Robert J. Glennon	1992	Field PM Specialist	Harrisburg, PA
Mark Stannard	1992	Agronomist	Pullman, WA
Ural Crase	1992	Biological Technician	Quicksand, KY
Larry Holzworth	2002	Field PM Specialist	Bozeman, MT

Meritorious Service Award			
Name	Year	Position[1]	Location
Dan Ogle	2003	Field PM Specialist	Boise, ID
Joe Scianna	2004	Horticulturalist	Bridger, MT
Scott Edwards	2005	Field PM Specialist	Alexandria, LA
Greg Fenchel	2006	PMC Manager	Los Lunas, NM
John Scheetz	2002	National PM Information Specialist	Bridger, MT
Dave Lorenz	2002	Regional PM Specialist	Chester, PA
John Dickerson	2003	Field PM Specialist	Syracuse, NY
Jimmy Henry	2003	PMC Manager	Elsberry, MO
Don Surrency	2004	Field PM Specialist	Athens, GA
Bob Joy	2006	Field PM Specialist	Ho'olehua, HI
Joel Douglas	2006	Regional PM Specialist	Fort Worth, TX
Nancy Jensen	2007	Agronomist	Bismarck, ND
Bruce Ayers	2007	Biological Technician	Big Flats, NY
Dianne Naylor	2007	Secretary	Big Flats, NY
Mary Anne Gonter	2008	Biological Technician	Brooksville, FL
Pam Stewart	2008	Secretary	Elsberry, MO
Russ Haas	2008	NRCS Technical Advisor to the National Park Service	Bismarck, ND
Chris Hoag	2009	Wetland Specialist	Aberdeen, ID
Jim Stevens	2009	PMC Manager	Nacogdoches, TX
Don Gohmert	2010	State Conservationist	Temple, TX
Steve Bruckerhoff	2010	PMC Manager	Elsberry, MO
Edwin Mas	2010	Field PM Specialist	Mayaguez, PR
Boyd Simonson	2010	Biological Technician	Aberdeen, ID
Dan Ogle	2010	Field PM Specialist	Aberdeen, ID
Dwight Tober	2011	Field PM Specialist	Bismarck, ND
Dave Burgdorf	2011	Field PM Specialist	East Lansing, MI
Notable Achievement Award			
Name	Year	Position[1]	Location
Bruce Munda	2002	Field PM Specialist	Tucson, AZ
Jody Holzworth	2003	Public Affairs Specialist	Boise, ID
Glenn Sakamoto	2003	PMC Manager	Ho'olehua, HI
Larry Holzworth	2004	Field PM Specialists	Bozeman, MT;
Chris Miller	2004	Field PM Specialists	Somerset, NJ

Notable Achievement Award			
Name	Year	Position[1]	Location
Jerry Kaiser	2005	Field PM Specialist	Elsberry, MO
Mark Stannard	2005	PMC Manager	Pullman, WA
John Englert	2006	PMC Manager	Beltsville, MD
Mimi Williams	2007	Field PM Specialist	Gainesville, FL
Leslie Glass	2007	Web Master	Bismarck, ND
Los Lunas PMC	2008	Unit Award	Los Lunas, NM
Hawaii PM Specialist and PMC	2009	Unit Award	State Office & Ho'olehua, HI
Derek Tilley	2010	Agronomist	Aberdeen, ID
Jerry Longren	2010	Biological Technician	Manhattan, KS
Ron Cordsiemon	2010	PMC Manager	Elsberry, MO
Special Service Award			
Name	Year	Position[1]	Location
Pearlie S. Reed	1988	State Conservationist, NRCS	Annapolis, MD
Deane R. Harrison	1989	State Resource Conservationist, NRCS	Salt Lake City, UT
Theodore Kelsey	1991	Soil Conservationist, NRCS	Durham, NH
Jerrell L. Lemunyon	1992	Conservation Agronomist, NRCS	Fort Worth, TX
Robert Glennon	2002	Water Quality Specialist, NRCS	Little Rock, AR
Calvin Ernst	2003	Seed Grower	Meadville, PA
Lee Brooks	2004	Assistant State Conservationist, NRCS	Boise, ID
Jay T. Mar	2004	RC&D Coordinator, NRCS	Fargo, ND
Nancy Dunkle	2004	Revegetation Specialist, NPS	Lakewood, CO
Allan Gustafson	2005	Area Resource Conservationist, NRCS	MN
David Wise	2006	Soil Conservationist, NRCS	Fond du Lac Tribal & Comm. College, Cloquet, MN
Berry Isaacs	2006	State Biologist, NRCS	Harrisburg, PA
Scott Edwards	2006	RC&D Coordinator, NRCS	Lafayette, LA
Niles Glasgow	2007	State Conservationist, NRCS	Columbia, SC
Alan Schlegel	2008	Agronomy Professor, KS State University	SW Research & Extension Ctr., KS State Univ.

Special Service Award			
Name	**Year**	**Position**[1]	**Location**
Steve Poppe	2008	Horticulture Coordinator	West Central Research & Outreach Ctr., Univ. of MN
Karen Clause	2009	Range Management Specialist, NRCS	Pinedale, WY
Constance Miller	2009	State Forester, NRCS	Lincoln, NE
Robert Rennolet	2009	District Conservationist, NRCS	Parkston, SD
William Bronder	2010	Soil & Water Cons. District	Sherburne, MN
Robert Kilian	2010	Area Range Specialist, NRCS	Miles City, MT
John Graham	2011	Soil Conservationist, NRCS	Lexington, KY
Plant Materials Newcomers Award			
Name	**Year**	**Position**[1]	**Location**
Jacy L. Gibbs	1986	Field PM Specialist	Boise, ID
James S. Alderson	1987	PMC Manager	Knox City, TX
Melvin E. Sams	1988	System Analysis	Beltsville, MD
David A. Dyer	1989	PMC Manager	Lockeford, CA
L. H. "Herby" Bloodworth	1990	Agronomist	Coffeeville, MS
Theresa R. Flessner	1991	Agronomist	Corvallis, OR
Mike M. Lane	1992	PMC Manager	Coffeeville, MS

[1] The position held at the time of the reward.

Chapter 10: IMPACTS OF THE PRE-VARIETAL RELEASE CERTIFICATION STANDARDS

While Richard White, and those that followed him, had some challenging times managing the budget, from the author's perspective it was not the only volatile aspect of the Plant Materials Program during the 1994 - 2010 period. From 1935 through 2010 the average number of cultivar and informal releases per year was a little less than five. From 1995 through 2010 just the pre-varietal releases averaged nearly twenty. Obviously, the change made in the January, 1994 Plant Materials Manual was overwhelmingly accepted, far in excess of the originators intent. Was this a totally good thing?

SCS had recognized the need for some flexibility in the release policy for some time. Other changes were taking place that increased the desirability of expanding the cultivar-only policy. These changes included:

1. There was increasing concern for preserving not only diversity of species, but also of the genetic diversity within each species.[668] The rational is that a native species varies genetically in its adaptation to the particular localities and environmental conditions under which it grows. Conservation plantings were being viewed as Ecological Landscaping, which emphasizes the desirability of matching genotypes to the environment being restored.[669] The convention then holds that the plant material which originates in, and is native to one geographic region is generally the best to use for replanting in that region. If a site was to be restored with a broadly adapted cultivar, which would re-vegetate the site more effectively, it would potentially introduce new germplasm. While this point of view is easily challenged on many fronts, it must be recognized.

2. Another motivation to expand the cultivar-only policy was the perception by some SCS customers and many within SCS that the development period for new cultivars was too long. Even when a clear need for a plant was recognized, and outstanding candidates were found, a minimum of five or more years were required before adequate data could be accumulated to warrant a cultivar release. While the real strengths of many cooperative releases have resulted from this broad-based testing, and it provides assurances of a high level of performance over time and geographic area, there was pressure to move faster.

3. While many of the outstanding SCS releases from the very beginning were introductions onto the North American Continent, objections to foreign introductions to solve conservation problems have become a hot political issue. There is ample documented evidence that many introduced plants became the work horse of solving erosion problems in major regions, when native plants could not. However, now that the erosion problems have been fixed, the work horses are seen as the villains.

4. All publicly funded conservation plantings require third-party certification, as exists with certified cultivars. If new plantings included ecotypes, some certification policy would be required for them.

5. The need for woody plant certification was apparent, but slow in coming, for two principal reasons. First, the long term evaluation period for woody plants made it difficult to develop a cultivar certification standard resembling the standards for grasses and forbs. Secondly, the flower and ornamental plants industry had several standards,[670] reducing the pressure for a soil conservation trees and shrubs standard.[671]

By the end of 1993, the framework of a policy had been reached by the three agencies involved in conservation plant development work; NRCS, U.S. Forest Service and ARS, with major assistance from

Stanford A. Young, Seed Certification Specialist, Utah State University, Logan, UT. These new standards were included in the Plant Materials Manual revision that was issued January 13, 1994, only days after Sharp's retirement.[672] The implementation of this policy over the next few years dramatically impacted the Plant Materials Program.

The Association of Official Seed Certifying Agencies (AOSCA) since 1919 has, among other things; assisted clients in developing standards for genetic purity and identity and recommending minimum standards for seed quality for the classes of certified seed. Any alteration to NRCS release standards needed to be done in compliance AOSCA standards.

The traditional AOSCA cultivar development track, referred to as the 'genetic manipulation' track, was generally followed by observational nurseries and PMCs that resulted in a cultivar. A comparison of the AOSCA and PMC tracks to cultivar release is shown in Table 10.1. These processes apply to both native and introduced plants.

Realistically, SCS tree and shrub cultivars, and many grasses and forbs, undergo little or no genetic manipulation during the evaluation process. However, through the use of large assemblies, they do undergo a selection process, and all undergo performance, site and climatic adaptation trials. Any new process needed to provide certifiable release classes at each of the four steps.

Table 10.1 AOSCA and PMC Release Process Comparison

AOSCA Step	PMC Step
1. Bulk population	Collection/Assembly
2. Selected	Initial Evaluation
3. Tested	Advanced and Final Evaluations
4. Cultivar	Cultivar

The result of the collaborative effort was the development of an AOSCA No Genetic Manipulation track, paralleling the 'genetic manipulation' track. Both provide the potential of a cultivar releases. However, the 'no genetic manipulation' track established three pre-cultivar categories and a forth cultivar category. Table 10.2 shows the nomenclature for the genetic and no genetic development tracks.[673] A brief definition of each certification standard from the 2010 National Plant Materials Manual is provided below.

Table 10.2 Nomenclature for both AOSCA and PMC Development Tracks

AOSCA Genetic Manipulation	PMC Traditional	AOSCA No Genetic Manipulation Classes
Bulk Populations	Collection/Assembly	Source identified Pre-Variety
Selected Germplasm	Initial Evaluation	Selected Pre-Variety
Tested Germplasm	**Advanced/Final Evaluations**	**Tested Per Variety**
Cultivar	Cultivar	Cultivar

Source-identified releases within the PMP should usually be used only under special circumstances, for example, where uses of local ecotypes are necessary. Selected or tested categories of pre-varietal releases are normally more appropriate release types and preferred for NRCS releases.

Selected releases are phenotypically selected plants of untested parentage that have promise but no proof of genetic superiority or distinctive traits. The propagating material of this release class should be produced with methods that ensure genetic purity and identity from either natural stands or seed production areas or seed/plant production fields or orchards.

Tested releases are the progeny of plants whose parentage has been tested and has proven genetic superiority or possesses distinctive traits for which the heritability is stable, as defined by the certifying agency. The seed or plants must be produced so as to assure genetic purity and identity. Such production could occur in either rigidly controlled, isolated natural stands or individual plants, or in seed/plant production fields or orchards.

Cultivar denotes an assemblage of cultivated plants that is clearly distinguished by any characters (morphological, physiological, cytological, chemical, or others), is uniform in these characteristics, and retains its distinguishing characters when reproduced (sexually or asexually). The terms "cultivar" and "variety" are often used interchangeably. The term "variety" is accepted by AOSCA; however, this term also refers to a botanical classification (a variety of a species). Because of this confusion, the PMP will use only the term "cultivar" when referring to cultivar releases.

Germplasm releases represent a fifth release option but it is only intended to make germplasm available to others for use in research, selection, or development and not for commercial production.

The 'no genetic manipulation' track with its three pre-variety options plus the cultivar option appears to meet the above identified needs. Using the source identified class allows the third-party certification of native collections, which also opens the door for ecotype certification. Most importantly, the new standards provide a process for certifying selected and tested trees and shrub species.

EVALUATING THE IMPACT

Was the pre-varietal releases concept desirable? Based on number of releases that quickly appeared the answer is yes. From the first release in 1939 through 2010, observational nurseries and PMCs have released about 720 plants.[674] Of this number, roughly 354 were cultivars, 45 informal, 14 germplasm and 307 pre-varietal releases. During the period of 1993 through 2010, there were seventy-one cultivars, 104 source identified, 183 selected, eighteen tested and three germplasm releases. The average number of cultivars per year is not far off of the norm. It is logical to assume many PMCs had several potential cultivars in the pipeline, well beyond the tested pre-varietal stage, and these continued until released. This is supported by the diminishing number of cultivars from fifteen in 1993, reaching zero in 2001. Cultivar release between 2001 and 2010 was twenty-five. Pre-varietal releases were replacing the thoroughly tested, broadly adapted, commercially produced cultivar. Table 10.3 provides a tabular view of this period. Table 10.4 covers the total release history of observational nurseries and PMCs for the 1939 -2010 periods.

Generally, each row in Table 10.4 is a ten-year period. The first one (1935-1950) includes those from the beginning of the nurseries. The 1981-1993 and 1994-2000 rows break on the pre-varietal release policy change.

The 1994 Plant Materials Manual states as a part of its comments on source identified releases, "This release method is expected to be used when there is a high priority and urgent need for identified plant materials; there is a lack of commercially available and adapted materials for this identified need; there is high potential for immediate use in the identified need area; and a local population source exists."[675] The 2010 Manual takes a different approach, stating, "Source identified releases within the Plant Materials Program should usually be used only under special circumstances, for example, where the use of local ecotypes is necessary. Selected or tested categories of pre-varietal releases are normally more appropriate release types and preferred for NRCS releases."[676]

Examining the pre-varietal releases from one PMC will provide insight to how the new procedure has changed the releasing norm and assisted in providing required (or desired) local ecotypes for its service area. During the 1995 and 2010 period, a PMC released one cultivar (in 1995) and eighty-one ecotypes, for five geographic regions in its service area. This involved twenty-nine species, which included up to seven releases of the same species. This number included one tested, fourteen selected and sixty-six source identified pre-variety releases.[677]

346

Table 10.3 Plant Release Types by Year, 1993 - 2010

Year	Total	Cultivars	Tested	Selected	Source identif.	Germp.	Total Pre-Varietal
1993	17	15				2	2
1994	15	12		2	1		3
1995	13	5			6	1	8
1996	19	4	1	4	10		15
1997	36	3		27	6		33
1998	25	3	1	16	5		22
1999	23	2	1	7	13		21
2000	23	2	2	16	8		21
2001	24	0	1	7	11		24
2002	29	3	3	11	12		26
2003	20	3	1	6	10		17
2004	14	1	1	10	2		13
2005	19	4	2	9	4		15
2006	29	3	3	22	1		26
2007	24	3	2	14	6		22
2008	20	5		11	5		16
2009	16	3		11	2		13
2010	11	0		9	2		11
Totals	377	71	18	182	104	3	306

Table 10.4 Release Types by Years

	Releases			Per-Varietal Releases				
Periods	Cultivars	Informal	Total Releases	Tested	Selected	Source identified	Germ-plasm	All Pre-Varietal
1935-1950	21	15	36	0	0	0	0	0
1951-1960	21	14	35	0	0	0	1	1
1961-1970	37	9	46	0	0	0	1	1
1971-1980	76	3	78	0	1	0	3	3
1981-1993	143	3	146	0	0	0	8	8
1994-2000	31	0	31	5	74	49	1	129
2001-2010	25	1	26	13	108	55	0	176
Totals	354	45	398	18	183	104	14	318

While the release record of this PMC is outside norm for the pre-varietal period, it is indicative of the impact of the new pre-varietal release policy on the Plant Materials Program and the questions it raises about how the new releasing procedure should be managed, both at the PMC and the national levels. The explosion of new releases raises other questions related to their maintenance and isolation requirements, plus the maintenance and isolation requirements of previous cultivar releases. All require maintenance. The policy manual requirements for each release includes 1) to maintain breeder or early generation pre-varietal production, 2) limited production of foundation and pre-varietal (G0, G1, and/or G2) seed, and 3) minimum isolation between like releases of identical species as prescribed by the certification standards. Additionally, there is the associated record keeping, machine cleaning, etc. for each release, compounded by multiple releases of the same species. Combined, these concerns would seem almost insurmountable given the size of the average PMC's physical plant and budget.

There may have been other factors driving the pre-varietal release activities. The Government Performance and Results Act was enacted in 1993, which contained the Performance Assessment Rating Tool (PART) to measure the effectiveness of government programs.[678][679] Details were developed to apply the tool to the Plant Materials Program. The resulting measurement was called the PMC Performance Index, and it was used for several years. Specifically, it was designed to monitor the performance of each PMC and Plant Materials Specialist to ensure they were engaged in all facets of the program. At one time it was used as a factor in allocating funds, which included some bonus funding for the highest index scores. After PMCs learned how to achieve a high score this part of the index was discontinued, and no extra funds were available for paying the bonuses.[680]

The maximum yearly score for a PMC is 100. Since releases are such a major part of the PMC products, it is not surprising that the index weighs them heavily. For example, if a PMC, over a ten-year period, assembles, evaluates and releases a well-documented superior performing cultivar, the maximum score they earn during the release year is a fifteen. A tested release also earns a score of fifteen, a selected release earns a thirteen and a source identified release earns a nine. Any release earns points over the period of years involved in its development for the collection, evaluation, etc. However, as in the case of source identified releases, all the required actions could be accomplished over a two-year period. One PMC released twelve source identified plants in one year, for a potential total score of 108.

In 2010, a decision was made to discontinue requiring the reporting of Performance Index data, because

- As mentioned above all PMCs had figured out how to reach the threshold for bonus money, but there was no money for them;

- OMB abandoned the requirements for agencies to submit Performance Assessment Rating Tool data.[681]

Keeping the 304 pre-varietal releases available in the marketplace has undoubtedly stretched the innovative genius of the plant materials teams. To get some idea on how well this was working, a survey of all PMCs was done.[682] Each PMC was asked whether their pre-varietal releases were

- Never in commercial production, or

- Had been in commercial production but was not now (as of 2012) or

- Is now being produced commercially.

Of the total 304 pre-varietal releases, 291 were included in the survey. Of these 291, two are now cultivars, five were discontinued by the PMC and twenty-two belong to two PMCs that did not respond, leaving 262 in the survey. These were distributed as follows:

- Never in commercial production   59

- Had been in commercial production but was not now   41

- Is now being produced commercially   162

The 162 pre-varietal releases currently reported to be in commercial production is impressive. However, resolving suppliers, etc. was problematic.

It must be recognized that the management of pre-varietal releases varied considerably between PMCs. The number of such releases varied between centers from over eighty to three or four. The Manhattan PMC had four pre-varietal releases, all in commercial production. They were released prior to 2005 when the recording of production data slowed. Other Centers have similar records.

Except for a germplasm release, the releasing of a new plant, cultivar or pre-varietal, is based on the assumption that some form of production will follow, thus allowing those for whom it was released to secure planting material.

Cultivars Under Pressure

The need for a certification process for trees and shrubs and local ecotypes of grasses and forbs, plus shifts in public thinking regarding the use of non-indigenous plants led to this major shift in how PMCs manage the plant release process.-The broadly adapted, superior performing cultivar was losing favor, and was replaced by locally-adapted, tested or untested ecotypes, which became certifiable. This was the intent of the policy change, and led to the explosion. It is logical to ask whether the new releases represent viable ecotypes that are truly unique to an ecosystem, or just a plant found growing in the area? The other side of that coin is how many are justifiably reaching cultivar status but aren't being released as a cultivar because of the stigma the word carries? The Plant Materials Manual states, "When a selection for a specific trait within a population is made, or when distinct populations are bulked, or individuals are crossed, the resulting population is then considered genetically manipulated," which takes it out of the realm of pre-varietal.[683] Consider these two releases:

- Itasca selected germplasm release of little bluestem. It is a composite of plants originally collected from seventy-two different sites within eastern North Dakota, north central South Dakota, and central and northeastern Minnesota. The following is from its documentation: "Selected for plants comprising the Itasca Germplasm were chosen for improved vigor, leafiness, and disease resistance." Does Itasca represent an original ecotype? No, it was "a selection for a specific trait within a population." As a composite of plants from the seventy-two sites, was the foundation seed produced from a crossing block? Most likely, resulting in purposeful manipulation, easily qualifying for cultivar status.

- Foothills Selected Class Germplasm Canada Bluegrass. Foothills is a composite of eight collections from Europe (Denmark, Romania, Netherlands, Czechoslovakia), Asia (former USSR), and the United States. A total of thirty-seven different accessions of Canada bluegrass were evaluated. These eight accessions were selected for their seedling vigor, rate of spread, forage production, seed production, and uniformity of phenology. Is this a 'natural' ecotype? "When a selection for a specific trait within a population is made, or when distinct populations are bulked, or individuals are crossed, the resulting population is then considered genetically manipulated."[684] Under existing political mania does the selection for 'rate of spread' spell invasive trouble down the road, or does its containing introduced (Denmark, etc.) germplasm indicate future complications?

It appears that the decision to release these plants as a natural track rather than a cultivar was deliberate. Politically and economically this may have been the correct decision, but was it the right technical decision? Both involved PMCs should be proud to place these two at the head of the class, i.e. release them as cultivars.

Summary

As the documentation of these pre-varietal release types is studied, it is obvious that many represent extremely valuable germplasm, while others are only a boilerplate of the species. The real question is whether there is any science-based logic that they can make a true contribution to natural resource conservation. This was the intent of the policy. In short they may represent what one adversary expressed when he said, "Anyone can release a plant." The first three native and certified releases from the Plant Materials Program were 'Vaughn' and 'El Reno' sideoats grama and 'Sherman' big bluegrass, each from separate observational nurseries. Even though all were widely tested, in the end they remain broadly adapted ecotypes that are commercially available sixty-five years later. Is this the future of the pre-varietal release? If the current release policy had been the policy from 1935, it is possible that few, if any, of the current cultivars would have been released as such. That may have been justified for some. The vast majorities were well-tested and most will meet the cultivar requirement of "distinguished by any characters (morphological, physiological, cytological, chemical, or others), is uniform in these characteristics, and retains its distinguishing characters when reproduced (sexually or asexually)."

The new policy in 1994 was needed and rational; it filled the identified viod. Viewing its application in hindsight it is logical to wonder if it was well crafted. W was its use appropriate and well managed or was it overused and poorly managed? The current National Plant Materials Specialist, John Englert, has resolved to bring the explosion under control. The most encouraging sign of change is contained in a letter from John when he wrote, "In general, the PM Program has not done a very good job transitioning into the pre-varietal release arena. We are in the process of refining our release procedures to ensure that no matter what the type of release, there is some science which goes into it, whether it is created for improved performance to solve a specific conservation need, or for ecological restoration needs."[685] Add to that a requirement that the 'release represents a unique and identifiable ecotype', then things will be back on track.

Chapter 11: GREAT INNOVATIONS AND TOP PERFORMING CULTIVARS

INTRODUCTION

From the beginning of the observational nurseries, innovative ways of helping conservation plants perform was a required component. In reality, the productive history of the Plant Materials Program is about innovations.

It is highly likely that most innovations occurred without any recognition that something special was happening. By the time they were accepted as significant accomplishments, the responsible individuals had moved on. This leaves the historian the responsibility to dig them out and acknowledge their contributions.

Each PMC section in Chapter 8 includes at least one Featured Vegetative Accomplishment other than a plant release. Many are innovations of one sort or another. Chapter 10 - Key Leaders acknowledges outstanding individuals and their accomplishments, which also include innovations. This chapter briefly mentions some of them and references the location of their discussion; and covers in more detail those not included elsewhere. In general, they are presented in chronological order.

GREAT INNOVATIONS

Evolution of the Observational Nursery concept in 1936

As we know, Dr. Crider is the father of this approach. The idea came from his groundbreaking work at the Boyce Thompson Arboretum.[686]

Crider was the person in charge of SCS Nurseries at the time the policy was written. He held the opinion that he was the author of this approach.[687] His career and contributions are discussed extensively in Chapter 3 and in Chapter 10 - Key Leaders.

The Concept of Outlying Nurseries

This innovation started even before SCS became an agency; in 1934 by Virgil B. Hawk at the Pullman Bureau of Plant Industry nursery. The section on the Pullman PMC in Chapter 8 details how outlying nurseries evolved.

Domesticating native grasses of the Great Plains in 1940

Throughout its existence the Manhattan Nursery, and later the PMC, were at the center of this evolving science. A thriving native grass seed industry stands as a testament to this effort, plus millions of re-grassed Great Plains acres. A 2002 Native Plants Journal confirms they used the correct approach.[688] See the expanded discussion in the Manhattan PMC in Chapter 8.

The Sand Dune Stabilization Project on the Coast of Oregon in 1942

This project is the Featured Vegetative Accomplishment for the Corvallis PMC in Chapter 8, and is discussed relative to introduced plants in Chapter 12.

Developing Machinery for Seedbed Preparation and Seeding on Southwestern Ranges in 1942

Southwestern rangeland, ravaged by abusive grazing for decades was clearly in need of new plants and some innovative way of getting the plants established. This is the Featured Vegetative Accomplishment of the Tucson PMC and is located in Chapter 8. James E. (Bud) Smith, Jr. experimented with a similar problem in the Southern Great Plains. His efforts are discussed in Chapters 4 and 5.

East, Midwest and West Mineland Reclamation Projects in 1947

In 1918, R. H. Cunningham began strip mining at McMasters Grove near the center of the farming village of Monroeville, PA. One local resident, writing in the 1950s, recalled that: "After the coal was taken out, this naturally left these coal pits in their destructive state, besides great heaps of soil, rock, slate, red dog, slack and other refuse remaining. Wherever you may be living, the chances are that there are one or more of these slag heaps in sight of your home."[689]

The need for plant material to stabilize surface mining refuse existed before there was a Soil Erosion Service or Soil Conservation Service. The first plant materials related solutions were not started until the late 1940s.[690] Although belated, the surface mines revegetation accomplishments in both the eastern and western coalfields was an historic leap forward. The section on the Bridger and Meeker PMCs in Chapter 8 and Key Person Ruffner in Chapter 10 cover the role played by the Plant Materials Program.

The Take Half and Leave Half Experiment in 1949

Dr. Crider may have given thought to conducting this experiment prior to joining SCS in 1935 or before he relocated to the Beltsville, MD National Observational Project in 1939.[691] However, once there, he initiated the Root growth stoppage experiments. It is the Featured Vegetative Accomplishment of the Beltsville Center in Chapter 8.

Streambank Erosion Control on the Winooski River of Vermont in 1949

The Winooski River of northern Vermont flows generally west into Lake Champaign. Like scores of other rivers in the Northeast, the Winooski has cut away its banks and over run its channel.[692] It has taken shortcuts or long meanders across farm fields. In the late 1940s, local landowners with the cooperation of SCS undertook a project to curb the destructive erosion of the stream. No observational studies personnel from the Big Flats, NY nursery were involved in the study. The lead author was the Region 1 Biologist who in many ways filled the role of a regional plant materials person, particularly as it related to biology. The production side of the nursery was involved to the extent of supplying cuttings, primarily the purple osier willow plant materials. The 1951 USDA Annual Reports took notice of the Big Flats Nursery developing a cost-saving method of rooting the purple osier willow cuttings they supplied, which in 1975 became the cultivar 'Streamco'.[693]

Measures used in the Winooski project included both mechanical and vegetative methods. Discussions of the mechanical practices are minimal. The land use at the time was predominantly, that is, eighty-five percent, dairy farming and clear-cut lumbering.

The first practice installed was fencing to keep the livestock out of the stream. This not only reduced the destructive nature of the animal crossing but also created conditions to allow the establishment of vegetation. Following this a variety of treatments were installed:

- Sloping and Planting – Banks were sloped to a 2:1 ratio on the lighter soils and 1:1.5 on heavier ones. Immediately following the sloping, selected areas were planted, based on the probable severity of water and ice action on the bank. This included areas where the stream current was offshore and the bank was not undercutting. These slopes were planted with black willow (*Salix nigra*) and purple osier willow (*Salix purpurea*). This gave fair to good control where the current was offshore but did not prohibit the undercutting of the banks when the water level reached the toe of the slope.

- Sloping, Planting and Brush Matting – This technique was used where additional protection was needed, however the brush matting did not prevent the banks from being undercut.

- Sloping, Riprapping at the Toe of the Slope, Brush Matting and Planting – This combination of techniques was the most successful practice. Hardwood brush from nearby was used as the matting material. Stems up to one inch thick were laid to form a thick mat, between twelve and eighteen inches thick, and staked down with wire. The mats were installed as quickly as possible following the sloping.

The plantings were made mostly of the local species of red osier dogwood (*Cornus stolonifera*) and box elder (*Acer negundo*), along with the purple osier willow. Some popular species were planted on flat areas above the bank.

The purple osier willow was the outstanding plant for streambank control on the Winooski River project. Nearly 89,000 cuttings were used. Good to excellent survival was obtained in most cases. They grew rapidly, especially the first four or five years, generally reaching the height of nine to ten feet. The local or white willow was used extensively. Considering the general undesirability of trees on streambanks, the brittle nature of white willow and its inferior survival made it less desirable than purple osier.

The use of speckled alder (*Alnus serrulata*) in the matting resulted in seedlings becoming established and impressed the authors enough for them to note that it required further study. Numerous other tree species were planted above the top of the slope.

In the concluding summary, the project was deemed a success and purple osier willow is identified as the superior streambank stabilizing species, with two native dogwood shrubs, red osier or silky cornel (*Cornus amomum)* also as desirable. Years later the Big Flats PMC released 'Ruby' red osier dogwood and the Appalachian PMC released 'Panbowl' speckled alder.

Using Rice Hull as Seed Diluents to Facilitate Seeding in 1950

Establishing conservation plantings that provide permanent vegetative cover is usually accomplished by direct seeding. Occasionally there are situations where a single species may be seeded, but to obtain better ground cover more rapidly and a more diverse plant community, seed mixtures including grasses, forbs and even woody species are preferred.

Grass, forbs and woody seeds generally end up feeding through a seed drill at variable rates. This is because of differences in seed size and seed weight. As a result, seed mixtures tend to separate in a drill with heavy seed migrating to the bottom as the drill bounces across the field. When planting a mixture of different-sized seeds or weight, or sometimes a single species, it is recommended that a carrier or diluents be used to facilitate more accurate drilling.

Lemmon and Hafenrichter tested several kinds of cracked cereals as diluents.[694] Cracked and screened barley proved most satisfactory. Southworth described how Hoglund developed the use of rice hulls and proved them superior to the other commonly used diluents.[695] O. K. Hoglund was the long time manager of the Pleasanton California nursery and PMC.

The 1949 report by the SCS Chief to the Secretary of Agriculture about what was going on at SCS nurseries nationally was mostly about Hoglund's innovation.[696]

The SCS nursery at Pleasanton developed an especially effective method for seeding mixtures of grass and legume seed by mixing the seed with rice hulls. The sowing of mixtures of different kinds of seeds in a single operation produced uniform distribution of all seeds, regardless of variations in shape and weight.

Hoglund had been working on this problem for some time. He discovered rice hulls as a carrier mainly by the trial and error method. The results first obtained from the use of this carrier were startling. Each hull acted as a tiny cup and held small clusters of the different seed in the mixture. Those not trapped in the cups seemed to float in the small spaces between the hulls. Fed through a grain drill, set to seeding barley at the rate of 160 pounds per acre, the seeds and rice hulls came through in an almost precise proportion to the rates of mixture. It made no difference whether the seeds were large or small, heavy or light. The rice hulls distributed them uniformly.

Hopeful but not wholly convinced, Hoglund resorted to a mechanical seed cleaner and separator. No amount of cleaning could separate more than fifty percent of the seeds from their possessive hulls.

Hoglund made his discovery in the fall of 1947. The first field planting with rice hull in their new role was made on the L. Z. Mitchell ranch near Corning, CA in October of that year. Thirty acres were seeded to a mixture of Harding grass, burnet, and subterranean clover, each having widely different sizes, shapes, and weights. The result was a vigorous, even stand of high-yielding forage. The uniform growth of all plants, evidenced eighteen months later, gave powerful support to Hoglund's conviction that rice hulls might eventually revolutionize the method of sowing small-seeded forage mixtures.

Figure 11.1 O. K. Hoglund

Rice hulls and seeds can be mixed in considerable quantity and stored in bags for later use. There is no danger of seed separation regardless of the amount of handling. Because of their bulk, however, one sack of rice hulls, or about six bushels, is all that can be handled efficiently at one mixing. Larger quantities make it difficult to get even distribution of seeds through the hulls.

Hoglund listed the advantages of using rice hulls for seeding forage mixtures with a grain drill. Most important was the even distribution of all seeds and the uniform forage stands that would result. The simplicity of the process was a strong point. A single-drill setting does the entire job. Farmers could forget grass-seeding attachments; the rice hulls and seed all went in the grain compartment together. Seeds of all kinds, sizes, shapes, and weights could be used with rice hulls. In sowing mixtures which include large seeds, such as vetch or bigger, the volume of rice hulls should be reduced by about one-half the total volume of the large seeds.

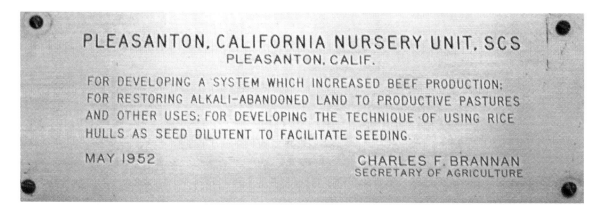

Figure 11.2 Plaque received by the Pleasanton PMC for the rice hulls innovation

Further testing led to the development of California Technical Note 16 by PM Specialist H. W. Miller in 1956.[697] It provided adequate details for use by field offices. Miller concluded that rice hulls are superior to cracked grain, sand or sawdust. The cup shape of rice hulls is largely responsible for their ability to hold seeds in a uniform suspension. "Even large seeds, such as 'Lana' vetch and 'Blando' brome feed evenly when thoroughly mixed with rice hulls."

According to St. John et al, it is highly recommended that U.S. #1-Grade rice hulls be used, as poorer quality ones are often broken, which reduces the cupping action to hold small-sized seeds together.[698] In May 2005 the Aberdeen, Bridger, Bismarck, Pullman and Upper Colorado PMCs joined forces to develop a technical note on the same subject. Although Miller's Technical Note is evident in the 2005 publication, the latter carries much more detail on calibrating the drill.

This excellent innovation has been used throughout the West. Ironically, it took on an additional meaning. Beginning in the SCS Nurseries and continuing into the 1950s and 1960s there was a stable group of individuals that became plant materials specialists after the 1954 reorganization. This was also during the international Cold War period, and the term Iron Curtin was well understood. Within the SCS Plant Materials Program, a similar understanding existed when the phrase 'Rice Hull Curtain' was used, meaning an invisible barrier existed between the west and the other regions relative to a free flow of technical information. Truth be known, it may have been a tinge of resentment against the forthright, and all too often correct West Regional Plant Materials Specialist, Dr. Hafenrichter.

Establishing Vegetation along Eroding Tidal Shores in 1960

In 1965 when the Cape May, NJ PMC became operational there were two clearly defined conservation problems the PMC needed to address. Number one priority was the plants and technology to build and stabilize coastal sand dunes. The second priority was how to use plants to halt or reduce erosion along tidal estuaries.

Although previous work by SCS plant materials specialists, primarily Marshall Augustine, gave a hint of the potential of a vegetative solution, the frequent failures left open the question as to whether any vegetative solution was realistic. In contrast to vegetating dunes, the nuances associated with the dynamic tidal beaches were much greater, each influencing the establishment and maintenance of vegetation. This work is the Featured Vegetative Accomplishment for the Cape May Center in Chapter 8.

Windbreak and Shelterbelt Protection Projects in the Northern Great Plains in 1965

If you are in North Dakota when the "wind comes sweepin' down the plain" most likely you would be looking for some shelter. One kind of shelter you would not have found a hundred years ago was a selection of woody plants for farm and home shelterbelts. That is because there were not very many of them, but now there are. This innovative work is discussed in detail in Chapter 8 as the Featured Vegetative Accomplishment of the Bismarck PMC and with Key Person Erling Jacobson in Chapter 10.

Cover Crops in California in 1975

In 2009, there were 2,550,500 acres of tree, vine and soft fruit crops in California.[699] Cover crops have been used in a part of these orchards and vineyards for over a hundred years. They are most prevalent in almond and walnut orchards, stone fruit orchards, and in table, raisin and wine grape vineyards. The need for this practice is increasing as more orchards and vineyards are planted on sloping land.

The vineyard or orchard crop, method of irrigation, method of harvest, topography and soil type, and available cover crops creates a myriad of potential combinations of cover cropping systems. Successful cover crop systems must take into account each of these variables and blend with the orchard or vineyard operating system. Plants useful under some conditions may be a liability under others. In the mid-1960s Clarence Finch, SCS Conservation Agronomist, and the state PM Specialist, Bob MacLauchlan, took on the task of evaluating and identifying the proper plants for each combination of management system and orchard or vineyard type. Finch, located in Fresno, was the linchpin, with the plant materials program supplying plant materials and evaluation assistance.

First, the most common management systems were identified.

1. Non-tillage systems where the cover crop is mowed four to seven times beginning in early spring

2. Non-tillage systems where the cover crop is infrequently clipped, usually in early spring for frost protection and late spring for residue control

3. Tillage systems where cover crop is fall-planted followed by summer fallow

4. Tillage systems where cover crop is annually seeded in the fall followed by volunteer summer annuals

5. Tillage systems of reseeding winter annual cover followed by summer fallow

6. Tillage systems of reseeding winter annual cover followed volunteer summer annuals

7. Tillage system of no winter cover followed by volunteer summer annuals

8. Tillage system of no winter cover followed by annually seeded summer annuals

9. Tillage system of no winter cover followed by reseeding summer annuals

The evaluated crops included citrus, fruit (apple, apricot, olive, pear and prune), nut (almond, walnut and pistachio) and vineyard crops.

All evaluations were on orchards and vineyards using strip cover management, which is growing cover crops in strips between tree or vine rows, with the row itself in a bare strip two to six feet wide.

Once these steps were resolved, all logical cover crops were planted in citrus, fruit and nut groves and vineyards over several years in the San Joaquin Valley.

The results through 1975 were published in *Cover Crops in California Orchards & Vineyards*.[700] It contains a detailed discussion of twenty-one useful cover cropping species. The most valuable tool is the Recommendations Table, which matches the above management system and orchard or vineyard type with recommended cover crop plants. For example, if the management is Non Tillage System and the crop is grapes for table wine, there are three recommended cover cropping choices. On the other hand, if the landowner is looking for a Management System for almonds there are two, each with multiple recommended cover crop species.

Finally, three commonly used management systems are discussed in detail. They are for almond orchards, raisin vineyards and citrus orchards.

From these examples, the recommended management system for any combination can be constructed for any vineyard or orchard crop grown in the San Joaquin valley.

Leveraging Automation Advancements for the Plant Materials Program in 1980s

Certain people are born to be leaders. How big or what they lead does not matter. One of those persons joined the Big Flats, NY PMC staff in 1974 as an agronomist. His name was Wendall Oaks. His zeal for the automation of information, and its machinery was apparent even then. For example, he told a superior, who was attempting to do an analysis of variance calculation with pen and paper, that he could do it on his wristwatch.

In 1978 he became manager of the Los Lunas, NM PMC where his juices for the automation and management of data had an opportunity to flourish. He was convinced the collection, management and evaluation of PMC plant data could and should be automated, and that all PMCs could be linked together as one. Not only did he believe that it could be done, but he knew the piece of equipment that could do it. That was revolutionary thinking in the early 1980s. In Biblical terms, Oaks was a prophet, in circus terminology he was the main event, in automation terminology he was the guru.

Good fortune shined on him when National PM Specialist Robert MacLauchlin believed he had come upon a financial windfall with the closing and sale of an old SCS nursery in Bellingham, WA. Oaks knew exactly how best to use the money. He had emerged not only as a leader of automation in the Plant Materials Program but in the entire agency. He was anxious to see PMCs be the first discipline in the agency to have a uniform standard computer operating system. At that time, each computer company had their own operating system. According to Oaks, the Hewlett Packard 250 would be best for PMCs. The Bellingham money was used to buy one for each PMC, fulfilling Oaks' vision. Over the years, the hardware and software technology have changed, but this early and continuing effort as a PMC manager at Los Lunas, influenced not only the PMC Program, but also the agency direction. In 1988, Wendall Oaks received the USDA Superior Service Award for this and other efforts.

Oaks joined the Information Technology Center in Fort Collins, CO in 1992 where he continued with the development of software for plant materials and other program automation. Others joined him in the discipline, principally John Scheetz, Manager of the Bridger, MT PMC, who had become a disciple of Oaks. He led much of the later day software development as center manager, and in 1998 worked full-time on this effort. As a result, the Plant Materials Program has been well served in this arena.

The Conversion of the National List of Scientific Plant Names (NLSPN) to Plant List of Attributes, Nomenclature and Symbols (PLANTS)

The initial efforts of Thomas N. Shiflet in developing the National List of Scientific Plant Names (NLSPN) [701], how it started down the road to being automated, and the employment of Dr. Scott Peterson is discussed in Chapter 6 during the late 1980s time frame. The processes used by Peterson to make it a USDA star are discussed here.

Scott initiated action by contacting the Flora of North America Association to determine if they would collaborate with SCS on the revision. At that time, the Association was totally focused on producing a multi-volume flora and did not want to undertake an overall U.S. plant checklist. His next contact was the Biota of North America Program directed by Dr. John Kartesz, who had developed a North American checklist for vascular plants. He was willing to participate.

The initial objective was to revise NLSPN into the Internet-based PLANTS system by 1991. The U.S. Forest Service was an initial partner in one revision of the NLSPN, and was a heavy user of plant symbols and standardized names. They provided some seed

Figure 11.3 Scott Peterson

money to assist Scott in getting the effort initiated. Collaborative meetings were set up in Beltsville with various other Federal agencies that had an interest in utilizing PLANTS. They are shown in Table 11.1.

A consensus was reached among these Federal agencies on taxonomic and data priorities and a process for developing PLANTS was approved. To initiate data development, cooperative agreements were made with the various data providers. Richard Roberts of the USDA Information Technology staff arranged for some funding, which was critical in getting this project underway.

Scott met with the staff of the USDA Information Office in Fort Collins, Colorado to initiate database design and development. Mary Lea Dodd led the initial software development team. Database and data development came together in 1991 to establish PLANTS. In 1994, to better service users, PLANTS was migrated to the World Wide Web, one of the first USDA applications to be placed there.

Table 11.1 Federal agencies interested in utilizing and helping to develop PLANTS

USDA Agricultural Research Service	Environmental Protection Agency
USDA Forest Service	USDI Bureau of Indian Affairs
USDA Animal and Plant Health Inspection Service	Natl. Oceanic and Atmospheric Adm.
USDA Farm Services Agency	Smithsonian Institution
USDA Rural Development	U.S. Geological Survey
USDI Bureau of Land Management,	USDI Fish and Wildlife Service
USDI National Park Service	USDD Army Corps of Engineers

By 1993, National PM Specialist Curtis Sharp had secured funding and a facility location for an SCS National Plant Data Center, administratively under the Ecological Sciences Division Director, and located it on the campus of Southern University, Baton Rouge, Louisiana. The Center continues the development and maintenance of PLANTS, working in collaboration with its partners.

In 2005, the Plant Data Center embarked on a bold new direction for updating and improving plant information. The need for different kinds of data and changes in Federal procurement rules led to this improved paradigm. Direct relationships with the botanical community evolved, and collaborations were expanded.

By 2008, PLANTS was the most heavily used scientific plant database in the world with over 50,000 users per day. Through PLANTS, more people are exposed to what is now the Natural Resource Conservation Service (NRCS) each day than any other venue. In 2009, the Plant Data Center was co-located with the NRCS Eastern National Technical Support Center in Greensboro, North Carolina.

Programs with Other Agencies – National Park Service

The National Park Service's (NPS) Denver Service Center works nationally with individual parks on revegetation of construction disturbances. NPS managers are challenged to control or arrest erosion and blend re-vegetated areas with the existing landscape, while maintaining genetic integrity and preventing the introduction of exotic species. The Federal Lands Highway Program provides funding for park road construction and reconstruction. An advantage offered by the Federal Lands Highway Program was that funds were available to obligate contracts for revegetation two to three years before construction began.

Local genetic stocks are always the first choice for revegetation and restoration. However, these plant materials were generally not available. NPS looked to the Plant Materials Program as a potential source for producing local native plants. Fortunately, this was possible with the Federal Lands Highway Program allowing the two to three years lead-time, creating a window in which the NPS could arrange with PMCs for the type of vegetation they wanted to use. In 1987, the Yellowstone and Glacier National Parks developed agreements with the Bridger, Montana PMC to produce seed of ecotypes collected on the parks. Next, starting in 1988, the Corvallis, Oregon PMC successfully

Figure 11.4 Wendell Hassell

358

provided locally collected ecotypes for a road rehabilitation project in Sol Duc Park. These experiences were so successful that Rocky Beavers of the NPS and Wendell Hassell, SCS PM Specialist in Denver, CO drafted an interagency MOU that would allow other parks to make similar agreements with other PMCs. The MOU was signed in March 1989. This cooperative agreement continues.

Two full-time National Technical Coordinators managed the program. The first pair was Hassell and Beaver. Both were stationed with the NPS in Denver. They coordinated the development of individual agreements between PMCs and parks. They also provided technical assistance for specific projects and studies–and organized service-wide workshops for revegetation/restoration training of park personal.

By 1990, project agreements had been enacted with fifteen parks and involved eleven PMC's as shown Table 11.2.

Table 11.2 National Park Service parks and PMCs with revegetation agreements

Park Projects	Park State(s)	PMC
Cumberland Gap National Historical Park	KY TN VA	Beltsville MD
Great Smoky Mountains National Park	TN	Quicksand KY
Natchez Trace Parkway	MS	Coffeeville MS
Big Bend National Park	TX	Knox City TX
Chickasaw National Recreation Area	OK	Knox City TX
Wuptaki National Monument	AZ	Los Lunas NM
Bryce Canyon National Park	UT	Meeker CO
Glacier National Park	MT	Bridger MT
Grand Teton National Park	WY	Meeker CO
Mesa Verde National Park	CO	Meeker CO
Yellowstone National Park	WY	Bridger MT
Grand Canyon National Park	AZ	Los Lunas NM
Yosemite National Park	CA	Lockeford CA
Mount Rainier National Park Hwy 123 410	OR	Corvallis OR
Mount Rainier National Park Sunrise/Paradise	OR	Corvallis OR

By 1995, there were thirty-six projects with twenty-nine parks cooperating with thirteen PMCs. By 2000, there were thirty-three active projects at twenty-three parks in cooperation with nine PMCs. In 2010, there were forty-six active projects at twenty-nine National parks in cooperation with eleven PMCs.

Wendell Hassell continued as NRCS National Coordinator until December until 1997 when he retired. Russell Haas replaced him, retired in August 2008, and was replaced by Pat Davey. The NPS coordinator, Rocky Beavers, resigned in May 1998; he was replaced by Nancy Dunkle who retired in January 2005. Sarah Wynn replaced Nancy.

Riparian and Wetland Establishment Techniques in 1990 and Beyond

Chris Hoag came to the Aberdeen, ID PMC in 1990 as a Plant Materials Center Trainee. He retired in 2010. His formal training was in range science, and had worked as a range conservationist with SCS before coming to the PMC. His contributions to riparian and wetland establishment techniques is well documented in Chapter 10. Chris is included in Chapter 9 as a Productive Scientist.

The Evolution of an expanded Release Process in 1994

This evolution is discussed in detail in Chapters 7 and 8.

Saline Seep Mitigation in 2004

The Northern Plains and Intermountain West are characterized by substantial areas of saline soils, typified of Figure 11.5. The original source of the salts is weathered bedrock and ancient saline sea-bottoms. The major factor responsible for the formation of salt-affected soils is the redistribution of salts within the soil, with water as the primary carrier. Where rainfall is high, most salts are leached out of the soil. In arid regions, typical of most western states, the salt levels accumulated in soils can be very high because of limited or reduced leaching. Of course, not all soils in arid regions are salt-affected because the soil parent materials are not contributing sources of salts.

Figure 11.5 Impacts of salt-affected soils

However, indirect sources of salts can exist from irrigation water that comes from saline sources or saline water that comes from groundwater wells.[702]

Wherever saline soils occur, they reduce the land's value for agriculture. Figure 11.6 is of Bozoisky Russian wildrye on a saline site.

Larry Holzworth, plant materials specialist for Montana provided the following background on how the Bridger Montana PMC became involved in the landmark work of identifying plants suitable for planting on saline soils.[703]

Mark Majerus was the first person to begin collecting saline/sodic tolerant plant materials, establishing initial evaluation plantings, developing the techniques of saline/sodic soil reclamation and releasing plant materials for this use. Mark was hired in 1976 by the Montana Soil and Water Conservation Districts, Inc. with soft money from the Old West Regional Commission.[704] Money for the saline research was passed through the MSWCD to the SCS Bridger Plant Materials Center to fund Mark. Mark's office was located at the Bridger PMC and he was supervised by the Center Manager. Later, he was hired by SCS and worked as a Soil Conservationist and then became manager. Mark made a large contribution, conducting on-center and off-center research trials, which resulted in plant materials and techniques for saline/sodic soil reclamation in the Northern Great Plains.

Figure 11.6 'Bozoisky-Select' Russian wildrye

Publications about plant performance on saline soils written by Majerus are impressive. The first, dealing specifically with his research was <u>Plant Materials for Saline-Alkaline Soils</u>, published in 1996.[705] In 2004, he co-authored an updated technical note titled, Plants for <u>Saline to Sodic Soil Conditions</u>.[706]

His 1996 Technical Note lists thirteen grass species that are suitable for planting in the saline-alkaline soils of the Northern Great Plains and Southern Canadian Prairie Provinces. One of the criteria for making the list was commercial availability, and all are available. Four are native grasses and nine introduced. All have good-to-excellent forage quality. The select group is shown in Table 11.3.

The Bridger PMC, building on the work of Majerus, turned their effort to identify tolerant woody plants that would prosper on saline soils. Their effort was undertaken because well-documented tests to determine the most tolerant woody plants was lacking. A mid-course progress report was in the PMCs 2010 Annual Technical Report.[707] The objective is, "To determine the relative salinity tolerance of eighteen different species of trees and shrubs used in various conservation applications in Montana and Wyoming." The report shows the conservation uses of woody species on saline soils for conservation applications. They include field windbreaks, shelterbelts, wildlife habitat improvement, mineland reclamation, water conserving landscaping and urban forestry. A major application of this knowledge will be revegetation with woody plants following Russian olive and salt-cedar removal on salt-affected sites. This will become more important as control efforts for these invasive species increase. While plant selection is not within the scope of this project, the results may suggest potential seed sources, genera, or species for future testing.

Table 11.3 Commercially available, saline-alkaline tolerant plants for the Northern Great Plains

Species	Common Name	Cultivars
Leymus multicaulus	beardless wildrye	Shoshone
Thinopyrum ponticum	tall wheatgrass	Alkar, Largo, Jose
Leymus angustus	Altai wildrye	Prairieland, Pearle, Eejay
Elytrigia repens X Pseudoroegneria spicata	hybrid wheatgrass	NewHy
Elymus trachycaulus	slender wheatgrass	Pryor
Festuca arundinacea	tall fescue	Kenmont, Fawn, Alta, Goar,
Psathyrostachys juncea	Russian wildrye	Bozoisky-Select, Swift, Mankota, Vinall
Pascopyrum smithii	western wheatgrass	Rosana, Rodan, Walsh
Alopecurus arundinaceus	creeping foxtail	Garrison, Retain
Agropyron cristarum	crested wheatgrass	Fairway, Ephraim
Agropyron cristatum X A. desertorum	crested wheatgrass hybrid	Hycrest
Agropyron desertorurn	desert wheatgrass	Nordan, Summit
Agropyron sibericum	Siberian wheatgrass	P-27, Vavilov

The woody planting was made in a salt-affected saline seep consisting of fluctuating levels of salts and water across the site. After five years, the mean survival for the eighteen species in the study was 49.6%. However, four species exceeded 80%. One was the Russian olive, with a 93% survival rate. The other three, all trees, were Siberian elm (*Ulmus pumila*) at 83.3%, green ash (*Fraxinus pennsylvanica*) at 93.3% and cottonwood (*Populus deltoids)* at 96.7%. Three shrubs exceeded 70% survival; blueleaf honeysuckle (*Lonicera korolkowii),* silverberry *(Elaeagnus commutate),* and seaberry (*Hippophae rhamnoides).* This study will be finalized and results reported in the 2011 Bridger PMC Annual Technical Report.

This outstanding innovation of finding and documenting plants for reclaiming soils impacted with salinity is an outstanding example of how the Bridger PMC has improved land use in the Northern Great Plains and Southern Canadian Prairie Provinces.

Use of Piligrass (*Heteropogon contortus*) Hay Bales for the Island of Kaho`olawe's Highly Erodible Sites in 2008

The application of this innovative idea may be limited but it warrants recognition.[708] It is discussed and presented with pictures in Chapter 8, under the section on the Ho'olehua PMC.

TOP PREFORMING CULTIVARS

All production data in the following tables came from the annual production data collected by the Plant Materials Program, starting in 1977. No data is included on production past 2005. All economic data is based on the economic analysis of the production data.[709] The methodology used to determine these values is discussed in detail in Appendix 4. While some of the cultivars released by PMCs have been discontinued, they are included in the following tables.

Table 11.4 Top 25 seed producing and the top 10 plant producing releases

Release Name	Common Name	Release Year	Unit	Primary PMC	Total Production
Pensacola	Bahiagrass	1944	LB	GA	36,813,261
Newport	Kentucky bluegrass	1958	LB	WA	22,508,470
Luna	pubescent wheatgrass	1963	LB	NM	11,117,885
Manchar	smooth brome	1943	LB	WA	9,775,273
Regar	meadow brome	1966	LB	ID	9,621,077
Critana	thickspike wheatgrass	1971	LB	MT	8,777,835
Emerald	crownvetch	1961	LB	MO	8,744,697
F-149	American joinvetch	1969	LB	FL	7,406,100
Selection 75	Klinegrass	1969	LB	TXJS	6,747,544
Blackwell	Switchgrass	1944	LB	KS	4,694,940
Secar	Snake River wheatgrass	1980	LB	WA	4,494,801
Sherman	big bluegrass	1945	LB	WA	4,455,236
Rimrock	Indian ricegrass	1996	LB	MT	4,411,570
Arriba	western wheatgrass	1973	LB	NM	4,359,759
Rosana	western wheatgrass	1972	LB	MT	4,338,058
Jose	tall wheatgrass	1965	LB	NM	4,280,519
El Reno	sideoats grama	1944	LB	KS	3,963,651
P-27	Siberian wheatgrass	1953	LB	ID	3,914,525
Latar	orchardgrass	1957	LB	WA	3,651,805
Sodar	streambank wheatgrass	1954	LB	ID	3,467,043
Magnar	basin wildrye	1979	LB	ID	3,189,719
T-4464	Buffelgrass	1949	LB	TXJS	2,927,283
Blando	soft chess	1954	LB	CA	2,910,000
Lana	wollypod vetch	1956	LB	CA	2,910,000
Cave-In-Rock	Switchgrass	1974	LB	MO	2,852,720
Cape	American beachgrass	1970	PL	NJ	179,250,874
Cardinal	autumn olive	1961	PL	NY	36,706,654
Tropic Lalo	Paspalum	1984	PL	HI	28,042,318
101	bicolor lespedeza	1947	PL	GA	18,087,900
Amquail	Thunberg's lespedeza	1987	PL	GA	15,085,257
Bigalta	Limpograss	1978	PL	FL	13,733,300
Streamco	purpleosier willow	1975	PL	NY	9,646,792
Imperial	Carolina poplar	1979	PL	MI	7,852,372
VA-70	shrub lespedeza	1952	PL	MD	7,446,713
Tropic Coral	tall erythrina	1985	PL	HI	7,109,000

* - LB = pound, PL = Plant

Nine of the top thirty-five producing cultivars in Table 11.4 entered the commercial market during the observational nursery days. Fifteen are native plants and twenty are introduced. Most surprising is that 'Rimrock' Indian ricegrass, released in 1996, is on the list. In addition to its conservation value, Native Americans in the Southwest and Great Basin regions commonly used Indian ricegrass as a food source. Flour made from seed of ricegrass, known as Wye or Wai to the Paiute, Shoshone and Ute tribes, was used to make a mush with a pleasing, nutlike flavor. Montana State University-Bozeman has determined that flour derived from Rimrock Indian ricegrass is gluten-free. This flour (Montina) is commercially available for use by people who cannot consume gluten without dire health consequences.[710]

Table 11.5 contains the top twenty-five producer benefitting cultivars, respectively. Although 'Pensacola' bahiagrass is the top producing cultivar pound wise (Table 11.4) its benefit to producers did not make Table 11.5. Three of the cultivars in Table 11.5 are sold as plants, American beachgrass, sawtooth oak and tall erythrina.

Table 11.5 Top 25 producer-benefiting cultivars

Cultivar	Common Name	Year Released	Release PMC	Cultivar Produced Value
Selection 75	Klinegrass	1969	TXPMC	$27,260,000
Critana	thickspike wheatgrass	1971	MTPMC	$23,568,000
Luna	pubescent wheatgrass	1963	NMPMC	$21,635,000
Nezpar	Indian ricegrass	1978	IDPMC	$20,421,000
Cape	American beachgrass	1970	NJPMC	$17,607,000
Emerald	Crownvetch	1961	MOPMC	$16,916,000
Magnar	basin wildrye	1979	IDPMC	$16,739,000
Blackwell	Switchgrass	1944	KSPMC	$16,130,000
Athens	sawtooth oak	1972	GAPMC	$15,968,000
Sherman	big bluegrass	1945	WAPMC	$15,466,000
Rimrock	Indian ricegrass	1996	MTPMC	$15,421,000
Arriba	western wheatgrass	1973	NMPMC	$15,335,000
Hachita	blue grama	1980	NMPMC	$14,352,000
Goldar	bluebunch wheatgrass	1989	IDPMC	$14,049,000
Cave-In-Rock	Switchgrass	1974	MOPMC	$12,760,000
Vaughn	sideoats grama	1940	NMPMC	$12,145,000
El Reno	sideoats grama	1944	KSPMC	$11,194,000
Emerald Sea	shore juniper	1971	NJPMC	$10,537,000
Rountree	big bluestem	1983	MOPMC	$10,514,000
Rosana	western wheatgrass	1972	MTPMC	$10,198,000
Corto	Australian saltbush	1977	AZPMC	$9,836,000
Secar	Snake River wheatgrass	1980	WAPMC	$9,646,000
Appar	prairie flax	1980	IDPMC	$8,359,000
Tropic Coral	tall erythrina	1985	HIPMC	$7,836,000
Haskell	sideoats grama	1983	TXPMC	$7,216,000

Table 11.6 has eighteen native cultivars and seven introduced. 'Rimrock' is again the most recent release, and only four are from the observational nurseries. The twenty-five represents the efforts of ten PMCs. Three Centers had four each. All except Bridger, MT had also been an observational nursery. Nine were the product, or near product of the observational nurseries.

Table 11.6 Top 25 ecological-benefiting cultivars

Cultivar	Common Name	Year Released	Release PMC	Cultivar Ecological Benefit
Selection 75	Klinegrass	1969	TXPMC	$139,044,000
Newport	Kentucky bluegrass	1958	WAPMC	$106,840,000
Sherman	big bluegrass	1945	WAPMC	$82,450,000
Critana	thickspike wheatgrass	1971	MTPMC	$45,220,000
Bigalta	Limpograss	1978	FLPMC	$36,073,000
Pensacola	Bahiagrass	1944	GAPMC	$31,203,000
Hachita	blue grama	1980	NMPMC	$30,286,000
T-4464	Buffelgrass	1949	TXPMC	$30,161,000
Blackwell	Switchgrass	1944	KSPMC	$28,539,000
Vaughn	sideoats grama	1940	NMPMC	$24,398,000
Luna	pubescent wheatgrass	1963	NMPMC	$24,302,000
El Reno	sideoats grama	1944	KSPMC	$21,722,000
Arriba	western wheatgrass	1973	NMPMC	$21,164,000
Haskell	sideoats grama	1983	TXPMC	$20,648,000
Rosana	western wheatgrass	1972	MTPMC	$19,823,000
Alamo	Switchgrass	1978	TXPMC	$19,191,000
Forestburg	Switchgrass	1987	NDPMC	$17,845,000
Cave-In-Rock	Switchgrass	1974	MOPMC	$17,308,000
P-27	Siberian wheatgrass	1953	IDPMC	$16,679,000
Manchar	smooth brome	1943	WAPMC	$16,576,000
Sodar	streambank wheatgrass	1954	IDPMC	$16,262,000
Rimrock	Indian ricegrass	1996	MTPMC	$16,245,000
Emerald	Crownvetch	1961	MOPMC	$14,360,000
Regar	meadow brome	1966	IDPMC	$14,134,000
Secar	Snake River wheatgrass	1980	WAPMC	$13,871,000

Table 11.7 includes the combined producer and ecological benefits of the top twenty-five cultivars. The observational nurseries are well represented with six from the 1940s.

There are eighteen cultivars of native origin Table 11.7 and seven introduced. All, but one of them are grasses. Most woody plants fall short in terms of ecological benefit. While they are produced in large numbers, when planted they protect much fewer acres. For example, 'Cape' American beachgrass is the largest producer of plants but only covers 309 acres while a few pounds of seed plant an acre.

Table 11.7 Top 25 Ecological- and Producer-Benefiting Cultivars

Cultivar	Common Name	Year Released	Release PMC	Unit	Total Producer and Ecological Value
Selection 75	klinegrass	1969	TXPMC	LB	$166,305,000
Newport	Kentucky bluegrass	1958	WAPMC	LB	$106,840,000
Sherman	big bluegrass	1945	WAPMC	LB	$97,916,000
Critana	thickspike wheatgrass	1971	MTPMC	LB	$68,789,000
Luna	pubescent wheatgrass	1963	NMPMC	LB	$45,937,000
Blackwell	switchgrass	1944	KSPMC	LB	$44,670,000
Hachita	blue grama	1980	NMPMC	LB	$44,637,000
Bigalta	Limpograss	1978	FLPMC	PL	$37,865,660
Vaughn	sideoats grama	1940	NMPMC	LB	$36,543,000
Arriba	western wheatgrass	1973	NMPMC	LB	$36,500,000
Pensacola	Bahiagrass	1944	GAPMC	LB	$36,018,000
T-4464	buffelgrass	1949	TXPMC	LB	$33,390,000
Rimrock	Indian ricegrass	1996	MTPMC	LB	$31,667,000
Emerald	crownvetch	1961	MOPMC	LB	$31,275,000
El Reno	sideoats grama	1944	KSPMC	LB	$30,727,000
Cave-In-Rock	switchgrass	1974	MOPMC	LB	$30,068,000
Rosana	western wheatgrass	1972	MTPMC	LB	$30,021,000
Magnar	basin wildrye	1979	IDPMC	LB	$29,565,000
Haskell	sideoats grama	1983	TXPMC	LB	$27,864,000
Secar	Snake River wheatgrass	1980	WAPMC	LB	$23,517,000
Nezpar	Indian ricegrass	1978	IDPMC	LB	$22,612,000
Sodar	streambank wheatgrass	1954	IDPMC	LB	$22,334,000
Alamo	switchgrass	1978	TXPMC	LB	$21,323,000
Forestburg	switchgrass	1987	NDPMC	LB	$21,245,000
Goldar	bluebunch wheatgrass	1989	IDPMC	LB	$21,166,000

The graph displays the relationship between the costs and the benefits of the observational nursery/plant materials centers from 1935 through 2005, as well graphically comparing the source of the benefits.

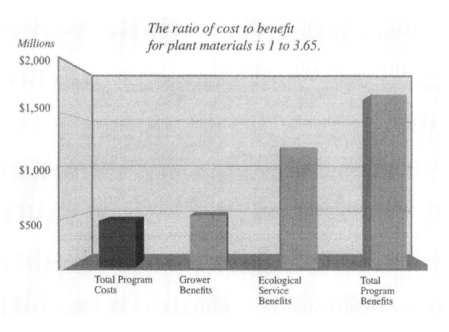

Chapter 12: THE CASE OF INTRODUCED PLANTS FOR CONSERVATION PURPOSES

INTRODUCTION

When looking at the issue of introduced plants, i.e., using plants that have evolved elsewhere, the most important quote to remember may be: "In 1492, Christopher Columbus reached the Western Hemisphere. The impact of that landing has dramatically altered every ecosystem in North America."[711] Was Columbas a good or bad introduction?

Remember Pogo's words, "We have met the enemy and he is us."[712]

Using introduced plants became a hot political issue in the late twentieth century. With increased regulatory and citizen-based concerns, this seems an appropriate point to take a broader look at introduced conservation plants. It will help if we can get inside the heads and understand the thinking of the earlier developers of conservation plants; like in the 1930, and 1940s. Their charge could be likened to that of a fireman confronting a burning home. Soil erosion in the Southeast was rampant, the Great Plains soil was passing over Washington and Western rangeland lay unprotected. What were their thoughts?

Finding conservation plants that could slow or stop this erosion was the number one priority. They were the mother lode; a brand new program had been created to find them. Imagine the pride swelling in the chest of James E. Smith, Jr. in 1960 when he wrote, "In 1935 T-4464 buffelgrass accession was received from South Africa by way of the Beltsville, Maryland nursery, and was planted in a rod row evaluation block at the San Antonio nursery. Growth was outstanding, and a small trial planting of it was made at Sutherland Springs, Texas in 1948. The first market supply of buffel seed was offered for sale in 1950. Four years later it was estimated that there was in excess of 500,000 acres of buffelgrass in range, pasture, and seed increase plantings in southern and southeastern Texas."[713] Smith knew soil conservation when he saw it, and no doubt smiled and said, "There's a half million acres that won't blow again."

T-4464 has fallen from grace, discontinued as a cultivar,[714] but Smith knew success when he saw it.[715] While the glimmer of a named, superior performing, widely adapted cultivar shines a little less than did the early ones, Smith's feeling of accomplishment must be appreciated. They had been told, and had every reason to believe, that the Great Plains soil landing in the Atlantic Ocean was the resource that must be saved. T-4464 is still doing that, but once the soil was safe the priority seemed to shift to saving the native flora, which had failed when the land resource fell in the path of human use.

PRE-SCS HISTORY OF PLANT INTRODUCTIONS INTO NORTH AMERICA

Plant introduction is an old activity.[716] From the dawn of time humans have brought back useful plants from the lands where they visited. It is also an ancient activity of governments. Charles Woolley gives the first recorded account of an introduction.[717] It is an inscription found in Mesopotamia on how Sargon crossed the Taurus and brought back specimens of trees, vines, figs and roses for "acclimatization in his own land." The Egyptians sent ships to the Land of Plum to get incense trees around 1500 B.C.[718]

The first Europeans settlers in America took up residence along the forested Atlantic seaboard, which was void of many plants they felt were needed for their survival in their new world. This included human food, as well as food for their livestock. Columbus had brought some plants with him on his first voyages to the West Indies, including wheat. Wheat crops were planted in the western hemisphere in 1494.[719] They arrived in Mexico in 1520 and in the colonies in the 1600s.[720] Red clover, a valuable forage legume, was cultivated in Massachusetts in 1747.[721] Rice arrived in 1685,[722] and soybeans arrived in 1765.[723]

Thomas Jefferson searched constantly for new crops adapted to the conditions of his land and climate.[724] While a United States envoy to France, he sent seeds of various grasses, acorns of the cork oak, olive plants and innumerable fruits and vegetable seeds to agricultural societies, farmers, and botanists in the fledgling United States. He is quoted as saying "The greatest service which can be rendered any country is the introduction of a new plant into its culture."[725] He smuggled Italian rice out of Italy and brought it to the planters of South Carolina which enabled them to "produce the best rice in the world."[726]

Other plants, such as the extensively distributed Kentucky bluegrass, were introduced in the early colonial days.[727] Native Americans called it "White man's tracks" because most everywhere white man went with his livestock and plows, they found Kentucky bluegrass.

Humans and plants travel together. Not only do humans like plants; plants are essential for their survival. Timothy (*Phleum pratense*), a common forage grass, has been traced to the early 1700s in colonial settlements in New England.[728] It was choice hay for horses, the fuel for colonial transportation. Well adapted to the cool, humid climate, it soon became distributed over much of the northern colonial area. It was initially called Herd's grass, named for the New Hampshire farmer who grew it. Later, the common name changed to Timothy, named after Timothy Hanson, another New Englander that started producing and selling seed. George Washington and Benjamin Franklin were both satisfied customers of Timothy Hanson's hay.[729]

The combination of introduced farming practices of Europeans, and cotton, native to tropical America, altered the landscape of much of the Southeast, just as the introduction of domestic livestock altered the Midwest and Western United States.[730] These introductions also changed other things. During the first century and a half after Columbus's voyages, the native human population of the Americas plummeted by an estimated eighty percent, from around fifty million in 1492 to eight million in 1650.[731] Native Americans comprised a hundred percent of the human population in North America in 1492; in 2000, less than 0.67 percent, according to U.S. Census data.[732] Native plants have survived this introduction better than the native humans. This is a low benchmark for tolerable invasiveness.

Of all the introductions that have altered the landscape of the Continent, humans have altered their environment a thousand times more than all other introduced species combined. Massive adjustments took place quickly during the founding of the United States and continue today. Pasture and cotton fields replaced forests, savannas became corn fields, plains became commodity crop production machines, and domestic horses, cattle and sheep now occupy grazing land where the deer and antelope once played.[733] Four-lane highways replaced Indian trails, rushing streams became mammoth lakes and pastoral landscapes became cities and towns. Introduced humans had found a niche.

WAS A SEARCH FOR CONSERVATION PLANTS WARRANTED?

Had all these changes warranted the search for conservation plants? Was there even a need to stop or slow the loss of top our soil? Did such a search justify the use of introduced plants? Chapter 1, "Why the Plant Materials Centers Program Was Needed?" makes a case for an affirmative answer. The North American continent ceased to be a virgin somewhere in the middle of the sixteenth century. The tipping point came when the country realized it was being raped, and was jolted into action. The time and the place can be pinpointed: April 27, 1935, soon after a dust cloud of Great Plains soil darkened the skis over the national capital and Hugh Hammond Bennett had testified before the Senate Public Lands Committee.[734]

FINDING THE BEST PLANT, NATIVE OR INTRODUCED

The first governmental recognition of the importance of plant importation came with the passage of the Treasury Circular Act of 1827.[735] Next, with the establishment of the USDA in 1862, the government became active in seed and plant procurement and distribution, some concentrating on conservation plants.[736] An organized search for better conservation plants, including introduced ones, started with the USDI Soil Erosion Service in 1934,[737] and continued in SCS observational nurseries in 1935.[738] A leader in this effort, Dr. Franklin Crider, thought "Nature has evolved a plant for every purpose."[739] On this premise, the Plant Materials Center Program was born. Dr. Crider's concept did not say "Nature has evolved a plant in North America for every purpose." Nature, of course, exists worldwide. If, or how long, he pondered his exact wording is unknown. Faced with the red, yellow and brown Southeast streams carrying the productive soil of a nation to the sea, or the dust storm passing overhead, transporting the most fertile top soil in the world to the Atlantic Ocean, he may not have pondered long, so the search began.

Observational study leaders laid their hands on any plant they thought might work to abate erosion. Soil erosion was the gorilla in the room, not introduced plants. Whatever plants they selected had to grow on harsh eroding or eroded sites, and had to stabilize the soil. These harsh conditions were foreign to most native plants. The opportunity to evolve a tolerance for such sites had not existed.

Most collections for superior plants came from native stands. Conservation plant-wise, this was indeed profitable in many regions of the U.S., but not all. In the densely forested regions of the East and Southeast, the kinds of herbaceous, ground covering plants that are essential to stop this kind of erosion and allow the re-invasion of natives were hard to find locally;[740] they had not evolved. Even though there were lots of such plants in the Western U.S., their ability to be propagated easily or re-established on overgrazed and eroded rangeland proved difficult. Faced with a 'stop the erosion' mandate, they jumped at whatever would do the job. The absence of native, soil-binding plants for stabilizing the strip mine spoil in Appalachia limited their options.

The first plant conservationists of the 1934-1935 eras acknowledged that all plants, native or introduced, had the potential of invading surrounding areas. Those that did not would become extinct. They were also acutely aware of the negative aspects of bringing a plant into general use that had the potential of adversely affecting the habitats they invaded. It was true in 1934 and it is true today. They were also aware that it took nature several millenniums to evolve a plant to fit the niches created by humankind in the past three hundred years.[741]

FRAMING THE DEBATE

There will continue to be a debate, relative to the Plant Materials Program, regarding the evaluating and placing of non-native cultivars in the commercial market. The potential opposition results from several circumstances.

1. First, of course, is the undesirable risk that a non-native cultivar might spread voluntarily beyond its anticipated and intended area of use. An example of a plant doing this was 'Pensacola' bahiagrass. It was first evaluated as a conservation plant on badly eroded and abandoned cotton land in the Southeast. Tests quickly showed that it out performed other grasses for this use, converting the land from useless to productive pasture. Over time it voluntarily left the pasture, showing up on highway shoulders and banks. Again its performance was such to make it the plant of choice for this use in many states. Then it began appearing in lawns. Some thought that was a good thing. One author wrote "Pensacola bahiagrass is a warm-season grass commonly used in lawns in regions that have warm winters. Pensacola is the most popular bahiagrass variety, mostly due to its resiliency and tolerance of

368

insects and drought."[742] Others preferred something else. Wasn't there a native grass that will do as good or better job than 'Pensacola' on these sites? Or should its use be forbidden, and native plants, although less desirable, be used? Of course the challenge of finding them remains, which the early conservationists were unable to do.

2. Strong objections are often generated when a cultivar volunteers off the intended use site onto a different land use where its presence is a determent, such as woody plants volunteering into pasture land. An example of this is autumn olive. It can stabilize acid, low fertility, surface coal mine spoil in Appalachia better than any native shrub, and, while doing so, it greatly enhances the available food and cover of all sorts of wildlife.[743] Had acid coal mine spoil existed when shrubs were evolving in Appalachia, autumn olive might have been one of them. Its attributes make it such a desirable conservation plant for such uses. It is easy to establish, tolerant to very acidic soils, competitive, produces abundant seed and, although not a legume, fixes soil nitrogen. Unfortunately, these attributes are exactly why it can invade other sites so easily. It does an excellent job for the intended use, but pasture isn't one of them. While the reinvasion of native woody plants into pastures that were carved out of previously forested areas is natural and will occur if the pasture is not well managed, the invasive ability of autumn olive exceeds what average management will deter.[744]

3. Even the native, broadly adapted conservation cultivars offer the potential for mixing their germplasm into ecosystems that contain the same species, thus compromising the purity of the local ecotype. 'Blackwell' switchgrass, from Blackwell County, Oklahoma, performs well through much of the northeast and southeast. While the species is not a dominate one in those regions, like it is in the Great Plains, 'Blackwell' planted there could contaminate the few scattered local ecotypes. Of course, there is a constant desire to make things better in most aspects of human existence, and 'Blackwell' might do that for the locals.

4. Sometimes introduced plants are the fall guy for no reason of their own, other than they are introduced. An example can be seen in parts of the central Great Plains. 'Lincoln' smooth brome and cultivars of naturalized Kentucky bluegrass found a niche and grow with great vigor in these deep fertile soils. The niche was created wherever the existing plant cover was diminished, by overgrazing, or other forms of destroying the native flora. These plants were competitive and tolerated overgrazing, prohibiting the return of native grasses and forbs.[745] Extensive areas of the native rangeland have been replaced through this process.[746] While the cause of the invasion of smooth brome and Kentucky bluegrass was poor resource management, the brome and bluegrass are viewed as the problem. However, nature evolved plants to fill an existing void. If fenced cattle and sheep had roamed the prairies, no doubt smooth brome would have evolved there.

5. Then there remains the classical example of not wanting strangers in the neighborhood. When the Europeans came to the new world, the Native Americans were not happy to see them. They were viewed for what they were, an introduced species. As the introduced humans took over their land and killed them off, their negative attitude became understandable. Then, when the Irish and Italians came with their rough ways and offensive religion, the English and German immigrants wished they had stayed home.[747] When the more palatable and higher producing 'Selection 75' Kline grass was introduced into the overgrazed rangeland of central and southern Texas , it replaced the less palatable native grasses and forbs, provided there were any left.[748] Farmers and ranchers loved it.[749] Others were less pleased.[750] Similar examples are cultivars of introduced crested wheatgrass. Widely used to re-stabilize western rangeland that had been overgrazed by cows and sheep, it was unwanted by many, even though its tolerance to overgrazing was better than the natives.[751]

369

EARLY SELECTION OF INTRODUCED PLANTS, BY REGION

From the beginning of the Plant Materials Program in 1934, there has been a vast regional difference between the types of conservation problems being studied. For example, re-vegetating strip mine spoil was a top priority in the Appalachian region, while stopping the wind erosion dominated the early work in the Great Plains. This obviously impacted the type of plants evaluated for solving the problems, including both native and introduced species.

When the humid east and south were occupied by Europeans, they created conditions similar to the ones they had left. Native Americans had not created such conditions, thus no plants for growing on such land existed. That did not mean that no such plants existed. SCS concluded the first priority was to heal the scars quickly. The concept of "Let nature take its course" was unacceptable. To intervene with the best tools available was the course they followed.

Humid East and South

The majority of herbaceous plants used for initial conservation work in the humid Eastern third of the nation were introduced. The native flora was nearly void of plants that the newly arrived residents could eat, or feed their livestock. The same was true when it came time to heal the scars on the landscape, which resulted from practices totally foreign to the North Americans continent. In both cases, they imported plants.

While some scorned the effort of these early conservationists as foolish for even trying, had they not developed the specifications required for re-vegetating mine spoil, the 1977 Surface Mining Act could not have been written.[752] The stabilizing tools were available, including many introduced plants.

Tall fescue is a most important conservation grass in the U.S. It provides the primary ground cover on approximately thirty-five million acres.[753] According to the Oklahoma Invasive Species site, tall fescue came into the U.S. in the late 1800s.[754] It is a versatile cool season perennial grass. In addition to being an erosion control plant, it is used for livestock forage and various turf purposes. Its path to wide spread use went through SCS observational nurseries.[755]

Mentioned earlier is bahiagrass, found in Florida in 1941 along the wharf in Pensacola, FL. Believing that it had pasture potential, SCS, began to promote it as an improved pasture grass for the Deep South. Today, it occupies well over a million acres, where it has been planted, and hundreds of acres, where it has been unintentionally spread by man and beast.

One introduced legume used extensively for erosion control and beautifications in the twenty-five-inch-and-up rainfall regions of the temperate U.S. is crownvetch, another loved and not loved introduction. Any highway traveler in the eastern states during May, June or July will have seen crownvetch protecting and beautifying the highway slopes. Three cultivars were on the market, 'Chemung', 'Emerald' and 'Penngift'.[756] The SCS PMC Program was associated with developing the first two, and The Pennsylvania State University developed 'Penngift' which was also the first to be commercially sold, beginning in 1955.

Many naturalists, conservationists and environmentalists have objected to crownvetch as an invasive plant. The Pennsylvania Department of Transportation (PennDOT) contends the campaign against crownvetch has been promoted by the Federal Highway Administration because of political pressure. From PennDOTs point of view, this decision was made without full realization of crownvetch's role in highway vegetation management. According to them, complaints from landowners adjacent to highway plantings have been almost non-existent over the nearly fifty years it has been used.-The fact that it is grazed out by livestock eliminates any potential of it being troublesome in pastures adjacent to the highway. Poor shade tolerance also limits its invasion of forested areas.

PennDOT felt so strongly about the use of crownvetch on their highway slopes, that to resist it being banned, on June 17, 1982 Governor Dick Thornburg signed Act 1982-150, Laws of Pennsylvania, declaring 'Penngift' crownvetch as the official State Beautification and Conservation Plant of the Commonwealth of Pennsylvania.[757]

The useable erosion coverage from a well-established stand of crownvetch is fifteen to twenty years. Like all monoculture stands, of either native or introduced plants, they will themselves be invaded. In the case of crownvetch planted in a thirty-inches-or-more rainfall zone, it will succumb to invading exotic and native trees, shrubs and vines.[758] Another reason the highway administrations like the plant is that a healthy stand restricts the reinvasion of trees on the banks and close to the road. While valued as a community asset due to their beauty and environmental benefits, trees are the single most commonly struck objects in serious roadside crashes.[759] Vehicle collisions with trees account for more than 4,000 fatalities and 100,000 injuries each year. Efforts by highway agencies to remove trees are often met with strenuous objections by local residents, concerned with preserving our natural resources and the aesthetics they bring to our surroundings.

The Great Plains

The Dust Bowl was the fire storm that helped bring SCS into existence. The big difference from the humid east was that native plants that could do the revegetation job abounded. Lacking was commercial availability and the know-how of seed production and required establishment techniques. New cultivars of native grasses and forbs were soon in production, and the process to establish them was as well.[760] Adapting ecotypes to ecological areas become the norm.

Introduced plants were not out of the picture, however. As discussed earlier, it was astounding how quickly and effectively Kentucky bluegrass and smooth brome adapted to the region. SCS participated in the expansion and use of smooth brome. This grass was first introduced into the U.S. by the University of California at Berkeley in about 1880, called Hungarian or awnless brome.[761]

Prior to 1994, there had been twenty-four cultivars of smooth brome on the commercial market in the U.S. and Canada.[762] They documented its range of useful adaptation, which was much of the U.S. north of the 38° latitude, except in the dryer areas of the Great Basin. Most of the cultivars were released from central U.S. State University Experiment Stations. SCS nurseries or PMCs participated in two releases: 'Elsberry' from the Missouri PMC in 1954 and 'Manchar' from the Pullman, WA PMC in 1943.

If rapid and easy establishment, longevity, excellent soil protection, tolerance to grazing and palatability are desirable, bluegrass and smooth brome measured up well.

The Semi-arid and Arid Intermountain West

The Westover-Enlow and the Roerich Expeditions brought in a wealth of new germplasm for evaluation. Additionally, during 1934, four teams of two men each spent the late summer collecting native plant seeds throughout the Pacific Northwest.[763] From these came many useful cultivars.

Crested wheatgrass and other introduced grasses that are widely used in the West had been exposed to thousands of years of similar conditions as was found in many parts of the west.[764] They had made some survival adjustments.[765] Not so with the native grasses and forbs. North American native herbivores ranged over millions of acres, taking a bite here, and another bite there. In a year or two they were back for another bite, resulting in zero grazing pressure. Blue bunch, thickspike or slender wheatgrasses, all natives, had experienced none of the grazing pressure imposed on them by the fenced-in alien livestock, and soon disappeared from the ranges, as well as many other native grassed and forbs.[766] Actually, the millions of acres of degraded western rangeland that have been planted with crested and other introduced wheatgrasses could have been planted with natives, except for the introduced grazing systems. Instead of adjusting the grazing system to the native flora, it was necessary to adjust the flora to the grazing system. Crested wheatgrass helped do this. Today it may be seen as the enemy.

On January 18, 1950, R. M. Ross, Chief, Nursery Division, sent a memorandum to Chief Bennett, the subject being "Native and Introduced Grasses and Legumes brought into Conservation Use." The memo contained an attachment listing these "outstanding plants and strains which, after careful investigation and observational trial, have been found to best do the conservation job". It also gave the estimated pound of seed produced and acres treated. There were twelve native grasses and legumes and twenty-three introduced varieties. See Table 12.1.

Table 12.1 Conservation Plant Production

Type of plant	Estimated pounds of seed	Estimated acres treated
Native	813,300	934,000
Introduced	4,439,600	7,745,000

Crested wheatgrass was introduced from central Asia by the Bureau of Plant Industry in 1908. The original planting was made at their station in Mandan, ND. It was evaluated favorably in the Northern Plains, but was not used significantly until it was promoted through Civilian Conservation Corps seedings on abandoned land. The number of acres seeded was considerably less than planned, but it put the species into the seed trade, and it became widely used by the U.S. Forest Service and Bureau of Land Management in the Intermountain West.[767][768]

It is estimated that more than ten million acres have been seeded. It out-competes cheatgrass and halogeton, providing more desirable ecosystem benefits, although perhaps not as desirable as the native sagebrush/needlegrass habitat. Some consider crested wheatgrass to be invasive; others think it is a well-behaved grass.

Mediterranean Climate of California

Here the approach changed. The invading annuals, which the Spaniards brought with their cattle, had, to a great extent, replaced the native range flora,[769] which contained some perennial grasses.[770] Although introduced, some were desirable, at least from a conservation point of view. Combining superior-producing, introduced annual grasses, plus introduced annual legumes, with good management, provided more forage than the pre-Spaniard native flora, and provided good conservation cover. Efforts to find superior, introduced, perennial grasses for this climate were successful, but their grazing management requirements exceeded what many ranchers were willing to provide.

Pacific Coastal Region

As with most regions, the Northwest has its hot button introductions. The Warrenton sand stabilization project fills the bill for this region.

The Warrenton dune project is discussed in details at the Featured Vegetative Accomplishment of the Corvallis PMC in Chapter 8. By the early twenty-first century, American beachgrass, an exotic, was invading and replacing the European beachgrass. [771] Both American and European varieties were now considered invasive exotics. Other questions have been raised: Was it even desirable to stabilize the site in the first place, since it impacted the ecological purity of native species? For example, it is suggested that any dune formation threatens the habitat of the Western snowy plover. The Native American dunegrass creates a hummocky landscape which may not threaten the snowy plover.[772]

Hindsight may suggest the original 1935 objectives of stabilizing sand that was threatening to inundate many facilities and ecological sites was wrong. Since the problem arose because of the jetty built at the mouth of the Columbia River in the late nineteenth century, which was scouring the channel bottom and dumping millions of cubic yards of sand on the beach south of the jetty, was it also wrong? Preserving nature within the context of a twenty-first century society is complex.

<u>Southwest</u>

One could easily picture the Southwest as the birthplace of the 'observational' process of evaluating plants for conservation use. As we know, Dr. Crider had his start down the path of his 'Nature has evolved a plant for every purpose' notion during his years as director of the Boyce Thompson Arboretum.[773] While no evidence has been found that Crider actually fostered the use of any introduced plants while at Boyce, he certainly did when he joined SCS at the Tucson, AZ Soil Erosion Service nursery as manager. Plantings were made in the greenhouse in the spring of 1935, at about the time it was becoming an SCS nursery. A large number of the items came from the recent Roerich expedition.[774] Crider left the Tucson nursery in late 1935 or early 1936. A report (author unknown) titled "Increasing Introduced Grasses", written in 1936 about work at the Tucson nursery, lists four accession numbers of *Eragrostis* species, as well as several native grasses, and states "A number of foreign introductions, outstanding in appearance and seed forming habits, have been increased as rapidly as possible."[775] In 1945, Crider published USDA Circular 730, <u>Three introduced lovegrasses for soil conservation</u>. Species included in the 1936 report were among the three in his publication.

Over time these species have lost favor because, for the most part, they did so well they were considered to be replacing the natives. One reason they were so widely used in the southwest during the 1940 - 1970 period was because the native grasses had disappeared due to overgrazing.[776] Dregne states, "The overgrazing that destroyed or severely altered the original grass cover of the rangelands of Mexico and the United States began in Mexico after the Spanish conquest and spread into the U.S. Southwest. By the early part of the nineteenth century, overgrazing was already a fact on both sides of the international boundary. With the explosive expansion of cattle numbers in the Southwest when the railroads arrived, range carrying capacities were greatly exceeded, and that situation continued well into the twentieth century."

GOOD NEWS

Bare soil erodes quickly. Easily established and quick starting plants are the most economical and effective way for preventing this. Many of the plants used for this purpose are short-lived introduced grasses and legumes, simply because marketable native plants with these characteristics are not available.

The long-term objective for many of these plantings is permanent, vegetative cover consisting of native plants typical of non-disturbed areas. One way to accomplish this is through the regeneration of the native flora. This happens whether wanted or not in high rainfall regions.-Concern exists, however, that this may not be the case in lower rainfall regions and the quick-starting plants may inhibit regeneration, and remain as an unwanted, introduced plant.

Roach, Talbott, Sheley, and Korfhage report on the fate of introduced seeded grasses during thirty-one years of post-fire forest regeneration in the state of Washington.[777] Forest fires in grand fir (*Abies grandis*)/pinegrass (*Calamagrostis rubescens*) associations characteristically result in a flush of lodgepole pine (*Pinus contorta*) regeneration that creates a dense tree monoculture. In their study, seven annual and perennial grasses were seeded to prevent erosion and increase forage production for wildlife and livestock, while having the effect of limiting tree regeneration. Tree regeneration, native and non-native species, and aboveground biomass were evaluated. The seeded species quickly established dominant cover two to three times the biomass level of native species. Density of tree regeneration was inversely correlated with perennial grass cover during the first ten years. During the next ten years the seeded grasses disappeared, long before tree canopy closure. Within fifteen to twenty years, native species had regained dominance, and after thirty years the last remnants of the non-native grasses were replaced in the seeded areas by a diverse mixture of native grasses, forbs, shrubs, and trees. In contrast, a monoculture of lodgepole pine dominated the unseeded areas. This study showed that non-native grasses seeded after wildfires do not always persist and can serve as a transition to restoring a more diverse serial community.

SUMMARY

Looking back there are a few cultivars placed on the market whose offspring wandered too aggressively. Some can be faulted with costing a farming enterprise, such as clearing autumn olive from pastures. By far, the greater objections to introduced plants fall into one or all of the following: [778]

- Lower quality habitat for wildlife

- Loss of biodiversity

- Modification of natural ecosystem processes

- Socioeconomic (fire intensity, highway mowing cost, lease value for wildlife recreation, aesthetic value)

- Increases in disturbance and fragmentation of the landscape.

Those concerns have shown up onto the radar screen in the last thirty years or so. They are not easy to get one's arms around. Comparing the magnitude of black clouds of Great Plains soil passing over Washington to these concerns begins to clarify the differences between a 1935 conservationist and a 2010 environmentalist. For these issues to be addressed with the same vigor as SCS attacked the black clouds, a Bennett-type crusader will be required to articulate them.

Chapter 13: FACTORS AFFECTING PRODUCTIVITY OF OBSERVATIONAL NURSERIES AND PLANT MATERIALS CENTERS

INTRODUCTION

The entire nursery program of SCS existed to provide plant materials for reducing soil erosion. Charles Enlow outlined for H. H. Bennett in November 1935 what the observational studies part of the old Soil Erosion Service nurseries was doing to accomplish this and, in his opinion, the SCS nurseries should do the same thing.[779]

Then Dr. Crider officially clarified the objective of the observational nurseries as "determining the relative erosion control and other economic value of outstanding native species... as well as introductions." Crider also put a little more detail on how to do it in his March 25, 1936 Field Memorandum #SCN-4 and the July 27, 1937 "Observational Phase of the Nursery Program."[780][781]

The products of the Enlow and Crider directions were to be new plants, (release, cultivar, etc.) that was better than what was currently available, how to use them successfully, and large scale production of them by the SCS nurseries and commercial growers. These were the major measuring sticks of progress.

As discussed elsewhere, developing a release took five or more years. The first new plants to appear by name were in 1939, with a rapid increase of others in the 1940s. As time passed and many new plants entered the large scale production mode, differences between the West, Midwest and the East began to appear in the number of releases, the magnitude of their use and acceptance, and their origin.

Why did these differences exist? Many factors could have caused it; a few will be considered.

IMPACT OF PRECIPITATION AND GERMPLASM SOURCE ON PRODUCTIVITY

During the nursery years (1935 - 1954) there were as many as sixty-seven nurseries in eleven regions in operation at one time or another. The number of regions shrank to seven by 1942. Those seven regions had twenty-three operating nurseries when they closed in 1953 (Beltsville, MD is excluded). The nurseries were distributed as shown in Table 13.1.

Table 13.1 Distribution of nurseries in 1953

Region 1 - Northeast (WV north and East)	1
Region 2 - Southeast (VA, KY and South) -	7
Region 3 - Upper central states (OH, IN, IL, MI, MN, MO, WI) -	4
Region 4 - Lower Great Plains plus LA - (TX, OK, CO, LA) -	1
Region 5 - Upper Great Plains (KS, NB, SD, ND, MT WY) -	3
Region 6 - Southwest (AZ, NM) -	2
Region 7 - Northwest (CA, OR, WA, ID) -	5

This represents a fair geographic distribution with possibly an overload in the Southeast, and an under weighting in the Northeast and the intermountain states of the West. Actually there were no nurseries in Nevada or Utah and none west of the Rocky Mountains in Colorado, Wyoming or Montana.

There are good records of all releases from observational nurseries, and sporadic production records beginning to appear in archive records by the mid-1940s. For example 'Sherman' big bluegrass was released in 1945 by the Pullman, WA observational nursery. Archive records show that in 1948

'Sherman' was listed by name, and 42,700 pounds of seed was produced "... through the efforts of the Soil Conservation Service."[782] In 1949 an additional 95,167 pounds were produced of big bluegrass, presumed to be 'Sherman', directly or indirectly through SCS efforts.[783] A 1948 report listed thirty-five production grass or legume species from observational nurseries that had been selected for some superiority. Eleven were named SCS releases by 1948, and at least a dozen more would be named, such as 'Durar' hard fescue (released in 1949) or 'Blando' brome (released 1954). The point of this is to identify what regions the new plants were coming from and to provide an idea of their production. Table 13.2 shows an estimate on how many of the thirty-five plants in production in 1948 were from each region.

Table 13.2 1948 Distribution of new plants in production among the seven regions

Region 1 - Northeast (WV north and East)	1
Region 2 - Southeast (VA, KY and South)	5
Region 3 - Upper central states (OH, IN, IL, MI, MN, MO, WI)	1
Region 4 - Lower Great Plains plus LA - (TX, OK, CO, LA)	3
Region 5 - Upper Great Plains (KS, NB, SD, ND, MT WY)	5
Region 6 - Southwest (AZ, NM)	0
Region 7 - Northwest (CA, OR, WA, ID)	20

One striking aspect of this somewhat unreliable report was the absence of any plants clearly identifiable from Region 6. Although Albuquerque, NM released 'Vaughn' sideoats grama and 'Grenville' switchgrass in 1940, no evidence as is found in the 1948 report to suggest their production, but of far greater importance is the number from Region 7 nurseries.

By 1955 there were more releases and they sorted out as shown in Table 13.3.

Table 13.3 1955 Distribution of new plants in production among the previous seven regions

Region 1 - Northeast (WV north and East)	0
Region 2 - Southeast (VA, KY and South)	7
Region 3 - Upper central states (OH, IN, IL, MI, MN, MO, WI)	0
Region 4 - Lower Great Plains plus LA - (TX, OK, CO, LA)	3
Region 5 - Upper Great Plains (KS, NB, SD, ND, MT WY)	4
Region 6 - Southwest (AZ, NM)	5
Region 7 - Northwest (CA, OR, WA, ID)	14

These types of regional differences are consistent, and increase over time, not only in terms of number of releases but production of releases. There may be many reasons in addition to moisture availability, but it appears to be a major one. To check this hypothesis, the country was divided into three major precipitation regions. Of course any national delineation limited to three regions will be extremely arbitrary, each having inclusions not representative of the region. However, the following do reflect significant moisture differences between them.

The moisture variables are as follows:

- Humid East plus Hawaii which included PMCs in HI, GA, MD, MS, NY, NJ, MI, FL and MO.

- Semiarid Midwest which included PMCs in KS, TX, ND and MT.

- Arid West which included PMCs in NM, ID, CA, AZ, OR and WA.

By design or otherwise, the nursery regions in 1950 came close to doing this. It would have been completed by moving Louisiana to SCS Region 2, combining Regions 1, 2 and 3 to become the Humid East, joining Region 4 and 5 to make the Semiarid Midwest and Regions 6 and 7 to become the Arid West.

The evaluation of the impact of moisture on productivity was done with two sets of data. The first set used the benefits derived from 1977 through 2005 production of the seventy-six plants that were released from 1939 through 1971. This represents the program's development years, the transition years from nurseries to PMCs and ten or so 'normal' operating years. Selecting 1971 also allows commercial production of the releases after 1971 to become well established in commercial markets before 1977, when the accumulation of production data started. The second period was the measure of production from 1977 through 2005 of 114 releases made from 1972 through 1985.

Results from 1939 – 1971 with 76 Releases

In Table 13.4 the Contrib. ON/PMC column shows the number of units (observational nursery or PMC) that contributed release(s). The data is sorted by the three moisture regions and by germplasm source, native or introduced. For example the humid east's nine contributing nurseries or PMCs produced twenty cultivars with a total value of $63 million.

Table 13.4 Influence of precipitation zone and species source on the value of cultivars released prior to 1971

Distribution	Contrib. ON/PMC	Total Value	Source (Value)		Source (Cultivars)		Total CVs
			Native	Introduced	Native	Introd.	
Humid East	9	$63,043,337	$10,004,620	$53,038,716	2	18	20
Semi-Arid MW	4	$241,861,467	$67,031,383	$174,830,084	11	6	17
Arid West	7	$393,030,983	$143,218,687	$249,812,296	10	29	39
Totals	20	$697,935,787	$220,254,691	$477,681,096	23	53	76

The data shows that during the release period of 1939 through 1971:

- The Humid East plus Hawaii contributed twenty cultivars for an average of 2.2 per PMC. The Semi-Arid Midwest contributed fifteen cultivars or an average of 3.8 per PMC. The Arid West contributed forty cultivars or an average of 5.7 per PMC.

- The total value of the releases from the Arid West was ten times, and the Semi-Arid Midwest was four times greater than the Humid East. It is worth noting that fifty percent of the total Humid East value came from 'Pensacola' bahiagrass.

- The effect of germplasm source was also striking. Introduced species were utilized 2.5 times more as conservation plant source than native species. Ninety percent of the Humid East releases were introduced plants.

- The use of natives in the Semi-Arid Midwest, percentage wise, was much greater than the other two.

While the data is unavoidably skewed due to the low number of contributing units (observational nursery or PMC) in the Semi-Arid Midwest, the value per contributing PMC or contributing cultivar within each unit reflects a more realistic picture. These differences are shown in Table 13.5.

The value of each contributing PMC in the Semi-Arid Midwest and Arid West were similar but about eight times more than the Humid East. However the value of each cultivar from Semi-Arid Midwest exceeded the Arid West by thirty-five percent and the Humid East by five times.

Table 13.5 Contributing Value per ON or PMC Unit and Cultivar

Distribution	Contrib. ON/PMC Unit	Value/ Each Contributing ON or PMC	Total CVs	Value/Each Contributing Cultivar
Humid East	9	$7,001,000	21	$3,003,000
Semi-Arid Midwest	4	$60,465,000	15	$16,124,000
Arid West	7	$56,147,000	40	$9,826,000
Average		$34,896,000		$9,651,000

Explaining the Differences

There may be many reasons for the geographic differences in the development and utilization of conservation plants. For example, other parts of this history refer to administrative difficulties associated with an observational nursery in the Humid East. However, the available moisture hypotheses appear valid. The areas of limiting moisture had a greater need, had the larger land mass needing treatment, and the public and political perception of need favored the lower moisture areas. After all, the Dust Bowl was, as the saying goes, the big kid on the block. The magnitude of the problem facing the Semi-Arid Midwest in 1935 was as clear cut as was degraded rangeland further west.

Where the precipitation is ample, the land can withstand a greater degree of misuse and recover. Overgrazing by domestic livestock was common in the humid east, but it rarely destroyed the soil covering vegetation, and if it did the more abundant rainfall lead to a quick recovery. In the increasingly dryer areas of the west, overgrazing reduced or eliminated the vegetative cover, and the limited moisture easily kept natural revegetation from occurring. Overgrazing plus the plow and limited moisture produced the increased need for conservation plants in Great Plains relative to the humid east.[784] In the southern Great Plains alone it was estimated in 1935 that 5.4 million acres, nearly twice the size of Connecticut,[785] had been affected by erosion and was in need of cover.[786]

In the humid east, the two most apparent conservation problems, to some degree paralleling the needs for conservation cover in the West and Midwest, were re-vegetating cotton and other abandoned farmland in the southeast, and mine land spoil revegetation in the Appalachian region. Both of these combined were small compared to the need further west. The abandoned cropland in the southeast succeeded quickly, with the development of two new 'wonder' grasses, tall fescue and Bahiagrass, along with ample rainfall.

Land owners of the abandoned mine land had no incentive to re-vegetate until they were required to, thus progress on that front had to wait until this happened. This was not until 1977.[787] The Plant Materials Program had developed the knowledge on how to deal with the problem, but to a great extent during this 1939 - 1971 time period, the limited planting was done with commercially available material.[788] Again, the acres of disturbed land were tiny by comparison.

The abundance of releases of introduced plants in the Humid East is logical for a number of reasons but primarily because the best vegetation for providing erosion protection are close growing grasses, and the heavily forested east was not conducive for their evolution, as contrasted to the Great Plains. As a result, stabilizing the exposed earth required plants from other sources, including other countries.

Results from 1971 - 1985, 114 Releases

Doing the same analysis for another period of plant releases will provide some additional sense as to the productiveness of the program and utilization of new plants. Table 13.6 is the same as the one above except it shows the magnitude of commercial production from 1977 through 2005 of the 114 new releases between 1971 and 1985. It does not include the production from prior releases.

Table 13.6 Influence of precept zone and species source on the value of cultivars released 1971 through 1985

Distribution	Contrib. ON/PMC	Total Value	Source (Value)		Source (Cultivars)		Total CVs
			Native	Introduced	Native	Introd.	
Humid East	8	$100,908,289	$32,396,268	$68,512,021	9	27	36
Semi-Arid Midwest	4	$87,047,288	$74,286,143	$12,761,146	26	8	34
Arid West	8	$184,432,850	$157,167,815	$27,265,034	31	13	44
Totals	20	$372,388,427	$263,850,225	$108,538,202	66	48	114

Comparing the two tables, the data shows the following:

- The total magnitude of use from this batch of releases was only a little more than half what it was from the 1939-1970 releases. However, the total value for the Humid East increased by about thirty percent. Sixty-five percent of the use of this increase came from two Florida and one Missouri introduced cultivars.

- The Arid West still led the way in number of releases and magnitude of production.

- There was a dramatic shift in the use of native plants from twenty-eight percent in the pre-1971 releases to fifty-seven percent between 1971 and 1985.

- The value per contributing unit or contributing cultivars within each unit reflects a narrowing of the difference seen for releases from an earlier period. However, an individual cultivar released in the Humid East or Semi-Arid Midwest produced only about seventy-five percent as much as the Arid West This is shown in Table 13.7.

- While each contributing PMC in the Humid East was still lagging, it had made progress against the other two, and the value between contributing cultivars had narrowed. However, the Arid West contributing PMCs continued to outshine the others.

Table 13.7 Contributing Value per ON or PMC Unit and Cultivar

Distribution	Contributing PMC Unit	Value/Contributing ON/PMC	Total CVs	Value/Contributing Cultivar
Humid East	8	$12,613,000	36	$2,803,000
Semi-Arid Midwest	4	$21,761,000	34	$2,560,000
Arid West	8	$23,054,000	44	$4,192,000
Average		$18,619,000		$3,185,000

IMPACT OF FOCUSING ON THE PLANT

Another reason for the observed regional differences on productivity, at least between the Humid East and the Arid West, deals with Crider's application of how observational nurseries should screen for outstanding plants. It can be argued that the procedure of the observational nurseries pointed directly to the concept that 'nature has evolved a plant for every purpose' and the evaluation process need not worry about the problem: Just find those superior plants and then fit them to the problem.

379

An assembly of a large numbers of plants was to be evaluated for "an improvement in erosion control value to materials now in use." The focus was on the plant, not the conservation problem.

For years some observational nurseries and PMCs assembled every type of herbaceous or woody plant into an observational planting (later called initial evaluations) and evaluated each for a host of characteristics, hoping that the process would tell the scientist which accessions were worth further study, including what conservation problem the plant might help solve. For many years prior to and following the nurseries closing, the Beltsville National Project and later a National PMC received hundreds of foreign accessions. They came either directly through contact established by Dr. Crider, or from other USDA offices, later consolidated in the Agriculture Research Service Plant Introduction Office. These accessions were sent directly to observational nurseries/PMCs around the country at the discretion of the Beltsville manager. The distribution logic was that the plant will grow in that region, and the evaluation logic seemed to be that if the trained scientist looked at enough plants one or more would have conservation value for some yet-to-be-identified problem. In later years this was despairingly called the shotgun approach.

The West region under the able leadership of Dr. A. L. Hafenrichter had developed a list of projects into which every observational nurseries/PMC evaluation would fit. It was used well into the 1970s and maybe beyond. The project titles were as follows:

RN-l. Observational Testing of Native and Introduced Grasses, Legumes and Forbs

RN-2. Seed Yields and Rate of Seeding Studies

RN-3. Mixtures of Grasses and Legumes

RN-4. Seedings of Trees and Shrubs to Determine Improved Methods of Culture

RN-5. Date and Rate of Seeding Grass Species

RN-6. The Effect of Previous Crops and Tillage on Establishment

RN-7. Method of Seeding Grasses

RN-8. Testing Trees and Shrubs for Conservation Use

RN-9. Woodlots, Snowbreaks and Shelterbelts

RN-200 Initial Seed Increase

RN-233 Large Scale Seed Increase

These projects appear to be designed in line with Crider's concept that the focus is on the plant and not the problem. "RN-1, Observational Testing of Native and Introduced Grasses, Legumes and Forbs" does not specify a conservation need, but it does specify the type of plant. The use of 'Observational Testing' is not mentioned in "RN-8 Testing Trees and Shrubs for Conservation Use." Actually RN-8 and RN-9 appear to be added to cover woody plants, which played, at best, a minor role during the observational nursery days in the West.

Hafenrichter presented an excellent paper at the 1937 Agronomy Society meeting in St. Louis, MO titled Observational Nursery Plantings: Grasses and Forage Crops.[789] In 1938 he presented an almost identical paper, at the Grass School held June 6-10 in Pullman, also titled Observational Nursery Plantings - Grasses and Other Forage Crops. The latter had been edited and adjusted for a different audience, in which he presented a more vigorous argument supporting the evaluation of grasses and legumes only. Both papers began by making the point that the Nursery Division had two obligations, and he was going to talk about the observational nursery one. Of course, the other part is the large scale production of grasses, forbs and woody plants.

He introduced his paper by saying, "This paper will deal primarily with the observational plantings in forage crops in Region XI, with occasional reference to observation plantings under way or complimented with woody plants." He proceeded in a way as to offer a justification for concentrating only on RN-1 at the expense of avoiding woody plants, "Observational plantings occupy an important place in the program of the Section of Nurseries in the Pacific Northwest. It is felt that this emphasis…is thoroughly justified and predicated by the needs of the SCS which the Section of Nurseries is obligated to serve. It was stated in a previous paper at this Grass School by another speaker that in the entire program in Region XI about equal emphasis is placed on work with herbaceous and woody plants."

Hafenrichter seemed to be referring to that observation and pointed out that "to date the observational plantings of herbaceous plants have exceed those of woody plants and it will probably be necessary to continue the emphasis in this manner." Bottom line: observational nursery plantings of grasses and other forage crops, the erosion stoppers, are logically the gorilla for observational nurseries in Region XI.

Hafenrichter then turned to the objectives of observational plantings. The first one was "Determining the value of species and varieties and strains of plants, especially with respect to their utilization in soil and moisture conservation." This was pure Crider; there was no mention of conservation needs whatsoever. The second objective was to "Determine methods of propagation" and third and last to "reduce the volume of such plantings by working out a system of correlation designed to increase the value of observations in relative few locations."

He proceeded to explain how the first step of establishing an observation nursery would be done. For example, "Such plantings are to be made in rows which are without exception to be one rod in length with sufficient additional planting to eliminate any 'border effect'." With regard to in-planting arrangements he said, "An attempt is made to arrange these plantings carefully, both with respect to site location and with respect to grouping so that species with known similarity in growth habit as well as varieties, ecological strains, etc. are grouped together." No mention was made of grouping according to intended use. He observed that a standard note taking form had been developed.

The next step was to separate the accessions that, "indicate promise in soil and moisture conservation. This is virtually a new field." He did not provide any detail on how to address this new field, but turned instead to describe the magnitude of the soil and moisture conservation problems in Region XI, including fifty-four million acres of eroded range lands. There it was. He finally identified the problem, observing that forage crop work prior to 1936 had been done on irrigated land and was badly needed for range land as well. From all this he concluded, "Consequently forage crops occupy a very important place in soil and moisture conservation in the region." He could have said that 'observational nurseries in Region XI will be of the RN-1 type and the problem will be soil and moisture conservation on range land'. End of conversation.

While the intent here is to evaluate the basis of focusing on the plant rather than the problem, it may be of significant historical interest to consider the magnitude of observational plantings in Region 11. Below is a table of Observational Rod Row Plantings of Grasses and Legumes in Region 11 during 1935 and 1936. This is shown in Table 13.8.

In the same 'Grass School' publication is a table listing, "Species being increased as a source of seed planting stock for soil and moisture conservation plantings at the Pullman Nursery Unit." His species list included twelve native grasses and nine introduced, and two legumes, one native and one introduced.[790]

Table 13.8 Magnitude of Observational Studies in Region 11

Nursery	Foreign Introductions		Native Collections		Cultivated Strains		Total
	1935	1936	1935	1936	1935	1936	
Pullman, WA	738	540	1576	875	495	210	3913
Union, OR	86	7	145	75	15	83	411
Pendleton, OR	1	3	121	19	0	26	170
Moro, OR	4	3	93	16	0	26	142
Lind, OR	3	1	110	13	12		139
Goldendale, WA	0	4	0	53	0	53	110
Dayton, WA	0	4	0	53	0	43	100
Condon, OR	0	4	0	55	0	38	97
Warrenton, WA	0	14	0	8	0	0	22
Totals	832	580	2045	1167	522	479	5104

Now back to the evaluation process. Even though an RN-1 project did not require the identification of the conservation need, in Region XI the default conservation need was eroded range lands. No other need was discussed in the observational nursery plantings paper. The massive amount of RN-1 observational testing at Pullman, WA and in outlying nurseries was for the revegetation of range lands, representing, not by design, but by default, a single focus on one conservation problem, not only at Pullman but at other nurseries under his supervision. In 1936 Pullman was the major nursery in the Northwest, joined in 1939 by Pleasanton, CA and Aberdeen, ID. After the reorganization in 1954, Los Lunas and Tucson were also in the West Region.

While the first nine RN projects listed above included references to other than traditional range species, and such planting did exist, the release record at Pullman reflected the 'forage for rangeland' priority. Their first non-grass release was in their fifty-sixth year of existence.

Was this a good thing? Over the years, on a national basis, the concept of how best to evaluate an assemblage of plants for conservation purposes shifted from a shotgun approach to a rifle approach. The shotgun approach evaluated each assembled plant for its potential for soil and moisture conservation, as described by Crider. The herbaceous initial observational nursery in the Humid East might contain multiple accessions of species commonly used for forage, for re-vegetating mine spoil, road banks, streambanks or wildlife food and cover. Those that were identified as superior were increased and their potential use resolved. The rifle approach assembled and evaluated only plants for a specific conservation need, and frequently only a single species.

Using Pullman as an example, by default they appear to have been using the rifle approach from their beginning. One might suspect it was Hafenrichter's approach to avoid the shotgun approach by the using the RN Projects. With the enormous need for rangeland revegetation, it certainly appears that it was a good thing. Considering the results it looks like a slam dunk. See the list of releases in Chapter 8 for the Pullman PMC for the release period of 1943 through the 1980s. While every release during that period was not strictly a forage species they all related to soil and moisture conservation on rangeland related problems.

Contrast this to PMCs in the Humid Northeast. As discussed above, the lack of that single, overwhelming need was a major unintended deterrent to plant materials productivity between west and east. This was true at least until the mid-1960s. Big Flats, the only PMC serving the Northeast for most of that period continued to use the shotgun approach. However, plant materials specialists, Joe

Ruffner and Marshall Augustine, led the region into the rifle approach for about the same reason as it was being used in the West. Each of these fellows had one overwhelming plant materials need to solve; Ruffner had revegetation of coal mine spoil and Augustine was fully employed stabilizing sand dunes and tidal river banks. Unfortunately, Big Flats did not serve either of these problems well. However, they might have done better on the coal mine spoil had they eliminated eighty percent of their shotgun approach to evaluations.

Abraham Stoesz, Chief Plant Materials Specialists in Washington, wrote a bit of a summary on <u>Development and Major Accomplishments During the Past Decade</u> on August 30, 1963.[791] One accomplishment was

> Changes in attitude in people towards the development of new plants often result in a shift in emphasis. It was common in parts of the country after discovering a good plant to raise the question 'what can it do for conservation?' Now the approach is: Here are our problems, what plants can be found to solve them? This wholesome shift in emphasis is now generally evident throughout the country.

The first exposure to the rifle approach by the author of this history happened on his way to a new position. He had been requested to see the state conservationist, Seldom Tinsley, before reporting to his work station. Tinsley, a pretty good plant person in his own right, told him, "Your first three weeks on the job will be spent collecting every American beachgrass plant you can find from Cape Cod to Kitty Hawk. And don't come dragging in a lot of junk. We need a superior beachgrass and we need it quick." (Sounds like James E. "Bud" Smith Jr.) This set the Cape May PMC, established in 1965 under the direction of Dr. Virgil Hawk, who had been trained by Hafenrichter, on the correct path, releasing 'Cape' American beachgrass in 1970.

SUMMARY

There are many factors that impact the productivity of the Plant Materials Program. Logic and ample evidence shows that available moisture lessened the need for conservation plants in the Humid East and accelerated the need in the Semi-Arid Midwest and Arid West. And the observational nurseries responded in excellent fashion. By the early 1980s, under excellent leadership, and with highly productive scientists, the solution to eroding, windblown or animal denuded rangeland was found, and the tools were developed to address the problem.

The value of introduced releases during its first thirty years was $448 million, compared to $220 million for native releases. The value of introduced releases between 1971 and 1985 fell to $109 million compared to $264 million for natives. Regionally, given the absence of soil conserving native species in the Humid East, the results are about as expected.

Dr. Crider's concept of how observational nurseries should screen for outstanding plants appears to have represented the shotgun approach: Focus on the plant, not the conservation problem. At least in the West it appears a rifle approach was used instead, to great success.

Chapter 14: A CONSTANT QUESTION — PMC RESEARCH AUTHORITY

BACKGROUND

It may be appropriate to discuss the history of PMC research authority. It is a subject referenced now and then, usually as a question. It became a more burning question when efforts to increase the technical capability of PMCs got underway. Many potential plant materials employees will raise the question. For example, bright young people just out of graduate school who want, as one person put it, 'to do good science', may be negatively influenced if he or she learns PMCs do not have research authority. A prospective employee with a PhD in agronomy might wonder, "What will I do with all those new tools I learned at the university if my employer does not have research authority?"

Legislative Background

Neither the Division of Nurseries, the observational studies nor the Plant Materials Centers have ever had research authority. There is a related legislative history that may create some confusion. To understand this it is necessary to return to 1933 when the National Industrial Recovery Act was enacted on June 6 and the Federal Emergency Administration of Public Works[792] came into existence. The latter could establish new agencies, one of which was the Soil Erosion Service.[793] It was established as a temporary agency in the Department of the Interior, to administer unemployment relief funds used for erosion control.

Departmental memorandums and a new act by Congress during the mid-1930s resulted in SCS by 1936 having a Nursery Section, later becoming a division, and a Division of Research.[794] [795] [796] The SCS Nursery Division co-existed with the Division of Research until 1953, one having research authority and one not. The Division of Research was abolished, effective January 16, 1953, with soil and water research functions transferred to Agricultural Research Service, pursuant to Secretary's Memorandum 1318, October 14, 1952.[797] The Nursery Division was also abolished and the observational studies part of the nurseries became the Plant Materials Program.

During the formation period of SCS nursery policy, Dr. Franklin Crider, Chief of the Nursery Section in 1936-1937 wrote the foundation documents that continue today to guide the observational nature of PMCs. The first document he prepared did not address the research subject at all.[798] This was logical because, in reality there was nothing to say. The second, however, Observational Phase of the Nursery Program highlighted indirectly the lack of nursery research authority by stating "The work is distinctly different than, and is not to be confused with, the research work of the Research Division of our Service nor that of the Bureau of Plant Industry. However, its relationships are such as to suggest close cooperation with these branches.[799] In a March 2, 1939 memo to Regional Conservators he wrote of observational nurseries "occupying an essential intermediary place between research and practical field application."[800]

On March 2, 1939 Dr. Crider, with the approval of C. B. Manifold, issued an unnumbered message to all Regional Conservators on Projecting Nursery Observational Work.[801] The purpose of this document was to provide additional details on how to develop and use cooperative agreements and work plans for conducting work with others. This document emphasizes that any cooperative activities requiring research will be spelled out in the work plan. Under the discussion of Work Plans Crider writes "Functionally the nursery observation work falls into four general classes, which constitutes the basis for the formation of work plans." They are A. Initial Observations, B. Supplemental Observations (adjuncts of major plant materials centers), C. Facilitating Studies, and D. Special Studies. The purpose of listing the four was to clearly identify what duties belong to SCS observational nurseries (A, B, and C) and which duties belong to the cooperator, which is item D. Expanding on item D he summarized that when cooperative plant evaluations with state and federal agencies is "of a distinctly specialized or research nature" the cooperating research agency will assume full leadership and responsibility for it.

Throughout this 1933 -1953 period no legislative authority can be found that authorized Soil Erosion Nurseries of the USDI Bureau of Plant Industry, or SCS Section (within Conservation Operations) or Division of Nurseries to conduct research. Granted, the agency had research authority in the Division of Research until 1953. Many of the research facilities were continued by ARS and others transferred to state experiment stations.[802]

In 1954 when observational studies in the Nursery Division became PMCs the lack of research authority of the nurseries became a part of the PMC's policy. In 1956 SCS Administrator wrote the Secretary of Agriculture, "It is the policy of the SCS to use the techniques of observation...in the work at Plant Materials Centers. Plant breeding and hybridization, on the other hand, are recognized research techniques and are the responsibilities of the technicians of research agencies."[803] The first SCS Plant Materials Program Policy statement under the heading of 'Functions'[804] includes as the last function "bring to the attention of research agencies the need for further plant improvement." The third SCS, Plant Materials Policy document, National Plant Materials Handbook, dated June 16, 1977,[805] states the "Basic authority for the SCS plant materials program is provided in the Soil Conservation Act of 1935 (Public Law 46, 74th Congress).[806]

THE REALITY

The charge to the Plant Materials Program from 1935 forward has been to find superior plants and techniques for their use that will help protect and conserve our natural resources. This charge lends itself to an observational approach. Based on the products produced by observational nurseries and PMCs, and the costs of those products, the scales are strongly tilted in favor of the Program being an immense success.[807] [808] Would it have been more productive had it had research authority? This is difficult to evaluate. Hafenrichter recognized the possible need for research type evaluations by insisting all work be conducted in association with research facilities.

What is research? In the broadest sense of the word, the definition of research includes any gathering of data, information and facts for the advancement of knowledge.[809] Used as a noun the definition is the systematic investigation into and study of materials and sources in order to establish facts and reach new conclusions.[810] The Random House Dictionary says "To search again" or "Systematic inquiry into a subject in order to discover or revise facts, theories, etc."[811] It is impossible to imagine what part of these definitions has not been used by the Plant Materials Program over and over again.

If we accept that the Plant Materials Program has produced some excellent products, it has done so by doing whatever was required to produce the product. Any innovative and productive plant materials facility will have used tools that met all the definitions of research. No evidence has been identified of internal or external concerns that the plant materials program was doing research. Limitations created by the lack of research authority have not appeared to exist. Limitations to accomplishments may have been more associated with personnel than the lack of research authority. The bottom line seems to be that PMCs need to do what is required to produce the product.

Appendix 1: ACRONYM DEFINITIONS

AOSCA	Association of Seed Certifying Agencies
CRP	Conservation Reserve Program
E&WP	Engineering and Watershed Planning
ECS	Ecological Science Division
ESCOP	Agreement of the Experimental Station Committee on Organization and Policy
GSA	General Services Administration
FPMT	Field Plant Materials Technician
MOU	Memorandum of Understanding
NLSPN	National List of Scientific Plant Names
NPDC	National Plant Data Center
NPMP	National Plant Materials Program
NRCS	National Resource Conservation Service
PART	Performance Assessment Rating Tool
PL	Plant Industries
PLANTS	Plant List of Attributes, Names, Taxonomy and Symbols
PMC	Plant Materials Center
PMP	Plant Materials Program
PM Specialist	Plant Materials Specialist
QIT	Quality Improvement Team
RTSC	Regional Technical Service Center
SCD	Soil Conservation District
SCS	Soil Conservation Service
SES	Soil Erosion Service
TSC	Technical Service Center
USDA	U.S. Department of Agriculture
USDI	U.S. Department of the Interior
W-F PMT	Washington-Field Plant Materials Technician

Appendix 2: PARTIAL LIST OF PUBLICATIONS BY SOIL CONSERVATION SERVICE NURSERY DIVISION AND PLANT MATERIALS PROGRAM EMPLOYEES AND OTHER SELECTED REFERENCES USED IN THIS HISTORY

This Appendix identifies published publications by SCS/NRCS authors or co-authors, except the extensive online publications found with each PMC. It may include a few online publications that are not on a PMC web page or that are on a PMC website.

Alderson, James and W. Curtis Sharp. 1994. Grass Varieties of the U.S., Agric. HB 170. 296.

Allen, Phillip and W. W. Steiner1965. Autumn Olive – For Wildlife and Other Conservation Uses. USDA Leaflet No. 458.

Anderson, Darwin and A. R. Swanson. 1949. J. of Rn. Mgt. Machinery for Seedbed Preparation and Seeding on Southwestern Ranges. Vol. 2, No. 2:64-66.

Archives of the James E. "Bud" Smith, Jr. Plant Materials Center, USDA, NRCS, Knox City, TX

Atkins, M. D. 1955. Plant the "go-back-land" to grass. J. Soil & Water Consv., 10 (5):233-235.

Atkins, M. D. 1958. Cover on watershed dams. J. Soil & Water Consv., 13 (5): 220-222.

Atkins, M. D. 1962. Conservation Plant Materials for the Great Plains J. Soil & Water Consv., 17 (5): September-October. 199-203.

Atkins, M. D. and James E. Smith Jr. 1967. Grass Seed Production and Harvest in the Great Plains, USDA Farmers' Bulletin 2226. Washington, DC. 30 p.

Atkins, M. D., and A. J. Longley. 1950. Airplane seeding of sand lovegrass. Soil Consv., 15 (11):258-260.

Atkins, M. D., and A. J. Longley. 1950. Sand lovegrass makes a comeback. Soil Consv., 14 (6):138-141.

Atkins, M. Donald and J. J. Coyle. 1960. Grass waterways in soil conservation. USDA, SCS. Washington, DC. Leaflet no. 477.

Atkins, Ozell A. and W. C. Young. 1942. The Partridge Pea, *Chamaecrista fasciculata*, a Promising Plant for Soil Conservation. Agron. J. 1941; 33: 471-472.

Augustine, Marshall and W. C. Sharp. 1969. Effect of Several Fertilizer Treatments on the Production of American Beachgrass Culms. Agron. J 61: 43-45.

Bagley, W. T., G. G. Long, and M. D. Atkins. 1970. Genetic variation of green ash in the Great Plains Region. Unpublished Paper No. 3136, Nebraska Agric. Exp. Sta., Lincoln, NE. 16 p.

Bailey, L. H. and Ethel Zoe Bailey. 1930. RUS, A biographical register of rural leadership in the United States and Canada. Ithaca, NY

Bailey, R. Y. and L. B. Scott. Using Tall Fescue in Soil Conservation. USDA Leaflet 254. 1949

Bailey, R. Y., L. B. Scott and L. J. Leffelman. 1948. Grasses and Legumes Tested on Land utilization Projects. Soil Consv., 13: 158-161, 168.

Ball, D., G. Lacefield, D. Nelson, S. Schmidt, C. Hoveland, and W. Young, III. 2004. Extension publications developed through university/seed industry cooperation. Proc. Fifth Intern. *Neotyphodium*/Grass Interactions Symp. May 23-26. Fayetteville, AR.

Barnes, O. and A. L. Nelson. 1945. Mechanical treatments for increasing the grazing capacity of shortgrass range. Wyoming Agric. Exp. Sta. Bull. 273. 35 P.

Beddoes, Jennifer, Dan Ogle, Rob Sampson and Chris Hoag. 2007. Riparian Buffer Design and Species Considerations. http://www.plant-materials.nrcs.usda.gov/pubs/idPM Specialisttn7248.pdf/.

Belcher, C. R., and W. C. Sharp. 1981. Evaluation of Two Cordgrasses for Use on Tidal Banks. Am. Soc. Agron. Atlanta, Georgia.

Belcher, C. R., W. C. Sharp, and D. W. Hamer. 1983. Salt Meadow Cordgrass Variety for Tidal Banks. Am. Soc. Agron. Washington, DC.

Belcher, Cluster R. and W. Curtis Sharp. 1979. Testy Lespedezas. Soil Consv., SCS, Washington, DC. p. 5-6
.

Belcher, Cluster R. and W. Curtis Sharp. Native Grasses Fight the Waves on Tidal Shorelines. USDA, SCS Soil & Water Conservation News. December 1981, Vol. 2, No. 9.

Bentrup, G. and J. C. Hoag. 1998. The Practical Streambank Bioengineering Guide. (PDF; 3,083K) USDA-NRCS Aberdeen Plant Materials Center, Aberdeen, ID. May 1998. 151

Bertramson, B. Rodney. 1985. History of the Forage program at W.S.U. Dept. of Agron. and Soils, WSU. Pullman, WA

Beutner, E. L., and Darwin Anderson. 1944, A method of seedbed preparation and reseeding deteriorated range lands. Agron. J., 36: 171-172.

Boyce Thompson Arboretum History. 2011 http://ag.arizona.edu/bta/history.html/.

Briggs, James and Jerry Hammond. SCS Searches Worldwide for Conservation Plants. Soil & Water Conservation News, March 1987.

Britt, Clarence S. 1966 Soil and water conservation research in the Northeastern States. USDA-ARS, Washington, DC.

Burgdorf, Dave, Christopher Miller, Stoney Wright, Carlos Morganti, Dale Darris, Chris Hoag, Glenn Sakamoto. 2007. Plant Species with Rooting Ability from Live Hardwood Materials for use in Soil Bioengineering Techniques. http://www.nrcs.usda.gov/Internet/FSE_DOCUMENTS/stelprdb1042291.pdf/

Byrd, Morris, Young W. C. and Verne E. Davison. 1963. Seed Yields of Shrub Lespedezas in Arkansas. The J. of Wildlife Management, Vol. 27, No. 1: 135-136.

C. R. Enlow to H. H. Bennett, November 25, 1936, File 215.2, Personnel, Central Files May 1935-June 1936, Box 71, Records of the NRCS, Record Group 114, National Archives at College Park, MD.

Carlson, J. R., Schwendiman, J. L. and C. A. Kelley. 1978. Improving ground cover on disturbed soils in the Steppe Region of Oregon and Washington. Proc. Amer. Soc. Agron. Meetings. Chicago, IL

Carlson, Jack, W. C. Sharp. 1975. Germination of High Elevation Manzanitas, Tree Planters Notes 26:3: p. 10-11

Cooper, H. W., J. E. Smith, Jr., and M. D. Atkins. 1957. Producing and harvesting grass seed in the Great Plains. Farmers Bull. No. 2112. U.S. Govt. Printing Office, Washington, DC.

Cooper, William S. and Abraham D. Stoesz. 1931. The Subterranean Organs of *Helianthus suberrimus*. Bulletin of the Torrey Botanical Club, 58:67-72.

Cornelius, Donald R. 1944. Revegetation in the Tall Grass prairie Region. Agron. J., Vol. 36, No. 5.

Cornelius, Donald R. 1946. Comparison of Soil Conserving Grasses. Amer. Soc. Agron. J. 38 (8):682-689.

Cornelius, Donald R. and M. Donald Atkins. 1946. Grass establishment and development studies in Morton County, Kansas. Ecology, Vol. 27, No. 4:342-353.

Crider, Franklin J. 1945. Three introduced lovegrasses for soil conservation. USDA Circular 730, Washington, DC. 90 p.

Crider, Franklin J. 1951. New Plants for the New Agric., Soil Conservation Magazine, Vol. 16, No. 9. p. 202 - 09.

Crider, Franklin J. 1952. Natob: A new bush Lespedeza for soil conservation. Circular No. 900. USDA, Washington, DC. 10 p.

Crider, Franklin J. 1955. Root growth stoppage resulting from defoliation of grass. Technical Bulletin 1102. USDA-SCS, Washington, DC.

Croeni, Kenneth and Mark Testerman. 1974. The Mark of 'Zorro'. Soil Consv., Magazine. USDA-SCS, Washington, DC.

Darris, D. C., E. T. Jacobson, and R. J. Haas. 1981. Native woodland species for surface mine reclamation. Restoration and Management Notes. Vol. 1 (1) June.

Davis, R. L. and W. C. Young. 1951. Kudzu-23 - a new fine-textured variety. *Soil Conservation*. 16: p. 279 - 280.

Dawson, David H. 1961. Medium Purple Willow for Muckland Windbreaks. J. Soil & Water Consv., Vol. 16, No. 6.

Dedication of the Tucson, AZ Plant Materials Center Building. 2000. http://www.nrcs.usda.gov/news/thisweek/2000/001110.html#anchor106943/.

Dedication, James E. "Bud" Smith, Knox City Plant Materials Center files, Knox City, TX, September 7, 1965.

Dickerson, J. A. 1993. Eastern gamagrass cultural studies-New York and New England. In Proceedings, Eastern gamagrass workshop, USDA-SCS, Manhattan, KS. 38 p.

Douglas, D. S., Schwendiman J. L. and A. L. Hafenrichter. 1953. Conservation in the Kickitat Using Grasses and Legumes. USDA, SCS. Pacific Region, Portland, OR. 40 p.

Dreesen, D. R. 2002. Evaluation of Containerized Legumes for Revegetation of Molycorp Overburden Poles - 1996 Trial of Source-Identified Germplasm. USDA-NRCS Los Lunas Plant Materials Center, Los Lunas, NM. Feb. 2002. 7 p.

Dreesen, D. R., J. T. Harrington, A. M. Wagner, L. Murray, and P. Sun. 2001. Testing Native Grasses for Survival and Growth in Low pH Mine Overburden. Proceedings of the ASSMR 18th National Meeting, June 3-7, 2001, Lexington, KY. Vol. 1:2-17, 2001. 14 p.

Dreesen, David R., Fenchel, Greg, Goodson, Danny G., and Keith White. 2006. Seeding Xeric Riparian Sites Following Removal of Invasive Phreatophytes. Riparian Management Course. USDA-NRCS, Los Lunas, NM. 8.

Dreesen, David. 2004. Tumbling for Seed Cleaning and Conditioning. Native Plants J., Vol. 5, No. 1, Spring 2004. 3 p.

Dreesen, David. 2006. Development of Legume Dalea for Use in Burn Rehab Seed Mixtures in Southwestern Pinyon/Juniper Communities. Los Lunas Plant Materials Center, Los Lunas, NM. 8 p.

Duebbert, H. F., E. T. Jacobson, K. F. Higgins, and E. B. Podoll. 1981. Establishment of seeded grasslands for wildlife habitat in the prairie pothole region. USDI Fish and Wildlife Service. Special Scientific Report-Wildlife No. 234, Washington, DC. 21 p

Enlow, C. R. 1936. Promising Introduced Species for dry-site Erosion Control Seeding and Planting in the West. Amer. Soil Survey Assoc., Bull. 17:118-121.

Enlow, C. R., and G. W. Musgrave. 1948. Grass and other Thick Growing Vegetation in Erosion Control. Grass, 1948 USDA YB of Agric., GPO. P. 615-633.

Ensminger, M. E., A. G Law, T. J., Cunha, and J. L. Schwendiman. 1947. Grain Feeding Cattle on Pasture. Wash. Agric. Expt. Stn. Bull 483.

Entenmann, F. M., Schwendiman, J. L. and J. K. Patterson. 1952. Cultural Methods of Establishing Grass and Sweet Clover in the Effects of Varying Percentage of Grass and Sweet Clover on Crop Yield. Agron. J. 44:514-516.

Fenchel, Greg, Dreesen, David R., Miller, Marcus, Lacy, Steve, Leiting, Ken and George Chavez. 2007. A Guide for Planning Riparian Treatments in New Mexico, USDA-NRCS, Albuquerque, NM. 40 p.

Fenchel, Greg, Goodson, Danny G., and Keith White. 2006. Southwest Riparian Tree and Shrubs Planting Methods that Require Minimal or No Irrigation. Seventeenth Biennial High Altitude Revegetation Workshop, Fort Collins, Colorado, March 7-9, 2006.

Fenchel, Gregory A. and David R. Dreesen. 2009. Longstem Transplants for Riparian Plantings in the Southwest. Soc. of Rn. Mgt., 62nd Annual Meeting, Albuquerque, NM.

Fenchel, Gregory, David Dreesen, Danny Goodson, Keith White, Hope Wood. 2007. The Los Lunas Plant Material Center Partners with New Mexico Soil & Water Consv., Districts to Restore Riparian Areas in the Southwestern United States. Tamerisk 2007 Symposium - October 24-26, Two Rivers Convention Center, Grand Junction, Colorado, Grand Junction, Colorado. October 26, 2007. 1 p.

Fenchel, Gregory, Dreesen, David, and Barbara Garrett. 2006. Conservation Showcase, Fall Planting of Native shrubs. USDA-NRCS New Mexico State Office, Albuquerque, NM.

Fenchel, Gregory, 2005. Alkali Muhly, A Common and Abundant New Mexico Riparian Grass Species. USDA-NRCS Los Lunas Plant Materials Center, Los Lunas, New Mexico. 2 p.

Finch, Clarence U. and W. Curtis Sharp. Cover Crops in California Orchards and Vineyards. USDA-SCS, Davis, CA. 1981.

Fine, G. L., F. I. Barnett, K. L. Anderson, R. D. Lippert, and E. T. Jacobson. 1990. Registration of Pete eastern gamagrass. Crop Sci. 30:741.

Flory, Evan L. and Charles G. Marshall. Regrassing for Soil Protection in the Southwest, USDA Farmers Bull. 1913. 1942

Floyd M Cossitt, C. A. Rindt and Harry A. Gunning. 1949. Production of Planting Stock. Trees, 1949 USDA YB of Agric., GPO.

Gaffney, F. B., W. C. Sharp, and M. W. Testerman. 1981. Potential for flatpea for forage. Am. Soc. Agron., Atlanta, Georgia.

Galgen, W. M., Green, W. D., Ensminger, M. E., Patterson, J. K., Law, A. G. and J. L. Schwendiman. 1956. Pastures for Horses. Wash. Agric. Expt. Stn. Cir. 289 p.

Glagin, M. W., Ensminger, M. E., Ham, W. E., Schneider, B. H. and J. L. Schwendiman. 1952. Grass and Grass-Alfalfa Pastures Supplement with Grain for Beef Production in Eastern Washington. Wash. Agric. Expt. Stn. Circ. 164 p.

Goldsmith, G. W. and A. L. Hafenrichter. 1932. Anthokinetics: the physiology and ecology of floral movements. Publication Number 420. Carnegie Institution of Washington, DC., W. F. Roberts Company, Washington, DC.

Graham, E., S. Majerus, M. Majerus, J. Scianna, and R. Hybner. 2009. Selection and Release of Indigenous Plant Materials for the Anaconda Superfund Site - 'Opportunity' Germplasm Nevada Bluegrass. Proceedings of the ASSMR - Land Reclamation Symposium, Lexington, KY.

Griffin, J. L., G. A. Jung, C. F. Gross, R. E. Kocher, and W. C. Sharp. 1978. IVDMD Forage Estimates of Warm-Season Grasses in the Northeast. Am. Soc. Agron., Chicago, IL.

Haas, R. J., E. T. Jacobson, and D. A. Tober. 1981. Woody natives selected, propagated for conservation use. Restoration and Management Notes. Vol. 1 (1).

Hafenrichter, A. L and May Z. Huntamer. 1933. The Ecology of 'Quincy Grass', *Oryzopsis hymenoides*, in Washington State. Tenth Annual Meeting, NW Scientific Assoc., Spokane, WA.

Hafenrichter, A. L. 1948. Getting new range plants into practice. J. Rn. Manage. 1:9-18.

Hafenrichter, A. L. 1951. Akaroa Orchardgrass. Westland Pasture J. 2 (4): 4.

Hafenrichter, A. L. and H. M. Wanser, 1935. Wind erosion on summer fallow on wheat lands of the west. Soil Consv., 1 (2):8-10.

Hafenrichter, A. L, Schwendiman, J. L. Harris, Harold R., MacLauchlan, Robert S. and Harold W. Miller. 1968. Grasses and Legumes for Soil Conservation in the Pacific Northwest and Great Basin States Agric. Handb. 339, USDA-SCS, Washington, DC.

Hafenrichter, A. L. and A. D. Stoesz. 1948. Domesticated Grasses in Conservation. Grass, 1948 USDA YB of Agric., GPO. P 354-356.

Hafenrichter, A. L., Foster, R. B. and J. L. Schwendiman. 1965. Effect of Storage at Four Locations in the West on Longevity of Forage Seeds. Agron. J. 57:142-147.

Hafenrichter, A. L., Mullen, L. A. and R. L. Brown. 1949. Grasses and Legumes for conservation in the Pacific Northwest. USDA Misc. Publ. 678. U.S. Gov. Print. Office, Washington, DC.

Hafenrichter, A. L., Schwendiman, J. L. and A. G. Law. 1964. Registration of Other Grasses, Volga Wildrye. Crop Sci. 4:116.

Hamilton, Lewis P. and W. M. Wooton. 1950. Grass Seed Production. Arizona Agric. Exp. Stn. Bull. 228. 40 p.

Hanson, A. A. 1959. Grass varieties in the United States. USDA, Washington, DC.

Harrington, J. T., D. R. Dreesen, A. M. Wagner, L. Murray, and P. Sun. 2001. The Influence of Seed Source and Stock Size on First-Year Performance of Direct Transplanted Conifer Seedlings. Proceedings of the ASSMR 18th National Meeting, Lexington, KY. Vol. 1:265-270.

Hawk, V. B., and J. L. Schwendiman. 1962. Other grasses for the North and West (Rev). In H. D. Hughes, M. E. Heath, and D. S. Metcalfe (eds.) Forages. Iowa State Univ. Press, Ames. p. 234-336.

Hawk, V. B., and W. C. Sharp. 1967. Sand Dune Stabilization along the North Atlantic Coast, J. of Soil & Water Consv., Vol. 22, No. 4.

Hawk, V. B. 1951 and J. L. Schwendiman. Other Grasses for the North and West, Forages, Iowa St. Univ. Press, Ames, Iowa. p. 379-91

Hawk, V. B. 1961. Crownvetch for Iowa. Iowa Certified Seed News, March. 6.

Hawk, V. B. 1962. Emerald Crownvetch – New Legume Fills Many Needs for Conservation Plans. Iowa Soil & Water, Vol. 6, No. 3, p. 10

Hawk, V. B. 1962. Emerald Crownvetch. Seed World, Vol. 90, No. 9. p. 30.

Hawk, V. B. and C. P. Wilsie. 1962. Emerald Crownvetch Released by SCS. Crops and Soils, Vol. 14 No. 6:19.

Hawk, V. B. and D. S. Douglas. 1962. Crownvetch – New Pasture Plant. Soil Consv., Vol. 27, No. 9: 206-7.

Hawk, V. B., and J. L. Schwendiman. 1962. Other Grasses for the North and West. Forages (2nd ed.), Iowa U. Press, Ch. 33:324-336.

Hawkins, A. C. Soil & Water Conservation in Maryland. Conservation in Maryland. 2001. www.mascd.net/handbook/MASCD7a.pdf/

Henry, D. S., H. W. Everett, and W. C. Sharp. 1976. Response to Three Warm Season Grasses to Clipping at Four Growth Stages. Am. Soc. Agron., Houston, TX.

Henson, J. F., W. R. Oaks, and S. Vail. 1991. Preliminary Comparison of Plant Species for Heavy Metal Concentration When Grown on Reclaimed Molybdenum Tailings. Proceedings, ASSMR, Durango, CO

Higgins, K. F., H. F. Duebbert, and E. T. Jacobson. 1982. Successful establishment of stands of cool-season native grasses. Restoration and Management Notes. Vol. 1(2).

Hoag, C., D. Tilley, D. Darris, and K. Pendergrass. 2008. Field Guide for the Identification and Use of Common Riparian Woody Plants of the Intermountain West and Pacific Northwest Regions. http://www.plant-materials.nrcs.usda.gov/pubs/idpmcpu7969.pdf/ 196 p.

Hoag, J. Chris and Dan Ogle. 2010. Willow Clump Plantings. http://www.plant-materials.nrcs.usda.gov/pubs/idPM Specialisttn10093.pdf/

Hoag, J. C., B. Simonson, B. Cornforth, and L. St. John. 2001. Waterjet Stinger - A tool to plant dormant unrooted cuttings of willows, cottonwoods, dogwoods, and other species. http://plant-materials.nrcs.usda.gov/idpmc/publications.html/

Hoag, J. C., S. K. Wyman, G. Bentrup, L. Holzworth, D. G. Ogle, J. Carleton, F. Berg, and B. Leinard. 2001. 2001. Users Guide to the Description, Propagation, and Establishment of Wetland Plant Species and Grasses for Riparian Areas in the Intermountain West. http://www.plant-materials.nrcs.usda.gov/pubs/idpmctn10749.pdf/.

Hoag, J. C., Wyman, S. K., Bentrup, G., Holzworth, L., Ogle, D. G., Carleton, J., Berg, F. and B. Leinard. 2001. Users Guide to the Description, Propagation, and Establishment of Wetland Plant Species and Grasses for Riparian Areas in the Intermountain West. http://www.plant-materials.nrcs.usda.gov/pubs/idpmctn10749.pdf/.

Hoag, J. C. 2007. How to plant willows and cottonwoods for riparian restoration. http://www.plant-materials.nrcs.usda.gov/pubs/idpmctn7064.pdf/.

Holzworth, L. K, Majerus, M., Scianna, J. and S. Winslow. 1999. Restoration of woody plants with native range communities. http://www.plant- materials.nrcs.usda.gov/pubs/mtpmctn1100.pdf/.

Holzworth, L. K. 2002. Establishment of Permanent Vegetation. http://www.plant-materials.nrcs.usda.gov/pubs/mtPM Specialisttn30402.pdf/.

Holzworth, L. K., H. Hunter, and S. R. Winslow. 2004. Disturbed Forestland Re-vegetation Effectiveness Monitoring - Results of 30 Years. Ninth Billings Land Reclamation Symposium & 20th Annual Meeting of Am. Soc. of Mining and Reclamation, Billings, MT. 28 p.

Holzworth, L. K., J. Schaefer, G. Green, and T. Wiersum. 1993. The city of Anaconda erosion control and stabilization of C hill. In the Proceedings of the 10th ASSMR annual meeting, Spokane, WA. 8 p.

Hoover, M. M., James E. Smith, Jr., A. E. Faber, and D. R. Cornelius: 1947. Seed for Regrassing Great Plains Areas, USDA Farmers' Bulletin 1985.

Hoover, M.M. 1939. Native and Adapted Grasses for Soil and Moisture Conservation in the Great Plains and Western States. USDA, SCS, Farmers Bulletin No. 1812, Washington, DC.

Hoover, M. M., J. E. Smith, Jr., A. E. Gerber and Donald R. Cornelius. 1947. Seed for Regrassing the Great Plains Area, USDA Farmers' Bull. 1965.

Hoover, Max M., M. A. Hein, William A. Dayton and C. O. Erlanson. 1948. The Main Grasses for Farm and Home. Grass, 1948 USDA YB of Agric., GPO. 637-700, illus.

Horner, G. M. Rasmussen, L. W. and J. L. Schwendiman. 1954. Natural brush Cover on Palouse Farms. Wash. Agric. Expt. Stn. C. 429 p.

Humphrey, E. G., D. A. Carroll, and W. C. Sharp. 1981. Permanent Legume Cover in No-Till Corn. Am. Soc. Agron., Atlanta, GA.

Hybner, R., E. Graham, M. Majerus, and S. Majerus. 2009. Comparative Evaluation of Grasses, Forbs, and Seed Mixtures from Local versus Non-Local Origins at Stucky Ridge, Anaconda, MT. Proceedings of the 11th Annual ASSMR, Lexington, KY.

Jacobson, E. T. 1975. Evaluation, Selection, and Increase of Prairie Wildflowers for Conservation Beautification. http://images.library.wisc.edu/EcoNatRes/EFacs/NAPC/NAPC04/reference/ econatres.napc04.ejacobson.pdf/.

Jacobson, E. T., D. A. Tober, R. J. Haas, and D. C. Darris. 1986. The performance of selected cultivars of warm season grasses in the northern prairie and plains states. http://images.library.wisc.edu/EcoNatRes/EFacs/NAPC/NAPC09/reference/econatres.napc09.ejaco bson.pdf/.

Jacobson, E. T. 1974. The evaluation, selection, and increase of prairie wildflowers for conservation beautification http://images.library.wisc.edu/EcoNatRes/EFacs/NAPC/NAPC04/reference/conatres.napc04.ejacob son.pdf/.

Jacobson, E. T., C. M. Taliaferro, C. L. DeWald, D. A. Tober, and R. J. Haas. 1985. New and old world bluestems. In Proceedings Soc. of Rn. Mgt., 38th Annual Mtg., Denver, CO. p. 148-158.

Johnson, D. A., Jigjidsuren, S., Sheehy, D. P., Majerus, M. E., Winslow, S. R. and L. K. Holzworth. 2006. Collection and Evaluation of Forage Germplasm Indigenous to Mongolia. Rangelands of Central Asia: http://www.treesearch.fs.fed.us/pubs/22868/.

Jones, C. L., J. T. Harrington, and D. R. Dreesen. 2002. Refinement and Stratification of Thinleaf Alder and Water Birch Seeds from New Mexico. Jones, C. L., J. T. Harrington, and D. R. Dreesen. 2002. Native Plants J., Moscow, Idaho. Vol. 3, No. 2. 9 p.

Jung, G. A., and W. C. Sharp. 1982. Agronomic Characteristics Essential for Adaptation into Systems of Utilization. Am. Soc. Agron., Anaheim, CA.

Jung, G. A., C. F. Gross, L. A. Burdette, and W. C. Sharp. 1978. Warm Season Range Grasses Extend Beef Cattle Forage. Sci. in Agric., Vol. 25, No. 2, Pennsylvania State University

Jung, G. A., C. F. Gross, R. E. Kocher, L. A. Burdette, and W. C. Sharp. 1978. Persistence and Productivity of Warm-Season Grasses Under Grazing in Pennsylvania. Am. Soc. Agron., Chicago, IL.

Jung, G. A., C. F. Gross, W. C. Sharp, R. E Kocher and L. A. Burnette. 1079. New Insights on Warm Season Grasses. Soil Consv., USDA-SCS, Washington, DC. p. 8-10.

Klien, L. M., Henderson, N. J. and A. D. Stoesz. 1961. Equipment for cleaning seeds. Seeds, 1961 USDA YB of Agric., GPO. P. 307–329.

Knudson, M. J., R. J. Haas, D. A. Tober, D. C. Darris, and E. T. Jacobson. 1990. Improvement of chokecherry, silver buffaloberry, and hawthorn for conservation use in the northern plains. http://www.fs.fed.us/rm/pubs_int/int_gtr276/int_gtr276_291_299.pdf/.

Law, A. G. and John L. Schwendiman. 1946. Bromar Mountain Bromegrass. Wash. Agric. Expt. Stn. Bull. 479 p.

Law, A. G., Goss, R. L. and J. L. Schwendiman. 1972. Registration of Cougar Kentucky Bluegrass. (Reg. No. 7). Crop Sci. 12:255.

Law, A. G., Schwendiman, J. L. and Jens. Clausen. 1964. Registration of Newport Bluegrass. Crop Sci. 4:114-116.

Law, A. G., Schwendiman, J. L. and M. E. Ensminger. 1949. Sweet Clover Grass Pasture in Eastern Washington. Wash. Agric. Expt. Stn. Bull. 509.

Law, A. G., Schwendiman, J. L., Goss, R. L. and J. K. Morrison. 1967. Cougar Kentucky Bluegrass. Wash. Agric. Expt. Stn. Circ. 352 p.

Lemmon, Paul E. and A. L. Hafenrichter. 1947. The Dilution Method for Plot or Field Seeding of Grassed and legumes Alone or in Mixtures. J. Am. Soc. Of Agron. Vol. 39.

Lippert, Robert D. and Edde D. Rhodes. 1965. Grass can Survive even if Flooded. KS Farmer Stockman Vol. 78, No. 1.

Lorenz, David G., Sharp, W. Curtis and Joseph D. Ruffner. 1991. Conservation plants for the Northeast. Program Aid 1154. USDA-SCS, Washington, DC. 43 p.

MacLauchlan, Robert S. 1980. Soil Conservation Service National study on alternatives financing, staffing and/or managing plant materials centers. USDA, NRCS, Washington, DC.

MacLauchlan, Robert S., Harold W. Miller and Oswald K. Hoglund 1970. Lana Vetch for Medusahead Control. J. of Rn. Mgt., Vol. 23, No. 5:351-353.

Majerus, M. 2000. Restoration with native indigenous plants in Yellowstone and Glacier National Parks. http://www.plant-materials.nrcs.usda.gov/pubs/mtpmcsylandrecl.pdf/.

Majerus, M. E., Reynolds, C., Scianna, J., Winslow, S., Holzworth, L. and B. Woodson. 2001. Creating Native Landscapes in the Northern Great Plains and Rocky Mountains. http://www.plant-materials.nrcs.usda.gov/pubs/mtpmcpunatland.pdf/.

Marburger, J. E., D. W. Burgdorf, M. D. Dominick, R. J. Haas, E. T. Jacobson, and R. L. Wynia. 1993. Plant materials technology for wetland restoration and creation in the Midwest. USDA-SCS, Bismarck, ND. Prairie Ecosystems: Wetland Ecology, Management and Restoration. Wetland Symposium. Jamestown, ND.

Marty, L. 2000. The use of local ecotypes for the revegetation of acid/heavy metal contaminated lands in western Montana. Proc. 2000 Billings Land Reclamation Symposium, Pages 216- 228. 13 p.

McClure, N. R., Hafenrichter, A. L. and J. L. Schwendiman. 1958. Grasses and Legumes in Conservation Farming in Central Oregon and Adjacent Areas. USDA-SCS, Portland, Oregon. 40 p.

McWilliams, Jesse L. Influence of Mechanical Treatment on Germination and Longevity of Seed of Various Grasses. SCS, Mandan, ND, Entry 215.0, Central Files, Nurseries General (October 1935 - March 1936) RG 114, Records of the Nursery Division, National Archives, College Park, MD.

Michels, C. A. and J. L. Schwendiman. 1934. Determining Yields on Experimental Plots by the square Yard Method. Agron. J. 26:993-1001.

Norris, Sharon L. 1989. History of the Aberdeen Plant Materials Center. USDA-SCS, Boise, ID.

Ogle, D. G., Majerus, Mark and L. St. John. 2004. Plants for Saline to Sodic Soil Conditions. http://www.plant-materials.nrcs.usda.gov/pubs/idPMSpecialisttn5465.pdf/.

Ogle, Dan, St John, Loren, Stannard, Mark and Larry Holzworth. 2007. Grass, Grass-Like, Forb, Legume and Woody Species. http://www.mt.nrcs.usda.gov/technical/ecs/plants/technotes/pmtechnoteMT59.html/.

Patterson, J. K., Schwendiman, J. L., Law, A. G. and H. H. Wolfe. 1956. Producing Grass seed in Washington. Wash. Agric. Ext. Stn. MP 41.

Phillips, Steven E. and Douglas Helms. 1994. Interviews with Chiefs of the SCS. USDA, Washington, DC. http://www.farmlandinfo.org/documents/34766/Interviews_with_Chiefs_Donald_Williams.pdf/.

Prodgers, R. A., T. Keck, and L. K. Holzworth. 2000. Revegetation Evaluations-How Long Must We Wait? http://www.plant-materials.nrcs.usda.gov/pubs/mtPM Specialistsy2448.pdf/.

Ranney, C. W., Schwendiman, J. L. and A. L. Hafenrichter. 1967. Grasses and Legumes for Conservation use in Semiarid Wheat-Fallow Areas of Eastern Washington. USDA, SCS, Portland Oregon. 89 p.

Release of the Cultivar 'Ruffner' Tall Oatgrass. 2009. http://plant-materials.nrcs.usda.gov/wvpmc/publications.html/ (February 4, 2011).

Richard, D. E. and V. B. Hawk. 1945. Palatability for Sheep and Yield of Hay and Pasture Grasses at Union, Oregon. Oregon. Agric. Exp. Stn., Bull. 431. 51 pp., illus.

Rogler, George A. 1951. Russian Wildrye. USDA. Leaflet 313. 8 p., illus.

Rosner, L. S., J. T. Harrington, D. R. Dreesen, and L. Murray. 2002. Effect of Gibberellic Acid and Standard Seed Treatments on Mountain Snowberry Germination. Native Plants J. Vol. 3, No. 2. 8 p.

Rosner, L. S., J. T. Harrington, D. R. Dreesen, and L. Murray. 2003. *Sulfuric Acid Scarification of Wax Current Seeds from New Mexico*. Native Plants J., Vol. 4, No. 1. 7 p.

Ruffner, Joseph D and John G. Hall. 1963. Crownvetch in West Virginia. Univ. Agric. Exp. Stn., Morgantown, WV. Bulletin 487. 19 p.

Ruffner, Joseph D. 1978. Plant Performance on Surface Coal Mine Spoil in the Eastern United States. USDA-SCS; SCS-TP-155. Washington, D.C.

Savage, D. A. and James E. Smith, Jr. 1944. Regrassing Methods for the Southern Great Plains. USDA Great Plains Field Stn. Woodward, OK. 16 p.

Scholten, H., D. D. Breitbach, R. J. Haas and E. T. Jacobson. 1992. Shrub species for single-row field windbreaks under center-pivot irrigation systems. http://www.extension.umn.edu/distribution/naturalresources/dd6042.html/.

Schumacher, C. M. and M. D. Atkins, 1965. Re-establishment and use of grass in Morton County, Kansas, land utilization project. USDA, SCS-TP-146. 14 p.

Schwendiman, J. L. 1946. Root Production of Grasses and Sweet Clover in Conservation Mixtures. Northwest Sci. 20: 3.

Schwendiman, J. K. 1946. Registration of Draylar Bluegrass. Crop Sci. 4:114-116.

Schwendiman, J. K. 1972. Registration of Alkar Tall Wheatgrass. (Reg. No. 7) Crop Sci. 12:260.

Schwendiman, J. K. 1972. Registration of Sherman Big Bluegrass. (Reg. No. 6) Crop Sci. 12:125.

Schwendiman, J. K. 1972. Registration of Topar Pubescent Wheatgrass. (Reg. No. 8) Crop Sci. 12:260.

Schwendiman, J. L. 1955. A Nursery Helps Put Conservation on the Land. J. Soil & Water Consv., Vol. 10, No. 4.

Schwendiman, J. L. 1956. Improvement of Native Range through Introduction. J. Rn. Mgt. 9:91-95.

Schwendiman, J. L. 1957. Well Managed Conservation Seedings Help Alfalfa in "Good Land Management Supports Wildlife". Wash. Agric. Exp. Stn. Cir. 295 p.

Schwendiman, J. L. 1959. Testing New Range Forage Plants. The Am. Assoc. for the Adv. of Sci. Grasslands Pub. 53:345-357.

Schwendiman, J. L. 1960. Tall Wheatgrass Gains Stature. Crops and Soils 12:5 -14.

Schwendiman, J. L. 1961. Orchard Cover Crops in Wash. Proc. 57th Annual Meeting, Wash. State Hort. Assoc.: 33-43.

Schwendiman, J. L. 1965. Production and Harvesting Forage Grass Seed in the Pacific Northwest, USA. 1965. Proc. 9th Grassland Congress, Sao Paulo, Brazil. P. 527-530.

Schwendiman, J. L. 1966. Introduced Grasses Used for Soil Conservation in the western U.S. Proc. 10th Int. Grassland Cong., Helsinki, Finland.

Schwendiman, J. L. 1977. Coastal and sand dune stabilization in the Pacific Northwest. Proc. of the International J. Biometeorology Cong., College Park, MD, Int. J.. Bio. V. 21(3):281-89.

Schwendiman, J. L. 1977. Vegetative Control of Inland Sand Dunes in the Pacific Northwest. Proc. of the International Biometeorology Cong., College Park, MD. Int. J.. Bio. V. 21(3): 290-298.

Schwendiman, J. L. 1986. Its First 50 Years. Pullman Plant Materials Center, USDA, SCS, Pullman WA. http://www.wsu.edu/pmc_nrcs/History.html/.

Schwendiman, J. L. and A. G. Law. 1946. Primar, A new Slender Wheatgrass for Conservation Use. Wash. Agric. Exp. Stn. Bull. 478 p.

Schwendiman, J. L. and A. L. Hafenrichter. 1954. Timothy Mite Becomes Problem for Seed Growers in the Northwest. Crops and Soils 6:5.

Schwendiman, J. L. and A. L. Hafenrichter. 1955. A Nursery Helps Put Conservation on the Ground. Soil & Water Consv., 10:189-196.

Schwendiman, J. L. and L. A. Mullins. 1944. Effects of Processing on Germinative Capacity of Seed of Tall Oatgrass (*Arrhenatherum elatius*). Agron. J. 36:783.

Schwendiman, J. L. and V. B. Hawk. 1973. Other Grasses for the North and West. Chapter 22 in 'Forages' textbook. Iowa State Univ. Press, Ames IA.

Schwendiman, J. L., Douglas, D. S. and A. L. Hafenrichter. 1961. Latar Orchardgrass for Conservation in the West. USDA, Prod. Res. Report 54:1-8.

Schwendiman, J. L., Foster, R. B. and O. K. Hoglund. 1960. The Influence of Climate, Soils, and Management on the Root Development of Grass Species in the Western States. Proc. Am. Forage and Grassland Council Joint Meeting with Soc. of Rn. Mgt., New Orleans, LA.

Schwendiman, J. L., Hafenrichter, A. L. and A. G. Law. 1943. The Production of Tops and Roots by Grass and Sweet Clover when Grown in Mixtures. Agron. J 45:110-114.

Schwendiman, J. L., Hafenrichter, A. L. and A. G. Law. 1964. Registration of Durar Hard fescue. Crop Sci. 4:114-116

Schwendiman, J. L., Sackman, R. F. and A. L. Hafenrichter. 1940. Processing Seed of Grasses and Other Plants to Remove Awns and Appendages. USDA Cir. 558. 15 p.

Scianna, J. D, E. C. Graham, R. W. Kilian, D. P. Zentner and R. Hybner. 2009. Effects of Sub-Irrigation Tubes and Cover Type on Woody Plant Establishment. Proceedings of the 11th Annual ASSMR-Land Reclamation Symposium, Lexington, KY.

Scianna, J. D., Holzworth, L., Ogle, D. G., Cornwell, J. and L. St. John. 2002. Restoration and Diversification of Plant Communities with Woody Plants Idaho NRCS State Office, Boise, ID. ID-TN 41, April 16, 2002. 7 p.

Scianna, J. D., L. Holzworth, D. G. Ogle, J. Cornwell, and L. St. John. 2002. Restoration and Diversification of Plant Communities with Woody Plants. Idaho NRCS State Office, Boise, ID. 7 p.

Sharp, W C., C. R. Belcher, and J. A. Oyler. 1980. Vegetation for Tidal Stabilization in the Mid-Atlantic States. http://www.plant-materials.nrcs.usda.gov/pubs/njpmcar2659.pdf/.

Sharp, W. Curtis, David L. Schertz and Jack R. Carlson. 1995. Forages for Conservation and Soil Stabilization. *Forages* Vol. II. P. 243-63. Iowa St. Univ. Press, Ames, IA

Sharp, W. Curtis, Geo. A. White and James A. Briggs. 1987. Our American Land, 1987 USDA YB of Agric. GPO. 54-58.

Sharp, W. Curtis. 1977. Conservation Plants for the Northeast. USDA, SCS Program Aid 1134. 40 p.

Sharp, W. Curtis. 1992, Selecting Plant Materials for Erosion Intervention. US – Central and Eastern European Agric. Environmental Program. p 236-44.

Sharp, W. C. 1965. Effect of Clipping and Nitrogen Fertilization on Seed Production of Red Fescue. Agron. J.; 57:252-52.

Sharp, W. C. 1970. New Plants for Conservation. Economic Botany. 24:53-4.

Sharp, W. C. 1970. Rem-Red Honeysuckle, A New Ornamental with Wildlife Value. Am. Nurseryman; 82:7.

Sharp, W. C. 1976. Role of SCS Plant Materials Program in Developing Plants for Hill Lands. International Hill Land Symposium, WVU, Morgantown, WV. P. 59.

Sharp, W. C. 1982. Best of Beach Vegetation, Part I-Availability and Use of Beachgrasses, Parks and Recreation Resources; Vol. I, No. 1

Sharp, W. C. 1982. Best of Beach Vegetation, Part III-Establishing and Managing Herbaceous Vegetation, Parks and Recreation Resources; Vol. I, No. 3.

Sharp, W. C. 1982. Best of Beach Vegetation, Part II-Types and Use of Herbaceous Vegetation, Parks and Recreation Resources; Vol. 1, No. 2.

Sharp, W. C. 1982. Best of Beach Vegetation, Part IV-Types and Use of Woody Vegetation, Parks and Recreation Resources; Vol. 1, No. 4.

Sharp, W. C. 1983. Use and Management of Tall Growing Warm Season Grasses in the Northeast. USDA-SCS, Broomall, PA. 17.

Sharp, W. C. 1984. Overview of SCS Plant Materials--Emphasizing Forage and Special Purpose Legume Work. Eight *Trifolium* Conference. Tiffon, GA.

Sharp, W. C. and Joseph D. Vaden. 1970. 10-Year Report on Sloping Technique Used to Stabilize Eroding Tidal River Banks. Shore and Beach; 38:31-5

Sharp, W. C., and V. B. Hawk. 1975. Establishment of Woody Plants for Secondary and Tertiary Dune Stabilization along the Mid-Atlantic States. Int. J. of Biometeorology; 21, 3:245-55.

Sharp, W. C., J. A. Oyler, and C. R. Belcher. 1981. Criteria for Identifying Eroding Tidal Shorelines with Vegetative Stabilization Potential. Am. Soc. Agron., Atlanta, GA.

Sharp, W. C., M. van der Grinten, R. S. Dayton, and C. R. Belcher. 1982. Effect of Production Location on Seed Yield and Quality of Four Switchgrasses. Am. Soc. Agron., Anaheim, California.

Sharp, W. C., R. S. Ross, M. W. Testerman, and R. Williamson. 1980. Ability of Crownvetch to Suppress Woody Plant Invasion. Jor. Soil & Water Consv., Vol. 35, No. 3:142-44.

Sharp, W. Curtis. 1969. Registration of 'Chemung' Crownvetch. Crop Sci. Vol. 9, No. 3:393-4.

Slinkard, A. E., Nurmi, E. O. and J. L. Schwendiman. 1970. Seeding Burned Over Lands in Northern Idaho. Currant Info. Series #139. Univ. of Idaho.

Smith, James E. "Bud" 1960-1962. Annual Reports, Plant Center Operations, USDA-SCS, Plant Materials Center, Knox City, TX.

Stark, R. H., Toevs, J. L. and A. L. Hafenrichter. 1946. Grasses and cultural methods of Great Basin Grasses. Functional Ecology. 1:139-143.

Stark, R. H., Toevs, J. L. and A. L. Hafenrichter. 1946. Grasses and Cultural Methods of Reseeding Abandoned Farm Land in Southern Idaho. ID Agric. Expt. Stn. Bull. 267.

Steiner, Wilmer W. 1963 Control of Soil Subject to Wind Erosion, Highway Research Board, Highway Res. Record No. 23:69-71.

Stevens, William Walton. 1999. History of Soil & Water Conservation in North Carolina, USDA-NRCS, Raleigh, NC

Stoesz, A. D. and Hugh Richwine. 1948. New Grass fills Gap in Northern Great Plains. Soil Consv. 13:241-243.

Stoesz, A. D. and Robert L. Brown. 1957. Stabilizing sand dunes. Soil, 1957 USDA YB of Agric. GPO. 321-326.

Stoesz, A. D. 1943. Mennonites and Soil Conservation. Conference on Mennonite. Cultural Problems, No. 2. pp. 67-72.

Stoesz, A. D. 1952. Harvesting, processing, and seeding of native grasses in the central and northern Great Plains. Agron. J., 44:378-383.

Stroh, James R. and Alvin G. Law. 1967. Effects of Defoliation on the Longevity of Stand, Dry Matter Yields and Forage Quality of Tall Wheatgrass, Agropyron elongatum (Host) Beauv. Agron. J. 59:432-435.

Stroh, James R. and Vernon P. Sunberg. 1970. Emergence of grass seedlings under crop residue culture. J. of Rn. Mgt. p. 226-27.

Swingle, Charles F. 1937. Experiments in Propagating Shipmast Locust. J. of Forestry, Vol. 35, No. 8:713-20

Swingle, Charles F. 1939. Seed Propagation of Trees, Shrubs and Forbs for Conservation Planting. USDA-SCS, Washington, DC.

Swingle, Charles F. 1940. Regeneration and Vegetative Propagation. The Botanical Review, Vol. VI, No. 7:301-43.

Tabor, Paul. 1935. Legions of lespedeza. Soil Consv., 1 (2): 6-7.

Tabor, Paul. 1950. Some Observations of Bahia Grass for Soil Conservation in the Southeastern United States. Agron. J. 42: 362–364

Tabor, Paul. 1951. Browntop Millet (*Panicum ramosum*). Agron. J. 43:100.

Tabor, Paul. 1952. Comments on Cogon and Torpedo Grasses: A Challenge to Weed Workers. Weed Science of America, Vol. 1, No. 4:374-375

Tabor, Paul. 1952. Comments on Cogon and Torpedo Grasses: A Challenge to Weed Workers. Weed Science of America, Publisher. *Weeds*, Vol. 1, No. 4 pp. 374-375

Tabor, Paul. 1961. The Early History of Annual Lespedeza in the United States. Agric. History Soc., Agric. History, Vol. 35, No. 2:85-89.

The Crider Memorial Garden of conservation plants. 1967. Soil Conservation Magazine U.S. GPO, Div. of Public Documents, Washington, DC.

The Stockman-Review and Spokane Chronicle, Wednesday, June 10, 1992, Spokane, Wash.

Thornburg Ashley A. 1976. Plant materials for use on surface-mined lands in arid and semiarid regions. USDA, SCS TP-157,. U.S. Environmental Protection Agency, Washington DC.

Thornburg, Ashley A. and James R. Stroh. 1968. Cultural and Mechanical Seed -Harvesting of Fourwing Saltbush Grown Under Irrigation. Soc. of Rn. Mgt., Annual Meeting, Albuquerque, NM.

Thornburg, Ashley. 1971. Grassland legume seed production in Montana. Agric. Expt. Stn. Bull. 333. Montana State Univ., Bozeman.

Tober, D. A., E. T. Jacobson, and R. J. Haas. 1981. Vegetative assembly and evaluation of little bluestem for conservation use in the Northern Great Plains. Soc. of Rn. Mgt., 34th Annual Mtg., Tulsa, OK. 10 p.

Tober, D. A., E. T. Jacobson, and R. J. Haas. 1984. Selection of superior little bluestem ecotypes for conservation use in the Northern Great Plains. Soc. of Rn. Mgt., 37th Ann. Mtg., Rapid City, SD.

USDA, NRCS, Los Lunas PMC. 2007. Deep Planting: Guidelines for Planting Dormant Whip Cuttings to Revegetate and Stabilize Streambanks. http://plant-materials.nrcs.usda.gov/nmpmc/publications.html

USDA, NRCS, Los Lunas PMC. 2007. Guidelines for Planting Longstem Transplants for Riparian Restoration in the Southwest: Deep Planting-The Ground Water Connection. http://www.plant-materials.nrcs.usda.gov/pubs/nmpmcbr7106.pdf/.

USDA, NRCS, Plant Materials Center Web Site. http://plant-materials.nrcs.usda.gov/releases/.

USDA, NRCS. 2006. Plant Materials Program Costs and Benefits 1935 – 2005. USDA, NRCS, Washington, D.C. http://www.nrcs.usda.gov/Internet/FSE_DOCUMENTS/stelprdb1042295.pdf/.

USDA, NRCS. 2011. Conservation Plant Releases sorted by Scientific Name. http://plant-materials.nrcs.usda.gov/releases/ releasesallbysci/.

USDA, SCS. 1979. Plant Materials for Conservation. Program Aid 1219.

USDA-NRCS PMC Field Day 2004. Plant Materials Center, Bismarck, ND, June 17.

Vogel, K. P., L. C. Newell, E. T. Jacobson, J. E. Watkins, P.E. Reece, and D. E. Bauer. 1996. Registration of Pronghorn prairie sandreed grass. Crop Science. 36:1712.

Voigt, Paul W. and W. Curtis Sharp. 1995. Forages for Conservation and Soil Stabilization. Forages Vol. I:395-409. Iowa St. Univ. Press, Ames, IA

Wenger, L. E., Cornelius, D. R., Smith, J. E. and A. D. Stoesz. 1943. Methods of harvesting, storing, and processing native grass seeds. Subcommittee reports of the Southern Great Plains Re-vegetation Committee. National Academy of Science, Nat. Research Council, Annual Report 1963-64. Super. Of Doc., US Gov. Printing Office, Washington, DC.

Winslow, S. R. 2002. Native Plant Seed Collection and Seed Production for Reclamation. http://www.plant-materials.nrcs.usda.gov/pubs/mtpmcsy3202.pdf/.

Wolfe, Laird P., and Henry M. Wolfe. 1950. Grass Seed Production in Nebraska. Neb. Extension Cir. 188 p.

Wolff, Simon E. 1951. Harvesting and Cleaning Grass and Legume Seed in the Western Gulf Region. USDA Handb. 24. 108 p., illus.

Woods, J. E., Hafenrichter, A. L., Schwendiman, J. L. and G. A. Law. 1953. The Effect of Grass on the Yield of Forage and Production of Roots of Alfalfa-Grass Mixtures with Special reference to Soil Conservation. Agron. J. 45:590-595.

Young, W. C. 1973. Plants for Shoreline Erosion Areas of the U.S. Man-Made Lakes: Their Problems and Environmental Effects. Geophysical Monograph Series No. 17, Am. Geophysical Union.

Young, W. C. and J. D. Powell. 1963. Runner Oak Shows promise for Wildlife Habitat Improvement. GA Agric. Res. Vol. 5, No. 2:4-5

Appendix 3: CHRONOLOGICAL NURSERY SYNOPSIS FROM SCS REPORTS TO USDA 1935 to 1953

Annually, SCS wrote a report of their nursery operations for the Secretary of Agriculture. Each report contained highlights of the production and observational nursery accomplishments. The following chronological synopsis of these reports for the 1933 – 1953 periods is primarily about observational nursery work. It omits most information about the production nursery operations.[812]

It is apparent that the annual reports were written by different people, and on occasion there are contradictions from year to year. On the other hand, some writers liked what was said the previous year so well they repeated it the next year. It presents an interesting account of what SCS nurseries thought of themselves at the time. The reader will find repetition from year to year, suggesting the writer may not always have kept abreast of the latest accomplishments to include in the report, and thus repeated, in a general way, what was done.

What is most striking is the transition of the Nursery Division from 1935 to 1953. In 1935, the nurseries existed to produce or collect large quantities of plants and seed for conservation plantings. Occasionally there were a few bread crumbs thrown to the work of observational nurseries. Over time that faded and, as Charles Enlow said, the observational studies become the main work of the nurseries.

Scientific plant names listed in the reports may not be the currently accepted name. They are included as listed in the reports. The few underlined phrases are provided to emphasize what the writer saw as the priority at that time.

The documentation for each year will include narrative copied or summarized from the Annual Reports. Excessive narratives from the reports have been condensed. Brief observations by the editor may be intermingled throughout the report narrative. Those observations are presented in italics. Individual citation notes for each year would be identical except for the year, and are omitted; therefore one note is provided which documents the reference material for all years. Any information included from other sources has a separate note.

<u>1935 Annual Report</u>

The Division of Nurseries was established in the SCS in April 1935 to administer the erosion-control nurseries transferred from the Bureau of Plant Industries.

At the time of the transfer the Bureau of Plant Industries was operating twenty nurseries. *This is in contrast to other sources of information. Fourteen were transferred to SCS.* Much of the work under way was experimental dealing with the collection of promising native and foreign erosion-control plants, and the development of propagation methods for immediate increase.

Since the transfer of the nurseries, quantity production of planting stock for the entire SCS has been emphasized, but the collection (*observational studies*) work continues.

The Division of Nurseries is divided in to three sections, (1) tree and shrub work, (2) grass work, and (3) purchases.

Actually, in 1935 the nurseries were a section in the Division of Conservation Operations, becoming a Division in 1940.

Six nurseries had been established in the Great Plains and Western States to serve as centers for the study of native vegetation and its use in erosion control. The studies include collection, identification, distribution, methods of propagation, and increase of all species having potential value as erosion-control plants. During the 1934 season, over 600 species of native plants were collected, identified, and grown in the erosion-control nurseries to determine their value for erosion control on field projects of the Service.

This designation of these six centers is not to be confused with observational studies. While there is overlap on studies between the two, the six designated centers were tasked to learn how to produce seed of natives and then to quickly start producing large quantities on the production side. They also produced large quantities of trees and shrubs and carried out observational studies.

Climatic conditions are such throughout most of the western Great Plains and other dry lands of the West that cultivated species of grass cannot be used in establishing vegetative cover on abandoned agricultural lands. For this reason, recourse must be made to native grass species which are able to withstand the prevailing extremes of temperature, moisture, and soil. Most of these native grasses occur only in mixed stands and in locations that make the task of harvesting a very difficult one. The demand for large quantities of native grass seed has led to the formation of a bulk seed-collection program which has developed into a major activity of the soil-conservation nurseries of the Western States.

In addition to the bulk-seed-collecting program, the nurseries will be centers for small-scale collections being made with the hope of finding all native plants having a potential positive value in erosion control. Plants collected during the season of 1934 are being grown in the nurseries during the present season, and notes are being made as to their agronomic characteristics.

Some of the transferred nurseries from the SES were open for no more than a year or two. The SES nursery at Placerville, CA was closed immediately.

1936

Opening and closing of nurseries was rampant in the first few years of SCS operation. All told, at least eighty-one existed at one time or another during this period but never all at the same time. No number is given in the 1936 report on the number operating.

The Section of Conservation Nurseries is primarily concerned with providing suitable planting materials for use in the various phases of soil-erosion control and general revegetation. Its major work includes the production of nursery stock and the collection of native seeds and plants in quantity, as well as technically supervising the procurement of commercial seeds, fertilizers, limestone, and allied agricultural products. Contributory to the success of these larger operations, however, are a number of specialized activities such as: (1) assembling and observing plants which may have greater usefulness in erosion control than those now used; (2) collecting small lots of seeds for interregional exchange and test; (3) making seed-germination and treatment tests; (4) working out appropriate, practical methods of propagation, and. (5) developing special -methods and machinery for harvesting native seeds. In all of these activities the closest cooperation is maintained with the Sections of Woodland Management, Wildlife Management and Agronomy in order to insure more fully the collection and production of suitable kinds and quantities of plant materials for all purpose of the Service.

Another important function of the nurseries, in a large measure inseparable from quantity production, is the collection of propagation material of plants that may have greater value for erosion control than those now in common use. Collectors of the Service have obtained many promising species and assembled them at the various nurseries. These plants are being grown and observed in respect to their habit of growth, soil-binding properties, drought resistance, ease of propagation and transplanting, and general adaptability for use in the soil conservation program. In the same manner, introduced plants, obtained through cooperation with the Division of Plant Exploration and Introduction, of the Bureau of Plant Industry, and through the efforts of the Service staff, are being assembled and grown as observational plantings at the nurseries. Some of these species have already shown themselves of outstanding value in erosion control and are being propagated in quantities sufficient for project utilization.

1937

In the spring of fiscal year 1937, there were fifty-four nurseries operating. They shipped 113 million trees and shrubs, and carried over 90 million. Several small nurseries were consolidated to larger ones. By June 30, forty-three were still operating.

Various quantities of seed were obtained from several new grasses grown in the nurseries for seed increase, notably two excellent species produced from South Africa, *Eragrostis curvula* and *E. lehmanniana*, of which 2,606 pounds of seed were harvested. *It is interesting to note here the production of these two grasses in 1937, yet they were not released as cultivars until 1950.*

Several thousand species and variations of native and exotic plants were under observation during the year. A number of them showed excellent characteristics for erosion-control purposes. Of particular note among those not heretofore in common use are *Juniperus astiei, Rubus·parvifolius, Astragalus ruybi, Pentzia incana, Ephedra sinica, Eragrostis curvula, E. lehmanniana, Agropyron pungens*, and *Hordeum bulbosum*, as well as outstanding strains of the native grasses, such as *Agropyron spicatum, A. inerme, Elymus canadensis, E. glaucus, E. triticoides* and *Poa ampla*.

1938

Nursery activities were curtailed and consolidated. Nineteen temporary nurseries were discontinued as a result of increased efficiency in the operation of larger and better equipped units. At the close of the year, the total number of nurseries in active operations had been reduced to thirty-six. Of these thirty-two are engaged in the production of woody stock and grass seed, and in observational work, the other four were used exclusively for seed production and observational purposes.

Since the Section of Conservation Nurseries has as its primary function the provision of <u>adequate quantities of planting materials</u> for erosion-control operations constant efforts, were made to improve the species in common use and to introduce new plants better suited to perform effective and economical erosion control. This was accomplished in part by the study and selection of seed trees and seed sources to insure that only seed of superior individuals would be used for the production of nursery stocks and for direct project plantings. Numerous examples of this work could be cited such as efforts to bring true shipmast locust into quantity production as a substitute for the common black locust. This variety indicates borer resistance, greater rapidity of growth and apparently will produce a more marketable product. A number of other plants received similar attention, particularly hackberry, honey locust and ash, and certain oaks and conifers. *The large scale production of the selected shipmast locust was never realized.*

A <u>significant activity</u> of the Section of Conservation Nurseries was the assembly, observation and testing of superior plants and methods for erosion-control purposes. Through cooperation with the Section of Hill Culture Research of the Division of Research this type of work became increasingly important in most of the nurseries. Plants were studied and tested from the standpoints of human food, forage value, and economic products, in addition to their erosion control value. Efforts were also made to determine their ability to survive and propagate under problem-area conditions.

The assembly of native plant materials such as grasses and legumes, the introduction of exotics and the study of plants that have economic as well as erosion control value were conducted cooperatively with the Bureau of Plant Industry, other bureaus of the Department and with a number of state agricultural experiment stations. This work resulted in many additions to the improved plant species available for use in the erosion control program.

<u>1939</u>

Many additional species and strains of plants of promising value in conservation work were assembled and planted in the nurseries for initial observation. A number of those which had been under observation for some time were selected as being worthy of increase and more extended trial under actual field conditions, while others of proven merit passed into the quantity-production category and were grown for general use. Approximately 40,000 pounds of seed of those grasses and legumes having particularly outstanding values for conservation purposes were produced in the nurseries. *Unfortunately the plants were not named.*

Confirmatory trial plantings on problem areas under actual field conditions were extended in most of the regions in collaboration with State experiment stations. Composed of the best selections from the nurseries, these plantings served not only as a means of determining the adaptation and usefulness of the plants for particular conservation purposes but as excellent demonstrations.

In 1939, thirty-four nurseries in twenty-eight states reported production of 249.5 million stock plants with a sustainable production of 163.2 million plants.[813] As the demand grew, the agency moved to expanding existing nurseries rather than opening new ones. The observational nurseries expanded their cooperation to include the Department of the Interior's Bureau of Plant Industries, the Division of Plant Exploration and Introduction, and the Division of Forage Crop Production and Dry Land Agriculture, and maintained working relations with several state agricultural experiment stations.

Of course a major change came at the end of 1939 when Dr. Franklin Crider moved from the Nursery Division Chief to the manager of the newly created National Observation Project at Beltsville, MD. This Project represented the establishment of another nursery, but it was involved solely with observational activities rather than being involved with production. Dr. Crider was replaced in the position of Nursery Division Chief by Dr. Harry A. Gunning.

One most noteworthy accomplishment not included in the report was the first nursery release of a new plant.

<u>1940</u>

The difficulty of establishing effective vegetative cover on all badly eroded lands and keeping sufficient cover on croplands, orchards, pastures, and rangelands continues to be an impediment to the conservation program and emphasizes the need for plants with special qualities for erosion control. The Service, therefore, made field plantings of new species and strains of plants with promising qualities in order to observe their adaptability and determine their cultural requirements and value for erosion control. As a result of such observations, kudzu (*Pueraria thunbergiana*) is being extensively planted and is proving to be of great value in the Southeast. European beachgrass (*Ammophila arenaria*) plantings are now a control measure on the maritime dunes in the Pacific Northwest. Many other grasses and legumes have been assembled on the nurseries for testing and evaluation. Several have characteristics of unusual promise and may soon be brought into extensive use more effectively to conserve the soils of the Nation. Some of the native grasses are already going into extensive use, although they had not been cultured before the Service brought them info the nurseries. Among the most important of these natives now in extensive use are little bluestem and western wheatgrass.

Sixty-four new selections were provided to the Hill Culture Section. Thirty-four nurseries were functional at the beginning of 1940, but only thirty-one were functioning by December, 1940.

<u>1941</u>

By the beginning of World War II there were thirty functioning nurseries furnishing 151 million plants to conservation projects and expanding the observational nurseries impact. The establishment of a national observational project, with headquarters at the Beltsville Agricultural Research Center, centralized the leadership for this work.

The processing of seed of native species has developed rapidly during the past year, giving considerable impetus to their use in revegetation. Many of our native grasses have awns or appendages that require special drills. Since seed of different species vary in amount of processing required to provide a product of standard quality, processing schedules giving duration of treatment and mill speed have been determined for various types of mills. Milling costs are very low considering the improvement obtained in the quality of seed.

Since the primary function of the nurseries is to provide adequate quantities of suitable planting material for soil conservation operations, a considerable effort has been made to improve the species in commercial use and to introduce new plants better suited to perform effective and economical erosion control. Those phases of nursery work designed to facilitate the technique of operations and improve plant materials are collectively referred to as the observational program. The establishment of a national nursery observational project, with headquarters at the Beltsville Research Center, near Washington, has centralized the leadership for this work at one point and should result in greater efficiency and progress.

As a result of the plant exploration of the Service among native species growing here in America, specifically to find better soil-conserving and range forage plants, a number of grasses not previously cultivated have been brought into use. The seed of a number of native grasses that could not be purchased anywhere seven years ago are now being sold on an important scale by seedsmen. The establishment of a new farm industry, collection of wild grass seeds, has been the result. Among the seed that have been brought into prominence in this manner are western wheatgrass, blue grama, buffalo grass, big and little bluestem, and side-oats grama.

1942

SCS nurseries in 1942 furnished 120 million plants and 1,000 pounds of seed to erosion control projects, from thirty nurseries in twenty-nine states.

Progress has been made in the selection and use of improved forage species of grasses for conservation plantings. Seed produced in this manner is available for further conservation plantings on cooperators' farms or may be sold commercially, thus providing a source of improved, adapted seed and at the same time providing the seed producer with material cash income.

Cooperative activities with state experiment stations and of agencies throughout the Department has resulted in rapid progress in plant testing work and in many instances has provided improved materials for Service operations.

1943

By 1943, the urgent demand for increased food and fiber and the shortage of farm labor had reduced the importance of tree plantings to a minimum. Nursery facilities were now being used for growing and maintaining foundation seed stocks of improved selections, which were distributed to farmers to be grown commercially, while making available sixty-five million plants.

The Service nurseries are providing plants and seed for the establishment and improvement of pastures, for hay meadows in the crop rotation, and for reseeding range lands. Kudzu plants and lespedeza seed continue to be our major contribution in the South. Their use is being reflected in improved yields of cultivated crops and greatly increased production of animal products. Native grass species of the West are being collected, processed, and thoroughly demonstrated by the nurseries for pasture and range reseeding. Improved strains and varieties of grasses and legumes developed by plant breeders of the state agricultural experiment stations and the Department of Agriculture are being increased by Service nurseries and distributed to farmers through soil conservation districts.

Cooperating with other Federal agencies and the state agricultural experiment stations, facilities and personnel of the Service nurseries have been made for growing and maintaining foundation seed stocks of improved selections, which in turn will be distributed to farmers to be grown for commercial use.

During the year, twenty-nine soil conservation nurseries were in operations, furnishing 65,000,000 plants for erosion control plantings. Operations involving the collection, production and purchase of a total of 1,400,000 pounds of seed of grass and legume seed were directed by the Nursery Division.

1944

The 1944 emphasis remained about the same as 1943. The shift from production and use of woody plants to grasses and legumes began.

The production of woody plant materials was curtailed in comparison with that of former years. Meanwhile, more attention was given to seed production of grasses and legumes that serve to protect the land from erosion and at the same time increase soil fertility and provide food and forage for livestock.

The Service supplied only a portion of the required planting stock and cooperators obtained the needed remainder from commercial or other sources. During the year, approximately sixty-one million plants were furnished to conservation districts.

Cooperating with other Federal agencies and the state agricultural experiment stations, the facilities and personnel of the Service nurseries were made available for growing and maintaining foundation seed stocks of improved selections to be distributed to farmers, and to be grown by them for commercial use. This program involved not only the increase of improved strains and varieties of grasses and legumes developed by plant breeders of the state agricultural experiment stations and the U.S. Department of Agriculture, but also the testing of these strains for soil and climatic adaptability, cultural requirements, disease resistance, and palatability.

Service nurseries continued to provide plants and seed in limited quantities for the establishment and improvement of pastures, for hay meadows in the crop rotation, and for reseeding range lands. Kudzu plants and lespedeza seed continued to be a major contribution in the South. During the year, an effort was made to establish a planting within each soil conservation district, to be used cooperatively as a source of plants and seed. Their use is now being reflected in improved yields of cultivated crops and greatly increased production of animal products.

Native grass species of the West were collected, were processed, and their value for pasture and range reseeding was thoroughly demonstrated. Among these were blue grama, side-oats grama, bluestem, and buffalo grass. As these species prove their practicability and seeds become commercially available, the Service discontinues their collection and distribution.

1945

As the war was ending in 1945, SCS nurseries provided fifty million plants and one million pounds of seed to conservation district cooperators. On the observation nursery side, expanded use of certain proven introduced plants was emphasized.

Among the leading grasses brought into use were western wheatgrass, blue grama, buffalo grass, sand lovegrass, and the bluestem grasses.

Expanded use of certain proved introduced legumes and grasses was emphasized. Successful establishment of crested wheatgrass on range lands formerly occupied by sage brush, juniper and scrub oak now exceeds two million acres in the Great Plains and intermountain areas of the West. Thus land productivity has been increased from two to eight times. In the Southeastern United States, kudzu plantings are now approaching one million acres. The use of lespedezas has been spread westward. Two introduced grasses, weeping lovegrass and Lehmann lovegrass, are finding general acceptance and use in the Southwest.

1946

This was the first year when these annual reports included information to the effect that SCS policy was to reduce to a minimum "material assistance to soil conservation districts. Whenever possible the Service limits its cooperation to supplying technical assistance." The increasing importance of observational nursery products was beginning to emerge. Commercial seed production of selected plants from the observational nurseries was rapidly increasing.

During the fiscal year 1946, the Soil Conservation Service supplied about twenty million trees and shrubs to soil conservation districts. This was less than half the number supplied districts the previous year. It is the policy to reduce to a minimum the material assistance to soil conservation districts. Wherever possible, the Service limits its cooperation by supplying technical services. Distribution was limited mainly to newly organized districts as demonstration plantings, to extremely critical eroding land areas, and to communities where economic conditions made it impossible for the farmers to purchase needed tree seedlings.

Coinciding with the curtailment of woody-stock production in Service nurseries, however, there is a need for quantity production, and of growing and bringing into general use new, superior soil-conserving plant species and strains.

There is at present a serious national shortage of grass and legume seeds. To relieve this condition and to promote soil conservation farming generally, the Service is cooperating with the Division of Forage Crops and Diseases of the Bureau of Plant Industry, Soils, and Agricultural Engineering, and the state agriculture experiment stations in producing and distributing seeds of improved soil-conserving forage crops.

The facilities and technical personnel of the nurseries of' the Service are being utilized for the growing of genetically pure foundation seed of improved plants. The resultant seed crops are distributed to soil conservation districts for conservation planting and for seed increase. Thus greater and greater quantities of improved varieties of grasses and legumes are reaching the farmers directly through commercial markets. During the fiscal year of 1946, approximately 500,000 pounds of high quality seed of this character were produced on Soil Conservation Service nurseries.

Having found out how to use many excellent but heretofore undomesticated native grasses for conservation purposes, the Service has continued to give attention to harvesting seed of many of these species. Approximately 800,000 pounds of seed of species such as blue grama, side-oats grama, galleta, little bluestem, and buffalo grass were collected during the year. In addition, through information furnished by the Service, farmers have been able to collect seeds of native grasses for their own use and to sell. This production is not from new varieties but is the product of learning how to produce them by the nurseries doing Grass Work.

Soil and moisture conservation and the consequent increase in farm income depend largely on the character of the vegetation used in soil conservation practices. As the agency responsible for supplying soil-conserving plant materials, therefore, the Service has given increased emphasis to growing the best possible species and strains and finding out how to establish them on the land. This work has entailed the collection and observation in nursery and field of many new and useful native and introduced plants. Conducted in close cooperation with Federal and State research agencies, it is making direct, practical contribution to conservation farming. As a result of these cooperative observational studies, many new and superior farm and range plants have been brought into general use in ever section of the country.

1947

By 1947, the narrative of these reports had switched almost entirely to the discussion of observational nurseries products. The number of operating nurseries in 1947 was twenty-nine, supplying about twenty-four million plants.

The continued scarcity of grass and legume seed is seriously delaying the conversion of many acres of continuous and heavily used cropland to permanent cover. Having found out how to use many excellent but heretofore undomesticated native grasses, the Service has continued to give attention to harvesting seed of many of these species. These grasses have proved invaluable in the arid sections of the country in converting abandoned cropland into useful and productive range. About 500,000 pounds of seed of blue grama, sideoats grama, bluestem and buffalo grass were collected during the year. In addition, through information and equipment furnished by the Service, many districts collected large quantities of native grass seed for use by their farmer cooperators. Also seed collectors and commercial seed firms harvested seed and are offering it for sale through many dealers. Available quantities are still relatively small, however, and continued encouragement and assistance is required of the Service.

While the native grasses have played an important part in providing needed plant materials for conservation plantings, the Service has also given a great deal of attention to materials introduced from foreign countries.

During 1947, the facilities of Service nurseries were used largely for maintaining foundation seed stocks and, the quantity production of newly evaluated conservation plants. The total seed production in the nurseries was 422,000 pounds. This seed was distributed to soil conservation districts for seed increase. In the Southeast, 730 five-acre district seed blocks of one selected grass were established in nine states.

Many species and strains of conservation plants are in process of evolution in the nurseries, Eighty-three were advanced during the past year from the initial-observational category to the field-trial and seed-increase stage. Typical outstanding species in process of evaluation in the nurseries include a cold-hardy kudzu; an early-fruiting, cold-resistant lespedeza from China; an extremely drought-resistant, soil-holding grass from South Africa; and a prostrate, compact indigo plant from South America.

Coupled with these evaluation studies has been the incorporation of native grasses into conservation-farming practices. Through careful study of their cultural requirements, seeding habits, and methods of harvesting, eighteen heretofore undomesticated species have been brought into use in the West, with seed available on the commercial market. They include such important grazing species as blue grama, buffalo grass, western wheatgrass, sand lovegrass, and the bluestems. To overcome the deficiency of legumes in conservation farming in the Great Plains, plant-observational studies were begun in 1946 to assemble and evaluate species suitable for such purpose. As a result, a large number of promising native and introduced legumes were brought together for evaluation in the nurseries of that section.

1948

The 1948 report continues to emphasize the desire of SCS to reduce the number of trees, shrubs and seed they provide soil conservation districts from the twenty-eight operating nurseries, and replace it with technical assistance.

The shortage of seed stocks continues to be a limiting factor in the rapidity with which nursery stock production can be stimulated, and it will be several years before the supply equals the demand. In this interval it will be the policy of the Service to supply starting quantities of planting stock to cooperating soil conservation districts. Goals have been set for the production of from thirty-five to forty million plants in the fiscal year 1949, with the expressed intention of supplying only the most needy soil conservation districts.

Only twenty of these nursery units produced tree and shrub nursery stock. All twenty-eight, however, produced grass and legume seed. During the year the Service supplied cooperating soil conservation districts with 825,000 pounds of grass and legume seed of species especially suited for conservation purposes and not available on the commercial market.

The Service has given a great deal of attention to grasses and other erosion control plants introduced from foreign counties. Exchange relationships have been established with South and Central America, Africa, Australia, New Zealand, Europe and Asia, whereby we supply seed of Native American grasses in exchange for promising species indigenous to 'other countries. In the past ten years several thousands of accession has been received and tested in Service nurseries. Hundreds of species have looked sufficiently promising to increase and test under field conditions and about thirty have been accepted into the agriculture of the United States.

1949

The SCS operated twenty-seven nurseries in 1949 and supplied about twenty-eight million plants to SCDs.

A major activity of the Service nurseries is to increase production of uncommon or new strains of grasses and legumes. For example, in the Pacific Coast Region, two strains of new and improved plants have been approved for release by cooperating agencies. One of these is the 'Cucamonga' brome, which is a new self-seeding annual grass especially adapted for control of wind erosion in the vineyards in southern California. The other plant was developed in the Bellingham, WA nursery. It is called 'Cascade', a strain of birdsfoot trefoil. This legume is particularly well suited for hay and pasture seedings in Washington and Oregon. The seed of both of these plants will be increased through the facilities of the nursery division until sufficient seed becomes available through the regular trade channels. The total amount of grass and legume seed produced or harvested through Service nursery facilities, during the year, amounted to more than 2,400,000 pounds.

Through seed exchange with interested technical workers in twenty-five foreign countries, 549 plant accessions were acquired for conservation trial. The countries most largely represented are the Union of South Africa, Australia, China, Argentina, Canada, Sweden, and Central America. Cooperative arrangements were recently developed whereby the Soil Conservation Service participates directly in plant introductions obtained by the Division of Plant Introduction and Exploration of the Bureau of Plant Industry, Soils, and Agricultural Engineering. After assembled plant materials are reviewed or initially evaluated, they are made available to the Service nurseries in the regions to which they appear to hold promise of being useful. During the year approximately 400 accessions of grasses, legumes, browse plants, and woody species were distributed in this way in cooperation with the American Association of Nurserymen.

The Soil Conservation Service nursery at Pleasanton, California developed an especially effective method for seeding mixtures of grass and legume seed by mixing the seed with rice hulls. The sowing of mixtures of different kinds of grass and legume seeds in a single operation get uniform distribution of all seeds, regardless of variations in shape and weight has long been a vexing problem. *The Annual report continued to devote several paragraphs outlining the details of the use of rice hull as a seed diluents, as developed by Oswald K. Hoglund, Pleasanton California agronomist. See Chapter 11 for expanded details on this process.*

1950

By 1950, SCS was considering how the needed conservation plants would be supplied if SCS discontinued their production. The Southeast was rapidly adapting the new grass called Suiter's tall fescue, produced primarily by the Chapel Hill, NC nursery. Two new lovegrasses, 'Wilman' and, Boer, show outstanding production in Arizona. Some of the thousands of pounds of grass and legume seed being produced by nurseries are from the observational studies, now functioning at most of the twenty-six nurseries.[814]

The Service has long recognized the fact that to produce the great amount of planting material needed annually to do the planned conservation work on farms and ranches in soil conservation districts will require the best efforts of both public and private enterprise. In woody plant production, our personnel have continued to assist the large expansion of forest-tree production by the States, the operation of nurseries by soil conservation districts, and increased production by commercial nurserymen of trees and shrubs for conservation purposes. While tree production is far short of the needs in most areas there has been a great increase in the production of tree seedlings by many State nurseries, particularly in the Southeastern Region.

The Service encourages district cooperators to produce shrubs and grass seed. Where needed, technical assistance on production and harvesting methods is provided.

The thousands of pounds of grass and legume seeds produced in Service nurseries are of species and strains which, through careful observational study, were found to have high soil-conserving qualities. Through our nursery observational work, soil conservation practices are improved by bringing into use better plant materials and methods. Under the leadership of Dr. Franklin J. Crider, who directs our National Observational Nursery Project, 454 accessions of potentially valuable soil-conserving plants were obtained from twenty-five foreign countries. Among these were 244 grasses, 142 herbaceous legumes, and sixty-eight miscellaneous species. Especially valuable contributions of seeds have come from foreign technical workers, many of whom have studied soil conservation with the field technicians of the Service.

In the Rock Hill, SC, nursery several plants such as red root and smartweed are being observed as to their possible value for wildlife purposes.

New and better methods of harvesting and processing seed are constantly being developed by Service technicians. For example, the hammer-milling of seed-bearing hay has become an established practice in the Western Gulf Region. It is most commonly used in connection with combine-harvested seed of the various bluestems and other native grasses that do not readily give up their seed in the combining operation. It is especially valuable for cleaning King Ranch bluestem and related species of Angleton and Caucasian bluestems. Whether the seed of these grasses are stripper-harvested or combine-harvested, there is a lot of stem and leaf material in the end product. If combined, the recovery of seed amounts to only twenty to thirty percent. The remainder is lost in the tailings unless these tailings are saved.

It has now become a standard practice when combine-harvesting these seed to catch the tailings on a canvas or in a sled pulled behind the combine. The material thus salvaged contains large quantities of seed but has too many stems to permit satisfactory planting, even with the trashy seed planters used in the Western Gulf Region. It has been found that the expense of cleaning the material can be eliminated by running the straw through a hammer mill. Here the impurities are cut into small pieces that readily pass through the trashy seed planter. The material can be easily sacked for shipment and handling.

Following the development of this hammer-mill seed-preparation method the practice has been rather generally adopted by soil conservation districts as a cheap, satisfactory means of processing seed for their local use. Since almost any type of hammer mill commonly used on farms and ranches can be used to process the "seed hay," it is easy for district cooperators to adopt the practice. This does away with the need for other cleaning equipment such as scalpers and standard cleaners. There is no accurate figure on the poundage of hammer-milled seed hay that has been processed and used by individuals and soil conservation districts. However, in 1949 the Land Utilization Project of the Soil Conservation Service near Decatur, TX harvested and processed by this method approximately 46,500 pounds of little bluestem seed material for planting on the project. The Soil Conservation Service Nursery at San Antonio, TX treated in this manner 3,900 pounds of King Ranch bluestem material from their foundation block that was mowed because the seed yield was too low to justify combining and cleaning. An additional 8,000 pounds was treated at this nursery by this means on a share-of-seed basis for a cooperating rancher who used his own share for reseeding additional acreage on his ranch. Most of the hammer-milled King Ranch bluestem hay from the San Antonio nursery was used in flood control operations for mulch seeding the earthen faces of various types of detention dams.

During the year, Service nursery personnel continued to develop and improve machines and methods used in nursery operations. For example, at the Big Flats, NY nursery, a new type of nursery-bed sander was constructed. This sander is used to cover newly sown seed with a thin layer of sand.

1951

Observational studies were functioning at full steam. Certified seed production increased. Production from the twenty-six nurseries included thirty-two million herbaceous plant parts, thirty-three million woody plants and 740,000 pounds of grass and legume seed.

The Service continued to encourage district cooperators to produce planting material, particularly grass and legume seed.

Much of this work is in furtherance of Service cooperation with State crop-improvement associations in increasing the production and use of the best seed and plant material of the best varieties and strains. In the Pacific Region, approximately 128,000 pounds certified seed were harvested during the war from farmer-district seed-production fields established with foundation seed furnished previous years. In this region more than 1,200 acres of new seed fields of twenty different strains of grasses and legumes were established on farms in districts.

Observational work with woody plants and grasses continued to yield promising results. A strain of bicolor lespedeza, 'Natob' appears to have greater winter hardiness and produces seed farther north than any other strain. A seed block of this strain has been established at Beltsville, MD in cooperation with the Fish and Wildlife Service for production of seed for the Northeast. In the Southeast, plantings of buffelgrass, Alyce clover, red fescue, and prostrate sericea look particularly promising and larger blocks for seed increase will be planed. Buffelgrass shows considerable promise over a wide area, good results having been reported from Texas and New Mexico. A combination of severe drought followed by very low temperatures and rust caused failure of King Ranch bluestem in some locations in north Texas and Oklahoma: This was a disappointment as records collected over a period of twelve years indicated that it was almost a perfect grass for the southern Plains.

In the Northeast methods of rooting cuttings of green-osier willow *(later released as 'Streamco')* have been developed which are expected to materially reduce the cost of production, cost of rooting cuttings, ordinarily more than twice as expensive as propagation from seed, has been reduced as much as two-thirds. If this method continues to be successful, it is expected to increase the use of rooted cuttings for streambank protection.

Technicians in the Northern Great Plains Region have developed a five-row transplanter with adjustable units for varying the spacing between rows in lining out seedlings. This was tested at Mandan, ND and found satisfactory. An adaptation of this transplanter in use at Manhattan, KS enables a seven-man crew to transplant 10,000 seedlings per hour at less cost and with less exposure of the seedlings than when conventional methods are used.

During the year, A. J. Johnston, working at the Southern California Nursery (San Fernando nursery), was given a $200 cash award for developing a vacuum seed harvester. This machine is particularly useful in harvesting seed from plants that produce seed over an eight to ten month period.

During the year the Service operated twenty-six nurseries. These nurseries produced about thirty-two million crowns, stolons or sprigs of herbaceous material.

1952

The essence of this report suggested that SCS either knew it must, or at least wanted to get out of the mass production business but save the observational studies at some of their twenty-four operating nurseries.

The policy of the Service continues to be that no planting material will be supplied where such can be obtained from private or other public sources. The demand for trees, shrubs herbaceous plants and seeds of grasses and legumes is far beyond the supply in many districts. The Service recognizing that it cannot supply all of the needed conservation planting materials, has centered its attention on the maximum production of the types most needed.

In Southern California stockmen have been looking for a plant that would produce green feed during the summer on a limited supply of moisture. Napier grass was introduced from central Africa. It is a vigorous perennial bunch grass best adapted for use in hot climates to meet this conservation need. During the last year the southern California nursery unit at San Fernando distributed 33,000 crown divisions to thirty-four cooperators in soil conservation districts. This planting stock was set out on farms to increase divisions for larger pasture plantings. The normal increase from this amount should be sufficient to plant 275 acres of this valuable grass next year.

A new strain of birdsfoot trefoil was released in the State of Washington in cooperation with the Washington State Agricultural Experiment Station. This strain Cascade lotus is a result of fifteen years' testing at the Service nursery at Bellingham, WA. One of the outstanding features of this new strain is its vigor in the seedling stage. This makes it well adapted for pasture and hay mixtures because of its ability to become established rapidly in competition with other plants, or with weeds. Cascade is expected to fill an important place in hay and pasture seedings in the Pacific coast area. It is not sufficiently winter hardy to be adapted east of the Cascade Mountains, and is recommended at present for use only on the west slope.

A new wheatgrass, 'Topar', developed by the SCS nursery at Aberdeen, Idaho, in cooperation with the Idaho Agricultural Experiment Station, was released as a new cultivar through the Idaho Crop Improvement Association. 'Topar' wheatgrass is adapted to range and dry-land pastures. It is relished by livestock more than any other wheatgrass and produces good yields with from eleven to twelve inches of rainfall. It stays green longer into the summer than crested wheat-grass. 'Topar' is a good seed producer. Under irrigation, when planted in three-foot rows and cultivated, 400 pounds of seed per acre can be expected.

'Topar' was developed by combining the best plants of eight different strains of pubescent wheatgrass from Turkestan. The nursery at Aberdeen has six acres devoted to the production of foundation seed. About 2,500 pounds of seed were produced in 1952 from this foundation-seed block, most of which was released to soil conservation districts for the production of registered and certified seed.

Two important grasses of this region, intermediate wheatgrass and 'Manchar' bromegrass, are used in alfalfa grass mixtures for hay and for pastures. Two others, 'Bromar' mountain bromegrass and 'Primar' slender wheatgrass are used with sweetclovers for green manures and pastures. These new varieties have been registered with the American Society of Agronomy (*Actually the Crop Science Society of America*). The seed produced in 1951 from material released by SCS, in addition to providing superior feed and cover, has returned to the seed growers of the Pacific Northwest more money than has been used by Service nursery located at Pullman, Washington since its establishment sixteen years ago. *The 2005 benefit analysis showed that releases from Pullman made prior to 1953 provided* *commercial growers a net profit of $24.3 million for the seed they produced of these releases from 1977 through 2005.*[815]

Seeds of several species and strains of grass produced by nurseries in New Mexico and Arizona are now being certified by the crop improvement associations of these two States. As most of the seed produced from these nurseries are foundation or registered quality, their increase is used by district farmer seed producers to meet certification standards.

The nursery at San Antonio, Texas released buffelgrass accession T-2264. This grass continues to show great promise and strong commercial demand in spite of difficulty in obtaining high germination from newly harvested seed. Considerable work continued to determine where in the Western Gulf Region this variety will best serve conservation. Smith reports widespread tests are underway to determine its limitations both as to use and adaptation to soils and site conditions.

Other promising varieties of buffelgrass are being tested in the nursery observational plots at San Antonio. Of these, blue buffelgrass from South Africa, accession T-3782, seems outstanding. It is strongly rhizomatous, very leafy, and appears to be highly palatable. Seed production is not as heavy as that of accession T-4464, but germination seems to present no particular problem.

Caucasian bluestem is making an excellent showing in the observational plantings in the San Antonio nursery and in the field observational trials carried on throughout the adapted areas of the Western Gulf Region. One important feature of Caucasian bluestem is its resistance to rust, which has been extremely serious on King Ranch bluestem and some of the native grasses. Although the use of Caucasian bluestem has been confined mainly to the cooler parts of this region, tests in south Texas during the year show it can resist insects and diseases and can withstand adverse heat and drought conditions as well as any of the other grasses tested in that area.

In the Southeast a selection of buffelgrass looks very promising at the nursery near Brooksville, FL. Considerable seed was produced during 1952 for distribution and testing in 1953.

The Arlington strain of sericea developed by SCS has now reached the point in production where no further grants will be made to soil conservation districts. This is in line with Service policy of discontinuing mass production and distribution of new plant materials and seed as soon as they are in commercial channels sufficient to meet local needs. This was the first observational nursery release, in 1939, but was not certified with the state seed certification program. *The last commercial production as reported by the Americus PMC was in 1999.*

During the year further observational increase blocks of Coastal bermudagrass were established in many districts. It is expected that by the end of 1953 it will be unnecessary to make further distribution of this grass from Service nurseries. *'Coastal' bermudagrass is not an SCS release; rather an Agriculture Research Service release from their Tifton, GA station. Apparently SCS nurseries were reproducing it for SCS use.*

During the year widespread observational trial plantings of native and introduced grasses were made on dry farm lands and depleted range lands in the Southwest. Through these trials and evaluation studies, many new strains have been screened from regular accessions, both native and exotic, for hardiness, drought resistance, and adaptation to special site conditions. The Albuquerque, New Mexico nursery established fifteen trial plantings with district cooperators. The planting sites ranged from abandoned farm lands in the southern Great Plains area to extremely arid and difficult sites in Arizona and Utah. From the Tucson, AZ nursery, eleven trial plantings were made to test species and methods on depleted range and abandoned land and on irrigated land with limited water supplies.

1953

In the last of these reports the agency was ready to make the move from a production/observational nursery program to just an observational one. Except for a few brief comments about weather-related damage, the 1953 nurseries report is only about observational nursery results.

Observational studies and cooperative plant testing, both at nurseries and under field conditions, were intensified during the year. More than sixty million trees, shrubs, and herbaceous transplants and 500 thousand pounds of grass, legume, tree, and shrub seed were produced for use by districts and other agencies.

The observational plant testing program continued to produce outstanding new species and strains of plant material. The National Observational Nursery Project at Beltsville, MD received 442 new plant accessions, 389 of which came from twenty-four foreign countries. These included 201 grasses, 167 legumes, and seventy-four other plants. In addition, 266 lots of seed and vegetative material were distributed to regional nurseries, eighty-two lots to domestic cooperating agencies, and exchange material to eleven foreign countries.

The 'Natob' lespedeza planting, made cooperatively with the Fish and Wildlife Service at Beltsville, is expected to prove of considerable usefulness in the biological work of SCS, to State game commissions and to commercial seed companies.

The Big Flats, NY nursery reports the most successful year in its history. In the observational program 178 accessions of grasses and legumes were tested, and twenty-two were found to have sufficient promise for initial seed increase. Studies were accelerated on the development of crownvetch selections in an effort to find more palatable forms of this promising legume. *In 1957 when the author arrived at Big Flats the twenty-two that were reputed to have promise were not found.* A total of twenty million trees and shrubs are now in the nursery beds at Big Flats, the majority of which will be mature enough for distribution during the 1953-54 shipping season.

In the Southeast Region the Paducah, KY, Chapel Hill, NC and Rock Hill, SC nurseries were closed during the year. The work at these units, which was on leased land, has been concentrated at four federally owned sites.

Observational studies in the Southeast continued to produce results. A stoloniferous form of buffelgrass looks very promising at the Brooksville, Florida nursery. Tupelo sericea, a low-growing, spreading strain, and Beltsville sericea, a vigorous upright form, are two perennial lespedezas that also show promise. The latter is now being increased for districts use. The Georgia State Agriculture Experiment Station made available two promising hybrid 'Pensacola' bahiagrass strains, which are now being increased. (*These were hybrid strains developed from the cultivar 'Pensacola', which was released in 1944).*Plants grown from this hybrid seed yield thirty percent more forage than other types. Other promising plant materials include rescue grass, cold-resistant white lupine, *Lespedeza japonica intermedia* 'VA-70', and a nearly seedless selection of multiflora rose.

Drought, high winds, and abnormal temperatures made operations difficult at San Antonio and Dalhart, Texas. But blue panicum, buffelgrass, Caucasian bluestem, and *Melilotus indica* were produced in quantity at these nurseries. Observational studies included cold hardy trials on buffelgrass and blue panicum strains. Medic bluestem continued to produce dense growth in spite of adversely dry weather during 1951-52. Its high degree of palatability and productiveness as shown by nursery trials has induced commercial seed companies to begin production. Blue buffelgrass, T-3782, was also placed in commercial seed production. This grass has shown an outstanding ability to persist in competition with other less desirable perennials and is better suited to heavy soils than the now-famous T-4464 buffelgrass.

In the Southwest, new cold hardy strains of Lehmann lovegrass are under test as successors to those that have already proved their ability to thrive under desert range conditions. Karoo grass, a new species from the twelve-inch rainfall areas of Africa, stays green at Tucson both winter and summer. Wilman lovegrass appears particularly promising and efforts are being made to develop a strain with additional cold hardiness. Imported strains of native grasses such as side oats grama and blue grama, plains lovegrass and pappusgrass are being studied.

Nurseries in the Pacific Coast Region have continued to develop a number of outstanding strains of native and introduced grasses and legumes, accepted for registration and certification. On central California ranges Harding grass is a proven perennial for area. It has shown so much promise that results have not yet been publicized for fear that a premature demand for seed would develop before supplies are available. Every effort is being made to assemble and increase promising strains of this grass.

At the San Fernando, CA nursery, perennial Veldt grass from Africa is being placed with soil conservation district seed growers on basis of results in field trials.

The work of SCS nurseries in developing and getting into use new and improved planting materials has opened up a whole new field of opportunity in conservation work. Many of these species and varieties are higher producers, more winter hardy, provide a longer green-feed season or are especially adapted to arid or other hazardous conditions where the establishment of vegetation for conservation purposes is difficult. The possibility of even greater advantages of these plants indicates that more attention needs to be given to this work.

On the other hand, it appears desirable to discontinue quantity production and distribution of trees, shrubs, and other improved varieties, many of which are now available through commercial channels. Accordingly, considerable realignment of nursery functions, personnel, and facilities is planned during the coming year. It is contemplated that SCS operation of nurseries no longer needed for quantity production will be discontinued. Other nurseries needed for the production of the limited materials required for observational studies and testing will be operated under contract. These plans will relieve SCS from the actual operation of nurseries and permit more attention to the development of better planting materials.

Appendix 4: METHODOLOGY USED TO DETERMINE THE NET VALUE OF PLANT RELEASES FROM THE NATIONAL PLANT MATERIALS PROGRAM

INTRODUCTION

As the National Plant Materials Program matured over the years, a distinct need for measuring productivity of its products emerged. Primarily, those products were the new and improved conservation plants and the methodology for producing and using them. Only one of these could be quantified, new conservation plant production. The first step to accomplish this was to collect and record the amount of seed and plants produced by commercial growers of each release. Starting in 1977, each PMC asked those commercial growers that were producing one of their releases the estimated price the grower was receiving for it. As soon as a reasonable estimate of the production of each cultivar was known, an attempt at estimating the gross value to the program was made by multiplying the amount of production by the price the grower received. Although of limited scope and accuracy, it did provide the first value estimate. An additional step of estimating the potential acres that could be planted by multiplying the gross production by the planting rate for the species gave an additional indication of value.

In 1995, the Cape May, NJ PMC recognized that their highest producing release, 'Cape' American beachgrass, was being produced in the millions of plants annually but only protecting a few acres of Atlantic Coast sand dunes, yet the dunes were protecting multi-million dollars' worth of housing and commercial real estate. Additionally, their other commercially produced cultivars were only creating a few acres of tidal marsh. The Center Manager, William Skaradek, asked the logical question: was the value of an acre of stabilized sand dune or rebuilt tidal marsh greater or less valuable to the well-being of society than the reestablishment of an acre of western rangeland? An acre of sand dunes require nearly 20,000 plants and the rangeland less than ten pounds of seed. By comparison of acres treated, Cape May wasn't even in the same league with most others. So Skaradek asked Curtis Sharp, a retired plant materials specialist, and a former employee at the Cape May Center, to attempt a more realistic approach to measuring the value of PMC cultivars. By 2007, a report was completed.[816] A useful paper, *The Value of the Tidal Marsh*, from the Center for Wetland Resources appeared in 1974.[817]

Fortunately, prior to and during the report development period, a body of work became available that greatly enhanced and advanced the measuring of value of conservation plants. A 1992 paper and a more definitive one in 1997 by the same lead author titled *"The value of the world's ecosystem services and natural capital"* provided a new analysis opportunity.[818] [819] Costanza, et al explained that the services of ecological systems, such as water supply or erosion control and sediment retention are critical to the functioning of the Earth's life-support system. They contribute to human welfare, both directly and indirectly, and therefore represent part of the total economic value of the planet. Actions that alter ecosystem functioning have economic consequences by altering the services they provide. Planting an acre of tidal marsh, or overgrazed rangeland or planting an acre of 'Pensacola' bahiagrass on abandoned cropland alter the services that ecosystem provides. These services are measurable, which Costanza et al provided in the 1997 paper.

In 2005, newly appointed National PM Specialist, Robert Escheman, asked Sharp if it would be possible to do such an analysis nationally. By 2007, a report was completed. It was summarized by Lynn Betts, former NRCS Public Affairs Specialist for Iowa, and published by NRCS National Office.[820] The measured benefits were

- The net benefit to commercial producers of PMC-developed cultivars.

- The value of the ecological service benefits resulting from the use by consumers of commercially produced PMC-developed cultivars.

It will be extremely valuable to the reader to secure online the paper by Costanza et al and study it thoroughly.

At the end of this document is a limited Data source Bibliography, as well as footnotes which were used for this analysis.

METHODS AND MATERIALS

Costs of the Plant Materials Center Program

Federal funds have been the primary funding source for observational nurseries and Plant Materials Centers. For the purposes of this study, costs are the sum of the annual funds appropriation by Congress for operating what is now the PMC Program from 1935 through 2005.

The first appropriated funds included in this analysis, for the operation of what later became PMCs, are from 1935. Many of the production nurseries had some sort of an observational nursery component. The amount of funds spent for them at the multiple locations was not separated in the nursery budgets, and, although the observational nurseries became PMCs in 1954, budgets for their operations were not available until 1965. However, archival records supplied some budget information for the nursery period and much more for the years between 1954 and 1965.[821][822][823] This information allowed funding estimates to be made for 1935 through 1965.[824] The actual amounts appropriated for PMC use for the 1966 through 2005 period were available.[825]

To give an indication of relativity, all final comparisons of financial data are presented in 2005 dollars. The Consumer Price Index-All Consumers (1982-84 = 100), was used for dollar comparisons between different years.[826]

Although some PMCs received funds from non-Federal sources, the vast majority came from Federal appropriations, and some of the appropriated funds were used for non-PMC activities. In the absence of a PMC Program, no funds would have been appropriated, nor would any funds from other sources been available. For these reasons, all costs in this analysis are from Federal funds appropriated for the purpose of operating observational nurseries and PMCs.

Data presented elsewhere shows when each PMC became operational. Table A4.1 shows estimated (1935-1965) or actual (1966-2005) annual Federal appropriation to establish and operate the observational nursery - PMC Program.[827][828]

Table A4.1 Annual Federal Funding for All Plant Materials Centers

Year	All PMCs	Year	All PMCs	Year	All PMCs
1935	$3,229,134	1959	$4,809,785	1982	$7,413,305
1936	$3,304,817	1960	$4,923,190	1983	$7,521,795
1937	$3,312,812	1961	$5,074,893	1984	$7,481,174
1938	$3,513,812	1962	$5,232,279	1985	$7,421,763
1939	$3,702,224	1963	$5,377,943	1986	$6,931,724
1940	$3,818,307	1964	$5,529,115	1987	$7,827,473
1941	$3,777,847	1965	$5,667,954	1988	$8,016,710
1942	$3,539,797	1966	$6,751,111	1989	$7,942,725
1943	$3,465,498	1967	$7,484,551	1990	$10,700,408
1944	$3,539,862	1968	$5,926,345	1991	$11,289,258
1945	$3,597,123	1969	$5,640,817	1992	$11,225,226
1946	$3,451,147	1970	$5,861,497	1993	$10,898,956
1947	$3,136,930	1971	$6,886,133	1994	$11,714,047

Year	All PMCs	Year	All PMCs	Year	All PMCs
1948	$3,017,490	1972	$6,878,092	1995	$10,341,673
1949	$3,176,732	1973	$6,936,379	1996	$11,047,084
1950	$3,261,944	1974	$7,380,910	1997	$10,738,458
1951	$3,144,110	1975	$8,697,747	1998	$10,573,758
1952	$3,208,071	1976	$8,316,554	1999	$10,579,727
1953	$3,311,606	1977	$8,782,054	2000	$10,349,085
1954	$3,419,000	1978	$8,638,730	2001	$10,062,747
1955	$3,569,926	1979	$7,244,393	2002	$10,149,304
1956	$3,659,393	1980	$6,551,083	2003	$11,358,181
1957	$4,115,458	1981	$6,757,079	2004	$10,640,697
1958	$4,652,016			2005	$10,454,000
Total Federal funding for all plant materials centers for all years				**$ 467,952,968**	

<u>Net Benefit to Commercial Producers of Plants Developed by the Plant Materials Center Program</u>

Estimates of commercial production of PMC releases by growers are available from 1977 to 2005.[829] This database has the quantity of commercial production for each year, by cultivar and producing state, as well as the price the producer received for the seed or plants. From this the gross value to the grower was determined. The price received each year was indexed to 2005 dollars. The Producer Price Index (1982 - 84 = 100): Farm products-Hay, Hayseed and Oils was used.[830] This index more closely represented PMC products than any other indices.

To determine the net value to producers, production costs were deleted from the gross value. To determine this, each PMC was asked to provide production costs by commercial growers by unit of production, such as price per pound or plant. These production costs were updated to 2005 costs, and deducted from each year's gross production value. From this, the net benefit or loss to the producer was calculated for each cultivar for each year in which there were production data available.

Because of a lack of data, values generated from commercial production of cultivars released and produced from the 1930s through 1976 are not included as a benefit in this study, thus under estimating producer value for those cultivars. Additionally, production data in the analysis include only releases for which NRCS was the principal releasing agency and which are included in the official NRCS listing of released cultivars.[831] This had the effect of deleting the value of the production of approximately seventy cultivars from this analysis, even though one or more PMCs contributed some of the efforts to developing and/or maintain the release. No cultivars released by the Alaska PMC were included in this analysis due to the lack of production and financial data, although they received some funding.

<u>Ecosystem Services Benefit of Plants Developed by the Plant Materials Center Program</u>

The services of ecological systems are critical to the functioning of the Earth's life-support system. They contribute to human welfare, both directly and indirectly, by providing goods (such as food) and services (such as erosion control or waste assimilation) to human populations.

Each PMC-developed cultivar should produce some ecological service benefit when established for one or more land uses. The ecological service benefit, as developed by Costanza et al, is a measure of the value of goods and services produced by ecosystems for human populations, such as regulation of global climate, retention of soil within an ecosystem or that portion of resources extracted from an ecosystem as human food.[832] For example, if a PMC-developed grass cultivar for rangeland restoration that is successfully established on one acre of land, Costanza estimated that that acre will result in an ecological benefit to human populations of $117 per acre per year. Of course the opposite would be true if one acre was denuded of its protective vegetative cover. This is the ecological service benefit for grass/rangeland land use. The benefit comes from the regulation of hydrologic flows, retention of soil within an ecosystem, soil formation processes, recovery and breakdown of nutrients, providing pollinators for the reproduction of plant populations, food production and recreational activities. Other land uses, such as an acre of tidal wetland, in 2005 produced $5,033 of ecological service benefit per acre annually, some from the same ecological functions and services as grass/rangeland, plus others such as the recovery of mobile nutrients and the removal and breakdown of excessive nutrients and compounds. Such an analysis begins to smooth out the inequities between an acre of rangeland and an acre of tidal marsh.

In a 2007 article, Costanza outlines some impacts of his 1997 paper, on which this analysis depends.[833] He concludes, "It was unique in that it not only asserted that ecosystems are important, but quantified how important they are in units (dollars) that were easy to compare with other things that support human welfare. The paper acknowledged the many difficulties, limitations, and controversies surrounding such an exercise. However, since its publication, the paper has been cited in the scientific literature almost one thousand times (as of October 2006), making it the second most highly cited article in the ecology/environment field in the last decade. He believes the high citation rate indicates that the paper achieved one of its principal goals of encouraging further discussion and research on the benefits of ecosystems and their components.

Table A4.2 shows the ecosystem function, the ecological services within the function and the ecological service benefit factor (dollar value) by land use, as developed by Costanza and used in this study. By summing each factor in the land use columns the 1996 ecological service benefit first is shown in 1996 dollars/hectare/year, then converted to dollars/acre/year in 2005 dollars, which was the figure used in the analysis. There are two additional listed land uses not included in Costanza's table: stabilized & habitat land, and grass/ range and habitat land, and appropriate dollar factors assigned based on what such sites would provide. For example, stabilized mine spoil provides not only the stabilization benefits but habitat as well. The same is true for re-vegetated rangeland. These two can be seen, separated from Table A4.2, in Table A4.3.

To measure the ecological service value of each cultivar, or each informal release that was commercially produced, the total number of acre-years of productive life from the 1977 - 2005 commercial production for each cultivar was determined. This was done by dividing the typical seeding or planting rate into the total production, which provided the maximum number of acres that could be established from the production. This figure was then reduced by the anticipated planting failure rate for each release, leaving the number of acres that could be successfully established with the produced plant materials. The number of acres established was multiplied by the anticipated productive life of a successful planting. This gave a total number of acre-years of productive life for the cultivar. Then, each cultivar was assigned to the land use for which it was most typically used. The ecological service benefit factor for that land use was multiplied by the acre-years of productive life for each cultivar. This provided the gross ecological service benefit value of that cultivar. The seeding or planting rates, anticipated planting failure rate, and anticipated productive life data was supplied by the releasing PMC or acquired from technical NRCS and other publications.

Table A4.2 Ecological Functions, Ecological Services and Benefit Factors Used in this Analysis

Ecological Function	Ecological Service	Land Use (all figures are in $/ha/year)				
		Forest-lands	Grass/range lands	Tidal Wet-lands	Upland wet-lands	Stabilized lands
Regulation of atmospheric chemical composition	Gas regulation	na	na	na	$265	$2
Regulation of global temperature, precipitation, etc.	Climate Regulation	$88	na	na	na	Na
Capacitance, dumping and integrity of the marsh to environmental fluctuations.	Disturbance regulation	na	na	$1,839	$7,280	Na
Regulation of hydrological flows.	Water regulation	na	$3	na	$30	$3
Storage and retention of water.	Water supply	na	na	na	$7,600	Na
Retention of soil within an ecosystem.	Erosion control	na	$29	na	na	$125
Soil formation processes	Soil formation	$10	$1	na	na	Na
Storage, initial cycling, processing and acquisition of nutrients.	Nutrient cycling	na	na	na	na	Na
Recovery of mobile nutrients and removal or breakdown of excess nutrients and compounds.	Waste treatment	$87	$87	$6,696	$1,659	$44
Movement of floral gemates.	Pollination	na	$25	na	na	$12
Regulation of non-human populations.	Biological Control	$4	$23	na	na	Na
Habitat for resident and transient populations.	Habitat refuge	na	na	$169	$439	$23
The portion of gross primary production extracted as food.	Food production	$50	$67	$466	$47	Na
The portion of gross primary prod. extracted as raw materials.	Raw materials	$25	na	$162	$49	Na
Sources of unique biological materials and products.	Genetic Resources	na	na	na	na	Na
Providing opportunities for recreational activities.	Recreation	$36	$2	$658	$491	Na
Providing opportunities for non-commercial uses.	Cultural	$2	na	na	$1,761	$2
	1996 US$ ha/yr	$302	$237	$9,990	$19,621	$211
Analysis Benefit Factors	2005 US$/ac/yr	$152	$117	$5,033	$9,886	$106

Table A4.2 Ecological Functions, Ecological Services and Benefit Factors Used in this Analysis (Continued)

Ecological Function	Ecological Service	Land Use (all figures are in $/ha/year)				
		Pasture-land	Habitat Land	Stabilized land & Habitat land	Temporary cover	Grass/ Rglnd & Habitat Land
Regulation of atmos. chemical composition	Gas regulation	$7	na	na	na	na
Regulation of global temp., precipitation, etc.	Climate Regulation	na	na	na	na	na
Capacitance, dumping and integrity of marsh environmental fluctuations.	Disturbance regulation	na	na	na	na	na
Regulation of hydrological flows.	Water regulation	na	na	na	na	$1
Storage and retention of water.	Water supply	na	na	na	na	na
Retention of soil within an ecosystem.	Erosion control	$17	$41	$63	$60	$35
Soil formation processes	Soil formation	na	na	na	na	na
Storage, initial cycling, processing and acquisition of nutrients.	Nutrient cycling	na	na	na	na	na
Recovery of mobile nutrients and removal or breakdown of excess nutrients and compounds.	Waste treatment	$87	na	$43	na	$43
Movement of floral gemates.	Pollination	na	na	na	na	$12
Regulation of non-human populations.	Biological Control	na	na	$16	na	$12
Habitat for resident and transient populations.	Habitat refuge	na	$220	$110	$6	$110
The portion of gross primary production extracted as food.	Food production	$90	na	na	na	$33
The portion of gross primary prod. extracted as raw materials.	Raw materials	na	na	na	na	na
Sources of unique biological materials and products.	Genetic Resources	na	na	na	na	na
Providing opport. for recreational activities.	Recreation	na	$49	$25	na	$25
Providing opportunities for non-commercial uses.	Cultural	na	$27	$14	na	$13
	1996 US$ ha/yr	$201	$337	$271	$66	284
Analysis Benefit Factors 2005 US$/ac/yr		$101	$109	$137	$34	145

Table A4.3 Ecological Functions, Ecological Services and Benefit Factors Used for two land uses (from table A4.2)

Ecological Function	Ecological Service	Land Use ($/ha/year)	
		Stabilized land & Habitat land	Grass/ Range land & Habitat Land
Retention of soil within an ecosystem.	Erosion control	$63	$35
Recovery of mobile nutrients and removal or breakdown of excess nutrients and compounds.	Waste treatment	$43	$43
Regulation of hydrological flows.	Water regulation		$1
Regulation of non-human populations.	Biological Control	$16	$12
Habitat for resident and transient populations.	Habitat refuge	$110	$110
The portion of gross primary production extracted as food.	Food production		$33
Providing opportunities for recreational activities.	Recreation	$25	$25
Providing opportunities for non-commercial uses.	Cultural	$14	$13
Analysis Benefit Factors	1996 US$ ha/yr	$271	$284
	2005 US$/ac/yr	$137	$145

Although they may not be as well suited, plants other than PMC cultivars could be used for the intended conservation purpose. This was addressed by reducing the ecological service benefit value of each PMC cultivar by ninety-five percent, leaving a five percent superiority factor over the anticipated performance of a plant of unknown origin, adaptation or performance. This is hereafter referred to as the 'PMC Advantage'. This five percent is based on the review of a numerous documents developed for many cultivars, conversations with persons most familiar with certain cultivars, and the cultivar's Release Notice for some, which was developed at the time the cultivar was released to commercial growers. The five percent is less than supported by most documents and personal experience. However, if the potential of error existed, the intent was to be sure it was on the conservative side of estimating cultivar benefits.

The superiority of PMC-developed plants over other commercially available plants of unknown origin, adaptation or performance, may be in productivity, forage quality, stabilizing value, speed of spread, increased seed production, heat or cold hardiness, longevity, tolerance to abusive grazing, seedling vigor, and adaptation to severe physical conditions, such as high or low pH or droughty soils. Alternatively, cultivar superiority may be the result of it being the only available cultivar to meet a specific conservation need. For example, for years 'Pensacola' Bahiagrass was the only source of this outstanding species; 'Tioga' deer-tongue is the only effective native grass for stabilizing spoils in the Eastern U.S. with a pH below 4.5.

The ecosystem services benefit was further reduced by subtracting the cost of establishing and maintaining each PMC Advantage acre-year. These costs were determined from a variety of sources, including EQIP cost share, state DNR agency figures, private companies, NRCS Practice Standards and specifications and documentation from Field PM Specialists and PMCs. The sum of this, after subtracting the establishment and management costs, provided the net ecological service benefit of that cultivar, which could be either positive or negative. The sum of these for each PMC release in the study provided the net ecological service benefit for the PMC.

Table A4.4 shows the calculation for one line of data. The plant is 'Cave-In-Rock' switchgrass, showing the analysis for the production in Missouri for 1992 of 90,000 pounds of commercially produced seed..

Table A4.4 Calculation of Producer Benefit and Ecological Services Benefit for the production of one cultivar, during one year in one state

Table Item	Data	Source/Explanation
cultivar	Cave-In-Rock	From PMC Data
common name	switchgrass	From PMC Data
year released	1974	From PMC Data
state produced	MO	From PMC Data
report year	1992	From PMC Data
Release PMC	MOPMC	From PMC Data
Amount Produced	90000	From PMC Data
unit	LB	From PMC Data
Production year Unit value	$2.50	From PMC Data
PPI Update from production year. unit price to 2009 unit price	2.88	1982 data updated to 1998 - i.e. 125.9/ 1982 PPI
Gross Value	$254,743	Amount Produced x 1999 Unit Value
1999 Unit production costs of $1.50 updated via PPI to 2005	$1.89	$1.50 x 125.9%
Total Production cost	$170,000	Amount Produced x 1999 Unit Prod. Costs
Net Producer Value	$89,500	Gross Prod. Value less Total Prod. Cost
seeding rate	5	From PMC Data
% fail rate	10%	From PMC Data
acres planted	18,000	Amount Produced/seed-plt rate
Gross Acres Established	16,200	acres planted less acres fail to est.
Acres from PMC Advantage of 0.05%	810	acres established due to superior PMC release
CV Land Use Benefit Code	GL (grazing)	From reference data
Land Use Benefit Value/Ac/Yr.	$117	From reference data
Useful Life (Yrs.)	8	From PMC Data
Gross Eco Benefit - Life of 810 acres for 8 years planting	$758,060	Acres established X PMC Release Adv.) x ecological land use factor/acre/yr x Useful life
Establishment and mgmt. costs for PMC Advantage acres planted	$243,900	From reference data
Net ecological benefit value	$514,260	

RESULTS

The total cost for the operation of the PMCs from 1935 through 2005, in 2005 dollars, was $467,952,968.

The net value to producers and the ecological services benefits for each cultivar are shown with the releasing PMC in Chapter 8. The net benefit to commercial producers from 1977 through 2005 was $518,309,667, for a cost to benefit ratio of 1 to 1.11 ($518,309,667/$467,952,968).

The net ecological service benefit value from 1977 through 2005 of commercial production was $1,189,376,488. This benefit, compared to costs from 1935-2005, produce a cost to benefit ratio of 1 to 2.54. The total benefits to producers and to ecosystems are $1,707,686,156 ($518,390,667 + $1,189,376,488), producing a cost to benefit ratio of 1 to 3.65. These results are summarized in Table A4.5.

Table A4.5 A Summary of the Cost of Establishing and Operating the PMC Program from 1935 through 2005 Relative to the Derived Economic Benefits

Measured Benefits	Value	Benefit to Cost
Cost of establishing and operating all Plant Materials Centers -1935-2005	$467,952,968	
Net benefits to producers of all released cultivars for 1977-2005 period	$518,309,667	1.11
Benefits to ecological systems of successfully established plantings from all released cultivars for the 1977-2005 period	$1,189,376,488	2.54
Benefits to producers and ecological systems from the use of successfully established plantings from all released cultivars for the 1977-2005 period	$1,707,686,156	3.65

DISCUSSION

Evaluating Methodology for Measuring Benefits

Approaches considered for measuring the consumer benefits of using the PMC-developed plants included placing dollar values on increases in forage production, ton of soil saved or benefits derived from aesthetically stabilized highway slopes or enhanced wildlife habitats. The absence of a logical methodology or supporting data for these approaches led instead to measuring the value that PMC products make to ecological systems when they are successfully established. Costanza et al gathered information and presented ways of measuring them.

Benefits Beyond Financial

Costanza acknowledges that there are limitations inherent with such estimates. They summarize however, that "Most of the problems and uncertainties we encountered indicate that our estimates represent a minimum value." A good example of this is the underestimating benefits of some plants that were developed for specific conservation jobs but play a much larger benefiting role. A separate case study summarizes the benefit of stabilizing Mid-Atlantic coastal sand dunes from Cape Cod, MA to Kitty Hawk, NC.[834]

> Ecologically, dunes are nature's way of protecting inland areas, recycling sand, and maintaining stability to the coastal zone, including the beaches. In the absence of human influence, dunes re-vegetate naturally following major storms. This analysis measures the ecological benefit of artificially re-vegetating dunes. However, the demand for dune stabilizing plants came not from the need to protect ecological values but to protect the multi-billion dollar housing and tourism industry along the coast. Dunes not only protect and enhance the ecology of the coastal region; they also protect the human developments, which this analysis does not capture.

This analysis shows that the commercial production from 1975 through 2005 of plants developed exclusively for dune stabilization from one PMC was enough to protect 3,127 acres for fifteen years, resulting in an ecological service benefit of $255,403, which is only a fraction of the value of one beach front home and lot which the vegetated dunes protect.

Any limitations to the methodology used to assign ecological service values to PMC products should be viewed in light of the methodology process. This can best be done by selecting a cultivar with a long history. For example, 'El Reno' sideoats grama, a native grass of the southern Great Plains, was released for commercial production in 1944 by the Kansas PMC. The ecological service benefit evaluation of this plants starts with the seed that was commercially produced from 1977 through 2005, which was 3,963,700 pounds, excluding all the seed that had been produced from 1945 through 1976. The total number of acres that could be planted with the 3,963,700 pounds of seed is 586,750. However, it was assumed fifteen percent of the plantings would fail, resulting is 510,215 acres being successfully established, each providing grazing land estimated by Costanza to produce $117 ecological service benefit per acre per year for the ten-year life of the planting. This figure was then reduced by ninety-five percent, recognizing that the land owner could have planted something else. The five percent of remaining benefits was further reduced by $207 per acre for establishment costs plus $8.00 per acre for annual maintenance cost. From this, plus the benefits of all the other plants released by the Kansas PMC, is subtracted the cost of operating the PMC, not from 1977, but from 1933. The sum of this methodology for all PMC released plants produced the ecological service benefit ratio, exclusive of the benefits derived by the seed producer of 2.54.

Although limitations to the methodology outlined by Costanza may exist, it is both rational and defensible, and represents the best identified approach to assigning dollar values to the use of PMC products. As the concept is further developed and refined, it will become even more useful.

SUMMARY

From its beginning in 1935, the SCS/NRCS/PMC Program has developed many successful tools for solving soil and water conservation problems. A major tool has been the development of new plants to meet specific conservation needs. The purpose of this analysis is to quantitatively measure the economic benefits of this work.

The costs are the total Federal appropriation for operating the Program from 1935 through 2005. The measured benefits, from 1977 through 2005, are the net value to the growers who produced the improved plants, and the benefit to ecosystems in which they are used.

Measurable benefits produce a positive ratio of 3.65.

Appendix 5: OBSERVATIONAL NURSERY LEADERS AND PLANT MATERIALS CENTER MANAGERS, 1934 - 2010

The nursery leaders and PMC managers are listed in alphabetical order by state location. If the Comments column is blank it means the information was not available.

Palmer, AK — 1st Plant Observations: 1973

Name	Tenure	Comments
James Stroh	1973 - 1980	1st mgr. provided by SCS, transferred to WA PM Specialist
Stoney J. Wright	1980 -	AK Dept. of Agri. Employee

Historical Comments

A new PMC was opened through a cooperative agreement between SCS and Alaska Department of Agriculture. The first Manger was provided by SCS, and thereafter by the AK Department of Agriculture. Since then SCS has had limited input, except funding, to the program or management

Booneville, AR — 1st Plant Observations: 1987

Name	Tenure	Comments
James A. Stevens	1987 - 1988	Center opened 4/12/1987. Promoted to KS PM Specialist
Randy King	1989 -	

Historical Comments

Established by congressional action based on the recognized needs.

Tucson, AZ — 1st Plant Observations: 1934

Name	Tenure	Comments
Joseph A. Downs	1935 - 1936	Became manager of Albuquerque, NM nursery
Charles G. Marshall	1936 - 1938	Promoted to Regional Nurseryman
Louis P. Hamilton, Jr.	1938 - 1953	SCS employee
Louis P. Hamilton, Jr.	1954 - 1961	Univ. of AZ Agri. Exp. Sta. Employee
Louis P. Hamilton, Jr.	1962 - 1966	Manager, SCS PMC, retired
Robert Slayback	1966 - 1972	Promoted to PM Specialist in NY
Wendell Hassell	1972 - 1975	Promoted to PM Specialist in CO
Larry Holzworth	1975 - 1979	Promoted to PM Specialist in MT
Patrick Williams	1979 - 1981	Illness
James Briggs	1981 - 1983	Promoted to NPMC PMC Mgr.
Scott Lambert	1984 - 1987	Promoted to PM Specialist in WA
Bruce Munda	1987 - 1995	Promoted to PM Specialist in AZ
Mark Pater	1996 - 2002	Transferred to BLM
Ramona Garner	2002 - 2008	Promoted to RPM Specialist in NC
Manuel Rosales	2008 -	

Historical Comments

Opened as a BPI 1934, with Franklin J. Crider as an employee. Transferred to SCS as a production and observational studies nursery in 1935. The nursery production part closed in 1954, and the observational studies continued through a cooperative agreement with the University of Arizona, who managed the PMC until 1961, when it returned to SCS.

Santa Paula/
Pleasanton/Lockeford, CA   1st **Plant Observations: 1939**

Name	Tenure	Comments
Oswald K. Hoglund	1936 - 1939	ON Manager at Santa Paula
Paul Dickey	1939 - 1946	Nursery Manager, Hoglund Assistant.
Harold Miller	1946 - 1953	Nursery Manager
Oswald Hoglund	1953 - 1968	Nursery Manager Santa Paula and Chief Agri. Aid at Pleasanton 1938 - PMC Manager 1953. Retired
Jerry Long	1968 - 1969	Resigned to become a veterinarian
Kenneth Croeni	1969 - 1973	Pleasanton
Kenneth Croeni	1973 - 1984	Lockeford, retired
Raimond R. Clary, Jr.	1984 - 1987	Lockeford, returned to field office
David Dyer	1987 - 2008	Retired
Derek Tilley	2008 - 2009	Returned to Aberdeen PMC
Rita Bickle	2009 - 2010	Acting
Margaret Smither-Kopperl	2010 -	

Historical Comments

In 1939 a sixty acre nursery site was purchased by SCS almost in downtown Pleasanton, California. The nursery closed in 1954, and Pleasanton continued as an SCS operated PMC. In 1973 congrees authorized its re-location to Lockeford.

Meeker, CO   1st **Plant Observations: 1975**

Name	Tenure	Comments
Glenn Carnahan	1975 - 1977	Transferred to BLM
Sam Stranathan	1977 - 1990	Transferred to PM Specialist in CO
Charles Holcomb	1990 - 1992	Acting
Gary Noller	1990 - 1992	Acting
Randy Mandell	1992 - 1995	Resigned
Gary Noller	1995 - 1996	Acting
Steve Parr	1997 -	

Historical Comments

Opened through the efforts of the White River and Douglas Creek Soil Conservation Districts, and is managed by them. SCS provides technical and financial support. Meeker was authorized.

Arcadia/Brooksville, FL   1st **Plant Observations: 1936, 1957 at Arcadia, 1963 at Brooksville**

Name	Tenure	Comments
G. B. Blickensderfer	1948 - 1953	Manager at Thorsby 1938, moved to Brooksville 1948. Became FL PM Specialist in 1954.
Harry Haynesworth	1957 - 1963	Haynesworth opened Arcadia in 1957, moved to Brooksville with the PMC, and to GA as PMS in 1963.
Robert (Bob) D. Roush	1963 - 1980	Retired
Robert Craig	1981 - 1982	Was acting while PM Specialist
Donald Smith	1982 - 1982	Retired
Robert Glennon	1982 - 1987	Transferred to NPMC
Samuel A. Sanders	1987 - 1991	Promoted to PM Specialist in FL
Clarence Maura	1991 - 2005	Retired
Janet M. Grabowski	2005 -	

Historical Comments

The earliest date identified for a production and observational studies nursery being at Brooksville, FL was in 1947. Closed in 1953. A PMC opened in Arcadia, FL in 1957, and relocated to Brooksville in 1967.

Jimmy Carter, Americus, GA — 1st Plant Observations: 1936

Name	Tenure	Comments
John D. Powell	1938 - 1954	SCS Nursery Manager.
John D. Powell	1954 - 1977	PMC Manager, employed by GA Agri. Exp. Sta.
John D. Powell	1977 - 1982	SCS PMC Manager, retired
Mike Owsley	1982 - 2013	Retired

Historical Comments

Opened as an SCS production and observational studies nursery in 1935. The nursery closed in 1954, and reopened as a PMC through a cooperative agreement with the GA Agri. Exp. Stn., This cooperative agreement was terminated in 1977 and the operations continued under SCS management. Americus has had only two managers in seventy-four years of operations. A 1935-37 manager was not identified.

Ho'olehua, HI — 1st Plant Observations: 1957

Name	Tenure	Comments
Lynn Guenther	1952 - 1962	Instrumental in getting PMC established. Promoted to PM Specialist in MI
Earl Lewis	1962 - 1971	Retired
Robert J. Joy	1972 - 1988	Served jointly as mgr. and PM Specialist, promoted to HI PMC
Glenn S. Sakamoto	1989 -	

Historical Comments

The PMC was authorized by congressional action based on the recognized needs. It was first established on Maui in 1957, and in 1972 relocated to Molokai.

Aberdeen, ID — 1st Plant Observations: 1939

Name	Tenure	Comments
Russell H. Stark	1939 - 1950	Transferred to other SCS position.
Donald S. Douglas	1950 - 1957	Promoted to PM Specialist in ID
Harold L. Harris	1957 - 1961	Promoted to PM Specialist in ID
Ronald B. Foster	1961 - 1966	Resigned to farm
Charles G. Howard	1966 - 1986	Retired
Gary L. Young	1986 - 1996	Transferred to Bureau of Reclamation
Loren St. John	1997 -	

Historical Comments

Opened as an SCS nursery in 1939, but only doing observational studies. The nursery closed in 1954, and the observational studies continued as an SCS operated PMC.

Manhattan, KS — 1st Plant Observations: 1936

Name	Tenure	Comments
William Giles	1938 - 1943	Giles later became president Mississippi State University.
Donald E. Cornelius	1936 - 1946	In charge of ON.
Charles F. Swingle	1939 - 1943	Nursery manager for this period
Fred P. Eshbaugh	1943 1948	Fred became manager in 1944, became head National Arboretum in 1954.
Fred P. Eshbaugh/M. Donald Atkins	1949 - 1953	Atkins ON Manager, maybe earlier; became regional PM Specialist
Clarence Swallow	1953 - 1964	KS State Agri. Experiment Station

Name	Tenure	Comments
Erling T. Jacobson	1965 - 1975	PMC returned to SCS mgt. Promoted to ND PM Specialist
John Dickerson	1975 - 1978	Resigned
Robert Dayton	1979 - 1984	Promoted to IA agronomist
Gary S. Fine	1986 - 1991	Transferred to LA PMC Manager
Richard L. Wynia	1991 -	First PMC Trainee.

Historical Comments

Opened as an SCS production and observational studies nursery in 1936. Closed as a nursery in 1953. The observational part continued through a cooperative agreement whereby the KS State Agriculture Experiment Station operated a PMC with SCS financial and technical assistance. It returned to SCS operations in 1965.

Golden Meadow, LA   1st Plant Observations: 1985

Name	Tenure	Comments
Tommy Biles	1989 - 1991	Changed PMC positions
Gary Fine	1991 - 2006	Retired
Richard Neill	2006 - 2008	Retired
Garret Thomassie	2009 -	

Historical Comments

Established by congressional action based on the recognized needs.

National, Beltsville, MD   1st Plant Observations: 1939

Name	Tenure	Comments
Franklin J. Crider	1939 - 1948	Headed up National Observational Project
Wilmer W. Steiner	1948 - 1953	Nursery Manager
Wilmer W. Steiner	1953 - 1955	PMC Manager. Promoted to RPM Specialist Horticulturist at Upper Darby, PA regional office in 1955.
Robert Thornton	1955 - 1968	Retired
Wayne Everett	1969 - 1973	Promoted to KY PM Specialist
Gilbert Lovell	1973 - 1978	Transferred to Asst. Natl. PM Specialist
Mike McCrary	1978 - 1979	Transferred to TX field office
Keith Salvo	1979 - 1983	Promoted to NC PM Specialist
James Briggs	1983 - 1989	Transferred to RC&D position
Eric Scherer	1989 - 1991	Transferred to CT field office
Scott Peterson	1991 - 1994	Promoted to Dir., Plant Data Center
John Englert	1994 - 2009	Promoted to National PM Specialist
Jeremy West	2010 -	Relocated to another USDA position.

Historical Comments

Opened as an SCS observational studies nursery in 1936. As the observational part of the nursery program developed, the Beltsville nursery soon became the central location for the distribution and of foreign introductions to regional nurseries. The evolving observational studies were under the direction of Franklin J. Crider, who was located at Beltsville during the earlier years. It was never a large production nursery. It closed in 1953, but continued as the National PMC under SCS operations.

Rose Lake, MI   1st Plant Observations: 1958

Name	Tenure	Comments
Charles McDaniels	1958 - 1959	
Dorian Carroll	1959 - 1969	Promoted to MI PM Specialist
Samuel Jackson	1970 - 1974	Died while in this position
Ellis (Bill) Humphrey	1975 - 1990	Retired
Phil Koch	1991 - 1999	

Name	Tenure	Comments
John Rissler	2000 - 2004	
John W. Leif	2005 -	

Historical Comments

Established by congressional action based on the recognized needs.

Elsberry, MO   1st Plant Observations: 1934 by BPI

Name	Tenure	Comments
Hugh Stevenson	1935 - 1939	Became local nurseryman. Unsure when left.
Roger E. Sherman		Sherman on staff in 1936, not listed in 1938
J. J. Pierre	1949	Unsure when came or years stayed
Roger E. Sherman	1954 - 1958	
William H. Billings	1958 - 1966	Promoted to OR PM Specialist
Charles Mowry	1966 - 1971	Promoted to NJ PM Specialist
Donald Smith	1971 - 1975	Promoted to FL PM Specialist
Jimmy Henry	1975 - 2003	Retired
Steven B. Bruckerhoff	2004 - 2010	Retired
Ronald L. Cordsiemon	2010 -	

Historical Comments

Elsberry opened as an SCS production and observational studies nursery in 1935. Closed as a nursery in 1953. The observational part continued as an SCS operated PMC. Manager for 1940 – 1949 unsure, maybe Sherman.

Jamie L. Whitten, Coffeeville, MS   1st Plant Observations: 1936

Name	Tenure	Comments
William G. Beatty	1938 - 1941	Date of nursery closing unsure, about 1943.
Vastine E. Ahlrich	1962 - 1969	
B. B. Billingsley	1969 - 1991	Transferred to PMC Agronomist
David L. Lane	1991 - 1997	Retired
Joel Douglas	1997 - 2005	Promoted to Regional PM Specialist
Paul Rodrigue	2006 - 2007	
Sherry Surrette, Acting	2008 - 2009	
Philip J. Barbour, Acting	2008 - 2009	
Lamar Burgess	2010 - 2012	

Historical Comments

A nursery opened here in 1936 and closed in the early 1940s. The Coffeeville PMC was authorized by Congress and began operations on August 8, 1960 functioning both as a PMC and a seed production unit for the Yazoo-Little Tallahatchie Flood Prevention Project.

Bridger, MT   1st Plant Observations: 1959

Name	Tenure	Comments
Ashley A. Thornburg	1959 - 1965	Promoted to RPM Specialist
James R. Stroh	1965 - 1973	Became first PMC manager at the new Alaska PMC
John Scheetz	1973 - 1998	Became National PM IT Coordinator
Mark Majerus	1998 - 2006	Retired
Roger Hybner	2006 - 2010	Switched positions with Scianna
Joseph D. Scianna	2010 -	

Historical Comments

Established by congressional action based on the recognized needs, primarily through the efforts of the Montana and Wyoming Association of Conservation Districts.

Cape May, NJ — 1st Plant Observations: 1965

Name	Tenure	Comments
Dr. Virgil B. Hawk	1965 - 1970	Retired
Fred Gaffney	1970 - 1973	Promoted to NY PM Specialist
Cluster R. Belcher	1973 - 1985	Promoted to NJ PM Specialist
Donald Hamer	1985 - 1995	Retired
Michael R. Fournier	1995 - 1997	Returned to NRCS Field Office work
William Skaradek	1997 - 2008	Transferred to other NRCS position
Christopher Miller	2009 -	

Established by congressional action based on the recognized needs, primarily resulting from the massive coastal storm which hit the mid-Atlantic coast in 1962.

Albuquerque/Los Lunas, NM — 1st Plant Observations: 1936 at Albuquerque, 1957 at current site

Name	Tenure	Comments
Joseph Downs	1936 - 1953	Promoted to NM 1st PM Specialist in 1954
Glenn Niner	1936 - 1969	SCS Nursery employee until 1954, on-site technical advisor PMC until 1969.
James E. Anderson	1957 - 1979	Univ. of NM Asst. Prof. Coop Agreement leader. Retired
Leaford Windle	1968 - 1977	SCS Technical advisor.
Larry Hamilton	1977 - 1978	SCS Technical advisor.
Wendall Oaks	1978 - 1991	First SCS employee to assumed PMC manager responsibilities. Joint PMC Mgr. and PM Specialist 1990-91. Promoted to NM PM Specialist,
Greg A. Fenchel	1992 -	

Historical Comments

An SCS production and observational nursery as established in Albuquerque, NM in 1936. The entire facility was closed in 1953. Selected plant materials and records were salvaged by former nursery employees. In 1957 a cooperative agreement with The University of NM for them to operate a PMC on their Middle Rio Grande Substation in Los Lunas, with financial and technical assistance from SCS. The agreement was adjustment in 1978 whereby SCS provided the manager.

Big Flats, NY — 1st Plant Observations: 1940

Name	Tenure	Comments
Kenneth L. Hovey/Dr. Gasper A. Loughridge	1940	Hovey may have been Mgr. of Nursery briefly, Loughridge Asst. Mgr. and Observational Nursery Mgr.
Dr. Gasper A. Loughridge/Dr. S. M. Raleigh	1940 - 1942	ON Managers Loughridge drafted in '42, replaced by Raleigh, who went to Penn State by 1946.
Dr. Gasper A. Loughridge	1946	Unsure how long served.
Dr. Maurice E. Heath	1947 - 1951	Heath came in about 1947, bringing strong support for ON work, which was lacking in NE. After leaving position may have stayed vacant for some time. The ON staff never exceeded 2, an agronomist and one aide Carlton Dody.
Harry Porter	1952 - 1953	Became PM Specialist for NY, PA
Edward Kenne	1953 - 1957	State University of NY, Alfred Agri. Tech. Institute, Alfred, NY, facility manager plus ON manager.
Curtis Sharp	1957 - 1960	State University of NY, Alfred Agri. Tech. Institute, Alfred, NY employee in charge of SCS PMC work.

Name	Tenure	Comments
Curtis Sharp	1960 - 1965	PMC returned to SCS management. Became NY PM Specialist in 1965.
Clifford Williams	1965 - 1969	Promoted to Agronomist in CO
Sheridan Dronen	1969 - 1975	Promoted to NC PM Specialist
Jack Carlson	1975 - 1977	Promoted to WA PM Specialist
Mark Testerman	1977 - 1981	NY Agronomist/Resigned
D. Mitchell Cattrell	1981 - 1983	Returned to field office
John Oyler	1983 - 1986	Promoted to PM Specialist in WV
Martin van der Grinten	1986 -	

Historical Comments

An SCS production and observational nursery was established in Big Flats in 1940. Charles M. Clements was Nursery Manager 1941 – 1953. During WW II the former CCC camp became a Civilian Public Service camp, which supplied the nursery labor. The nursery production part closed in 1954 and a cooperative agreement with State University of NY, Alfred, NY was developed for them to operate a PMC, with financial and technical assistance from SCS. This arrangement was terminated in 1960, and management returned to SCS.

Bismarck, ND   1st Plant Observations: 1934 an Mandan

Name	Tenure	Comments
Dr. Ernie George	1934 - 1937	Nursery Manager, Bureau of Plant Industry
Dr. George Rogler	1936 - 1953	Head of grass nursery, i.e. ON.
Arthur E. Ferber/Laird G. Wolfe	1936 - 1953	Nursery Manager. He was ON Mgr. at Waterloo, NE nursery in 1949.
Buck Worthington	1953 - 1954	Nursery Manage, ND Association of Conservation Districts r
John McDermand	1954 - 1967	SCS Technical Advisor. Promoted to ND PM Specialist
George Kary	1954-1963	ND Association of Conservation Districts Nursery Manager
Lee Hines	1964 - 1967	ND Association of Conservation Districts Nursery Manager
Sheridan Dronen	1967 - 1970	First SCS manager. Promoted to NY PMC manager
David Lorenz	1971 - 1974	Promoted to TX PMC manager
Russell Haas	1974 - 1984	Promoted to ND PM Specialist
Dwight A. Tober	1984 - 1998	Promoted to ND PM Specialist
Wayne Duckwitz	1999 -	

Historical Comments

An SCS production and observational nursery as established in Mandan, ND in 1936, which continued until 1953, when it relocated out of a flood plain to Bismarck, ND. The nursery production soon closed. The observational part continued through a cooperative agreement whereby the ND Association of Conservation Districts operated a PMC with SCS financial and technical assistance. It returned to SCS operations in 1967, but still maintains a close cooperative agreement with the Association.

Warrenton, Astoria, Bellingham/Corvallis, OR   1st Plant Observations: 1937

Name	Tenure	Comments
Robert L. Brown	1938 - 1942	Manager at Warrenton
Wilber E. Chapin	1938 - 1954	Bellingham Manager
Lynn E. Guenther	1943 - 1953	At Astoria 1938 as Asst. Became manager at Bellingham, WA. Became 1st manager of HI PMC.
Thomas A. Bown	1957 - 1962	Promoted to HI PM Specialist
Stanley L. Swanson	1962 - 1978	Retired
Jack O. Peterson	1978 - 1987	Retired

Name	Tenure	Comments
Dale C. Darris	1987 - 1995	Transferred to PMC Agronomist
Roy Carlson	1995 - 2002	State Resource Conservationist, State Office, Corvallis, OR, acting.
Robert Tracey	2002 - 2006	
Joe Williams	2006 – 2013	Transferred to other NRCS position.

Historical Comments

Nurseries that served Western WA and OR prior to the opening of Corvallis include Bellingham, WA which operated from 1937 until 1953, and Astoria, (Warrenton) OR which opened in 1937 and closed in about 1950. These can be viewed as forerunners of Corvallis, which opened in 1957. Between 1995 and 2001 there was a shared management responsibility. Manager's responsibilities were actually divided among several persons. Theresa Flessner was to coordinate/direct daily work assignments and to coordinate with the SRC (Roy Carlson) and State Office staff on budget and personnel matters. Roy was made the supervisor of record for all PMC employees. Dale Darris retained oversight/management responsibilities for physical facilities and equipment as the conservation agronomist. This arrangement ended in 2001.

Great Basin, Fallon, NV — 1st Plant Observations: 2008

Name	Tenure	Comments
Steve Perkins	2006 - 2008	Resigned, became reclamation specialist
Eric Eldredge	2008	

Historical Comments

Established by congressional action based on the recognized needs.

Nacogdoches, TX — 1st Plant Observations: 1982

Name	Tenure	Comments
James A. Stevens	1983 - 1987	Promoted to AR PMC manager
Melvin Adams	1987 - 1999	Retired
James Alderson	1999 - 2000	Temporary while PM Specialist
James A. Stevens	2000 - 2010	Retired
R. Alan Shadow	2011 -	

Historical Comments

Through cooperative agreement between Stephen Austin University, Deep East Texas, and Northeast Texas Associations of Soil and Water Conservation Districts, NRCS, U.S. Forest Service, and a local Resource Conservation & Development Council.

Kika de la Garza, Kingsville, TX — 1st Plant Observations: 1981

Name	Tenure	Comments
James D. Ledbetter	1981 - 1985	
Dan Larson	1985 - 1987	Promoted to MO PM Specialist
Patrick Conner	1987 - 1991	
John Lloyd-Reilley	1992 -	

Historical Comments

In 1981 the Caesar Kleberg Wildlife Research Institute, the South Texas Association of Soil and Water Conservation Districts and SCS signed a cooperative agreement to operate a PMC. The Center has not been authorized by congress.

San Antonio/Spur/James E. "Bud" Smith, Knox City, TX		1934 - 1953 at San Antonio, 1954 - 1965 sporadic evaluations by PM Specialist at Spur and San Antonio, Knox City in 1965
Name	**Tenure**	**Comments**
George T. Ratliffe	1936 - 1938	San Antonio
Emery A. Telford	1938 - 1943	San Antonio nursery manager
Dennis E. Griffiths	1938 - 1943	San Antonio
James E. Smith	1950 - 1953	At San Antonio as nursery manager
James E. Smith	1953 - 1965	As TX PM Specialist conducted some evaluations at Spur
Arnold Davis	1965 - 1966	Promoted to TX PM Specialist
Howard A. Carleton	1968 - 1969	
Jacob Garrison	1969 - 1974	Promoted to AZ PM Specialist
David Lorenz	1974 - 1984	Promoted to PA PM Specialist
Jon Moncries	1984 - 1985	
James Alderson	1986 - 1990	Promoted to TX PM Specialist
Morris J. Houck, Jr.	1990 - 2006	Promoted to MS PM Specialist
Raymond T. Cragar	2007 - 2008	Retired
Gary L. Rea	2008 -	

Historical Comments

In 1935 a BPI nursery in San Antonio, TX was transferred to SCS. The nursery was predominantly producing and evaluating grasses. The facility closed in 1953, and the land was transferred to the TX Agricultural Experiment Station. Many of the desirable plants from the San Antonio had, and continued to be, under evaluation by SCS employees at the TX Agricultural Experiment Station in Spur, TX. When the Knox City PMC was established in 1965, resulting from a recognized need, these valuable plants were the first items planted there. Four plants were released by the PMC from the San Antonio work, and one from work at Spur.

Pullman, WA		1st Plant Observations: 1934. BPI Nursery
Name	**Tenure**	**Comments**
A. L. Hafenrichter	1935 - 1939	It is unclear exactly who was nursery manager 1935 - 1939. Virgil Hawk is listed as Outlying Nursery manager, and Arthur J. Johnson as Farm Manager. Hafenrichter served as Regional Nursery Mgr. 1935 - 1953, then promoted to West RPM Specialist
John L. Schwendiman	1939 - 1940	Temporary Manager
Paul Lemmon	1940 - 1943	Nursery Manager 1943 in San Fernando, CA
Virgil B. Hawk	1943 - 1944	Nursery Manager, Returned to Graduate School, Iowa State in 1944
John L. Schwendiman	1945 - 1954	Promoted to WA PM Specialist
Robert J. Olson	1954 - 1959	Promoted to WA State Forester
Edwin O. Nurmi	1959 - 1968	Retired
Frank Webb	1968 - 1975	Promoted to NJ PM Specialist
Clarence Kelley	1975 - !994	Retired
Mark E. Stannard	1994 -	Acting 1994-96.

Historical Comments

Opened as a BPI 1934, transferred to SCS as a production and observational studies nursery in 1935. The nursery production part closed in 1954, and the observational studies continued as an SCS operated PMC.

Quicksand, KY/Alderson, WV		1st Plant Observations: 1967
Name	**Tenure**	**Comments**
Norvel Colbert	1967 - 1970	Promoted to KY PM Specialist
Donald Henry	1970 - 1977	Promoted to KY PM Specialist

Name	Location	Tenure	Comments
William Kuenstler		1977 - 1980	Promoted to Agronomist Position
Charles Gilbert		1980 - 1988	Resigned
Laura Ray		1988 - 1993	Resigned
Raymond T. Crager		1994 - 1997	Transferred to TX PMC manager
John C. Vandevender		1997 -	

Historical Comments

Established by congressional action based on the recognized needs. The PMC was established in Quicksand, KY and in 1994 initiated the re-location the Alderson, WV,

Appendix 6: FIELD, REGIONAL AND NATIONAL PLANT MATERIALS SPECIALISTS AND COOPERATIVE COORDINATORS

Plant Materials Technician/Specialists positions were established in 1954-55. Initially they were called Technicians and later changed to Specialist. This Appendix only uses specialist.

While the name of the positions changed over the years, their duties remained fairly consistent. There was a national PM Specialist, three to six regional PM Specialists and a varying number of field PM Specialists serving at the state level. Service areas changed often over the years in some parts of the country, making a listing of positions by location difficult. As a result, the field PM Specialist positions is listed in their general service area. Field PM Specialists are listed first, followed by cooperative agreement coordinators, Assistant National PM Specialists and National PM S.

Field Plant Materials Specialists

Northeastern Northeast

Name	Location	Tenure	Comments
Wilson Hill	Amherst, MA	1955 - 1964	Served NE States, Retired
Harry Porter	Morgantown, WV & Big Flats, NY	1953 - 1960	Promoted to regional non PM position
Ernest McPharron	Syracuse, NY	1960 - 1965	Retired
Curtis Sharp	Big Flats, NY	1965 - 1965	Transferred to PM Specialist in NJ.
Jesse McWilliams	Syracuse, NY	1965 - 1970	Transferred to NV Agronomist
Robert Slayback	Syracuse, NY	1970 - 1974	Transferred to PM Specialist in CA
Fred Gaffney	Syracuse, NY	1974 - 1981	Transferred to NY Agronomist.
John Dickerson	Syracuse, NY	1981 - 2003	Retired
Paul R. Salon	Syracuse, NY	2004 - present	

Southeastern Northeast

Name	Location	Tenure	Comments
Marshall Augustine	College Park, MD	1953 - 1968	Retired
Curtis Sharp	Cape May CH, NJ	1965 - 1970	Transferred to CA PM Specialist
Charles Mowry	Somerset, NJ	1970 - 1974	Transferred to ID PM Specialist
Frank Webb	Somerset, NJ	1974 - 1983	Transferred to VT agronomist.
Cluster Belcher	Somerset, NJ	1983 - 1992	Retired
Christopher Miller	Somerset, NJ	1992 -	Joint PMC Mgr. and PM Specialist post 2008

Central and Southwestern Northeast

Name	Location	Tenure	Comments
Frank Glover	Morgantown, WV	1954- 1955	Became state agronomist and SRC in WV
Joseph Ruffner	Morgantown, WV	1955 - 1970	Promoted to regional PM Specialist
H. Wayne Everett	Lexington, KY	1973 - 1977	Transferred to TX PM Specialist
Ralph Williamson	Morgantown, WV	1978 - 1980	Returned to a FO position in VA.
John Spitzer	Harrisburg, PA	1981 - 1984	Agronomist/PM Specialist. Retired
David Lorenz	Harrisburg, PA	1984 - 1985	Promoted to regional PM Specialist.
John Oyler	Morgantown, WV	1986 - 1987	Resigned.
Donald Henry	Lexington, KY	1978 - 1989	Retired
Robert Glennon	Harrisburg, PA	1988 - 1995	Transferred to another NRCS position.
John C. Vandevender	Morgantown, WV	1995 - 1997	Transferred to WV PMC manager.

South Atlantic

Name	Location	Tenure	Comments
Karl E. Graetz	Raleigh, NC	1953 - 1974	Manager Chapel Hill, NC Nursery. Retired.
Sidney Dronen	Raleigh, NC	1974 - 1978	Promoted to SD SRC.
J. V. McDonald	Raleigh, NC	1978 - 1980	Retired
Foy Hendricks	Raleigh, NC	1980 - 1983	Agronomist & PM Specialist. Promoted to Regional Agronomist.
Keith Salvo	Raleigh, NC	1983 - 1994	Retired to fishing
Roger Hansard	Raleigh, NC	1994 - 2006	Water Quality & PM Specialist.
Matt Flint	Raleigh, NC	2006 - 2008	Was Biologist but did some PMS work.
Josh Spencer	Raleigh, NC	2008 -	Was Water Quality Specialist but did some PMS work.

Florida and Caribbean

Name	Location	Tenure	Comments
C. B. Blickensderfer	Palmetto, FL	1953 - 1963	Sarasota Nursery Mgr. through 1953. Retired.
A. H. Quintero	Mayaguez, PR/Gainesville, FL	1963 -1969	1957 - 1964 PM Specialist Caribbean, 1964 -1969 PM Specialist FL and Caribbean. Promoted to STC Caribbean Area.
Robert M. Craig	Gainesville, FL	1969 - 1976	Served FL and PR. Retired
Donald Smith	Brooksville, FL	1976 - 1987	Served FL and PR.

Name	Location	Tenure	Comments
Samuel A. Sanders	Gainesville, FL	1987 - 2005	Served FL and PR. Retired
Mary J. Williams	Gainesville, FL	2005 -	Serves FL
Carlos E. Morganti	Mayaguez, PR	2009 -	Serves PR

Central Gulf State

Name	Location	Tenure	Comments
Paul Tabor	Athens, GA	1953 - 1962	Retired
Harry Haynesworth	Athens, GA	1963 -1984	Retired
Charles Donald Surrency	Thomson, GA	1984 - 2006	Retired

Lower Mississippi Valley

Name	Location	Tenure	Comments
Morris Byrd	Little Rock, AR	1955 - 1966	Retired
Thomas A. Bown	Jackson, MS	1966 - 1978	
Kenneth Blan	Jackson, MS	1978 - 1980	Promoted to MW Regional PM Specialist
James A. Wolfe	Jackson/Coffeeville, MS	1985 - 1992	Retired
Joel Douglas	Coffeeville, MS	1993 - 1997	Promoted to PMC Manager
Sherry Surrette	Jackson, MS	2006 - 2007	Changed employers

Mississippi Tidal Region

Name	Location	Tenure	Comments
Michael Materne	Alexander, LA	1989 - 2001	Returned to non PM SCS position.
Scott D. Edwards	Alexander, LA	2002 - 2006	Transferred to RC&D Coord.
Morris J. Houck, Jr.	Alexander, LA	2006 -	

Great Lakes Region

Name	Location	Tenure	Comments
Ernest McPharron	Madison, WI	1955 - 1960	Transferred to NY PM Specialist
Dave Dawson	East Lansing, MI	1958 - 1962	
Lynn Guenther	East Lansing, MI	1962 - 1968	Died in the position.
William M. Briggs	Madison, WI	1960 - 1968	
Dorian Carroll	East Lansing, MI	1969 - 1988	Retired
David W. Burgdorf	East Lansing, MI	1989 - 2012	Retired

Corn Belt Region

Name	Location	Tenure	Comments
Virgil B. Hawk	Ames, IA	1955 -1965	Transferred to NJ PMC Mgr.
Billie H. Rountree	Columbia, MO	1965 - 1975	Was Asst. Nursery Mgr. Minden, LA 1948. Retired
James R. Brown	Columbia, MO	1976 - 1986	Retired

Name	Location	Tenure	Comments
Dan D. Lawson	Columbia, MO	1987 - 1990	Transferred to EPA liaison position
Darrell Dominick	Columbia, MO	1990 - 1992	Became a state conservationist later
John L. Reid	Columbia, MO	1992 - 1995	
Jerry U. Kaiser	Elsberry, MO	1996 -	

Northern Great Plains

Name	Location	Tenure	Comments
John McDermand	Bismarck, ND	1965 - 1974	Retired
Erling Jacobson	Bismarck, ND	1975 - 1984	Promoted to MW Regional PM Specialist
Russell Haas	Bismarck, ND	1984 - 1998	Promoted to NPS liaison
Dwight A. Tober	Bismarck, ND	1998 - 2010	Retired
Wayne Markegard	Bismarck, ND	2010 -	

Central Great Plains - OK, KS and NB

Name	Location	Tenure	Comments
Robert D. Lippert	Salina, KS	1957 - 1977	Retired
Charles M. Schumacher	Lincoln, NE	1960 - 1965	Dates are approximate. Serving NE and Eastern SD.
J. W. Walstrom	Salina, KS	1977 - 1985	Retired
John T. Nicholson	Salina, KS	1986 -1988	Transferred to A MW state agronomist
James A. Stevens	Salina, KS	1989 - 1991	Transferred to East TX PMC Manager.
Jerry B. Lee	Salina, KS	1992 - 1993	
Steve Myers	Salina, KS	1994 - 1995	Acting
Terry M. Conway	Salina, KS	1995 - 2004	Promoter to SRC
Mark A. Janzen	Salina, KS	2004 -	

Southern Great Plains

Name	Location	Tenure	Comments
James E. Smith	Temple, TX	1953 - 1965	Former Reg. Nurseryman. Retired
Arnold Davis	Temple, TX	1965 - 1973	Promoted to South Regional PM Specialist.
DeReath N. Palmer	Temple, TX	1973 - 1977	Retired
H. Wayne Everett	Temple, TX	1977 - 1979	Promoted to West Region PM Specialist
Richard Heizer	Temple, TX	1979 - 1989	Promoted to OK SRC
James Alderson	Temple, TX	1990 - 2005	Retired
Robert Ziehr	Temple, TX	2006 -	

Montana and Wyoming

Name	Location	Tenure	Comments
Jesse McWilliams	Casper, WY	1960 - 1965	Transferred to Algeria, then to Big Flats, NY as PM Specialist
Ashley Thornburg	Bridger/Bozeman, MT	1965 - 1974	Promoted to Regional PM Specialist
R. G. Lohmiller	Bozeman, MT	1974 - 1979	Promoted to SRC
Larry K. Holzworth	Bozeman, MT	1979 - 2007	Retired
James Jacobs	Bozeman, MT	2007 -	

Northern Great Basin

Name	Location	Tenure	Comments
Donald H. Douglas	Aberdeen, ID	1957 - 1960	Promoted to Regional PM Specialist
Harold L. Harris	Aberdeen, ID	1961 - 1973	Retired
Charles A. Mowry	Boise, ID	1974 - 1981	Retired
George R. James	Boise, ID	1981- 1984	Retired
Jacy Gibbs	Boise, ID	1984 - 1992	Promoted to Regional PM Specialist
Daniel G. Ogle	Boise, ID	1993 - 2012	Retired

Central and Southern Great Basin

Name	Location	Tenure	Comments
Joseph A. Downs	Albuquerque, NM	1936 - 1953 1953 - 1962	Mgr. Albuquerque Nursery 1935-54. PM Specialist in 1953 - 1962. Retired
Sherrill H. Fuchs	Albuquerque, NM	1963 - 1966	Went to Tunesia, returned to NE Regional agronomist
Glenn C. Niner	Los Lunas/ NM	1966 - 1969	Fill in PM Specialist for Fuchs, and SCS PMC Advisor to cooperator, retired
Daniel Merkel	Santa Fe/Albuquerque, NM	1969 - 1975	Acting 1968 - 1970 ??
Wendell Hassell	Denver, CO	1975 - 1989	Became NPS liaison
Robert Bruce	Albuquerque, NM	1984 - 1986	Duel PM Specialist/Forester in NM while Denver PM Specialist.
William Fuller	Albuquerque, NM	1984 - 1988	Duel PM Specialist/Agronomist in NM
Wendall Oaks	Albuquerque, NM	1990 - 1992	Also served as PMC manager 1990-91. Promoted to Fort Collins, CO IT position.
Sam Stranathan	Denver, CO	1990 - 1994	May have served CO only. Retired.
Kenneth Lair	Denver, CO	1995 - 1996	May have served CO only.

Name	Location	Tenure	Comments
Herman Garcia	Denver, CO	1998 - 2001	May have served CO only.
Gary Finstad	Denver, CO	2001 - 2004	May have served CO only.
Pat Davey	Lakewood, CO	2004- 2008	May have served CO only.
Christine Taliga	Lakewood, CO	2009 -	May have served CO only.

Southwestern

Name	Location	Tenure	Comments
Darwin Anderson	Phoenix, AZ	1953 - 1964	Killed while on duty; plane crash.
Clinton Renney	Phoenix, AZ	1965 - 1972	Retired
Jesse McWilliams	Reno, NV	1970- 1974	May have been an agronomist, retired
Jake C. Garrison	Phoenix, AZ	1974 - 1987	Retired
Steve Carmichael	Phoenix, AZ	1988 - 1990	
James Briggs	Phoenix, AZ	1990 - 1996	Promoted to AZ SRC and Regional PM Specialist
Bruce Munda	Tucson, AZ	1996 -	

Pacific Northwest

Name	Location	Tenure	Comments
John Schwendiman	Pullman, WA	1954 - 1976	Retired
Jack Carlson	Spokane, WA	1977 - 1980	NTC PM Specialist
James Stroh	Spokane, WA	1980 - 1987	Retired
Scott Lambert	Spokane, WA	1988 - 2002	Left the Service - BLM
Gary A. Kuhn	Spokane, WA	2004 - 2008	Retired
Richard Fleenor	Spokane, WA	2008 -	

California

Name	Location	Tenure	Comments
Harold Miller	Pleasanton, CA	1954 - 1966	Promoted to CA SRC
Robert MacLauchlan	Pleasanton, CA	1966 - 1970	Promoted to MW Regional PM Specialist
Curtis Sharp	Pleasanton/Lockeford, CA	1970 - 1974	Promoted to NE Regional PM Specialist
Robert Slayback	Lockeford/Davis, CA	1974 - 1995	Retired. Vacant since then

Hawaii

Name	Location	Tenure	Comments
Thomas A. Bown	Honolulu, HI	1962 - 1966	Promoted to PM Specialist in AR
DeReath N. Palmer	Honolulu, HI	1966 - 1973	Transferred to HI
Robert J. Joy	Ho'olehua, HI	1976 - 2012	Retired

Regional Plant Materials Specialists

Northeast Regional Plant Materials Specialists

Name	Location	Tenure	Comments
C. B. Manifold	Harrisburg, PA	1953 - 1955	Was Chief of Operations in 1936, Chief Forestry Division in 1948
Wilmer W. Steiner	Upper Darby, PA	1955 - 1970	Former Beltsville Nursery Manager. Promoted to National PM Specialist
Joseph Ruffner	Upper Darby, PA	1970 - 1973	Retired
Curtis Sharp	Broomall/Chester, PA	1974 - 1985	Promoted to National PM Specialist
David Lorenz	Chester, PA	1985 - 1996	Transferred to US Army Liaison. Retired
Liva Marques	Greensboro, NC	2005 - 2007	Moved to US Forest Service.
Ramona Garner	Greensboro, NC	2008 -	

Southern Regional Plant Materials Specialists

Name	Location	Tenure	Comments
M. Crawford Young	Athens, GA/Fort Worth, TX	1954 - 1973	Former Manager Thorsby, GA Nursery. Retired
Arnold Davis	Fort Worth, TX	1973 - 1983	Retired
H. Wayne Everett	Fort Worth, TX	1984 - 1996	Retired
Joel Douglas	Fort Worth, TX	2005 -	

Upper Mid-West Regional Plant Materials Specialists   Discontinued after 1965

Name	Location	Tenure	Comments
Kenneth Welton	East Lansing, MI	1955 - 1959	Retired, former STC in IN
Arthur D. Fladin	Milwaukee, WI	1960	Date approximate.
Donald S. Douglas	Milwaukee, WI	1960 - 1965	Promoted to National PM Specialist

Midwest Regional Plant Materials Specialists

Name	Location	Tenure	Comments
Harold Cooper	Lincoln, NB	1954 - 1955	Later STC in WY
Donald Atkins	Denver/Lincoln, NB	1955 - 1970	Agronomist at Manhattan in 1946. Retired
Robert MacLauchlan	Lincoln, NB	1970 - 1974	Promoted to National PM Specialist. Retired
Ashley Thornburg	Lincoln, NB	1974 - 1978	Retired
Vacant filled by NE & S PM Specialist		1978 - 1982	
Kenneth Blan	Lincoln, NB	1982 1984	
Erling Jacobson	Lincoln, NB	1984 - 1994	Retired

West Regional Plant Materials Specialists

Name	Location	Tenure	Comments
A. L. Hafenrichter	Portland, OR	1935 - 1967	Retired
Harold Miller	Portland, OR	1967 - 1970	Retired
Donald S. Douglas	Portland, OR	1970 - 1974	Retired
Sherrill H. Fuchs	Portland, OR	1974 - 1978	Became regional agronomist
Donald Robertson	Portland, OR	1979 - 1980	Promoted to Asst. NTC Director
H. Wayne Everett	Portland, OR	1980	Promoted to Asst.NPMSt
Kenneth Blan	Portland, OR	1980 - 1980	Transferred to MW NTC
Jack R. Carlson	Portland, OR	1980 - 1992	Promoted to Fort Collins, CO IT position, later to NHQ SES position.
Jacy Gibbs	Portland, OR	1992 - 1995	Retired
James Briggs	Portland, OR	2005 -	

Coordinators

NRCS Plant Materials Coordinator with National Park Service

Name	Location	Tenure	Comments
Wendell Hassell	Denver, CO	1989 - 1997	Retired
Russell Haas	Denver, CO/Bismarck, ND	1998 - 2009	Retired
Pat Davey	Denver, CO	2008 - 2013	Retered

NRCS Plant Materials Liaison to the US Army Environmental Center

Name	Location	Tenure	Comments
David Lorenz	Aberdeen Proving Ground, MD	1996 -2002	Retired

NRCS Plant Materials Information Technology Coordinator

Name	Location	Tenure	Comments
John Scheetz	Bridger, MT	1998 - 2002	Retired

Assistant National Plant Materials Specialists

Name	Location	Tenure	Comments
Robert Thornton	Washington, D.C.	1968 - 1969	Retired
Gilbert Lovell	Washington, D.C.	1978 - 1980	Transferred to ARS
H. Wayne Everett	Washington, D.C.	1980 - 1984	Transferred To South Regional PM Specialist

National Plant Materials Specialists

Name	Location	Tenure	Comments
A. D. Stoesz	Washington, D.C.	1954 - 1964	Retired
Donald Douglas	Washington, D.C.	1965 - 1970	Transferred to West Regional PM Specialist
Wilmer W. Steiner	Washington, D.C.	1971 - 1973	Retired
Robert S. MacLauchlan	Washington, D.C.	1974 - 1984	Retired
Curtis Sharp	Washington, D.C.	1985 - 1993	Retired
Richard S. White	Colby, KS/Washington, D.C.	1994 - 2005	Retired
Robert Escheman	Washington, D.C.	2005 - 2008	Retired
John Englert	Washington, D.C.	2009 -	

Appendix 7: QIT CRITICAL ISSUES AND REQUIRED ACTION TO ADDRESS CRITICAL ISSUES

Critical Issues	Required Action to Address Critical Issues

1. Accountability/ Evaluation

Revise management matrices to reflect priorities with appropriate milestones

Stated commitment to use management matrices for accountability

Development criteria for use in rating success of PMC and PM Specialist

Have periodic review of PMC program by regional team

Assess customer satisfaction with questionnaires and surveys

Develop/implement single plan for all plant science endeavors

Review/examine management matrices and communicate concerns to RC and STC

2. Assessment of Customer needs

System to ID needs, Field Office priorities, & integrate

Recognize Field Office as customer

Use new structure to operate

Include external customers in needs determination

Complete and maintain assessment of customer groups

3. Budget

Provide increased funding for PM based on % of total NRCS budget

Develop standard process to identify PMC needs and develop workload analysis procedure

Evaluate PMC programs for minimum productivity

Review offset policy with PMC's annually

Establish linkages and protocol for allocation and management of CO-46 funds

Provide budgeting flexibility for a national CO-46 reserve

Incorporate plant materials needs into strategic planning process

Evaluate sale of PMC products to offset development costs

Establish policy that other funds support plant materials efforts that support them

4. Commitment by Management /Advisory Process

Implement/support national structure

Use consistent accountability/ evaluation process annually

Ensure/support responsibility to implement and use tech development and transfer structure.

Ensure plant materials participation in detailed processes of tech development and transfer

5. Coordination/ Management of Resources

Initiate recommended structure to improve coordination and management

Implement actions in Accountability/Evaluation Section, especially items 5 & 6

Hold common-interest PMC and multi-discipline meetings and/or teleconferences

Consider/use in-house capability prior to external use

Create Plant Sciences Technical Coordinators (new positions)

6. Holistic Approaches for Land management

Participate with partners on priority ecosystem studies consistent with strategic plan

Ensure that holistic principals are considered in tech voids and priorities at PMC's

Critical Issues	Required Action to Address Critical Issues

7. Integration

Involve all stakeholders in tech development and transfer structure

Use tools available to ensure integration

Ensure STC's take active role in integration and participation

Secure electronic equipment and FOCS training essential for integration

8. Marketing and Visibility

Use strategic planning process to identify customer needs, product development, tech transfer, and marketing

Develop procedure for marketing products, using 7 phases

Publish PM documents in multiple formats

Develop standard PM logo or registered trademark

Change working title of Plant Materials Specialist to Plant Science Specialist

Establish dedicated marketing specialist

9. Meeting New Challenges

Identification and articulation of high priority needs by top management

Identify new challenges within service area

Evaluate present program to adequately address national and local priorities

Incorporate priority challenges into PMC operations

Implement administrative structure with accountability, authority, priority aspects

Summarize progress of low priority studies and then drop w/ product outputs

Train staff to meet mission & new challenges/needs of customers

Secure state of the art equipment

10. Native Species

Adopt national NRCS policy on using native plants

List additional recommended native species in FOTG

Assign PM Specialist's responsibility for development and maintenance of FOTG sections

Focus studies on regional priority native species

Establish steering committee for national native species plan

Encourage use of AOSCA procedures for native releases

Encourage use of AOSCA procedures for native releases

Participate on Federal Native Plant Conservation Committee

Address native species in "Marketing and Visibility"

11. Partner Participation

Include partners in advisory and decision process

Develop checklist of partners by subject area

Empower decision making at lower levels

12. Products and Functions

Top priority on completion of products. Field Office should receive minimum of 1/year

All products need to give NRCS and PM full credit

Have active partner participation in foundation seed production

Increase electronic capability for acquiring, transferring, analyzing data

Obtain PVP for releases when feasible

Develop quality products, sell when appropriate

Promote opportunities for providing "hands-on" training and experience at PMC's

13. Service Area

Base service area on MLRA or similar Eco regions

PMC and PM Specialist serve same area with a PM Specialist in each service area

Ensure each state in service area has equitable assistance

Designate or assign area of expertise to each PMC

14. Staffing

Staff to meet PS needs relative to national and regional strategic plans

Recognize responsibilities of NPM Specialist (National Program Manager) in today's NRCS

Create position in each region to coordinate all plant science technology

Establish PM Specialist for each service area

15. Structure and Linkages

Decide on national technology structure for plant science

Identify organizational structure within Regions

Implement decisions on structure

Integrate structure into strategic planning process

Utilize Beltsville for something other than a National PMC, establish team to explore alternatives

Establish national technology integration team

16. Technology Transfer - Role of PM Specialist

Define role of PM Specialist in development and transfer of technology

Develop technology transfer standards

Evaluate proposed technology transfer scenarios and identify potential variances

Evaluate field planting program to focus on real tech transfer functions

Evaluate and provide training to improve PM Specialist skills

Designate/assign each professional staff an area of expertise

Provide at least one PM Specialist for each PMC service area

Appendix 8: DISCONTINUED CONSERVATION PLANTS

The Plant Materials Program strives to maintain the most effective plants for natural resource conservation activities. The Program officially discontinues plant releases for a variety of reasons, including (1) the plant has been replaced by newer, more effective materials, (2) there is little or no commercial production or no demand from commercial growers, or (3) the plant has become or has the potential to become invasive. Discontinued plant releases are no longer produced by the Plant Materials Program.

Abbreviations used in the table:

Column Release Type: C = Cultivar, IF = Informal, GP = Germplasm, PV = Pre-Varietal;

Column Origin: N = Native, I = Introduced, NL = Naturalized

Release Name	Scientific Name	Common Name	Release Year	Release type	Origin	Reason for Discontinuing
Arlington	*Lespedeza cuneata*	sericea lespedeza	1939	IF	I	no longer produced
Tupelo	*Lespedeza cuneata*	sericea lespedeza	1939	IF	I	no longer produced
King Ranch	*Bothriochloa ischaemum var. songarica*	yellow bluestem	1941	IF	I	no longer produced
Manchar	*Bromus inermis*	smooth brome	1943	C	I	potentially invasive
Prairie	*Bromus catharticus*	rescuegrass	1946	C	I	no longer produced; replaced by others
Primar	*Elymus trachycaulus ssp. trachycaulus*	slender wheatgrass	1946	C	N	no longer produced; replaced by others
Goar	*Lolium arundinaceum*	tall fescue	1946	C	I	no longer produced; replaced by others
-unnamed-	*Phalaris aquatica*	Hardinggrass	1946	IF	I	no longer produced; replaced by others
100	*Lespedeza bicolor*	bicolor lespedeza	1947	IF	I	no longer produced
-unnamed-	*Piptatherum miliaceum*	smilograss	1947	IF	I	no longer produced; replaced by others
T-4464	*Pennisetum ciliare*	buffelgrass	1949	IF	I	no longer produced
A-84	*Eragrostis curvula*	Boer lovegrass	1950	C	I	no longer produced
A-68	*Eragrostis lehmanniana*	Lehmann's lovegrass	1950	C	I	no longer produced; potentially invasive
A-130	*Panicum antidotale*	blue panicgrass	1950	C	I	no longer produced
Tombigbee	*Sorghum bicolor*	chicken corn	1950	IF	NL	no longer produced

Release Name	Scientific Name	Common Name	Release Year	Release type	Origin	Reason for Discontinuing
Wild	*Sorghum bicolor ssp. drummondii*	Sudangrass	1950	IF	NL	no longer produced
Browntop	*Urochloa ramosa*	millet	1950	IF	I	replaced by other releases
Draylar	*Poa glauca ssp. glauca*	upland bluegrass	1951	C	I	replaced by others
Natob	*Lespedeza bicolor*	bicolor lespedeza	1952	C	I	no longer produced; potentially invasive
Asheville	*Lolium arundinaceum*	tall fescue	1952	IF	I	no longer produced
Blue	*Pennisetum ciliare*	buffelgrass	1952	IF	I	no longer produced
Amur	*Thinopyrum intermedium*	intermediate wheatgrass	1952	C	I	no longer produced
Mike	*Trifolium michelianum*	clover	1952	IF	I	no longer produced
Ball	*Trifolium nigrescens*	clover	1952	IF	I	no longer produced
P-27	*Agropyron fragile*	Siberian wheatgrass	1953	C	I	replaced by others
Topar	*Thinopyrum intermedium*	pubescent wheatgrass	1953	C	I	no longer produced; replaced by others
Elsberry	*Bromus inermis*	smooth brome	1954	C	NL	no longer produced; replaced by others
Kleberg	*Dichanthium annulatum*	bluestem	1954	IF	I	no longer produced
Pretoria 90	*Dichanthium annulatum*	bluestem	1954	IF	I	no longer produced
Medio	*Dichanthium aristatum*	bluestem	1954	IF	I	no longer produced
Thorsby	*Lespedeza bicolor*	bicolor lespedeza	1954	IF	I	no longer produced
Cascade	*Lotus corniculatus*	birdsfoot trefoil	1954	C	I	no longer produced
Caucasian	*Bothriochloa bladhii*	Caucasian bluestem	1955	IF	I	no longer produced; potentially invasive
El Kan	*Bothriochloa ischaemum*	yellow bluestem	1956	IF	I	no longer produced; potentially invasive
P-4874	*Poa bulbosa*	bulbous bluegrass	1956	C	NL	replaced by others; potentially invasive
Greenar	*Thinopyrum intermedium*	intermediate wheatgrass	1956	C	I	no longer produced; replaced by others
Gordo	*Dichanthium aristatum*	bluestem	1957	IF	I	no longer produced

Release Name	Scientific Name	Common Name	Release Year	Release type	Origin	Reason for Discontinuing
Newport	*Poa pratensis*	Kentucky bluegrass	1958	C	NL	replaced by others; potentially invasive
Nakuru	*Bromus catharticus*	rescuegrass	1959	IF	I	no longer produced; potentially invasive
Artex	*Urochloa texana*	Texas millet	1960	PV	N	no longer produced
Cherry	*Andropogon hallii*	sand bluestem	1961	C	N	replaced by other releases
Emerald	*Coronilla varia*	crownvetch	1961	C	I	replaced by others; potentially invasive
Cardinal	*Elaeagnus umbellata*	autumn olive	1961	C	I	potentially invasive
Mission	*Ehrharta calycina*	perennial veldtgrass	1962	C	I	no longer produced; replaced by others
Davis	*Indigofera hirsuta*	hairy indigo	1962	IF	NL	replaced by other releases
Orlando	*Lupinus angustifolius*	blue lupine	1963	IF	N	no longer produced
Chemung	*Coronilla varia*	crownvetch	1964	C	I	replaced by others; potentially invasive
Thorsby	*Vigna unguiculata*	cowpea	1964	IF	I	no longer produced
Mandan-759	*Thinopyrum intermedium*	intermediate wheatgrass	1965	IF	I	replaced by others
Pomar	*Dactylis glomerata*	orchardgrass	1966	C	I	no longer produced
A-67	*Eragrostis curvula*	Boer Lovegrass	1967	C	I	no longer produced
F-149	*Aeschynomene americana*	American joinvetch	1969		N	no longer produced
Catalina	*Eragrostis curvula*	Boer lovegrass	1969	C	I	no longer produced
Arnot	*Robinia hispida var. fertilis*	bristly locust	1969	C	N	no longer produced
Dadeville	*Vicia lutea*	smooth yellow vetch	1969	IF	NL	no longer produced
Rem Red	*Lonicera maackii*	Amur honeysuckle	1970	C	I	potentially invasive
Ambro	*Lespedeza virgata*	virgata lespedeza	1971	C	I	no longer produced
Cling-Red	*Lonicera maackii*	Amur honeysuckle	1971	C	I	replaced by others; potentially invasive
Mackinaw	*Lotus corniculatus*	birdsfoot trefoil	1971	C	I	no longer produced; replaced by others
Marshfield	*Lotus pedunculatus*	big trefoil	1971	C	I	no longer produced
Wilmington	*Paspalum notatum*	Bahiagrass	1971	IF	NL	no longer produced; replaced by others
Palar	*Eragrostis superba*	Wilman lovegrass	1972	C	I	no longer produced

Release Name	Scientific Name	Common Name	Release Year	Release type	Origin	Reason for Discontinuing
Lathco	Lathyrus sylvestris	flatpea	1972	C	NL	potentially invasive
PMK-24	Tripsacum dactyloides	eastern gamagrass	1974	GP	N	same genetic material as 'Pete'
Puhuima	Eragrostis lehmanniana	Lehmann's lovegrass	1976	C	I	no longer produced; potentially invasive
Kalo	Lotus corniculatus	birdsfoot trefoil	1976	C	I	no longer produced
Corto	Atriplex semibaccata	Australian saltbush	1977	C	I	no longer produced
Kuivato	Eragrostis lehmanniana	Lehmann's lovegrass	1977	C	I	no longer produced
King Red	Elaeagnus angustifolia	Russian olive	1978	C	I	no longer produced; potentially invasive
Bigalta	Hemarthria altissima	Limpograss	1978	C	I	no longer produced; replaced by others
Greenalta	Hemarthria altissima	Limpograss	1978	C	I	no longer produced; replaced by others
Redalta	Hemarthria altissima	Limpograss	1978	C	I	no longer produced; replaced by others
Ganada	Bothriochloa ischaemum var. ischaemum	yellow bluestem	1979	C	I	no longer produced; potentially invasive
Elsberry	Elaeagnus umbellata	autumn olive	1979	C	I	replaced by others; potentially invasive
Cochise	Eragrostis trichophora	Atherstone lovegrass	1979	C	I	no longer produced; potentially invasive
Athens	Quercus acutissima	sawtooth oak	1980	IF	I	no longer produced
Brazos	Cynodon dactylon	bermudagrass	1982	C	I	replaced by others
Sea Isle	Carex kobomugi	Japanese sedge	1984	C	I	potentially invasive
GSF-I	Tripsacum dactyloides	eastern gamagrass	1984	GP	N	no longer able to identify clonal material
GSF-II	Tripsacum dactyloides	eastern gamagrass	1984	GP	N	no longer able to identify clonal material
Panoche	Bromus rubens	red brome	1985	C	NL	no longer produced; potentially invasive
Tierra	Colutea arborescens	bladdersenna	1985	C	I	no longer produced; replaced by others

Release Name	Scientific Name	Common Name	Release Year	Release type	Origin	Reason for Discontinuing
Redwing	*Elaeagnus umbellata*	autumn olive	1985	C	I	no longer produced; potentially invasive
Late	*Indigofera hirsuta*	hairy indigo	1985	IF	NL	no longer produced
Ellagood	*Elaeagnus umbellata*	autumn olive	1986	C	NL	potentially invasive
Long	*Salix barclayi*	mountain willow	1986	C	N	no longer produced
Wilson	*Salix bebbiana*	Bebb willow	1986	C	N	no longer produced
Oliver	*Salix brachycarpa*	grayleaf willow	1986	C	N	no longer produced
Roland	*Salix lucida ssp. lasiandra*	Pacific willow	1986	C	N	no longer produced
Amquail	*Lespedeza thunbergii*	Thunberg's lespedeza	1987	C	I	potentially invasive
Service	*Poa secunda*	big bluegrass	1990	C	N	no longer produced
Rocker	*Heteropogon contortus*	tanglehead grass	1992	C	N	no longer produced
Georgia 5	*Lolium arundinaceum*	tall fescue	1992	C	NL	no longer produced; replaced by others
Sumter Orange	*Hemerocallis fulva*	daylily	1993	C	NL	no longer produced
ND-WWG931	*Pascopyrum smithii*	western wheatgrass	1993	PV	N	no longer produced
ND-WWG932	*Pascopyrum smithii*	western wheatgrass	1993	PV	I	no longer produced
Doncorae	*Paspalum nicorae*	Brunswickgrass	1993	C	I	no longer produced
Schwendimar	*Elymus lanceolatus ssp. lanceolatus*	thickspike wheatgrass	1994	C	N	unable to maintain seed purity in production
Centennial Selection	*Carex nebrascensis*	Nebraska sedge	1997	PV	N	no demand
Modoc Selection	*Carex nebrascensis*	Nebraska sedge	1997	PV	N	no demand
Ruby Lake Selection	*Carex nebrascensis*	Nebraska sedge	1997	PV	N	no demand
Sterling Selection	*Carex nebrascensis*	Nebraska sedge	1997	PV	N	no demand
CJ Strike Selection	*Eleocharis palustris*	creeping spikerush	1997	PV	N	no demand
Malheur Selection	*Eleocharis palustris*	creeping spikerush	1997	PV	N	no demand
Mud Lake Selection	*Eleocharis palustris*	creeping spikerush	1997	PV	N	no demand
Ruby Lake Selection	*Eleocharis palustris*	creeping spikerush	1997	PV	N	no demand
Roswell Selection	*Juncus balticus*	Baltic rush	1997	PV	N	no demand

Release Name	Scientific Name	Common Name	Release Year	Release type	Origin	Reason for Discontinuing
Sterling Selection	*Juncus balticus*	Baltic rush	1997	PV	N	no demand
Stillwater Selection	*Juncus balticus*	Baltic rush	1997	PV	N	no demand
Marfa	*Leptochloa dubia*	green sprangletop	1997	IF	N	no longer produced
Camas Selection	*Schoenoplectus acutus var. acutus*	hardstem bulrush	1997	PV	N	no demand
Hagerman Selection	*Schoenoplectus acutus var. acutus*	hardstem bulrush	1997	PV	N	no demand
Ogden Bay Selection	*Schoenoplectus acutus var. acutus*	hardstem bulrush	1997	PV	N	no demand
Stillwater Selection	*Schoenoplectus acutus var. acutus*	hardstem bulrush	1997	PV	N	no demand
Bear Lake Selection	*Schoenoplectus maritimus*	alkali bulrush	1997	PV	N	no demand
Bear River Selection	*Schoenoplectus maritimus*	alkali bulrush	1997	PV	N	no demand
Fort Boise Selection	*Schoenoplectus maritimus*	alkali bulrush	1997	PV	N	no demand
Stillwater Selection	*Schoenoplectus maritimus*	alkali bulrush	1997	PV	N	no demand
Fort Boise Selection	*Schoenoplectus pungens var. pungens*	common threesquare	1997	PV	N	no demand
Malheur Selection	*Schoenoplectus pungens var. pungens*	common threesquare	1997	PV	N	no demand
Market Lake Selection	*Schoenoplectus pungens var. pungens*	common threesquare	1997	PV	N	no demand
Corinth GP	*Cornus drummondii*	roughleaf dogwood	1998	PV	N	no longer produced
Jefferson GP	*Cornus drummondii*	roughleaf dogwood	1998	PV	N	no longer produced
Nicholson GP	*Cornus drummondii*	roughleaf dogwood	1998	PV	N	no longer produced
Tazewell GP	*Cornus drummondii*	roughleaf dogwood	1998	PV	N	no longer produced
Railroad Valley Selection	*Juncus balticus*	Baltic rush	1998	PV	N	no demand
Wayne Kirch Selection	*Schoenoplectus pungens var. pungens*	common threesquare	1998	PV	N	no demand
Riley GP	*Chamaecrista fasciculata*	partridge pea	1999	PV	N	re-released as cultivar 'Riley'

Release Name	Scientific Name	Common Name	Release Year	Release type	Origin	Reason for Discontinuing
Jackson	*Tripsacum dactyloides*	eastern gamagrass	1999		N	no demand
Medina	*Tripsacum dactyloides*	eastern gamagrass	2000		N	replaced by others
Snake River Plains GP	*Atriplex canescens*	fourwing saltbush	2001	PV	N	no demand
Northern Cold Desert GP	*Krascheninnikovia lanata*	winterfat	2001	PV	N	no demand
Durham GP	*Panicum virgatum*	switchgrass	2005	PV	N	no longer produced

Appendix 9: COMMON & AND SCIENTIFIC PLANT NAMES

Common Name	Scientific Name	Common Name	Scientific Name
alkali bulrush	Schoenoplectus maritimus	Aweoweo	Chenopodium oahuense
alkali muhly	Muhlenbergia asperifolia	awnless bush sunflower	Simsia calva
alkali sacaton	Sporobolus airoides	Bahiagrass	Paspalum notatum
alpine bluegrass	Poa alpina	Baltic rush	Juncus balticus
alpine milkvetch	Astragalus alpinus	Barley	Hordeum vulgare
alpine sweetvetch	Hedysarum alpinum	basin wildrye	Leymus cinereus
American beachgrass	Ammophila breviligulata	alkali bulrush	Schoenoplectus maritimus
American black currant	Ribes americanum	beach fleabane	Senecio pseudoarnica
American dunegrass	Leymus mollis	beach lovage	Ligusticum scoticum
American joinvetch	Aeschynomene americana	beach plum	Prunus maritima
American plum	Prunus americana	beach sunflower	Helianthus debilis ssp. debilis
American sloughgrass	Beckmannia syzigachne	beach wildrye	Elymus arenarius
Amur honeysuckle	Lonicera maackii	beardless wildrye	Leymus multicaulis
Amur maple	Acer ginnala	beardless wildrye	Leymus triticoides
annual fescue	Vulpia myuros	Bebb willow	Salix bebbiana
annual ryegrass	Lolium rigidum	bermudagrass	Cynodon dactylon
antelope bitterbrush	Purshia tridentata	bicolor lespedeza	Lespedeza bicolor
Arctic Wild Chamomile	Tripleurospermum maritima	big bluestem	Andropogon gerardii
Arizona cottontop	Digitaria californica	big sacaton	Sporobolus wrightii
Arizona fescue	Festuca arizonica	big sagebrush	Artemisia tridentata ssp. vaseyana
Arnold hawthorn	Crataegus anomala	big saltbush	Atriplex lentiformis
aromatic sumac	Rhus aromatica var. serotina	big trefoil	Lotus pedunculatus
arrowleaf clover	Trifolium vesiculosum	birdsfoot trefoil	Lotus corniculatus
arroyo willow	Salix lasiolepis	bitter panicum	Panicum amarum
Atherstone lovegrass	Eragrostis trichophora	black chokeberry	Photinia melanocarpa
Australian saltbush	Atriplex semibaccata	black chokecherry	Prunus virginiana
autumn olive	Elaeagnus umbellata	black grama	Bouteloua eriopoda
black locust	Robinia pseudoacacia	California brome	Bromus carinatus
black mangrove	Avicennia germinans	California buckwheat	Eriogonum fasciculatum

Common Name	Scientific Name	Common Name	Scientific Name
black-eyed Susan	Rudbeckia hirta	California bulrush	Schoenoplectus californicus
bladderpod	Cleome isomeris	California oatgrass	Danthonia californica
bladdersenna	Colutea arborescens	Canada bluegrass	Poa compressa
blanketflower	Gaillardia aristata	Canada wildrye	Elymus canadensis
blanketflower	Pappophorum bicolor	cane bluestem	Bothriochloa barbinodis
blazing star	Liatris elegans	Carolina poplar	Populus canadensis
blue elderberry	Sambucus nigra ssp. cerulea	Caucasian bluestem	Bothriochloa bladhii
blue grama	Bouteloua gracilis	ceanothus	Ceanothus flexilis
blue lupine	Lupinus angustifolius	cereal rye	Secale cereale
blue panicgrass	Panicum antidotale	chalky bluestem	Andropogon glaucopsis
blue wildrye	Elymus glaucus ssp. jepsonii	Chickasaw plum	Prunus angustifolia
bluebunch wheatgrass	Pseudoroegneria spicata ssp. spicata	chickencorn	Sorghum bicolor
bluestem	Dichanthium aristatum	Cicer milkvetch	Astragalus cicer
Boer Lovegrass	Eragrostis curvula	clover	Trifolium michelianum
boreal yarrow	Achillea millefolium var. borealis	clover	Trifolium nigrescens
bottlebrush squirreltail	Elymus elymoides	coastal little bluestem	Schizachyrium littorale
bristly locust	Robinia hispida var. fertilis	coastal panicgrass	Panicum amarum
Brunswickgrass	Paspalum nicorae	Columbia river willow	Salix sessilifolia
buffalograss	Buchloe dactyloides	common elderberry	Sambucus nigra ssp. canadensis
buffelgrass	Pennisetum ciliare	common reed	Phragmites australis
bulbous bluegrass	Poa bulbosa	common snowberry	Symphoricarpos albus
bur oak	Quercus macrocarpa	common threesquare	Schoenoplectus pungens var. pungens
butterfly weed	Asclepias tuberosa	cornelian cherry dogwood	Cornus mas
buttonbush	Cephalanthus occidentalis	cotoneaster	Cotoneaster integerrimus
caley pea	Lathyrus hirsutus	cowpea	Vigna unguiculata
coyote willow	Salix exigua	Engelmann daisy	Engelmannia peristenia
crabapple	Malus coronaria	erect willow	Salix ligulifolia
creeping burhead	Echinodorus cordifolius	false indigo bush	Amorpha fruticosa
creeping foxtail	Alopecurus arundinaceus	false Rhodes grass	Chloris crinita
creeping spikerush	Eleocharis palustris	false sunflower	Heliopsis helianthoides

Common Name	Scientific Name	Common Name	Scientific Name
crested wheatgrass	Agropyron cristatum	feltleaf willow	Salix alaxensis var. alaxensis
crested wheatgrass	Agropyron cristatum × A. desertorum	field oxytrope	Oxytropis campestris
crested wheatgrass	Agropyron cristatum ssp. pectinatum	field oxytrope	Oxytropis campestris
crested wheatgrass	Agropyron desertorum	firecracker penstemon	Penstemon eatonii
crimson clover	Trifolium incarnatum	flatpea	Lathyrus sylvestris
crownvetch	Coronilla varia	Florida hopbush	Dodonaea viscosa
daylily	Hemerocallis fulva	Florida paspalum	Paspalum floridanum
deertongue	Dichanthelium clandestinum	foothill needlegrass	Nassella cernua
desert saltbush	Atriplex polycarpa	forage kochia	Kochia prostrata
desert willow	Chilopsis linearis	Four flower trichloris	Chloris pluriflora
desert zinnia	Zinnia acerosa	fourwing saltbush	Atriplex aptera
desmodium	Desmodium aparines	fourwing saltbush	Atriplex canescens
Dillenius' ticktrefoil	Desmodium glabellum	fuzzytongue penstemon	Penstemon eriantherus var. eriantherus
Douglas spirea	Spiraea douglasii	Galleta grass	Pleuraphis jamesii
Drummond willow	Salix drummondiana	giant bulrush	Schoenoplectus californicus
dune willow	Salix hookeriana	giant cutgrass	Zizaniopsis miliacea
Dusty Miller Artemisia	Artemisia stelleriana	golden chinquapin	Castanea pumila
dwarf fireweed	Chamerion latifolium	grayhead prairie coneflower	Ratibida pinnata
dwarf intermediate wheatgrass	Thinopyrum intermedium	grayleaf willow	Salix brachycarpa
dwarf sand cherry	Prunus pumila var. depressa	green ash	Fraxinus pennsylvanica
dwarf willow	Salix cottetii	green needlegrass	Nassella viridula
eastern gamagrass	Tripsacum dactyloides	green sprangletop	Leptochloa dubia
greenleaf manzanita	Arctostaphylos patula	Jacob's ladder	Iris setosa
gulfhairawn muhly	Muhlenbergia capillaris var. filipes	Jakutsk snow parsley	Cnidium cnidiifolium
hackberry, common	Celtis occidentalis	Japanese millet	Echinochloa frumentacea
hairawn muhly	Muhlenbergia capillaris	Japanese sedge	Carex kobomugi
hairy grama	Bouteloua hirsuta	junglerice	Echinochloa colona
hairy indigo	Indigofera hirsuta	kawelu	Eragrostis variabilis
hairy vetch	Vicia villosa	Kentucky bluegrass	Poa pratensis
hairy wedelia	Wedelia texana	kleingrass	Panicum coloratum

456

Common Name	Scientific Name	Common Name	Scientific Name
Hall's panicum, Filly panic	Panicum hallii var. filipes	koleagrass	Phalaris aquatica
hard fescue	Festuca trachyphylla	kori-yanagi willow	Salix koriyanagi
Hardinggrass	Phalaris aquatica	Kura clover	Trifolium ambiguum
hardstem bulrush	Schoenoplectus acutus var. acutus	lace bark elm	Ulmus parvifolia
hazel alder	Alnus serrulata	late lilac	Syringa villosa
hazelnut	Corylus americana	laurel willow	Salix pentandra
herbaceous mimosa	Mimosa strigillosa	Lehmann's lovegrass	Eragrostis lehmanniana
highbush cranberry	Viburnum opulus var. americanum	Lemmon's willow	Salix lemmonii
hooded windmill grass	Chloris cucullata	Lewis' mock orange	Philadelphus lewisii
Hookers plantain	Plantago hookeriana	Limpograss	Hemarthria altissima
hybrid crabapple	Malus	little bluestem	Schizachyrium scoparium
hybrid plum	Prunus	littleleaf lead tree	Leucaena retusa
hybrid poplar	Populus deltoides × P. niga	longawn sedge	Carex macrochaeta
hybrid popular	Populus	lopsided indiangrass	Sorghastrum secundum
Illinois bundleflower	Desmanthus illinoensis	Louisiana sage	Artemisia ludoviciana
Indian ricegrass	Achnatherum hymenoides	Mackenzie willow	Salix prolixa
indiangrass	Sorghastrum nutans	maidencane	Panicum hemitomon
inland saltgrass	Distichlis spicata	mammoth wildrye	Leymus racemosus
intermediate wheatgrass	Thinopyrum intermedium	Manchurian crabapple	Malus mandshurica
marshhay cordgrass	Spartina patens	Pacific willow	Salix lucida ssp. lasiandra
Maximilian sunflower	Helianthus maximiliani	pale purple coneflower	Echinacea pallida
meadow barley	Hordeum brachyantherum	Palmer's penstemon	Penstemon palmeri var. palmeri
meadow brome	Bromus biebersteinii	panicledleaf ticktrefoil	Desmodium paniculatum
Mexican lupine	Lupinus elegans	partridge pea	Chamaecrista fasciculata
Mexican teosinte	Zea mexicana	paspalum	Paspalum hieronymi
millet	Urochloa ramosa	perennial forage peanut	Arachis glabrata
Mongolian cherry	Prunus fruticosa	perennial pea	Lathyrus latifolius
mountain brome	Bromus marginatus	perennial peanut	Arachis glabrata
mountain mahogany	Cercocarpus montanus	perennial soybean	Neonotonia wightii
mountain whitethorn	Ceanothus cordulatus	perennial veldtgrass	Ehrharta calycina
mountain willow	Salix barclayi	piligrass	Heteropogon contortus

Common Name	Scientific Name	Common Name	Scientific Name
Muhlenberg maidencane	*Amphicarpum muehlenbergianum*	pitcher sage	*Salvia azurea var. grandiflora*
narrow leaf penstemon	*Penstemon angustifolius*	plains bristlegrass	*Setaria leucopila*
narrow-leaved coneflower	*Echinacea angustifolia*	plains bristlegrass	*Setaria vulpiseta*
Nebraska sedge	*Carex nebrascensis*	plains lovegrass	*Eragrostis intermedia*
New England aster	*Symphyotrichum novae-angliae*	Polargrass	*Arctagrostis latifolia*
New Mexico forestiera	*Forestiera pubescens var. pubescens*	ponderosa pine	*Pinus ponderosa*
nodding locoweed	*Oxytropis deflexa*	powdery thalia	*Thalia dealbata*
Nootka alkaligrass	*Puccinellia nutkaensis*	prairie acacia	*Acacia angustissima*
nootka reedgrass	*Calamagrostis nutkaënsis*	prairie coneflower	*Ratibida columnifera*
northern geranium	*Geranium erianthum*	prairie cordgrass	*Spartina pectinata*
northern goldenrod	*Solidago multiradiata*	prairie coreopsis	*Coreopsis palmata*
northern white cedar	*Thuja occidentalis*	prairie flax	*Linum lewisii*
Old World bluestem	*Dichanthium*	prairie flax	*Linum perenne*
orchardgrass	*Dactylis glomerata*	prairie Junegrass	*Koeleria macrantha*
oxeye false sunflower	*Heliopsis helianthoides*	prairie sandreed	*Calamovilfa longifolia*
proso millet	*Panicum miliaceum*	Russian olive	*Elaeagnus angustifolia*
pubescent intermediate wheatgrass	*Thinopyrum intermedium*	Russian wildrye	*Psathyrostachys juncea*
pubescent wheatgrass	*Thinopyrum intermedium*	saltmeadow cordgrass	*Spartina patens*
purple needlegrass	*Nassella pulchra*	sand bluestem	*Andropogon hallii*
purple prairieclover	*Dalea purpurea*	sand dropseed	*Sporobolus cryptandrus*
purple prairieclover	*Dalea purpurea var. purpurea*	sand lovegrass	*Eragrostis trichodes*
purpleosier willow	*Salix purpurea*	sandbar willow	*Salix interior*
purpletop	*Tridens flavus*	Sandberg bluegrass	*Poa secunda*
rattlesnake master	*Eryngium yuccifolium*	Sargent crabapple	*Malus sargentii*
red brome	*Bromus rubens*	Saskatoon serviceberry	*Amelanchier alnifolia*
red fescue	*Festuca rubra*	sawtooth oak	*Quercus acutissima*
redosier dogwood	*Cornus sericea ssp. sericea*	scratchgrass	*Muhlenbergia asperifolia*
redseed plantain	*Plantago rhodosperma*	seacoast bluestem	*Schizachyrium maritimum*
reed canarygrass	*Phalaris arundinacea*	seaoats	*Uniola paniculata*
rescuegrass	*Bromus catharticus*	seashore paspalum	*Paspalum vaginatum*
reseeding soybean	*Glycine soja*	seaside goldenrod	*Solidago sempervirens*

Common Name	Scientific Name	Common Name	Scientific Name
Rio Grande clammyweed	Polanisia dodecandra ssp. riograndensis	sericea lespedeza	Lespedeza cuneata
riverbank lupine	Lupinus rivularis	sheep fescue	Festuca ovina
Rocky Mountain juniper	Juniperus scopulorum	shore juniper	Juniperus conferta
Rocky Mountain penstemon	Penstemon strictus	shortspike windmill grass	Chloris subdolichostachya
rose clover	Trifolium hirtum	showy tick trefoil	Desmodium canadense
rough blazing star	Liatris aspera	shrub lespedeza	Lespedeza thunbergii
roughleaf dogwood	Cornus drummondii	Siberian wheatgrass	Agropyron fragile
roundhead lespedeza	Lespedeza capitata	sideoats grama	Bouteloua curtipendula
RS wheatgrass	Elymus hoffmannii	silky dogwood	Cornus amomum
rugosa rose	Rosa rugosa	silky willow	Salix sericea
Russian almond	Prunus tenella	silver buffaloberry	Shepherdia argentea
silverberry	Elaeagnus commutata	sulphur flower buckwheat	Eriogonum umbellatum var. polyanthum
Sitka alder	Alnus viridis ssp. sinuata	sun hemp	Crotalaria juncea
Sitka willow	Salix sitchensis	sweetgrass	Hierochloe odorata
skunkbush sumac	Rhus trilobata	switchgrass	Panicum virgatum
slender grama	Bouteloua repens	tall dropseed	Sporobolus compositus
slender wheatgrass	Elymus trachycaulus ssp. trachycaulus	tall erythrina	Erythrina variegata
small burnet	Sanguisorba minor	tall fescue	Lolium arundinaceum
smilograss	Piptatherum miliaceum	tall oatgrass	Arrhenatherum elatius var. elatius
smooth brome	Bromus inermis	tall wheatgrass	Thinopyrum ponticum
smooth cordgrass	Spartina alterniflora	tanglehead grass	Heteropogon contortus
smooth yellow vetch	Vicia lutea	Texas dropseed	Sporobolus texanus
Snake River wheatgrass	Elymus wawawaiensis	Texas grama	Bouteloua rigidiseta
snow buckwheat	Eriogonum niveum	Texas millet	Urochloa texana
soaptree yucca	Yucca elata	Texas swampmallow	Pavonia lasiopetala
soft chess	Bromus hordeaceus ssp. hordeaceus	thickspike gayfeather	Liatris pycnostachya
Soft Rush	Juncus effusus	thickspike wheatgrass	Elymus lanceolatus ssp. lanceolatus
soybean	Glycine	thickspike wheatgrass	Elymus lanceolatus
spike muhly	Muhlenbergia wrightii	Thunberg's lespedesa	Lespedeza thunbergii
spike trisetum	Trisetum spicatum	tick clover	Desmodium perplexum

Common Name	Scientific Name	Common Name	Scientific Name
splitbeard bluestem	Andropogon ternarius	Tilesy sage	Artemisia tilesii
squirreltail	Elymus elymoides ssp. elymoides	trailing wildbean	Strophostyles helvula
staghorn cinquefoil	Potentilla bimundorum	tufted hairgrass	Deschampsia caespitosa
stiff goldenrod	Oligoneuron rigidum var. rigidum	tufted wheatgrass	Elymus macrourus
stiff sunflower	Helianthus pauciflorus ssp. pauciflorus	tufted wheatgrass	Leymus innovatus
streambed bristlegrass	Setaria leucopila	upland bluegrass	Poa glauca ssp. glauca
Sudangrass	Sorghum bicolor ssp. drummondii	Ussurian pear	Pyrus ussuriensis
Utah serviceberry	Amelanchier utahensis	whiplash pappusgrass	Pappophorum vaginatum
Utah sweetvetch	Hedysarum boreale	white prairie clover	Dalea candida
velvet bundleflower	Desmanthus velutinus	wild bergamont	Monarda fistulosa
velvet rosettegrass	Dichanthelium scoparium	wild lupine	Lupinus perennis
Venus penstemon	Penstemon venustus	wild plum	Prunus
vetivergrass	Vetiveria zizanioides	Wilman lovegrass	Eragrostis superba
virgata lespedeza	Lespedeza virgata	winterberry euonymus	Euonymus bungeanum
Virginia wildrye	Elymus virginicus	winterfat	Krascheninnikovia lanata
Viviparous arctic bluegrass	Poa arctica ssp. lanata	woolgrass	Scirpus cyperinus
viviparous fescue	Festuca viviparoidea	woollypod vetch	Vicia villosa ssp. varia
western clematis	Clematis ligusticifolia	yellow bluestem	Bothriochloa ischaemum
western dogwood	Cornus sericea ssp. occidentalis	yellow bluestem	Bothriochloa ischaemum var. ischaemum
western needlegrass	Achnatherum occidentale	yellow bluestem	Bothriochloa ischaemum var. songarica
western snowberry	Symphoricarpos occidentalis	yellow indiangrass	Sorghastrum nutans
western wheatgrass	Pascopyrum smithii		
western yarrow	Achillea millefolium var. occidentalis		

About the Author

Curtis Sharp grew up on a small farm in Southern West Virginia, learning his first agronomic lesson when a county agent told his father "If you expect to send these boys to college you better get some super phosphate on those pastures". His father did and the super phosphate helped replace the native broom sedge with the introduced Kentucky bluegrass.

Sharp earned a Bachelor of Science degree from West Virginia University in 1953, participating in the SCS trainee program during the summers; and a Masters in Agronomy from The Pennsylvania State University in 1955. After a two year military obligation he became the SCS advisor to the Alfred Agricultural and Technical institute, which operated the Big Flats, NY PMC through a cooperative agreement. The agreement ended in 1960, and Sharp returned to SCS as PMC manager until 1965.

He spent the balance of his professional career at various locations in the SCS/NRCS Plant Materials Program, retiring in 1993. His positions and accomplishments, as well as his contributions to the development and use of conservation plants, are referenced in this history, as is that of hundreds of others that worked within the Program.

Although started by others, Sharp views his contribution to stabilizing coastal sand dunes and tidal shorelines along the mid-Atlantic coast as his most rewarding, hands-on, plant materials effort.

Index

464

End Notes:

Acknowledgements

[1] NRCS Plant Materials Centers, http://www.nrcs.usda.gov/wps/portal/nrcs/main/national/plantsanimals/plants/centers (February 5, 2011).

Introduction

[2] Alfred W. Crosby, *The Columbian Exchange: Biological and Cultural Consequences of 1492*, (Westport, CT: Greenwood Press 1972).

[3] Studymode, Columbian Exchange, http://www.studymode.com/essays/Columbian-Exchange-510625.html/ (May 1, 2013).

[4] Joseph Stromberg, "The Era of Our Ways", *Smithsonian* (January, 2013): 17.

[5] "National Industrial Recovery Act (1933)", http://www.ourdocuments.gov/doc.php?doc=66&page=transcript/ (April 30, 2013).

[6] Douglas Helms, *Readings in the History of the Soil Conservation Service Historical Notes No 1:1992*, SCS, USDA, http://www.nrcs.usda.gov/Internet/FSE_DOCUMENTS/stelprdb1043484.pdf/ (November 13, 2011).

[7] *National Plant Materials Program Manual*, http://plant-materials.nrcs.usda.gov/technical/references.html/3/1/2912/ (June 12, 2010).

[8] *PLANTS Database*, http: //plants.usda.gov/java/ (April 12, 2010).

Chapter 1: Why the Plant Materials Program was needed

[9] *History of the Enoree and Long Cane Ranger Districts*, http://www.fs.usda.gov/detail/scnfs/home/?cid=fsbdev3/037408/ (May 20, 2010).

[10] Ibid.

[11] *History of American Agriculture, Chapter 3 - The new Nation*, http://www.teach1.cses.vt.edu/Hist3124/ch3.html/ (October 13, 2011).

[12] Robert H. Jeffries, *Early Jasper County: Life in Jasper County Between 1810 – 1900*, http://www.rootsweb.ancestry.com/~gajasper/bios/jeffriesfampart2.html/ (October 13, 2011).

[13] *The New Georgia Encyclopedia, Land and Resources, Geography, Piedmont*, http://www.georgiaencyclopedia.org/nge/Home.jsp/ (June 25, 2004).

[14] H. H. Bennett and W.R. Chapline, "Soil Erosion a National Menace", *USDA Cir. 33* 1928, USDI, Washington DC.

[15] Walter Ebeling, *The Fruited Plain: The Story of American Agriculture*, (Berkeley: University of California Press, 1979), 153.

[16] Bennett and Chapline, loc. cit.

[17] Stanley W. Trimble, *Man-Induced Soil Erosion on the Southern Piedmont: 1700-1970*, (Soil and Water Conservation Society, 1974, Ankeny, IA).

[18] *Economic History in Appalachian Ohio*, http://www.firstohio.com/Economic/ED/history.aspx/ (May 6, 2010).

[19] *Dust Bowl Trough*, http://www.dustbowltough.com/home.html/ (December 3, 2009).

[20] William Lockeretz, "The Lessons of the Dust Bowl," *American Science*, Vol. 66, (1978), 560-569.

[21] *The Great Plains and Prairies*, http://countrystudies.us/united-states/geography-17.html/ (February 6, 2010).

[22] USDA, *The second RCA appraisal: soil, water, and related resources on nonfederal land in the United States* (Washington, DC: GPO, 1989).

[23] L. J. Hagen, *Wind Erosion in the United States*. Proc. of Wind Erosion Symposium, (Poznan, Poland, CCLX: 25, 1994).

[24] L. J. Hagen and N. P. Woodruff, "Air pollution from dust storms in the Great Plains", *Atmos. Environ.* (1973) 7:323-332.

[25] National Drought Mitigation Center, "Drought In The Dust Bowl Years", http://drought.unl.edu/DroughtBasics/DustBowl/DroughtintheDustBowlYears.aspx/.

[26] *Dust Bowl Trough*, loc. cit.

[27] *The Encyclopedia of Earth*, http://www.eoearth.org/article/Dust_Bowl/ (March 21, 2011).

[28] *Perspectives on Biodiversity: Valuing Its Role in an ever changing World* (1999), http://www.nap.edu/openbook.php?record/id=9589&page=14/ (May 22, 2011).

[29] Richard N. Mack, "Invasion of *Bromus tectorum* L. into Western North America," *Agro-Ecosystems*, Vol. 7:2 (August 2, 1981) 145-165.

[30] H. A. Wallace to President of the U.S., "The western range, A Great but Neglected Natural Resource" in response to Senate Res. 289, September 29, 1936, Washington, DC, 620 pp.

[31] *Ranching in Montana: A Brief History*, http://dnrc.mt.gov/cardd/mtgrasscommission/ranching.asp/ (June 30, 2004).

[32] Forest Management Policies, "Land Use History of North America, Colorado Plateau", http://cpluhna.nau.edu/Change/forest_management_policies.html/ (March 16 2011).

[33] William S.Abruzzi, "The Social and Ecological Consequences of Early Cattle Ranching in the Little Colorado River Basin." *Human Ecology* 23 (1995) 75-98.

[34] "Desertification in developed countries", *International Symposium and Workshop on Desertification in Developed Countries*, Reprinted from *Environmental Monitoring and Assessment*, Vol. 37, 1-3, (Netherlands: Kluwer Academic Publishers, 1995).

[35] Forest Management Policies, loc. cit.

[36] P. H. Roberts, *Hoof prints on Forest Ranges* (San Antonio, TX: Thew Naylor Company, 1963)

[37] *Ranching in Montana: A Brief History*, loc. cit.

[38] Sheila Barry, Stephanie Larson, and Melvin George, *California Native Grasslands: A Historical Perspective*, http://californiarangeland.ucdavis.edu/Publications%20pdf/CRCC/California%20Native%20Grasslands%20-%20A%20Historical%20Perspective.pdf/ (March 17, 2010).

[39] S. F. Enloe, J. M. DiTomaso, S. B. Orloff, and D. Drake. "Soil water dynamics differ among rangeland plant communities dominated by yellow starthistle (*Centaurea solstitialis*), annual grasses, or perennial grasses", *Weed Science* 52, 6 (2004), 929-935.

[40] Janneke HilleRisLambers, Stephanie G Yelenik, Benjamin P Colman, and Jonathan M Levine, "California annual grass invaders: the drivers or passengers of change?" *J Ecol*. 98, 5 (September 2010), 1147–1156.

[41] *History of the Enoree and Long Cane Ranger Districts*, loc. cit.

[42] W. W. Woodhouse, Jr., "Dune Building and Stabilization with Vegetation" *U.S. Army Corps of Engineers*, Vol. 3 (1978), 9-104

[43] Stephen W. Broome, *Restoration and Management of Coastal Dune Vegetation*, Bulletin # AG-591, NC State Univ., Dept. of Soil Science, Raleigh, NC, http://www.soil.ncsu.edu/lockers/Broome_S/ram.html/ (May 3, 2011).

[44] Virginia Agriculture Exp. Sta., "The Virginia tidal riverbank erosion study", Research Report 65 (Blacksburg, VA: VPI, 1962).

[45] W. Curtis Sharp, Cluster R. Belcher and John Oyler, *Vegetation for Tidal Stabilization in the Mid-Atlantic States*, (Washington, DC: USDA-SCS, 1981), 19.

[46] Pennsylvania streams, http://www.dcnr.state.pa.us/brc/rivers/riversconservation/registry/CrumCreek/XIII.%20MAJOR%20ISSUES.final.pdf/ (September 3, 2011).

[47] James J. Hoorman and Jeff McCutcheon, *Understanding the Benefits of Healthy Riparian Areas*, http://ohioline.osu.edu/ls-fact/0001.html/ (January 18, 2011).

[48] Samantha Volz, *Native Trails in Ohio*, http://traveltips.usatoday.com/native-american-trails-ohio-22510.html/ (June 27, 2010).

[49] Upper Sprague Watershed Assessment, Chapter 12, *Terrestrial Wildlife Species and Habitat* http://www.klamathpartnership.org/pdf/sr_watershed_assessment/sr_12-terrestrialwildlife.pdf/ (November 7, 2010).

Chapter 2: Early Erosion Control Efforts

[50] Guide's Guide, "The Province Lands", *Cape Cod National Seashore*, http://www.nps.gov/caco/planyourvisit/upload/FinalGGPlands.pdf/ (September 13, 2011).

[51] Angus McDonald. *Early American Soil Conservationists*, USDA Misc. Publication No. 449, (GPO, Washington, DC, 1941).

[52] John Vincent Ford, "The Economic Philosophy of John Taylor", *The William and Mary Quarterly*, Vol. 9, No. 3, (Omohundro Institute of Early American History and Culture, July 1929) p. 221

[53] Frederick Doveton and Ralph E. Griswold, "Thomas Jefferson Landscape Architect," *J. of the Society of Architectural Historians*, Vol. 40, No. 1, (Univ. of VA Press 1978) 78-80.

[54] Richard Bardolo, *Agricultural literature and the early Illinois Farmer*, Volume 29, (Univ. VA Press, 1948) 19-20, 28.

[55] J. S. Cates, *Mangum Terrace and Its Relation to Efficient Farm Management*, 1912, http://www.ncmarkers.com/Markers.aspx?ct=ddl&sp=search&k=Markers&sv=H-58%20-%20MANGUM%20TERRACE/ (February 2, 2011).

[56] Edmund Ruffin, Agricultural, *Geological, and Descriptive Sketches of Lower North Carolina, and the Similar Adjacent Lands* (Institution for the Deaf & Dumb & the Blind, 1861) 296.

[57] W. J. Mcgee, "Soil Erosion", USDA Bur. Soils, Bull. No. 71, (GPO, 1911).

[58] Mark Stromberg and Paul Kephart, *Hastings Natural History Reservation, Landowners Guide to Native Grass Enhancement and Restoration*, http://www.hastingsreserve.org/nativegrass/NatGrasBackgrnd.html (October 31, 2010).

[59] Janneke HilleRisLambers, Stephanie G Yelenik, Benjamin P Colman, and Jonathan M Levine, "California annual grass invaders: the drivers or passengers of change?" *J Ecol*., (September 2010), 5 1147–1156.

[60] George A. Rogler and Russell J. Lorenz, "Crested Wheatgrass - Early History in the U.S.," *J. Range Mgt*. (1983), 36, No. 1, 91   93.

[61] Dept. of Botany, Smithsonian Institution, "Learn More About: U.S. Exploring Expedition", *Botanical Exploration, Yesterday, Today, Tomorrow*, http://www.sil.si.edu/digitalcollections/usexex/learn/Kress.html/ (March 21, 2010).

[62] Jack Carlson, Frank Rickendorf and Wilbur Ternyik, "Stabilizing Coastal Sand Dunes in the Pacific Northwest", *Agri. HB* 687, USDA-SCS, 1991, Washington, DC.

[63] Richard J. Blaustein, *Kudzu's invasion into Southern United States life and culture*, USDA, http://www.srs.fs.usda.gov/pubs/ja/ja_blaustein001.pdf/, Retrieved August 20, 2007 (June 13, 2010).

[64] Wikipedia, *Kudzu in the United States*, http://en.wikipedia.org/w/index.php?title=Kudzu_in_the_United_States&oldid=445326103/ (September 10, 2011).

[65] Marston Taylor Bogert, "The Function of Chemistry in the Conservation of Natural Resources", *Journal of the American Chemical Society*, Vol. 31, 1909, 135.

[66] *The Grass Whisperer, Bishop Family Farm*, http://www.thegrasswhisperer.com/content/12016/ (July 30, 2011).

[67] Arnel Hallauer, *Corn Breeding*, Iowa State Univ., ISRF08-13, 2008, http://www.ag.iastate.edu/farms/08reports/Northeast/CornBreeding.pdf/ (September 20, 2011).

[68] F. Lamson-Scribner, *Grasses as Soil and Soil Binder*, Yearbook of Agriculture (Washington, DC: GPO, 1894) 4:141-142.

[69] Frank S Crosswhite, "History, Geology and Vegetation of Picketpost Mountain", *Desert Plants*, Vol. 6, No. 2 (Tucson, AZ: Univ. of Arizona Press).

[70] *Chronology of Federal Soil and Water Conservation Involvement*, 1929, Buchanan amendment to agriculture appropriations bill for fiscal year 1930 provides $160,000 to study causes of soil erosion and methods of control, http://www.ciesin.org/docs/002-475/002-475.html/ (November 21, 2012).

[71] Bennett and Chapline, loc. cit.

[72] "National Industrial Recovery Act (1933)", loc. cit.

[73] C. R. Enlow, "Memo to H.H Bennett, November 1935", Entry 254, RG 114.5.2, Natl. Archives, College Park, MD.

Chapter 3: Creation Of SCS And Evolution Of A Plant Evaluation Concept

[74] Maurice G. Cook, *Hugh Hammond Bennett: The Father of Soil Conservation*, http://www.soil.ncsu.edu/about/century/hugh.html/ (June 1, 2009).

[75] *Denver Public Library EAD Project*, http://eadsrv.denverlibrary.org/sdx/pl/doc-dm.xsp?id=CONS9_d0e38&fmt=text&base=fa/ (December 1, 2011).

[76] John T. Phelan and Donald L. Basinger, *Engineering in the Soil Conservation Service, History Notes No. 2*, Economics and Social Science Div., (USDA-SCS, Washington, DC, 1993).

[77] Lawrence C. Kelly, "Anthropology in the Soil Conservation Service", *Agricultural History*, Vol. 59, No. 2, The History of Soil and Water Conservation: A Symposium (April 1985), 136-147.

[78] Douglas Helms, *Readings in the History of the Soil Conservation Service Historical Notes No. 1*, SCS, USDA, 1992, http://www.nrcs.usda.gov/Internet/FSE_DOCUMENTS/stelprdb1043484.pdf/ (November 6, 2011).

[79] D. Chongo Mundende, *Encyclopedia of Oklahoma History & Culture, Soil and Water Conservation*, http://digital.library.okstate.edu/encyclopedia/ (May 16, 2009).

[80] *Dust Bowl Trough*, loc. cit.

[81] George A. Cevasco, Richard P. Hammond, Everett Mendelsohn, *Modern American Environmentalist, A Biographical Encyclopedia* (Baltimore: Johns Hopkins Univ. Press, 2009).

[82] Eugene C. Buie, *History of Water Resource Activities of the USDA-SCS*, (USDA- NRCS, Washington, DC, 1973).

[83] Prevention of soil erosion; surveys and investigations; preventive measures; cooperation with agencies and persons; acquisition of land, U.S. Code, Title 16, Chapter 3B, 590a.

[84] The National Industrial Recovery Act (NIRA; Pub. L. 73-90, 48 Stat. 195, enacted June 16, 1933, codified at 15 U.S.C. § 703)

[85] *Soil Conservation and Domestic Allotment Act of 1936*, Gale's Major Acts of Congress, http://www.answers.com/topic/soil-conservation-and-domestic-allotment-act#ixzz1Y1rV16vs/ (September 24, 2011).

[86] Ibid.

[87] Douglas Helms, "The Civilian Conservation Corps: Demonstrating the Value of Soil Conservation". *J. Soil Water Consv* 40 (March-April 1985), 184-188.

[88] Douglas Helms, *Briefing Paper on the Plant Materials Centers*, (USDA,-NRCS, Washington, DC, April 7, 2008).

[89] Frank N. Meyer Memorial Medal, "Charles R. Enlow receives award" *J. of Heredity*, Vol. 61, No. 6 (1970) 259-260.

[90] "Plant Materials Introduced by the Division of Plant Exploration and Introduction", BPI, April 1 to June 30, 1935, USDA Inventory No. 123, January 1940, Washington, DC.

[91] C.R. Enlow Memo to H. H Bennett, November 1935, Entry 254, RG 114.5.2, Natl. Archives, College Park, MD.

[92] Dr. Virgil Hawk to John Schwendiman March 21 1983, included in John L. Schwendiman, The First Fifty Years, The Plant Materials Center, Pullman, WA, (USDA-SCS, 1987). Hawk states "On April 15 I was transferred to the new USDA, SCS organization with Charlie Enlow in charge in Washington, DC".

[93] A Brief History of the Development of the Seed Industry, http://seedstory.wordpress.com/a-brief-history-of-the-seed-industry/ November 30, 2012.

[94] C. B. Manifold Memo to H. H Bennett, December 18, 1935, Entry 254, RG 114.5.2, Natl. Archives, College Park, MD.

[95] Robert L. Geiger, Jr., *A Chronological History of the Soil Conservation Service and Related Events*, (USDA-SCS, Washington, DC, 1955), 7.

[96] Boyce Thompson Arboretum, http://ag.arizona.edu/bta/history.html/ (Dec. 6, 2011).

[97] Fischer Scientific, Feb. 10, 1961, p. 373, http://www.sciencemag.org/content/133/3450/local/front-matter.pdf/ (Dec 6, 2012).

[98] Field Memorandum #SCN-4, "Functions and Activities of Nurseries to Regional Conservators and Nurserymen", Entry 254, RG 114.5.2, Natl. Archives, College Park, MD.

[99] "New Regent U. of A. Specialist in Southwestern Horticulture", *Casa Grande Valley Dispatch*, January 21, 1927.

[100] AZ 420, University of Arizona Office of the President records, 1914-1937, Box 21, Folder 8, Commencement, 1929-1936.

[101] "Dr. Crider Speaks Here Monday Night" *Prescott Evening Courier,* June 30, 1930, http://news.google.com/newspapers?nid=897&dat=19300613&id=kJ4nAAAAIBAJ&sjid=9k8DAAAAIBAJ&pg=4492,667580/ (May 5, 2011).

[102] J. R. Cox and G.B. Ruyle, *Influence of Climate and Edaphic Factors on the Distribution of Eragrostis lehmanniana*, Nees Arizona, USA, Grassland Society of Southern Africa, 1986.

[103] F. J. Crider, *Three introduced lovegrasses for soil conservation*, USDA Circular No. 730, (GPO, 1945).

[104] Kimberly Matas, "Frank Crosswhite: Legacy of botanist lives on at Boyce Thompson Arboretum," *Arizona Daily Star,* January 12, 2009, http://azstarnet.com/news/local/education/college/article_501a7619-387c-5ca5-9149-e70fab336051.html/ (August 17, 2010).

[105] Sylvia Lee, in an e-mail while she was writing an anniversary history of the Boyce Thompson Arboretum.

[106] Frank S Crosswhite , *Studies of Simmondsia chinensis at the Boyce Thompson Southwestern Arboretum*, Office of the Arid Lands Studies, Univ. AZ, Tucson. http://www.pssurvival.com/ps/Crops/Jojoba/_And_Its_Uses_1972.pdf (June 3, 2012)

[107] Charles Enlow personnel file, available through Douglas Helms NRCS Historian (retired).

[108] C.R. Enlow memo to Mrs. Murray, June 24, 1935, Box 12, Entry 254, RG-114.5.2, Natl. Archives, College Park, MD.

[109] F. J. Crider, Memo to Regional Conservationists and Nurserymen, March 25, 1936, Box 10, Entry 254, RG 114.5.2, Natl. Archives, College Park, MD.

[110] Wilmer W. Steiner letter to F. Joy Hopkins, June 22, 1967, Box 23, Entry 254, RG 114.5.2, Natl. Archives, College Park, MD.

[111] Franklin J. Crider, *Root growth stoppage resulting from defoliation of grass*, Tech. Bul. 1102, USDA, SCS (GPO, Washington, DC, 1955).

[112] H. H. Bennett request to all Regional Directors "I would now like to have" October 26, 1949, Box 6, Entry 254, RG 114.5.2, Natl. Archives, College Park, MD.

[113] Records of the Hill Culture Research Section and the Hill Culture Division, RG 114.4.8, Records of the NRCS, Natl. Archives, College Park, MD.

[114] C. B. Manifold Memo to All Regional Conservators and Nurserymen, March 25, 1936, Box 10, Entry 254, RG 114.5.2, Natl. Archives, College Park, MD.

[115] Robert L. Geiger, op. cit., 8.

[116] Franklin J. Crider Memo to Regional Conservators, July 27, 1937, Entry 215.0, Central Files, Natl. Archives, College Park, MD.

[117] Calif. Crop Imp. Assoc., History of seed certification in Calif. 1900 - 1958, http://www.ccia.ucdavis.edu/html/history.html/ (December 28, 2012).

[118] All Ranking Field Offices, Regional Memorandum 559, Re: "Functions and Procedures of nursery Division", February 4, 1941, Box 14, Entry 254, RG 114.5.2, Natl. Archives, College Park, MD.

[119] F. J. Crider, "Observational Planting", *Soil Conservation Magazine*, Vol., 3, (December, 1939) 146-151.

[120] Douglas Helms, *Briefing Paper on the Plant Materials Centers*, loc. cit.

[121] Field Memorandum #SCS 730, "Coordination of activities to promote the use of superior plants and methods in erosion control", November 14, 1938, Entry 254, RG 114.5.2, Natl. Archives, College Park, MD

[122] F. J. Crider to All Ranking Field Offices, "Projecting Nursery Observational Work", March 2, 1939, Entry 254, RG 114.5.2, Natl. Archives, College Park, MD.

[123] Ibid.

[124] Wilmer W. Steiner letter to F. Joy Hopkins, loc. cit.

[125] Robert L. Geiger, op. cit., 8

[126] F. J. Crider, Memo to Maurice E. Heath, SCS, Big Flats, NY, April 13, 1949, Box 5, Entry 254, RG 114.5.2.

Chapter 4: Production And Observational Nurseries - Their People, Products, Processes And Performance

[127] Regional and Annual Reports, "Observational nursery results at Paducah, KY", Entry 254, RG 114.5.2 and Box 71, Entry 215.0, RG-114, Natl. Archives, College Park, MD.

[128] Nurseries and Headquarters, "List #2 – SCS Nurseries – 1936, Regions", Entry 254, RG 114.5.2, Natl. Archives, College Park, MD.

[129] Guy C. Fuller, "Machinery that Facilitates the Harvesting of Grass Seed," Soil Conservation Magazine, Vol., 1, (December 1935), 12.

[130] "Planned Use of Land in Soil Conservation Service Nurseries", May, 1951, Entry 254, RG 114.5.2, Natl. Archives, College Park, MD.

[131] "Status and Use of Plant Materials Centers formerly and Presently Operated by Soil Conservation Service", February 1960, Entry 254, RG 114.5.2, Natl. Archives, College Park, MD.

[132] "Soil Conservation Service Annual Administrative Report - FY. 1952", Nursery Division, Region I, August 1952, Entry 254, RG 114.5.2, Natl. Archives, College Park, MD.

[133] A. L. Hafenrichter to A.D. Stoesz, inquiring of nurseries doing grass work, January 15, 1963, Entry 254, RG 114.5.2, Natl. Archives, College Park, MD.

[134] A. D. Stoesz to A. L. Hafenrichter replying to request of nurseries doing grass work, January 9,1963, Entry 254, RG 114.5.2, Natl. Archives, College Park, MD.

[135] Richard P. White, Executive Secretary, American Association of Nurserymen, Washington, D.C. letter to Chief Bennett from March 29, 1939., RG 114, Box 1, General Files, 101.2.

[136] "Nursery Division Report for 1952", Entry 254, RG 114.5.2, Natl. Archives, College Park, MD.

[137] "History of SCS Nursery, Paducah, KY", May 23, 1949, Entry 254, RG 114.5.2, Natl. Archives, College Park, MD.

[138] "Permanent Employees of Soil Conservation Service Nurseries", January 30, 1936, Entry 215.0, RG-114, Natl. Archives, College Park, MD.

[139] Kearney.com, This Week in History, http://www.kearneyhub.com/news/local/this-week-in-history/article_caab89de-d303-11df-a7ef-001cc4c03286.html (September 29, 2012).

[140] "New Nurseries Established", Soil Conservation Magazine, Vol., 1, (September 1935), 10.

[141] "Annual Reports of Department of Agriculture, SCS, 1935", (USDA, Washington, DC, 1935), 18-19.

[142] "Annual Reports of Department of Agriculture, SCS, 1936", (USDA, Washington, DC, 1936), 25-26.

[143] "Annual Reports of Department of Agriculture, SCS, 1937", (USDA, Washington, DC, 1937), 31-32.

[144] C. R. Enlow Memo to H. H Bennett, November 1935, Entry 254, RG 114.5.2, Natl. Archives, College Park, MD.

[145] "Annual Reports of the Department of Agriculture, 1941", Nursery Operations NRCS, (GPO, Washington, DC, 1941), 44-45.

[146] The number of nurseries operating in 1941 according to the "1941 Annual Reports to Dept. by SCS" is two less than shown in Table 4.1.

[147] Harry A. Gunning letter to A. E. Jones about situation at Big Flats, NY, August 5, 1946, Entry 254, RG 114.5.2, Natl. Archives, College Park, MD.

[148] Harry A. Gunning letter to A. E. Jones about situation at Big Flats, NY, August 5, 1946, Entry 254, RG 114.5.2, Natl. Archives, College Park, MD.

[149] Robert M. Ross to John W. Kellar, Region 1 Nurseryman, February 10, 1949, Entry 254, RG 114.5.2, Natl. Archives, College Park, MD.

[150] "Annual Report of Regional Nursery, Division Region I, July 1, 1950 – June 30, 1951", Entry 254, RG 114.5.2, Natl. Archives, College Park, MD.

[151] Paul Lemmon memo to Nursery Division Chief Grover Brown, March 6, 1952, Entry 254, RG 114.5.2, Natl. Archives, College Park, MD.

[152] USDA, NRCS, Plant Materials Program Costs and Benefits 1935 – 2005, http://prod.nrcs.usda.gov/Internet/FSE_DOCUMENTS/stelprdb1042295.pdf/ (February 1, 2011).

[153] Ibid.

[154] Annual Technical, and Other Reports from Regional Nurseries, 1934-67, "Summary of Nursery Operations", Entry 254, RG 114.5.2, Natl. Archives, College Park, MD.

[155] Personal communications by authors with former employees, libraries, PMC and SCS other offices.

[156] "Nursery Observational Program Personnel", March 1, 1949, Entry 254, RG 114.5.2, Natl. Archives, College Park, MD.

[157] Personal communications by authors with former employees.

[158] "Classified Field Personnel by Nurseries, April 1939", Entry 254, RG 114.5.2, Natl. Archives, College Park, MD.

[159] "Annual Technical, and Other Reports from Regional Nurseries, 1934-67", Appendix 40, Entry 254, RG 114, Records of the Nursery Division, National Archives, College Park, MD.

[160] F.J. Crider, memo to Regional Conservationists and Nurserymen, March 25, 1936, Entry 254, RG 114.5.2, Natl. Archives, College Park, MD.

[161] Online Language Dictionary, http://www.wordreference.com/es/translation.asp?tranword=cultivar%20%5Bcultivated%20variety%5D/ (June 13, 2010).

[162] "Increased Grass Production, Mainly Through Districts", Entry 254, RG 114.5.2, Natl. Archives, College Park, MD.

[163] Proposed Procedure for Distribution of Foundation Seed Stock of Promising Plants, 1938, Entry 254, RG 114.5.2, Natl. Archives, College Park, MD.

[164] When SCS officially releases a selection with unique and identifiable attributes, following SCS requirements, it becomes a cultivar, (cultivated variety), so designated by single quotation marks, such as 'Vaughn'. Other forms of releases where the plant has unique and identifiable attributes but the agency requirements are not followed and the plant is not officially released, is not considered a cultivar, and the given name is not enclosed in single quotation marks.

[165] "Improved Conservation Plant Materials Released by NRCS and Cooperators through September 1999", (USDA, NRCS, Washington, DC, 1999).

[166] Franklin J. Crider Memo to Regional Conservators, July 27, 1937, Entry 215.0, Central Files, Natl. Archives, College Park, MD.

[167] NM State University Seed Certification, http://seedcertification.nmsu.edu/ (May 14, 2011).

[168] *Sericea Lespedeza, Introduction*, http://www.fs.fed.us/database/feis/plants/forb/lescun/all.html#Introductory (August 12, 2010).

[169] *Sericea Lespedeza, A Pasture, Hay and Conservation Plant*, Alabama Coop. Ext. System, http://www.aces.edu/pubs/docs/A/ANR-1318/ANR-1318.pdf/ (August 12, 2010).

[170] North Carolina Crop Improvement Association, http://www.nccrop.com/programs.php/Seed_Certification/7/ (August 14, 2011).

[171] M. M. Hoover memo to H. A. Gunning, October 22, 1942, Central Files, Entry 1, RG 114, Natl. Archives, College Park, MD.

[172] PLANTS Database, http://plants.usda.gov/java/ (April 12, 2010).

[173] "Annual Report, SCS Nurseries, Reg. 1, July 1, 1936", Entry 254, RG 114.5.2, Natl. Archives, College Park, MD.

[174] "Work project, A Section of Conservation Nurseries", Washington, D.C. March 11, 1936, Entry 254, RG 114.5.2, Natl. Archives, College Park, MD.

[175] Ibid.

[176] John L. Schwendiman, The First Fifty Years, The Plant Materials Center, Pullman, WA, (Pullman, WA 1987).

[177] Release Notice, 'Manchar' smooth brome, http://public.wsu.edu/~pmc_nrcs/ Releases/Manchar.pdf/ (August 12, 2012).

[178] Release notice 'Sherman' big bluegrass, http://public.wsu.edu/~pmc_nrcs/ Releases/Sherman.pdf/ (August 12, 2012).

[179] Release notice 'Primar' slender wheatgrass, http://public.wsu.edu/~pmc_nrcs/ Releases/Primar.pdf/ (August 12, 2012).

[180] NRCS Plant Guide, Bluebunch Wheatgrass, http://plants.usda.gov/plantguide/pdf/pg.pssps.pdf/ (August 12, 2012).

[181] Alderson and Sharp, Grass Varieties of the U.S., USDA, HB 170, (GPO, Washington, DC, 1994) 249-50.

[182] Release notice 'Alkar' tall wheatgrass, http://public.wsu.edu/~pmc_nrcs/Releases/Alkar.pdf/ (August 12, 2012).

[183] "Annual Administrative Report, Nursery Division, Pacific Southwest Region", August 1, 1941, Entry 254, RG 114.5.2. Natl. Archives, College Park, MD.

[184] Alderson. loc. cit., 104.

[185] "Akaroa orchardgrass" Clatskanie Chief, Clatskanie, OR, April 3, 1953, 7.

[186] Viticulture Practices & Cover Crops, http://www.youtube.com/watch?v=hsHRpoReg-Q/ (September 9, 2012).

[187] Great Basin Seed, Pubescent Wheatgrass, http://greatbasinseeds.com/ecom-prodshow/Elytrigia_intermedia_trichophorum.html/ (August 14, 2012).

[188] Lehmann lovegrass (Eragrostis lehmanniana), http://www.saguaro-juniper.com/i_and_i/invasive_spp/lehmann_lovegrass.html/ (August 14, 2012).

[189] USDA, NRCS, Plant Materials Program Costs and Benefits.

[190] Release brochure, Mandan Canada wildrye (*Elymus canadensis*,) (USDA NRCS, Bismarck, ND, 2005).

[191] Release brochure, Nordan crested wheatgrass (Agropyron desertorum), (USDA NRCS, (Bismarck, ND, rev. 2011).

[192] Robert Newhall, Phil Rasmussen and Boyd Kitchen, "Introducing Big Sagbrush into a Crested Wheatgrass Monoculture", undated, https://extension.usa.edu/rangelands/files/uploads/Sagebrush%20intro%20Crested%20WG.pdf/ (September 9, 2012).

[193] Robert Newhall, Phil Rasmussen and Boyd Kitchen, Introducing Big Sagebrush into a Crested Wheatgrass Monoculture, undated, http://extension.usu.edu/rangelands/files/uploads/Sagebrush/Sagebrush%20into%20Crested%20WG.pdf/ (September 19, 2012).

[194] Sharp Seed Co., (Panicum virgatum) 'Blackwell', http://www.buffalobrandseed.com/index.cfm/fuseaction/plants.plantDetail/plant_id/100323/index.html/ (August 14, 2012).

[195] Sharp Bros. Seed Co. Healy, KS, http://www.sharpseed.com/pdf/sideoatsgrama.pdf/ (August 14, 2012).

[196] "Report of the Regional Nursery, Division Region 4, January 1, 1942 – January 1, 1944", Entry 254, RG 114.5.2, Natl. Archives, College Park, MD.

[197] J. R. Harlen, King Ranch bluestem, Okla. Agr. Exp. Sta., Forage Crops Leaflet, No. 11, (Okla. Agr. Exp. Sta., 1952).

[198] James E "Bud" Smith, 1960, loc. cit.

[199] Buffel Grass Seed Company, Inc. The grass is always greener on our side of the fence, Buffel Grass T-4464, http://www.buffelgrassseed.com/new_page_15.html/ (August 14, 2012).

[200] USDA, Forest Service, Environmental Assessment for Integrated Treatment of Noxious or Invasive Plants, http://a123.g.akamai.net/7/123/11558/abc123/forestservic.download.akamai.com/11558/www/nepa/4482_FSPLT2_118055.pdf/ (August 14, 2012).

[201] Diego Valdez-Zamudiol and D. Philip Guertin, Soil Erosion Studies in Buffelgrass Pasture, http://www.fs.fed.us/rm/pubs/rmrs_p013/rmrs_p013_282_286.pdf/ (August 14, 2012).

[202] Status of Introduced Plants in Southern Arizona Parks, http://www.buffelgrass.org/sites/default/files/pennfacts.pdf/ (August 14, 2012).

[203] USDA-NRCS Discontinued Conservation Plant Releases, http://plant-materials.nrcs.usda.gov/releases/discontinued.html (August 14, 2012).

[204] Glenn W. Burton, *A Search for the Origin of Pensacola Bahia grass*. USDA, ARS and The Univ. of GA College of Agric., Coastal Plain Station, Tifton GA. Journal Series Paper No. 19, 1967, 397.

[205] Personal conversations between author and Dr. Hawk.

[206] "Work project, A Section of Conservation Nurseries".

[207] H. H. Bennett note to Regional Nurserymen listing 'I would like to have' October 26, 1949, Entry 254, RG 114.5.2, Natl. Archives, College Park, MD.

[208] R. M. Ross Memo to H. H. Bennett containing "Main Work of the Soil Conservation Service for Fiscal Year 1949", October 24, 1949, Entry 254, RG 114.5.2, Natl. Archives, College Park, MD.

[209] R. M. Ross to, H. H. Bennett, Item 7 Undated, approximately Nov. 1949, Entry 254, RG 114.5.2, Natl. Archives, College Park, MD.

[210] *Conservation Plant Releases sorted by Scientific Name*, http://plant-materials.nrcs.usda.gov/releases/ releasesallbysci.html/ (November 15, 2011).

[211] M. M. Hoover, Memo A. E. Jones, January 2, 1946, Central Files, Box 295, Entry 1, RG 114, Natl. Archives, College Park, MD.

[212] USDA-NRCS, "Conservation Plant Releases," http://plant-materials.nrcs.usda.gov/releases/releasesallbysci.html (December 12, 2011).

[213] Franklin J. Crider memo to Regional Conservators, July 27, 1937, Nursery Division, Entry 215.0, Central Files, Natl. Archives, College Park, MD.

[214] F. J. Crider, March 25, 1936, loc. cit.

[215] James E "Bud" Smith , 1960, loc. cit.

[216] L. E. Wenger, et al, "Methods of harvesting, storing, and processing native grass seeds", Subcommittee reports of the Southern Great Plains Re-vegetation Committee, Natl. Academy of Sci., Nat. Res. Council, Annual Report 1963-64. (Nat. Res. Council, Washington, DC, 1964).

[217] D. A. Savage and James E. Smith, Jr., *Regrassing Methods for the Southern Great Plains*. USDA-ARS, Southern Great Plains Field Sta., (USDA, Woodward, Okla. 1944), 16.

[218] R. H. Stark, J. L. Toevs, and A. L. Hafenrichter. *Grasses and Cultural Methods of Reseeding Abandoned Farm Land in Southern Idaho*, ID Agr. Exp. Sta. Bul. 267, (ID Agr. Exp. Sta., Boise, ID, 1946).

[219] R.H. Stark, J. L. Toevs, and A. L. Hafenrichter. "Grasses and cultural methods of Great Basin Grasses", *Functional Ecology* 1, (1964) 139-143.

[220] C. F. Swingle, *Seed Propagation of Trees, Shrubs and Forbs for Conservation Planting*, (USDA, SCS, Washington, DC, 1939).

[221] "Region 5 Observational Nurseries Policy", Entry 254, RG 114.5.2, Natl. Archives, College Park, MD, undated.

[222] Franklin J. Crider Memo to Regional Conservators, July 27, 1937.

[223] *Improved Conservation Plant Materials*, 1999.

[224] M. M. Hoover Memo A. E. Jones, January 2, 1946, Central Files, Box 295, Entry 1, RG 114, Natl. Archives, College Park, MD.

[225] Seed Biology Program, Ohio State University, http://seedbiology.osu.edu/production.html/ (December 12, 2011).

[226] Soil Conservation and Domestic Allotment Act of 1936. Gale's Major Acts of Congress, http://www.answers.com/topic/soil-conservation-and-domestic-allotment-act#ixzz1Y1rV16vs (September 24, 2011).

[227] J. Douglas Helms, Technical Assistance – The Engine of Conservation, http://www.nrcs.usda.gov/wps/portal/nrcs/main/national/programs/technical (March 15, 2005).

[228] Douglas Helms, Readings in the History of the Soil Conservation Service, Coon Valley, WI, A Conservation Success Story, (USDA-SCS, Washington, DC, 1992) 51-53.

[229] James E "Bud" Smith, 1960.

[230] Vic Ruhland, "Through these eyes: The First 70 Years of Soil and Water Conservation in Minnesota", (USDA-NRCS, St. Paul, MN. 2005).

[231] *Conservation History, Oklahoma*, http://www.ok.gov/conservation/documents/Jan07nl-web.pdf (July 3, 2012).

[232] USDA, NRCS, Technical Assistance, http://www.nrcs.usda.gov/wps/portal/nrcs/main/national/programs/technical (November 5, 2011).

[233] John L. Schwendiman, *The First Fifty Years,* loc. cit.

[234] "Regional Grass School," SCS, Region XI, Pullman, WA June 6-10, 1938, Entry 254, RG 114.5.2, Natl. Archives, College Park, MD.

[235] "The Observational Cottonwood Study, 1936-1939", Entry 254, RG 114.5.2, Natl. Archives, College Park, MD.

[236] "Technical Reports, Region 2, 1941- 1946", Entry 254, RG 114.5.2. Natl. Archives, College Park, MD.

[237] "Annual Reports of Department of Agriculture, SCS, 1939", (USDA, Washington, DC., 1939), 38-39.

[238] "Annual Reports of Department of Agriculture, SCS, 1947", (USDA, Washington, DC, 1947), 44-45.

[239] "Annual Reports of Department of Agriculture", SCS, 1947.

[240] This toast was made available by Robert McLachlan, who had received it from John Schwendiman in 1984.

[241] "Soil Conservation Service Annual Administrative Report - FY. 1952, Nursery Division, Region I", August 1952, p 31, Entry 254, RG 114.5.2, Natl. Archives, College Park, MD.

[242] Soil Conservation Service Nurseries, "Stock Production - CY 1937", July 1938, Entry 254, RG 114.5.2, Natl. Archives, College Park, MD.

[243] "Annual Production Summaries, Plant Materials Produced and Shipped from SCS Nurseries", During Fiscal Years Ending June 31, 1948, 1949, 1950, 1951, Entry 254, RG 114.5.2, Natl. Archives, College Park, MD.

Chapter 5: TRANSITION PERIOD FROM OBSERVATIONAL NURSERIES TO PLANT MATERIALS CENTERS

[244] Douglas Helms, *Briefing Paper on the Plant Materials Centers*, (USDA,-NRCS, Washington, D.C., April 7, 2008).

[245] John T. Phelan and Donald L. Basinger, *Engineering in the Soil Conservation Service, History Notes No. 2*, Economics and Social Science Div., (USDA-SCS, Washington, DC, 1993).

[246] U.S. Congress, House, Testimony by Dr. Salter before the House Sub-Committee, April 1, 1953, Entry 254, RG 114.5.2, Natl. Archives, College Park, MD.

[247] Ibid.

[248] R. M . Ross to H. H. Bennett, October 24, 1949 "Main Work of the Soil Conservation Service for Fiscal Year 1949", Entry 254, RG 114.5.2, Natl. Archives, College Park, MD.

[249] Helms, April 7, 2008, loc. cit.

[250] National Agriculture Library Collection Number 350, Beltsville, MD.

[251] U.S. Congress, House, 1954a. Subcommittee of the Committee on Appropriations, Department of Agriculture Appropriations for 1955, 83rd Cong., 2nd session, part 3, 1328.

[252] Agricultural Appropriations Bill, 1954, "Report No. 382", Entry 254, RG 114.5.2, Natl. Archives, College Park, MD.

[253] J. W. Christ, memo to Dr. Robert Salter, Washington, D.C., April 17, 1953, Entry 254, RG 114.5.2 Natl. Archives, College Park, MD.

[254] Agricultural Appropriations Bill, 1954, "Report No. 382", Entry 254, RG 114.5.2, Natl. Archives, College Park, MD.

[255] Helms, April 7, 2008, loc. cit.

[256] Throughout the transition period of 1953-54, memorandums, testimony, etc. were inconsistent in identifying the number of operating nurseries. Correct numbers appear to be 1948 = 27, 1949 = 26 (Astoria, OR closed), 1950 until April 1, 1951 = 26, May 1, 1951 = 24 (Minden, LA and Woodward, OK closed or were removed from SCS listings). These number of nurseries was taken from 1948 "Plant Materials Produced and Shipped listing, 1949", "Use of Land SCS Nurseries; 1950", "Plant Materials Produced and Shipped", April 1, 1951, "Estimate of Plants and Trees Shipped from SCS Nurseries;" May 1, 1951, all in Entry 254, RG 114.5.2.0, Natl. Archives, College Park, MD.

[257] "Nursery Division Report for 1952", Entry 254, RG 114.5.2, Natl. Archives, College Park, MD.

[258] F. G. Renner memo to A.D. Stoesz, September 3, 1953, Entry 254, RG 114.5.2, , Natl. Archives, College Park, MD.

[259] A. M. Limburg, "Current Status of SCS Nurseries, September 1, 1954", Entry 254, RG 114.5.2, Natl. Archives, College Park, MD.

[260] U.S., Congress, Senate, Subcommittee of the Committee on Appropriations, Agricultural Appropriations for 1955, 83rd Cong., 2nd session, 1954, 649.

[261] H. R. Wells letter to J. H. Christ, October 26, 1952, Entry 254, RG 114.5.2, Natl. Archives, College Park, MD.

[262] J. H. Christ memo to Robert M. Salter, October 26, 1953, Entry 254, RG 114.5.2, Natl. Archives, College Park, MD.

[263] U.S. Congress.

[264] A. M. Limburg.

[265] John D. Snow, Chairman Aberdeen, ID Chamber of Commerce to D.A. Williams, December 7, 1953 Entry 254, RG 114.5.2, Natl. Archives, College Park, MD.

[266] Helms, April 7, 2008.

[267] U.S. Congress.

[268] Helms, April 7, 2008.

[269] William Walton Stevens, History of Soil and Water Conservation in North Carolina, (USDA-NRCS, Raleigh, NC., 1999).

[270] Ernest McPharron personal conversations with author, 1961-1965 about visits to Winona, MN and La Crosse, WI.

[271] A. H. Moseman memo to R. M. Salter, June 10, 1953, Entry 254, RG 114.5.2, Natl. Archives, College Park, MD.

[272] L. B. Scott, Regional Nurseryman to Karl Graetz, Sandy Level, VA, Sept. 8, 1953, Entry 254, RG 114.5.2, Natl. Archives, College Park, MD.

[273] "Statement of Important Developments in Nurseries, Southwest Region", July 1, 1952 to June 30, 1953", July 9, 1953, Albuquerque, NM, Entry 254, RG 114.5.2, Natl. Archives, College Park, MD.

[274] J. H. Christ, memo to Robert M. Salter.

[275] Clyde L. Patton, Wildlife Resource Commission, NC, exchange of letters with R. Y. Bailey, SCS Regional Office, Spartanburg, SC, Nov. 6 and Nov. 16, 1993, Entry 254, RG 114.5.2, Natl. Archives, College Park, MD.

[276] Robert M. Salter memo to Secretary of Agriculture after August 2, 1953, Entry 254, RG 114.5.2, Natl. Archives, College Park, MD.

[277] James G. Maddox, The Bankhead-Jones Farm Tenant Act, Law and Contemporary Problems Vol. 4, No. 4, Farm Tenancy (Oct., 1937), 434-455.

[278] Federal Register, Volume 19, January 28, 1954, 467.

[279] "Status of Nurseries as of February 1, 1955", loc. cit.

[280] Bismarck, ND Plant Materials Center Field Day, June 17, 2004, (USDA-NRCS, 2004).

[281] H. R. Wells letter to J. H. Christ, loc. cit.

[282] "Status of Nurseries as of February 1, 1955", Entry 254, RG 114.5.2 Natl. Archives, College Park, MD.

[283] W. C. Young memo A.D. Stoesz, July 22, 1954, Entry 254, RG 114.5.2, Natl. Archives, College Park, MD.

[284] D. A. Williams Memorandum to E. L. Peterson, July 16 1956, "Soil Conservation Service Plant Materials Center (Nurseries)", Entry 254, RG 114.5.2, Natl. Archives, College Park, MD.

[285] F. C. Crider, "Projecting Nursery Observational Work" March 2, 1939, Entry 254, RG 114.5.2, Natl. Archives, College Park, MD.

[286] Dr. Salter testimony before the House Sub-Committee, April 1, 1953, Entry 254, RG 114.5.2.

[287] Memorandum from W.C. Young to Dr. A.D. Stoesz, July 2, 1954, Box 5, Entry 254, RG 114.5.2.

[288] Douglas Helms, *He Loved to Carry the Message: The Collected Writing of Douglas Helms*, 1967-2010, Edited by Sam Stalcup (Published by Lulu.com, January 2012), 639-648.

[289] Ibid. 77.

[290] Hugh Hammond Bennett, "They've Cut the Heart Out of Soil Conservation", *The Country Gentleman*, January 1955.

[291] USDA-SCS, Administrator's Memo. SCS, "Policies, Objectives, and Functions I Plant Materials", Draft 3-14-1956, Washington, D.C., Entry 254, RG 114.5.2, Natl. Archives, College Park, MD.

[292] John T. Phelan and Donald L. Basinger. *Engineering in the Soil Conservation Service*. History Notes No. 2, Economics and Social Science Div., (USDA-SCS, Washington, DC, 1993).

[293] B. R. Bertramson, *History of Agronomy and Soils*, WSU, Pullman, WA. 1984,http://css.wsu.edu/overview/history/State_History/V_Research--2.2_Forage.pdf/ (January 13, 2011).

[294] "Nursery Personnel Likely to become Surplus", July 1, 1953, Entry 254, RG 114.5.2, Natl. Archives, College Park, MD.

[295] T. S. Buie, memo to SCS Chief Robert M. Salter, July 24, 1953, Entry 254, RG 114.5.2, Natl. Archives, College Park, MD.

[296] Robert Donahue was a personnel clerk at the Big Flats nursery and advanced to Assistant Administrative Officer in the NY SCS state office, and remained a friend of the new PMC.

[297] "Nursery Observational Program Personnel. March 1, 1949, Nursery Division", Entry 254, RG 114.5.2, Natl. Archives, College Park, MD.

[298] Personal papers of H. Wayne Everett, Burleson, TX.

[299] J. W. Christ, memo to Dr. Robert Salter, Washington, D.C., April 17, 1953, Entry 254, RG 114.5.2 Natl. Archives, College Park, MD.

[300] John L. Schwendiman, *The First Fifty Years, The Plant Materials Center, Pullman, W*A. (USDA-SCS, Pullman, WA, 1987).

[301] See Appendix 2 for details on the publications.

[302] James E "Bud" Smith, 1960, loc. cit.

[303] "Annual Administrative Report, Fiscal Year 1953" SCS, San Antonio, TX, Box 13, Entry 254, RG 114.2, Natl. Archives, College Park, MD, pp. 12, 13.6.

[304] PLANTS Database, http: //plants.usda.gov/java/ (April 12, 2010).

[305] James E. "Bud" Smith, 1960, loc. cit.

[306] Ibid.

[307] *Elsberry Plant Materials Center 2005 ATR*, http://plant-materials.nrcs.usda.gov/mopmc/index.html/ (March 12, 2012).

[308] R. S. MacLauchlan, SCS, "The Adaptation, Cultural and Management Requirements of Cascade Lotus", *Northwest Science*, (1957), No. 31, 170.

[309] "Annual Report, Nursery Division, Fiscal year 1953", Entry 254, RG 114.5.2, Natl. Archives, College Park, MD.

[310] D. A. Williams, memo to E. L. Peterson, July 16, 1956, Entry 254, RG 114.5.2, Natl. Archives, College Park, MD.

[311] USDA-SCS, Administrator's Memo, SCS, "Policies, Objectives, and Functions - Plant Materials", Draft 3-14-1956, Washington, DC, Entry 254, RG 114.5.2, Natl. Archives, College Park, MD.

[312] Field Memorandum #SCN-4, loc. cit.

[313] B. R. Bertramson, History of Agronomy and Soils, WSU, Pullman, WA. 1984, http://css.wsu.edu/overview/history/State_History/V_Research--2.2_Forage.pdf/ (January 13, 2011).

[314] "Status of Nurseries as of February 1, 1955", loc. cit.

[315] A. M. Limburg, "Current Status of SCS Nurseries, September 1, 1954", Entry 254, RG 114.5.2, Natl. Archives, College Park, MD.

[316] "Estimated Distribution of 1954 Funds for Nursery Work", July 31, 1953, Natl. Archives, College Park, MD.

[317] "Summary of Nursery Operations", Entry 254, RG 114.5.2, Natl. Archives, College Park, MD.

[318] "Status of Nurseries as of February 1, 1955", loc. cit.

[319] F. G. Renner memo to A.D. Stoesz, September 3, 1953, Entry 254, RG 114.5.2, Natl. Archives, College Park, MD.

[320] D. A. Williams, memo to E. L. Peterson.

[321] Edward H. Graham memo to J.C. Dykes, March 31, 1954, Entry 254, RG 114.5.2, Natl. Archives, College Park, MD.

[322] D. A. Williams memo H. G. Bobst, April 3, 1954, Entry 254, RG 114.5.2, Natl. Archives, College Park, MD.

[323] C. Dorney memo to Edward H. Graham, April 29, 1959, 1954, Box 23, Entry 254, RG 114.5.2, Natl. Archives, College Park, MD.

[324] "Status of Nurseries as of February 1, 1955", loc. cit.

[325] *Notice Release of Brooksville 68 Germplasm Perennial Peanut Tested Class of Natural Germplasm*, http://www.plant-materials.nrcs.usda.gov/pubs/flpmcrnargl18br68.pdf/ (September 29, 2012).

[326] "Status of Nurseries as of February 1, 1955", loc. cit.

[327] Ibid.

[328] D. A. Williams, memo to J. H. Christ, Honolulu, HI, January 4, 1957, Entry 254, RG 114.5.2, Natl. Archives, College Park, MD.

[329] "Estimated Distribution of 1954"

[330] Nursery Division Report for 1952, Entry 254, RG 114.5.2, Natl. Archives, College Park, MD.

[331] Ibid.

[332] "Summary of Nursery Operations".

[333] P. C. McGrew, memo A. L. Hafenrichter, December 31, 1959, Entry 254, RG 114.5.2, Natl. Archives, College Park, MD.

[334] Hearne Seeds, *Cover Crops & Erosion Control Mixes, Lana Vetch Wollypod*, http://www.hearneseed.com/product-info.php?Lana_Vetch-pid195.html/ (October 14, 2012).

[335] Robert S. MacLauchlan, Harold W. Miller and Oswald K. Hoglund 1970." Lana Vetch for Medusahead Control", J. of Rn. Mgt. (1970), 23, No 5, pp. 351-353.

[336] Clarence U. Finch and W. Curtis Sharp, *Cover Crops in California Orchards and Vineyards*. (USDA-SCS, Davis, CA, 1981).

[337] James E "Bud" Smith, 1960, loc. cit.

[338] "The Period of Reconstruction," A. L. Hafenrichter, 1962, Entry 254, RG 114.5.2, Natl. Archives, College Park. MD.

[339] "National PMC Annual Report, 1959," Entry 254, RG 114.5.2, Natl. Archives, College Park. MD.

[340] Ibid.

[341] Memo from A. D Stoesz to Washington-Field PM Tech. Aug. 3, 1959, Entry 254, RG 114.5.2, Natl. Archives, College Park. MD.

[342] Edward Graham , "Report of Plant Technology Division conference of Jan. 19-23", Shreveport, LA, Entry 254, RG 114.5.2, Natl. Archives, College Park. MD.

[343] This situation changed slowly. In 1984 a regional PM Specialist was given a toy cement truck for pointing out a at training design session that the engineers had twice as much time on the regional training agenda for a pouring concrete class than did all plant science for establishing protective vegetation.

[344] W.C. Young , memo to Dr. A.D. Stoesz, October 19, 1959, Entry 254, RG 114.5.2, Natl. Archives, College Park, MD.

[345] A. D. Stoesz, memo to W. C. Young, October 12, 1959, Entry 254, RG 114.5.2, Natl. Archives, College Park, MD.

[346] D. A. Williams draft memo to W. B. Davey, Nov. 12, 1959, Entry 254, RG 114.5.2, Natl. Archives, College Park, MD.

Chapter 6: Plant Materials Program, 1960 - 1993

[347] "Plant Materials: Table 1 – Plant Materials Centers, budget breakdown by PMC", 1959, 1960, Entry 254, RG 114.5.2, Natl. Archives, College Park, MD.

[348] Ibid.

[349] USDA, NRCS, *Plant Materials Program Costs and Benefits*, loc. cit.

[350] D. A. Williams, memo to Frank J. Welch, March 7, 1961, Box 24, Entry 254, RG 114.5.2, Natl. Archives, College Park, MD.

[351] F. J. Hopkins, memo to D.A. Williams, Report of Committee, January 9, 1961, Box 24, Entry 254, RG 114.5.2.

[352] In the early 1970s an author moved to a western PM Specialist position and was surprised to see the size of the inventories of several PMCs of released plants; far in excess of any rational evaluation needs. This was confirmed somewhat in a conversation with Robert S. MacLauchlan, an SCS employee who worked at and with PMCs in the west from 1953 until 1974.

[353] Donald S. Douglass, memo to Dr. A.D. Stoesz, February 7, 1961, Entry 254, RG 114.5.2, Natl. Archives, College Park, MD.

[354] Dr. Abraham Stoesz, "Development and Major Accomplishments During the Past Decade, 1963", Entry 254, RG 114.5.2, Natl. Archives, College Park, MD.

[355] Hugh Hammond Bennett, "They've Cut the Heart Out of Soil Conservation", loc. cit.

[356] Donald S. Douglas, untitled presentation, April 17, 1961. Entry 254, RG 114.5.2, Natl. Archives, College Park, MD.

[357] F. J. Crider, "Memorandum to Regional Conservationists and Nurserymen," March 25, 1936, loc. cit.

[358] D. A. Williams, memo to F. C. Edminster, August 23, 1961, Entry 254, RG 114.5.2, Natl. Archives, College Park, MD.

[359] D. M. Whitt, memo to Washington Field Plant Tech., October 23, 1963, Entry 254, RG 114.5.2 Natl. Archives, College Park, MD.

[360] D. S. Douglas, memo to A. D. Stoesz, December 30, 1963, Entry 254, RG 114.5.2, Natl. Archives, College Park, MD.

[361] D. S. Douglas, memo to D. M. Whitt, November 7, 1963, Entry 254, RG 114.5.2, Natl. Archives, College Park, MD.

[362] D. S. Douglas, memo to A. D. Stoesz, December 30, 1963, loc. cit.

[363] Douglas Helms, Inventory of the Records of the NRCS, RG-114, "Introduction and Administrative History of the Natural Resources Conservation Service", Complied by Renée M. Jaussaud, unpublished.

[364] Dr. Abraham Stoesz, "Development and Major Accomplishments During the Past Decade, 1963", loc. cit..

[365] USDA-SCS, The Plant Materials Program, *Finding Plant Solutions for Conservation Needs*, http://workflow.den.nps.gov/8_Transportation/March2009wkshp/March17_Tuesday/3.17WorkingwithPlantMaterialCenters.pdf/ (November 9, 2011).

[366] V. B. Hawk, "Registration of Emerald Crownvetch", Crop Science, (May, 1965), 5 No. 3, p. 290-290.

[367] USDA, NRCS, *Plant Materials Program Costs and Benefits*, loc. cit.

[368] "Annual Technical Report, PMC Western States," Entry 254, RG 114.5.2, Natl. Archives, College Park, MD.

[369] "Conservationist Killed" Yuma Dailey Sun, Monday, November 23.1964, p. 2, http://newspaperarchive.com/yuma-daily-sun/1964-11-23/page 2/ (November 5, 2012).

[370] John L. Schwendiman, *The First Fifty Years*, loc. cit.

[371] These observations are based on knowing several of the "Hafenrichter boys" and conversations with them about others.

[372] "Annual Plant Materials Progress Report", PMC, USDA, SCS, 1965, Entry 254, RG 114.5.2, Natl. Archives, College Park, MD.

[373] Green Acres Program, NJ Dept. Env. Prot., http://www.nj.gov/dep/greenacres/bondact.html/ (June 24, 2012).

[374] D. S. Douglas, memo to A.D. Stoesz attachment contained statement on page 4, 12/30/1963, Entry 254, RG 114.5.2, Natl. Archives, College Park, MD.

[375] D. S. Douglas, "Annual Report FY 1966, Plant Materials in SCS", Washington, DC, Entry 254, RG 114.5.2, Natl. Archives, College Park, MD.

[376] W. W. Steiner, memo to Donald S. Douglas, Entry 254, RG 114.5.2, Natl. Archives, College Park, MD.

[377] Assoc. of Retired Conservation Service Employees, http://www.arscse.org/qannounC.html/ (November 11, 2012).

[378] Donald Douglas, based on a statement he made in the interview with Douglas Helms that John Schwendiman had retired a couple years ago.

[379] USDA, NRCS, *Plant Materials Program Costs and Benefits*, loc. cit.

[380] Honey locust, *Gleditsia triacanthos L.*, http://www.na.fs.fed.us/pubs/silvics_manual/volume_2/gleditsia/triacanthos.html/ (November 15, 2012), 6.

[381] D. S. Douglas, "Annual Report FY 1966".

[382] Northern Latitude PMC web site, http://plants.alaska.gov/. (November 12, 2012).

[383] Hill Culture Research Section and the Hill Culture Division, Records of the Conservation Experiment Stations Division, RG 114.4.2, Natl. Archives, College Park, MD.

[384] Theodore C Scheffer and Henry Hopp, *Decay Resistance of Black Locust*, Tech. Bul. 984 (GPO, Washington DC, 1949).

[385] Edward H. Wollerman, "Strains of Black Locust Resistant to Borer", (USDA-FS, Columbus, OH August, 1955).

[386] Steiner Group Black Locusts 'Appalachia' 'Allegheny' 'Algonquin', (USDA-NRCS, Washington, DC, 2007).

[387] *Black Locust (Pseudoacacia)*, http://www.gardenguides.com/taxonomy/black-locust-robinia-pseudoacacia/ (November 14, 2012).

[388] Much of the information dealing with the Plant Materials Program from 1974 through 1984 was supplied by Robert S. MacLauchlin, who was the National Plant Materials Specialist during that period.

[389] Greensheets Report – Plant Materials Program, File code 190, November 8, 2002, NRCS, Washington, DC.

[390] Energy Research Information System quarterly report, http://archive.org/details/energyresearchin002001surfrich/ (January 14, 2013).

[391] P. L. 99-198, The Food Security Act of 1985

[392] USDA, Farm Service Agency, Conservation Programs, http://www.fsa.usda.gov/FSA/webapp?area=home&subject=copr&topic=crp-st/ (May 23, 2013).

[393] Prior to 1994 a germplasm release meant the PMC was releasing germplasm only for use by others in development work.

[394] Parts of the Plant Materials History between 1985 and 1993 were provided by W. Curtis Sharp who was the National Plant Materials Program Leader for that period.

[395] Booneville PMC Booneville, AR, http://plant-materials.nrcs.usda.gov/arpmc/ (June 27, 2011).

[396] *Golden Meadow Annual Tech. Report, 2001*, http: //www.plant-materials.nrcs.usda.gov/pubs/lapmctr11233.pdf/ (July 12, 2010).

[397] Inflation Calculator, Bureau of Labor Statistics, *CPI Inflation Calculator*, http: //www.bls.gov/data/inflation_calculator.html/ (November 17, 2012).

[398] Houston Chronicle, Sat. March 3, 1992, Sec. A, p. 32

[399] Tyrus R. Timm Honor Registry, Mack Gray, http: //tyrustimmregistry.org/?q=content/mack-gray/ (November 11, 2012).

[400] Dale Darris, personal letter, January 29, 2013.

[401] *Plant Science Quality Improvement Team*, (NRCS, Washington, DC, 1996).

[402] Ibid.

[403] Gu Anlin and Wang Zongli, Atlas of Rangeland Plants in Northern China, China Agri. and Technology Press, 2009.

[404] Michael Van Valkenburgh, Stephen Noone, Ted Zoli and Don Lavender, *Black Locust Lumber: A Sustainable Alternative*, http://www.asla.org/uploadedFiles/CMS/Business_Quarterly/ASLA_Black_Locust_Lumber_Presentation.pdf/ (December 13, 2012).

[405] USDA-SCS, *Plant Materials Program Strategic Plan, February 1992* (NRCS, Washington, DC, 1992), 1-11.

[406] USDA, Agriculture Marketing Service, http://www.ams.usda.gov/AMSv1.0/getfile?dDocName=STELDEV3002796/ (December 12, 2012).

Chapter 7: Years of Change 1994 – 2010

[407] *Federal Personnel Handbook*, http://www.federalhandbooks.com/fedbooks/Personnel.pdf/ (December 13, 2012).

[408] When Hassell and Donald Hamer made their trip to Hungary in 1989, Peter Smith was there also, as an economic and resource team member, along with his wife. Normally, the teams went their separate ways but on one occasion both teams joined together for a mining reclamation meeting. Mining company executives presented an overview orientation and then all were to travel to a mine. Wendell and Don, the visiting revegetation specialist, were escorted to the mine via limousine with company officials. The rest of the entourage, including the Smith's, crowded into a van. Whether it was this incident or others, Smith shared some observations in writing with his supervisor, James Newman, upon his return. From Smith's point of view Hassell and Hamer were poor representatives of their country, primarily in their demeanor and personal conduct. Newman conducted some inquiries about the character and typical conduct of Hassell and Hamer and concluded it was a non issue. Did this encounter impact the selection of the new National Leader of the Plant Materials Program? Did this influence the decision to go outside the agency for the new National Leader while an excellent one was available from within? The decision certainly impacted the PM Program.

[409] The December 1996 Plant Science OIT Final Report list Dr. White's location as Kansas.

[410] *Plant Science Quality Improvement Team*, loc. cit.

[411] Quoting from *The First Fifty Years* by John Schwendiman "Virgil B. Hawk, graduate student in WSU agronomy department, made the first plantings on the Pullman nursery in 1934. He was appointed manager of the outlying nursery unit...He made the first grass-legume alternate row plantings and originated the concept of field plantings."

[412] Delaware State Univ. wrote a Status Report on July 30, 2001 on the herbarium progress.

[413] *Conservation Technical Assistance Program Funds – Fiscal Year 2004*, http://www.nrcs.usda.gov/wps/portal/nrcs/detail/national/programs/technical/?cid=nrcs143_008250/.

[414] *Conservation Technical Assistance Program Funds – Fiscal Year 2010*, http://www.nrcs.usda.gov/wps/portal/nrcs/detail/national/programs/technical/cta/?cid=stelprdb1044456/.

[415] Supplied by National PM Specialist.

[416] *Consumer Price Index*, http://www.bls.gov/cpi/

[417] Plant Materials Program Task Force Report, February 2000 (Revised May 2000).

[418] *National Plant Materials Program Manual*, 1994, loc. cit.

[419] USDA, NRCS, *Plant Materials Program Costs and Benefits*, loc. cit.

[420] *The Lawn Place*, http://thelawnplace.com/files/bahia1.html/ (February 5, 2012).

[421] Email from John Englert, July 20, 2013.

[422] Resource Concepts, Inc., "NRCS Plant Materials Program Public Awareness Project Report" (Carson City, NV: December 2001).

[423] USDA, NRCS, Publications - *Aberdeen Plant Materials Center*, http://plant-materials.nrcs.usda.gov/idpmc/publications.html/ (December 10, 2012).

[424] Robert Escheman, Agency Profile, USDA/NRCS, Plant Materials Program, http://www.docstoc.com/docs/1100028/Agency-Profile-USDA-NRCS-Plant-Materials-Program/ (February 21, 2013).

[425] Robert Costanza, Ralph d'Arge, R.de Groot, S. Farber, M. Grasso, B. Hannon, K. Limburg, S. Naeem, R. V. O'Neill, J. Paruelo, R. G. Raskins, P. Sutton and Marjan van den Belt, "The value of the world's ecosystem services and natural capital", *Nature*, (1997), 387: 253-260.

[426] USDA, NRCS, *Plant Materials Program Costs and Benefits*.

[427] Robert Costanza, loc. cit.

[428]

[429] USDA, NRCS, Plant Materials Centers, (Washington, DC, April 2007) 55.

[430] American Customer Satisfaction Index, http://www.theacsi.org/ (November 15, 2011).

[431] John Englert, personal letter, January 11, 2013.

[432] *Reassessment of the NRCS Plant Materials Program*, USDA, NRCS, September 18, 2009.

Chapter 8: Overview Of Each Plant Materials Center

[433] USDA, NRCS, *Plant Materials Program Costs and Benefits 1935 – 2005*, loc. cit.

[434] USDA, NRCS, *Discontinued Conservation Plant Releases*, http://plant-materials.nrcs.usda.gov/releases/discontinued.html/ (August 14, 2012).

[435] NRCS Plant Materials Centers, http://www.nrcs.usda.gov/wps/portal/nrcs/main/national/plantsanimals/plants/centers (February 5, 2011).

[436] Northern Latitude PMC web site, http://plants.alaska.gov/ (November 12, 2012).

[437] NRCS budget data for the Plant Materials Program, (NRCS, Washington, DC).

[438] Climate Regions of Alaska, http://climate.gi.alaska.edu/ClimTrends/30year/regions1.html/ (November 12, 2012).

[439] Booneville PMC Booneville, AR, http://plant-materials.nrcs.usda.gov/arpmc/ (November 12, 2012).

[440] L. Tharel, Litter, *Dry-Matter Production of Eight Grass Species with Three Levels of Poultry Litter*, Booneville PMC Research, (Booneville AR, 2007), 6.

[441] H. Allen Tolbert, Thomas J. Gerik, Wyatte L. Harman, Jimmy R. Williams and Melanie Magre, *EPIC Evaluation of the Impact of Poultry Litter Application Timing on Nutrient Losses,* http://digitalcommons.unl.edu/usdaarsfacpub/598/ (November 13, 2011).

[442] Dedication of the Tucson, AZ Plant Materials Center Building. 2000, http://www.nrcs.usda.gov/news/thisweek/2000/001110.html#anchor106943/ (June 11, 2010).

[443] "Annual Administrative Reports, Regions 1-9, 1939-40", Entry 254, RG 114.5.2, Natl. Archives, College Park, MD.

[444] Robert L. Geiger, Jr., *A Chronological History of the Soil Conservation Service and Related Events*, (USDA-SCS, Washington, DC, 1955).

[445] F. J. Hopkins, memo to A. E. Jones, August 10, 1948, Entry 254, RG 114.5.2, Natl. Archives, College Park, MD.

[446] Geiger, *A Chronological History of the Soil Conservation Service and Related Events*, loc. cit., 2.

[447] Temper Archaeological Research Services, Inc., http://lcweb2.loc.gov/pnp/habshaer/az/az0200/az0286/data/az0286data.pdf/ (August 9, 2010).

[448] F. J. Crider, *Three introduced lovegrasses for soil conservation*, USDA Circular No. 730, (GPO, 1945).

[449] Darwin Anderson and A. R. Swanson, Machinery for Seedbed Preparation and Seeding on Southwestern Ranges, *J. Rn. Mgt.*, (April, 1949), 2, No. 2 , 64-66.

[450] "Annual Reports of Department of Agriculture", SCS, 1949, (GPO, Washington, DC, 1949), 42-43.

[451] J. R. Carlson, W.C. Sharp, "Germination of high elevation manzanitas", *Tree Planters' Notes* (1975), 26(3), 10–11, 25.

[452] Gary L. Noller, and Marti Walsh, *Maybell Antelope Bitterbrush*, UCEPC, (USDA-NRCS, Meeker, CO, 2006).

[453] "UCEPC Progress Report of Activities", (USDA, NRCS, Meeker, CO, 2000).

[454] Robert Hammon and Gary L. Noller, 2004, *Fate of Fall-Planted Bitterbrush Seed at Maybell Colorado*, USDA, NRCS, Meeker, CO, http://www.plant- materials.nrcs.usda.gov/pubs/compcpo6393.pdf/ (August 9, 2010).

[455] S. Pfaff, M. A. Gonter, and C. Maura, *Florida Native Seed Production Manual*, (USDA-SCS, Brooksville, FL, 2002), 65 p.

[456] "Annual Administrative Reports, Regions 1-9, 1939-40", RG 114.5.2, Entry 254, Natl. Archives, College Park, MD.

[457] "Observational Planting, General Information, 1937", RG-114, Entry 254, Natl. Archives, College Park, MD.

[458] U.S. Congress, House, 1954a. Subcommittee of the Committee on Appropriations, *Department of Agriculture Appropriations for 1955*, 83rd Cong., 2nd session, pt 3, p. 1328.

[459] "Nursery Division Region 1, 1947-53", RG 114, Entry 254, Natl. Archives, College Park, MD.

[460] Mike Owsley and Jim Latham, *Georgia Native Plant Material Guide for Longleaf Pine Understory*, (USDA, NRCS, Athens, GA, July 2007).

[461] Donald Surrency, and Mike Owsley, *Plant Materials Program Assisting Small Farmers,* (USDA, NRCS, Athens, GA, 2006), 79 p.

[462] Glenn Sakamoto, *Progress Report on the Use of Piligrass (Heteropogon contortus) Hay Bales for the Island of Kaho`olawe's Highly Erodible Sites*, http://www.plant-materials.nrcs.usda.gov/pubs/hipmcpr8078.pdf/ (June 15, 2009).

[463] David Duvauchelle, Piligrass: Mulching Rates with Seeded Hay-Bale, Ho'olehua, HI, (USDA, NRCS, 2002).

[464] Sharon L. Norris, *History of the Aberdeen Plant Materials Center*, (USDA, SCS, Boise, ID, 1989).

[465] Charles Bair and Derek J. Tilley, *The Jet Harvester, A Shop Built Tool for Harvesting Forb and Shrub Seed*, ftp://ftp-fc.sc.egov.usda.gov/ID/programs/technotes/tn55_jet_harvester.pdf/ (May 24, 2010).

[466] Derek J. Tilley, Dan Ogle and Brent Cornforth, *Quick Methods to Estimate Seed Quality*, ftp://ftp-c.sc.egov.usda.gov/ID/programs/technotes/tn35_estimating_seed_quality_1110.pdf/ (June 6, 2012).

[467] B. Hamaker, *Whistler Center for Carbohydrate Research*, Dept. of Food Science, (Purdue Univ., 2010).

[468] D. Ogle and B Cornforth, *A quick method to estimate germination percentages for seed species*, PM Tech. Note No. 35, (USDA, NRCS. Boise, ID, 2000), 3.

[469] Soil Conservation Service Notes, *Lawrence Daily Journal - World of Lawrence, KS*, May 6, 1937, http://news.google.com/newspapers?nid=2199&dat=19370506&id=7XZdAAAAIBAJ&sjid=WlwNAAAAIBAJ&pg=5459,1260032/ (April 9, 2011).

[470] Donald R. Cornelius and Newell C. Melcher, "Estimating the Yield of Blue Grama Seed," *KS Acad. Of Sci.*, (1942), 45.

[471] F.C. Gates, *Grasses in Kansas* (Kansas State Board of Agr., 1936).

[472] Warren Whitman, 1941. *Grasses of North Dakota*, Bul. 300 (ND Agr. Exp. St., 1941).

[473] M. M. Hoover, J. E. Smith, Jr., A. E. Ferber, and D. R. Cornelius, *Seed for regressing Great Plains areas*, Farmers Bulletin (USDA, Washington, DC, 1947).

[474] A. L. Hafenrichter, A.D. Stoesz, *Domesticated Grasses in Conservation*. (USDA Yearbook, 1948), 354-356.

[475] H. B. Cooper, James E. Smith, Jr. and M. D. Atkins, *Producing and harvesting grass seed in the Great Plains*, Farmers Bul. 2112. (USDA, Washington, DC, 1957), 30 p.

[476] M. D. Atkins and James E. Smith, Jr., *Grass Seed Production and Harvest in the Great Plains,* Farmers Bul. 2226, (USDA, Washington, DC, 1967), 30 p.

[477] S. Ray Smith Jr. and R. D. B. Whalley, "Model for Expanded Use of Native Grasses", *Native Plants J,* (Spring 2002), 3, no. 1, 38-49.

[478] USDA, NRCS, *Plants for Gulf of Mexico Coastal Restoration*, http://www.la.nrcs.usda.gov/technical/PM/golden_meadow.html/ (May 3, 2011).

[479] Soil and Water Conservation Research in the Northeastern States, prepared by Clarence S. Britt, Soil Scientist, Soil and Water Conservation Research Division, ARS, Beltsville, MD, 1965.

[480] "Annual Administrative Reports, Regions 1-9, 1939-40", Entry 254, RG 114.5.2, Natl. Archives, College Park, MD.

[481] "Plant Materials Produced and Shipped from the SCS Nurseries", 1949-1950, RG 114, Entry 254, RG 114.5.2, Natl. Archives, College Park, MD.

[482] "Annual Reports, Nursery Division, 1950", Entry 254, RG 114.5.2, Natl. Archives, College Park, MD.

[483] National Plant Germplasm System, USDA, ARS, http://www.ars-grin.gov/npgs/ (June 30, 2009).

[484] Franklin J. Crider, *Root growth stoppage resulting from defoliation of grass*, Tech. Bul. 1102, (GPO, Washington, DC, 1955).

[485] Thomas Cogger, Vijai Pandian and David Burgdorf, *Community Garden Guide Vegetable Garden Planning and Development*, http://www.plant-materials.nrcs.usda.gov/pubs/mipmcot9407.pdf/ (June 19, 2009).

[486] *Nurseries*, File 215.0, General, Central Files, October 1935-March 1936, Records of the NRCS, Record Group 114, Natl. Archives at College Park, MD.

[487] *Integrated Roadside Vegetative Management*, http: //www.uni.edu/irvm/ (January 29, 2013).

[488] *Iowa Ecotype Project*, http://www.uni.edu/ecotype/ (January 29, 2013).

[489] Jerry Kaiser and Steve Bruckerhoff, *Switchgrass for Biomass Production by Variety Selection and Establishment Methods for Missouri, Illinois, and Iowa*, TN MO-372009, (USDA- NRCS, Columbia, MO, 2009).

[490] "Annual Administrative Reports, Regions 1-7, 1936-37", Entry 254, RG 114.5.2, Natl. Archives, College Park, MD.

[491] J. Grabowski, *Seed Propagation Techniques for Wetland Plants*, USDA, Jamie L. Whitten PMC, Coffeeville, MS (USDA, SCS, Jackson, MS, 1997).

[492] E. W. Garbisch, and S. McIninch, "Seed information for wetland plant species of the northeast United States", *Restor. And Manage Notes*, (1992) 10(1), 85-86.

[493] R.E. Hybner, M. Graham, M. Majerus and S. Majerus, *Comparative Evaluation of Grasses, Forbs, and Seed Mixtures from "Local" versus "Non-Local" Origins at Stucky Ridge*, Anaconda, MT. (Billings Land Reclamation Symposium, Lexington, KY, 2009), 1 p.

[494] Green Acres Program, NJ Dept. Env. Prot., http://www.nj.gov/dep/greenacres/bondact.html/ (June 24, 2012).

[495] W. C. Sharp and Joseph H. Vaden, "Ten-year report on sloping techniques used to stabilize eroding tidal bank", Shore and Beach, (April 1970), 38, 31-35.

[496] W. Curtis Sharp, Cluster R. Belcher and John Oyler, *Vegetation for Tidal Stabilization, In the Mid-Atlantic States*, (USDA, SCS, 1981), 19.

[497] *The New York Standards and Specifications for vegetating sand dunes and tidal banks*, http://www.dec.ny.gov/docs/water_pdf/sec3part4.pdf/ (February 14, 2010).

[498] D. A. Williams, memo to E. L. Peterson, July 16, 1956, Entry 254, RG 114.5.2, Natl. Archives, College Park, MD.

[499] "Annual Administrative Reports, Regions 1-9, 1939-40", Entry 254, RG 114.5.2, Natl. Archives, College Park, MD.

[500] David Dreesen, "Tumbling for Seed Cleaning and Conditioning," *Native Plants J.* (Spring 2004), 5, No. 1, 3 p.

[501] L. S. Rosner, J. T. Harrington, D. R. Dreesen, and L. Murray, "Effect of Gibberellic Acid and Standard Seed Treatments on Mountain Snowberry Germination," *Native Plants J.* (Fall 2002), 3, No. 2, 8 p.

[502] C. L. Jones, J. T. Harrington, and D. R. Dreesen. 2002. 'Refinement and Stratification of Thinleaf Alder and Water Birch Seeds from New Mexico," *Native Plants J.* (Fall 2002), 3, No. 2, 9 p.

[503] Ibid

[504] Gregory A. Fenchel, and David R. Dreesen, "Longstem Transplants for Riparian Plantings in the Southwest," *J. Rn. Mgt.* (February, 2009), 1 p.

[505] "Annual Administrative Reports, Regions 1-9, 1939-40", Entry 1, RG 114. Natl. Archives, College Park, MD.

[506] "Evaluation Studies and Field Tests, Regions 1-11, 1937-39", Entry 1, RG 114. Natl. Archives, College Park, MD.

[507] Swarthmore College Peace Collection, Swarthmore, PA, http://www.swarthmore.edu/library/peace/DG051-099/dg056cpspers.html/ (November 2, 2004).

[508] W. C., Sharp, Robert S. Ross, M. W. Testerman, and R. Williamson, "Ability of crownvetch to suppress woody plant invasion," *J. of Soil and Water Consv.,* (May/June 1980), 35 (3), 142-43.

[509] Varietal Differences in Crownvetch Cotyledon Size, https://www.agronomy.org/publications/aj/abstracts/62/6/AJ0620060711?access=0&view=pdf/ (March 10, 2012).

[510] Annual Technical Reports, Big Flats PMC, (USDA, SCS, Big Flats, NY, 1962).

[511] USDA-NRCS *Plant Materials Center Field Day*, June 17, 2004, Bismarck PMC, (SCS, Bismarck, ND, 2004).

[512] Stan Stelter, Tribune West, *Breath held all across the wide Missouri*, Dec. 10, 1985.

[513] Erling Jacobson, personal communications, 2011.

[514] Henry Nash Smith, "Rain Follows the Plow: The Notion of Increased Rainfall for the Great Plains, 1844-1880," *Huntington Library Quarterly* 10 (1947), 174.

[515] B. E. Fernow, *What is Forestry?,* Bul. 5, 1891, 34-35, (USDA, Forest Service).

[516] Charles A. Scott, "The Plains Shelterbelt Project," *Report of the Kansas State Board of Agriculture for the Quarter Ending March*, (KSU, Manhattan, KS, 1935), 47.

[517] Ibid.

[518] Wilmon H. Droze, *Trees, Prairies, and People: A History of Tree Planting in the Plains States* (Denton, TX, Texas Woman's University, 1977).

[519] J. F. Arden, *Farm Forestry*, (John Wiley & Sons, Inc. NY, NY).

[520] W. T. MacLaughlin, "Planting for Topographic Control on the Warrenton Oregon Coastal Dune Area," *Northwest Science*. (1939), 13-2, 26-32.

[521] R. E. HIckson and F. W. Rodolf, *History of Columbia River Jetties,* (Dept. of the Army, Corps of Engineers, Portland, OR, October, 1950), Chapter 32.

[522] Willard T. McLaughlin and Robert L. Brown, *Controlling coastal sand dunes in the Pacific Northwest*, Circ. No. 660. (USDA-SCS, Washington, DC, 1942).

[523] Ibid.

[524] Douglas Helms, "The Civilian Conservation Corps: Demonstrating the Value of Soil Conservation", *J. of Soil and Water Consv.* 40 (March-April 1985), 184-188.

[525] Willard T. McLaughlin and Robert L. Brown, loc. cit.

[526] R .L. Brown and A. L. Hafenrichter, "Factors Influencing the production and Use of Beachgrass and Dunegrass Clones for Erosion Control: Effect of Date and Planting," *J. ASA*, (1948), 40(6), 512-521.

[527] R. L. Brown and A. L. Hafenrichter, *Stabilizing sand dunes on the Pacific coast with woody plants*. Misc. Pub. 892. (USDA, SCS, Washington, DC, 1962), 18 p.

[528] J. L. Schwendiman. "Coastal and sand dune stabilization in the Pacific Northwest", *International J. Biometeorology* (1977), 21:281-89.

[529] Helms, 1985, loc. cit.

[530] Jack Carlson, Frank Reckendorf and Wilbur Ternyik, *Stabilizing Coastal Dunes in the Pacific Northwest*, AH 687, (USDA- SCS, Washington, DC, 1991), 52 p.

[531] Frank Reckendorf, Don Leach, Robert Baum, Jack Carlson, "Stabilization of Sand Dunes in Oregon," *Agricultural History*, (April 1985), pp. 262-263.

[532] Gale Thomson, "The sand man of Florence", *The Register Guard, Eugene, OR*, May 1, 2006.

[533] Carlson, 1991, loc. cit.

[534] Gale Thomson, loc. cit.

[535] Andrea J. Pickart, "Restoring the Grasslands of Northern California's Coastal Dunes", *Grasslands*, CA Native Grasslands Assoc., (2008), XVIII, No. 1.

[536] *Recovery Plan for the Pacific Coast population of the Western Snowy Plover*, http://www.fws.gov/arcata/es/birds/WSP/documents/RecoveryPlanWebRelease_09242007/WSP%20Final%20RP%2010-1-07.pdf/ (June 25, 2012).

[537] *Constructed Wetlands for On-site Septic Treatment*, http://www.plant-materials.nrcs.usda.gov/pubs/etpmcbrconwet.pdf/ (May 1, 2011).

[538] George Farek and John Lloyd-Reilley, *A Bioengineering System for Coastal Shoreline Stabilization*, http://www.plant-materials.nrcs.usda.gov/pubs/stpmcjm0869.pdf/ (June 24, 2010).

[539] Dickens County Biographies, http://www.rootsweb.ancestry.com/~txdicken/spur/c/conner_genevieve_bob.html/ (October 14, 2009).

[540] Native American Seed, *Consulting the Elders... What If?* <http://www.seedsource.com/medicine/elders.asp/ (March 10, 2010).

[541] Lee Stone and Arnold Davis, *Seed Bed Preparation: The Johnson Grass Wars*, <http://texasprairie.org/index.php/manage/restoration_entry/seed_bed_preparation_the_johnson_grass_wars/ (October 14, 2010).

[542] James E "Bud" Smith, "Material for special report on grass to D.A. Williams via Frank Harper", 1960, Entry 254, RG 114.5.2. Natl. Archives, College Park, MD.

[543] Fact Sheet: *Windbreaks and Shelterbelts - Conservation Practices 380 and 650*, http://plant-materials.nrcs.usda.gov/txpmc/publications.html/ (March 24, 2009).

[544] John L. Schwendiman, *History of the Pullman PMC - Its First 50 Years*, USDA, SCS Plant Material Center, Pullman, WA, 1990, http://www.wsu.edu/pmc_nrcs/History.html/ (March 13, 2009).

[545] Ibid.

[546] Ibid.

[547] National Plant Materials Manual, 2010 edition.

[548] Personal conversations with fellow employee, Curtis Sharp.

[549] John L. Schwendiman, *History of the Pullman PMC - Its First 50 Years*, loc. cit.

[550] Robert S. MacLauchlan and A. L. Hafenrichter, "Alternate-Row Grass-Legume Seedings". *J. of Soil and Water Consv.* (1961), 16, 61-64.

[551] Frank C. Edminster, Walter S. Atkinson, and Arthur C. McIntyre, *Streambank Erosion Control on the Winooski River, Vermont*, Cir. No. 837, (GPO, Washington, DC, 1949) 54 p.

[552] USDA, NRCS, http://plant-materials.nrcs.usda.gov/wvpmc/ (January 6, 2011).

Chapter 9: Key Leaders, Productive Scientists, Productive Teams, Other Major Contributors and Awards

[553] L. H Bailey and Ethel Zoe Bailey. A biographical register of rural leadership in the United States and Canada, (Mason Printing Corp.), 1925 1930.

[554] AZ 420, University of Arizona Office of the President records, 1914-1937, Box 21, Folder 8, Commencement, 1929-1936.

[555] *Boyce Thompson Arboretum State Park*, http://ag.arizona.edu/bta/history.html/ (January 7, 2011).

[556] *History of Boyce Thompson Arboretum State Park*, http://azstateparks.com/parks/BOTH/history.html/ (November 13, 2011).

[557] Frank S Crosswhite , *Studies of (Simmondsia chinensi)s at the Boyce Thompson Southwestern Arboretum*, Office of the Arid Lands Studies, Univ. AZ, Tucson, http://www.pssurvival.com/ps/Crops/Jojoba_And_Its_Uses_1972.pdf/ (June 3, 2012).

[558] "New Regent, Univ. of AZ, Specialist in Southwest Horticulture" *Casa Grande Valley Dispatch*, January 21, 1927, p 3.

[559] Aldo Leopold, *Comes Alive*, April 4 at Boyce Thompson Arboretum State Park, 2011, http://azbw.com/Aldo_Leopold%20.php/ (November 17, 2011).

[560] Frank S Crosswhite, "History, Geology and Vegetation of Picketpost Mountain", *Desert Plants*, Vol. 6, No. 2 Tucson, (AZ Univ. of Arizona Press).

[561] Mark Siegwarth, Aridus, *What is in a Name? Legumes of Arizona –An Illustrated Flora and Reference*, Vol. 21, No. 2, http://cals.arizona.edu/desertlegumeprogram/pdf/aridus_21_2.pdf/ (May 3, 2010).

[562] Dedication of the Tucson, AZ Plant Materials Center Building, 2000, http://www.nrcs.usda.gov/news/thisweek/2000/001110.html#anchor106943/ (June 3, 2010).

[563] Frank S. Crosswhite, loc. cit.

[564] C. R. Enlow Memo to H. H Bennett, November 1935, Entry 254, RG 114.5.2, Natl. Archives, College Park, MD.

[565] F.J. Hopkins to H. H Bennett, December 18, 1935, File 215.0, Nurseries, General, central Files, October 1935-March 1936, Entry 254, RG 114.5.2, Natl. Archives, College Park, MD.

[566] "Field Memorandum #SCN-4, Functions and Activities of Nurseries to Regional Conservators and Nurserymen", Entry 254, RG 114.5.2, Natl. Archives, College Park, MD.

[567] "Policies and Procedures Historical, 1936-61" *nomination of Dr. Franklin J. Crider for a Superior Service Award*, Annual Administrative reports, Regions 1-7, 1946-47, Entry 254, RG 114.5.2, Natl. Archives, College Park, MD.

[568] H. H. Bennett Memo to F. J. Crider April 15, 1949, Entry 254, RG 114.5.2, Natl. Archives, College Park, MD.

[569] The Crider Memorial Garden.

[570] Wilmer W. Steiner letter to F. Joy Hopkins, June 22, 1967, regarding Franklin J. Crider, Entry 254, RG 114.5.2, Natl. Archives, College Park, MD.

[571] "The Crider Memorial Garden of conservation plants", *Soil Consv.,. Magazine*, 1967, p. 24.

[572] B. R. Bertramson, *History of Agronomy and Soils, WSU, Pullman, WA*, 1984, http://css.wsu.edu/overview/history/State_History/V_Research--2.2_Forage.pdf/ (January 13, 2011).

[573] J. L. Schwendiman, *The First 50 Years: Pullman Plant Materials Center*, USDA, SCS, Pullman WA, 1986, http://www.wsu.edu/pmc_nrcs/History.html/ (June 7, 2010).

[574] B.R. Bertramson, *History of Agronomy and Soils, WSU, Pullman, WA*, loc. cit.

[575] J. L. Schwendiman, *The First 50 Years:*, loc. cit.

[576] USDA, NRCS, *Conservation Plant Releases sorted by Scientific Name*, 2011, http://plant-materials.nrcs.usda.gov/releases/releasesallbysci.html/ (May 7, 2010).

[577] Congressional Inquiries regarding Nurseries, 1953, Entry 254, RG 114.5.2, Natl. Archives, College Park, MD.

[578] U.S. Congress, House, 1954a. Subcommittee of the Committee on Appropriations, *Department of Agriculture Appropriations for 1955*, 83rd Cong., 2nd session, pt 3, p. 1328.

[579] U.S. Congress, Senate, 1954. Subcommittee of the Committee on Appropriations, *Department of Agricultural Appropriations for 1955*, 83rd Cong., 2nd session, pt 3, p. 659.

[580] Steven E Phillips and Douglas Helms. *Interviews with Chiefs of the Soil Conservation Service*, USDA, Washington, D.C. 1994, http://www.farmlandinfo.org/documents/34766/Interviews_with_Chiefs_Donald_Williams.pdf (May 14, 2010).

[581] USDA, NRCS, *Conservation Plant Releases sorted by Scientific Name*, 2011, loc. cit.

[582] Steven E Phillips and Douglas Helms. *Interviews with Chiefs of the Soil Conservation Service*, loc. cit.

[583] Robert S MacLauchlan conversations with author, 2010 -12.

[584] USDA, Soil Conservation Service, *National study on alternatives financing, staffing and/or managing plant materials centers*, (USDA-SCS, Washington, DC, 1980).

[585] Ibid.

[586] B. R. Bertramson, *History of Agronomy and Soils, WSU, Pullman, WA*, loc. cit., 112-14.

[587] John L. Schwendiman, interview by Douglas Helms Washington, DC, September 19, 1981.

[588] Ibid, p 3.

[589] "Obituaries", *Stockman-Review and Spokane Chronicle*, Wednesday, June 10, 1992, Spokane, WA.

[590] J .L. Schwendiman, *The First 50 Years*. Loc. cit.

[591] USDA, NRCS, *Plant Materials Program Costs and Benefits 1935 – 2005*, http://prod.nrcs.usda.gov/Internet/FSE_DOCUMENTS/stelprdb1042295.pdf/ (February 1, 2011).

[592] John L. Schwendiman, interview by Douglas Helms, loc. cit.

[593] "Annual Administrative Reports", Regions 1-7, 1946-47, Entry 254, RG 114.5.2, Natl. Archives, College Park, MD.

[594] "Annual Report, Observational Studies" Archives of the USDA-NRCS, James E. "Bud" Smith, Jr. Plant Materials Center, Knox City, TX (undated).

[595] James E "Bud" Smith, 1960, loc. cit.

[596] *Annual Reports, Plant Center Operations*, Calendar Years 1960, 1961, 1962, James E. "Bud" Smith PMC, (USDA, NRCS Knox City, TX).

[597] "New Accessions", Archives of the James E. "Bud" Smith, Jr. Plant Materials Center, USDA, NRCS, Knox City, TX.

[598] "New Plant Canter", *Abilene Reporter*, Abilene, Texas, September 8, 1967.

[599] "Dedication, James E. "Bud" Smith", Archives of the James E. "Bud" Smith, Jr. Plant Materials Center, USDA, NRCS, Knox City, TX.

[600] J. C. Hoag, Harvesting, *Propagating, and Planting Wetland Plants*, Technical Note 13, 2003, http://plant-materials.nrcs.usda.gov/idpmc/publications.html/ (June 24, 2010).

[601] Chris Hoag and Dan Ogle, *The Stinger*, October, 2011, http://plant-materials.nrcs.usda.gov/idpmc/publications.html/ (December 13, 2011).

[602] J. C. Hoag, *Willow Clump Plantings*, Technical Note 42, 2003, http://plant-materials.nrcs.usda.gov/idpmc/publications.html/ (February 6, 2011).

[603] J. C. Hoag, *Vertical Bundles: a streambank bioengineering treatment to establish willows and dogwoods on streambanks*, 2010, http://plant-materials.nrcs.usda.gov/idpmc/publications.html/ (February 6, 2011).

[604] D. J. Tilley, and J.C. Hoag, *Pre-soaking hardwood willow cuttings for fall versus spring dormant planting*, 2009. Information Series 25, http://plant-materials.nrcs.usda.gov/idpmc/publications.html/ (June 24, 2010).

[605] J. C. Hoag, *Wetland Sodmats* Aberdeen, ID. Tech Note 22, 2008, , http://plant-materials.nrcs.usda.gov/idpmc/publications.html/ (February 6, 2011)..

[606] Hoag Riparian & Wetland Restoration, LLC, http://www.idahotrout.org/bioengineering_course_agenda.pdf/ (December 4, 2012).

[607] Frank S Crosswhite, *Desert Plants*, loc. cit.

[608] Ibid.

[609] "Annual Administrative Reports, Regions 1-9, 1939-40", Entry 254, RG 114.5.2, Natl. Archives, College Park, MD.

[610] "Annual Administrative Reports", Regions 1-7, 1946-47, loc. cit.

[611] "Annual Administrative Reports", Regions 1-9, 1939-40", loc. cit.

[612] James Alderson and W. Curtis Sharp, *Grass Varieties of the U.S.*, USDA, HB 170, (GPO, Washington, DC, 1994) 249-50.

[613] USDA, NRCS, *Plant Materials Program Costs and Benefits 1935 – 2005,* loc. cit.

[614] Dan Merkel, telephone conversation, June 20, 2011.

[615] Douglas Helms, *Briefing Paper on the Plant Materials Centers*, (USDA-NRCS, Washington, DC, 2008).

[616] Beltsville, MD, National Agricultural Library Collection Number 350.

[617] Heritage Centre, Winnipeg, Manitoba, 2003, www.mennonitechurch.ca/.../Stoesz,%20Abraham%20D.%20fonds.htm (April 13 2010).

[618] Beltsville, MD Collection No. 350, op. cit.

[619] U.S. Congress, House, Testimony by Dr. Salter before the House Sub-Committee, April 1, 1953, Box 5, Entry 254, RG 114.5.2, Natl. Archives, College Park, MD.

[620] Douglas Helms, *Briefing Paper*, loc. cit.

[621] Beltsville, MD, Collection Number 350, loc. cit.

[622] U.S. Congress, House, Testimony by Dr. Salter, loc. cit.

[623] U.S., Congress, House, 1954b. p. 3, p. 1326.

[624] USDA, NRCS, *Plant Materials Program Costs and Benefits,* loc. cit.

[625] Frank S Crosswhite, *Desert Plants,* loc. cit.

[626] Sharon L Norris, *History of the Aberdeen Plant Materials Center*. (USDA-SCS, Boise, ID, 1989).

[627] Assoc. of Retired Conservation Service Employees, http://www.arscse.org/qannounC.html/ (November 11, 2012).

[628] Steiner is identified with a publication, *Gleditsia triacanthos L.*, Honeylocust, which he was associated with, and was of interest to the Hill Culture Program of SCS at Beltsville, MD, 1944, http://www.na.fs.fed.us/pubs/silvics_manual/volume_2/gleditsia/triacanthos.html/ (November 15, 2012).

[629] Robert L. Geiger, Jr., *A Chronological History of the Soil Conservation Service and Related Events*, (USDA-SCS, Washington, DC, 1955).

[630] "Evaluation Studies and Field Tests, Regions 1-11", 1937-39, Box 18, RG 114, Entry 254.

[631] M. Owsley, email, May 2010.

[632] Glenn W. Burton, "A Search for the Origin Pensacola Bahia grass", *Economic Botany*, Vol. 21, No. 4, (1967), 379-382.

[633] William Walton Stevens, *History of Soil and Water Conservation in North Carolina*, (NRCS, Raleigh, NC, 1999).

[634] R. M. Ross to H. H. Bennett, October 24, 1949 "Main Work of the Soil Conservation Service for Fiscal Year 1949", Entry 254, RG 114.5.2, Natl. Archives, College Park, MD.

[635] Athens, GA, Hargrett Library, University of Georgia, Collection Number MS2163.

[636] USDA, NRCS, *Plant Materials Program Costs and Benefits,* loc. cit.

[637] Edward K. Twidwell, LSU AgCtr, Bahia Grass Production and Management, http://www.lsuagcenter.com/NR/rdonlyres/82A096A6-7F6F-4306-853B-F49A1D98AFEF/78032/pub2697 BahiagrassHIGHRES.pdf/ (Jun 17, 2013).

[638] Dwight Tober NRCS, Bismarck, ND Plant Materials Specialist (retired) prepare the bulk of this.

[639] E. T. Jacobson, "The evaluation, selection, and increase of prairie wildflowers for conservation beautification" In *Prairie: A multiple view*, M. K. Wali, American Prairie Conf. No. 4, (Grand Forks, ND, Univ. of ND Press, 1974), 349-404.

[640] Curtis Sharp developed this from personal knowledge and association with Ruffner, plus interviews with him and others.

[641] Ross H Mellinger, Frank W Glover and John G Hall, *Results of revegetation of strip mine spoil by soil conservation districts in West Virginia*, (WVU Exp. Sta., Morgantown, WV, 1966).

[642] David G. Lorenz, W. Curtis Sharp, Joseph D. Ruffner, *Conservation plants for the Northeast*, (USDA-NRCS, Washington, DC, 2008).

[643] Joseph D. Ruffner, *Plant Performance on Surface Coal Mine Spoil in the Eastern United States*, SCS-TP-155, (USDA, SCS; Washington, DC, 1978).

[644] Surface mining control and reclamation act of 1977, http://www.eoearth.org/article/Surface_Mining_Control_and_Reclamation_Act_of_1977,_United_States/ (March 2, 2013).

[645] USDA, NRCS, *Conservation Plant Releases sorted by Scientific Name*, 2011, loc. cit.

[646] Erling T. Jacobson, Regional Plant Materials Specialist (retired), Lincoln, NE prepared much of this.

[647] Curtis Sharp developed this from personal knowledge and association with Augustine.

[648] A .C. Hawkins, Soil & Water Conservation in Maryland, Conservation in Maryland (undated). www.mascd.net/handbook/MASCD7a.pdf/ (February 12, 2011).

[649] Ibid.

[650] Erling T. Jacobson, Regional Plant Materials Specialist (retired), Lincoln, NE prepared much of this, assisted by David Lorenz, Regional Plant Materials Specialist (retired).

[651] Bismarck, ND Plant Materials Center Field Day, June 17, 2004, (USDA-NRCS, 2004).

[652] Erling T. Jacobson, Regional Plant Materials Specialist (retired), Lincoln, NE prepared much of this, with assistance from Peter Jensen, State Range Conservationist (retired), Lincoln, NE.

[653] C. R. Enlow, Memo to H. H Bennett, 1935, loc. cit..

[654] Charles Enlow personnel file, available through Douglas Helms NRCS Historian (retired).

[655] Walter C. Lowdermilk memo to Max M. Hoover, Spencer, WV, Feb. 12,1935, Nursery Division Trip Reports, Entry 254, RG 114.5.2, Natl. Archives, College Park, MD.

[656] Robert L. Geiger, Jr., *A Chronological History of the Soil Conservation Service and Related Events,* loc. cit.

[657] J. L. Schwendiman, *The First 50 Years. Pullman Plant Materials Center, USDA, SCS, Pullman WA*, loc. cit.

[658] M. M. Hoover to H. A. Gunning, October 22, 1942. Central Files, Box 295, Entry 1, RG 114, Natl. Archives, College Park, MD.

[659] M. M. Hoover to A. E. Jones, January 2, 1946, Central Files, Box 295, Entry 1, RG 114. Natl. Archives, College Park, MD.

[660] *Annual Report of the 1954 North Central Regional Project*, (USDA, PI Station, Ames, IA).

[661] Harry A. Gunning, "Permanent Personnel of Soil Conservation Nurseries", January 30, 1936, Entry 254, RG 114.5.2, Natl. Archives, College Park, MD.

[662] Univ. of AZ. Herbarium collection results, Harry A. Gunning May 1, 1936, http://loco.biosci.arizona.edu/herbarium/db/get_one_specimen.php?id=150517/ (June 4, 2012).

[663] USDA Misc. Publication 304, *Directory of Organization and Field Activities of the Dept. of Agr.*, (GPO, Washington, DC, 1938), 89.

[664] Ibid.

[665] "Annual Reports of Department of Agriculture, SCS", 1940 – 1948, Entry 254, RG 114.5.2, Natl. Archives, College Park, MD.

[666] Floyd M Cossitt, C.A. Rindt and Harry A. Gunning. *Production of Planting Stock: Trees,* Yearbook of Agriculture, (GPO, Washington, D.C., 1949).

[667] Employee Awards and Recognition Program, http://www.ocio.usda.gov/directives/doc/DR4040-451-1.html/ (January 20, 2011).

Chapter 10: Impacts of the Pre-Varietal Release Certification Standards

[668] *Guidelines for Selecting Native Plants: The Importance of Local Ecotype*, http://for-wild.org/download/idensele/guidsele.html/ (November 4, 2012).

[669] *Guidelines For Landscaping To Protect Native Vegetation From Genetic Degradation*, http://www.cnps.org/cnps/archive/landscaping.php/ (November 4, 2012).

[670] GLOBALGAP *Flower and Ornamental standard*, http://www.globalgap.org/cms/front_content.php?idcat=9/ (November 4, 2012).

[671] AOSCA, The AOSCA Native Plant Selection, 2011, http://www.aosca.org/aoscanativeplantbrochure.pdf/ (May 12, 2012).

[672] *National Plant Materials Program Manual*, 1994 Edition (NRCS, Washington, DC, 1994).

[673] Ibid.

[674] John Englert, data formulated 2010.

[675] *National Plant Materials Program Manual, 1994*, loc. cit.

[676] *National Plant Materials Program Manual, 2010*, http://plant-materials.nrcs.usda.gov/technical/references.html/ 3/1/2912 (June 12, 2010).

[677] *Conservation Plant Releases, Elsberry PMC*, http://plant-materials.nrcs.usda.gov/mopmc/releases.html/ (July 25, 2012).

[678] *National Plant Materials Program Manual*, 2010.

[679] Government Performance and Result Act, OMB, http://www.whitehouse.gov/omb/mgmt-gpra/index-gpra/ (January 14, 2013).

[680] Conversation with John Englert, National PM Specialist.

[681] John Englert, personal letter, January 11, 2013.

[682] Survey was conducted by the author via email with PMCs.

[683] *National Plant Materials Program Manual, 2010*.

[684] Ibid.

[685] John Englert, personal letter, January 11, 2013.

Chapter 11: Great Innovations and Top Performing Cultivars

[686] Boyce Thompson Arboretum, http://ag.arizona.edu/bta/history.html/ (December 6, 2011).

[687] F. J. Crider, memo to Maurice E. Heath, April 13, 1949, Entry 254, RG 114.5.2, Natl. Archives, College Park, MD.

[688] S. Ray Smith Jr. and R. D. B. Whalley, "Model for Expanded Use of Native Grasses", *Native Plants J*, (Spring 2002), 3, no. 1, 38-49.

[689] Louis A. Chandler, *Monroeville Historical Society, Coal Mining*, http://monroevillehistorical.org/index.php?option=com_content&task=view&id=164&Itemid=200/ (December 3, 2012).

[690] Ross H Mellinger, Frank W Glover and John G Hall, *Results of revegetation of strip mine spoil by soil conservation districts in West Virginia*, (WVU Exp. Sta., Morgantown, WV, 1966).

[691] Franklin J. Crider, *Root growth stoppage resulting from defoliation of grass*. Technical Bulletin 1102. (GPO, Washington, DC, 1955).

[692] Frank C. Edminster, Walter S. Atkinson, and Arthur C. McIntyre, *Streambank Erosion Control on the Winooski River, Vermont*, Cir. No. 837, (GPO, Washington, DC, 1949) 54 p.

[693] *Annual Reports of Department of Agriculture*, SCS, 1951, (GPO, Washington, DC, 1941), 61-62.

[694] Paul E. Lemmon and A. L. Hafenrichter, "The Dilution Method for Plot or Field Seeding of Grassed and legumes Alone or in Mixtures", *Agron. J.* (Sept. 1947), 39:817-821.

[695] William L. Southworth, "Rice hulls for seeding", *Soil Consv.*, (1949), 14:280-282.

[696] *Annual Reports of Department of Agriculture*, SCS, 1949, (GPO, Washington, DC, 1949), 42-43.

[697] H. Miller, *Seed dilution with rice hulls*. TN 16. (USDA-SCS, Davis, CA, March, 1966).

[698] L. St. John, D. Ogle, D. Tilley, M. Majerus, and L. Holzworth, *Mixing Seed with Rice Hulls*, TN 7, (USDA-NRCS, Boise, ID, 2005), 15.

[699] *California Fruit and Nut Review 2009*, http://www.nass.usda.gov/Statistics_by_State/California/Publications/Fruits_and_Nuts/201207frtrv.pdf/ (December 21, 2012).

[700] Clarence U. Finch and W. Curtis Sharp, *Cover Crops in California Orchards & Vineyards*, (USDA-SCS, Davis, CA Aug. 1976).

[701] *PLANTS Database*, http://plants.usda.gov/java/ (December 21, 2012).

[702] D.G. Ogle, M. Majerus, and L. St. John, *Technical Note 9: Plants for Saline to Sodic Soil Conditions*, (USDA-NRCS, Boise, ID, 2004), 12 p.

[703] Personal communications with the authors.

[704] William J. Fogarty, *Report on Saline Seep to the Old West Regional Commission*, 1974, http://www.amazon.co.uk/Report-saline-seep-Regional-Commission/dp/B00072GDN4/ (July 18, 2012).

[705] M. Majerus, *Technical Note No. 26 Plant Materials for Saline-Alkaline Soils*, (USDA-NRCS, Bozeman, MT, 1996), 5 p.

[706] D.G. Ogle, M. Majerus, and L. St. John, *Technical Note 9: Plants for Saline to Sodic Soil Conditions*, (USDA-NRCS, Boise, ID, 2004), 12 p.

[707] *Effects of Soil Salinity Level on the Survival and Growth of Trees and Shrubs Adapted to the Northern Plains and Intermountain West*, (USDA-NRCS, Bozeman, MT, May 2011), p 76-79.

[708] Glenn Sakamoto, *Progress Report on the Use of Piligrass (Heteropogon contortus) Hay Bales for the Island of Kaho`olawe's Highly Erodible Sites*. http://www.plant-materials.nrcs.usda.gov/pubs/hipmcpr8078.pdf/ (June 15, 2009).

[709] USDA, NRCS, *Plant Materials Program Costs and Benefits 1935 – 2005*, https://prod.nrcs.usda.gov/Internet/FSE_DOCUMENTS/stelprdb1042295.pdf/ (February 1, 2011).

[710] *Bridger Plant Materials Center*, http://plant-materials.nrcs.usda.gov/mtpmc/index.html/ (December 28, 2012).

Chapter 12: The Case of Introduced Plants for Conservation Purposes

[711] Charles C. Mann, 1493, *Uncovering the New World Columbus Created* (Knopf Doubleday Pub. Group, 2011).

[712] *I go Pogo*, http://www.igopogo.com/we_have_met.html/ (November 16, 2012).

[713] James E "Bud" Smith, "Material for special report on grass to D.A. Williams via Frank Harper," 1960, Entry 254, RG 114.5.2. Natl. Archives, College Park, MD.

[714] USDA-NRCS *Discontinued Conservation Plant Releases*, http://plant-materials.nrcs.usda.gov/releases/discontinued.html (Aug. 14, 2012).

[715] *The Dust Bowl and Black Sunday*, http://www.altereddimensions.net/earth/DustBowlAndBlackSunday.aspx/ (December 28, 2012).

[716] Knowles A. Ryerson, *History of the Significance of the Plant Introduction work of the USDA*, (Agriculture History Society, Washington, DC, 1933).

[717] Charles Leonard Woolley, *The Sumerians*, (Oxford: Clarendon Press, 1928).

[718] *Francis Marion and Sumter National Forests*, http://www.fs.usda.gov/ (September 5, 2011).

[719] Caribbean Archeology, FL Museum of Natural History, *Christopher Columbus*, http://www.flmnh.ufl.edu/caribarch/columbus.html/ (February 24, 2011).

[720] *Triticum Introduction*, http://www.gramene.org/species/triticum/wheat_intro.html/ (March 14, 2010).

[721] M.E. Heath and C. K. Kaiser, "Forages in a Changing World" in *Forages 4th ed.*, Ames: Iowa State Univ. Press, 3-11, 1985.

[722] C. Wayne Smith and Robert H. Dilday, *Rice, Origin, History, Technology and Production* (New York: John Wiley & Sons, Inc., 2002).

[723] *The History of Soybeans*, http://www.ncsoy.org/ABOUT-SOYBEANS/History-of-Soybeans.aspx/ (August 11, 2009).

[724] M.D. Peterson, 1984. *The Writings of Thomas Jefferson* (New York: Literary Classics of the United States, Inc., 1984), 702-704.

[725] *Jefferson Farm and Garden*, http://www.jeffersonfarm.org/support_us.php/ (May 12, 2011).

[726] *Rice*, http://www.monticello.org/site/house-and-gardens/rice/ (October 12, 2011).

[727] Utah State University, *Kentucky Bluegrass*, http://extension.usu.edu/range/Grasses/kentuckybluegrass.html/ (July, 27 2011).

[728] *Easy Ranch, The History of Timothy Grass Hay*, http://www.estyranch.com/timothy-grass-hay-history.html/ (December 10, 2011).

[729] Ibid.

[730] *Cotton*, http://en.wikipedia.org/wiki/Cotton/ (November 6, 2011).

[731] *European colonization of the Americas*, http://en.wikipedia.org/wiki/European_colonization_of_the_Americas#cite_note-Histoire-2#cite_note-Histoire-2/ (January 15, 2012).

[732] CensusScope, *Ethnic and racial Heritage*, 2000, http://www.censusscope.org/us/s16/chart_ancestry.html/ (November 11, 2012).

[733] PLANTS Database, *autumn olive*, http://plants.usda.gov/java/noxious?rptType=Federal/ (May 5, 2012).

[734] *Dust Bowl Trough*, loc. cit.

[735] A History: The USDA. *Longwood Ornamental Plant Exploration Program*, http://dspace.udel.edu:8080/dspace/handle/19716/2918/ (November 20, 2011).

[736] Hanson, A. A. 1959. *Grass varieties in the United States*, U.S. Department of Agriculture Washington, DC.

[737] C. R. Enlow Memo to H. H Bennett, November 1935, loc. cit.

[738] "Increasing Introduced Grasses, Tucson, AZ Nursery, 1936," Entry 254, RG 114.5.2, Natl. Archives, College Park, MD.

[739] The Plant Materials Program, *Finding Plant Solutions for Conservation Needs*, http://workflow.den.nps.gov/8_Transportation/March2009wkshp/March17_Tuesday/3.17WorkingwithPlantMaterialCenters.pdf/ (March 17, 2011).

[740] Wikipedia, The Free Encyclopedia, *Appalachian mixed mesophytic forests*, http://en.wikipedia.org/wiki/Appalachian_mixed_mesophytic_forests/ (October 10, 2011).

[741] Charles Reagan Wilson and William R. Ferris, *Encyclopedia of Southern culture* (Univ. of North Carolina, Raleigh, September 1989).

[742] Garden Guides, *How to care for Pensacola Bahia Grass*, http://www.gardenguides.com/94002-care-pensacola-bahia-grass.html/ (November 15, 2011).

[743] Joseph D. Ruffner, 1978. *Plant Performance on Surface Coal Mine Spoil in the Eastern United States*, SCS-TP-155, (USDA-SCS, Washington, DC, 1978).

[744] PLANTS Database, loc. cit.

[745] T. O. Dill, S.S. Waller, K.P. Vogel, R.N. Gates and W.W. Stroup, "Renovation of seeded warm-season grasses with atrazine," *J. of Rn. Mgt.* (January, 1986): 39, No. 1, pp. 72-75.

[746] P.L. Grilz and J.T. Romo. 1994. "Water Relations and Growth of Bromus inermis Leyss (Smooth Brome) Following Spring or Autumn Burning in a Fescue Prairie", *American Midland Naturalist*, (October, 1994): 132, No. 2 pp. 340-348

[747] *Race and Ethnic Relations, European Americans*, http://www.angelfire.com/nv/verbigerate/europeanamericans.html/ (May 5, 2012).

[748] Tropical Forages, *Panicum coloratum*, http://www.tropicalforages.info/key/Forages/Media/Html/Panicum_coloratum.html/ (May 7, 2012).

[749] Norman Martin, *Perennial forages look promising on the plains*. CASNR NewsCenter, 2008, http://www.depts.ttu.edu/agriculturalsciences/news/ (December 6, 2011).

[750] *The Invasive Grass Phenomenon*, http://ckwri.tamuk.edu/fileadmin/user_upload/docs/STN/Presentations/Invasive_Grass_Phenomenon.pdf/ (December 15, 2011).

[751] R. N. Mack and J.N Thompson, "Evolution in steppe with few large hooved mammals." *American Naturalist* (1982): 119: 757-773.

[752] Office of Surface Mining Reclamation and Enforcement, http://www.osmre.gov/topic/smcra/smcra.shtml/ (August 3, 1977).

[753] Garry D. Lacefield and Jimmy Henning, *Alternatives for fungus infected tall fescue*, 1986, http://www.ca.uky.edu/agc/pubs/agr/agr119/agr119.html/ (November 1, 2012).

[754] Oklahoma Invasive Species, *Tall Fescue*, http://oklahomainvasivespecies.okstate.edu/tall_fescue.html/ (November 15, 2012).

[755] William Walton Stevens, *History of Soil and Water Conservation in North Carolina*, USDA-NRCS, Raleigh, NC, 1999).

[756] John T. Whaley, *Crownvetch's Role in Vegetation Management*, http://www.propertyrightsresearch.org/2004/articles/crownvetch.html/ (November 1, 2012).

[757] An act declaring and adopting Penngift Crownvetch (*Coronilla varia L*. Penngift) as the State Beautification and Conservation Plant of Pennsylvania. 1982, June 17, P.L. 526, No. 151.

[758] W.C. Sharp, R. S. Ross, M. W. Testerman and R. Williamson, "Ability of crownvetch to suppress woody plant invasion." *J. Soil and Water Consv.* (1980): 35 No. 3, 142-144.

[759] Safety and Trees: *The Delicate Balance*, http://safety.fhwa.dot.gov/roadway_dept/clear_zones/fhwasa0612/ (November 12, 2011).

[760] "Committee Report of the Southern Great Plains Revegetation Committee, Instituted Meade, KS", Entry 254, RG 114, Natl. Archives, College Park, MD.

[761] F. Lamson-Scribner, *American grasses*, USDA, Div. of Agrostology, Circular No. 18, (GPO, Washington, DC, 1897): p. 308.

[762] James Alderson and W. Curtis Sharp, *Grass Varieties of the U.S.*, USDA, HB 170, (GPO, Washington, DC, 1994) 249-50.

[763] *Pullman Plant Materials History*, http://public.wsu.edu/~pmc_nrcs/History.html/ (December 3, 2011).

[764] George A. Rogler and Russell J. Lorenz, "Crested Wheatgrass - Early History in the U.S." *J. Range Mgt.* (1983): 36, No. 1, .p 91 – 93.

[765] T. O. Dill, et al, "Renovation of seeded warm-season grasses with atrazine", loc. cit.

[766] John Hendrickson and Bret Olson, *Understanding Plant Response to Grazing*, Chapter 4, http://www.cnr.uidaho.edu/rx-grazing/handbook/Chapter_4_Targeted_Grazing.pdf/ (November 25, 2011).

[767] Reynolds, H. G., 1918, *Reseeding southwestern range lands with crested wheatgrass*, http://digital.library.unt.edu/ark:/67531/metadc9474/ (December 21, 2011).

[768] George A. Rogler and Russell J. Lorenz, "Crested Wheatgrass - Early History in the U.S. ", loc. cit.

[769] Janneke HilleRisLambers, Stephanie G Yelenik, Benjamin P Colman, and Jonathan M Levine, "California annual grass invaders: the drivers or passengers of change?" *J Ecol.*, (Sep. 2010): 5 1147–1156.

[770] Kurt J. Vaughn, Carmen Biel, Jeffrey J. Clary, Felicidad de Herralde, Xavier Aranda Richard Y. Evans, Truman P. Young and Robert Savé, "California perennial grasses are physiologically distinct from both Mediterranean annual and perennial grasses", *Plant Soil* (March 2011): 345:37–46.

[771] W. E. Ternyik, conversations with the author.

[772] U.S. Fish & Wildlife Service, *Western Snowy Plover*, http://www.fws.gov/arcata/es/birds/WSP/plover.html/ (December 15, 2012).

[773] Frank S Crosswhite, History, Geology and Vegetation of Picketpost Mountain, *Desert Plants*, Vol. 6, No. 2 Tucson, (AZ Univ. of Arizona Press).

[774] "Roerich Expedition to Mongolia in search of drought resistant grasses, 1934-37", General Records of the Bureau of Plant Industries, RG 54.2, 1879-1972. 1934-36.

[775] "Increasing Introduced Grasses, Tucson, AZ Nursery, 1936", loc. cit.

[776] H. E. Dregne, "Desertification of arid lands", in *Physics of desertification*, ed. F. El-Baz and M. H. A. Hassan, (Dordrecht, The Netherlands: Martinus, Nijhoff, 1986).

[777] Cindy Talbot Roche, Roger Sheley and Robert C. Korfhage, "Native Species Replace Introduced Grass Cultivars Seeded following Wildfire", *Ecological Restoration*, (2008): 26, no. 4, p. 321-330.

[778] The Invasive Grass Phenomenon, loc. cit.

Chapter 13: Factors Affecting Productivity of Observational Nurseries and Plant Materials Centers

[779] C. R. Enlow Memo to H. H Bennett, November 1935, Entry 254, RG 114.5.2, Natl. Archives, College Park, MD.

[780] F. J. Crider, Memo to Regional Conservationists and Nurserymen, March 25, 1936, Box 10, Entry 254, RG 114.5.2, Natl. Archives, College Park, MD.

[781] Franklin J. Crider Memo to Regional Conservators, July 27, 1937, Entry 215.0, Central Files, Natl. Archives, College Park, MD.

[782] Table II "Grasses and legumes brought into conservation use through the efforts of the Soil Conservation Service --. 1949", Entry 254, RG 114.5.2, Natl. Archives, College Park, MD.

[783] "Estimate of Native Domesticated grass and Legume Seed Harvested Calendar Year 1949", January 25, 1950, Entry 254, RG 114.5.2, Natl. Archives, College Park, MD.

[784] Timothy Egan, *The Worst Hard Times*, (New York: Houghton Mifflin Co., 2006).

[785] Connecticut, Facts, *Map and State Symbols*, http://www.enchantedlearning.com/usa/states/connecticut/ (March 1, 2012).

[786] *About The Dust Bowl*, http://www.english.illinois.edu/maps/depression/dustbowl.html/ (February 26, 2012).

[787] Surface Mining Control and Reclamation Act of 1977, Public Law 95-87, http://www.osmre.gov/topic/SMCRA/publiclaw95-87.shtm/ (February 26. 2012).

[788] Joseph D. Ruffner, 1978. *Plant Performance on Surface Coal Mine Spoil in the Eastern United States*, SCS-TP-155, (USDA-SCS, Washington, DC, 1978).

[789] "Observational Nursery Plantings -- Grasses and Other Forage Crops", A. L. Hafenrichter, March, 1937, Entry 254, RG 114.5.2, Natl. Archives, College Park, MD.

[790] John L. Schwendiman, *The First Fifty Years, The Plant Materials Center, Pullman, WA*, (Pullman, WA 1987).

[791] Dr. Abraham Stoesz, "Development and Major Accomplishments During to Past Decade," 1963, Entry 254, RG 114.5.2, Natl. Archives, College Park, MD.

Chapter 14: A Constant Question – PMC Research Authority

[792] The National Industrial Recovery Act (NIRA; Pub. L. 73-90, 48 Stat. 195, enacted June 16, 1933, codified at 15 U.S.C. § 703)

[793] 114.2 General Records of the Soil Erosion Service and the Soil Conservation Service 1915-77 http://www.archives.gov/research/guide-fed-records/groups/114.html/ (December 14, 2009).

[794] Eugene C. Buie, *A History of Water Resource Activities of the USDA*, Soil Conservation Service (USDA-SCS, Washington, DC, 1979).

[795] (49 Stat. 163), April 27, 1935.

[796] Records of the NRCS, (Record Group 114) 1875-1977, 1988-95 (bulk 1935-53), http://www.archives.gov/research/guide-fed-records/groups/114.html#114.4/ (December 14, 2009).

[797] Ibid.

[798] F. J. Crider, memo to Regional Conservationists and Nurserymen, March 25, 1936, Entry 254, RG 114.5.2, Natl. Archives, College Park, MD.

[799] Franklin J. Crider Memo to Regional Conservators, July 27, 1937, Entry 215.0, Central Files, Natl. Archives, College Park, MD.

[800] Douglas Helms, *Briefing Paper on the Plant Materials Centers*, (USDA,-NRCS, Washington, D.C., April 7, 2008).

[801] F. J. Crider to All Ranking Field Offices, "Projecting Nursery Observational Work", March 2, 1939, Entry 254, RG 114.5.2, Natl. Archives, College Park, MD.

[802] Curtis Sharp conducted his graduate studies at such a station, The Pennsylvania State Univ., University Park, PA.

[803] D. A. Williams memo to E. L. Peterson on SCS Plant Materials Centers. July 16, 1956, Entry 254, RG 114.5.2, Natl. Archives, College Park, MD.

[804] Administrator's Memorandum, Service Policies, Objectives, and Functions in Plant Materials, Draft 3-14-1956, Entry 254, RG 114.5.2, Natl. Archives, College Park, MD.

[805] USDA, NRCS, *National Plant Materials Handbook*, June 16, 1977, Washington, DC.

[806] E. B. Nixon, Jr. 1957. "Franklin D. Roosevelt & Conservation, 1911-1945", Vol. 1, General Services Administration, National Archives and Records Service, Franklin D. Roosevelt Library, Hyde Park, NY.

[807] USDA, NRCS, *Plant Materials Program Costs and Benefits 1935 – 2005*, https://prod.nrcs.usda.gov/Internet/FSE_DOCUMENTS/stelprdb1042295.pdf/ (February 1, 2011).

[808] See Appendix 5, "Methodology of 2005 Economic Analysis".

[809] Definition of Research, http://explorable.com/definition-of-research.html/ (October 22, 2012).

[810] Definition of Research, http://www.google.com/#hl=en&spell=1&q=definition+research&sa=X&ei=LzWFULmUMJLV0gGi_oCIBQ&ved=0CBsQvwUoAA&bav=on.2,or.r_gc.r_pw.r_qf.&fp=4624fb5637c33ac3&bpcl=35466521&biw=1049&bih=590/ (October 22, 2012).

[811] The Random House Dictionary of the English Language, (Random House, New York, NY, 1968).

[812] Primarily from the Annual Reports of Department of Agriculture, Soil Conservation Service for years 1933 through 1953.

[813] "Statement of Nursery Annual Production, Capacity" SCS, October 31, 1939, Entry 254, RG 114.5.2, Natl. Archives, College Park, MD.

[814] "Statement of Nursery Annual Production, Capacity" SCS, October 31, 1939, Entry 254, RG 114.5.2, Natl. Archives, College Park, MD.

[815] USDA, NRCS, *Plant Materials Program Costs and Benefits*, loc. cit.

[816] Developing Conservation Plants for USDA Programs: Benefits for Society, Wildlife and the Environment, A Comparison of Benefits and Costs 1965-1997, W. Curtis Sharp, 1997, http://www.plant-materials.nrcs.usda.gov/pubs/njpmcbr390.pdf/ (February 24, 2012).

[817] Gosselink, J.G., E.P. Odem and R.M. Pope. *The Value of the Tidal Marsh*, (Center for Wetland Resources, LSU, Baton, 1974).

[818] R. Costanza and H. E. Daly 1992, "National capital and sustainable development", *Consv. Biol.*, (1992), 6:37-46.

[819] Costanza, R., R. d'Arge, R.de Groot, S. Farber, M. Grasso, B. Hannon, K. Limburg, S. Naeem, R.V. O'Neill, J. Paruelo, R.G. Raskins and P. Sutton. 1997. "The value of the world's ecosystem services and natural capital." *Nature*, (1997), 387: 253-260.

[820] USDA, NRCS, *Plant Materials Program Costs and Benefits 1935 – 2005*, https://prod.nrcs.usda.gov/Internet/FSE_DOCUMENTS/stelprdb1042295.pdf/ (February 1, 2011) 4.

[821] "Annual Report of Regional Nursery, Division Region I, July 1, 1950 – June 30, 1951," Entry 254, RG 114.5.2, Natl. Archives, College Park, MD.

[822] "Estimated Distribution of 1954 Funds for Nursery Work", July 31, 1953, Natl. Archives, College Park, MD.

[823] Nursery Division Report for 1952, Entry 254, RG 114.5.2, Natl. Archives, College Park, MD.

[824] Review of historical USDA, SCS financial records for the 1935 - 1965 period.

[825] Personal communications with NHQ Administrative Services, Washington, DC.

[826] Bureau of Labor Statistics. Consumer Price Index - All Consumers, Series ID:CUUR0000AA0. Washington, DC. http://www.bls.gov/cpi/ (September 3, 2010).

[827] Several PMCs had breaks in service, such as NM from 1953 until 1957. Funding adjustments were made for these periods.

[828] All figures are in 2005 dollars.

[829] This data was extracted from the NRCS Plant Materials Database, Activities and Accomplishments by the National PMC, Beltsville, MD Staff.

[830] Bureau of Labor Statistics. 2000b. Producer Price Index - Commodities, Series ID: WPU018. Washington, DC.

[831] Conservation Plants by Scientific Name, NRCS, http://plant-materials.nrcs.usda.gov/releases/releasesallbysci.html/, (February 27, 2011).

[832] Costanza, R., et al. 1997, "The value of the world's ecosystem services and natural capital.", loc. cit.

[833] Value of the world's ecosystem services: the influence of a single paper, The Encyclopedia of Earth, August 9, 2007, http://www.eoearth.org/article/Value_of_the_world%E2%80%99s_ecosystem_services:_the_influence_of_a_single_paper/ (February 26, 2012).

Made in the USA
Columbia, SC
20 November 2020